HIGHER
GCSE Modular Mathematics for Edexcel

ALAN SMITH

SERIES CONSULTANT: JEAN LINSKY

U3 U4

Hodder Murray
www.hoddereducation.co.uk

Acknowledgements

The Publishers would like to thank the following for permission to reproduce copyright material:

p.207 © akg-images / ullstein bild

Every effort has been made to trace all copyright holders, but if any have been inadvertently overlooked the Publishers will be pleased to make the necessary arrangements at the first opportunity.

Although every effort has been made to ensure that website addresses are correct at time of going to press, Hodder Murray cannot be held responsible for the content of any website mentioned in this book. It is sometimes possible to find a relocated webpage by typing in the address of the home page for a website in the URL window of your browser.

Hodder Headline's policy is to use papers that are natural, renewable and recyclable and made from wood grown in sustainable forests. The logging and manufacturing processes are expected to conform to the environmental regulations of the country of origin.

This high quality material is endorsed by Edexcel and has been through a rigorous quality assurance programme to ensure that it is a suitable companion to the specification for both learners and teachers. This does not mean that its contents will be used verbatim when setting examinations nor is it to be read as being the official specification – a copy of which is available at www.edexcel.org.uk

Orders: please contact Bookpoint Ltd, 130 Milton Park, Abingdon, Oxon OX14 4SB. Telephone: (44) 01235 827720. Fax: (44) 01235 400454. Lines are open 9 a.m to 5 p.m., Monday to Saturday, with a 24-hour message answering service. Visit our website at www.hoddereducation.co.uk

© Alan Smith 2006
First published in 2006 by
Hodder Murray, an imprint of Hodder Education,
a member of the Hodder Headline Group
338 Euston Road
London NW1 3BH

Impression number   10 9 8 7 6 5 4 3 2 1
Year   2011 2010 2009 2008 2007 2006

All rights reserved. Apart from any use permitted under UK copyright law, no part of this publication may be reproduced or transmitted in any form or by any means, electronic or mechanical, including photocopying and recording, or held within any information storage and retrieval system, without permission in writing from the publisher or under licence from the Copyright Licensing Agency Limited. Further details of such licences (for reprographic reproduction) may be obtained from the Copyright Licensing Agency Limited, 90 Tottenham Court Road, London W1T 4LP.

Cover illustration © David Angel @ Début Art
Illustrations © Barking Dog Art

Typeset in 10/12 Times by Tech-Set Ltd, Gateshead
Printed in Great Britain by CPI Bath.
Personal Tutor CD: © Alan Smith; with contributions from Andy Sturman; developed by Infuze Limited; cast: Nicolette Landau; recorded at Alchemy Soho.

A catalogue record for this title is available from the British Library

ISBN-10: 0340940689
ISBN-13: 978 0340 940 686

CONTENTS

Introduction	**vii**

Unit 3

1	**Working with whole numbers**	**1**
	Starter: Four 4's	1
	1.1 Addition and subtraction without a calculator	2
	1.2 Multiplication without a calculator	4
	1.3 Division without a calculator	7
	1.4 Positive and negative integers	9
	1.5 Factors, multiples and primes	11
	1.6 Highest common factor (HCF)	12
	1.7 Lowest common multiple (LCM)	14
	Key points	18
	Internet Challenge 1: Prime time	19
2	**Fractions and decimals**	**20**
	Starter: Half and half	20
	2.1 Equivalent fractions	21
	2.2 Arithmetic with decimals	23
	2.3 Decimals and fractions	26
	2.4 Rounding and approximation	29
	Key points	34
	Internet Challenge 2: Fraction vocabulary	35
3	**Percentages**	**36**
	Starter: How many per cent?	36
	3.1 Simple percentages	36
	3.2 Finding a percentage of an amount	38
	Key points	40
	Internet Challenge 3: What percentage …?	41
4	**Powers, roots and reciprocals**	**42**
	Starter: Roman numerals	42
	4.1 Basic powers and roots	43
	4.2 Higher powers and roots	45
	4.3 Fractional (rational) indices	46
	4.4 Negative powers and reciprocals	47
	4.5 The laws of indices	49
	4.6 Standard index form	52
	4.7 Calculating with numbers in standard form	53
	Key points	57
	Internet Challenge 4: Astronomical numbers	58
5	**Working with algebra**	**59**
	Starter: Right or wrong?	59
	5.1 Substituting numbers into formulae and expressions	59
	5.2 Working with indices	62
	5.3 Expanding brackets	64
	5.4 Multiplying two brackets together	66
	5.5 Factorising – common factors	68
	5.6 Factorising – quadratic expressions	69
	5.7 Factorising – harder quadratic expressions	71
	5.8 Factorising – difference of two squares	71
	5.9 Simplifying algebraic fractions (rational expressions)	73
	Key points	77
	Internet Challenge 5: The language of algebra	78
6	**Coordinates and straight line graphs**	**79**
	Starter: Matchstick puzzles	79
	6.1 Coordinates in all four quadrants	80
	6.2 Graphs of linear functions	83
	6.3 The midpoint of a line segment	85
	6.4 Coordinates in 3-D	86
	Key points	89
	Internet Challenge 6: Coordinates and maps	90
7	**Number sequences**	**91**
	Starter: Circles, lines and regions	91
	7.1 Number sequences	92
	7.2 Describing number sequences with rules	94
	7.3 Arithmetic sequences	96
	Key points	102
	Internet Challenge 7: Fibonacci numbers	103

8 Working with shape and space		**104**
Starter: Alphabet soup		104
8.1	Corresponding and alternate angles	105
8.2	Angles in triangles and quadrilaterals	108
8.3	Areas and perimeters of simple shapes	113
8.4	Surface area and volume	120
Key points		128
Internet Challenge 8: The four-colour theorem		129

9 Properties of circles		**130**
Starter: Circle vocabulary		130
9.1	Tangents, chords and circles	131
9.2	Constructing regular polygons inside a circle	135
Key points		137
Internet Challenge 9: Circles		138

10 Working with units		**139**
Starter: Leap years		139
10.1	Basic metric units	140
10.2	Choosing and using metric and imperial units	141
10.3	Compound measures	142
10.4	Angles and bearings	145
Key points		149
Internet Challenge 10: Definitions of units		150

11 Using a calculator efficiently		**151**
Starter: Big numbers		151
11.1	Powers, roots and reciprocals	152
11.2	Using brackets	154
11.3	Using the fraction key	156
Key points		158
Internet Challenge 11: Computing crossword		159

Unit 4

12 Fractions, ratios and percentages		**163**
Starter: Equivalent fractions		163
12.1	Adding and subtracting with fractions	164
12.2	Multiplying and dividing with fractions	166
12.3	Working with ratios	169
12.4	Percentage increase and decrease	172
12.5	Reverse percentage problems	175
12.6	Simple and compound interest	177
12.7	Using the ANS key	179
Key points		183
Internet Challenge 12: Investigating inflation		184

13 Algebraic equations		**185**
Starter: Triangular arithmagons		185
13.1	Expressions, equations and identities	186
13.2	Simple equations	187
13.3	Harder linear equations	188
13.4	Equations and brackets	190
13.5	Equations with fractional coefficients	191
13.6	Using equations to solve geometry problems	193
13.7	Generating formulae	195
13.8	Changing the subject of a formula	197
13.9	Trial and improvement	200
Key points		206
Internet Challenge 13: Carl Friedrich Gauss		207

14 Graphs of straight lines		**208**
Starter: Number sequences		208
14.1	Gradient and intercept of linear functions	209
14.2	Equations and graphs	213
14.3	Parallel lines	215
Key points		219
Internet Challenge 14: Parallels		220

15 Simultaneous equations		**221**
Starter: Fruity numbers		221
15.1	Solving simultaneous equations by inspection	222
15.2	Solving simultaneous equations by algebraic elimination	223
15.3	Solving simultaneous equations by a graphical method	227
15.4	Setting up and solving problems using simultaneous equations	228
Key points		232
Internet Challenge 15: Magic squares		233

16 Inequalities — 234
- Starter: Treasure hunt — 234
- 16.1 Whole-number solutions to inequalities — 235
- 16.2 Using algebra to solve linear inequalities — 236
- 16.3 Illustrating inequalities on a number line — 237
- 16.4 Graphs of linear inequalities in two variables — 239
- Key points — 244
- Internet Challenge 16: Investigating mathematical symbols — 245

17 Travel and other graphs — 246
- Starter: Animal races — 246
- 17.1 Modelling with straight line graphs — 247
- 17.2 Distance–time graphs — 252
- 17.3 Velocity–time graphs — 256
- Key points — 264
- Internet Challenge 17: Faster and faster — 265

18 Circles and cylinders — 266
- Starter: Three and a bit … — 266
- 18.1 Circumference and area of a circle — 267
- 18.2 Sectors of a circle — 272
- 18.3 Circumference and area in reverse — 274
- 18.4 Surface area and volume of a cylinder — 276
- 18.5 Exact calculations using pi — 279
- Key points — 285
- Internet Challenge 18: Measuring the Earth — 286

19 Constructions and loci — 287
- Starter: Round and round in circles — 287
- 19.1 Constructing triangles from given information — 288
- 19.2 Constructions with line segments — 295
- 19.3 Locus constructions — 300
- 19.4 Bearings — 305
- Key points — 310
- Internet Challenge 19: In perspective — 311

20 Transformation and similarity — 312
- Starter: Monkey business — 312
- 20.1 Reflections — 313
- 20.2 Rotations — 319
- 20.3 Combining transformations — 324
- 20.4 Enlargements — 328
- 20.5 Similar shapes and solids — 333
- Key points — 342
- Internet Challenge 20: Geometrical definitions — 343

21 Pythagoras' theorem — 344
- Starter: Finding squares and square roots on your calculator — 344
- 21.1 Introducing Pythagoras' theorem — 345
- 21.2 Using Pythagoras' theorem to find a hypotenuse — 347
- 21.3 Using Pythagoras' theorem to find one of the shorter sides — 348
- 21.4 Pythagoras' theorem in three dimensions — 350
- Key points — 354
- Internet Challenge 21: Investigating Pythagorean triples — 355

22 Introducing trigonometry — 356
- Starter: A triangular spiral — 356
- 22.1 The sine ratio — 357
- 22.2 The cosine ratio — 360
- 22.3 The tangent ratio — 364
- 22.4 Choosing the right trigonometrical function — 366
- 22.5 Finding an unknown angle — 368
- 22.6 Multi-stage problems — 370
- Key points — 377
- Internet Challenge 22: Famous geometers — 378

23 2-D and 3-D objects — 379
- Starter: Making cubes — 379
- 23.1 Angles in polygons — 380
- 23.2 Drawing and constructing 3-D objects — 384
- 23.3 Volume and surface area of pyramids, cones and spheres — 390
- 23.4 Converting between units of area and volume — 394
- 23.5 Dimensional analysis — 395
- 23.6 Upper and lower bounds — 398
- Key points — 405
- Internet Challenge 23: Investigating polyhedra — 406

24 Circle theorems	**407**
Starter: Scrambled words	407
24.1 Pythagoras' theorem and circles	408
24.2 Angle properties inside a circle	411
24.3 Further circle theorems	417
Key points	426
Internet Challenge 24: The nine-point circle theorem	427
25 Direct and inverse proportion	**428**
Starter: A sense of proportion	428
25.1 Direct proportion	429
25.2 Inverse proportion	432
25.3 Graphical representation of direct and inverse proportion	435
Key points	440
Internet Challenge 25: The planets and their orbits	441
26 Quadratic equations	**442**
Starter: Solutions of equations	442
26.1 Solving quadratic equations – factorising	443
26.2 Solving quadratic equations – formula	445
26.3 Problems leading to quadratic equations	446
26.4 Completing the square	448
Key points	452
Internet Challenge 26: Conic sections	453
27 Advanced algebra	**454**
Starter: How many shapes?	454
27.1 Working with surds	455
27.2 Algebraic fractions and equations	458
27.3 Simultaneous equations, one linear and one quadratic	460
27.4 Changing the subject of an equation where the symbol appears twice	462
27.5 Exponential growth and decay	463
Key points	467
Internet Challenge 27: Famous formulae	468
28 Further trigonometry	**469**
Starter: How tall is the church?	469
28.1 The sine rule	470
28.2 The ambiguous case of the sine rule	474
28.3 The cosine rule	477
28.4 Area of a triangle using $\frac{1}{2}ab \sin C$, and segments of circles	481
28.5 Trigonometry in 3-D	484
28.6 Frustums	487
Key points	491
Internet Challenge 28: Heron's formula	492
29 Graphs of curves	**493**
Starter: Making waves	493
29.1 Tables of functions	494
29.2 Plotting and using graphs of curves	496
29.3 Graphs of sine, cosine and tangent functions	501
29.4 Transformations of graphs	504
Key points	515
Internet Challenge 29: Famous curves	516
30 Vectors	**517**
Starter: Knight's tours	517
30.1 Introducing vectors	518
30.2 Adding and subtracting vectors	519
30.3 Multiplying a vector by a number (scalar multiplication)	521
30.4 Using vectors	522
Key points	529
Internet Challenge 30: Queens on a chessboard	530
31 Mathematical proof	**531**
Starter: $1 = 2$	531
31.1 Congruent triangles	532
31.2 Algebraic proofs	535
31.3 Use of counter-examples	537
Key points	540
Internet Challenge 31: Proofs and theories	541
32 Introducing coordinate geometry	**542**
Starter: Coded message	542
32.1 Pythagoras' theorem on a coordinate grid	542
32.2 Coordinate geometry of a circle	545
32.3 Gradients of parallel and perpendicular lines	548
Key points	552
Internet Challenge 32: Shapes on spotty paper	553
Index	**554**

Introduction

This series has been written to provide complete coverage of the new two-tier Edexcel GCSE Modular Mathematics specification (Higher) for first teaching from September 2006. This book has been written with reference to Units 3 and 4. A separate Hodder Murray book, *Foundation and Higher GCSE Modular Mathematics for Edexcel: U2,* in the same series, covers the Data Handling content for Unit 2.

Students following the Higher course may have differing individual target grades for the GCSE, and this is reflected in the structure of the book. Some of the content in U3 reaches well back into earlier work forming a bridge with Key Stage 3 material. These topics are:

- Chapter 1 – Working with whole numbers
- Chapter 2 – Fractions and decimals
- Chapter 5 – Working with algebra
- Chapter 8 – Working with shape and space.

Some of the early work covered in these four chapters may be skipped, or used as revision material as appropriate.

The first part of this book, up to Chapter 11, covers all the work needed in order to be ready for the Unit 3 test, while Chapters 12 to 32 cover the content for U4. Note that knowledge of U3 is assumed for U4.

For the examinations, you will require a good quality scientific calculator for some of the papers – calculators are not permitted in others. All the exercises in this book have an icon to indicate whether calculators are permitted or not, and you should follow this advice carefully in order to build up the necessary mixture of calculator and non-calculator skills before the examination. There are many differences between calculators, so make sure that you are fully familiar with your own particular model – do not buy a new calculator (or borrow one) just before the examination!

Each chapter begins with a 'starter'. This is an exercise, activity or puzzle designed to stimulate thinking and discussion about some of the ideas that underpin the content of the chapter. The main chapter contains explanations of each topic, with numerous worked examples, followed by a corresponding exercise of questions. At the end of each chapter there is a 'review exercise' made up of questions on the content for the whole chapter, followed by a set of 'key points'. Many of the review questions are from past Edexcel GCSE examination papers – this is indicated in the margin.

Each chapter concludes with an 'internet challenge' that is intended to be done (either at school or at home) using an internet search engine, such as *Google*. Much of the internet challenge material goes beyond the boundaries of the GCSE specification, providing enrichment and leading to a deeper understanding of mainstream topics. The challenges look at the history of mathematics and mathematicians, or the role of mathematics in the real world. When doing these, it is hoped that you will not just answer the written questions, but also take some time to explore the subject a little deeper – the

internet contains a vast reservoir of very well-written information about mathematics. However, the reliability of internet information can be variable, so it is best to check your answers by referring to more than one site if possible.

When an exercise contains questions covering different levels, a 'walker' icon is used to indicate a suitable jumping-off point for those wishing to avoid higher-level questions. Occasionally an exercise will revert back to lower-level questions again, in which case a 'walker' icon facing the other way indicates that it is a suitable jumping-on point.

All the content has been checked very carefully against the new GCSE specification to ensure that all examination topics are suitably covered. If you have mastered all the relevant topics covered in this book then you should be able to approach the examinations confident in the knowledge that you are fully prepared. Additional practice exam-style question papers, with full mark schemes, are available in Hodder Murray's accompanying assessment pack.

Finally, it is hoped that you will consider studying mathematics as a sixth form subject. Many of the topics encountered in the early months of an A-level course are natural developments of the content of the later chapters in this book, and if you are able to handle these confidently then you should feel well-prepared for A-level should you choose to study it.

Good luck on exam day!

Alan Smith

Christ's Hospital
West Sussex

July 2006

UNIT 3

CHAPTER 1

Working with whole numbers

In this chapter you will **revise earlier work on**:
- addition and subtraction without a calculator
- multiplication and division without a calculator
- using positive and negative whole numbers (integers)
- factors and multiples.

You will **learn how to:**
- decompose integers into prime factors
- calculate highest common factors (HCFs) and lowest common multiples (LCMs) efficiently.

You will also be **challenged to**:
- investigate primes.

Starter: Four 4's

Using exactly four 4's, and usual mathematical symbols, try to make each whole number from 1 to 100. Here are a few examples to start you off.

$$1 = \frac{44}{44}$$

$$2 = \frac{4 \times 4}{4 + 4}$$

$$3 = \frac{4 + 4 + 4}{4}$$

$$4 = 4 + 4 \times (4 - 4)$$

$$5 = \frac{4 \times 4 + 4}{4}$$

$$6 = 4 + \frac{4 + 4}{4}$$

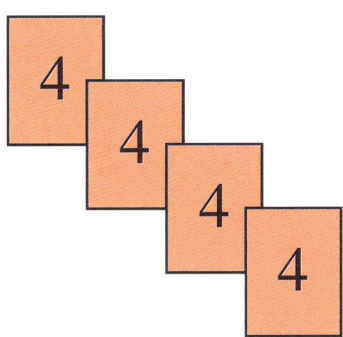

You should try to stick to basic mathematical symbols such as $+$, $-$, $\times$, $\div$ and brackets, wherever possible, but you may need to use more complicated symbols such as $\sqrt{\ }$ and $!$ to make some of the higher numbers. Ask your teacher if you need some help with these symbols.

1.1 Addition and subtraction without a calculator

You will sometimes need to carry out simple addition and subtraction problems in your head, without a calculator. These examples show you some useful shortcuts.

EXAMPLE

Work out the value of $19 + 6 + 21 + 4$.

> When adding a string of numbers, look for combinations that add together to give a simple answer. Here, $19 + 21$ and $6 + 4$ both give exact multiples of 10.

SOLUTION

$$19 + 6 + 21 + 4 = 19 + \ldots + 21$$
$$ + 6 \ldots + 4$$
$$= 40 + 10$$
$$= \underline{50}$$

EXAMPLE

Work out the value of $199 + 399$.

> Both these numbers are close to exact multiples of 100, so you can work out $200 + 400$ and then make a small adjustment.

SOLUTION

$$199 + 399 = 200 - 1 + 400 - 1$$
$$= 200 \ldots + 400$$
$$ - 1 \ldots - 1$$
$$= 600 - 2$$
$$= \underline{598}$$

EXAMPLE

Work out $257 - 98$.

> 98 is close to 100, so it is convenient to take away 100, then add 2 back on.

SOLUTION

$$257 - 98 = 257 - 100 + 2$$
$$ = 157 + 2$$
$$= \underline{159}$$

Harder questions may require the use of pencil and paper methods, and you should already be familiar with these. Remember to make sure that the columns are lined up properly so that each figure takes its correct place value in the calculation.

EXAMPLE

Work out 356 + 173.

SOLUTION

```
   3 5 6
 + 1 7 3
   ─────
     2 9
   1
```

Work from right to left.
Add the units: 6 + 3 = 9
Next, the 10s column: 5 + 7 = 12
The digit 2 is entered, and the 1 is carried to the next column.

```
   3 5 6
 + 1 7 3
   ─────
   5 2 9
   1
```

Finally, the 100s column: 3 + 1 + 1 = 5

So 356 + 173 = <u>529</u>

Here are two slightly different ways of setting out a subtraction problem.
You should use whichever of these methods you prefer.

EXAMPLE

Work out 827 − 653.

SOLUTION

Method 1

```
   8 2 7
 − 6 5 3
   ─────
       4
```

For the units: 7 − 3 = 4
For the 10s: 2 − 5 cannot be done directly.

```
   7 1
   8̸ 2 7
 − 6 5 3
   ─────
   1 7 4
```

Exchange 10 from the 82 to give 70 and 12.
Now 12 − 5 = 7 and 7 − 6 = 1

So 827 − 653 = <u>174</u>

Method 2

```
   8 2 7
 − 6 5 3
   ─────
       4
```

The first part is the same as method 1.

```
     1
   8 2 7
 − 7̸6 5 3
   ─────
   1 7 4
```

Instead of dropping 82 down to 72, you can make 65 up to 75.

Now 12 − 5 = 7 and 8 − 7 = 1

So 827 − 653 = <u>174</u>

EXERCISE 1.1

Work out the answers to these problems in your head.

1 $46 + 19 + 54 + 11$
2 $198 + 357 + 2$
3 $66 + 111 + 14$

4 $345 + 187 + 55$
5 $23 + 24 + 25 + 26 + 27$
6 $39 + 48 + 61 + 52$

7 $59 + 69 + 79$
8 $144 - 99$
9 $149 + 249$

10 $376 - 199$

Use any written method to work out the answers to these problems. Show your working clearly.

11 $274 + 89$
12 $456 + 682$
13 $736 - 473$

14 $949 - 477$
15 $1377 + 2557$
16 $3052 - 1644$

17 $6355 - 2471$
18 $2005 - 1066$

19 An aircraft can carry 223 passengers when all the seats are full, but today 57 of the seats are empty. How many passengers are on the aircraft today?

20 The attendances at a theatre show were 475 (Thursday), 677 (Friday) and 723 (Saturday). How many people attended in total?

1.2 Multiplication without a calculator

You will sometimes need to carry out simple multiplication problems in your head. This example shows one useful shortcut.

EXAMPLE

Work out the value of 49×3.

49 is almost 50, so you can work out 50×3 then take off the extra 3.

SOLUTION

$49 = 50 - 1$
So $49 \times 3 = 50 \times 3 - 1 \times 3$
$= 150 - 3$
$= \underline{147}$

Harder questions will require pencil and paper methods. Here is a reminder of how **short multiplication** works.

EXAMPLE

Work out the value of 273×6.

SOLUTION

```
   2 7 3
 ×     6
       8
     1
```
Begin with 3 × 6 = 18. Enter as 8 with the 1 carried.

```
   2 7 3
 ×     6
     3 8
   4 1
```
Next, 7 × 6 = 42, plus the 1 carried, makes 43. Enter as 3 with the 4 carried.

```
   2 7 3
 ×     6
 1 6 3 8
 1 4 1
```
Finally, 2 × 6 = 12, plus the 4 carried, makes 16. Entered as 6 with the 1 carried; enter this 1 directly into the 1000s column.

So 273 × 6 = <u>1638</u>

When working with bigger numbers, you will need to use **long multiplication**. There are two good ways of setting this out – use whichever one you are most confident with.

EXAMPLE

Work out the value of 492 × 34.

SOLUTION

Method 1

```
     4 9 2
 ×     3 4
   1 9 6 8
   1 3
```
First, multiply 492 by 4 to give 1968.

```
     4 9 2
 ×     3 4
   1 9 6 8
           0
```
Next, prepare to multiply 492 by 30, by writing a zero in the units column. This guarantees that you are multiplying by 30, not just 3.

```
     4 9 2
 ×     3 4
   1 9 6 8
 1 4 7 6 0
     2
```
492 times 3 gives 1476.

```
     4 9 2
 ×     3 4
   1 9 6 8
 1 4 7 6 0
 1 6 7 2 8
   1 1
```
Finally, add 1968 and 14 760 to give the answer 16 728.

So 492 × 34 = <u>16 728</u>

Method 2

First, write 492 and 34 along the top and down the end of a rectangular grid.

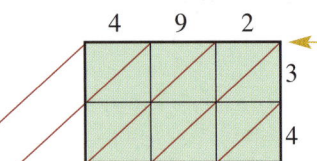

Next, add diagonal lines, as shown.

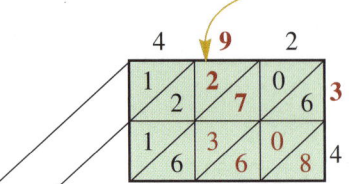

Within each square of the grid, carry out a simple multiplication as shown. For example, 9 times 3 is 27.

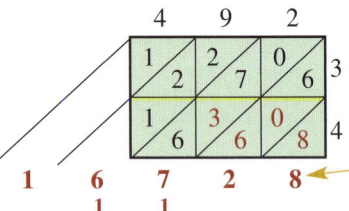

Finally, add up the totals along each diagonal, starting at the right and working leftwards.

EXERCISE 1.2

Use short multiplication to work out the answers to these calculations.

1 144×3
2 254×4
3 118×6
4 227×8
5 326×7
6 420×5
7 503×4
8 443×9

Use any written method to work out the answers to these problems. Show your working clearly.

9 426×12
10 255×27
11 308×21
12 420×49
13 866×79
14 635×42
15 196×88
16 623×65

17 A company has 23 coaches and each coach can carry 55 passengers.
What is the total number of passengers that the coaches can carry?

18 I have a set of 12 encyclopaedias. Each one has 199 pages.
How many pages are there in the whole set?

19 Joni buys 16 stamps at 19 pence each and 13 stamps at 26 pence each.
How much does she spend in total?

20 A small camera phone has a rectangular chip of pixels that collect and form the image.
The chip size is 320 pixels long and 240 pixels across.
Calculate the total number of pixels on the chip.

1.3 Division without a calculator

Division is usually more awkward than multiplication, but this example shows
a helpful method if the number you are dividing into (the **dividend**) is close to a
convenient multiple of the number you are dividing by (the **divisor**).

EXAMPLE

Work out the value of $693 \div 7$.

> 693 is almost 700, so you can work out
> $700 \div 7$ then take off the extra $7 \div 7$

SOLUTION

693 is $700 - 7$
So $693 \div 7 = 700 \div 7 - 7 \div 7$
$= 100 - 1$
$= \underline{99}$

In most division questions you will need to use a formal written method.
Here is an example of **short division**, with a remainder.

EXAMPLE

Work out the value of $673 \div 4$.

SOLUTION

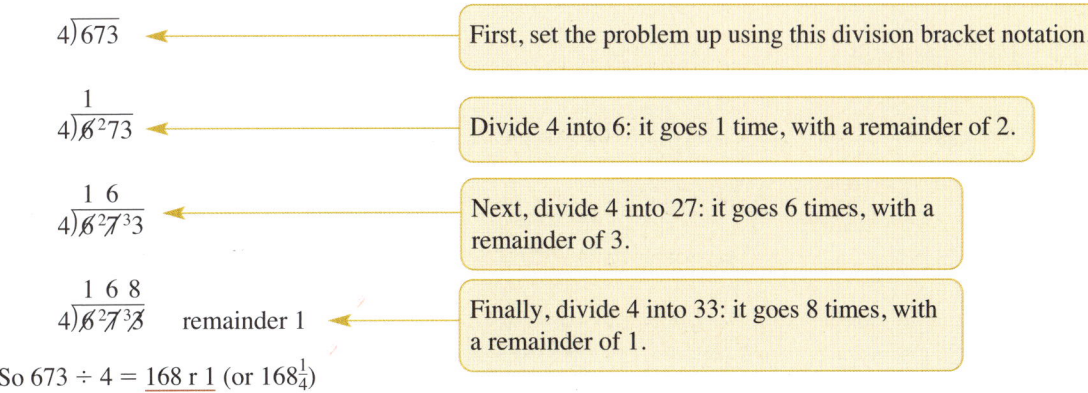

So $673 \div 4 = \underline{168 \text{ r } 1}$ (or $168\frac{1}{4}$)

When dividing by a number bigger than 10, it is usually easier to set the working out as a **long division** instead. The next example reminds you how this is done.

EXAMPLE

Work out the value of 3302 ÷ 13.

SOLUTION

$$13\overline{)3302}$$

Begin by setting up the problem using division bracket notation.

$$\begin{array}{r} 2 \\ 13\overline{)3302} \\ \underline{26} \\ 7 \end{array}$$

13 will not divide into 3, so divide 13 into 33. This goes 2 times, with remainder 7.

$$\begin{array}{r} 2 \\ 13\overline{)3302} \\ \underline{26} \\ 70 \end{array}$$

Bring down the next digit, 0 in this case, to make the 7 up to 70.

$$\begin{array}{r} 25 \\ 13\overline{)3302} \\ \underline{26}\downarrow \\ 70 \\ \underline{65} \\ 5 \end{array}$$

13 divides into 70 five times, with remainder 5.

$$\begin{array}{r} 254 \\ 13\overline{)3302} \\ \underline{26} \\ 70 \\ \underline{65}\downarrow \\ 52 \\ \underline{52} \\ 0 \end{array}$$

Finally, bring down the digit 2 to make 52. 13 divides into 52 exactly 4 times, with no remainder.

So 3302 ÷ 13 = <u>254</u> exactly

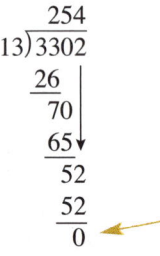

EXERCISE 1.3

Use short division to work out the answers to these calculations. (Four of them should leave remainders.)

1 329 ÷ 7
2 977 ÷ 5
3 2686 ÷ 9
4 28 845 ÷ 3
5 1530 ÷ 6
6 2328 ÷ 8
7 1090 ÷ 4
8 400 ÷ 7

Use long division to work out the answers to these problems. Show your working clearly.
(Only the last two should leave remainders.)

9 7684 ÷ 17
10 7581 ÷ 19
11 3315 ÷ 15
12 4956 ÷ 21
13 5771 ÷ 29
14 3600 ÷ 25
15 7890 ÷ 23
16 3250 ÷ 24

17 750 grams of chocolate is shared out equally between 6 people. How much does each one receive?

18 In a lottery draw the prize of £3250 is shared equally between 13 winners. How much does each receive?

19 Seven children share 100 sweets in as fair a way as possible. How many sweets does each child receive?

20 On a school trip there are 16 teachers and 180 children. The teachers divide the children up into equal-sized groups, as nearly as is possible, with one group per teacher. How many children are in each group?

1.4 Positive and negative integers

It is often convenient to visualise positive and negative whole numbers, or integers, strung out in order along a number line. The positive integers run to the right of zero, and negative integers to the left:

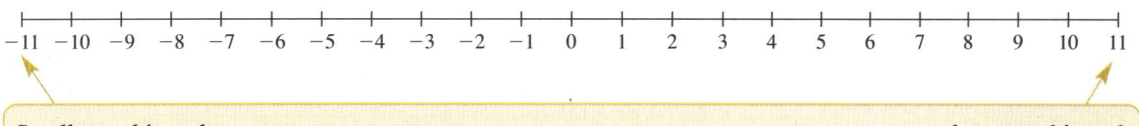

Smaller at this end…   … larger at this end.

Mathematicians describe numbers on the right of the number line as being larger than the numbers on the left. This makes sense for positive numbers, where 6 is obviously bigger than 4, for example, but care must be taken with negative numbers. 4 is bigger than -6, for example, and -8 is smaller than -7.

You need to be able to carry out basic arithmetic using positive and negative numbers, with and without a calculator. Many calculators carry two types of minus sign key: one for marking a number as negative, and another for the process of subtraction. So, in a calculation such as $-6 - 5$, you have to start with the quantity -6 and then subtract 5. Subtraction means moving to the *left* on the number line, so the answer is $-6 - 5 = -11$.

Take care when two minus signs are involved: the rule that 'two minuses make a plus' is not always trustworthy. For example, $-3 + -5 = -8$ (two minuses make even more minus!), whereas $-3 - -5 = -3 + 5 = 2$. So two *adjacent* minus signs are equivalent to a single plus sign.

If two adjacent signs are the *same* $(+\ +$ or $-\ -)$ then the overall sign is *positive*.

And if the signs are *different* $(+\ -$ or $-\ +)$ then the overall sign is *negative*.

EXAMPLE

Without using a calculator, work out the values of:
a) $6 - 9$
b) $-4 + 5$
c) $-8 + -3$
d) $5 - -6$

SOLUTION

a) $6 - 9 = \underline{-3}$
b) $-4 + 5 = \underline{1}$
c) $-8 + -3 = \underline{-11}$
d) $5 - -6 = 5 + 6 = \underline{11}$

When multiplying or dividing with positive or negative numbers, it is usually simplest to ignore the minus signs while you work out the numerical value of the answer. Then restore the sign at the end.

If an *odd* number of negative numbers is *multiplied* or *divided*, the answer will be *negative*.

If an *even* number of minus signs is involved, the answer will be *positive*.

EXAMPLE

Without using a calculator, work out the values of:
a) $(-5) \times (4)$
b) $(-4) \times (-3)$
c) $(-8) \div (-2)$
d) $5 \times (-4) \times (-2)$

SOLUTION

a) $(-5) \times (4) = \underline{-20}$
b) $(-4) \times (-3) = \underline{12}$
c) $(-8) \div (-2) = \underline{4}$
d) $5 \times (-4) \times (-2) = \underline{40}$

$5 \times 4 \times 2 = 40$ and there are two minus signs, so the answer is positive.

EXERCISE 1.4

Without using a calculator, work out the answers to the following.

1. $4 + (-6)$
2. $6 + (-3)$
3. $-3 - (-2)$
4. $2 - (-1)$
5. $-4 + 6$
6. $-4 + (-5)$
7. $-8 + 13$
8. $-3 - -15$
9. $(5) - -5$

10 $5 + {-5}$
11 $6 - {-2}$
12 $-3 - 4$
13 $4 + {-8}$
14 $-10 - {-1}$
15 $3 \times {-6}$
16 $-4 \times {-5}$
17 -2×8
18 $12 \div {-6}$
19 $-18 \div 3$
20 $-36 \div {-3}$

21 Arrange these in order of size, smallest first: $8, 3, -5, -1, 0$.

22 Arrange these in order of size, largest first: $12, -13, 5, 9, -4$.

23 What number lies midway between -4 and 12?

24 What number lies one-third of the way from -10 to 2?

1.5 Factors, multiples and primes

You will remember these definitions from earlier work:

A **multiple** of a number is the result of multiplying it by a whole number.

The multiples of 4 are $4, 8, 12, 16, \ldots$

A **factor** of a number is a whole number that divides exactly into it, with no remainder.

The factors of 12 are $1, 2, 3, 4, 6, 12$.

A **prime** number is a whole number with exactly two factors, namely 1 and itself. The number 1 is not normally considered to be prime, so the prime numbers are $2, 3, 5, 7, 11, \ldots$

If a large number is not prime, it can be written as the product of a set of prime factors in a unique way. For example, 12 can be written as $2 \times 2 \times 3$.

A **factor tree** is a good way of breaking a large number into its prime factors. The next example shows how this is done.

EXAMPLE

Write the number 180 as a product of its prime factors.

SOLUTION

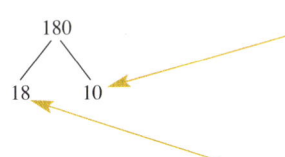

Begin by splitting the 180 into a product of two parts. You could use 2 times 90, or 4 times 45, or 9 times 20, for example. The result at the end will be the same in any case. Here we begin by using 18 times 10.

Since neither 18 nor 10 is a prime number, repeat the factorising process.

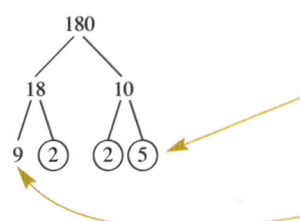

18 has been broken down into 9 times 2, and 10 into 2 times 5. The 2's and the 5 are prime, so they are circled and the tree stops there.

The 9 is not prime, so the process can continue.

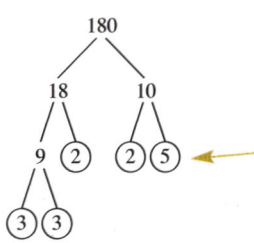

The factor tree stops growing when all the branches end in encircled prime numbers.

Thus $180 = 2 \times 2 \times 3 \times 3 \times 5$
$= 2^2 \times 3^2 \times 5$

2^2 means the factor 2 is used twice (two squared). If it had been used three times, you would write 2^3 (two cubed).

EXERCISE 1.5

1. List all the prime numbers from 1 to 40 inclusive.
   You should find that there are 12 such prime numbers altogether.

2. Use your result from question **1** to help answer these questions:
   a) How many primes are there between 20 and 40 inclusive?
   b) What is the next prime number above 31?
   c) Find two prime numbers that multiply together to make 403.
   d) Write 91 as a product of two prime factors.

3. Use the factor tree method to obtain the prime factorisation of:
   a) 80   b) 90   c) 450

4. Use the factor tree method to obtain the prime factorisation of:
   a) 36   b) 81   c) 144
   What do you notice about all three of your answers?

5. When 56 is written as a product of primes, the result is $2^a \times b$ where a and b are positive integers. Find the values of a and b.

1.6 Highest common factor (HCF)

Consider the numbers 12 and 20. The number 2 is a factor of 12, and 2 is also a factor of 20. Thus 2 is said to be a **common factor** of 12 and 20.

Likewise, the number 4 is also a factor of both 12 and 20, so 4 is also a common factor of 12 and 20.

It turns out that 12 and 20 have no common factor larger than this, so 4 is said to be the **highest common factor (HCF)** of 12 and 20. You can check that 4 really is the highest common factor by writing 12 as 4×3 and 20 as 4×5; the 3 and 5 clearly share no further factors.

EXAMPLE

Find the highest common factor (HCF) of 30 and 80.

SOLUTION

By inspection, it looks as if the highest common factor may well be 10.

Check: $30 = 10 \times 3$, and $80 = 10 \times 8$

and clearly 3 and 8 have no further factor in common.
 So HCF of 30 and 80 is 10

> By inspection means that you can just spot the answer by eye, without any formal working.

There is an alternative, more formal, method for finding highest common factors. It requires the use of **prime factorisation**.

EXAMPLE

Use prime factorisation to find the highest common factor of 30 and 80.

SOLUTION

By the factor tree method: $30 = 2 \times 3 \times 5$

Similarly, $80 = 2^4 \times 5$

So HCF of 30 and 80 $= 2 \times 5$
$ = 10$

> Look at the 2's: 30 has one of them, 80 has four. Pick the lower number: one 2
>
> Look at the 3's: 30 has one of them, but 80 has none. Pick the lower number: no 3's
>
> Look at the 5's: 30 has one of them, and 80 has one. Pick the lower number: one 5

The prime factorisation method involves a lot of steps, but it is particularly effective when working with larger numbers, as in this next example.

EXAMPLE

Use prime factorisation to find the highest common factor of 96 and 156.

SOLUTION

By the factor tree method: $96 = 2^5 \times 3$
 and $156 = 2^2 \times 3 \times 13$

HCF of 96 and 156 $= 2^2 \times 3$
$ = 4 \times 3$
$ = 12$

It is important to practise the prime factorisation method and master it, because some GCSE examination questions will ask you to use this method. If the question allows you to use any method, then you might like to try this ingenious alternative approach. A Greek mathematician named Euclid used it 3500 years ago, so it is often known as **Euclid's method**.

EXAMPLE

Use Euclid's method to find the HCF of 96 and 156.

SOLUTION

[96, 156] → [60, 96] → [36, 60] → [24, 36] → [12, 24] → [12, 12]

> Begin by writing the two numbers in a square bracket.

> Each new bracket contains the smaller of the two numbers, and their difference.

> Stop when both numbers are equal.

So HCF (96, 156) = 12

EXERCISE 1.6

1 Use the method of inspection to write down the highest common factor of each pair of numbers. Check your result in each case.
   a) 12 and 18
   b) 45 and 60
   c) 22 and 33
   d) 27 and 45
   e) 8 and 27
   f) 26 and 130

2 Write each of the following numbers as the product of prime factors. Hence find the highest common factor of each pair of numbers.
   a) 20 and 32
   b) 36 and 60
   c) 80 and 180
   d) 72 and 108
   e) 120 and 195
   f) 144 and 360

3 Use Euclid's method to find the highest common factor of each pair of numbers.
   a) 12 and 30
   b) 24 and 36
   c) 96 and 120
   d) 90 and 140
   e) 78 and 102
   f) 48 and 70

1.7 Lowest common multiple (LCM)

Consider the numbers 15 and 20.

The multiples of 15 are 15, 30, 45, 60, 75,...

The multiples of 20 are 20, 40, 60, 80,...

Any multiple that occurs in both lists is called a **common multiple**.

The lowest of these is the **lowest common multiple (LCM)**. In this example, the LCM is 60.

There are several methods for finding lowest common multiples. As with highest common factors, one of these methods is based on prime factorisation.

EXAMPLE

Find the lowest common multiple of 48 and 180.

SOLUTION

First, obtain the prime factorisations, using a factor tree if necessary.

$48 = 2^4 \times 3$
$180 = 2^2 \times 3^2 \times 5$

Look at the powers of 2:

$48 = 2^4 \times 3$
$180 = 2^2 \times 3^2 \times 5$

> There are 4 factors of 2 in 48, but only 2 in 180. Pick the higher of these: 4

Next, the powers of 3:

$48 = 2^4 \times 3$
$180 = 2^2 \times 3^2 \times 5$

> There is 1 factor of 3 in 48, but 2 in 180. Pick the higher of these: 2

Finally, the powers of 5:

$48 = 2^4 \times 3$
$180 = 2^2 \times 3^2 \times 5$

> There is no factor of 5 in 48, but 1 in 180. Pick the higher of these: 1

Putting all of this together:

$$\begin{aligned} \text{LCM of 48 and 180} &= 2^4 \times 3^2 \times 5 \\ &= 16 \times 9 \times 5 \\ &= 144 \times 5 \\ &= \underline{720} \end{aligned}$$

An alternative method is based on the fact that the product of the LCM and the HCF is the same as the product of the two original numbers. This gives the following result:

$$\text{LCM of } a \text{ and } b = \frac{a \times b}{\text{HCF of } a \text{ and } b}$$

This can be quite a quick method if the HCF is easy to spot.

EXAMPLE

Find the lowest common multiple of 70 and 110.

SOLUTION

By inspection, HCF is 10
So:

$$\begin{aligned} \text{LCM} &= \frac{70 \times 110}{10} \\ &= 7 \times 110 \\ &= \underline{770} \end{aligned}$$

It is also possible to find the HCF and LCM of three (or more) numbers. The prime factorisation method remains valid here, but other shortcut methods can fail. This example shows you how to adapt the factorisation method when there are three numbers.

EXAMPLE

Find the HCF and LCM of 16, 24 and 28.

SOLUTION

Write these as products of prime factors:
$16 = 2^4$
$24 = 2^3 \times 3$
$28 = 2^2 \times 7$
HCF of 16, 24 and 28 is $2^2 = \underline{4}$
LCM of 16, 24 and 28 is $2^4 \times 3 \times 7 = 16 \times 21 = \underline{336}$

The lowest number of 2's from 2^4 or 2^3 or 2^2 is 2^2

The highest number of 2's from 2^4 or 2^3 or 2^2 is 2^4

EXERCISE 1.7

Find the lowest common multiple (LCM) of each of these pairs of numbers. You may use whichever method you prefer.

1 12 and 20
2 16 and 26
3 18 and 45
4 25 and 40
5 36 and 48
6 6 and 20
7 14 and 22
8 30 and 50
9 36 and 60
10 44 and 55
11 16 and 36
12 28 and 42
13 18 and 20
14 14 and 30
15 27 and 36
16 33 and 55

17 a) Write 60 and 84 as products of their prime factors.
    b) Hence find the LCM of 60 and 84.

18 a) Write 66 and 99 as products of their prime factors.
    b) Hence find the LCM of 66 and 99.
    c) Find also the HCF of 66 and 99.

19 a) Write 10, 36 and 56 as products of their prime factors.
    b) Work out the highest common factor of 10, 36 and 56.
    c) Work out the lowest common multiple of 10, 36 and 56.

20 a) Write 40, 48 and 600 as products of their prime factors.
    b) Work out the highest common factor of 40, 48 and 600.
    c) Work out the lowest common multiple of 40, 48 and 600.

21 Virginia has two friends who regularly go round to her house to play. Joan goes round once every 4 days and India goes round once every 5 days. How often are both friends at Virginia's house together?

22 Eddie owns three motorcycles. He cleans the Harley once every 8 days, the Honda once every 10 days and the Kawasaki once every 15 days. Today he cleaned all three motorcycles. When will he next clean all three motorcycles on the same day?

REVIEW EXERCISE 1

Work out the answers to these arithmetic problems, using mental methods. Written working not allowed!

1 $315 + 198$
2 $467 - 99$
3 $17 + 88 + 83$
4 $455 + 379 + 145$
5 $1005 - 997$
6 43×11
7 599×3
8 $396 \div 4$
9 $456 \div 12$
10 $53 \times 7 + 53 \times 3$

Use pencil and paper methods (not a calculator) to work out the answers to these arithmetic problems.

11 $866 + 372$
12 $946 - 268$
13 124×7
14 144×23
15 44×77
16 651×37
17 $2484 \div 9$
18 $6812 \div 13$
19 $7854 \div 21$
20 $1000 \div 16$

Work out the answers to these problems using negative numbers. Do not use a calculator.

21 $(-7) + (-14)$
22 $6 - (-3)$
23 $(-10) - (-13)$
24 $12 + {-9}$
25 $13 - {-6}$
26 -5×-8
27 $-144 \div 16$
28 $256 \div (-8)$
29 -7×-4
30 $(-3)^3$

31 Use a factor tree to find the prime factorisation of:
   a) 70
   b) 124
   c) 96
   d) 240

32 a) Find the highest common factor of 24 and 56.
   b) Find the lowest common multiple of 24 and 56.

33 a) Write down the highest common factor of 20 and 22.
   b) Hence find the lowest common multiple of 20 and 22.

34 a) Write 360 in the form $2^a \times 3^b \times 5^c$
   b) Write $2^4 \times 3^2 \times 5$ as an ordinary number.

35 Who is right? Explain carefully.

If the HCF of two numbers is 1, then they must both be primes.

Not necessarily true.

Chuck   Lilian

36 Pens cost 25p each. Mr Smith spends £120 on pens.
Work out the number of pens he gets for £120. [Edexcel]

37 The number 1104 can be written as $3 \times 2^c \times d$, where c is a whole number and d is a prime number.
Work out the value of c and the value of d. [Edexcel]

38 a) Express 72 and 96 as products of their prime factors.
b) Use your answer to part a) to work out the highest common factor of 72 and 96. [Edexcel]

KEY POINTS

1. Mental methods can be used for simple arithmetic problems. When adding up strings of whole numbers, look for combinations that add up to multiples of 10.

2. Harder addition and subtraction problems require formal pencil and paper methods. Make sure that you know how to perform these accurately.

3. Simple multiplication problems may be done mentally or by short multiplication. For harder problems, you need to be able to perform long multiplication reliably. If you find the traditional columns method awkward, consider using the rectangular box method instead — both methods are acceptable to the GCSE examiner.

4. Long division is probably the hardest arithmetic process you will need to master. The traditional columns method is probably the best method — there are modern alternatives, but they can be clumsy to use. If you have a long division by 23, say, then it may be helpful to write out the multiples 23, 46, 69, ..., 230 before you start.

5. Exam questions may require you to manipulate and order negative numbers. Remember to treat the 'two minuses make a plus' rule with care; for example, $-2 \times -3 = 6$, but $-2 + -3 = -5$.

6. Non-prime whole numbers may be written as a product of primes, using the factor tree method. This leads to a powerful method of working out the highest common factor or lowest common multiple of two numbers.

7. Sometimes you may be able to spot HCFs or LCMs by inspection. This result might help you to check them:

$$\text{LCM of } a \text{ and } b = \frac{a \times b}{\text{HCF of } a \text{ and } b}$$

Internet Challenge 1

Prime time

Here are some questions about prime numbers. You may use the internet to help you research some of the answers.

1. Find a list of all the prime numbers between 1 and 100, and print it out. How many prime numbers are there between 1 and 100?

2. Find a list of all the prime numbers between 1 and 1000. How many prime numbers are there between 1 and 1000?

Compare your answers to questions **1** and **2**. Does it appear that prime numbers occur less often as you go up to larger numbers?

3. Why is 1 not normally considered to be prime?

4. How many Prime Ministers has the UK had? Is this a prime number?

5. Is there an infinite number of prime numbers?

6. What is the largest known prime number?

7. Is there a formula for finding prime numbers?

8. Where is the Prime Meridian?

9. Find out how the Sieve of Eratosthenes works, and use it to make your own list of all the primes up to 100. Check your list by comparing it with the list you found in question **1**.

10. Some primes occur in adjacent pairs, which are consecutive odd integers, for example, 11 and 13, or 29 and 31. Find some higher examples of adjacent prime pairs. How many such pairs are there?

CHAPTER 2

Fractions and decimals

In this chapter you will **revise earlier work on**:

- equivalent fractions
- adding and subtracting decimals
- changing fractions to decimals and vice versa
- rounding and approximation.

You will **learn how to**:

- multiply and divide using decimals
- order a list of fractions and decimals
- change recurring decimals into exact fractions.

You will also be **challenged to**:

- practise and extend your fraction vocabulary.

Starter: Half and half

Here are some puzzles on the theme of a half.

1 A climbing plant grows 50 cm in week 1. Each following week it grows half as much as it grew the week before. How tall will the plant become if it grows for ever?

2 What fraction is a half of a half of a half?

3 Shade half the squares to divide the shape into two symmetrical halves.

4 Two people wish to share a cake equally. They have a knife with which to cut it. How can they divide the cake so that each person is happy that he has at least half?

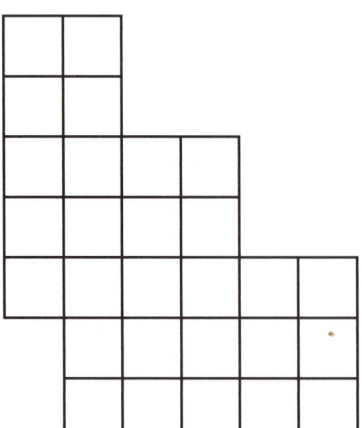

2.1 Equivalent fractions

You should already have met fraction diagrams like these:

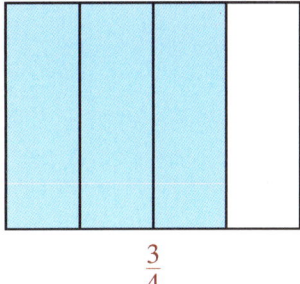
$\frac{3}{4}$

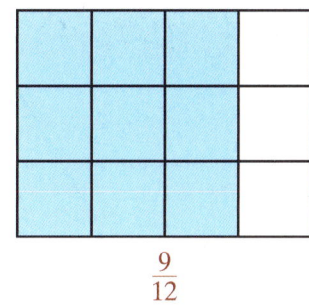
$\frac{9}{12}$

The diagram on the left shows 3 shaded parts out of 4, and the one on the right shows 9 shaded parts out of 12. Clearly, both diagrams indicate the same shaded proportion of the large rectangle. Thus you can conclude that $\frac{3}{4}$ and $\frac{9}{12}$ are identical in value.

Fractions with identical values are called **equivalent fractions**.
It is easy to create a pair of equivalent fractions – you simply multiply (or divide) the top (numerator) and bottom (denominator) of a given fraction by the same number:

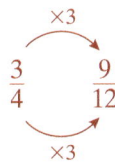

It is often helpful to apply this procedure in reverse:

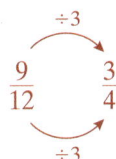

This process is known as **cancelling down**. When a fraction has been cancelled as fully as possible, it is said to be written in its **simplest terms**.

EXAMPLE

Cancel down the following fractions into their simplest terms.

a) $\dfrac{6}{10}$ b) $\dfrac{18}{54}$ c) $\dfrac{144}{360}$

SOLUTION

a) $\dfrac{6}{10} = \dfrac{3}{5}$ ← 6 and 10 are both even, so divide each of them by 2.

b) $\dfrac{18}{54} = \dfrac{\cancel{18}^{9}}{\cancel{54}_{27}}$ ← You can cancel 18 and 54 by dividing by 2…

$= \dfrac{\cancel{9}^{1}}{\cancel{27}_{3}}$ ← …but 9 and 27 are still both divisible by 9…

$= \dfrac{1}{3}$ ← …so cancel again.

c) $\dfrac{144}{360} = \dfrac{\cancel{144}^{12}}{\cancel{360}_{30}}$

$= \dfrac{\cancel{12}^{6}}{\cancel{30}_{15}}$

$= \dfrac{\cancel{6}^{2}}{\cancel{15}_{5}}$

$= \dfrac{2}{5}$ ← Always continue the cancelling procedure until there are no common factors remaining.

Equivalent fractions are a helpful tool when wanting to compare the sizes of fractions written with different denominators, as in the next example.

EXAMPLE

Arrange these fractions in order of size, smallest first.

$\dfrac{3}{5}, \dfrac{1}{4}, \dfrac{7}{10}, \dfrac{1}{2}$

SOLUTION

Rewriting the fractions with denominator 20, we have:

$\dfrac{12}{20}, \dfrac{5}{20}, \dfrac{14}{20}, \dfrac{10}{20}$ ← Examine the denominators. 5, 4, 10 and 2 all divide into 20.

So, in increasing order, the fractions are:

$\dfrac{5}{20}, \dfrac{10}{20}, \dfrac{12}{20}, \dfrac{14}{20}$

Restoring them to fractions in their lowest terms, the required order is:

$\dfrac{1}{4}, \dfrac{1}{2}, \dfrac{3}{5}, \dfrac{7}{10}$

EXERCISE 2.1

Write these fractions in their simplest terms.

1. $\frac{9}{36}$ 2. $\frac{15}{35}$ 3. $\frac{8}{82}$ 4. $\frac{13}{52}$ 5. $\frac{11}{55}$ 6. $\frac{42}{56}$

7. $\frac{24}{40}$ 8. $\frac{12}{20}$ 9. $\frac{8}{14}$ 10. $\frac{9}{15}$ 11. $\frac{49}{91}$ 12. $\frac{35}{45}$

Arrange these fractions in order of size, smallest first.

13. $\frac{11}{20}, \frac{1}{2}, \frac{3}{5}, \frac{5}{8}$ 14. $\frac{2}{3}, \frac{7}{8}, \frac{5}{6}, \frac{3}{4}$ 15. $\frac{13}{15}, \frac{5}{6}, \frac{2}{3}, \frac{4}{5}$

2.2 Arithmetic with decimals

You will already have met the idea of addition or subtraction with decimals. You simply line the numbers up at the decimal point, and then use the same methods that work for integers.

Multiplication is a little more difficult. A good method is to remove the decimal points temporarily, and use ordinary long multiplication to obtain the correct digits. Then insert the decimal point into the answer, using either estimation or a formal method to make sure it is in the right place.

EXAMPLE

Work out 14.2×2.4.

SOLUTION

Removing the decimal point, we have 142×24
Ordinary long multiplication gives:

```
      1 4 2
    ×   2 4
      5 6 8
    2 8 4 0
    3 4 0 8
```

The original problem contained two digits in total after the decimal points.
The answer must have the same number.

> You could use estimation instead:
> 14.2×2.4 is approximately $14 \times 2 = 28$, so 34.08 must be the correct decimal placement.

Thus the answer is 34.08

EXAMPLE

Work out 0.0035×0.02.

> Estimation is not so easy here, so the formal method of counting digits after the decimal point is probably simpler.

SOLUTION

Removing the decimal point, we have:

$$35 \times 2 = 70$$

The original problem contained six digits in total after the decimal points; so there must be six digits in the answer.
Thus the answer is:

0.000 070

That is: 0.000 07

For division, you can also remove the decimal point, and then replace it using the estimation method. Another approach is illustrated in the next example.

EXAMPLE

Work out $29.472 \div 1.6$.

SOLUTION

Multiplying both numbers by 10:

$$29.472 \div 1.6 = 294.72 \div 16$$

> Making both numbers 10 times bigger does not change the answer to the resulting division….
>
> …but it does now mean you are dividing by a whole number.

```
        .
16 ) 294.72
```

```
       18.42
16 ) 294.72
     16
     ---
     134
     128
     ---
      67
      64
      --
      32
```

> Put the decimal point here, to line up with the decimal point in the number underneath…
>
> …then carry out the long division in the normal way.

> As a final check, $29.472 \div 1.6$ is roughly $30 \div 2 = 15$, which looks consistent with 18.42

Answer: $29.472 \div 1.6 = \underline{18.42}$

Some examination questions may give you the numerical answer to a calculation using integers, then ask you to adapt it when decimals are involved.

EXAMPLE

Using the result that $1586 \times 13 = 20\,618$, obtain the values of:
a) 15.86×1.3 b) 0.1586×0.13 c) $206.18 \div 0.013$

SOLUTION

a) $15.86 \times 1.3 = \underline{20.618}$
b) $0.1586 \times 0.13 = \underline{0.020\,618}$
c) $206.18 \div 0.013$ is the same as:
$$\frac{206.18}{0.013} = \frac{206\,180}{13}$$
$$= \frac{20\,618}{13} \times 10$$
$$= 1586 \times 10$$
$$= \underline{15\,860}$$

Parts **a)** and **b)** may be done just by counting the digits after the decimal points.

For **c)**, multiply the top and bottom by 1000 to clear away the decimal points – this makes it easier to see what to do next.

EXERCISE 2.2

Work out the answers to these calculations without a calculator.

1 14.2×3
2 16.8×1.2
3 1.37×1.4
4 1.2×1.5
5 13.6×2.8
6 1.4×0.8
7 156×0.2
8 0.2×0.3
9 $61.12 \div 8$
10 $1.758 \div 8$
11 $25.6 \div 1.6$
12 $0.21 \div 0.7$
13 $17.16 \div 1.1$
14 $0.912 \div 1.2$
15 $33.88 \div 2.2$
16 $142.4 \div 0.32$

17 Given that $624 \times 23 = 14\,352$, work out the values of:
   a) 6.24×2.3 b) 62.4×23 c) 6240×230

18 Given that $144 \times 12 = 1728$, work out the values of:
   a) 1.44×1.2 b) 1440×0.12 c) $17.28 \div 1.2$

19 Given that $365 \times 24 = 8760$, work out the values of:
   a) 3.65×0.24 b) 36.5×2.4 c) $8.76 \div 36.5$

20 Given that $9022 \div 26 = 347$, work out the values of:
   a) $9.022 \div 26$ b) $9022 \div 0.26$ c) 3470×260

2.3 Decimals and fractions

There are three types of decimal numbers.

Terminating decimals stop after a finite number of decimal places. 0.32 is an example of a terminating decimal. Terminating decimals can be written as exact fractions.

Recurring decimals do not stop after a finite number of decimal places, but they do settle into a pattern of digits that repeats indefinitely.

0.316 316 316 316 316 316... is an example of a recurring decimal. It would normally be written as $0.\dot{3}1\dot{6}$, with a dot over the start and finish of the repeating pattern. Recurring decimals can be written as exact fractions.

Other decimals neither stop nor recur; 0.101 001 000 100 001... is an example of such a decimal. These decimals cannot be expressed as exact fractions, so they are called **irrational** numbers (that is, non-fractional). The number π is irrational.

EXAMPLE

Express 0.32 as an exact fraction. Give your answer in its lowest terms.

SOLUTION

0.32 means $\dfrac{32}{100}$

$= \dfrac{16}{50}$

$= \dfrac{8}{25}$

> 32 and 100 are both divisible by 2, to give 16 and 50 ... and they are divisible by 2 again, to give 8 and 25.

EXAMPLE

Express $0.\dot{4}$ as an exact fraction.

SOLUTION

Let $x = 0.\dot{4}$

Multiply both sides by 10:

$10x = 4.\dot{4}$

Write these results one below the other, and subtract:

$10x = 4.\dot{4}$
$x = 0.\dot{4}$
$9x = 4$

> Make sure you line up the decimal points. When you do the subtraction, the recurring decimals should disappear.

Divide both sides by 9:

$x = \dfrac{4}{9}$

You may need to multiply both sides by 100, or 1000, if the pattern of repeating digits is of length 2, or 3. Choose the right multiplier so that the digits move left by one full pattern.

EXAMPLE

Express $2.\dot{3}9\dot{6}$ as an exact mixed number. Give your answer in its lowest terms.

SOLUTION

> Since there are three figures in the recurring pattern, use a multiplier of $10 \times 10 \times 10 = 1000$

First, detach the whole number, 2, and consider the decimal part, 396

Let $x = 0.\dot{3}9\dot{6}$

Multiply by a power of 10 large enough to move all the digits along by one pattern, which in this case would be $\times 1000$.

Then $1000x = \dot{3}9\dot{6}$

Writing these results one below the other, and subtracting:

$$\begin{aligned} 1000x &= 396.\dot{3}9\dot{6} \\ x &= 0.\dot{3}9\dot{6} \\ \hline 999x &= 396 \end{aligned}$$

Thus

$$x = \frac{396}{999}$$
$$= \frac{132}{333}$$
$$= \frac{44}{111}$$

Finally, restore the whole number part, of 2, so $2.\dot{3}9\dot{6} = \underline{2\frac{44}{111}}$

When you convert a fraction into a decimal, the answer will be either a terminating decimal or a recurring decimal.

EXAMPLE

Write $\frac{1}{8}$ as an exact decimal.

SOLUTION

$$\begin{array}{r} 0.125 \\ 8\overline{)1.000} \\ \underline{8} \\ 20 \\ \underline{16} \\ 40 \\ \underline{0} \end{array}$$

> The remainder of 0 here tells you that the decimal has terminated.

So $\frac{1}{8} = \underline{0.125}$

EXAMPLE

Write $\frac{1}{7}$ as a recurring decimal.

SOLUTION

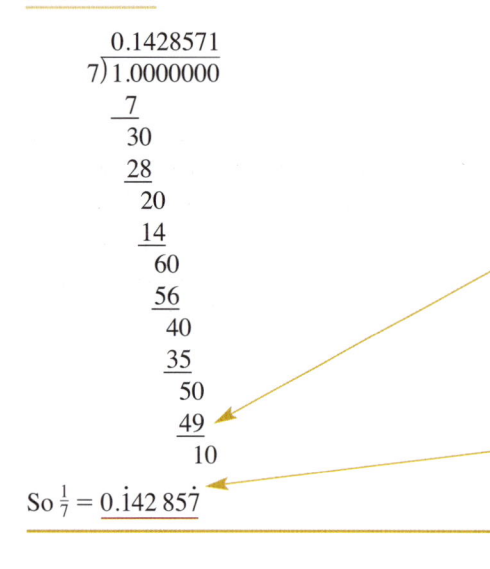

$$
\begin{array}{r}
0.1428571 \\
7{\overline{\smash{\big)}\,1.0000000}} \\
\underline{7} \\
30 \\
\underline{28} \\
20 \\
\underline{14} \\
60 \\
\underline{56} \\
40 \\
\underline{35} \\
50 \\
\underline{49} \\
10
\end{array}
$$

At this stage you are dividing 7 into 10 again, so the same pattern of remainders develops. This means the decimal will recur.

So $\frac{1}{7} = 0.\dot{1}42\,85\dot{7}$

Place a dot above the first and last digits of the repeating pattern.

EXERCISE 2.3

Write these terminating decimals as exact fractions. Give each answer in its lowest terms.

1 0.24   **2** 0.72   **3** 0.3   **4** 0.625

5 0.91   **6** 0.025   **7** 1.94   **8** 0.38

9 2.125   **10** 0.303

Write these recurring decimals as exact fractions, in their lowest terms. Show your method clearly.

11 $0.\dot{7}$ **12** $0.2\dot{9}$ **13** $1.\dot{3}$ **14** $0.5\dot{2}0\dot{4}$

15 $0.\dot{4}\dot{3}$ **16** $0.5\dot{4}$ **17** $0.3\dot{2}\dot{1}$ **18** $1.3\dot{4}\dot{2}$

Write these fractions as decimals.

19 $\frac{5}{8}$ **20** $\frac{3}{7}$ **21** $\frac{4}{9}$ **22** $\frac{9}{20}$

23 Which is larger: $0.\dot{2}\dot{7}$ or 0.28?

24 Andy says, '$0.\dot{7}$ is exactly twice as big as $0.\dot{3}\dot{5}$.' Is Andy right or is he wrong? Explain your answer carefully.

2.4 Rounding and approximation

Whole numbers are sometimes **rounded** to the nearest 10, 100 or 1000. For example, if the population of a small village is exactly 2721, it might make sense to round this to 2720 (nearest 10) or even 2700 (nearest 100).

EXAMPLE

a) Round 3474 to the nearest 10

b) Round 8483 to the nearest 100

SOLUTION

a) 3474 = 3470 to the nearest 10

b) 8483 = 8500 to the nearest 100

'To the nearest 10' means we must choose between 3470 and 3480. 3470 is nearest.

'To the nearest 100' means we we must choose between 8400 and 8500. 8500 is nearest.

When quantities are written using decimals, it is often sensible to round them to a certain number of figures. Rounding may be described using either **decimal places** (d.p.) or **significant figures** (s.f.).

EXAMPLE

Round these numbers to 3 decimal places:
a) 14.2573 **b)** 0.0258 **c)** 0.14962

SOLUTION

a) 14.2573 = 14.257 | 3 = 14.257 (3 d.p.)

b) 0.0258 = 0.025 | 8 = 0.026 (3 d.p.)

c) 0.149 62 = 0.149 | 62 = 0.150 (3 d.p.)

Make the cut after three decimal places. The first digit after the cut, 3, is *less than 5*, so round *down*.

When the first digit after the cut is *5 or more*, then round *up*. Here it is 8, so the 0.025 rounds up to 0.026

Rounding to a certain number of significant figures can be confusing. The best way is to look at the number from the left-hand direction, and pick out the first non-zero digit – this is the first significant figure. Then count the significant figures across to the right.

The confusing thing is whether 0's should be counted as 'significant'. These illustrations show some different cases you might encounter:

Number	Comment	Significant figures
24 000	The 2 and the 4 are significant figures, telling you that the number contains 2 lots of 10 000 and 4 lots of 1000. The three zeros are not significant figures; they merely act as placeholders. This number has 2 significant figures.	**24** 000
305 000	The first zero is a significant figure, because it is embedded between the 3 and 5. The other zeros are placeholders only. This number has 3 significant figures.	**305** 000
0.000 27	The first significant figure is the 2. The previous zeros merely show you which decimal column the 2 goes in to (they are placeholders). So this number has 2 significant figures.	0.000 **27**
0.014 03	Plainly the 1, 4 and 3 are significant figures. The 0 among them also is, but the other zeros are not. This number contains 4 significant figures.	0.0**1403**
0.250	Watch out! You might think only the 2 and the 5 are significant. The final zero, however, has no role as a placeholder – instead, it tells you that this number contains 0 thousandths. This means it is a significant figure, so this one has 3 significant figures.	**0.250**

EXAMPLE

Round these numbers to the indicated number of significant figures.
a) 156 230 (2 s.f.)   b) 0.0896 (2 s.f.)   c) 10.09 (3 s.f.)

SOLUTION

a) 156 230 = 15|6230 = 160 000 (2 s.f.)
b) 0.0896 = 0.089|6 = 0.090 (2 s.f.)
c) 10.09 = 10.0|9 = 10.1 (3 s.f.)

Rounding is also used in a slightly different way to establish **upper** and **lower bounds** for calculations. The next example illustrates a straightforward case. You will meet some harder examples in Chapter 23 on page 398.

EXAMPLE

A rectangular sports field measures 21 metres wide by 83 metres long; each dimension is measured correct to the nearest metre.
a) Write down the smallest value that the width of the sports field could be.
b) Work out the smallest possible perimeter for the field.
c) Calculate the maximum possible value for the area of the field.
    State your answer correct to 3 significant figures.

SOLUTION

a) 21 metres to the nearest metre means the width lies between 20.5 and 21.5 metres.
Thus the smallest possible width is 20.5 metres.

b) Smallest perimeter = 20.5 + 82.5 + 20.5 + 82.5
= 206 metres

c) The maximum possible area is computed using a rectangle 21.5 metres by 83.5 metres.
Area = 21.5 × 83.5
= 1795.25 square metres
= 1800 square metres (3 s.f.)

Note that it would not be right to use, say, 21.49 × 83.49, because these numbers are too low, so you have no choice but to use 21.5 × 83.5, even though these numbers would not round to 21 and 83. In effect you are establishing a kind of upper limit, called an upper bound, which the true area of the field cannot actually quite attain. This is quite an advanced concept, and is addressed again in Chapter 23.

EXERCISE 2.4

Round these whole numbers to the indicated level of accuracy.

1 1732 (to the nearest 10)

2 12 399 (to the nearest 100)

3 7621 (to the nearest 1000)

4 878 (to the nearest 10)

5 15 249 (to the nearest 100)

Round the following decimal numbers to the indicated number of decimal places.

6 3.141 59 (3 d.p.)   **7** 3.141 59 (4 d.p.)   **8** 16.237 (1 d.p.)

9 0.2357 (2 d.p.)   **10** 14.08 (1 d.p.)   **11** 14.80 (1 d.p.)

12 6.224 02 (4 d.p.)   **13** 1.895 (2 d.p.)

Round the following to the specified number of significant figures.

14 15.42 (3 s.f.)   **15** 15.42 (1 s.f.)   **16** 14.257 (3 s.f.)

17 359 262 (4 s.f.)   **18** 365.249 (2 s.f.)   **19** 9.8 (1 s.f.)

20 0.002 07 (2 s.f.)   **21** 10.99 (3 s.f.)

22 An equilateral triangle measures 12 cm along each side, to the nearest cm. Work out the smallest possible perimeter it could have.

23 A square measures 146 mm along each side, to the nearest mm. Work out the largest possible area it could have, giving your answer correct to 3 significant figures.

24 Last week, the number attending City's home soccer game was 25 000, correct to the nearest thousand. The week before it was 24 400, correct to the nearest hundred. Is it possible that the same number of people attended both weeks? Explain your answer.

25 In a museum there is a dinosaur bone. This notice is attached:

> **This bone came from a dinosaur that was born 75 000 000 years ago.**
> **The dinosaur lived for 20 years.**

Charlie says, 'That means the dinosaur died 74 999 980 years ago.' Is Charlie right?

REVIEW EXERCISE 2

Write each of these fractions in its lowest terms.

1 $\frac{14}{16}$ **2** $\frac{14}{21}$ **3** $\frac{5}{25}$ **4** $\frac{16}{20}$

5 $\frac{18}{20}$ **6** $\frac{50}{70}$ **7** $\frac{84}{96}$ **8** $\frac{44}{50}$

9 Arrange these fractions in order of size, smallest first.
$\frac{5}{8}, \frac{3}{4}, \frac{5}{6}, \frac{7}{12}$

10 Arrange these fractions in order of size, smallest first.
$\frac{11}{15}, \frac{7}{10}, \frac{2}{3}, \frac{3}{5}$

Work out the answers to these decimal calculations.

11 16.8 × 4   **12** 1.25 × 6   **13** 0.015 × 30   **14** 0.4 × 0.6

15 16.4 × 2.5   **16** 0.8 × 1.31   **17** 19.4 ÷ 4   **18** 13.2 ÷ 0.3

19 13.5 ÷ 2.5   **20** 5.76 ÷ 1.2

21 Arrange these numbers in order of size, smallest first.
$\frac{3}{4}$, 0.65, $\frac{5}{8}$, $0.\dot{6}$

22 a) Write the decimal 0.875 as a fraction in its lowest terms.
  b) Convert the recurring decimal $0.\dot{4}\dot{5}$ to a fraction in its simplest terms.

23 Write these numbers in order of size. Start with the smallest number.
  a) 0.56, 0.067, 0.6, 0.65, 0.605
  b) 5, −6, −10, 2, −4
  c) $\frac{1}{2}, \frac{2}{3}, \frac{2}{5}, \frac{3}{4}$ [Edexcel]

24 Ann wins £160. She gives $\frac{1}{4}$ of £160 to Pat, $\frac{3}{8}$ of £160 to John and £28 to Peter.
What fraction of the £160 does Ann keep?
Give your answer as a fraction in its simplest form.   [Edexcel]

25 Write down two different fractions that lie between $\frac{1}{4}$ and $\frac{1}{2}$.   [Edexcel]

26 Nick takes 26 boxes out of his van. The weight of each box is 32.9 kg.
Work out the *total* weight of the 26 boxes.   [Edexcel]

27 1.54 × 450 = 693

Use this information to write down the answer to:
  a) 1.54 × 45   b) 1.54 × 4.5   c) 0.154 × 0.45   [Edexcel]

28 Each side of a regular pentagon has a length of 101 mm, correct to the nearest millimetre.
  a) Write down the *least* possible length of each side.
  b) Write down the *greatest* possible length of each side.   [Edexcel]

29 Using the information that: 97 × 123 = 11 931

write down the value of:
  a) 9.7 × 12.3
  b) 0.97 × 123 000
  c) 11.931 ÷ 9.7   [Edexcel]

30 Convert the recurring decimal $0.2\dot{\dot{9}}$ to a fraction.   [Edexcel]

31 Change to a single fraction:
  a) the recurring decimal $0.\dot{1}\dot{3}$
  b) the recurring decimal $0.5\dot{1}\dot{3}$ [Edexcel]

32 a) Convert the recurring decimal $0.\dot{3}\dot{6}$ to a fraction.
  b) Convert the recurring decimal $2.1\dot{3}\dot{6}$ to a mixed number.
     Give your answer in its simplest form.   [Edexcel]

33 Express the recurring decimal $2.0\dot{6}$ as a fraction.
Write your answer as a fraction in its simplest form.   [Edexcel]

34 a) Express $0.\dot{2}\dot{7}$ as a fraction in its simplest form.
  b) x is an integer such that $1 \leq x \leq 9$. Prove that $0.0\dot{x} = \dfrac{x}{99}$ [Edexcel]

KEY POINTS

1. Fractions such as $\frac{2}{3}$ and $\frac{4}{6}$ are called equivalent fractions, because they have the same values. If you have to sort a list of fractions into numerical order it can be helpful to re-write them as equivalent fractions with a common denominator.

2. To multiply two decimals, remove the decimal points and carry out a normal integer multiplication. Then restore the decimal point, using either a formal method or estimation.

3. To divide one decimal by another, begin by multiplying both numbers by 10, or 100, or 1000, until the number you are dividing by has become a whole number (integer).

4. You will often need to convert terminating or recurring decimals into fraction form.

5. Terminating decimals may easily be expressed as fractions with denominator 10, 100, 1000, etc. and are then cancelled down where possible.

6. Recurring decimals are more awkward. Make sure you have studied the multiply/subtract method that reduces them to fractions with denominator 9, 99, 999, etc. Once again, cancel down at the end where possible.

7. Calculations involving decimals often require rounding to a sensible number of decimal places or significant figures. Make sure you understand how to do this. Significant figures, in particular, can sometimes be a little awkward to count.

Internet Challenge 2

Fraction vocabulary

Find the answer to each clue. You can use the internet and the list of 12 answers (in no particular order) given at the foot of the page.

1 A fraction in which the top number is larger than the bottom number, sometimes also called a top-heavy fraction. $\frac{11}{4}$ is an example of one.

2 A number made up by combining a whole number and a simple fraction. $3\frac{1}{2}$ is an example of one.

3 The top number of a simple fraction.

4 The bottom number of a simple fraction.

5 Two fractions with the same value, such as $\frac{1}{4}$ and $\frac{5}{20}$.

6 Fractions in which the top number is always 1, sometimes called unit fractions.

7 A slanting line used to separate the two parts of a simple fraction, for example in 3/4.

8 A horizontal line used to separate the two parts of a simple fraction, for example in $\frac{3}{4}$.

9 The result of interchanging the top and bottom numbers of a simple fraction.

10 A phrase describing a fraction that is written using the smallest possible numbers.

11 Another name for fractional numbers.

12 The process of simplifying a fraction by dividing a common factor into the top and bottom numbers.

CANCELLING	DENOMINATOR	EGYPTIAN FRACTIONS
EQUIVALENT FRACTIONS	IMPROPER FRACTION	VINCULUM
MIXED FRACTION	NUMERATOR	RATIONAL NUMBERS
RECIPROCAL	IN ITS SIMPLEST TERMS	SOLIDUS

CHAPTER 3

Percentages

In this chapter you will **revise earlier work on how to**:
- convert fractions to percentages and vice versa.

You will **learn how to**:
- find a percentage of an amount.

You will also be **challenged to**:
- investigate some percentages.

Starter: How many per cent?

Look at the hexagonal honeycomb shape below.
How many different paths can you find that spell PERCENT?
The paths must be continuous.
You could use a counting method, but a calculating method is more likely to be accurate.

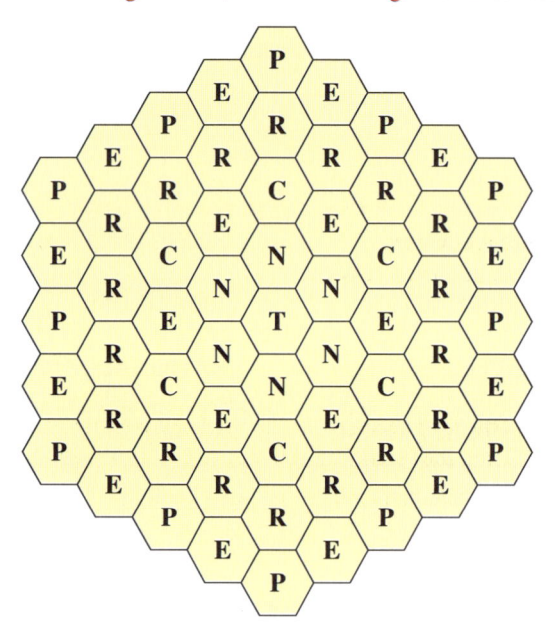

3.1 Simple percentages

A **percentage** simply means a number of parts per 100. For example, 15% means 15 parts per 100. You can convert percentages into simple fractions by writing them as fractions out of 100.

EXAMPLE

Write 45% as a fraction in its lowest terms.

SOLUTION

45% means 45 out of 100, so, as a fraction:

$$45\% = \frac{\cancel{45}^{9}}{\cancel{100}^{20}} = \frac{9}{20}$$

This example reminds you how to find a percentage of an amount.

EXAMPLE

Write $\frac{4}{5}$ as a percentage.

SOLUTION

Using equivalent fractions, write $\frac{4}{5} = \frac{?}{100}$

5 needs to be multiplied by 20 to make 100

4 multiplied by 20 is 80

So $\frac{4}{5} = \frac{80}{100}$

So $\frac{4}{5}$ is $\underline{80\%}$

Sometimes you need to convert fractions into percentages.

EXAMPLE

A local factory employs 1200 people. 720 of these are women.
a) What fraction are women? Give your answer in its lowest terms.
b) Write your answer to part a) as a percentage.

SOLUTION

a) As a fraction:

$$\frac{720}{1200} = \frac{72}{120}$$
$$= \frac{6}{10}$$
$$= \frac{3}{5}$$

> You can check this by entering $\frac{720}{1200}$ into your calculator, using the fraction key.
>
> The calculator will automatically cancel the fraction down.

Thus $\frac{3}{5}$ of the employees are women.

b) Using equivalent fractions, $\frac{3}{5} = \frac{6}{10} = \frac{60}{100}$
So $\underline{60\%}$ are women.

EXERCISE 3.1

Write these percentages as fractions, in their lowest terms.

1 40% **2** 36% **3** 5% **4** 30%
5 33% **6** $33\frac{1}{3}$% **7** $12\frac{1}{2}$% **8** $\frac{1}{2}$%

Express these fractions as percentages.

9 $\frac{3}{4}$ **10** $\frac{2}{5}$ **11** $\frac{3}{10}$ **12** $\frac{17}{20}$
13 $\frac{21}{25}$ **14** $\frac{19}{20}$ **15** $\frac{7}{8}$ **16** $\frac{3}{40}$

17 Arrange these quantities in order of size, smallest first.
   $0.7, 66\%, \frac{2}{3}, 0.67, \frac{5}{7}, 69\%$

18 An examination is out of 250 marks.
   a) Sonja scores 210 marks. What percentage is this?
   b) Peter scores 62%. How many marks out of 250 did he receive?

   The marks are then converted to a UMS (uniform mark system) score. The UMS marks are out of a total of 600.

   c) Callum scores 426 UMS marks. What percentage of 600 is this?

19 Ashley has just taken two mathematics test papers. In Arithmetic he scored 56 out of 80, while in Algebra he scored 64 out of 90. His friends are talking about the results.

> You did *much better* in the Algebra test.

Ami

> You did *about the same* in both tests.

Marcus

Use percentage calculations to explain who is right.

20 Naomi buys 8 CDs at a car boot sale. She pays £2.50 for each one. She sells them on the internet for a total of £24. Work out Naomi's percentage profit.

3.2 Finding a percentage of an amount

An easy way to find a percentage of an amount is to work out 1% first. Then multiply up to find the required percentage.

EXAMPLE

Find 24% of 350

SOLUTION

First find 1% (by dividing by 100):
1% is 350 ÷ 100 = 3.5
Now find 24%:
24% = 3.5 × 24 = <u>84</u>

EXERCISE 3.2

1 Find 8% of 600

2 Find 30% of 240

3 Find 12% of 300

4 Find 28% of 1600

5 Find 65% of £320

6 Find 7% of $900

7 Find 98% of 250 kg

8 Find 44% of 350 metres

9 Minnie scored 64% in a mathematics test. The test was out of 75 marks. How many marks did Minnie score?

10 In a school there are 350 boys and 450 girls. 60% of the boys travel to school by bus. 72% of the girls travel to school by bus.
   a) Work out the number of boys who travel by bus.
   b) Work out the total number of boys and girls who travel by bus.

REVIEW EXERCISE 3

Solve these problems without using a calculator. Show your working clearly.

1 Write 85% as a fraction in its lowest terms.

2 Write $\frac{7}{20}$ as a percentage.

3 Work out 15% of 360°.

4 Alan scores 38 out of 40 in a mathematics test. What percentage is this?

5 Write $\frac{13}{25}$ as a percentage.

6 Write 24% as a fraction in its lowest terms.

7 Clive has to walk 40 km on a two day mountain hike. He walks 16 km on the first day.
   a) How far must Clive walk on the second day?
   b) What percentage of the total distance must Clive walk on the second day?

8 Eddie is buying a new car. The cost of the car is £8500. Eddie has to pay a 20% deposit. Work out the size of Eddie's deposit.

9 A school has 975 students. 351 of them are in the sixth form.
   a) What fraction of the students are in the sixth form? Give your answer in its lowest terms.
   b) What percentage of the students are in the sixth form?

10 A customer who cancels a holiday with Funtours has to pay a cancellation charge. The cancellation charge depends on the number of days before the departure date the customer cancels the holiday.

The cancellation charge is a percentage of the cost of the holiday.
The table shows the percentages.

The cost of Amy's holiday was £840.
She cancelled her holiday 25 days before the departure date.

Number of days before the departure date the customer cancels the holiday	Cancellation charge as a percentage of the cost of the holiday
29–55	40%
22–28	60%
15–21	80%
4–14	90%
3 or less	100%

a) Work out the cancellation charge she had to pay.

The cost of Carol's holiday was £600. She cancelled her holiday and had to pay a cancellation charge of £480.

b) Work out £480 as a percentage of £600.

Ravi cancelled his holiday 30 days before the departure date. He had to pay a cancellation charge of £272.

c) Work out the cost of his holiday.

[Edexcel]

KEY POINTS

1 Percentages may be thought of as fractions out of 100.

2 To convert a percentage to a fraction, simply write the given percentage over a denominator of 100, then cancel down if appropriate.

3 To convert a fraction into a percentage, rewrite the given fraction as an equivalent fraction with denominator 100. The numerator then tells you the value of the percentage.

4 To find a percentage of a given amount, first work out 1% by dividing the original amount by 100. Then to find, for example 14%, multiply the 1% figure by 14.

Internet Challenge 3

What percentage . . .

1 ... of the Earth's surface is land?

2 ... of an iceberg lurks underwater?

3 ... of the Sun's mass is helium?

4 ... of the Earth's atmosphere is nitrogen?

5 ... of genius is inspiration, according to Edison?

6 ... is UK higher rate income tax charged at?

7 ... of gold is found in 18 carat jewellery?

8 ... of the Earth's water is in the oceans?

9 ... of the UK population is female?

10 ... of the Moon's surface is visible from the Earth?

Here are the answers (in order of size) to these questions.

1%   25%   30%   40%   51%   59%   75%   79%   90%   97%

Use the internet to help you match each question with its correct answer.

CHAPTER 4

Powers, roots and reciprocals

In this chapter you will **learn how to**:
- work with simple powers and roots using mental methods
- use a calculator to compute harder powers and roots
- work with fractional and negative powers, and reciprocals
- use the laws of indices to simplify numerical expressions
- write large and small numbers using standard form
- calculate using standard form.

You will also be **challenged to**:
- investigate astronomical numbers.

Starter: Roman numerals

The Romans used letters for numbers.

I = 1
V = 5
X = 10
L = 50
C = 100
D = 500
M = 1000

To add two letters, write the smaller one after the larger one. For example, VI = 5 + 1 = 6. To subtract two letters, write the smaller one before the larger one. For example, XL = 50 − 10 = 40.

Task 1
Turn these Roman numbers into ordinary numbers.
a) XVII
b) XIV
c) XLV
d) LXX
e) XCII
f) DCIX

Task 2
Write these ordinary numbers as Roman numerals.
a) 21
b) 24
c) 39
d) 212
e) 319
f) 47

Task 3
Film makers often use Roman numerals in their credits. *Star Wars* was originally released in MDCCCCLXXVII. *The Lion King* was released in MDCCCCXCIV. Write these two years as ordinary numbers.

4.1 Basic powers and roots

When a number is multiplied by itself, the result is called the **square** of the original number. For example, 5 squared is $5 \times 5 = 25$.

Reversing this process gives the **square root**. The square root of 25 is 5. This can be written using the $\sqrt{}$ symbol as $\sqrt{25} = 5$.

In a sense, 25 has two different square roots, because -5 times -5 also makes 25, so you might say that -5 is another square root of 25. To distinguish between these two cases, we say that 5 is the **positive square root** of 25 and -5 is the **negative square root** of 25.

When a number is multiplied by itself and then by itself again, the result is called the **cube** of the original number. For example, 5 cubed is $5 \times 5 \times 5 = 125$.

Reversing this process gives the **cube root**. The cube root of 125 is 5. This can be written using the $\sqrt[3]{}$ symbol as $\sqrt[3]{125} = 5$. (There is no negative cube root for 125.)

The GCSE examiner will expect you to know the squares and cubes of some basic whole numbers, and to recognise the corresponding square roots and cube roots. Here are the squares you should learn.

$2^2 = 4$ $7^2 = 49$ $12^2 = 144$
$3^2 = 9$ $8^2 = 64$ $13^2 = 169$
$4^2 = 16$ $9^2 = 81$ $14^2 = 196$
$5^2 = 25$ $10^2 = 100$ $15^2 = 225$
$6^2 = 36$ $11^2 = 121$

You should also learn these cubes:

$2^3 = 8$ $4^3 = 64$ $10^3 = 1000$
$3^3 = 27$ $5^3 = 125$

The squares, cubes, square roots and cube roots of other numbers will normally be found using a calculator. Make sure that you know how to use the keys for this on your calculator; most calculators use similar keys but their locations on the keypad vary between different models.

EXAMPLE

Without using a calculator, obtain the values of:
a) 13^2 **b)** 5^3 **c)** $\sqrt{121}$ **d)** $\sqrt[3]{27}$

SOLUTION

a) $13^2 = \underline{169}$
b) $5^3 = \underline{125}$
c) $\sqrt{121} = \underline{11}$
d) $\sqrt[3]{27} = \underline{3}$

> Make sure that you have learnt the basic squares and cubes so you can spot these answers by eye.

EXAMPLE

Fred is answering an algebra problem. He has worked out that $x^2 = 81$. Give two possible values of x that would complete Fred's answer.

SOLUTION

$x^2 = 81$

So $x = \sqrt{81}$ or $-\sqrt{81}$
$= 9$ or -9

You will meet this idea again later in the book, when you are working with quadratic equations.

EXAMPLE

Use your calculator to work out the values of:
a) 9.4^2 b) 2.5^3 c) $\sqrt{109}$ d) $\sqrt[3]{44.8}$

Round your answer to a sensible level of accuracy where appropriate.

SOLUTION

a) $9.4^2 = 88.36$

b) $2.5^3 = 15.625$

c) $\sqrt{109} = 10.440\,306\,51$
$= 10.44$ (4 s.f.)

d) $\sqrt[3]{44.8} = 3.551\,616\,007$
$= 3.552$ (4 s.f.)

a) and b) are calculated using the x^2 and x^3 keys on a calculator. No rounding is needed.

c) and d) are calculated using the $\sqrt{}$ and $\sqrt[3]{}$ keys on a calculator. The calculator generates a full screen of decimals.

A good exam habit is to show your full calculator result… …as well as the rounded answer.

EXERCISE 4.1

Find the values of the following, without using a calculator.

1 5^2
2 2^3
3 7^2
4 3^3

5 9^2
6 4^3
7 12^2
8 10^3

9 $\sqrt{144}$
10 $\sqrt{225}$
11 $\sqrt[3]{64}$
12 $\sqrt{36}$

13 $\sqrt{196}$
14 $\sqrt[3]{125}$
15 $\sqrt{81}$
16 $\sqrt[3]{1000}$

Use your calculator to work out the values of the following expressions. Round your answers to 3 significant figures where appropriate.

17 19^2
18 1.8^2
19 14.6^2
20 9^3

21 16.3^3
22 1.2^3
23 $\sqrt{13}$
24 $\sqrt{300}$

25 $\sqrt[3]{24}$
26 $\sqrt[3]{50}$
27 $\sqrt{2.5}$
28 $\sqrt[3]{6.8}$

29 Find x if $x^2 = 72$. Give your answers to 3 s.f.

30 Find y if $y^3 = 38$. Give your answer to 4 s.f.

4.2 Higher powers and roots

Although squares and cubes occur frequently in mathematics, other (higher) whole number powers and roots may also be used. The notation x^n represents n factors of x multiplied together so, for example, 6^4 means $6 \times 6 \times 6 \times 6 = 1296$.

Similarly, higher roots may be obtained too, using this idea in reverse.
The 5th root of 32 is 2, because $2 \times 2 \times 2 \times 2 \times 2 = 32$.
Roots are denoted using fractional powers, so you would write this as $32^{\frac{1}{5}} = 2$.
The notation $x^{\frac{1}{n}}$ represents the nth root of x.

As with basic powers, you will solve simple problems by sight, but may use a calculator for harder ones. Make sure that you know how to use your calculator's power and root keys.

EXAMPLE

Without using a calculator, obtain the values of:
a) 7^3 **b)** 2^8 **c)** $81^{\frac{1}{4}}$ **d)** $125^{\frac{1}{3}}$

SOLUTION

a) $7^3 = 7 \times 7 \times 7$
$= 49 \times 7$
$= \underline{343}$

b) $2^8 = 2 \times 2 \times 2 \times 2 \times 2 \times 2 \times 2 \times 2$
$= 4 \times 4 \times 4 \times 4$
$= 16 \times 16$
$= \underline{256}$

c) Since $3 \times 3 \times 3 \times 3 = 81$,
$$81^{\frac{1}{4}} = \underline{3}$$

d) Since $5 \times 5 \times 5 = 125$,
$$125^{\frac{1}{3}} = \underline{5}$$

EXAMPLE

Use your calculator to obtain the values of:
a) 14^4 **b)** 1.5^6 **c)** $1045^{\frac{1}{4}}$ **d)** $125^{\frac{1}{6}}$
Round your answers to 3 significant figures where appropriate.

SOLUTION

a) $14^4 = 38\,416$

b) $1.5^6 = 11.390\,625$
   $= 11.4$ (3 s.f.)

c) $1045^{\frac{1}{4}} = 5.685\,636\,266$
   $= 5.69$ (3 s.f.)

   Remember to show the full calculator values as well as your final rounded answer.

d) $125^{\frac{1}{6}} = 2.236\,067\,977$
   $= 2.24$ (3 s.f.)

EXERCISE 4.2

Without using a calculator, find the exact values of:

1. 3^4
2. 100^3
3. $216^{\frac{1}{3}}$
4. 10^4
5. 9^3
6. 2^5
7. $32^{\frac{1}{5}}$
8. 2^{10}
9. $1000^{\frac{1}{3}}$
10. $400^{\frac{1}{2}}$
11. 12^3
12. $16^{\frac{1}{4}}$

Use your calculator to find the value of each expression. Round your answers as indicated.

13. 12^5 (3 s.f.)
14. 9.8^4 (4 s.f.)
15. 1.3^7 (3 d.p.)
16. 0.95^4 (4 d.p.)
17. $6^{\frac{1}{3}}$ (4 s.f.)
18. $12^{\frac{1}{4}}$ (3 s.f.)
19. $6.3^{\frac{1}{5}}$ (3 d.p.)
20. $41.6^{\frac{1}{3}}$ (3 s.f.)

4.3 Fractional (rational) indices

Some expressions contain fractional indices, for example $8^{\frac{2}{3}}$. These require two processes to be applied together – you need to raise to a power, and also apply a root.

The top of the fraction tells you what power to apply – squaring in this case.

The bottom of the fraction tells you what root to apply – cube root in this case.

EXAMPLE

Find the value of $8^{\frac{2}{3}}$, without using a calculator.

SOLUTION

Method 1

$8^{\frac{2}{3}}$ = 8 squared and then cube rooted
   = 64 cube rooted
   = 4

Method 2

$8^{\frac{2}{3}}$ = 8 cube rooted and then squared
= 2 squared
= <u>4</u>

Notice that the order of the two processes did not affect the final result. Method 2 is probably more efficient, because the intermediate numbers you are working with are smaller.

EXERCISE 4.3

Without using a calculator, write the following expressions as simply as possible.

1. $4^{\frac{3}{2}}$
2. $27^{\frac{2}{3}}$
3. $25^{\frac{3}{2}}$
4. $9^{\frac{5}{2}}$
5. $36^{\frac{3}{2}}$
6. $64^{\frac{3}{2}}$
7. $64^{\frac{2}{3}}$
8. $100^{\frac{5}{2}}$
9. $81^{\frac{3}{4}}$
10. $125^{\frac{4}{3}}$
11. $16^{\frac{3}{2}}$
12. $16^{\frac{3}{4}}$

4.4 Negative powers and reciprocals

So far you have used *positive* powers: for example 10^3 tells you to *multiply* by 10, then by 10 again, and then by 10 again, so $10^3 = 1000$.

Negative powers are also used for numerical expression. For example, 10^{-3} tells you to *divide* by 10, then by 10 again, and then by 10 again, so $10^{-3} = 1/1000$.

Here is a general rule for negative powers:

$$x^{-n} = \frac{1}{x^n}$$

(This rule may be used as long as x is not zero; if x is zero then $\frac{1}{x^n}$ is not defined.)

EXAMPLE

Work out the values of:
a) 2^{-3}
b) 10^{-4}
c) 6^{-2}

SOLUTION

a) $2^{-3} = \frac{1}{2^3}$

$= \frac{1}{2 \times 2 \times 2}$

$= \underline{\frac{1}{8}}$

b) $10^{-4} = \dfrac{1}{10^4}$

$= \dfrac{1}{10 \times 10 \times 10 \times 10}$

$= \dfrac{1}{10\,000}$

c) $6^{-2} = \dfrac{1}{6^2}$

$= \dfrac{1}{6 \times 6}$

$= \dfrac{1}{36}$

The **reciprocal** of a whole number is 1 divided by that number. For example, the reciprocal of 2 is $\tfrac{1}{2}$, and the reciprocal of 4 is $\tfrac{1}{4}$.

Using power notation, reciprocals are indicated by a power of -1. So $2^{-1} = \tfrac{1}{2}$, and $4^{-1} = \tfrac{1}{4}$.

EXAMPLE

Work out the values of:
a) 8^{-1}　　　　　　**b)** 25^{-1}　　　　　　**c)** 3^{-1}

SOLUTION

a) $8^{-1} = \tfrac{1}{8}$ (or 0.125)

b) $25^{-1} = \tfrac{1}{25}$ (or 0.04)

c) $3^{-1} = \tfrac{1}{3}$

> Fractions are usually preferable to decimals in this type of question, since they are exact; decimals might not be.

> Note that $\tfrac{1}{3}$ does not have an exact terminating decimal form, so this answer is best given as a fraction.

Fractions, too, have reciprocals. To find the reciprocal of a fraction, simply interchange the top and bottom of the fraction.

To raise a fraction to a negative power, use the equivalent positive power and then interchange the top and bottom.

EXAMPLE

Work out the values of:
a) $\left(\dfrac{2}{3}\right)^{-1}$　　　　**b)** $\left(\dfrac{5}{7}\right)^{-2}$　　　　**c)** $\left(\dfrac{16}{25}\right)^{-\frac{1}{2}}$

SOLUTION

a) $\left(\dfrac{2}{3}\right)^{-1} = \dfrac{3}{2}$

b) $\left(\dfrac{5}{7}\right)^{-2} = \left(\dfrac{7}{5}\right)^2$

$= \dfrac{7^2}{5^2}$

$= \dfrac{49}{25}$

c) $\left(\dfrac{16}{25}\right)^{-\frac{1}{2}} = \left(\dfrac{25}{16}\right)^{\frac{1}{2}}$

$= \dfrac{25^{\frac{1}{2}}}{16^{\frac{1}{2}}}$

$= \dfrac{5}{4}$

EXERCISE 4.4

Work out the values of these, leaving your answers as exact fractions.

1. 3^{-2}
2. 10^{-3}
3. 5^{-2}
4. 4^{-1}
5. 9^{-2}
6. 4^{-2}
7. 2^{-5}
8. 10^{-1}
9. 5^{-1}
10. 20^{-2}

Evaluate these expressions, giving your answers as exact fractions.

11. $\left(\dfrac{3}{5}\right)^{-1}$
12. $\left(\dfrac{4}{3}\right)^{-1}$
13. $\left(\dfrac{25}{4}\right)^{-\frac{1}{2}}$
14. $\left(\dfrac{4}{5}\right)^{-2}$
15. $\left(\dfrac{2}{3}\right)^{-3}$
16. $\left(\dfrac{1}{2}\right)^{-1}$
17. $\left(\dfrac{9}{64}\right)^{-\frac{1}{2}}$
18. $\left(\dfrac{5}{3}\right)^{-2}$
19. $\left(\dfrac{100}{49}\right)^{-\frac{3}{2}}$
20. $\left(\dfrac{27}{64}\right)^{-\frac{2}{3}}$

4.5 The laws of indices

Another name for a power is an **index**, so powers are often called **indices**.
There are several laws of indices that can help you to simplify index problems.

EXAMPLE

Write $10^3 \times 10^5$ as a single power of 10.

SOLUTION

$10^3 = 10 \times 10 \times 10$

and $\quad 10^5 = 10 \times 10 \times 10 \times 10 \times 10$

so $\quad 10^3 \times 10^5 = (10 \times 10 \times 10) \times (10 \times 10 \times 10 \times 10 \times 10)$
$= 10 \times 10 \times 10 \times 10 \times 10 \times 10 \times 10 \times 10$
$= \underline{10^8}$

You could have solved this example much more efficiently just by adding the indices to give the final result: $10^3 \times 10^5 = 10^{3+5} = 10^8$.

EXAMPLE

Write $2^9 \div 2^6$ as a single power of 2.

SOLUTION

$2^9 = 2 \times 2 \times 2 \times 2 \times 2 \times 2 \times 2 \times 2 \times 2$

and $\quad 2^6 = 2 \times 2 \times 2 \times 2 \times 2 \times 2$

so $\quad 2^9 \div 2^6 = \dfrac{2 \times 2 \times 2 \times 2 \times 2 \times 2 \times 2 \times 2 \times 2}{2 \times 2 \times 2 \times 2 \times 2 \times 2}$

$= \dfrac{\cancel{2}^1 \times \cancel{2}^1 \times \cancel{2}^1 \times \cancel{2}^1 \times \cancel{2}^1 \times \cancel{2}^1 \times 2 \times 2 \times 2}{\cancel{2}^1 \times \cancel{2}^1 \times \cancel{2}^1 \times \cancel{2}^1 \times \cancel{2}^1 \times \cancel{2}^1}$

$= \dfrac{2 \times 2 \times 2}{1}$

$= \underline{2^3}$

Once again, there is a more efficient method. You could have just subtracted the indices to give the final result: $2^9 \div 2^6 = 2^{9-6} = 2^3$.

EXAMPLE

Write $(5^4)^2$ as a single power of 5.

SOLUTION

$5^4 = 5 \times 5 \times 5 \times 5$
so $\quad (5^4)^2 = (5 \times 5 \times 5 \times 5) \times (5 \times 5 \times 5 \times 5)$
$= 5 \times 5 \times 5 \times 5 \times 5 \times 5 \times 5 \times 5$
$= \underline{5^8}$

Again, it would be quicker to multiply the indices to give the final result: $(5^4)^2 = 5^{4 \times 2} = 5^8$.

The three examples above illustrate three general laws of indices, which may be expressed symbolically like this:

$x^a \times x^b = x^{a+b}$ when *multiplying*, *add* the indices
$x^a \div x^b = x^{a-b}$ when *dividing*, *subtract* the indices
$(x^a)^b = x^{ab}$ when *raising to a power*, *multiply* the indices.

You should look for opportunities to use these rules whenever you are simplifying numerical expressions involving indices.

The laws of indices allow you to assign a meaning to a power 0, such as 7^0. For example, using the laws of indices, $7^5 \div 7^5 = 7^{5-5} = 7^0$, but since $7^5 \div 7^5 = 1$ the value of 7^0 must be 1. More generally, $x^0 = 1$, for any value of x (provided x is not 0). Do not confuse this with x^1, which is just x.

This is loosely stated in words as 'anything to the power zero equals 1'. This rule covers all cases except 0^0, which is not defined to have a value. To summarise:

$x^1 = x$
$x^0 = 1$ provided x is not 0
0^0 is not defined.

EXAMPLE

Use the laws of indices to write these expressions as simply as possible.
a) $8^3 \times 8^4$ **b)** $5^{10} \div 5^8$ **c)** $(4^3)^2$ **d)** 8^0

SOLUTION

a) $8^3 \times 8^4 = 8^{3+4}$
              $= \underline{8^7}$

b) $5^{10} \div 5^8 = 5^{10-8}$
               $= \underline{5^2}$

c) $(4^3)^2 = 4^{3 \times 2}$
            $= \underline{4^6}$

d) $8^0 = \underline{1}$

> Although you can do each of these in your head, it is good discipline to write down the steps of the simplification as shown here.
>
> This helps you to master the laws of indices, and also lets your teacher follow your reasoning clearly.

EXERCISE 4.5

Simplify each of these expressions, giving your answer as a number to a single power.

1 $2^3 \times 2^4$ **2** $5^4 \times 5^3$ **3** $8^2 \times 8^7$ **4** $6^5 \div 6^2$

5 $9^4 \div 9^3$ **6** $3^{10} \div 3^9$ **7** $(2^3)^4$ **8** $(3^2)^3$

9 $3^2 \times 3^0$ **10** $2^{\frac{1}{2}} \times 2^{\frac{1}{2}}$ **11** $3^5 \times 3^3$ **12** 6×2^0

Work out each of these, giving your answer as an ordinary number.

13 $2^3 \times 2^2$ **14** $3^6 \div 3^5$ **15** $10^3 \times 10^3$ **16** $4^8 \div 4^6$

17 $(2^2)^3$ **18** $3^2 \times 3^3$ **19** $2^3 \times 2$ **20** $7^6 \div 7^4$

21 $3^{12} \div 3^9$ **22** $(3^0)^4$ **23** $(10^2)^3$ **24** $(5^2)^0$

4.6 Standard index form

Standard index form, or **standard form** as it is often called, is a very convenient way of writing very large or very small quantities. You start with a number between 1 and 10, and multiply (or divide) by a suitable number of powers of 10. For example, the number 3 000 000 could be written as 3×10^6, meaning that the 3 has to be multiplied by six powers of 10.

EXAMPLE

Write these numbers in standard form.
a) 4 000 000 000 b) 36 000 c) 14 300 000

SOLUTION

a) $4\,000\,000\,000 = 4 \times 10^9$
b) $36\,000 = 3.6 \times 10^4$ ← Note that 36×10^3 would not be right here, because 36 does not lie between 1 and 10.
c) $14\,300\,000 = 1.43 \times 10^7$

For numbers smaller than 1 you divide by powers of 10, instead of multiplying. This gives rise to a negative index of 10, instead of a positive one.

EXAMPLE

Write these numbers in standard form.
a) 0.0006 b) 0.000 000 25 c) 0.000 000 000 001 8

SOLUTION

a) $0.0006 = 6 \times 10^{-4}$
b) $0.000\,000\,205 = 2.05 \times 10^{-7}$
c) $0.000\,000\,000\,001\,8 = 1.8 \times 10^{-12}$

Count the number of hops needed to restore the 2.05 to the original number:
0.0000002.05
There are 7 altogether.

Remember that numbers in standard form *always* have the decimal point after the first non-zero digit.

EXERCISE 4.6

Write these numbers in standard index form.

1. 350 000
2. 40 000
3. 352 000 000
4. 19 300 000
5. 765
6. 0.0045
7. 0.8
8. 0.002 03
9. 0.000 000 000 827
10. 0.000 33

Write these as ordinary numbers.

11. 7.4×10^6
12. 2.15×10^7
13. 1.05×10^5
14. 2×10^9
15. 8.4×10^3
16. 5×10^{-3}
17. 2.5×10^{-6}
18. 1.004×10^{-7}
19. 8.3×10^{-11}
20. 5.05×10^{-4}

4.7 Calculating with numbers in standard form

In order to add or subtract two numbers in standard form, you have to make sure that the digits line up in their correct place values. You can do this either by converting them into ordinary numbers, or adjusting them so they both have the same power of 10. This latter method means that your working contains index numbers that are not 'standard', but this does not matter provided the final answer is expressed correctly.

EXAMPLE

Add together 4.2×10^4 and 7.3×10^5. Write your answer in standard form.

SOLUTION

Method 1
$4.2 \times 10^4 = 42\,000$ and $7.3 \times 10^5 = 730\,000$

so $\quad 4.2 \times 10^4 + 7.3 \times 10^5 = 42\,000 + 730\,000$
$\qquad\qquad\qquad\qquad\qquad = 772\,000$
$\qquad\qquad\qquad\qquad\qquad = \underline{7.72 \times 10^5}$

Method 2
Write both numbers using the lower power (10^4):

$7.3 \times 10^5 = 73 \times 10^4$

Thus $4.2 \times 10^4 + 7.3 \times 10^5 = 4.2 \times 10^4 + 73 \times 10^4$
$\qquad\qquad\qquad\qquad\qquad = 77.2 \times 10^4$
$\qquad\qquad\qquad\qquad\qquad = \underline{7.72 \times 10^5}$

Standard form numbers lend themselves to multiplication or division quite readily.

EXAMPLE

Multiply 3×10^5 and 2.5×10^7.

SOLUTION

$$3 \times 10^5 \text{ and } 2.5 \times 10^7 = 3 \times 2.5 \times 10^5 \times 10^7$$
$$= 7.5 \times 10^{5+7}$$
$$= \underline{7.5 \times 10^{12}}$$

> Multiply the two number parts, and multiply the two power terms.

Sometimes the final answer is not in standard index form, however, and needs a little adjustment.

EXAMPLE

Work out $(4 \times 10^8) \div (5 \times 10^2)$.

SOLUTION

$$(4 \times 10^8) \div (5 \times 10^2) = (4 \div 5) \times (10^8 \div 10^2)$$
$$= 0.8 \times 10^6$$
$$= 8.0 \times 10^{-1} \times 10^6$$
$$= \underline{8 \times 10^5}$$

> Divide the two number parts, and divide the two power terms.

> Note the adjustment into standard form here.

The GCSE examination requires you to know how to multiply and divide simple standard form numbers, using the methods in the examples above. For harder problems, a calculator may be appropriate.

A good calculator will allow you to type in the numbers using standard form. Some older models require the use of an $\boxed{\text{EXP}}$ key to do this, but on the latest models you will find a $\boxed{\times 10^x}$ key that allows a more natural entry notation. Make sure you know how your calculator works!

EXAMPLE

If $a = 3.55 \times 10^8$ and $b = 2.065 \times 10^9$ use your calculator to work out the values of each of these expressions. Give your answer in standard form, correct to 3 significant figures.

a) ab b) $\dfrac{a}{b}$ c) $\sqrt{a + 2b}$

SOLUTION

a) $ab = 3.55 \times 10^8 \times 2.065 \times 10^9$
$= 7.330\,75 \times 10^{17}$
$= \underline{7.33 \times 10^{17}}$ (3 s.f.)

b) $\dfrac{a}{b} = (3.55 \times 10^8) \div (2.065 \times 10^9)$
   $= 0.171\,912\,8329$
   $= \underline{1.72 \times 10^{-1}}$ (3 s.f.)

c) $a + 2b = 3.55 \times 10^8 + 2 \times (2.065 \times 10^9)$
   $= 4\,485\,000\,000$

   Thus $\sqrt{a + 2b} = \sqrt{4\,485\,000\,000}$
   $= 66\,970.1426$
   $= 67\,000$ (3 s.f.)
   $= \underline{6.70 \times 10^4}$ (3 s.f.)

> First work out just $a + 2b$…
> …then square root it.

EXERCISE 4.7

Work out the answers to these calculations without using a calculator.

Give your answers in standard form.

1. $(4 \times 10^6) + (7 \times 10^8)$
2. $(2.4 \times 10^5) + (1.8 \times 10^6)$
3. $(7 \times 10^7) - (5 \times 10^5)$
4. $(3 \times 10^5) - (8 \times 10^4)$
5. $(1.2 \times 10^{10}) \times (5 \times 10^7)$
6. $(7 \times 10^6) \times (6 \times 10^7)$
7. $(4 \times 10^{10}) \div (8 \times 10^7)$
8. $(3 \times 10^6) \div (4 \times 10^{-3})$

9. In the year 2004 a total of 2.17×10^8 passengers passed through UK airports. 6.7×10^7 of these passengers passed through Heathrow Airport. How many of the UK passengers did not pass through Heathrow? Give your answer as an ordinary number.

Use your calculator to evaluate these expressions.

Give your answers in standard form, correct to 3 significant figures.

10. $(2.45 \times 10^7) \div (8.22 \times 10^{11})$
11. $\dfrac{(3.5 \times 10^7) + (4.8 \times 10^9)}{8.4 \times 10^6}$
12. $184\,000 \div 0.0023$
13. $(1.5 \times 10^7)^2$
14. $\dfrac{(1.2 \times 10^6) - (4.8 \times 10^4)}{7 \times 10^{-5}}$
15. $(2.8 \times 10^{10}) \div 0.15$

REVIEW EXERCISE 4

1. Write down the values of:
   a) 5^3
   b) $\sqrt{144}$
   c) 15^2

2. Find the reciprocals of:
   a) 10
   b) $\tfrac{1}{4}$
   c) 2

3. Work out the values of:
   a) 10^{-2}
   b) 4^{-3}
   c) $8^{\frac{2}{3}}$

4. Write each of these using a single power.
   a) $6^3 \times 6^2$
   b) $3^{10} \div 3^7$
   c) $(4^3)^2$

5 Arrange these numbers in order of size, smallest first:
$3.2 \times 10^8, 7.6 \times 10^{-2}, 1.4 \times 10^9, 15\,300$

6 Find the value of $\sqrt{(2 \times 2 \times 3 \times 3 \times 5 \times 5)}$. [Edexcel]

7 Evaluate:
 a) 3^{-2}
 b) $36^{\frac{1}{2}}$
 c) $27^{\frac{2}{3}}$
 d) $\left(\dfrac{16}{81}\right)^{-\frac{3}{4}}$ [Edexcel]

8 Work out:
 a) 4^0
 b) 4^{-2}
 c) $16^{\frac{3}{2}}$ [Edexcel]

9 Work out the values of
 a) $(2^2)^3$
 b) $(\sqrt{3})^2$
 c) $\sqrt{2^4 \times 9}$ [Edexcel]

10 a) Write 84 000 000 in standard form.
 b) Work out:
 $$\dfrac{84\,000\,000}{4 \times 10^{12}}$$
 Give your answer in standard form. [Edexcel]

You may use your calculator for the remaining questions.

11 a) Work out the value of 5^3.
 b) Work out the value of
 (i) $\sqrt{(4.5^2 - 0.5^2)}$
 Write down all the figures on your calculator display.
 (ii) Write your answer correct to 2 decimal places. [Edexcel]

12 Calculate the value of
$$\dfrac{5.98 \times 10^8 + 4.32 \times 10^9}{6.14 \times 10^{-2}}$$
Give your answer in standard form correct to 3 significant figures. [Edexcel]

13 420 000 carrot seeds weigh 1 gram
 a) Write the number 420 000 in standard form.
 b) Calculate the weight, in grams, of one carrot seed.
 Give your answer in standard form, correct to 2 significant figures. [Edexcel]

14 A floppy disk can hold 1 440 000 bytes of data.
 a) Write the number 1 440 000 in standard form.
 A hard disk can hold 2.4×10^9 bytes of data.
 b) Calculate the number of floppy disks needed to store the 2.4×10^9 bytes of data. [Edexcel]

15 $y^2 = \dfrac{ab}{a+b}$
 $a = 3 \times 10^8$
 $b = 2 \times 10^7$
 Find y. Give your answer in standard form correct to 2 significant figures. [Edexcel]

KEY POINTS

1. Powers tell you how many times a number is to be multiplied by itself.
   For example, $2^4 = 2 \times 2 \times 2 \times 2$.
   Powers are also called indices.

2. The reverse of raising to a power is taking a root.
   So, for example, the fourth root of 16 is 2.
   This may be written as $\sqrt[4]{16}$ or $16^{\frac{1}{4}}$.

3. Fractional powers indicate a combination of raising to a power and taking a root.
   The power $\frac{3}{2}$, for example, tells you to cube and also square root the number.

4. n^{-1} indicates the reciprocal of n and takes the value $\frac{1}{n}$.
   The reciprocal of $\frac{a}{b}$ is $\frac{b}{a}$.

5. Negative powers indicate reciprocals, thus $3^{-2} = \frac{1}{3^2}$.

6. There are three key laws of indices:

   $x^a \times x^b = x^{a+b}$ when multiplying, add the indices
   $x^a \div x^b = x^{a-b}$ when dividing, subtract the indices
   $(x^a)^b = x^{ab}$ when raising to a power, multiply the indices.

7. Remember also that:

   $x^1 = x$
   $x^0 = 1$ (provided x is not 0)
   0^0 is not defined.

8. Very large or very small numbers may be written in the form $a \times 10^n$, where n is a whole number and $1 \leq a < 10$.
   This is called standard (index) form.

9. The GCSE examination will expect you to be able to manipulate standard form numbers both with and without a calculator.

Internet Challenge 4

Astronomical numbers

Astronomers work with very large numbers, so they often use standard index form, sometimes alternatively called scientific notation.

Here are some astronomical statements with missing values. The values are given, in jumbled-up order, to the right. Use the internet to help you decide which answer belongs with which statement.

1 Astronomers have calculated that the mass of the Sun is about ☐☐☐☐☐☐ kg.

2 The Sun is thought to have formed about ☐☐☐☐☐☐ years ago.

3 Each second the Sun's mass decreases by about ☐☐☐☐☐☐ tonnes.

4 The surface temperature of the Sun has been measured to be about ☐☐☐☐☐☐ degrees C.

5 It takes our solar system about ☐☐☐☐☐☐ years to make one revolution around the Milky Way galaxy.

6 Light travels through space at a speed of ☐☐☐☐☐☐ metres per second.

7 Visible light has a wavelength of about ☐☐☐☐☐☐ metres.

8 X-rays can have wavelengths as short as ☐☐☐☐☐☐ metres.

9 The Andromeda galaxy is so remote that light from it takes ☐☐☐☐☐☐ years to reach us.

10 It is thought that the Universe contains about ☐☐☐☐☐☐ individual galaxies.

Values:

2.998×10^8

10^{-9}

6×10^3

10^{11}

2×10^{30}

2.25×10^8

4×10^6

2.8×10^6

5×10^9

5.5×10^{-7}

CHAPTER 5

Working with algebra

In this chapter you will **revise and extend earlier work on how to**:

- substitute numbers into formulae and expressions
- work with indices
- expand brackets and collect like terms.

You will **learn how to**:

- factorise algebraic expressions
- add two algebraic fractions
- simplify algebraic fractions by factorising.

You will also be **challenged to**:

- investigate the language of algebra.

Starter: Right or wrong?

Each question is followed by two possible answers. Identify the right one – and explain what slip might have caused the wrong one in each case.

1 3×0	3	or	0
2 $6 - 5 + 1$	0	or	2
3 5^2	10	or	25
4 $2 + 3 \times 4$	20	or	14
5 $4 + 10 \div 2$	9	or	7
6 $(-3)^2$	9	or	-9

5.1 Substituting numbers into formulae and expressions

In this chapter you will be using letters in expressions to stand for mathematical quantities. Sometimes you are told the numerical value of each letter. It is then possible to work out the value of the corresponding expression.

For example, $x + 3$ is an algebraic expression. If x has the value 5 then, clearly, $x + 3$ has the value 8.

Care must be taken when substituting given numbers into more intricate expressions. In particular, be careful with minus signs and squares, cubes, etc. Remember the order of priorities described by BIDMAS – you should work out Brackets first, then Indices (squares, cubes, etc.). Next come Division and Multiplication, together, and finally Addition and Subtraction, also together.

EXAMPLE

If $p = 5$, $q = 2$ and $r = -4$, work out the values of
a) $3p + 4q$ **b)** $2p^2$ **c)** $pq - 5r$

SOLUTION

a) $3p + 4q = 3 \times (5) + 4 \times (2)$ ← Multiply before adding: BID**MA**S
$= 15 + 8$
$= \underline{23}$

b) $2p^2 = 2 \times (5)^2$ ← Indices before multiplying: B**ID**MAS
$= 2 \times 25$
$= \underline{50}$

c) $pq - 5r = (5) \times (2) - 5 \times (-4)$ ← Multiply before subtracting: BID**MA**S
$= 10 - -20$
$= 10 + 20$
$= \underline{30}$

EXAMPLE

If $x = 4$, $y = -1$ and $z = 3$, work out the values of
a) $3(x + 2z)^2$ **b)** $\dfrac{2x + 3y}{z + y}$

SOLUTION

a) $3(x + 2z)^2 = 3 \times (4 + 2 \times 3)^2$ ← Brackets first, then indices, then multiplying: **BID**MAS
$= 3 \times (4 + 6)^2$
$= 3 \times (10)^2$
$= 3 \times 100$
$= \underline{300}$

b) $\dfrac{2x + 3y}{z + y} = \dfrac{2 \times 4 + 3 \times (-1)}{3 + (-1)}$ ← In an algebraic fraction, you should evaluate the top and bottom separately first. Then do the division.
$= \dfrac{8 + -3}{3 + -1}$
$= \dfrac{5}{2}$
$= \underline{2\tfrac{1}{2}}$

Sometimes you need to substitute values into a **formula** rather than an **expression**. The only practical difference is that a formula contains an *equals sign*, so the final numerical answer can tell you the value of another algebraic letter, as in the next example.

EXAMPLE

The distance s travelled by a particle is given by the formula $s = ut + \frac{1}{2}at^2$.
a) Use your calculator to work out the value of s when $a = 9.8$, $t = 3.5$ and $u = 2.4$. Write down all the figures from your calculator display.
b) Round your answer to part a) correct to 2 significant figures.

SOLUTION

a) $s = ut + \frac{1}{2}at^2$
   $= 2.4 \times 3.5 + (1 \div 2) \times 9.8 \times 3.5 \;\boxed{x^2}$
   $= \underline{68.425}$

b) Correct to 2 significant figures, $\underline{s = 68}$

EXERCISE 5.1

If $p = 6$, $q = 5$ and $r = 2$, find the value of:

1 $3p - 2q$ **2** $5pq + 10q$ **3** $r^2 - 3p$ **4** $(2p - 3r)^2$

If $x = 4$, $y = 6$ and $z = -2$, find the value of:

5 $x^2 + z^2$ **6** $3x - z$ **7** $2z - 3y$ **8** $(y - 2z)^2$

If $f = 3$, $g = -1$ and $h = 2$, find the value of:

9 $4f^2$ **10** $5(f + g)$ **11** $f^2 + gh$ **12** $3g^2$

13 The number of bacteria N in a colony is modelled by the formula $N = 2500(1 + kt)$ where t is the time and k is a growth factor.
  a) Find the value of N when $k = 0.3$ and $t = 1.5$.
  b) Write down the number of bacteria at time $t = 0$.

14 The velocity v of a particle is given by the formula $v^2 = u^2 + 2as$.
  a) Find the value of v^2 when $u = 5$, $a = -3$ and $s = 2$.
  b) Find the corresponding value of v, correct to 3 significant figures.

15 The voltage V in an electronic circuit is given by the formula $V = IR$.
  a) Find the exact value of V when $I = 13$ and $R = 20$.
  b) Find the value of R when $V = 240$ and $I = 13$, giving your answer to 3 significant figures.

5.2 Working with indices

Indices are used in algebra as a short notation when a quantity is multiplied by itself repeatedly. In the previous section you used x^2 (said as 'x squared') to mean $x \times x$. In a similar way, x^3 (said as 'x cubed') is a short way of writing $x \times x \times x$. The number 2 or 3 is a power, or index. Sometimes you will meet higher indices too.

EXAMPLE

Simplify:
a) $f \times f \times f$
b) $t \times t \times t \times t$
c) $2 \times m \times m$

SOLUTION

a) $f \times f \times f = \underline{f^3}$
b) $t \times t \times t \times t = \underline{t^4}$
c) $2 \times m \times m = \underline{2m^2}$

You have probably already met the idea of simplifying algebraic expressions using indices, which are powers such as squares or cubes. For example, you may have been asked to simplify $x^2 \times x^3$, or, perhaps, $(y^4)^3$.

The rules for simplifying such expressions are quite straightforward, but they can appear confusing at first, so you should practise in order to be able to apply them confidently and correctly.

Here are the rules for multiplication and division.

Multiplication	Division
$x^a \times x^b = x^{a+b}$	$x^a \div x^b = x^{a-b}$

EXAMPLE

Simplify these expressions:
a) $x^2 \times x^3$
b) $x^7 \div x^3$

SOLUTION

a) $x^2 \times x^3 = x^{2+3}$
$= \underline{x^5}$

b) $x^7 \div x^3 = x^{7-3}$
$= \underline{x^4}$

Sometimes the algebraic terms will have whole-number multiples in front of them – these are known as **coefficients**. If these are present, you simply multiply or divide the coefficients in the usual way, and then multiply or divide the algebraic terms as well.

EXAMPLE

Simplify these expressions:
a) $5x^2 \times 4x^3$
b) $12x^7 \div 4x^3$

SOLUTION

a) $5x^2 \times 4x^3 = 5 \times 4 \times x^{2+3}$
$= 20 \times x^5$
$= \underline{20x^5}$

Multiply the two number coefficients… …and multiply the two pieces of algebra.

b) $12x^7 \div 4x^3 = (12 \div 4) \times x^{7-3}$
$= 3 \times x^4$
$= \underline{3x^4}$

Divide the two number coefficients… …and divide the two pieces of algebra.

Take care with an expression such as $(x^3)^2$ – it does not simplify to x^5. This is because $(x^3)^2$ means x^3 times x^3 which gives x^{3+3}, in other words, x^6. This gives us another rule for indices:

$(x^a)^n = x^{a \times n}$

EXAMPLE

Simplify these expressions:
a) $(x^2)^5$
b) $(2x^3)^4$

SOLUTION

a) $(x^2)^5 = x^{2 \times 5}$
$= \underline{x^{10}}$

b) $(2x^3)^4 = 2^4 \times (x^3)^4$
$= 16 \times x^{12}$
$= \underline{16x^{12}}$

Remember to raise 2 to the power 4… …as well as working out x^3 to the power 4.

EXERCISE 5.2

Write these expressions using indices.

1 $k \times k \times k$

2 $u \times u$

3 $x \times x \times x \times x \times x$

4 $n \times n \times n \times n$

5 $2 \times g \times g$

6 $5 \times t \times t \times t$

Simplify these expressions using the index laws $x^a \times x^b = x^{a+b}$ and $x^a \div x^b = x^{a-b}$.

7 $x^3 \times x^5$

8 $y^{10} \div y^3$

9 $z^4 \times z^3 \times z^2$

10 $2x^3 \times 5x^4$

11 $4x \times 6x^5$

12 $12y^6 \div 6y^3$

13 $4y^2 \times 2y^4$

14 $18z^6 \div 3z$

15 $2x^2 \times 3x^3 \times x^4$

16 $10z^6 \div 20z^4$

Simplify these expressions using the index law $(x^a)^n = x^{a \times n}$.

17 $(x^4)^2$ **18** $(y^2)^3$ **19** $(3z^3)^2$

20 $(4x^5)^2$ **21** $(y^{10})^3$ **22** $(2z^2)^4$

23 $(2x^4)^2$ **24** $(5x^2)^3$ **25** $(4xy)^3$

26 $(6x^2y)^2$

Simplify these expressions.

27 $3x^2 \times 5x^3$ **28** $4y^2 \div 2y$ **29** $(3z^2)^3$

30 $12y^{10} \div 12y^9$ **31** $4x^3 \times 10x^2$ **32** $48x^4 \div 16x$

33 $10x^7 \times 10x^3$ **34** $(x^3y)^2$ **35** $(x^3y^2)^3$

36 $4x^4 \times 3x$

5.3 Expanding brackets

In this section you will learn how to expand and simplify brackets. The instruction 'simplify' tells you to collect together like terms where possible. The next example reminds you how to collect like terms.

EXAMPLE

Simplify
a) $8x + 3y + 5x + 2y$ b) $3x + 2y + 9x - 6y$ c) $5c - 3e - 8c + 4e$

SOLUTION

a) $8x + 3y + 5x + 2y = 8x \qquad + 5x$
$\qquad\qquad\qquad\qquad\qquad + 3y \qquad + 2y$
$\qquad\qquad\qquad\qquad = \underline{13x + 5y}$

b) $3x + 2y + 9x - 6y = 3x \qquad + 9x$
$\qquad\qquad\qquad\qquad\qquad + 2y \qquad - 6y$
$\qquad\qquad\qquad\qquad = \underline{12x - 4y}$

c) $5c - 3e - 8c + 4e = 5c \qquad - 8c$
$\qquad\qquad\qquad\qquad\qquad - 3e \qquad + 4e$
$\qquad\qquad\qquad\qquad = \underline{-3c + e}$

Some algebraic expressions are written with brackets. It may be possible to 'expand' the brackets, which means that you multiply them out and rewrite the result without using brackets.

EXAMPLE

Expand $3(2x + 5)$.

'Expand' means *'clear away the brackets'*.

SOLUTION

$3(2x + 5) = 3 \times (2x) + 3 \times 5$
$= \underline{6x + 15}$

The bracket contains two terms, namely $2x$ and $+5$. Each term gets multiplied by the 3.

Examination questions often require you to do this twice, and then collect like terms to write the result in a neater form. In such a case you will be told to 'expand and simplify', as in the next example.

EXAMPLE

Expand and simplify $4(3x + 7) + 5(x + 2)$.

SOLUTION

First you multiply out the brackets…

$4(3x + 7) + 5(x + 2) = 12x + 28 + 5x + 10$
$= \underline{17x + 38}$

…then collect up $12x + 5x$ to make $17x$… and $+28$ and $+10$ to make $+38$.

Sometimes there are minus signs inside one or more of the brackets.

EXAMPLE

Expand and simplify $4(3x - 7) + 5(2 - x)$.

SOLUTION

Again, multiply out the brackets …

$4(3x - 7) + 5(2 - x) = 12x - 28 + 10 - 5x$
$= \underline{7x - 18}$

… then collect up $12x - 5x$ to make $7x$ … and -28 and $+10$ to make -18.

Watch carefully when there is a minus sign *in front of* one of the brackets, because the multiplication is much more tricky. This is a popular topic with GCSE examiners!

EXAMPLE

Expand and simplify $5(4x + 3) - 2(x + 3)$.

Multiply the terms in the second bracket by -2.

SOLUTION

$5(4x + 3) - 2(x + 3) = 20x + 15 - 2x - 6$
$= \underline{18x + 9}$

Then collect up $20x - 2x$ to make $18x$ … and $+15$ and -6 to make $+9$.

Notice that the minus outside the bracket ends up changing all the signs inside the bracket.

Finally, watch for a double minus multiplying to give a positive term, as in this example.

EXAMPLE

Expand and simplify $2(4x - 1) - 3(x - 2)$.

SOLUTION

$2(4x - 1) - 3(x - 2) = 8x - 2 - 3x + 6$
$ = \underline{5x + 4}$

The -3 multiplies with -2 to give $+6$.

EXERCISE 5.3

In questions **1** to **10** you are to multiply out the brackets and simplify the results. These are straightforward questions, without any awkward sign problems.

1 $2(x + 5) + 5(x + 2)$ **2** $3(2x + 1) + 2(x + 5)$ **3** $4(2x + 5) + 3(x + 3)$

4 $2(x + 5) + 3(2x + 5)$ **5** $10(x + 1) + 6(2x + 1)$ **6** $3(x + 5) + 4(x - 1)$

7 $2(x - 1) + 7(2x + 3)$ **8** $3(x + 2) + 2(2x - 1)$ **9** $5(x + 1) + 4(3x - 1)$

10 $6(3x - 2) + 5(4x + 3)$

In questions **11** to **20**, expand and simplify the result. Take special care when there is a negative number in front of the second bracket.

11 $6(2x - 1) + 3(3x - 1)$ **12** $4(x + 3) - 2(x + 1)$ **13** $6(2x + 1) - 3(3x + 1)$

14 $8(2x - 5) + 5(3x - 2)$ **15** $16(10x - 5) + 5(3x - 2)$ **16** $12(x + 2) - 3(2x + 4)$

17 $5(2x + 5) - 4(x - 2)$ **18** $6(x + 1) - 2(x - 3)$ **19** $7(x - 1) - 2(2x + 1)$

20 $4x + 3(2x - 1) - 5x$

5.4 Multiplying two brackets together

It is possible to expand the product of a pair of brackets multiplied together. There are several possible methods, all leading to the same end result. These include 'smiles and eyebrows', 'FOIL' and a grid method. They are demonstrated in the following examples.

EXAMPLE

Expand and simplify $(x + 3)(2x + 5)$.

SOLUTION

$(x + 3)(2x + 5) = 2x^2 + 6x + 5x + 15$

$= 2x^2 + 11x + 15$

> Each term in the first bracket is multiplied by each term in the second one. The 'smiles and eyebrows' show which pairs of terms are multiplying at each stage.

EXAMPLE

Expand and simplify $(2x + 3)(3x - 1)$.

SOLUTION

$(2x + 3)(3x - 1) = 6x^2 - 2x + 9x - 3$

$= 6x^2 + 7x - 3$

> Here we are using 'FOIL'.
> **F**irst $2x$ times $3x$ gives $6x^2$
> **O**utside: $2x$ times -1 gives $-2x$
> **I**nside: $+3$ times $3x$ gives $+9x$
> **L**ast: $+3$ times -1 gives -3

EXAMPLE

Expand and simplify $(4x - 1)(2x - 5)$.

SOLUTION

	$4x$	-1
$2x$	$8x^2$	$-2x$
-5	$-20x$	$+5$

> The two terms from the first bracket are written along one edge of the grid, and the terms from the other bracket down the other edge. The grid is then filled in by multiplying corresponding pairs of terms, for example $4x$ times -5 gives $-20x$.

$(4x - 1)(2x - 5) = 8x^2 - 2x - 20x + 5$

$= 8x^2 - 22x + 5$

You may use whichever of these methods you prefer – or even a combination of them. They are different ways of obtaining the same list of terms prior to collecting like terms.

EXERCISE 5.4

Expand and simplify these products of brackets. You may use any valid method of your choice, but you should show all the steps in your working.

1 $(x + 3)(3x + 4)$ 2 $(x + 2)(4x + 5)$ 3 $(x + 4)(2x + 1)$

4 $(x + 5)(2x - 1)$ 5 $(x - 3)(2x + 2)$ 6 $(2x + 11)(2x + 1)$

7 $(3x + 4)(x + 2)$ 8 $(x - 6)(6x + 1)$ 9 $(2x + 5)(2x - 3)$

10 $(x + 13)(4x - 1)$ 11 $(3x + 2)(2x + 3)$ 12 $(4x - 1)(2x + 5)$

13 $(7x + 3)(2x - 3)$ **14** $(x - 3)(x - 4)$ **15** $(2x + 3)(3x - 2)$

16 $(x - 3)(2x - 5)$ **17** $(x + 7)(x - 7)$ **18** $(2x - 3)(2x + 3)$

19 $(x + 3)^2$ **20** $(3x - 4)^2$

Note that, in question **19**, $(x + 3)^2$ means $(x + 3)(x + 3)$.

5.5 Factorising – common factors

Sometimes it is desirable to apply the reverse of expanding brackets – this is known as factorising. The idea is to take an expression that does not contain brackets, and rewrite it as some kind of product of factors, so that brackets are required in the final answer. There are several different types of factorisation on the GCSE specification, and you should learn to recognise when it is appropriate to use each type.

The simplest type of factorisation is to extract a common factor. You examine the terms of the expression one at a time, and look for the highest numerical and/or algebraic factors of each term, as in these two examples.

EXAMPLE

Factorise $16x + 20y$.

SOLUTION

$16x + 20y = \underline{4(4x + 5y)}$

> $16x$ and $20y$ are both multiples of 4, so you divide out 4 as a common factor.

EXAMPLE

Factorise $18x + 24x^2$.

SOLUTION

$18x + 24x^2 = \underline{6x(3 + 4x)}$

> Although $18x$ and $24x^2$ are both multiples of 2, you can do better – they are both multiples of 6. Also, it is possible to factor x out of both $18x$ and $24x^2$, so the highest common factor is $6x$.

Even if there are more terms, and more letters, the same overall principle applies. Find the highest common factor of the numerical coefficients first, then the highest common factor of the x parts, then the y parts, and so on.

EXAMPLE

Factorise $22x^2y^3 + 33x^3y^2 - 44x^4y$.

SOLUTION

The highest common factor of all three terms is $11x^2y$.

Thus $22x^2y^3 + 33x^3y^2 - 44x^4y = 11x^2y(\ldots + \ldots - \ldots)$
$= \underline{11x^2y(2y^2 + 3xy - 4x^2)}$

> Look at 22, 33, 44 to select 11
> Next, look at x^2, x^3 and x^4 to select x^2
> Finally, look at y^3, y^2 and y to select y
> Thus the HCF is $11x^2y$

EXERCISE 5.5

Factorise these expressions. They may all be done using the common factor method.

1. $x^2 + 6x$
2. $2x^2 + 6x$
3. $2x^2 + 6xy$
4. $y^2 - 10y$
5. $2y^2 - 10y$
6. $6x + 9x^2$
7. $12y^2 + 8$
8. $12y^2 + 8y$
9. $fg + 3g^2$
10. $9y^2 + 12y$
11. $5x^5 - 4x^4$
12. $12x^2 - 6x^3$
13. $14a^2 + 21ab$
14. $5xy + 10y$
15. $14 + 10y$
16. $15xy - 9x^2y$
17. $8y^2 - 20y^3$
18. $12y^2 - 8y$
19. $6 + 18x^2$
20. $12pq^3 - 12pq^2 + 15pq$

5.6 Factorising – quadratic expressions

Earlier in this chapter you practised multiplying out the products of two brackets. For example, $(x + 1)(x + 3)$ could be multiplied out to make $x^2 + 4x + 3$. It is possible to reverse this process, in order to factorise some kinds of algebraic expressions, known as **quadratics**.

EXAMPLE

Factorise $x^2 + 7x + 6$.

SOLUTION

$x^2 + 7x + 6 = (x + \ldots)(x + \ldots)$
$= \underline{(x + 6)(x + 1)}$

Check:
$(x + 6)(x + 1) = x^2 + 6x + x + 6$
$= x^2 + 7x + 6$ as required.

> Each bracket must contain an x, to give a product of x^2 …
> … and there must be two numbers in here which multiply together to make $+6$.

> They cannot be $+2$ and $+3$, since these would contribute $2x$ and $3x$, which do not combine to make $7x$.
> They could be $+6$ and $+1$, since these would contribute $+6x$ and $+x$, which do combine to make $+7x$.

This method of factorising can involve some experimentation before you find the right solution, especially when there are minus signs involved too. It is a good idea to check your final answer by multiplying the brackets back out again.

Here is another way in which the signs sometimes occur.

EXAMPLE

Factorise $x^2 - 7x + 12$.

SOLUTION

$x^2 - 7x + 12 = (x - ...)(x - ...)$
$= (x - 3)(x - 4)$

> To give a product of x^2, each bracket must contain an x.
> Both the signs must be negative, in order to generate $-7x$ but multiply to $+12$.
>
> You could try 12 and 1, or 6 and 2, but 4 and 3 look more promising.

Check:
$(x - 3)(x - 4) = x^2 - 3x - 4x + 12$
$= x^2 - 7x + 12$ as required.

Sometimes the final number term is negative, indicating that one of the factors is positive and the other negative. Take care to match them the right way round.

EXAMPLE

Factorise $x^2 + 3x - 28$.

SOLUTION

$x^2 + 3x - 28 = (x - ...)(x + ...)$
$= (x - 4)(x + 7)$

> One sign is positive, and one negative, in order to generate -28 at the end.
> Factors of 4 and 7 look good, since they multiply to make 28, and they differ by 3.
>
> Try $(x - 4)(x + 7)$ and $(x - 7)(x + 4)$. They both give -28, but one gives $-3x$ and the other $+3x$.

Check:
$(x - 4)(x + 7) = x^2 - 4x + 7x - 28$
$= x^2 + 3x - 28$ as required.

EXERCISE 5.6

Factorise these quadratic expressions.

1. $x^2 + 8x + 7$
2. $x^2 + 9x + 14$
3. $x^2 + 5x + 6$
4. $x^2 + 11x + 30$
5. $x^2 + 10x + 16$
6. $x^2 - 4x + 3$
7. $x^2 - 7x + 10$
8. $x^2 - 11x + 30$
9. $x^2 - 3x + 2$
10. $x^2 - 7x + 12$
11. $x^2 + 3x - 4$
12. $x^2 + x - 6$
13. $x^2 - x - 6$
14. $x^2 - 4x - 5$
15. $x^2 - x - 12$
16. $x^2 - 8x + 12$
17. $x^2 + 12x + 32$
18. $x^2 - x - 72$
19. $x^2 + 7x + 12$
20. $x^2 - 7x - 44$

5.7 Factorising – harder quadratic expressions

Suppose you need to factorise a quadratic such as $2x^2 + x - 3$. This is a little harder than the examples you have tried so far. Exactly the same methods are used, but there are more possibilities to consider, because the $2x^2$ can factorise as $2x$ in one bracket and x in the other.

EXAMPLE

Factorise $2x^2 + x - 3$. *(Means $1x$.)*

To give a product of $2x^2$, one bracket must contain an x, and the other $2x$.

SOLUTION

$2x^2 + x - 3 = (2x \ldots)(x \ldots)$
$ = (2x + 3)(x - 1)$

One of the signs must be positive, and the other negative, to get a product of -3.

Check:
$(2x + 3)(x - 1) = 2x^2 + 3x - 2x - 3$
$ = 2x^2 + x - 3$ as required.

The numbers must be 3 and 1, and after some experimentation, this combination of $+3$ and -1 is seen to work.

EXERCISE 5.7

Factorise these quadratic expressions.

1 $2x^2 + 3x + 1$
2 $2x^2 + 5x + 3$
3 $2x^2 + 5x + 2$
4 $3x^2 - 5x + 2$
5 $3x^2 - 2x - 1$
6 $5x^2 + 4x - 1$
7 $2x^2 - x - 1$
8 $5x^2 - 9x - 2$
9 $3x^2 - 8x + 4$
10 $2x^2 + 11x - 6$
11 $2x^2 - 9x + 9$
12 $6x^2 + x - 1$
13 $6x^2 - 5x - 25$
14 $12x^2 + 8x + 1$
15 $15x^2 + 19x + 6$
16 $4x^2 - 4x + 1$
17 $6x^2 - 13x + 2$
18 $2x^2 + 9x + 7$
19 $4x^2 + 12x + 9$
20 $2x^2 - 3x - 9$

5.8 Factorising – difference of two squares

Finally, you may meet a quadratic expression with no middle term, such as $x^2 - 25$. This is like having $x^2 + 0x - 25$. In this case the two factors are symmetric, one with a positive sign and one negative, to give the result $x^2 - 25 = (x + 5)(x - 5)$.

More generally,

$$x^2 - a^2 = (x + a)(x - a)$$

This is a result known as the **difference of two squares**.

EXAMPLE

Factorise $x^2 - 144$.

SOLUTION

$x^2 - 144 = \underline{(x + 12)(x - 12)}$

EXAMPLE

Factorise $10x^2 - 360$.

SOLUTION

$10x^2 - 360 = 10(x^2 - 36)$
$= \underline{10(x + 6)(x - 6)}$

First, take out a common factor … … then apply the difference of two squares.

EXERCISE 5.8A

Factorise these expressions, using the difference of two squares method.

1. $x^2 - 1$
2. $y^2 - 121$
3. $x^2 - 81$
4. $y^2 - 400$
5. $3x^2 - 75$
6. $2x^2 - 18$
7. $7y^2 - 63$
8. $10x^2 - 40$
9. $3x^2 - 27$
10. $4y^2 - 100$

The next exercise contains a mixture of all the different factorising methods you have learnt so far.

EXERCISE 5.8B

Factorise these expressions.

1. $x^2 + 6x + 5$
2. $x^2 + 8x$
3. $y^2 + 15y + 44$
4. $x^2 + 11x + 30$
5. $x^2 + 7x$
6. $y^2 + 3y - 10$
7. $4x^2 - 9x + 2$
8. $y^2 - y - 30$
9. $x^2 - 3x + 2$
10. $x^2 - 8x + 15$
11. $y^2 - 16$
12. $5xy - 10y^2$
13. $4x^2 - 8x + 3$
14. $7y^2 - 700$
15. $x^2 + 2x - 24$
16. $2y^2 + y - 10$
17. $4z^2 - 4z$
18. $2x^2 + 3x + 1$
19. $3x^2 - 12$
20. $2x^2 + 5x - 3$

5.9 Simplifying algebraic fractions (rational expressions)

Two algebraic fractions may be added together into a single fraction, but care must be taken to do this correctly. An important first step is to rewrite both fractions so that they have the same denominator.

EXAMPLE

Simplify $\dfrac{2x+1}{3} + \dfrac{x}{2}$

SOLUTION

Both fractions can be expressed with denominator 6.

$$\dfrac{2x+1}{3} + \dfrac{x}{2} = \dfrac{4x+2}{6} + \dfrac{3x}{6}$$
$$= \dfrac{4x+2+3x}{6}$$
$$= \dfrac{7x+2}{6}$$

The same method may be used when the denominators contain algebraic terms, though the working is a little harder, as in this next example.

EXAMPLE

Simplify $\dfrac{5}{x} + \dfrac{2}{x+1}$

SOLUTION

Both fractions can be expressed with denominator $x(x+1)$.

$$\dfrac{5}{x} + \dfrac{2}{x+1} = \dfrac{5(x+1)}{x(x+1)} + \dfrac{2x}{x(x+1)}$$
$$= \dfrac{5(x+1) + 2x}{x(x+1)}$$
$$= \dfrac{5x+5+2x}{x(x+1)}$$
$$= \dfrac{7x+5}{x(x+1)}$$

Finally, you may sometimes be able to simplify an algebraic fraction by cancelling a common factor in the denominator and the numerator. This example shows how this is done.

EXAMPLE

Simplify $\dfrac{x^2 + 3x}{x^2 + 4x + 3}$

SOLUTION

$$\dfrac{x^2 + 3x}{x^2 + 4x + 3} = \dfrac{x(x + 3)}{(x + 1)(x + 3)}$$

$$= \dfrac{x\cancel{(x + 3)}}{(x + 1)\cancel{(x + 3)}}$$

$$= \dfrac{x}{x + 1}$$

EXERCISE 5.9

Simplify these by adding the two fractions using a common denominator.

1. $\dfrac{x}{4} + \dfrac{x}{5}$
2. $\dfrac{2x}{3} + \dfrac{x}{4}$
3. $\dfrac{x}{2} + \dfrac{x + 1}{3}$
4. $\dfrac{x - 2}{4} + \dfrac{x}{2}$
5. $\dfrac{x + 1}{5} + \dfrac{x}{2}$
6. $\dfrac{5x + 3}{12} + \dfrac{3x}{8}$
7. $\dfrac{4}{x} + \dfrac{3}{x + 1}$
8. $\dfrac{1}{x + 2} + \dfrac{1}{x}$
9. $\dfrac{5}{x + 1} + \dfrac{2}{x + 2}$
10. $\dfrac{3}{x} + \dfrac{2}{x + 4}$

Simplify these algebraic fractions, by factorising the denominator and/or the numerator.

11. $\dfrac{x^2 + 2x}{x^2 + 3x + 2}$
12. $\dfrac{x^2 - 3x}{2x - 6}$
13. $\dfrac{6x + 9}{8x + 12}$
14. $\dfrac{6x + 9}{8x^2 + 12x}$
15. $\dfrac{x^2 + 5x}{x^2 + 6x}$
16. $\dfrac{x^2 + 5x}{x^2}$
17. $\dfrac{3(x - 1)^2}{x - 1}$
18. $\dfrac{x^2 - 16}{x - 4}$
19. $\dfrac{x^2 - 9}{x^2 + 3x}$
20. $\dfrac{x^2 + 5x + 4}{x^2 + 6x + 5}$

REVIEW EXERCISE 5

1. If $p = 4$, $q = 2$ and $r = -5$, find the values of:
   a) $3pq$
   b) $2p^2$
   c) $4p - 3r$
   d) pqr

2. If $x = 3$, $y = -2$ and $z = 10$, find the values of:
   a) $2x^2$
   b) y^3
   c) $3z - xy$
   d) $z(x + y)$

3. If $s = 1$, $t = 4$ and $u = -1$, find the values of:
   a) su
   b) $t^2 + 3u$
   c) $2s + 3t + 4u$

Simplify each of these algebraic expressions:

4. $x^2 \times x^5$
5. $3x^4 \times x^2$
6. $4x^3 \times 3x^2$
7. $10y^8 \div 2y^5$
8. $8z^5 \div 2z^4$
9. $12xy^8 \div 4y^5$
10. $(x^2)^3$
11. $(5xy^2)^2$
12. $(3xy)^2 \div y^2$
13. $(3x^2)^3 + 3x^6$
14. $\dfrac{5x^4 \times 6x^2}{3x^3}$
15. $\dfrac{(3xy) \times (4x^2y^3)}{6x^3y^2}$

Expand and simplify the following expressions:

16. $5(x + 2) + 2(x + 3)$
17. $2(y + 5) + 3(y + 1)$
18. $3(z + 1) + 5(z - 2)$
19. $7(x - 1) + 6(x + 2)$
20. $4(2x - 2) + 2(x - 3)$
21. $2(2x + 5) - 2(x + 1)$
22. $7(3x + 1) + 9(x - 1)$
23. $4(x - 2) - 2(x + 4)$
24. $3(2x + 4) + 4(x - 3)$
25. $5(2x + 2) - 2(5x - 1)$

Expand and simplify these expressions:

26. $(x + 5)(x + 1)$
27. $(y + 5)(y + 7)$
28. $(z + 4)(2z + 1)$
29. $(x - 5)(x + 4)$
30. $(2x - 3)(x + 5)$
31. $(2x - 1)(x - 1)$
32. $(3x + 2)(x - 3)$
33. $(2x - 3)(2x + 3)$
34. $(x + 4)(x - 4)$
35. $5(x + 1)(x - 1)$

Factorise the following expressions. You might need to use common factors, quadratic factorisation, or the difference of two squares.

36. $24x^2 + 10x$
37. $16xy - 20y^2$
38. $x^2 + 10x + 21$
39. $y^2 + 2y + 1$
40. $z^2 - 64$
41. $2y^2 + 9y - 5$
42. $2x^2 - 9x + 4$
43. $12x^2 - 10x$
44. $2y^2 + 7y + 6$
45. $4x^2 - 36$

46 a) Simplify $5p - 4q + 3p + q$

   b) Simplify $\dfrac{x^7}{x^2}$

   c) Factorise $4x + 6$
   d) Multiply out and simplify $(x + 3)(x - 2)$
   e) Simplify $2x^3 \times x^5$ [Edexcel]

47 a) Simplify $y^3 \times y^4$.
   b) Expand and simplify $5(2x + 3) - 2(x - 1)$.
   c) (i) Factorise $4a + 6$.
   (ii) Factorise completely $6p^2 - 9pq$. [Edexcel]

48 Tayub said, 'When $x = 3$, then the value of $4x^2$ is 144.'
   Bryani said, 'When $x = 3$, then the value of $4x^2$ is 36.'
   a) Who was right? Explain why.
   b) Work out the value of $4(x + 1)^2$ when $x = 3$. [Edexcel]

49 Simplify

   a) $3a^2b \times 4a^3b^2$ **b)** $\left(\dfrac{5p^3}{q}\right)^3$ **c)** $\dfrac{12t^5}{u^4} \times \dfrac{u^3}{3t^2}$ [Edexcel]

50 a) Expand and simplify $(x + 5)(x - 3)$
   b) Factorise completely $6a^2 - 9ab$ [Edexcel]

51 a) Expand and simplify $(x + y)^2$.
   b) Hence or otherwise find the value of $3.47^2 + 2 \times 3.47 \times 1.53 + 1.53^2$. [Edexcel]

52 Simplify fully:

   a) $(p^3)^3$ **b)** $\dfrac{3q^4 \times 2q^5}{q^3}$ [Edexcel]

53 a) Simplify $k^5 \div k^2$
   b) Expand and simplify:
   (i) $4(x + 5) + 3(x - 7)$
   (ii) $(x + 3y)(x + 2y)$
   c) Factorise $(p + q)^2 + 5(p + q)$
   d) Simplify $(m^{-4})^{-2}$
   e) Simplify $2t^2 \times 3r^3t^4$ [Edexcel]

54 Simplify **a)** $\dfrac{(x + 3)^2}{x^2 + 5x + 6}$ **b)** $\dfrac{2x + 6}{5x^2 + 15x}$

55 Write as a single fraction
   a) $\dfrac{x + 1}{5} + \dfrac{x}{3}$ **b)** $\dfrac{2x + 4}{9} + \dfrac{x}{6}$

KEY POINTS

1. When substituting numbers into expressions, remember the BIDMAS sequence – Brackets, then Indices, followed by Division/Multiplication and, finally, Addition/Subtraction.

2. In particular, remember that, for example, the value of $2x^2$ when $x = 3$ is 2 times $9 = 18$, and not $6^2 = 36$; the squaring must be done before the multiplication by 2.

3. There are three algebraic laws of indices:

   $x^a \times x^b = x^{a+b}$
   $x^a \div x^b = x^{a-b}$
   $(x^a)^b = x^{ab}$

4. When expanding brackets, watch for a minus sign in front of a bracket – this will change the sign of all the terms inside the bracket, for example:

   $-3(2x + 5) = -6x - 15$

5. In algebra, factorising is the reverse process of expanding. It can be confusing because there are several different methods, so make sure you have studied them all. You need to know the common factor method, the quadratic method and the difference of two squares, and when it is appropriate to apply each approach.

6. To add two algebraic fractions, first write them as equivalent fractions with the same denominator. Then just add the two numerators to complete the calculation.

7. Some algebraic fractions may be simplified by cancelling down. To do this, it is necessary first to factorise the denominator and numerator fully, then do the cancelling if a common factor is available.

Internet Challenge 5

The language of algebra

The wordsearch below contains 20 algebraic words for you to find. Once you have located them, use the internet to check the precise meaning of each word.

T	E	Q	U	A	T	I	O	N	N	D	P	O	R	I
V	X	S	P	G	F	E	N	Y	M	Z	S	E	R	Y
B	P	O	W	E	R	F	T	L	A	C	I	D	A	R
Q	R	X	O	Y	U	O	M	K	P	P	M	S	T	L
U	E	S	N	E	O	A	N	T	P	N	P	C	I	H
O	S	L	D	R	U	S	A	O	I	S	L	D	O	S
T	S	A	O	D	E	R	L	U	N	F	I	V	N	J
I	I	N	O	E	X	Y	E	A	G	I	F	A	A	Y
E	O	J	E	L	N	C	D	U	H	C	Y	R	L	T
N	N	D	N	O	I	T	C	N	U	F	E	I	Q	I
T	E	R	M	G	E	O	W	L	A	H	A	F	T	
A	R	I	L	T	C	U	D	O	R	P	N	B	A	N
V	A	D	J	H	Y	T	E	D	W	T	X	L	B	E
L	Y	T	S	F	A	C	T	O	R	I	S	E	L	D
C	I	T	A	R	D	A	U	Q	F	V	H	I	Y	I

Here are the words to find. They may run left, right, up, down or diagonally.

EQUATION	EXPAND	EXPRESSION	FACTORISE	FUNCTION
IDENTITY	INDEX	MAPPING	POLYNOMIAL	POWER
PRODUCT	QUADRATIC	QUOTIENT	RADICAL	RATIONAL
ROOT	SIMPLIFY	SURD	TERM	VARIABLE

CHAPTER 6

Coordinates and straight line graphs

In this chapter you will **revise earlier work on**:

- using coordinates in all four quadrants.

You will **learn how to**:

- plot graphs of linear functions defined implicitly or explicitly
- find the coordinates of the midpoint of a line segment
- work with coordinates in 3-D.

You will also be **challenged to**:

- investigate coordinates and maps.

Starter: Matchstick puzzles

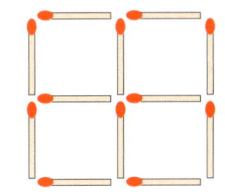

1 Starting with these twelve matches, remove two matches so that only two squares remain.

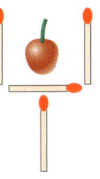

2 These four matches make a cocktail glass containing a cherry. Move two matches so that the cherry is outside the glass.

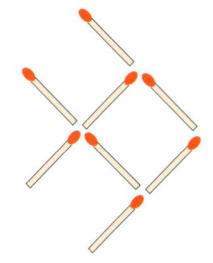

3 Move three matches so that the fish swims in the opposite direction.

4 Move one match to make a square.

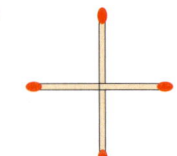

6.1 Coordinates in all four quadrants

You will already be familiar with the idea of using *x* and *y* coordinates like this:

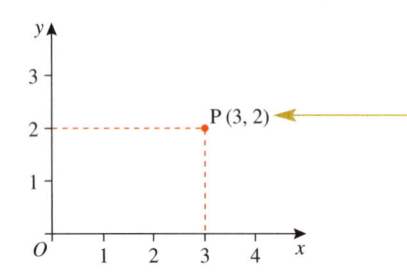

(3, 2) indicates 3 across in the *x* direction and 2 up in the *y* direction.

These are sometimes called *Cartesian* coordinates, after the French mathematician and philosopher René Descartes, although he was not the first mathematician to use them.

You can extend the basic Cartesian coordinate system into four regions, or quadrants, by using negative coordinates, like this:

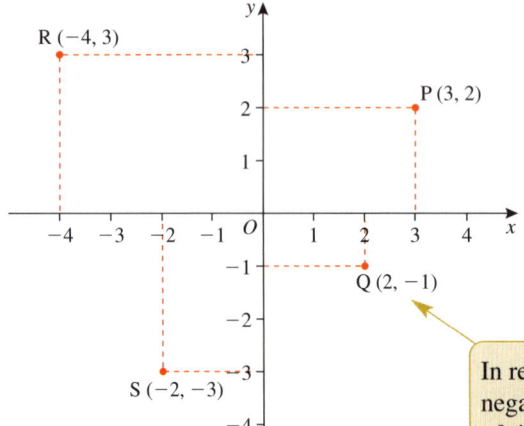

In relation to the origin:
negative coordinates indicate left instead of right (*x*) …

… or below instead of above (*y*).

EXAMPLE

Plot the points A (4, 2), B (−1, 3), C (−2, −1), D (3, −2) on a coordinate grid, and join them up in order, to form a closed shape. What shape is the result?

SOLUTION

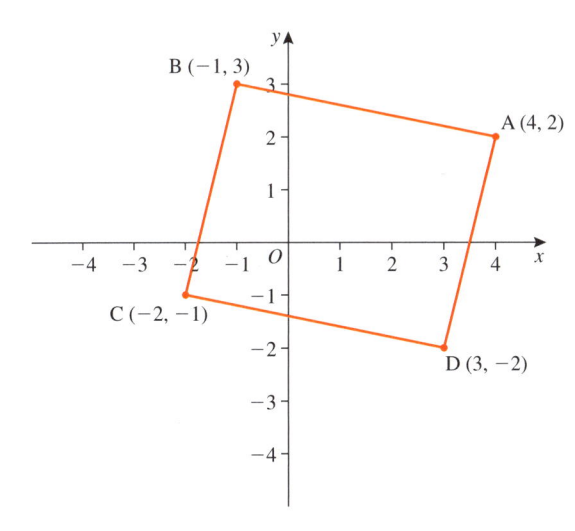

The shape ABCD is a parallelogram.

EXERCISE 6.1

1. Using the diagram below, write down the coordinates of A, B, C, D and E.

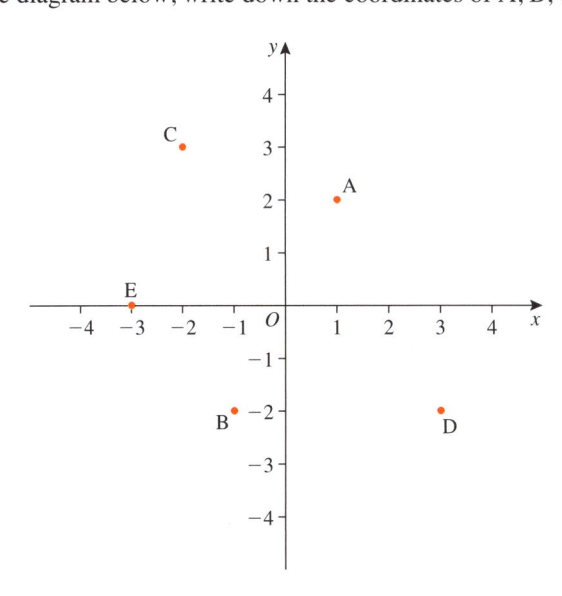

2 The questions refer to the diagram below:
   a) Which point is at $(-3, 1)$?
   b) What are the coordinates of E?
   c) Which point has the same x and y coordinates?
   d) Which point is midway between $(-2, 5)$ and $(4, 3)$?
   e) What are the coordinates of H?
   f) Which point has the largest y coordinate?
   g) Which point has the smallest x coordinate?

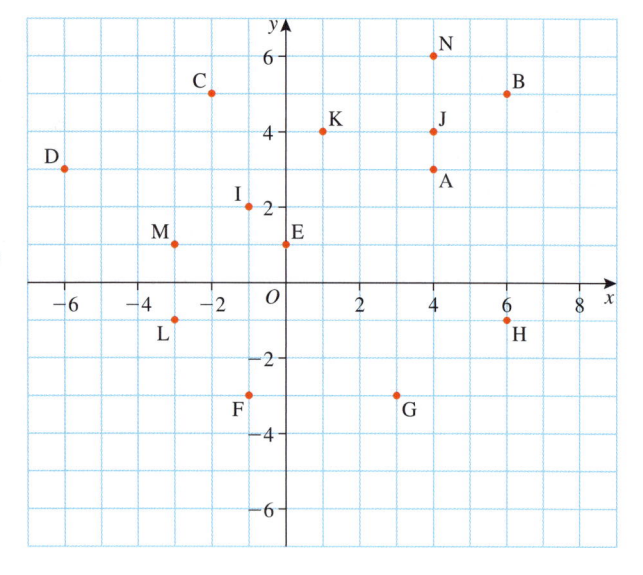

3 Here is a matchstick puzzle using a coordinate grid.
   Draw a coordinate grid so that x and y may both run from -6 to 6.
   Now draw 16 matches with heads and tails in the following positions:

Head $(3, 3)$	Tail $(3, 1)$	Head $(-1, 1)$	Tail $(-1, -1)$
Head $(3, 1)$	Tail $(1, 1)$	Head $(-1, 1)$	Tail $(-1, 3)$
Head $(1, 3)$	Tail $(1, 1)$	Head $(-3, 1)$	Tail $(-1, 1)$
Head $(1, 1)$	Tail $(1, -1)$	Head $(-3, -1)$	Tail $(-1, -1)$
Head $(1, 3)$	Tail $(-1, 3)$	Head $(-5, 1)$	Tail $(-3, 1)$
Head $(1, 1)$	Tail $(-1, 1)$	Head $(-5, -1)$	Tail $(-3, -1)$
Head $(1, 3)$	Tail $(3, 3)$	Head $(-5, 1)$	Tail $(-5, -1)$
Head $(1, -1)$	Tail $(-1, -1)$	Head $(-3, 1)$	Tail $(-3, -1)$

   Now you are ready to solve the puzzle! Your matches should make five squares. The puzzle is to move two matches so the matches form exactly four squares.

4 Follow these instructions carefully.
   Draw a coordinate grid so that x and y both run from -5 to 5.
   Now draw line segments as follows:

   From $(-5, 5)$ to $(5, 5)$ From $(-5, 5)$ to $(-5, -4)$
   From $(-5, -5)$ to $(5, -5)$ From $(5, -5)$ to $(5, 4)$
   From $(3, 5)$ to $(3, -1)$ From $(4, 4)$ to $(4, -4)$
   From $(2, 4)$ to $(2, 0)$ From $(-4, 4)$ to $(-4, 0)$
   From $(-4, 4)$ to $(2, 4)$ From $(-4, 0)$ to $(2, 0)$
   From $(-4, -1)$ to $(-1, -1)$ From $(-1, -1)$ to $(-1, -4)$
   From $(-5, -4)$ to $(-1, -4)$ From $(0, 0)$ to $(0, -5)$
   From $(3, -1)$ to $(1, -1)$ From $(1, -4)$ to $(4, -4)$
   From $(1, -1)$ to $(1, -4)$

   You should find that you have made a maze puzzle. Enter the maze at the top right corner, and find a route through to exit at the bottom left corner.

6.2 Graphs of linear functions

Expressions such as $3x + 5$ and $4 - 2x$ are called **linear expressions**. They must not contain any terms such as x^2, x^3 or $1/x$. Linear expressions are always of the form $ax + b$, where a and b are numbers. Although a and b often take positive whole number values, this is not always the case – they may be fractional, negative or even zero.

A relation of the form $y = ax + b$ is called a **linear function**. Linear functions are so called because, when you plot their graphs, the result is a straight line.

EXAMPLE

Plot the graph of $y = 2x + 3$ for values of x from -5 to 5.

SOLUTION

When $x = -5$, $y = 2 \times (-5) + 3 = -10 + 3 = -7$.

When $x = 0$, $y = 2 \times (0) + 3 = 0 + 3 = 3$.

When $x = 5$, $y = 2 \times (5) + 3 = 10 + 3 = 13$.

> Use the formula to work out matching x and y values for a low value of x (-5), a middle value (0) and a high value (5).

x	-5	0	5
y	-7	3	13

> It is convenient to store these values in a table, like this.

> After plotting the points, use a see-through ruler to check that the points form a straight line.
>
> In fact you need only two points to define a straight line …
>
> … but the third point acts as a check.

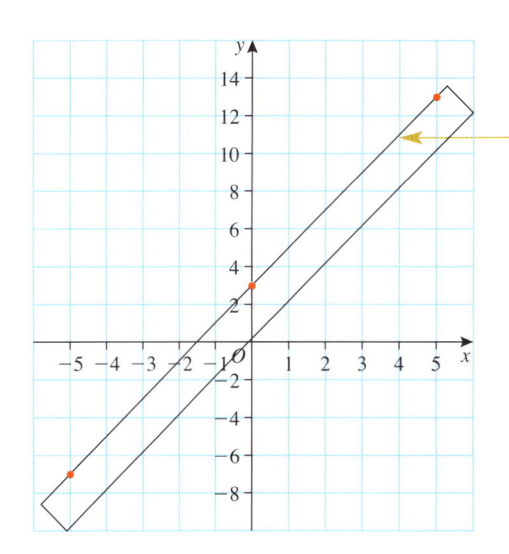

6 Coordinates and straight line graphs U3

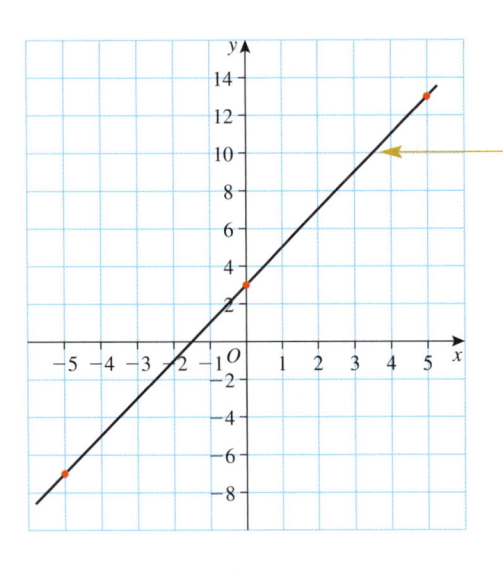

> Now join them with a single neat line.
> Note that the line continues slightly beyond the end-points at (5, 13) and (−5, −7).

Strictly speaking, the line $y = 2x + 3$ is infinitely long, since it extends indefinitely in both directions. The portion of this line cut off between $x = -5$ and $x = 5$ is more correctly known as a *line segment*.

EXERCISE 6.2

For questions **1** to **8** you are given a linear function and an incomplete table of values. Work out the missing values to complete the table, and then plot the graph of the corresponding line segment. You may use either graph paper or squared paper.

1 $y = 2x + 1$

x	−4	0	4
y	−7	1	

2 $y = x + 4$

x	−5	0	5
y	−1		

3 $y = 3x − 1$

x	−4	0	5
y			

4 $y = 2x − 3$

x	−2	0	4
y			

5 $y = \frac{1}{2}x + 4$

x	−6	0	4
y			

6 $y = x + 1$

x	−5	0	5
y			

7 $x + y = 10$

x	0	5	10
y			

8 $2x + y = 5$

x	−2	0	4
y			

9 Draw up a set of coordinate axes so that x can run from -10 to 10 and y from -25 to 25.
   a) Calculate the coordinates of three points that lie on the line $y = 2x$. Hence plot the line $y = 2x$ on your coordinate axes.
   b) Now calculate the coordinates of three points that lie on the line $y = 2x - 1$. Plot the line $y = 2x - 1$ on the same set of coordinate axes.
   c) Look at your two graphs. What do you notice?

10 Draw up a set of coordinate axes so that x can run from 0 to 10 and y from -5 to 10.
   a) Calculate the coordinates of three points that lie on the line $x + y = 8$.
   Hence plot the line $x + y = 8$ on your coordinate axes.
   b) Now calculate the coordinates of three points that lie on the line $x + y = 5$.
   Plot the line $x + y = 5$ on the same set of coordinate axes.
   c) Look at your two graphs. What do you notice?

6.3 The midpoint of a line segment

Suppose you wish to know the coordinates of the midpoint of a line segment joining the points A and B, without measuring it from a diagram. There is a simple way of doing this, namely, taking the average of the coordinates at each end.

The midpoint of the line segment joining (a, b) to (p, q) is

$$\left(\frac{a+p}{2}, \frac{b+q}{2}\right)$$

EXAMPLE

The points A, B and C have cooordinates $(3, 10), (5, 2)$ and $(-1, 7)$ respectively.
Work out the coordinates of

a) the midpoint of AB
b) the midpoint of AC.

SOLUTION

a) Midpoint is $\left(\frac{3+5}{2}, \frac{10+2}{2}\right) = (4, 6)$

b) Midpoint is $\left(\frac{3+-1}{2}, \frac{10+7}{2}\right) = (1, 8.5)$

EXERCISE 6.3

Find the coordinates of the midpoint of the line segment between these points.

1 A(6, 4) and B(10, 6)

2 C(5, 5) and D(9, 3)

3 E(4, −4) and F(11, 0)

4 G(3, −1) and H(6, −5)

5 I(−2, −7) and J(12, 3)

6 K(8, 8) and L(1, 1)

7 M(−2, 16) and N(12, −1)

8 P(4, 11) and Q(−1, −1)

6.4 Coordinates in 3-D

Coordinates can be used to specify the position of a point in 3-D, in a similar way to 2-D. You use x and y axes to mark out a horizontal grid, and a z axis to specify height above the horizontal grid (or below, if negative).

EXAMPLE

The diagram shows a cuboid ABCOPQRS.
AB = 5 units, BC = 2 units, AP = 8 units.

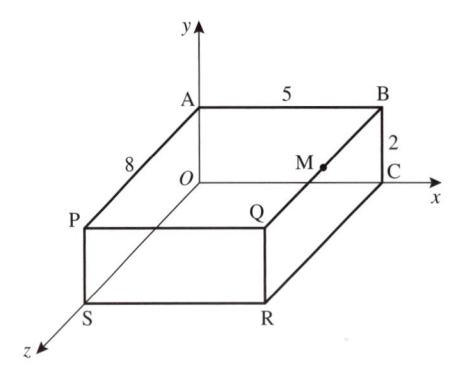

a) Write down the coordinates of B, C, P and Q.
b) M is the midpoint of BQ. State the coordinates of M.

SOLUTION

a) B is at (5, 2, 0).
C is at (5, 0, 0).
P is at (0, 2, 8).
Q is at (5, 2, 8).
b) M is midway between B (5, 2, 0) and Q (5, 2, 8).
Thus M is at (5, 2, 4).

As a general rule, you can find the coordinates of the midpoint of a line segment in 3-D by taking the average of the coordinates at each end:

The midpoint of the line segment joining (a, b, c) to (p, q, r) is:

$$\left(\frac{a+p}{2}, \frac{b+q}{2}, \frac{c+r}{2}\right)$$

EXERCISE 6.4

1. The diagram shows a cuboid $OABCSRQP$.

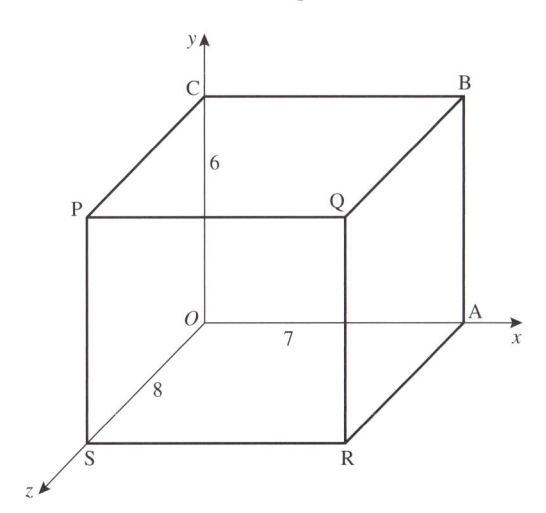

   A has coordinates $(7, 0, 0)$. P has coordinates $(0, 6, 8)$.
   a) Write down the coordinates of the points B, C, Q, R and S.
   b) Point M is midway between O and Q. Find the coordinates of M.
   c) Point N is midway between B and P. Find the coordinates of N.

2. The diagram shows a solid $OABC$.

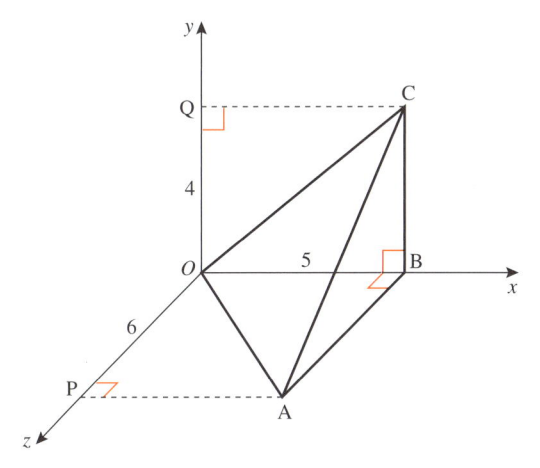

   PA and QC are parallel to the x axis, BC is parallel to the y axis, BA is parallel to the z axis.
   $OB = 5$ units, $OQ = 4$ units, $OP = 6$ units.
   a) Write down the coordinates of A, B and C.

   M is the midpoint of BC, and N is the midpoint of AC.
   b) Find the coordinates of M and N.
   c) Use your answers to b) to explain how you can tell the line segment MN is horizontal.
   d) What name best describes the solid $OABC$?

6 Coordinates and straight line graphs   U3   87

3   The diagram shows a building at a sports complex.
    A is (50, 0, 0), P is (0, 10, 0), C is (0, 0, 80), with
    all units in metres. Points U and V are 8 metres
    higher than the plane formed by points P, Q, R and S.
    a) Write down the coordinates of R and S.
    b) Find the coordinates of V.
    A swimming pool is built centrally in the building.
    The deepest point is at the centre of the pool.
    The surface of the pool is at the same vertical level
    as the plane formed by points O, A, B and C. The
    pool is 2 metres deep.
    c) Find the coordinates of the deepest point of
       the pool.

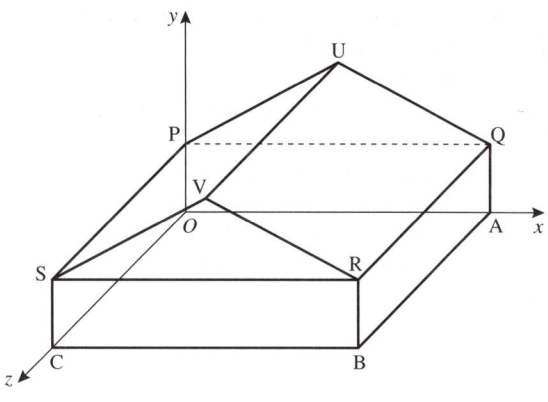

4   Point A is at (5, 2, 4), B is at (7, 2, 0) and C is at (6, 0, 6).
    M is the midpoint of line segment AB. N is the midpoint of line segment MC.
    a) Work out the coordinates of the point M.
    b) Work out the coordinates of the point N.

5   Here are the coordinates of six points:
          P (4, 0, 2)   Q (2, 0, 4)   R (6, 1, 1)   S (2, 0, 3)   T (3, 0, 3)   U (1, 1, 6)
    a) Which of the points is the midpoint of the line segment PQ?
    b) What can you say about the triangle QST?

REVIEW EXERCISE 6

For questions **1** to **4** you are given a linear function and an incomplete table of values. Copy and complete the table, and then plot the graph of the corresponding line segment.

1 $y = x + 4$

x	−5	0	2
y	−1		6

2 $y = \frac{1}{2}x + 1$

x	−2	0	6
y		0	

3 $y = 2x − 5$

x	−6	0	6
y			

4 $x + y = 20$

x	0	8	20
y			

5   This question is about eight points on a 2-D coordinate grid. The points are
        A (2, 2)   B (3, 6)
        C (5, 2)   D (7, 7)
        E (5, 6)   F (3, 10)
        G (4, 6)   H (1, 1)
    Without drawing a diagram, answer the following questions.
    a) Which point is one unit to the right of G?
    b) Which point lies on the line $y = 3x + 1$?
    c) How many points lie on the line $y = x$?
    d) Which point is closest to the origin?
    e) Which point is the midpoint of the line segment BC?
    f) Now draw a diagram to check if your answers were correct.

6 The diagram shows a set of coordinate axes and three points A, B, C.
OA = 4 units, OB = 3 units, OC = 6 units.
A cuboid is to be drawn with OA, OB and OC as three of its sides.
a) Copy the grid, and complete a sketch of the cuboid.
b) Write down the coordinates of A, B and C.
c) M is the midpoint of the line segment BC.
   Find the coordinates of M.

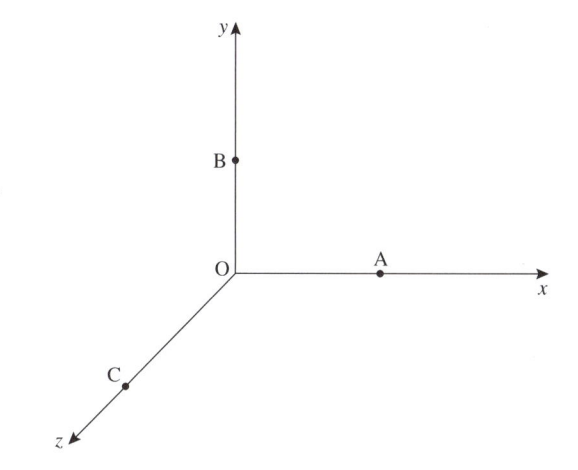

KEY POINTS

1. Points in a 2-D (two-dimensional) plane may be described using a coordinate system in which x runs from left to right and y from bottom to top. The coordinate axes cross over at the origin. x values to the left of the origin are negative; so, too, are y values below the origin.

2. Linear functions such as $y = 3x + 1$ may be plotted accurately by drawing a table of values. Although two points are sufficient to define a line, it is customary to plot three points as this helps detect errors caused by a slip in the working.

3. Points in 3-D (three dimensions) may be described using a coordinate system with three numbers (x, y, z).

4. A line segment is a straight line joining two points.

5. In 2-D, the midpoint of the line segment joining (a, b) to (p, q) is $\left(\dfrac{a+p}{2}, \dfrac{b+q}{2}\right)$

6. In 3-D, the midpoint of the line segment joining (a, b, c) to (p, q, r) is $\left(\dfrac{a+p}{2}, \dfrac{b+q}{2}, \dfrac{c+r}{2}\right)$

Internet Challenge 6

Coordinates and maps

Here are ten sentences about coordinates and maps. Unscramble the anagrams to complete each sentence. You might want to use the internet for checking, and for help with the harder ones.

1 Positions on the Earth are measured using DELOUTING and DUILATTE.

2 Places in the UK are given six-figure positions using the ANITONAL DRIG.

3 Many navigators now use GPS to find their position; this stands for LABLOG IGNIPOTIONS MYTESS.

4 Air traffic controllers might use the GARBINE and NOELATIVE of an aircraft to help guide it onto the flight path.

5 An astronomer describes the positions of objects in the sky using a coordinate system of GIRTH INCASNOSE and INDELACTION.

6 Some cartographers use a CREAMROT PORJETONIC to make maps of the world.

7 Map makers show height above sea level by using RONCUOT SENIL.

8 Elizabethan sailors like Sir Francis Drake used a method called EDDA NECKORING to help work out their position.

9 The x and y coordinate system we use in mathematics was developed by French mathematician ERNE SCRATEDES.

10 The zero line of longitude is called the CHEERWING DEMIRANI.

CHAPTER 7

Number sequences

In this chapter you will **learn how to**:

- recognise and use common number sequences
- use rules to generate number sequences
- find a general formula for the nth term of an arithmetic sequence.

You will also be **challenged to**:

- investigate Fibonacci numbers.

> **Starter:** Circles, lines and regions

Look at the sequence of circles below.

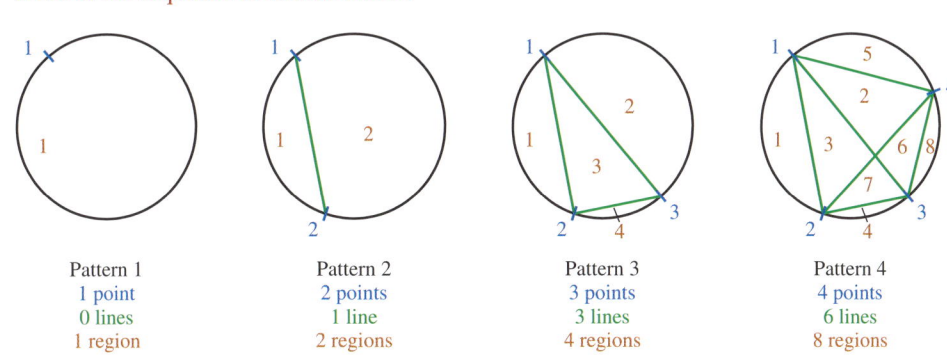

Pattern 1
1 point
0 lines
1 region

Pattern 2
2 points
1 line
2 regions

Pattern 3
3 points
3 lines
4 regions

Pattern 4
4 points
6 lines
8 regions

The diagram shows a sequence of circles. Each circle has some points marked around its circumference. Each point is joined to every other point by a line.

The lines and regions are then counted. The lines and regions are not all the same size.

Task 1
Describe a rule for how the number of points increases in this sequence.

Task 2
Describe a rule for how the number of lines increases.

Task 3
Describe a rule for how the number of regions increases.

Task 4

Now draw pattern 5 and pattern 6, and see if your rules seem correct. You should space out the points so that no triple intersections can occur, otherwise you lose a region. For example:

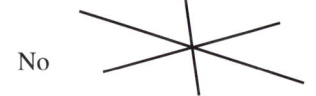

No   Yes

7.1 Number sequences

Here are some number sequences that occur often in mathematics.

Name of sequence	First six terms	Formula for the nth term
Positive integers	1, 2, 3, 4, 5, 6	n
Even numbers	2, 4, 6, 8, 10, 12	$2n$
Odd numbers	1, 3, 5, 7, 9, 11	$2n - 1$
Square numbers	1, 4, 9, 16, 25, 36	n^2
Cube numbers	1, 8, 27, 64, 125, 216,	n^3
Powers of 2	2, 4, 8, 16, 32, 64	2^n
Powers of 10	10, 100, 1000, 10 000, 100 000, 1 000 000	10^n
Triangular numbers	1, 3, 6, 10, 15, 21	$\dfrac{n(n+1)}{2}$

You may encounter these number patterns when solving mathematical problems based on counting patterns.

EXAMPLE

Look at this pattern of squares.

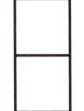

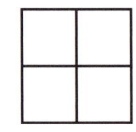

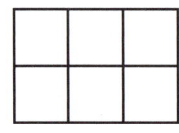

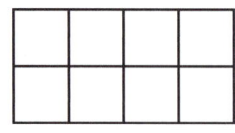

Pattern 1   Pattern 2   Pattern 3   Pattern 4

a) How many squares would there be in pattern 5?
b) Find a formula for the number of squares in pattern n.
c) Use your formula to find the number of squares in pattern 100.

SOLUTION

The number of squares forms a pattern 2, 4, 6, 8, that is, the even numbers.
a) Pattern 5 contains 2 × 5 = 10 squares.
b) Pattern n contains 2n squares.
c) Pattern 100 contains 2 × 100 = 200 squares.

Some number sequences are disguised versions of the common ones, perhaps with a constant number added or multiplied.

EXAMPLE

Find the next three terms in this number sequence. Find also a formula for the nth term.

    101, 104, 109, 116, 125, …

SOLUTION

101, 104, 109, 116, 125, … are all 100 more than the square numbers.

The next three terms are 100 + 36, 100 + 49 and 100 + 64,
that is, 136, 149, 164

The nth term is $100 + n^2$

EXERCISE 7.1

Write down the next two terms in each of these number sequences, and explain how each term is worked out. Give an expression for the nth term in each case.

They are all related to the list of common sequences in the table opposite.

1 10, 20, 30, 40, 50, 60, …

2 5, 7, 9, 11, 13, 15, …

3 51, 53, 55, 57, 59, 61, …

4 4, 8, 12, 16, 20, 24, …

5 2, 8, 26, 80, 242, …

6 0.1, 0.01, 0.001, 0.0001, …

7 10, 30, 60, 100, 150, 210, …

8 2, 8, 18, 32, 50, 72, …

9 Look at this pattern of triangles.

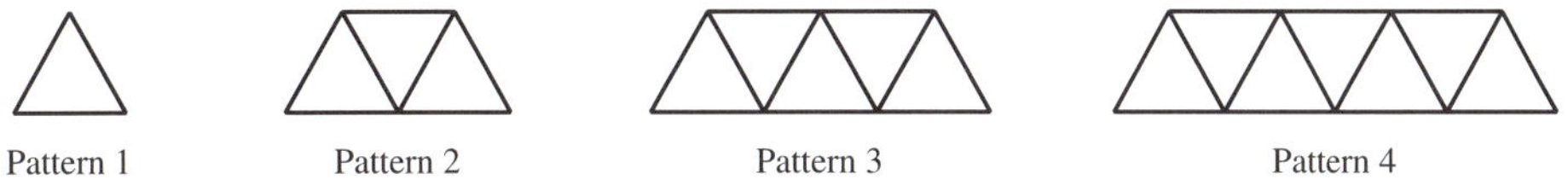

Pattern 1   Pattern 2   Pattern 3   Pattern 4

a) How many triangles would there be in pattern 7?
b) Find a formula for the number of triangles in pattern n.

10 Look at this pattern of spots.

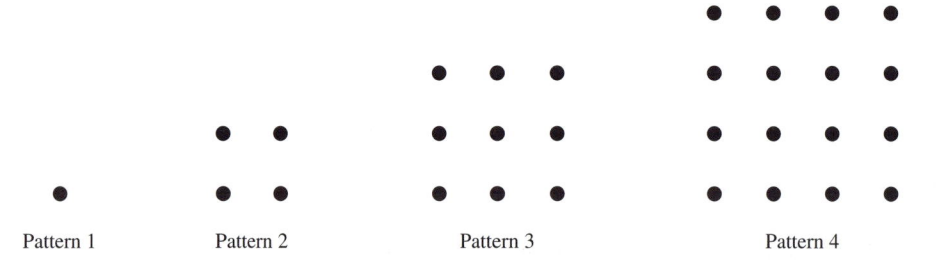

Pattern 1   Pattern 2   Pattern 3   Pattern 4

a) Find an expression for the number of spots in pattern n.
b) How many spots would there be in pattern 30?

7.2 Describing number sequences with rules

It can be very useful to be able to describe number sequences using rules. One way of doing this is to say how each term is connected to the next one in the sequence. (This is sometimes called a **term-to-term rule**, because it explains the link between one term and the next.)

EXAMPLE

A number sequence is defined as follows:
- The first term is 3.
- Each new term is double the previous one.

Use this rule to generate the first five terms of the number sequence.

SOLUTION

Start with 3:

$3 \times 2 = 6$
$6 \times 2 = 12$
etc.

The first five terms of the sequence are 3, 6, 12, 24, 48

EXAMPLE

A number sequence is defined as follows:
- The first term is 7.
- Each new term is 3 more than the previous one.

Use this rule to generate the first six terms of the number sequence.

SOLUTION

Start with 7:

$7 + 3 = 10$
$10 + 3 = 13$
etc.

The first six terms of the sequence are 7, 10, 13, 16, 19, 22

If you wanted to work out the 100th number in a sequence, it would be very tedious to have to write out all 100 numbers, one at a time. In this case it is better if you can use an algebraic expression for the nth term. (This is sometimes called a **position-to-term rule**, since you can work out the value of any term as long as you know its position in the sequence.)

EXAMPLE

The nth term of a number sequence is given by the expression $2n^2 + 1$.

a) Write down the first four terms of the sequence.
b) Find the value of the 20th term.

SOLUTION

a) $n = 1$ gives $2 \times 1^2 + 1 = 2 + 1 = 3$
$n = 2$ gives $2 \times 2^2 + 1 = 8 + 1 = 9$
$n = 3$ gives $2 \times 3^2 + 1 = 18 + 1 = 19$
$n = 4$ gives $2 \times 4^2 + 1 = 32 + 1 = 33$

The first four terms are 3, 9, 19, 33

b) When $n = 20$, $2 \times 20^2 + 1 = 800 + 1 = 801$.

EXERCISE 7.2

1 A number sequence is defined as follows:
- The first term is 5.
- Each new term is 2 more than the previous one.

Use this rule to generate the first five terms of the number sequence.

2 A number sequence is defined as follows:
- The first term is 1.
- To find each new term, add 1 to the previous term, and double this total.

Use this rule to generate the first four terms of the number sequence.

3 The nth term of a number sequence is given by the expression $8n - 1$.
a) Write down the values of the first five terms.
b) Work out the value of the 20th term.

4 The nth term of a number sequence is given by the expression $\dfrac{3n+1}{2}$.
   a) Write down the values of the first six terms.
   b) Work out the value of the 23rd term.

5 Andy has been doing an investigational GCSE coursework task. He gets this sequence of numbers:

   12, 15, 18, 21, 24, …

   a) Describe Andy's pattern in words.
   b) Find the 10th term in Andy's number sequence.

6 The nth term of a number sequence is given by the expression $100 - n$.
   a) Write down the values of the first five terms.
   b) Work out the value of the 50th term.

7 In a certain number sequence, the first term is 3. Each new term is found by multiplying the previous term by 3.
   a) Write down the first five terms of the number sequence.
   b) What name is given to this particular number sequence?

8 The nth term of a number sequence is given by the formula $7n + 3$.
   a) Work out the first three terms.
   b) Find the value of the 10th term.
   c) One of the numbers in the sequence is 1053. Which term is this?

9 The nth term of a number sequence is given by the expression $\dfrac{n(n+1)}{2}$.
   a) Write down the values of the first four terms.
   b) Work out the value of the 30th term.
   c) Explain why all the terms in this sequence are integers.
   d) What name is often given to the number sequence generated by this rule?

10 David is working with a number sequence. The nth term of his sequence is given by the expression $6n + 7$. He gets the number 2770 as one of his terms. Show that David must have made a mistake.

7.3 Arithmetic sequences

A number sequence in which the terms go up in equal steps is called an **arithmetic sequence**. The graph of an arithmetic sequence is a straight line, so it may alternatively be called a **linear sequence**. The size of the step is called the **common difference**.

EXAMPLE

For each sequence, say whether it is arithmetic or not. State the value of the common difference for each arithmetic sequence.
   a) 2, 3, 5, 8, 12, …
   b) 2, 5, 8, 11, 14, …
   c) 1, 2, 4, 8, 16, …
   d) 40, 36, 32, 28, 24, …

SOLUTION

a) 2, 3, 5, 8, 12, ... is not an arithmetic sequence (the terms go up by 1, then 2, then 3, etc.).
b) 2, 5, 8, 11, 14, ... is an arithmetic sequence with common difference 3.
c) 1, 2, 4, 8, 16, ... is not an arithmetic sequence (the terms go up by 1, then 2, then 4, etc.).
d) 40, 36, 32, 28, 24, ... is an arithmetic sequence with common difference -4.

An arithmetic sequence may be generated by an algebraic rule that gives a general formula for the nth term of the sequence.

EXAMPLE

Each of these rules describes the nth term of a number sequence. Write out the first four terms of each sequence, and hence pick out the ones that are arithmetic sequences.

a) $3n + 1$ b) $n^2 + n$ c) $5n - 1$ d) $10 - n$

SOLUTION

a) $3n + 1$ gives 4, 7, 10, 13, ... which is an arithmetic sequence with common difference 3.
b) $n^2 + n$ gives 2, 6, 12, 20, ... which is not an arithmetic sequence.
c) $5n - 1$ gives 4, 9, 14, 19, ... which is an arithmetic sequence with common difference 5.
d) $10 - n$ gives 9, 8, 7, 6, ... which is an arithmetic sequence with common difference -1.

The GCSE examination may require you to carry out this process in reverse, i.e. work out a formula for a given arithmetic sequence.

The formula for the nth term of an arithmetic sequence will always be of the form $an + b$. Here a and b represent coefficients, or numbers, whose values are to be determined. They may be positive, negative or zero.

The value of a is easy to spot – it is simply the value of the common difference. A good way to find b is to compute the value of the zeroth term, i.e. compute the value of an imaginary term one place before the actual first term. This will automatically generate the required value of b.

EXAMPLE

Find a formula for the nth term of the arithmetic sequence:

7, 10, 13, 16, 19, …

SOLUTION

Let the required formula be $an + b$.

The common difference is $10 − 7 = 3$, so $a = 3$.

Insert the zeroth term:

(4), 7, 10, 13, 16, 19, …

Hence $b = 4$.

Thus the nth term is given by the formula $3n + 4$

The same method can be used for problems set in a more practical context, as in the next example.

EXAMPLE

The table shows the cost of hiring a van. It is made up of a fixed hire charge plus a daily amount.

Number of days for which the van is hired (n)	Charge for hire (C) in £
1	50
2	80
3	110
4	140

a) Work out the cost of hiring the van for 10 days.
b) Express C in terms of n.
c) Carlos hired the van and paid £530. For how many days did he hire the van?

SOLUTION

a) Continuing the pattern in the table:

5	170
6	200
7	230
8	260
9	290
10	320

So the cost for 10 days is £320

b) The common difference is 30, so the formula must be of the form
$C = 30n + b$.
The sequence begins (20), 50, 80, 110, 140, ….
Therefore $b = 20$.
The formula is therefore $C = \underline{30n + 20}$

c) Now if $C = 530$, the formula gives:
$$30n + 20 = 530$$
$$30n = 530 - 20$$
$$30n = 510$$
Dividing by 30, $n = 17$.
Thus Carlos hired the van for $\underline{17 \text{ days}}$

EXERCISE 7.3

1 The first five terms in an arithmetic sequence are:

   12, 17, 22, 27, 32, …

   a) Find the value of the 10th term.
   b) Write down, in terms of n, an expression for the nth term of this sequence.

2 The first four terms in an arithmetic sequence are:

   58, 50, 42, 34, …

   a) Find the value of the first negative term.
   b) Write down, in terms of n, an expression for the nth term of this sequence.

Here are some arithmetic sequences. For each one, find, in terms of n, an expression for the nth term of the sequence.

3 8, 11, 14, 17, 20, …   **4** 2, 7, 12, 17, 22, …   **5** 10, 9, 8, 7, 6, …

6 4, 9, 14, 19, 24, …   **7** 21, 24, 27, 30, 33, …   **8** 12, 10, 8, 6, 4, …

9 Nina has been making patterns with sticks. Here are her first three patterns.

Pattern 1
4 sticks

Pattern 2
7 sticks

Pattern 3
10 sticks

   a) Work out the number of sticks in pattern 6.
   b) Write down, in terms of n, an expression for the nth term of this sequence.
   c) Explain how the coefficients in your formula are related to the way the sticks fit together.

10 The 10th term of an arithmetic sequence is 68 and the 11th term is 75.
   a) Write down value of the common difference for this sequence.
   b) Work out the value of the first term.
   c) Write down, in terms of n, an expression for the nth term of this sequence.

   Check that your formula works when $n = 10$ and $n = 11$.

REVIEW EXERCISE 7

Find the next three terms in each of these number sequences. For those that form arithmetic sequences, write down, in terms of n, an expression for the nth term of the sequence.

1 11, 22, 33, 44, 55, …

2 2, 4, 8, 16, 32, …

3 2, 5, 8, 11, …

4 1, 4, 9, 16, 25, …

5 10, 9, 8, 7, 6, …

6 100, 99, 97, 94, 90, …

7 A number sequence is defined as follows:
   - The first term is 7.
   - To get each new term, multiply the previous one by 3 and subtract 15.

   Work out the first four terms of this sequence.

8 The nth term of a number sequence is given by the expression $\dfrac{n^2 + 3n}{2}$.

   a) Work out the first five terms of this sequence.
   b) Do the first five terms form an arithmetic sequence?

9 Timothy has been drawing patterns. Here are his first three patterns.

   Pattern 1 — 6 sticks
   Pattern 2 — 11 sticks
   Pattern 3 — 16 sticks

   a) Write down the number of sticks in pattern 5.
   b) Work out the number of sticks in pattern 12.
   c) Write down, in terms of n, an expression for the nth term of this sequence.

10 Here are the first five terms of a sequence.

   30, 29, 27, 24, 20, …

   a) Write down the next two terms in the sequence.

   Here are the first five terms of a different sequence.

   1, 5, 9, 13, 17, …

   b) Find, in terms of n, an expression for the nth term of the sequence. [Edexcel]

11 Here are some patterns made with crosses.

   Pattern number 1
   Pattern number 2
   Pattern number 3
   Pattern number 4

   The table shows the number of crosses in pattern numbers 1, 2, 3 and 4.

Pattern number (n)	1	2	3	4
Number of crosses (C)	5	8	11	14

   Write down a formula for the number of crosses, C, in terms of the pattern number, n. [Edexcel]

12 Here are the first five numbers of a simple sequence.

   1, 5, 9, 13, 17

   a) Write down the next two numbers of the sequence.
   b) Write down, in terms of n, an expression for the nth term of this sequence. [Edexcel]

13 Here are the first five terms of an arithmetic sequence.

   6, 11, 16, 21, 26

   Find an expression, in terms of n, for the nth term of this sequence. [Edexcel]

14 The table shows some rows of a number pattern.

Row 1	1	$= \dfrac{1 \times 2}{2}$
Row 2	1 + 2	$= \dfrac{2 \times 3}{2}$
Row 3	1 + 2 + 3	$= \dfrac{3 \times 4}{2}$
Row 4		
Row 5		
Row 6		
Row 7		
Row 8		

Make a copy of the table.
a) Complete row 4 of the table.
b) Complete row 8 of the table.
c) Work out the sum of the first 100 whole numbers.
d) Write down an expression, in terms of n, for the sum of the first n whole numbers. [Edexcel]

15 The diagram shows patterns made of dots.

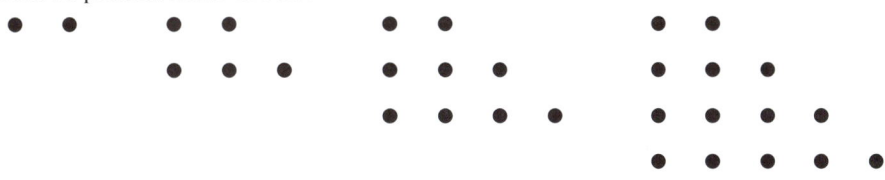

   Pattern number   1   2   3   4

The number of dots in each pattern is shown in the table below.

Pattern number	1	2	3	4	5	6
Number of dots	2	5	9	14		

a) Copy and complete the table.

b) (i) Work out the number of dots in pattern number 10.
  (ii) Give a reason for your answer.

The first four triangular numbers are 1, 3, 6, 10.

An expression for the nth triangular number is $\dfrac{n(n+1)}{2}$.

c) Use this to write down an expression for the number of dots in pattern number m.

d) Work out the number of dots in pattern number 99.

[Edexcel]

KEY POINTS

1. Common number sequences include the positive integers, the even numbers and the odd numbers. Others you should learn to recognise are:

Square numbers	1, 4, 9, 16, 25, 36, …
Cube numbers	1, 8, 27, 64, 125, 216, …
Powers of 2	1, 2, 4, 8, 16, 32, …
Powers of 10	1, 10, 100, 1000, 10 000, 100 000, …
Triangular numbers	1, 3, 6, 10, 15, 21, …

2. Some number sequences may be defined in words, by stating how each term is connected to the previous one. This type of definition can be inefficient in practice, since to find the 50th term, for example, you have to find all the intermediate terms too.

3. Some number sequences may also be described by means of an expression that allows you to find the nth term of the sequence directly. This type of rule is quite efficient, because you can find any term in the sequence directly, without having to compute all the intermediate ones.

4. An arithmetic sequence is one that goes up in equal steps; the formula for the nth term of such a sequence will be of the form $an + b$. The coefficient a is equal to the step size, and b is equal to the value of the imaginary zeroth term.

Internet Challenge 7

Fibonacci numbers

Fibonacci numbers are used to model the behaviour of living systems. Fibonacci numbers also lead to the Golden Ratio, widely used in classical art and architecture. In this challenge you will need to use a spreadsheet at first, before looking on the internet to complete your work.

Here is the Fibonacci number sequence:

$$1, 1, 2, 3, 5, 8, 13, 21, \ldots.$$

1. Type these numbers into a computer spreadsheet, such as Excel. (It is a good idea to enter them in a vertical list, rather than a horizontal one.)

2. Each term (apart from the first two) is found by adding together the two previous ones, for example, $13 = 8 + 5$. Use your spreadsheet replicating functions to automatically generate a list of the first 50 Fibonacci numbers.

3. Divide each Fibonacci number by the one before it, for example $8 \div 5 = 1.6$. Set up a column on your spreadsheet to do this up to the 50th Fibonacci number. What do you notice?

The quantities you found in question **3** approach a limit called the Golden Ratio, ϕ.

4. Using your spreadsheet value for ϕ, calculate $1 - \phi$ and $\dfrac{1}{\phi}$. What do you notice?

Now use the internet to help answer the following questions. Find pictures where appropriate.

5. How was the Golden Ratio used by the builders of the Parthenon in Athens?

6. Whose painting of 'The Last Supper' was based on Golden Ratio constructions?

7. Which painter was said to have 'attacked every canvas by the golden section'?

8. When was Fibonacci born? When did he die?

9. Is there a position-to-term rule for Fibonacci numbers, that is, is there a formula for finding the nth number?

10. What sea creature has a spiral shell that is often (mistakenly) said to be based on a Golden Ratio spiral?

CHAPTER 8

Working with shape and space

In this chapter you will **revise earlier work on**:

- lines and angles.

You will **learn how to**:

- use corresponding and alternate angles
- work with angles in triangles and quadrilaterals
- find areas of triangles and quadrilaterals
- calculate surface areas and volumes of solids.

You will also be **challenged to**:

- investigate the four-colour theorem.

Starter: Alphabet soup

Work out the values of the angles at the letters.

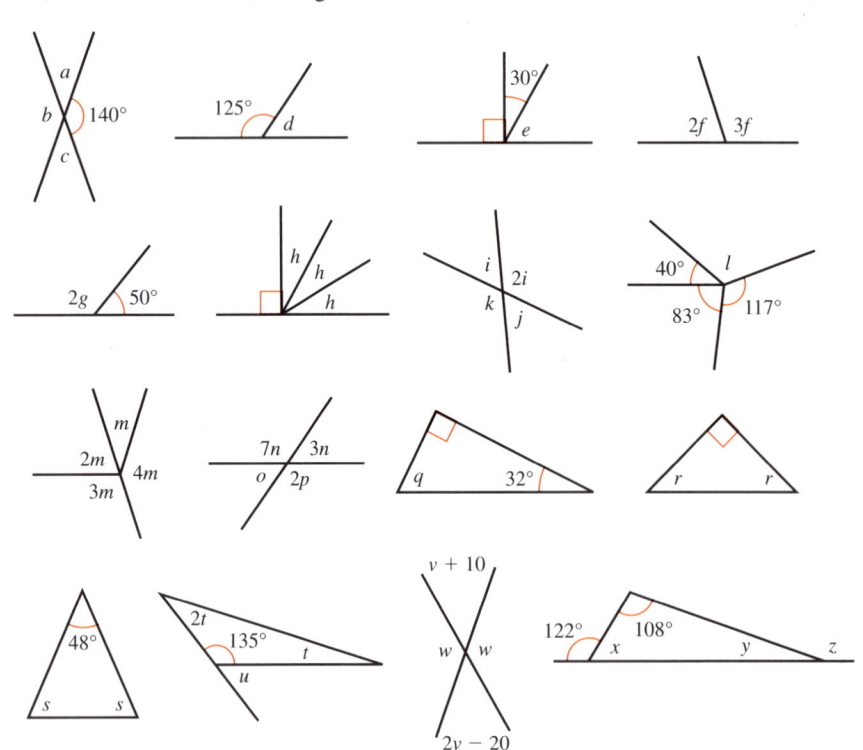

8.1 Corresponding and alternate angles

Imagine an infinitely long railway track, made up of two rails and a set of sleepers.

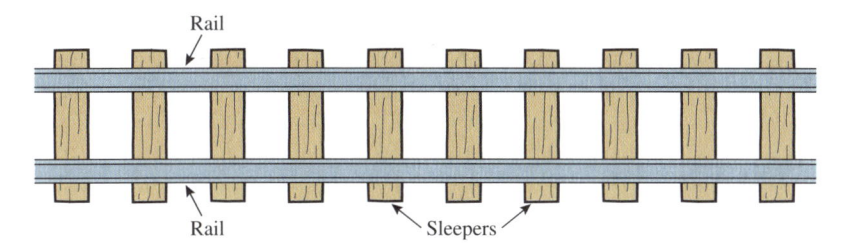

The rails and the sleepers are made up of straight lines, but there is a subtle mathematical distinction between them.

The rails are infinitely long straight lines. The rails are **lines**.

The sleepers are pieces of straight line, with definite start and finish points, so they are finite in length. The sleepers are **line segments**.

In this chapter you will be revising and practising your knowledge of geometry with straight lines and line segments.

The diagram shows two parallel lines and two line segments, or **transversals**, that cross the parallel lines at an angle.

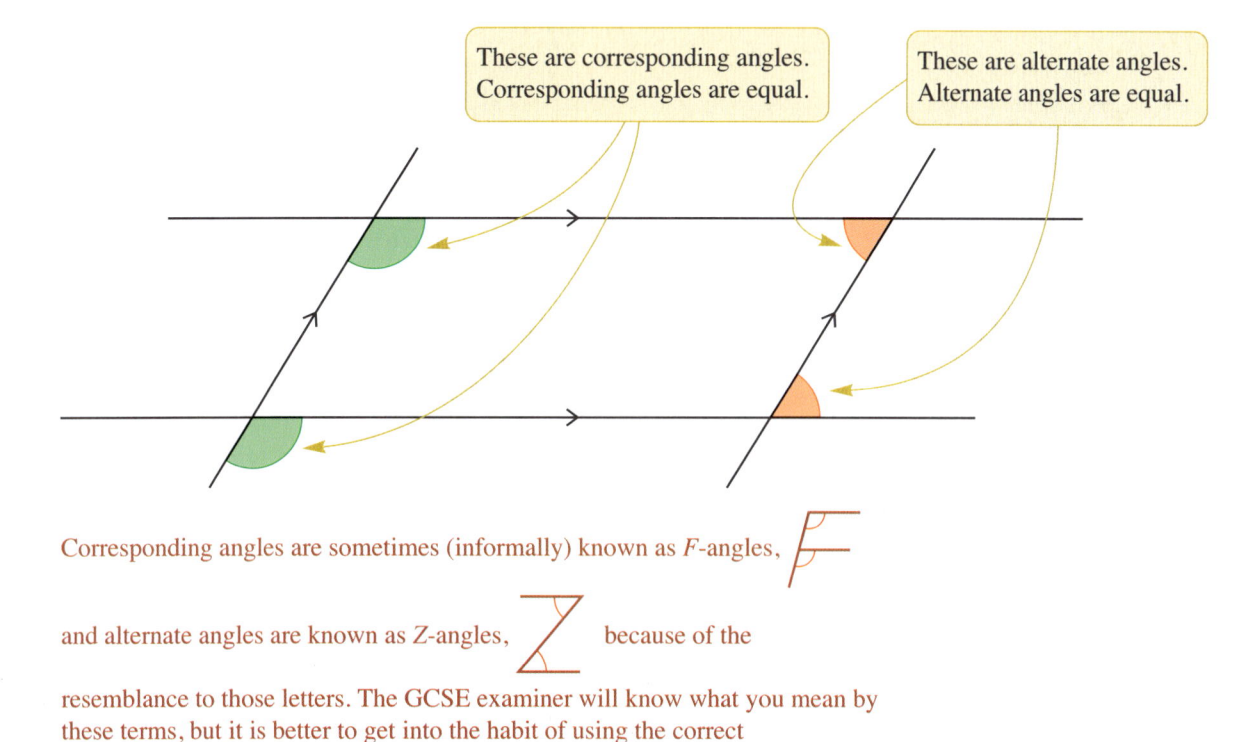

> These are corresponding angles. Corresponding angles are equal.

> These are alternate angles. Alternate angles are equal.

Corresponding angles are sometimes (informally) known as *F*-angles,

and alternate angles are known as Z-angles, because of the resemblance to those letters. The GCSE examiner will know what you mean by these terms, but it is better to get into the habit of using the correct mathematical names for them.

EXAMPLE

Find the angles represented by letters in the diagram below. Give a reason in each case.

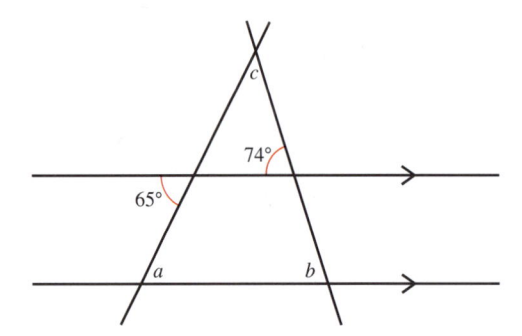

SOLUTION

$a = 65°$ (alternate to marked 65° angle)
$b = 74°$ (corresponding to marked 74° angle)
Angles a, b, c are at the three vertices of a triangle, so they add up to 180°.
Therefore $c = 180° − (65° + 74°)$
            $c = 180° − 139°$
            $c = 41°$

> Always explain your reasons.

Here are two other results about equal angles that you have probably met before.

> Angles on opposite sides of a vertex are equal; they are called **vertically opposite**.
> $a = b$

> Angles inside two parallels add up to 180°; they are called **co-interior angles** (or **allied angles**).
> $x + y = 180°$

In this next exercise you may use any angle properties you know, including those about vertically opposite angles, allied angles, alternate angles and corresponding angles.

EXERCISE 8.1

Find the values of the angles represented by the letters in each question.

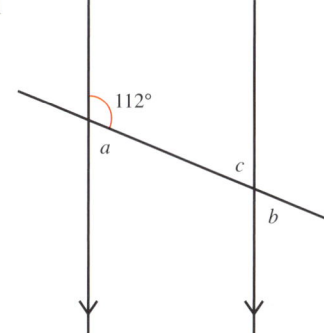

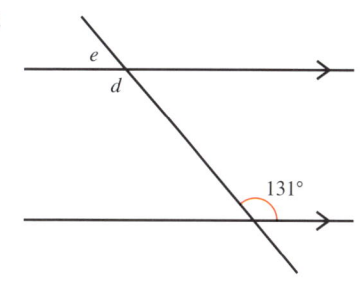

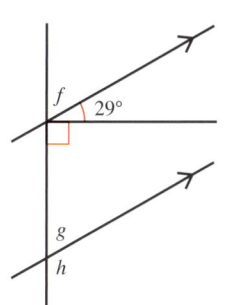

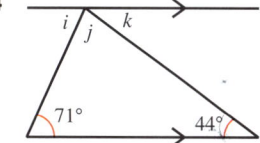

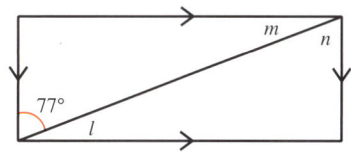

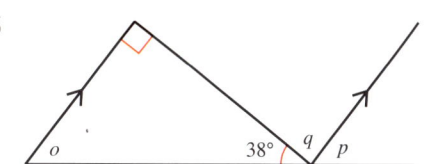

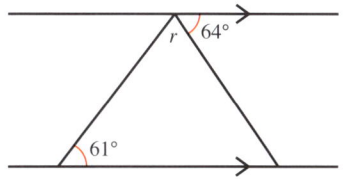

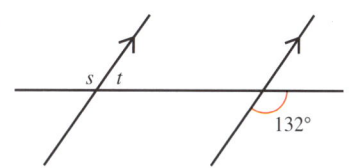

1

2

3

4

5

6

7

8

8.2 Angles in triangles and quadrilaterals

Here are three important results about angles in triangles and quadrilaterals. You could be asked to prove them in an exam.

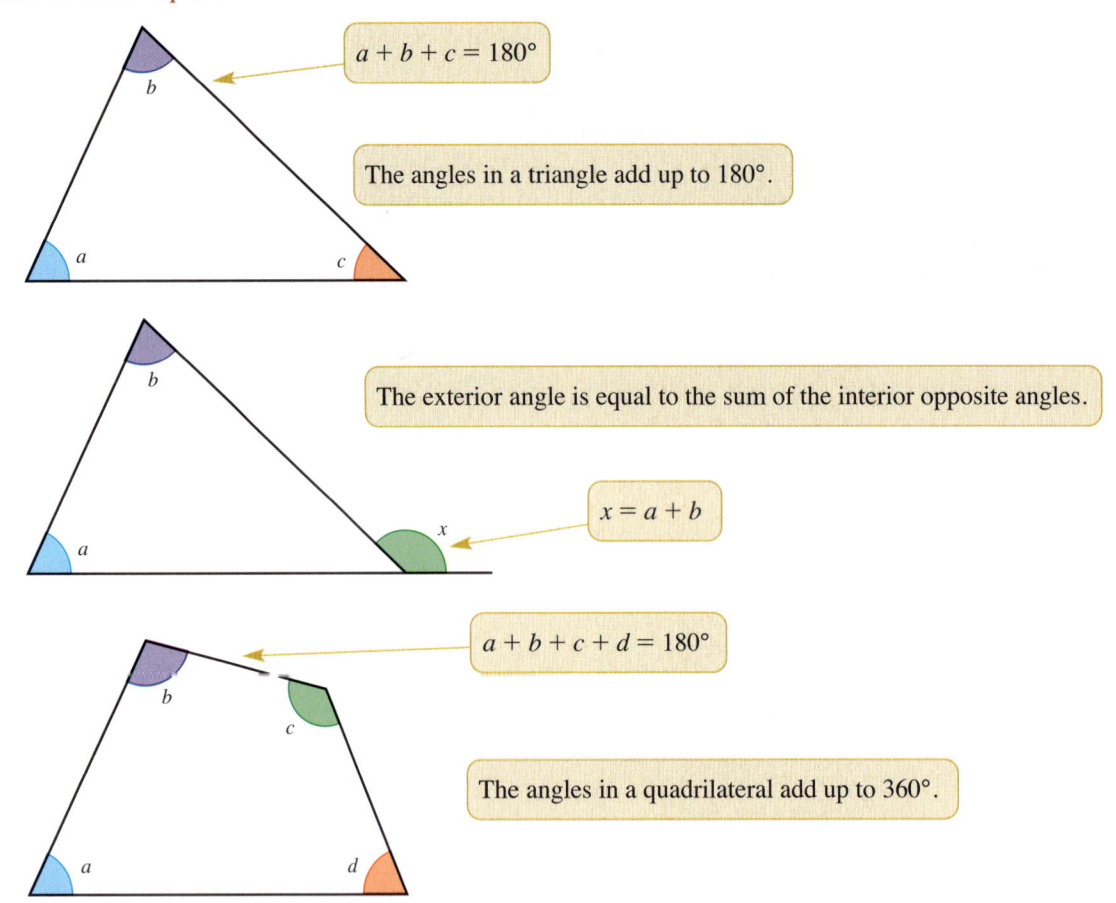

$a + b + c = 180°$

The angles in a triangle add up to 180°.

The exterior angle is equal to the sum of the interior opposite angles.

$x = a + b$

$a + b + c + d = 360°$

The angles in a quadrilateral add up to 360°.

Here are proofs of these results.

THEOREM

The angles in a triangle add up to 180°.

PROOF

Construct a line through one vertex, parallel to the opposite side.

Angles x and a are alternate, so $x = a$. Likewise, angles y and c are alternate, so $y = c$.

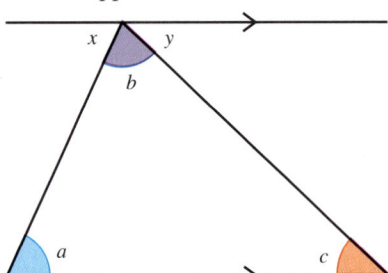

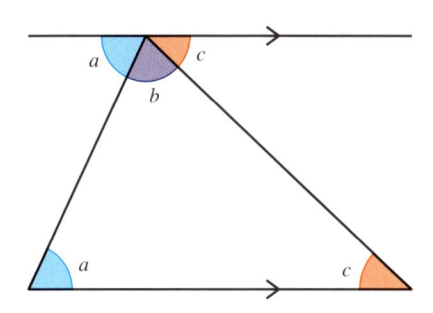

Now angles a, b and c form a straight line at the top of the diagram.
Therefore $a + b + c = 180°$.
So the angles in the triangle add up to 180°

THEOREM

The exterior angle at the vertex of a triangle is equal to the sum of the interior opposite angles.

PROOF

Construct a line through one vertex, parallel to the opposite side.

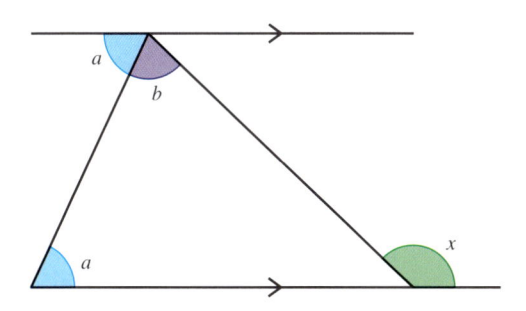

The angle alongside b is equal to a (alternate angles).
The angle x is alternate to the combined angle $a + b$.
Therefore $x = a + b$

THEOREM

The angles in a quadrilateral add up to 360°.

PROOF

Consider any quadrilateral PQRS, and draw the diagonal PR, so as to divide it into two triangles.

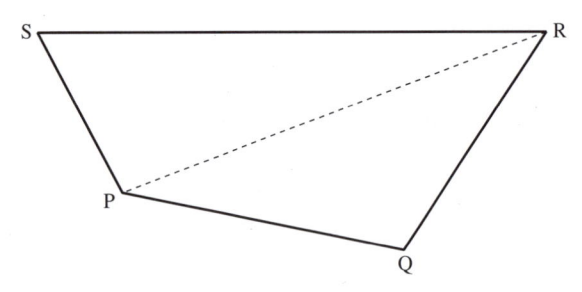

Now consider the angles inside each of the two triangles.

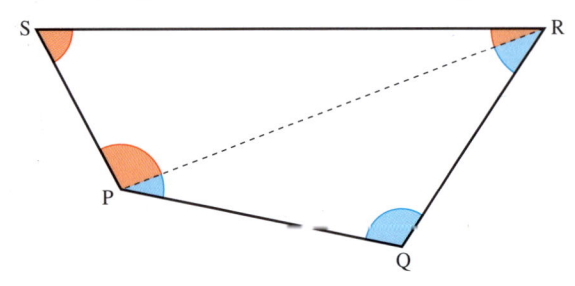

Clearly, the total of the angles inside quadrilateral PQRS is equal to the sum of the angles in triangle PSR plus the sum of the angles in triangle PQR. Hence:

Sum of angles in quadrilateral PQRS = 180° + 180°
= 360°

EXAMPLE

The diagram shows a quadrilateral PQRS. Find the value of the angle x.

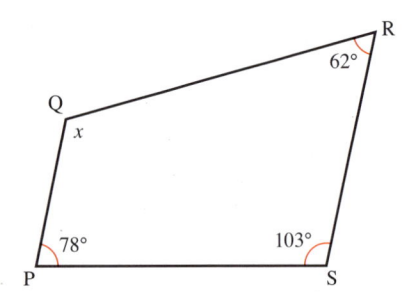

SOLUTION

The angles in a quadrilateral add up to 360, so
$$x + 78 + 103 + 62 = 360$$
$$x + 243 = 360$$
$$x = 360 - 243$$
$$x = 117°$$

EXERCISE 8.2

1. Find the value of a.

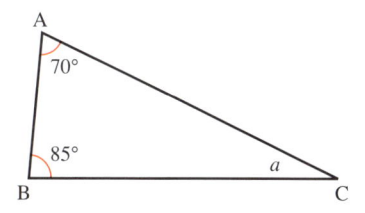

2. Find the value of x.

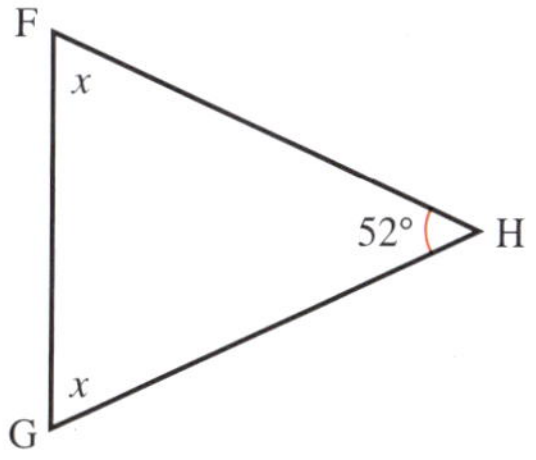

3. Find the value of x.

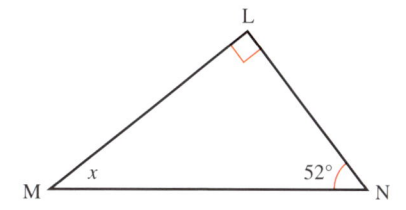

4. Find the value of y.

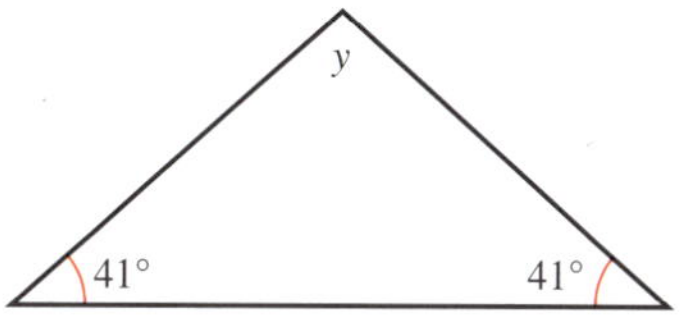

5. Find the value of x.

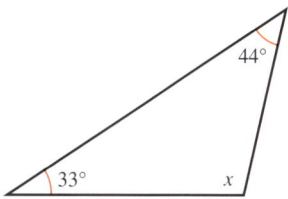

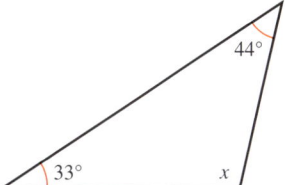

6. Two of the angles in a triangle are 44° and 92°.
   a) Work out the size of the third angle.
   b) What kind of triangle is this?

7. The angles in a triangle are $4c + 4°$, $5c - 7°$ and $7c + 7°$.
   a) Set up an equation in c.
   b) Solve your equation, to find the value of c.
   c) Work out the sizes of the angles in the triangle.
   d) What kind of triangle is this?

8 The diagram shows a quadrilateral. Work out the size of the angle *m*.

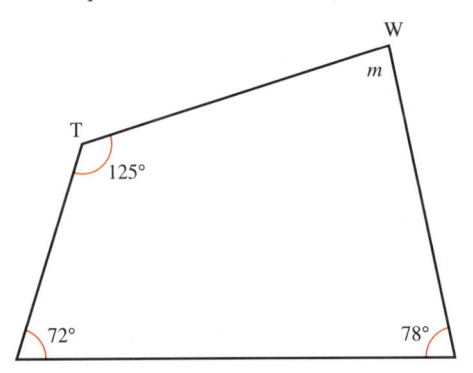

9 The diagram shows a quadrilateral. Work out the size of the angle *y*.

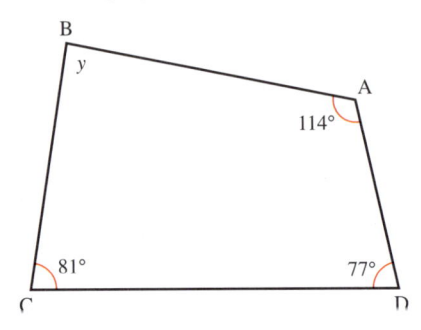

10 Find the size of the angle marked *x*.

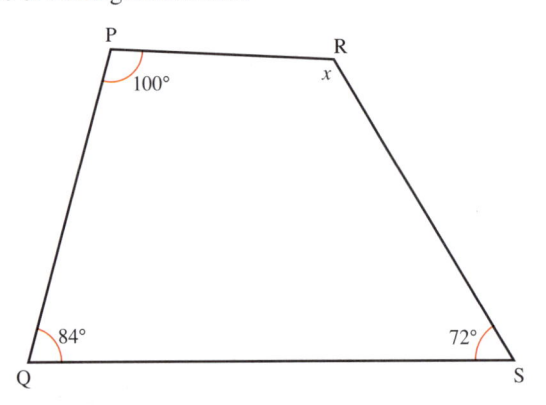

11 Find the size of each angle marked *z*.

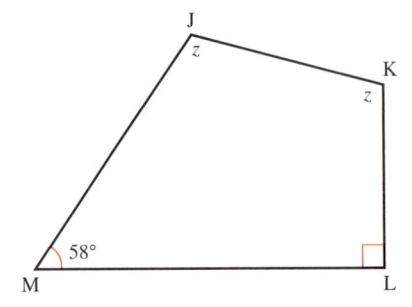

8.3 Areas and perimeters of simple shapes

A quadrilateral shape drawn at random will have four unequal sides, and the angles will all be different.

In practice, quadrilaterals with some sides (or angles) the same tend to be more useful, so these have special names. You will have met them before, but here is a reminder of the special quadrilaterals, and their geometric properties.

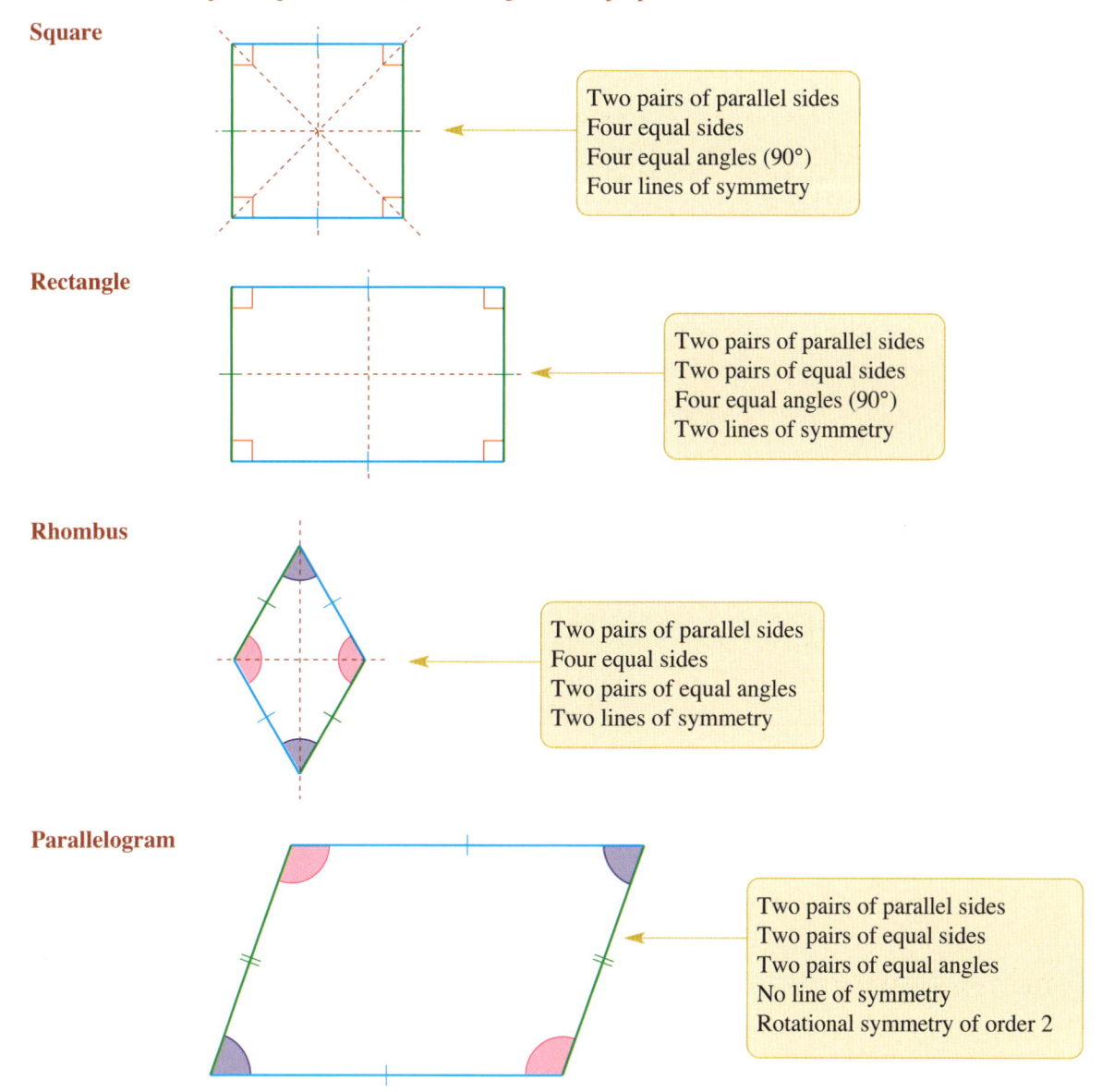

Square

Two pairs of parallel sides
Four equal sides
Four equal angles (90°)
Four lines of symmetry

Rectangle

Two pairs of parallel sides
Two pairs of equal sides
Four equal angles (90°)
Two lines of symmetry

Rhombus

Two pairs of parallel sides
Four equal sides
Two pairs of equal angles
Two lines of symmetry

Parallelogram

Two pairs of parallel sides
Two pairs of equal sides
Two pairs of equal angles
No line of symmetry
Rotational symmetry of order 2

Kite

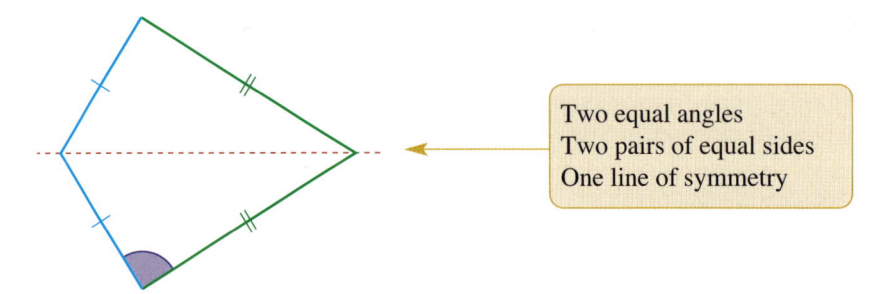

Two equal angles
Two pairs of equal sides
One line of symmetry

Arrowhead

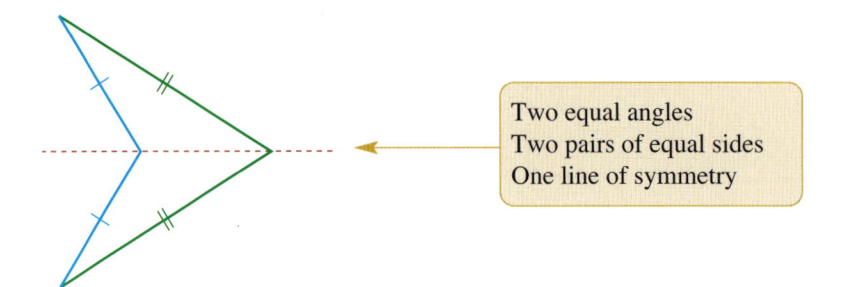

Two equal angles
Two pairs of equal sides
One line of symmetry

Trapezium

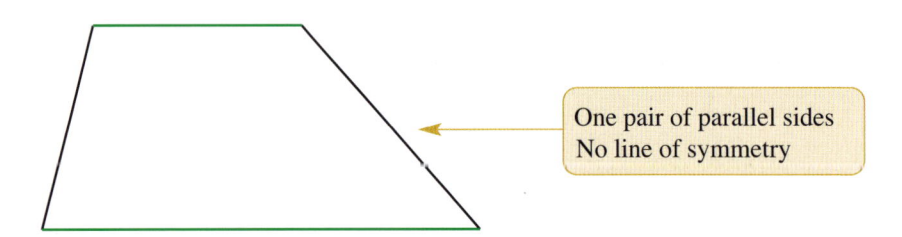

One pair of parallel sides
No line of symmetry

Isosceles trapezium

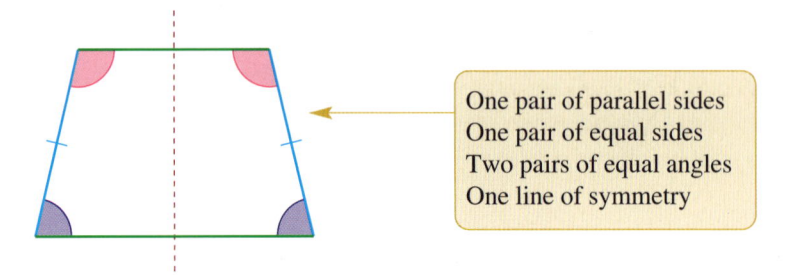

One pair of parallel sides
One pair of equal sides
Two pairs of equal angles
One line of symmetry

At GCSE you will need to know how to find the area of a square, rectangle, triangle, parallelogram and trapezium.

You may already be familiar with some of these results for calculating areas:

Rectangle
Area = base × height
$A = bh$

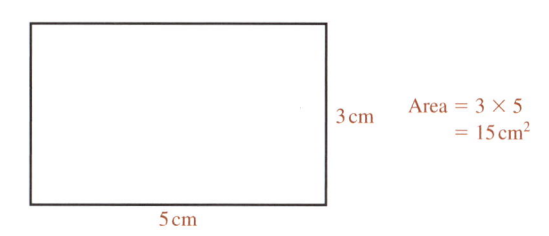

Area = 3 × 5
= 15 cm²

Triangle
Area = half × base × height
$A = \frac{1}{2}bh$

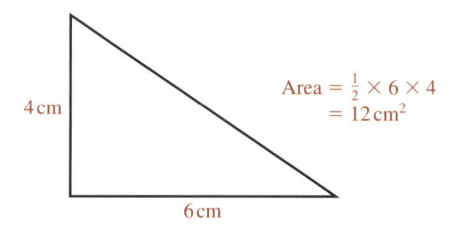

Area = $\frac{1}{2}$ × 6 × 4
= 12 cm²

Parallelogram
The area of a parallelogram can be found by using the triangle formula twice:

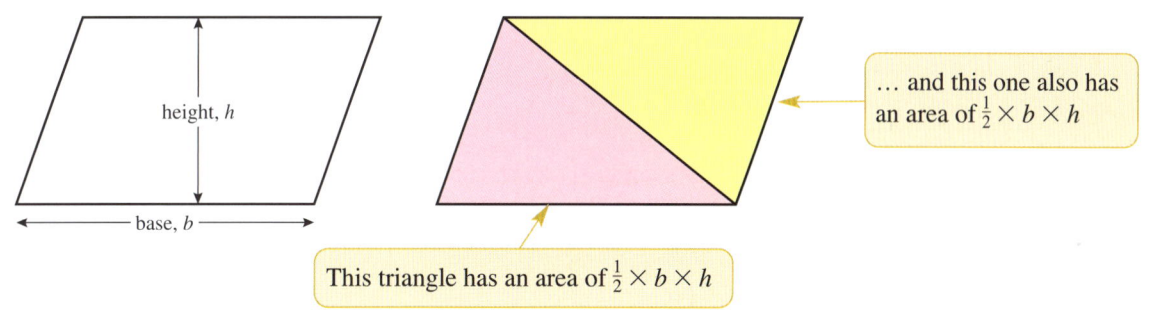

This triangle has an area of $\frac{1}{2} \times b \times h$

… and this one also has an area of $\frac{1}{2} \times b \times h$

Area of **parallelogram** = $\frac{1}{2} \times b \times h + \frac{1}{2} \times b \times h$
$A = b \times h$

EXAMPLE

Find the area of this parallelogram.

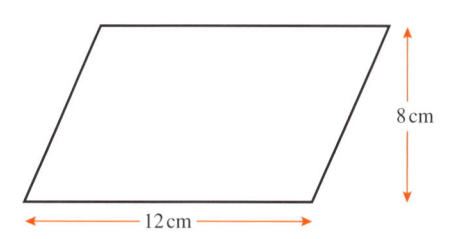

SOLUTION

The parallelogram has a base $b = 12$ cm and a height $h = 8$ cm.

Therefore area = $b \times h$
= 12 × 8
= 96 cm²

Remember to include the units in your answer

8 Working with shape and space U3

Finally, there is a formula for finding the area of a trapezium. The trapezium requires some surgery:

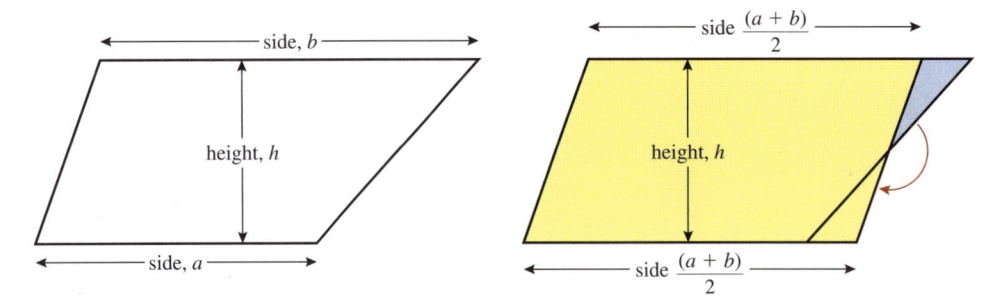

By slicing off and swivelling a triangle, as shown, the trapezium can be converted into a parallelogram with the equivalent area. The original trapezium had two different lengths of a and b. The length of the new parallelogram is found by taking the average of these, namely $\dfrac{a+b}{2}$.

Thus the area of the parallelogram is base × height = $\dfrac{a+b}{2} \times h$, and the trapezium must have the same area. This formula is often written using bracket notation:

Area of trapezium = $\tfrac{1}{2}(a + b)h$

EXAMPLE

Find the area of this trapezium.

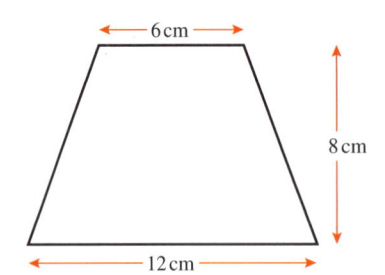

SOLUTION

The trapezium has parallel sides $a = 6$ cm and $b = 12$ cm, and a height $h = 8$ cm.

$$\begin{aligned}\text{Therefore area} &= \tfrac{1}{2}(a+b)h \\ &= \tfrac{1}{2} \times (6 + 12) \times 8 \\ &= \tfrac{1}{2} \times 18 \times 8 \\ &= 9 \times 8 \\ &= \underline{72 \text{ cm}^2}\end{aligned}$$

Areas of simple shapes such as triangles, rectangles, parallelograms and trapeziums may be found directly, by using the appropriate formulae. Make sure you learn them! You may also need to work out the areas of compound shapes, by breaking them down to two or more simpler pieces.

EXAMPLE

The diagram shows a shape made from two rectangles and a triangle.

a) Calculate the perimeter of the shape.
b) Calculate the area of the shape.

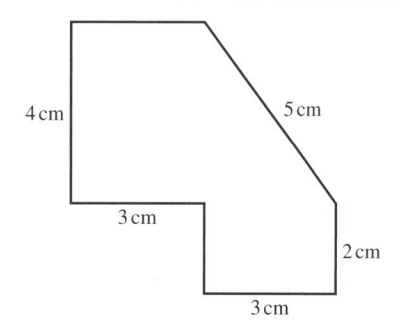

SOLUTION

a) Marking the missing lengths:
Perimeter = 3 + 4 + 3 + 2 + 3 + 2 + 5
= <u>22 cm</u>

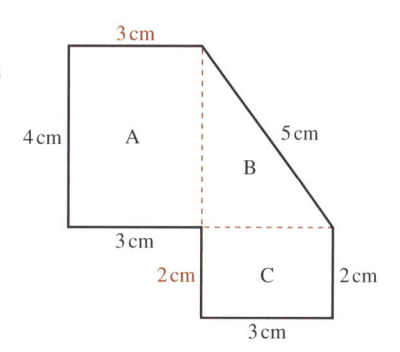

b) Denoting the three parts as A, B, C (see diagram above), then:
Area of A = 4 × 3 = 12 cm².
Area of B = $\frac{1}{2}$ × 4 × 3 = 6 cm².
Area of C = 3 × 2 = 6 cm².
Total area = 12 + 6 + 6 = <u>24 cm²</u>

Some questions on perimeters may be suitable for solving with algebra.

EXAMPLE

This rectangle has a length of $x + 5$ and a width of x.
Find an expression for its perimeter in terms of x.

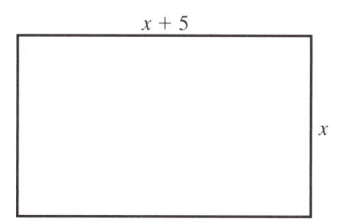

SOLUTION

The rectangle has sides of length $x, x + 5, x$ and $x + 5$.
Its perimeter is $x + x + 5 + x + x + 5 = \underline{4x + 10}$.

8 Working with shape and space U3

EXERCISE 8.3

Find the perimeter and the area of each shape. You may use standard formulae to help.

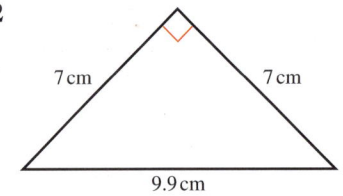

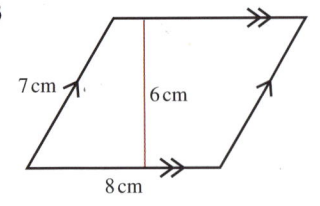

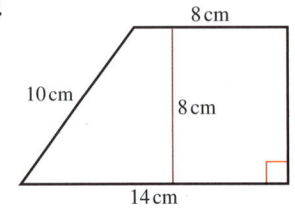

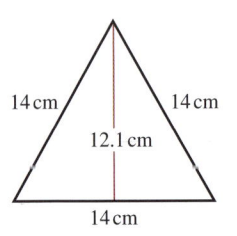

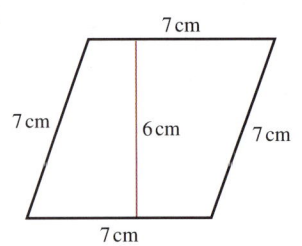

1 Right triangle with legs 6 cm and 8 cm, hypotenuse 10 cm.

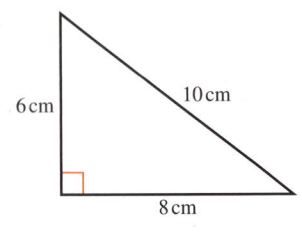

2 Right-angled triangle at apex, two equal sides of 7 cm, base 9.9 cm.

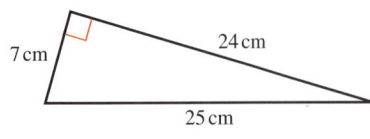

3 Parallelogram with slant side 7 cm, base 8 cm, perpendicular height 6 cm.

4 Trapezium with parallel sides 8 cm (top) and 14 cm (bottom), slant side 10 cm, perpendicular height 8 cm.

5 Isosceles triangle with two sides 14 cm, base 14 cm, perpendicular height 12.1 cm.

6 Parallelogram with slant sides 7 cm, parallel sides 7 cm, perpendicular height 6 cm.

7 Right-angled triangle with sides 7 cm, 24 cm, and 25 cm.

8 Trapezium with parallel sides 3.4 cm (top) and 5 cm (bottom), slant sides 1.7 cm, perpendicular height 1.5 cm.

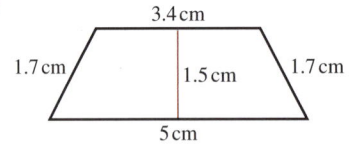

Calculate the perimeter and area of each shape. State your units in each case.

9 L-shaped figure with outer dimensions: top 7 cm, right side 4 cm, left side 6 cm, bottom 4 cm.

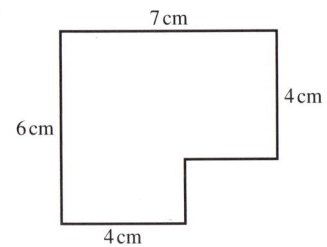

10 C-shaped figure with outer bottom 8 cm, right side with notch: 2 cm, 3 cm, 2 cm, 3 cm, 2 cm.

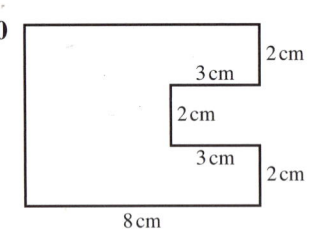

11

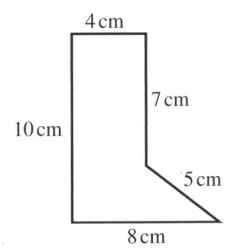

4 cm, 7 cm, 10 cm, 5 cm, 8 cm

12

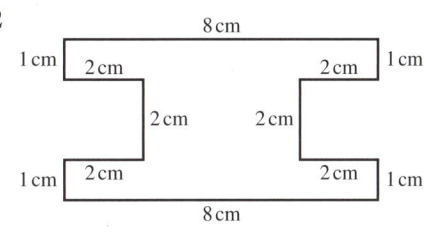

8 cm, 1 cm, 2 cm, 2 cm, 1 cm, 2 cm, 2 cm, 1 cm, 2 cm, 2 cm, 1 cm, 8 cm

13

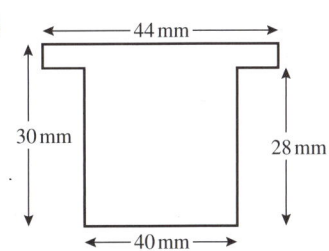

44 mm, 30 mm, 28 mm, 40 mm

14

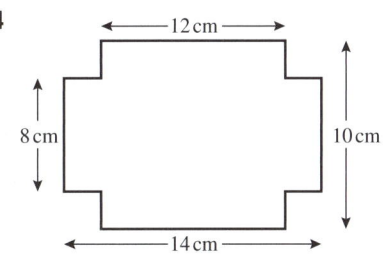

12 cm, 8 cm, 10 cm, 14 cm

15 A quadrilateral has exactly one set of parallel sides. What type of quadrilateral is it?

16 A quadrilateral has all four sides the same length. Tina says: 'It must be a square'.
Is Tina right? Explain your answer.

17 The diagram shows a rectangle.
All lengths are in centimetres.
The perimeter of the rectangle is 32 cm.
 a) Work out the value of x.
 b) Work out the area of the rectangle.

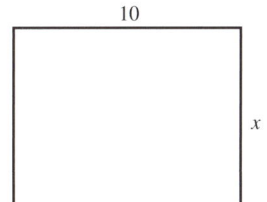

18 The diagram shows a triangle. Lengths are in centimetres.

Triangle with sides: x (AC), $x + 8$ (AB), $2x + 5$ (CB)

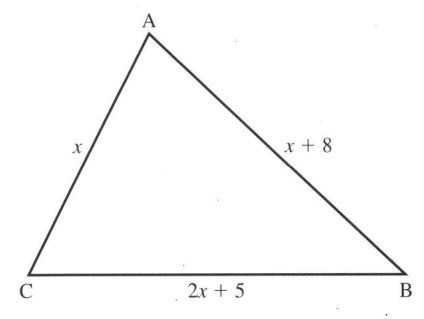

 a) Find an expression for the perimeter of the triangle, in terms of x.
 b) Given that $x = 3$ cm, work out the perimeter of the triangle.

8.4 Surface area and volume

The **surface area** of a cuboid is found by calculating the areas of its six separate faces, and then adding them together. The **volume of a cuboid** is found by multiplying the three dimensions of the cuboid together.

EXAMPLE

Find **a)** the surface area and **b)** the volume of this solid cuboid.

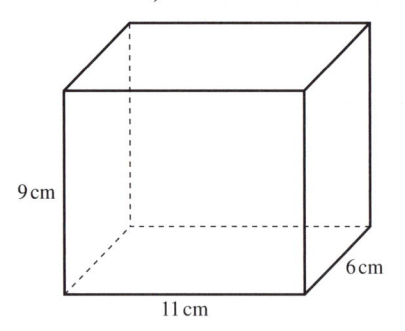

SOLUTION

a) Consider the left and right ends:

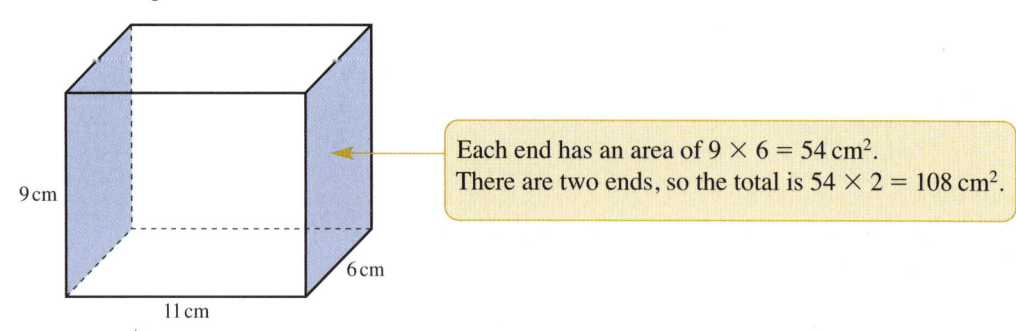

Each end has an area of $9 \times 6 = 54$ cm^2.
There are two ends, so the total is $54 \times 2 = 108$ cm^2.

Similarly for the top and bottom:

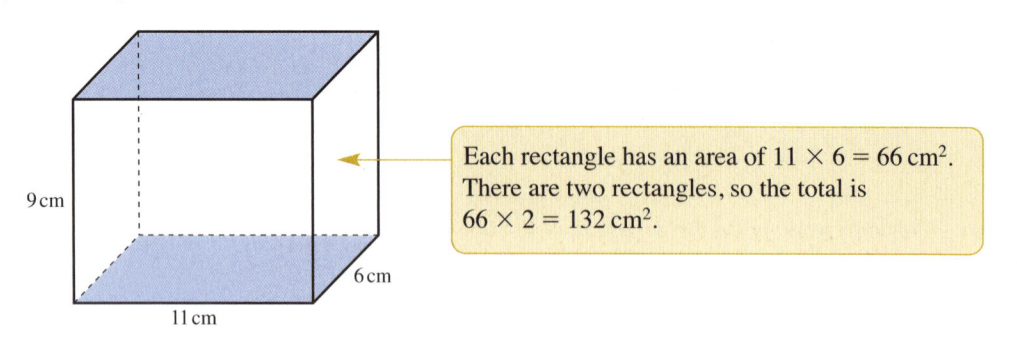

Each rectangle has an area of $11 \times 6 = 66$ cm^2.
There are two rectangles, so the total is $66 \times 2 = 132$ cm^2.

Finally, look at the front and back:

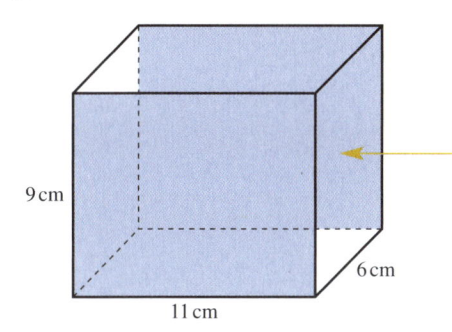

Each rectangle has an area of $11 \times 9 = 99 \text{ cm}^2$.
There are two rectangles, so the total is $99 \times 2 = 198 \text{ cm}^2$.

So the total area is $9 \times 6 \times 2 + 11 \times 6 \times 2 + 11 \times 9 \times 2$
$= 108 + 132 + 198$
$= \underline{438 \text{ cm}^2}$

b) The volume is $11 \times 6 \times 9 = \underline{594 \text{ cm}^3}$

A cuboid is a simple example of a **prism**. Prisms are three-dimensional solids with a constant cross-section. To find the volume of a prism, multiply its cross-sectional area by its length.

Volume of prism = area of cross section × length

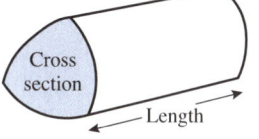

Sometimes you will be told the cross-sectional area, and you can then simply multiply it by the length.

EXAMPLE

The diagram shows a prism of length 10 cm and cross-sectional area 8 cm². Calculate its volume.

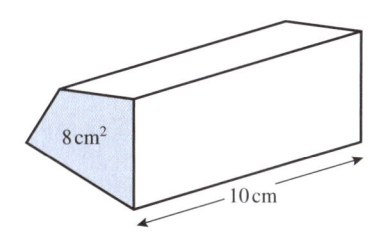

SOLUTION

Volume = area of cross section × length
= 8 × 10
= $\underline{80 \text{ cm}^3}$

$\text{cm}^2 \times \text{cm} = \text{cm}^3$

If the cross section is a simple shape, such as a triangle, then you might be asked to work its area out first.

8 Working with shape and space   U3

EXAMPLE

The diagram shows a prism. The cross section of the prism is a right-angled triangle.

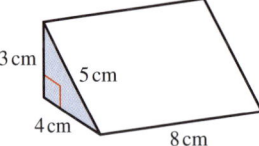

a) Calculate the area of the cross section.
b) Find the volume of the prism.
c) Work out the surface area of the prism.

SOLUTION

a) Area of cross section $= \frac{1}{2} \times 4 \times 3$
   $= \underline{6 \text{ cm}^2}$

b) Volume of prism $= 6 \times 8$
   $= \underline{48 \text{ cm}^3}$

c) The two triangular ends have areas of 6 cm² each.
   Top rectangle has area $5 \times 8 = 40 \text{ cm}^2$.
   Base has area $4 \times 8 = 32 \text{ cm}^2$.
   Back has area $3 \times 8 = 24 \text{ cm}^2$.
   Total surface area $= 6 + 6 + 40 + 32 + 24 = \underline{108 \text{ cm}^2}$

EXERCISE 8.4

1 The diagram shows a cube of side 10 cm.
  Calculate its surface area and also its volume.
  State the units in your answers.

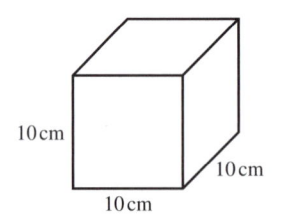

2 The diagram shows a cuboid, with dimensions 8 cm, 12 cm and 15 cm.
  a) Work out the surface of the cuboid, in cm².
  b) Work out the volume of the cuboid, in cm³.

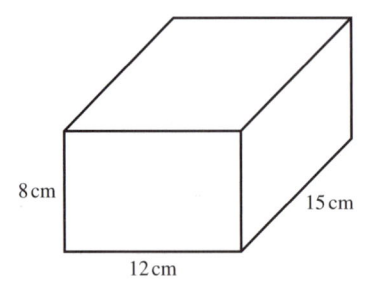

3 The diagram shows a prism. Its cross section is formed by a right-angled triangle of sides 5 cm, 12 cm, 13 cm.
  The prism has a length of 6 cm.
  a) Calculate the area of the cross section, shaded in the diagram.
  b) Work out the volume of the prism.
  c) Calculate the surface area of the prism.

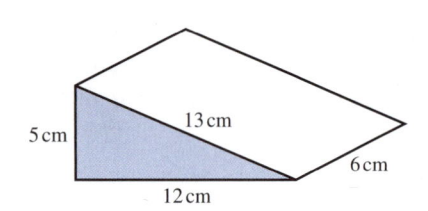

122   U3   8 Working with shape and space

4 The cross section of a steel girder is in the shape of a letter L. The cross section is shown in the diagram below.

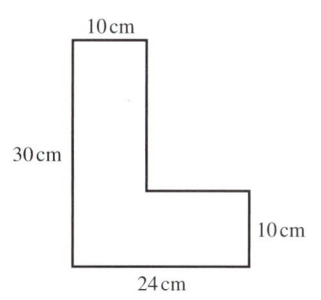

a) Work out the area of the L-shaped cross section.

The girder is 80 cm long.

b) Work out the volume of the girder.

5 A cube measures 12 cm along each side.
a) Work out the volume of the cube.
b) Work out the surface area of the cube.

6 A cuboid measures 15 cm by 20 cm by 30 cm.
a) Work out the volume of the cuboid.
b) Work out the surface area of the cuboid.

7 The diagram shows a water tank. It is in the shape of a cuboid. It has no lid.

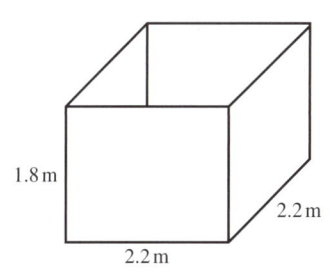

a) Work out the volume of the tank, correct to 3 significant figures.
b) Work out the total surface area of the inside of the tank.

8 The diagram shows a sketch of a swimming pool.

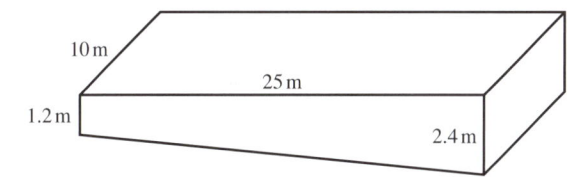

The pool is 1.2 m deep at the shallow end, and 2.4 m deep at the deep end.
The pool is 25 m long, and is 10 m wide.
a) Work out the volume of the pool.

1 cubic metre = 1000 litres.

b) Work out the number of litres of water in the pool when it is full.

8 Working with shape and space   U3

9   A cube has a volume of 10 648 cm^3.
   a) Work out the dimensions of the cube.
   b) Calculate the surface area of the cube.

10 A cuboid has a volume of 455 cm^3. Its dimensions are all different.
   Each dimension is a whole number of centimetres. Each dimension is greater than 1 cm.
   a) Work out the dimensions of the cuboid.
   b) Calculate the surface area of the cuboid.

REVIEW EXERCISE 8

In some of the questions that follow, you may find three capital letters being used to describe an angle, e.g. angle PQR. This means the angle formed by the line segment PQ joining the line segment QR, i.e. the angle Q.

1 Find the size of the angles marked a and b on the diagram.

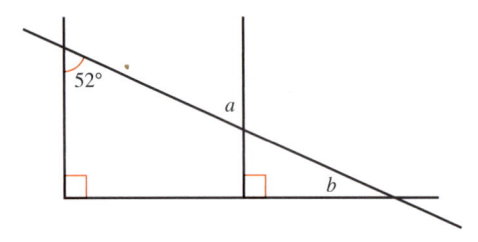

2 PQ is a straight line.

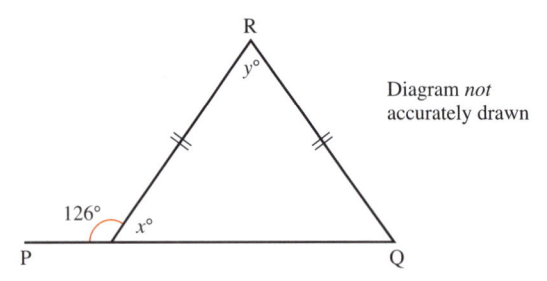

   Diagram *not* accurately drawn

   a) Work out the size of the angle marked $x°$.
   b) Work out the size of the angle marked $y°$. Give reasons for your answer.   [Edexcel]

3 A certain quadrilateral has all its angles equal, but its sides are not all the same length.
   a) Is it regular?
   b) What type of quadrilateral is this?

4 A cuboid has a volume of 175 cm^3. Two of its dimensions are 2.5 cm and 3.5 cm.
   Work out the remaining dimension.

5 Three different rectangles each have an area of 28 cm^2. The lengths of all the sides are whole numbers of centimetres. For each rectangle work out the lengths of the two sides.   [Edexcel]

6 PQRS is a parallelogram. Angle QSP = 47°. Angle QSR = 24°. PST is a straight line.

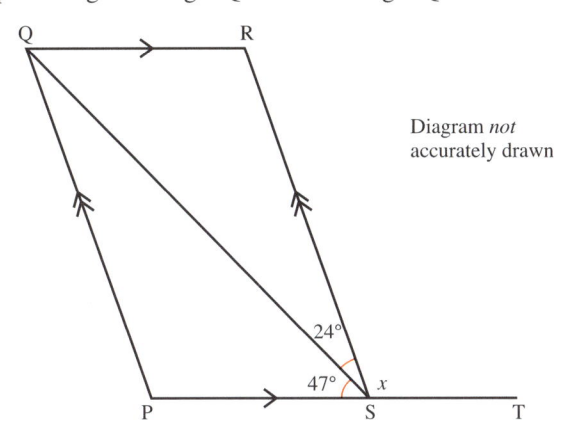

Diagram *not* accurately drawn

a) **(i)** Find the size of the angle marked *x*.
   (ii) Give a reason for your answer.
b) **(i)** Work out the size of angle PQS.
   (ii) Give a reason for your answer.

[Edexcel]

7 The diagram shows a prism.
The cross section of the prism is a trapezium.
The lengths of the parallel sides of the trapezium are 8 cm and 6 cm.
The distance between the parallel sides of the trapezium is 5 cm.
The length of the prism is 20 cm.
a) Work out the volume of the prism.
The prism is made out of gold. Gold has a density of 19.3 grams per cm^3.
b) Work out the mass of the prism. Give your answer in kilograms.

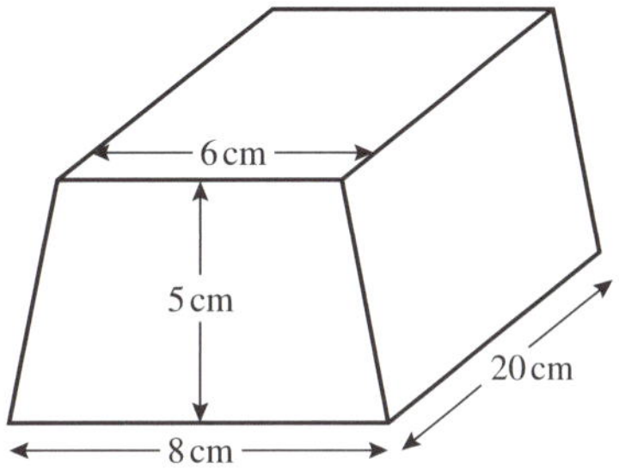

Diagram *not* accurately drawn

[Edexcel]

8 ABC and EBD are straight lines. BD = BC. Angle CBD = 42°.

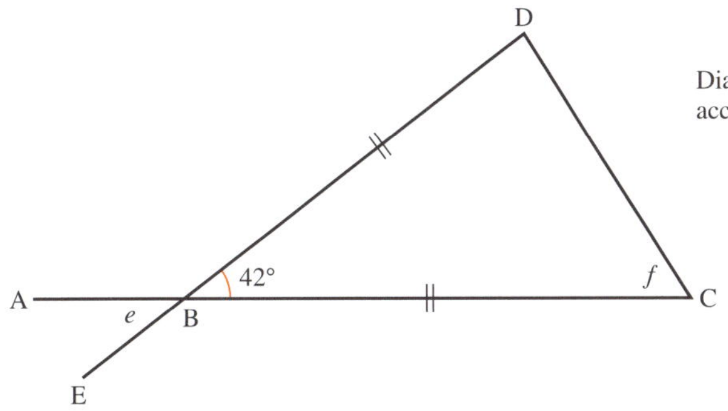

Diagram *not* accurately drawn

a) Write down the size of the angle marked *e*.
b) Work out the size of the angle marked *f*.

[Edexcel]

8 Working with shape and space   U3   125

9 In this diagram, the lines AB and CD are parallel.

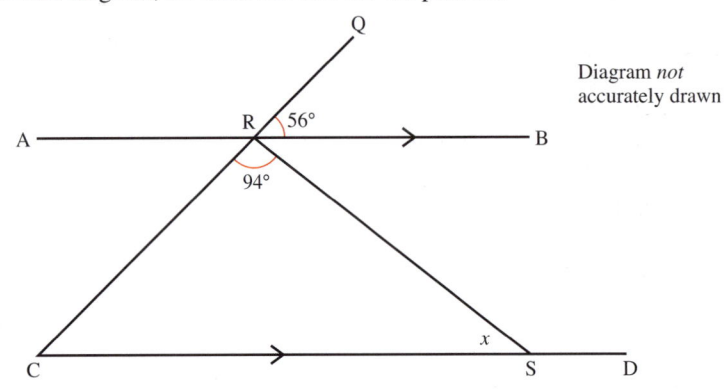

Diagram *not* accurately drawn

CRQ is a straight line. Angle CRS = 94°. Angle QRB = 56°. Angle RSC = x°.
Find the value of x. [Edexcel]

10 The diagram shows a prism.

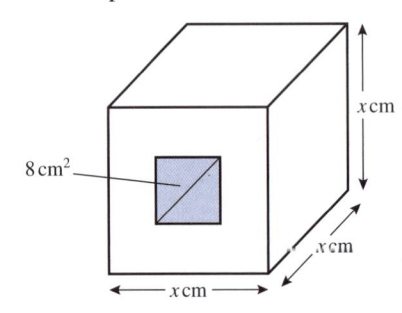

Diagram *not* accurately drawn

The prism is made from a cube of side x cm. A hole of uniform cross-sectional area 8 cm² is cut through the cube. Find, in terms of x, an expression for the volume of the prism. [Edexcel]

11 The diagram shows a trapezium ABCD.

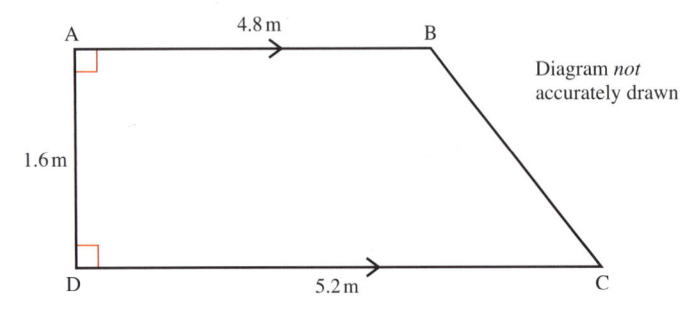

Diagram *not* accurately drawn

AB is parallel to DC. AB = 4.8 m, DC = 5.2 m, AD = 1.6 m.
Angle BAD = 90°, angle ADC = 90°.
Calculate the area of the trapezium. [Edexcel]

12 The diagram shows a water tank in the shape of a cuboid. The measurements of the cuboid are 20 cm by 50 cm by 20 cm.

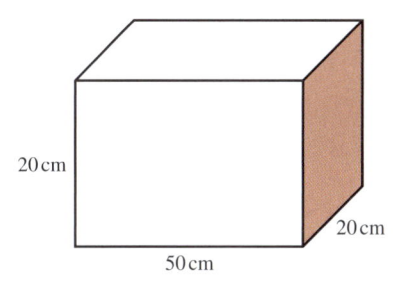

Diagram *not* accurately drawn

a) Work out the volume of the water tank.
Water is poured into the tank at a rate of 5 litres per minute. 1 litre = 1000 cm^3.
b) Work out the time it takes to fill the water tank completely. Give your answer in minutes.   [Edexcel]

13 The diagrams show a paperweight.

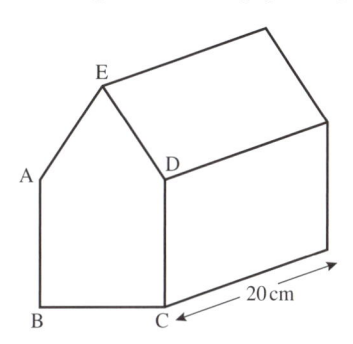

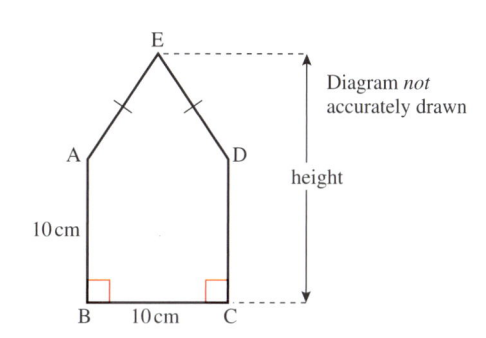

Diagram *not* accurately drawn

ABCDE is a cross section of the paperweight.
AB, BC and CD are three sides of a square of side 10 cm. AE = DE.
The area of the cross section is 130 cm^2.
a) Work out the height.
The paperweight is a prism of length 20 cm.
b) Work out the volume of the paperweight. Give the units with your answer.   [Edexcel]

14 The diagram shows a shape.

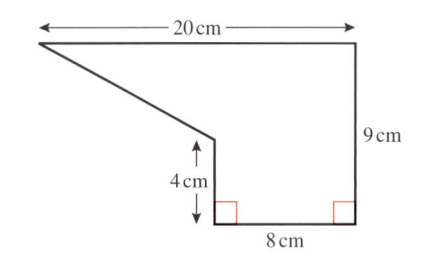

Diagram *not* accurately drawn

Work out the area of the shape.   [Edexcel]

15 The diagram represents a large tank in the shape of a cuboid.

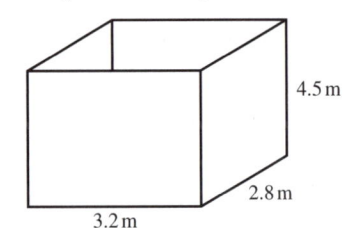

Diagram *not* accurately drawn

4.5 m
2.8 m
3.2 m

The tank has a base. It does not have a top.
The width of the tank is 2.8 metres, the length is 3.2 metres, the height is 4.5 metres.
The outside of the tank is going to be painted. 1 litre of paint will cover 2.5 m² of the tank.
The cost of the paint is £2.99 per litre.
Calculate the total cost of the paint needed to paint the outside of the tank. [Edexcel]

KEY POINTS

1 Corresponding (F) angles are equal.   Alternate (Z) angles are equal.

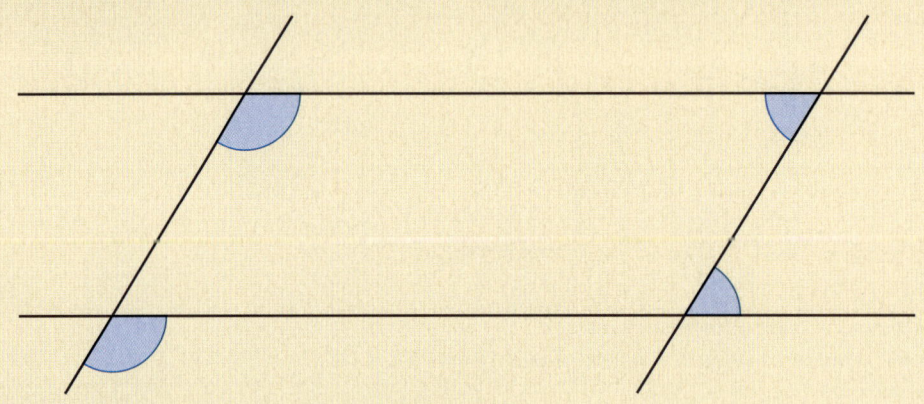

2 The angles in any triangle add up to 180°.

3 The angles in any quadrilateral add up to 360°.

4 Areas:

Area of a rectangle $= bh$

Area of a triangle $= \frac{1}{2}bh$

Area of a parallelogram $= bh$

Area of a trapezium $= \frac{1}{2}(a + b)h$

5 Remember to include units in your answers to numerical problems.

6 The volume of a cuboid is found by multiplying its three dimensions, so $V = abc$

7 A prism has constant cross-sectional area.

8 Volume of a prism = cross-sectional area × length

9 To find the surface area of a solid, work out the area of each separate flat surface, then add them up.

Internet Challenge 8

The four-colour theorem

The four-colour theorem claims that four colours are sufficient to colour in a map, in such a way that no two regions share the same colour along a boundary (except at a point).

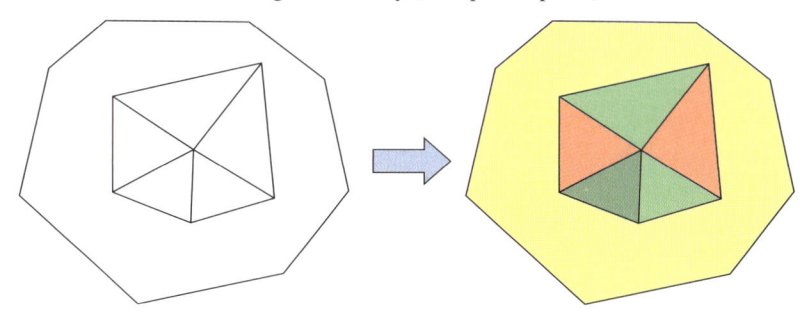

Try drawing some maps of your own, and colouring them in. Does the four-colour theorem appear to be true?

Now use the internet to help answer these questions.

1 Who first proposed this theorem, in 1852/3?

2 Who presented a flawed proof, in 1879?

3 Who presented another flawed proof, in 1880?

4 When was the four-colour theorem first successfully proved?

5 Who achieved this first proof?

6 What major innovation was used to support the proof?

7 Supposing a map is drawn on a sphere instead of a plane. How many colours are sufficient now?

8 Mathematicians refer to a three-dimensional ring doughnut shape as a *torus*. How many colours are sufficient to colour in any map on a torus?

9 What April Fool's joke concerning the four-colour theorem was perpetrated by the mathematician and mathematical games writer Martin Gardner in 1975?

10 Why might a real map-maker need to use more than four colours?
   Clue: What is unusual about Alaska?

CHAPTER 9

Properties of circles

In this chapter you will **learn how to**:
- use correct vocabulary associated with circles
- use tangent properties to solve problems
- construct regular polygons inside circles.

You will also be **challenged to**:
- investigate different meanings of 'circles'.

Starter: Circle vocabulary

Here are some words you will often encounter when working with circles:

  Centre   Radius   Chord   Diameter   Circumference
  Tangent   Arc   Sector   Segment

Try to match the correct words to the nine diagrams below:

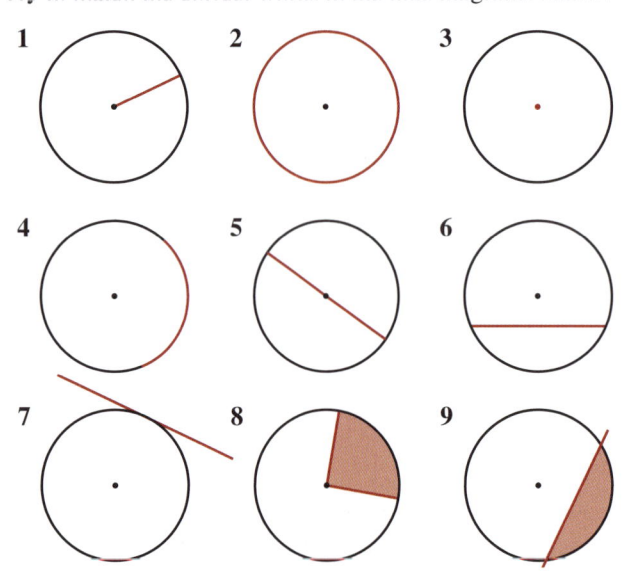

10 a) The French call a rainbow an '*arc-en-ciel*' (*ciel* = sky).
Do you think this is a good name?

b) The English call a piece of an orange a 'segment'.
Do you think this is a good name?

9.1 Tangents, chords and circles

In this section you will learn some theorems about circles, and then use them to solve problems. The theorems are concerned with tangents and chords.
A **chord** is a line segment joining two points on the circumference of a circle.
A **tangent** is a straight line that touches a circle only once.

A line segment drawn from the centre of a circle to the midpoint of a chord will intersect the chord at right angles.

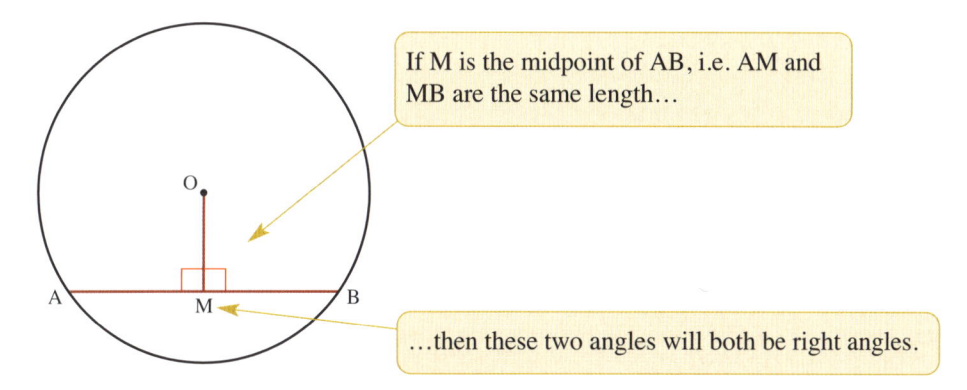

If M is the midpoint of AB, i.e. AM and MB are the same length…

…then these two angles will both be right angles.

A tangent and radius meet at right angles.

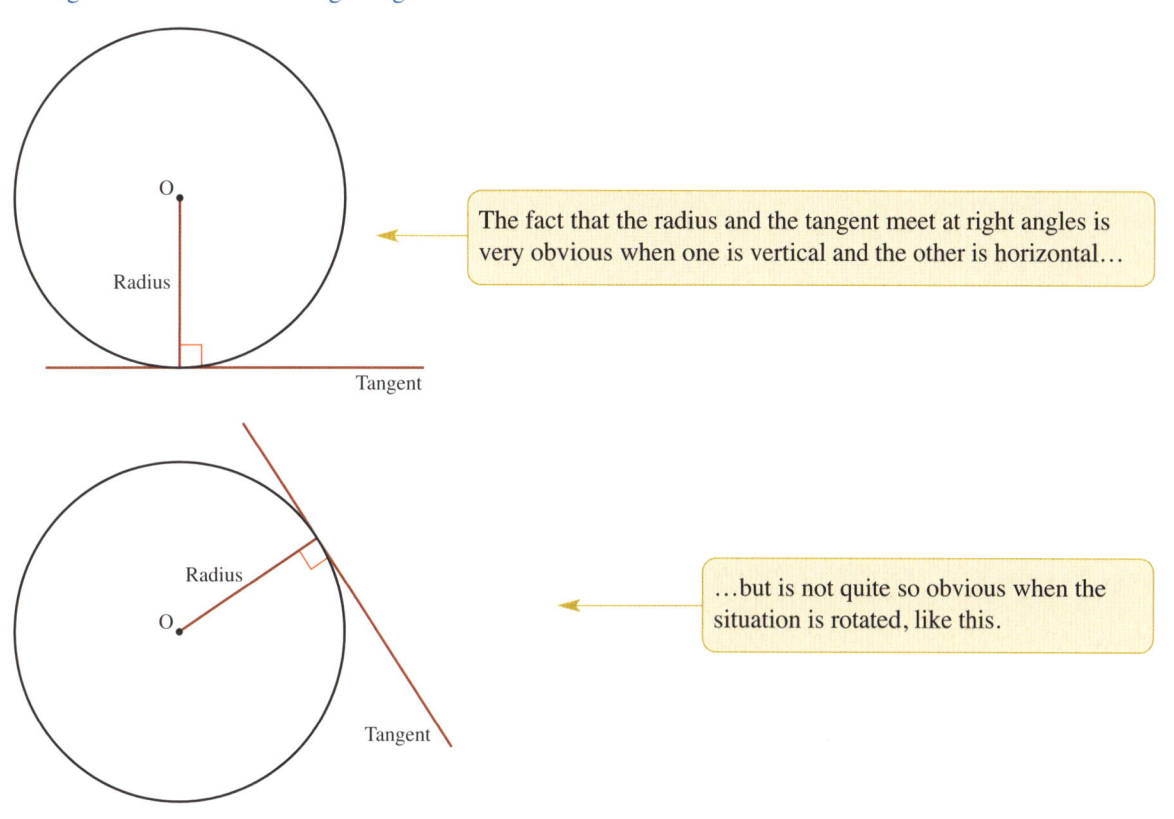

The fact that the radius and the tangent meet at right angles is very obvious when one is vertical and the other is horizontal…

…but is not quite so obvious when the situation is rotated, like this.

9 Properties of circles U3

The two tangents from a given point to a circle are equal in length.

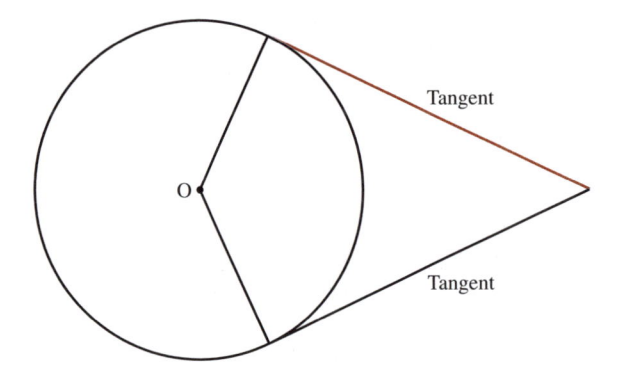

These theorems may be used to help you determine the values of missing angles in circles. When you use them, remember to tell the examiner which theorem(s) you have used.

EXAMPLE

The diagram shows a circle, centre O. PT is a tangent to the circle. Find the value of x.

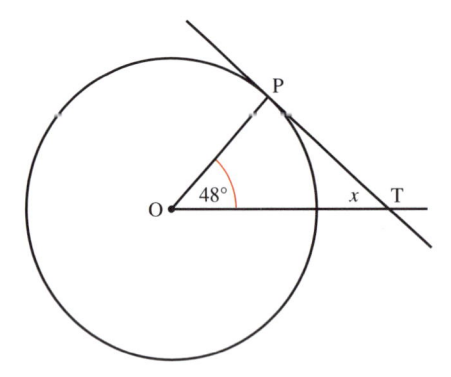

SOLUTION

Angle OPT = 90° (angle between the radius and tangent is 90°).

The angles in triangle TOP add up to 180°, so:

$$x = 180° - (48° + 90°)$$
$$= 180° - 138°$$
$$= \underline{42°}$$

EXAMPLE

The diagram shows a circle, centre Q.
AB is a chord across the circle.
M is the midpoint of AB.
Find the value of y.

SOLUTION

Angle AMQ = 90° (radius bisecting chord).

The angles in triangle AMQ add up to 180°.

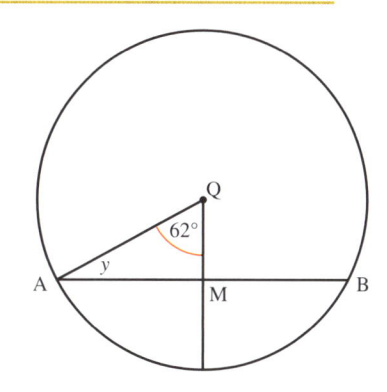

So: $y = 180° - (62° + 90°)$
   $= 180° - 152°$
   $= \underline{28°}$

EXERCISE 9.1

1 PT is a tangent to the circle, centre O. Angle PTO = 29°.

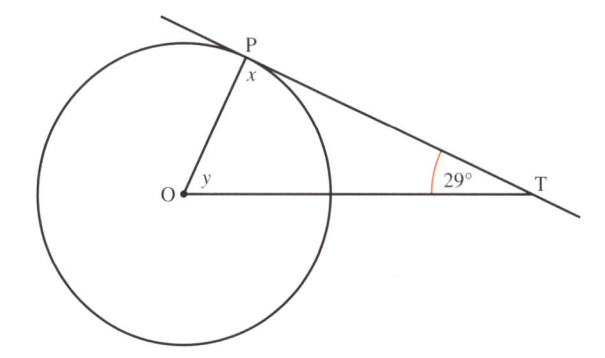

  a) State, with a reason, the value of the angle marked x.
  b) Work out the value of the angle marked y.

2 AP and BP are tangents to the circle, centre O. Angle APO = 33°.
  The length of the tangent AP is 12 cm.

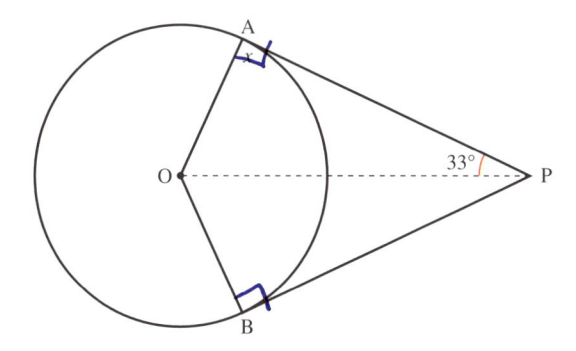

  a) Write down the length of the tangent BP.
  b) Write down the size of angle OAP, marked x.
  c) Work out the size of angle AOB.

9 Properties of circles U3   133

3 TP and TR are tangents to the circle, centre O. Angle PTR is 44°.

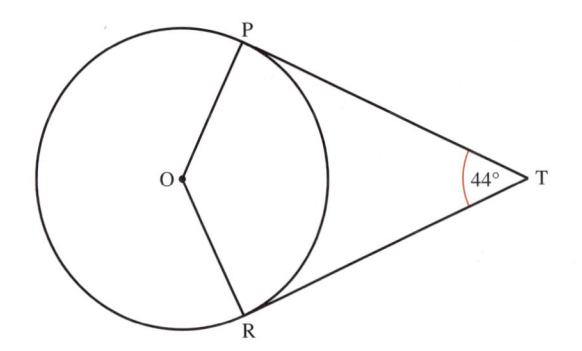

  a) Work out the size of angle POR. Give reasons.
  b) What type of quadrilateral is OPTR? Explain your reasoning.

4 TP and TR are tangents to the circle, centre O. Angle POR is 130°.

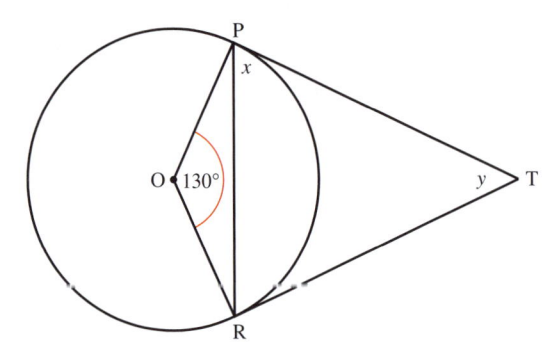

  a) What type of triangle is triangle OPR?
  b) Work out the value of x.
  c) Work out the value of y.

5 From a point T, two tangents TP and TQ are drawn to a circle, centre O.
  a) Make a sketch to show this information.

  The length TQ is measured, and found to be exactly the same as the length PO.
  b) What type of quadrilateral is TPOQ?

9.2 Constructing regular polygons inside a circle

You can construct a regular polygon inside a circle using compasses and a protractor. The idea is to divide the 360° angle at the centre of the circle into equal parts, according to how many sides you want the polygon to have. The angle of one of the parts at the centre is given by

Angles at centre = 360° ÷ number of sides

Here are some instructions for making a regular hexagon.

Step 1 Draw a circle of a convenient radius – say 6 cm.
Step 2 360° ÷ 6 = 60°, so measure and draw an angle of 60° at the centre of the circle.
Step 3 Repeat Step 2 to form a set of 60° sectors.

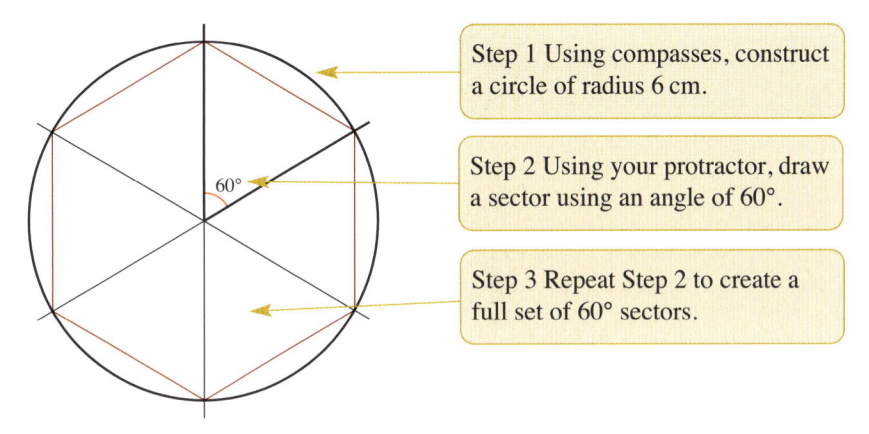

Step 1 Using compasses, construct a circle of radius 6 cm.

Step 2 Using your protractor, draw a sector using an angle of 60°.

Step 3 Repeat Step 2 to create a full set of 60° sectors.

Complete the construction by joining the six points around the circumference of the circle, as shown above.

EXERCISE 9.2

1 Follow the instructions given above, to construct a regular hexagon inside a circle of radius 6 cm.

2 a) Use the rule, angle at centre = 360° ÷ number of sides, to work out the angle at the centre in order to construct a regular octagon inside a circle.
 b) Use compasses to draw a circle of radius 7 cm.
 c) Using a protractor, construct a regular octagon inside the circle.

3 a) Use compasses to make a circle of radius 6 cm.
 b) Using a protractor, construct a regular pentagon inside the circle.

4 a) Use compasses to make a circle of radius 8 cm.
 b) Using a protractor, construct a regular ten-sided polygon (*decagon*) inside the circle.

5 a) Use compasses to make two copies of a circle of radius 8 cm.
 b) Using a protractor, construct nine points at equal intervals around the circumference of each circle.
 c) On the first circle, join the points up to make a regular nine-sided polygon (*nonagon*) inside the circle.
 d) On the second circle, join the points up in a different way, to make a nine-pointed star.

REVIEW EXERCISE 9

1 PQ is a tangent to the circle, centre O. Angle POQ = 61°.

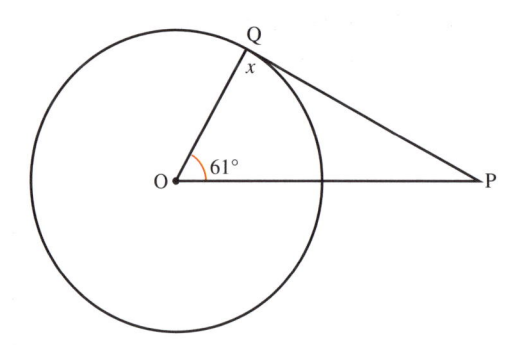

a) Write down the size of angle OQP, marked x.
b) Work out the size of angle OPQ.

2 AP and BP are tangents to the circle, centre O. Angle APO = 33°. The length of the tangent AP is 8 cm. The length of OA is 6 cm.

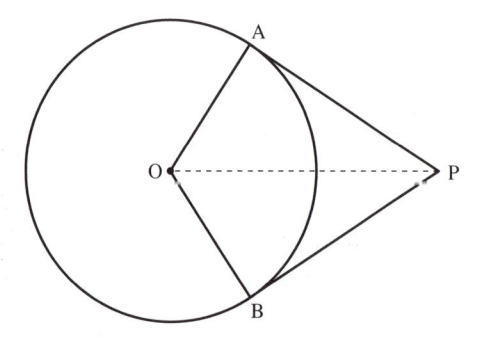

a) Write down the length of the tangent BP.
b) Explain why angle OAP must be a right angle.
c) Work out the area of triangle OBP.

3 AB is a chord inscribed in the circle, centre O. M is the midpoint of AB. Angle MOB is 37°.

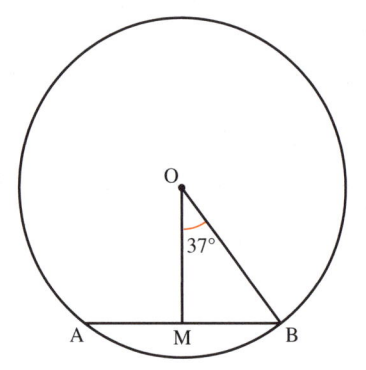

a) State the value of angle OMB.
b) Work out the size of angle OBM.

4 a) Using compasses, construct a circle of radius 8 cm.
   b) Using a protractor, construct a regular 12-sided polygon (*dodecagon*) inside the circle.

5 Jawad has a set of identical plastic isosceles triangles. He fits them together to make a regular polygon, centre O. The diagram shows how the first two triangles fit together.

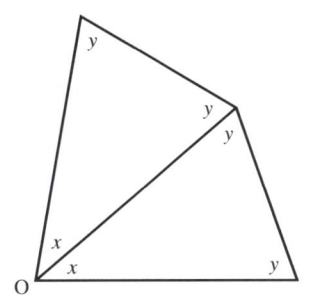

Given that $y = 70°$, work out the value of x.

KEY POINTS

1 Tangent and chord properties of a circle

A line segment drawn from the centre of a circle to the midpoint of a chord will intersect the chord at right angles.	A tangent and radius meet at right angles.	The two tangents from a given point to a circle are equal in length.

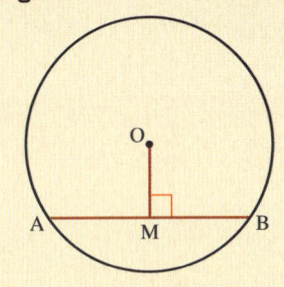

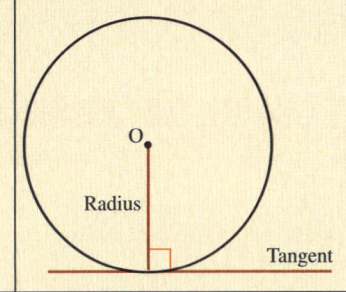

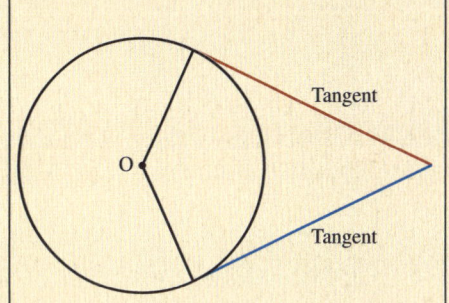

2 To construct a regular polygon inside a circle, use the rule

Angles at centre = 360° ÷ number of sides

Then use a protractor to divide the circle into equal sectors. Join the points around the circumference of the circle to complete the polygon.

Internet Challenge 9

Circles

Each clue has a two-word answer. Use the internet to help with the harder ones.

1. Line of latitude at approximately 66.7 degrees North passing through parts of Russia, Alaska, Canada, Greenland, Norway, Sweden and Finland.

2. A Londoner might use this to travel from Victoria to South Kensington.

3. International organisation whose motto, *Indolicis private loqui*, means 'not apt to disclose secrets'.

4. A group of individuals who are given special status within a religious or secret society; also the name of a Jamaican reggae band known for the song 'Bad Boys'.

5. A false type of logic, in which the conclusion is actually embedded within the premise.

6. Path on a sphere joining two points by the shortest route.

7. An unpleasant cycle of events from which there appears no escape – also part of the title of a 1994 movie about the writer Dorothy Parker.

8. The world's largest one of these is found at Avebury, Wiltshire.

9. 2004 novel by US-Canadian fantasy author Sean Stewart.

10. These curious patterns are found in some cereal fields. Although sometimes claimed to be formed by flying saucers or alien microwave signals, many of them have now been confirmed as elaborate hoaxes.

CHAPTER 10

Working with units

> In this chapter you will **revise earlier work on**:
> - basic metric units.
>
> You will **learn how to**:
> - choose appropriate metric units
> - make approximate conversions between metric and imperial units
> - work with compound measures such as speed and density
> - convert between systems of units
> - work with bearings.
>
> You will also be **challenged to**:
> - investigate the definitions of some units.

Starter: Leap years

A year is defined as the time it takes the Earth to complete one orbit around the Sun – this is approximately 365.2424 days. Our calendar assigns 365 days to most years, but every so often a leap year of 366 days is used, by adding a 29th day to February.

Here are the rules for deciding whether a year is a leap year or not:

- If the year is not a multiple of 4, then it has only 365 days.
- If the year is a multiple of 4, then it is a leap year with 366 days, unless it is a centennial year (i.e. ending in -00).
- Centennial years are leap years only if the year is a multiple of 400.

1 Use the rules to decide which of these years were leap years.

    1800   1824   1900   1939   1966   1984   2000

2 Use the rules to decide which of these years will be leap years.

    2024   2060   2100   2150   2200   2340   2400

3 How many leap years are there in any consecutive period of 400 years?

4 Use your answer to question **3** to show that the average length of a year using these leap rules is 365.2425 days.

10.1 Basic metric units

You should already be familiar with these metric units.

Distance
1 centimetre = 10 millimetres
1 metre = 100 centimetres
1 metre = 1000 millimetres
1 kilometre = 1000 metres

Mass
1 gram = 1000 milligrams
1 kilogram = 1000 grams
1 tonne = 1000 kilograms

Volume
1 litre = 1000 millilitres
1 millilitre = 1 cubic centimetre

Time
1 second = 1000 milliseconds
1 minute = 60 seconds
1 hour = 60 minutes

You can use these facts to convert between different metric units.

EXAMPLE

Convert:
a) 2.4 metres to centimetres
b) 1250 grams to kilograms
c) 0.35 litres to millilitres.

SOLUTION

a) 2.4 m = 2.4 × 100 cm
       = 240 cm

b) 1250 g = 1250 ÷ 1000 kg
          = 1.25 kg

c) 0.35 l = 0.35 × 1000 ml
          = 350 ml

EXAMPLE

Convert:
a) half a second into milliseconds
b) 5 minutes into seconds
c) half an hour into seconds.

SOLUTION

a) $\frac{1}{2}$ s = 0.5 × 1000 milliseconds
       = 500 milliseconds

b) 5 min = 5 × 60 s
         = 300 s

c) $\frac{1}{2}$ hour = 0.5 × 60 minutes
           = 30 minutes
           = 30 × 60 s
           = 1800 s

EXERCISE 10.1

1. Convert 3500 metres into kilometres.

2. Convert 42 000 kilograms into tonnes.

3. Write 2.75 kilograms in grams.

4. Express 450 milligrams in grams.

5. Work out how many seconds there are in 20 minutes.

6. A jug holds 250 millilitres of water. How many jugs must be used to fill a pond holding 45 litres?

7. A car journey lasts for 210 minutes. Convert this time into hours.

8. A rectangle measures 800 millimetres by 600 millimetres. Work out the perimeter of the rectangle. Give your answer in metres.

9. A drinks machine sells 200 drinks. Each drink has a volume of 330 millilitres. Work out the total volume of all 200 drinks sold. Give your answer in litres.

10. A square has a perimeter of 2.8 metres. Find the length of one side. Give your answer in centimetres.

10.2 Choosing and using metric and imperial units

If you wanted to write down the distance to the Moon you would probably not use millimetres, since the number would be very large! Likewise you would not want to measure the mass of an insect in tonnes.

The GCSE examination will expect you to be able to choose sensibly when selecting a unit for measurement. You also need to be able to convert between metric and imperial units, using the following approximations.

Distance

Metric	Imperial
2.5 centimetres	1 inch
30 centimetres	1 foot
8 kilometres	5 miles

Mass

Metric	Imperial
1 kilogram	2.2 pounds

Volume

Metric	Imperial
1 litre	1.75 pints
4.5 litres	1 gallon

EXAMPLE

a) Suggest a sensible metric unit for measuring:
  (i) the length of a garden   **(ii)** the mass of a sparrow.
b) A jogger runs 20 kilometres. Approximately how many miles is this?

SOLUTION

a) **(i)** The length of a garden might be best measured in metres.
  (ii) The mass of a sparrow might be best measured in grams.
b) 20 km = 8 + 8 + 4 km
        = 5 + 5 + 2.5 miles
        = 12.5 miles approximately

EXERCISE 10.2

1 Suggest a suitable metric unit for measuring the mass of a bicycle.

2 A carpenter says a piece of wood is 1 foot 6 inches long and 2 inches thick. Convert these quantities into approximate metric equivalents.

3 The distance from London to Brighton is 50 miles. Roughly how many kilometres is this?

4 Suggest a suitable metric unit for measuring the volume of a rucksack.

5 A sculpture has a mass of 40 kilograms. Roughly how many pounds is this?

6 Suggest a suitable metric unit for measuring the height of a mountain.

7 At an airport check-in, a suitcase is weighed and found to be 33 pounds. Roughly how many kilograms is this?

8 A petrol station sells unleaded petrol for £1.12 a litre. Roughly how much does one gallon of unleaded petrol cost?

9 Suggest a suitable metric unit for measuring the volume of a dose of liquid medicine.

10 A telescope lens has a diameter of 8 inches. Convert this into an approximate metric equivalent.

10.3 Compound measures

Compound measures arise when you combine two basic measures, usually by multiplication or division. Two of the more common ones are

  Speed = distance ÷ time
  Density = mass ÷ volume

The units of a compound measure will depend upon the units of the two components. For example, if you work out a speed by dividing a distance in metres by a time in seconds, then the result will be in metres per second.

EXAMPLE

An athlete can run 810 metres at a steady speed in two and a half minutes. Work out his speed in metres per second.

SOLUTION

Two and a half minutes is 150 seconds.
Speed = distance ÷ time
      = 810 metres ÷ 150 seconds
      = 5.4 m/s

EXAMPLE

A block of metal has a volume of 240 cm^3. Its mass is 1.56 kilograms.
a) Express the mass of the block in grams.
b) Work out the density of the block, in grams per centimetre.

A second block of metal has a volume of 310 cm^3 and a density of 5.5 g/cm^3.
c) Work out the mass of this block. Give your answer in kilograms.

SOLUTION

a) Mass = 1.56 × 1000 g
       = 1560 g
b) Density = 1560 g ÷ 240 cm^3
           = 6.5 g/cm^3
c) Mass = volume × density
       = 310 cm^3 × 5.5 g/cm^3
       = 1705 g
       = 1.705 kg

Some questions about speed may be based on a **distance–time graph** (or **travel graph**). This is a diagram with distance plotted along the vertical axis, and time along the horizontal axis. Take care to read the units carefully.

EXAMPLE

The diagram shows a car journey, comprising three sections marked A, B, C.
a) Work out the speed of the car during the section marked A.
b) Describe what was happening during the section marked B.
c) Work out the speed of the car during the section marked C.

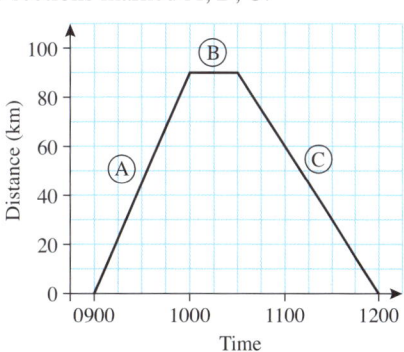

10 Working with units U3 143

SOLUTION

a) Section A takes 1 hour, and covers 90 km.
   Speed = distance ÷ time
        = 90 km ÷ 1 hour
        = 90 km/h

b) During Section B the car was stationary.
c) Section C takes 1.5 hours, and covers 90 km.
   Speed = 90 km ÷ 1.5 hours
        = 60 km/h

EXERCISE 10.3

1. A train travels 180 kilometres in one and a half hours. Work out its average speed, in km/h.

2. A solid ball has a mass of 966 grams and a volume of 420 cm^3. Work out its density, in g/cm^3.

3. A hiker walks 33.6 kilometres in 8 hours. Work out her average speed, in kilometres per hour.

4. A foam pad has a mass of 450 grams and a volume of 600 cm^3. Work out its density, in g/cm^3.

5. A rifle bullet can travel 2250 metres in 2.5 seconds. Work out its speed, in metres per second.

6. Two ornaments are made of the same metal. The smaller ornament has a volume of 120 cm^3 and a mass of 456 grams. The larger ornament has a volume of 150 cm^3.
   a) Work out the density of the metal. Give your answer in g/cm^3.
   b) Work out the mass of the larger ornament.

7. A long distance runner travels 3.24 kilometres in 12 minutes.
   a) Convert these quantities into metres and seconds.
   b) Hence work out his speed, in metres per second.

8. A solid cuboid measures 25 cm by 50 cm by 10 cm.
   a) Work out the volume of the cuboid. Give your answer in cm^3.
   The cuboid has a density of 5.2 g/cm^3.
   b) Work out the mass of the cuboid. Give your answer in kilograms.

9. Rob cycles at a steady speed for 40 minutes and travels 14 kilometres.
   a) Work out how far he could travel in 20 minutes.
   b) Hence work out his speed in km/h.

10. Tim has been measuring objects in a physics lab. His results are shown in the table.
    a) Copy and complete the table to show the densities. Tim has read in a book that objects will float in water if (and only if) their density is less than 1 g/cm^3.
    b) Use this rule to decide which of these objects would float in water.

	Mass	Volume	Density
Object A	240 g	150 cm^3	
Object B	600 g	800 cm^3	
Object C	125 g	50 cm^3	
Object D	720 g	160 cm^3	
Object E	85 g	125 cm^3	

11 The distance–time graph shows an aircraft journey.
  a) Work out the speed between 1400 and 1500.
  b) Work out the speed between 1530 and 1630.
  c) Explain what the aircraft was doing between 1500 and 1530.

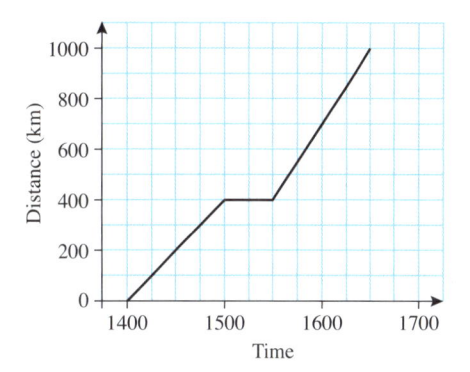

12 The travel graph shows a long train journey.
  a) Work out the speed of the train on each of the sections marked A, B, C.
  Give your answers in km/h.
  b) Between which times was the train travelling at the fastest speed?

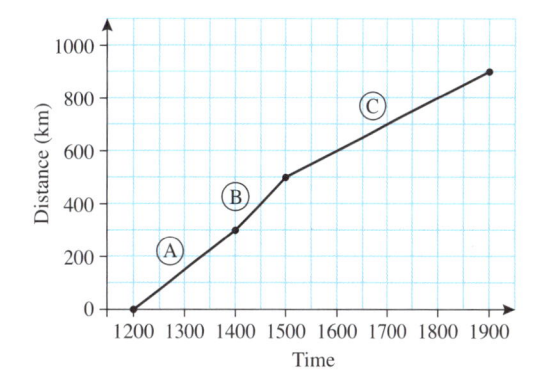

10.4 Angles and bearings

Directions in a plane are often described using bearings. Bearings are measured clockwise from North, and should be written using three figures, for example:

North is 000°, East is 090°, South is 180°, West is 270°

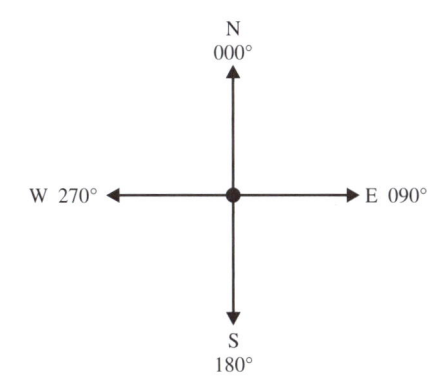

10 Working with units   U3   145

EXAMPLE

The diagram below shows a map with three towns marked P, Q, R.

P •

Q •

R •

Using a protractor, find:
a) the bearing of Q from P
b) the bearing of P from R.

SOLUTION

a) The bearing is 'from P' so draw a North line at P.
Draw a line joining P and Q.
Then measure the angle (clockwise), starting from due North.

Bearing of Q from P = 068°

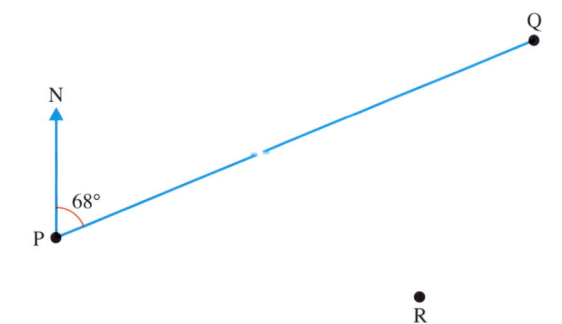

b) The bearing is 'from R' so draw a North line at R.
Draw a line joining R and P.
Then measure the angle (clockwise), starting from due North.
This is a reflex angle, so it is best to break it into two parts:

Bearing of P from R = 180° + 99°
= 279°

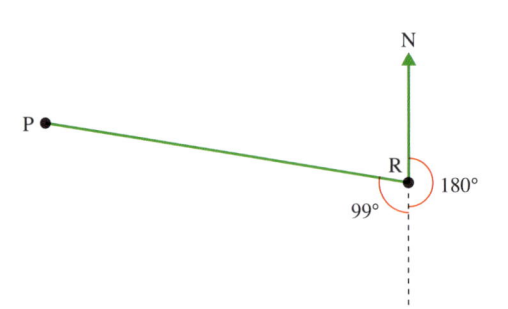

EXERCISE 10.4

1 The diagram shows three points K, L, M.
  a) Copy the diagram and measure the bearing of M from L.
  b) Measure the bearing of K from M.

2 The diagram shows an aircraft carrier A and five ships P, Q, R, S and T.

Work out the bearing of each of the five ships from the aircraft carrier A.

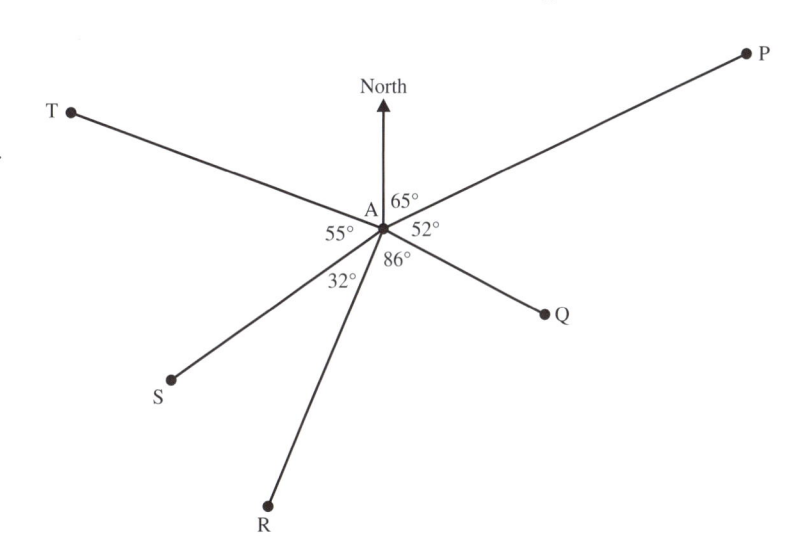

3 The diagram shows two towns, X and Y.
  a) Copy the diagram and measure the bearing of Y from X.
  b) Measure the bearing of X from Y.
  c) What do you notice about your answers to **a)** and **b)**?

4 Three towns A, B and C are at the vertices of an equilateral triangle.
Town B is directly due East of Town A. Town C is at a bearing of 060° from Town A.
  a) Illustrate this information on a sketch.
  b) Find the three-figure bearing of
    (i) Town A from Town B   **(ii)** Town C from Town B.

5 A pilot takes off and flies his aircraft on a bearing of 124° until he lands at his destination. On what bearing should he fly in order to make the return journey?

REVIEW EXERCISE 10

1. Convert:
   a) 450 centimetres into metres
   b) 350 grams into kilograms
   c) 75 litres into millilitres.

2. Chocolate bars weigh 65 grams each. Find the total weight of 360 bars. Give your answer in kilograms.

3. Use approximate conversion factors to convert:
   a) 6 inches into centimetres.
   b) 14 litres into pints.

4. Convert:
   a) 12.5 tonnes into kilograms
   b) 230 kilometres into metres
   c) 3200 millilitres into litres.

5. A television programme is scheduled to last for half an hour. A recordable DVD has 2040 seconds of unused time remaining. Does the DVD have enough room to record the programme? Show your method in full.

6. A bar of metal has a volume of 1260 cm^3 and a mass of 3.15 kg.
   a) Express the mass of the bar in grams.
   b) Work out the density of the bar, in g/cm^3.

7. A cyclist travels 24 kilometres in 90 minutes. Work out his speed, in km/h.

8. A stone block has a density of 3.1 g/cm^3, and its volume is 640 cm^3. Work out its mass. Give your answer in kilograms.

9. The travel graph shows an athlete running in a sprint race.

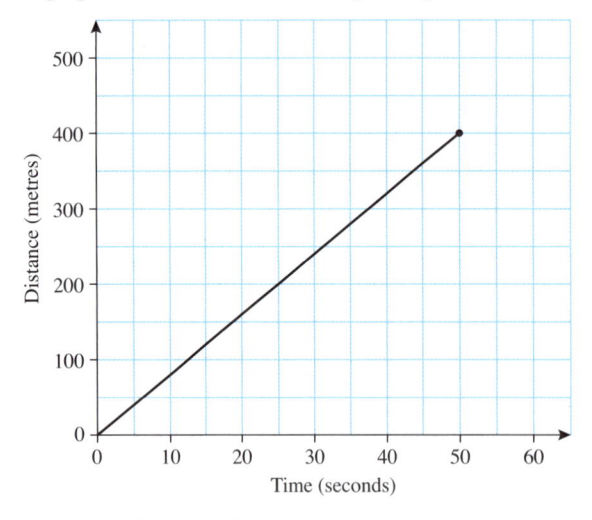

   a) Write down the distance of the race.
   b) Write down the time taken to complete the race.
   c) Work out the athlete's speed, in m/s.

10. a) Suggest a sensible metric unit for measuring the length of a pencil.
    b) A poster is 60 centimetres long. Roughly how many inches is this?

11 The diagram shows a map of four ships, W, X, Y and Z.
Use your protractor to measure:
a) the bearing of W from X
b) the bearing of Y from Z.

12 a) A pack of butter weighs half a pound. Roughly how many grams is this?
b) A tape measure is 2 metres long. Roughly how many inches is this?

KEY POINTS

1. Make sure you are confident at using the metric units for distance, mass and volume. The basic units are divided into 1000 smaller parts (milli-), or combined to make a unit 1000 times bigger (kilo-).

2. Compound units, such as speed and density, arise from a combination of two basic units. If a distance in metres is divided by a time in seconds, then the resulting speed will be in metres per second (m/s).

    Speed = distance ÷ time
    Density = mass ÷ volume

3. You need to learn approximate conversion factors between metric and commonly-used imperial units. The most important ones are:

    2.5 centimetres = 1 inch
    30 centimetres = 1 foot
    8 kilometres = 5 miles
    1 kilogram = 2.2 pounds
    1 litre = 1.75 pints
    4.5 litres = 1 gallon

4. Bearings are measured from North, in a clockwise direction.
    North is 000°, East is 090°, South is 180°, West is 270°.

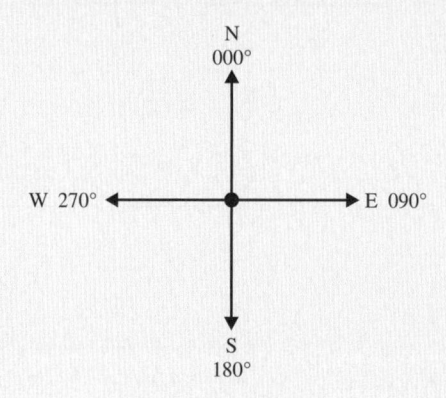

Internet Challenge 10

Definitions of units

Here are the definitions of some units. Use the internet to help solve the clues and identify them.
Each ☐ indicates a missing letter.

Some of the units are well known; others are more obscure.

#	Letters	Clue
1	☐☐☐☐	Originally the length of three barleycorns, this imperial unit is now defined to be 2.54 cm.
2	☐☐☐☐	Once defined as the distance from the King's nose to his outstretched hand, this unit is 36 inches or three feet.
3	☐☐☐☐☐	This unit of weight is abbreviated to the letters 'lb' from the Latin *libra*, meaning 'scales'. It is now defined to be exactly 0.45359237 kg.
4	☐☐☐☐	Still used to measure the heights of horses, this unit is equivalent to four inches.
5	☐☐☐☐	Unit of area – 'as much land as a pair of oxen could plough in one day' equivalent to 4840 square yards or about 0.4 hectare.
6	☐☐☐	An old measure of length, equal to sixteen and a half feet. Also called a pole or perch.
7	☐☐☐☐☐	Metric unit of capacity, equivalent to one thousand cubic centimetres.
8	☐☐☐☐☐☐	Unit of time, once expressed as a fraction of the Earth's rotation period, now defined using properties of the caesium atom.
9	☐☐☐☐☐☐	The *SI* unit of force, named after an English mathematician who lived from 1642 to 1727.
10	☐☐☐☐☐☐	Scale of temperature measurement, in which 0 corresponds to *absolute zero*.
11	☐☐☐☐☐☐☐☐	A non-*SI* metric unit of length, historically used in optics. It has the symbol Å, and is equal to 0.1 nanometre.
12	☐☐☐☐☐☐	Unit of electric current, named after a French scientist who was one of the main discoverers of electromagnetism.

CHAPTER 11

Using a calculator efficiently

In this chapter you will **revise earlier work on**:
- finding powers, roots and reciprocals efficiently.

You will **learn how to**:
- use brackets and the fraction key.

You will also **be challenged to**:
- solve a computing/calculating crossword.

Starter: Big numbers

What is the largest number you can make using the numbers 1, 2, 3, 4 only once, and without using any other mathematical symbols?

At first, you might think the answer is 4321.

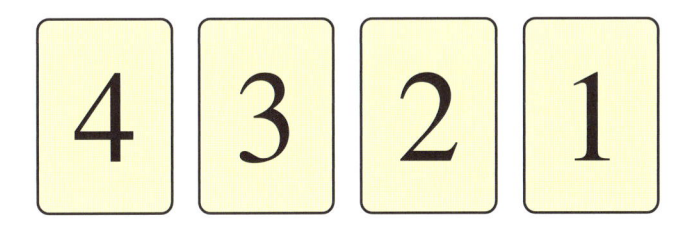

| 4 | 3 | 2 | 1 |

However, there are much bigger numbers that can be made!
For example, 134^2 is much larger than 4321.

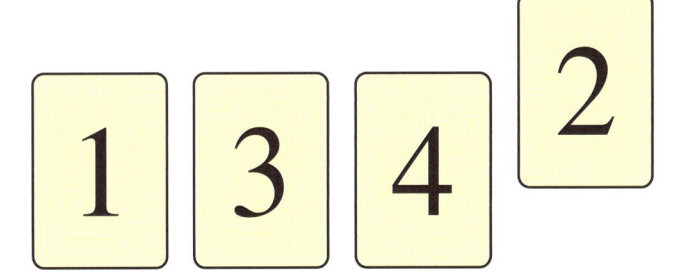

| 1 | 3 | 4 | ^{2} |

Try some other ideas based on powers.

In the GCSE 'calculator allowed' examination paper, you will need to demonstrate your ability to use a wide variety of calculator functions efficiently. This chapter will help you to practise some of these functions, but will not give exact instructions about which keys to press, since this can vary between different models and manufacturers. For the same reason, you should avoid borrowing or buying a calculator the day before the examination! You must take time to master the particular keys, functions and display modes of your own calculator, so that you can use it confidently on exam day.

11.1 Powers, roots and reciprocals

Your calculator should have a 'square' key, x^2, and also a more general power key, typically labelled as x^y or y^x. Make sure that you know where these keys are on your calculator. Work carefully through all the examples to make sure that you can reach the correct answer using your own calculator.

EXAMPLE

Using your calculator, work out the values of:
a) 12.3^2
b) 2^5
c) 3^7

SOLUTION

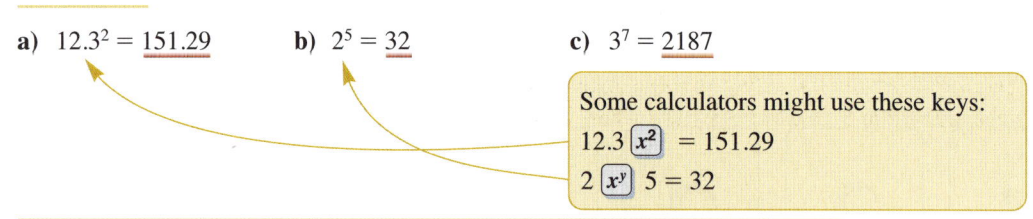

a) $12.3^2 = \underline{151.29}$
b) $2^5 = \underline{32}$
c) $3^7 = \underline{2187}$

Some calculators might use these keys:
12.3 x^2 = 151.29
2 x^y 5 = 32

If the answer to a calculation is very large (or very small) the display will automatically switch over to standard form. For example, older calculators may write 1.23 E +67 to represent the number 1.23×10^{67}. Newer calculators can display standard form in a more familiar way.

EXAMPLE

Work out the value of 2451^4. Give your answer in standard form, correct to 3 significant figures.

SOLUTION

$2451^4 = 3.608886677 \times 10^{13}$
$= \underline{3.61 \times 10^{13}}$ (3 s.f.)

Your calculator should also have a square root key, $\sqrt{}$, and it may have a cube root key, $\sqrt[3]{}$. In addition, it should have a more general root key, perhaps labelled as $\sqrt[n]{}$ or $x^{1/n}$ – they both mean the same thing. Once again, check these examples with your own particular calculator.

EXAMPLE

Giving your answers correct to 3 significant figures, work out the values of:
a) $\sqrt{42}$
b) $\sqrt[4]{21}$
c) $20^{\frac{1}{5}}$

SOLUTION

a) $\sqrt{42} = \underline{6.48}$ (3 s.f.)
b) $\sqrt[4]{21} = \underline{2.14}$ (3 s.f.)
c) $20^{\frac{1}{5}} = \underline{1.82}$ (3 s.f.)

You will recall from earlier work that the reciprocal of 2 is $\frac{1}{2}$, the reciprocal of 5 is $\frac{1}{5}$ and so on. Reciprocals are calculated by using the reciprocal key, which is usually labelled as $\boxed{x^{-1}}$ or $\boxed{1/x}$.

EXAMPLE

Find, to 3 significant figures, the values of:
a) $\frac{1}{7}$
b) the reciprocal of 11
c) 2.4^{-1}

SOLUTION

a) $\frac{1}{7} = \underline{0.143}$ (3 s.f.)
b) $\frac{1}{11} = \underline{0.0909}$ (3 s.f.)
c) $2.4^{-1} = \underline{0.417}$ (3 s.f.)

EXERCISE 11.1

Use your calculator to work out the values of these quantities.
Give your answers correct to 3 significant figures where appropriate.

1 144^2
2 15^3
3 667^5
4 95^7
5 $\sqrt{32}$
6 $\sqrt[3]{36}$
7 $\sqrt[4]{66}$
8 $\sqrt{80}$
9 34^{-1}
10 2.5^{-1}
11 0.2^{-1}
12 $\frac{1}{9}$
13 $\sqrt[3]{45}$
14 $12^{\frac{1}{3}}$
15 $144^{\frac{3}{4}}$
16 $14^{-\frac{1}{2}}$

17 Find the square of the square of 75.

18 Find the square root of the square root of 48.

19 Find the cube root of the square of 64.

20 Find the reciprocal of the reciprocal of 9.

11.2 Using brackets

For the GCSE examination, a calculator should have bracket keys. Bracket keys allow you to type in the value of a bracketed expression directly, exactly as it is written. Practise the next example on your calculator to make sure you know how the bracket keys work on your calculator.

As a check, you should also work out the values of some intermediate steps in the calculation and write them down in the exam. This allows the examiner to award marks for the method you have used if your final answer is not correct.

EXAMPLE

Work out the value of $2.4 \times (3.8 - 1.1 \times 1.2)^2$, correct to 3 significant figures.

SOLUTION

$$\begin{aligned}
2.4 \times (3.8 - 1.1 \times 1.2)^2 &= 2.4 \times 2.48^2 \\
&= 2.4 \times 6.1504 \\
&= 14.760\ 96 \\
&= \underline{14.8}\ (3\ \text{s.f.})
\end{aligned}$$

Sometimes the brackets are implied rather than written down, for example in a square root problem, or when dividing one expression by another. It is good practice to write the implied brackets into the expression before working out its value. Remember to show some of the intermediate steps to secure marks for the method you have used.

EXAMPLE

Use your calculator to find the values of:

a) $\sqrt{2.2 + 3.5 \times 4.2}$ b) $\dfrac{3.6 + 2.2^3}{4.8 - 1.2^2}$

Give each answer correct to 3 significant figures.

SOLUTION

a) $\begin{aligned}\sqrt{2.2 + 3.5 \times 4.2} &= \sqrt{(2.2 + 3.5 \times 4.2)} \\
&= \sqrt{16.9} \\
&= 4.110\ 960\ 958 \\
&= \underline{4.11}\ (3\ \text{s.f.})\end{aligned}$

b) $\begin{aligned}\dfrac{3.6 + 2.2^3}{4.8 - 1.2^2} &= \dfrac{(3.6 + 2.2^3)}{(4.8 - 1.2^2)} \\
&= \dfrac{14.248}{3.36} \\
&= 4.240\ 476\ 19 \\
&= \underline{4.24}\ (3\ \text{s.f.})\end{aligned}$

> It is a good idea to process the top and bottom of the fraction separately, and write down the results, so the examiner can award method marks.

Questions may also involve working with standard form on your calculator. You should be able to enter standard form numbers directly into your calculator display. The key for this is labelled [EXP] on some models, and [×10ˣ] on others.

EXAMPLE

Use your calculator to work out the value of $\dfrac{3.5 \times 10^4 + 2.8 \times 10^5}{6.6 \times 10^{-7}}$

Give your answer in standard form correct to 3 significant figures.

SOLUTION

There are implied brackets that are shown in red here:

$$\dfrac{(3.5 \times 10^4 + 2.8 \times 10^5)}{(6.6 \times 10^{-7})}$$

Keying this expression into a calculator gives the result:

$$\dfrac{(3.5 \times 10^4 + 2.8 \times 10^5)}{(6.6 \times 10^{-7})} = \dfrac{315000}{0.00000066}$$

$$= 4.77272727273 \times 10^{11}$$
$$= \underline{4.77 \times 10^{11}} \text{ (3 s.f.)}$$

EXERCISE 11.2

Use your calculator to work out the values of the following expressions. Write down all the figures on your calculator display, then round the answer to 3 significant figures, where appropriate.

1 $(16.2 - 2.8 \times 2.05) \times 2.3$

2 $(2.8 \times 3.5 - 4.9)^2$

3 $\sqrt{22.3 + 2.4 \times 1.5}$

4 $\dfrac{5.4 + 4.5}{5.4 - 4.5}$

5 $\dfrac{2.8 - 1.1^2}{3.4 \times 1.6}$

6 $\sqrt{5.4 \times 4.5}$

7 $\dfrac{6.5 - 2.3 \times 1.4}{1.4}$

8 $\dfrac{2.4 + 3 \times 2.2}{10 - 1.5^2}$

9 $2.6 \times (8.45 - 1.3^2)$

10 $(6.5 - 2.3) \times 1.4$

11 $\sqrt{2.5^2 + 3.5^2}$

12 $\dfrac{2^2 + 5^2}{3^2 + 4^2}$

13 $\dfrac{4.2 + 3.5^2}{3.5^2 - 4.6}$

14 $\sqrt{10.8^2 - 9.1^2}$

15 $\dfrac{2.4 \times 1.4 + 1.8 \times 2.3}{4.5}$

16 $\dfrac{250}{12.1 + 5.1}$

17 Use your calculator to work out the value of $\dfrac{2.4 \times 10^{17} + 3.1 \times 10^{18}}{7.2 \times 10^5}$

Give your answer in standard form correct to 2 significant figures.

18 Use your calculator to work out the value of $(4.55 \times 10^4)^3$

Give your answer in standard form correct to 3 significant figures.

19 Use your calculator to work out the value of $\sqrt{7.2 \times 10^5 + 3.3 \times 10^6}$

Give your answer in standard form correct to 2 significant figures.

20 Use your calculator to work out the value of $\dfrac{8.23 \times 10^5}{4.85 \times 10^{-6} + 2.05 \times 10^{-5}}$

Give your answer in standard form correct to 3 significant figures.

11.3 Using the fraction key

Your calculator should be equipped with a fraction key, probably labelled $\boxed{a^b/c}$. You should practise entering simple fractions like $\tfrac{2}{3}$ and mixed fractions like $4\tfrac{2}{3}$ using this key. Many calculators will allow you to enter a fraction, and then, by pressing the fraction key again, will show you the decimal equivalent. Most calculators will also automatically convert mixed fractions into top-heavy (improper) fractions, and back again. Try your calculator to see how to do this.

You can also use the fraction key to cancel a fraction into its simplest form. For example, $\tfrac{144}{180}$ would be entered as 144 $\boxed{a^b/c}$ 180 $\boxed{=}$ to obtain $\tfrac{4}{5}$.

EXAMPLE

Work out $1\tfrac{3}{4} \times 2\tfrac{5}{6}$, giving your answer as **a)** a mixed fraction and **b)** a top-heavy (improper) fraction.

SOLUTION

a) Using the fraction key, $1\tfrac{3}{4} \times 2\tfrac{5}{6} = 4\tfrac{23}{24}$

b) Using the fraction key, $4\tfrac{23}{24} = \tfrac{119}{24}$

> On some calculators, you press $\boxed{\text{SHIFT}}$ and $\boxed{a^b/c}$ to change a mixed fraction to a top-heavy fraction.

EXAMPLE

Work out 2.4×2.8, giving your answer as a mixed fraction.

SOLUTION

Using a 'standard' calculator, key $2.4 \times 2.8 = 6.72$
Then press the fraction key, to convert this to $6\tfrac{18}{25}$

> Note: Some calculators, such as Casio's *Natural Display* models, will compute the answer as a fraction automatically.

EXERCISE 11.3

Use your calculator's fraction key to work out the answers to the following calculations.
Give your answers as ordinary fractions or mixed fractions as appropriate.

1 $\tfrac{2}{7} + \tfrac{4}{11}$ **2** $\tfrac{2}{3} \times \tfrac{5}{13}$ **3** $\tfrac{2}{3} - \tfrac{5}{13}$ **4** $\tfrac{2}{5} \div \tfrac{14}{15}$ **5** $3\tfrac{2}{7} + 7\tfrac{9}{10}$

6 $15\tfrac{1}{4} - 11\tfrac{3}{5}$ **7** $2\tfrac{4}{5} \times 1\tfrac{1}{7}$ **8** $1\tfrac{3}{8} \div 2\tfrac{1}{4}$ **9** $(1\tfrac{1}{2})^2$ **10** $\sqrt{6\tfrac{1}{4}}$

Use your calculator to find the answers to these calculations as decimals.
Then convert the answers into exact fractions, using your fraction key.

11 2.5×3.5 **12** 13.2×0.86 **13** $56.64 \div 6.4$ **14** $\sqrt{1.8225}$ **15** $9.7 - 1.2^2$

16 $4.5^2 + 4.2$ **17** $4.8^2 - 3.6^2$ **18** $2.7 \times (4.4 + 3.2)$ **19** $\sqrt[3]{0.274625}$ **20** $71.34 \div 12.3$

REVIEW EXERCISE 11

1 Use your calculator to work out the value of:
$$\frac{\sqrt{12.3^2 + 7.9}}{1.8 \times 0.17}$$
Give your answer correct to 1 decimal place. [Edexcel]

2 a) Use your calculator to find the value of:
$$\sqrt{(47.3^2 - 9.1^2)}$$
Write down all of the figures on your calculator display.
b) Write your answer to part **a)** correct to 2 significant figures. [Edexcel]

3 Work out:
$$\frac{4.07 \times 10^3 \times 2.17 \times 10^5}{5.1 \times 10^{-4}}$$
Give your answer in standard form, correct to 2 significant figures. [Edexcel]

4 a) Use your calculator to work out the value of:
$$\frac{\sqrt{(1.3^2 + 4.2)}}{5.1 - 2.02}$$
Write down all the figures on your calculator display.
b) Give your answer to part **a)** to an appropriate degree of accuracy. [Edexcel]

5 a) Use your calculator to work out:
$$(2.3 + 1.8)^2 \times 1.07$$
Write down all the figures on your calculator display.
b) Copy out the expression and then insert brackets so that its value is 45.024

$$1.6 \ + \ 3.8 \ \times \ 2.4 \ \times \ 4.2$$ [Edexcel]

6 Work out the value of:
$$\sqrt{\frac{8.35 \times 978}{1025 + 222}}$$
Give your answer correct to 3 significant figures. [Edexcel]

7 a) Use your calculator to work out the value of:
$$\frac{32.6 \times 12.4}{21.4 - 13.9}$$
Write down all the figures on your calculator display.
b) Write your answer to part **a)** to an appropriate degree of accuracy. [Edexcel]

KEY POINTS

1. For the GCSE examination calculator paper you will need a good scientific calculator, which should include the following functions:

    Ordinary arithmetic keys ($+$, $-$, $\times$, $\div$)
    Square, square root, general power keys
    Reciprocal key
    Trig functions (sin, cos, tan)
    π key
    Fraction key
    Standard form key and display (Exp or $\times 10^x$)

2. Ideally your calculator should have a dual line display, so you can read what you have typed in as well as seeing the final answer. A replay key will allow you to correct any typing errors. Make sure that you have practised using all of these functions before exam day.

Internet Challenge 11

Computing crossword

Your teacher will give you a speed-up sheet to complete this challenge. Solve the clues about computers and calculations, and enter the answers into the grid. The shaded squares will reveal something that your calculator should have if it is suitable for the GCSE exam. You will already know some of the answers, but you may use the internet to help find the others.

1 This British mathematician died in 1954, and is considered the father of modern computer science.

2 6, 28 and 496 are examples of this type of number.

3 These indicate the part of a calculation that should be worked out first.

4 This quantity tells you how many times one number divides into another.

5 This graphics file format is often used as a way of compressing images for website display.

6 This computer chooses winning Premium Bond numbers.

7 Very large number, 10^{100}

8 A computing language devised in 1963 by Kemeny and Kurtz.

9, 12 _____ _____ form is a convenient way of writing very large (or small) numbers.

10 After oxygen, this is the most abundant element in the Earth's crust.

11 Person who breaks into computer security systems.

12 See **9**.

13 Liquid _____ Display, or LCD, is used on most modern calculators.

UNIT 4

CHAPTER 12

Fractions, ratios and percentages

In this chapter you will **revise earlier work on**:
- equivalent fractions.

You will **learn how to**:
- add and subtract using fractions
- multiply and divide using fractions
- simplify and use ratios
- work with percentage increase and decrease
- solve reverse percentage problems
- perform calculations using simple and compound interest.

You will also be **challenged to**:
- investigate inflation.

Starter: Equivalent fractions

Arrange these fractions into equivalent pairs. One pair has been done for you.

$\frac{2}{3}$ $\frac{1}{2}$ $\frac{3}{10}$ $\frac{5}{8}$ $\frac{4}{5}$

$\frac{12}{40}$ $\frac{12}{15}$ $\frac{36}{54}$ $\frac{9}{16}$ $\frac{36}{44}$

$\frac{18}{48}$ $\frac{3}{4}$ $\frac{15}{20}$ $\frac{18}{32}$ $\frac{15}{30}$

$\frac{5}{6}$ $\frac{3}{8}$ $\frac{9}{11}$ $\frac{20}{32}$ $\frac{25}{30}$

12.1 Adding and subtracting with fractions

Equivalent fractions are used when adding (or subtracting) fractions with different denominators. The fractions must be rewritten to have the same denominator before starting the addition.

EXAMPLE

Work out $\dfrac{2}{7} + \dfrac{1}{4}$.

SOLUTION

7 and 4 both divide into 28, so:

$$\dfrac{2}{7} + \dfrac{1}{4} = \dfrac{2 \times 4}{7 \times 4} + \dfrac{1 \times 7}{4 \times 7}$$

$$= \dfrac{8}{28} + \dfrac{7}{28}$$

$$= \dfrac{8 + 7}{28}$$

$$= \dfrac{15}{28}$$

> Add 8 and 7 to give 15. *Do not* try to add 28 and 28!

The same principle is used for subtraction.

EXAMPLE

Work out $\dfrac{7}{10} - \dfrac{1}{4}$.

SOLUTION

10 and 4 both divide into 20, so:

$$\dfrac{7}{10} - \dfrac{1}{4} = \dfrac{7 \times 2}{10 \times 2} - \dfrac{1 \times 5}{4 \times 5}$$

$$= \dfrac{14}{20} - \dfrac{5}{20}$$

$$= \dfrac{14 - 5}{20}$$

$$= \dfrac{9}{20}$$

Some fraction problems may require the use of mixed numbers, made up of part whole number and part fraction. For addition and subtraction you can often process the whole number parts separately from the fraction parts, and then combine everything at the end.

EXAMPLE

Work out $1\frac{3}{5} + 2\frac{3}{4}$.

SOLUTION

Add the whole numbers first: $1 + 2 = 3$
Now add the fractions:
$$\frac{3}{5} + \frac{3}{4} = \frac{12}{20} + \frac{15}{20}$$
$$= \frac{27}{20}$$
$$= 1\frac{7}{20}$$

$\frac{27}{20} = \frac{20}{20} + \frac{7}{20}$ to give $1\frac{7}{20}$

So the total is $3 + 1\frac{7}{20} = \underline{4\frac{7}{20}}$

EXAMPLE

Work out $7\frac{3}{10} - 3\frac{4}{5}$.

SOLUTION

$$7\frac{3}{10} - 3\frac{4}{5} = 4 + \frac{3}{10} - \frac{4}{5}$$
$$= 3 + 1\frac{3}{10} - \frac{4}{5}$$
$$= 3 + \frac{13}{10} - \frac{4}{5}$$
$$= 3 + \frac{13}{10} - \frac{8}{10}$$
$$= 3 + \frac{13 - 8}{10}$$
$$= 3 + \frac{5}{10}$$
$$= \underline{3\frac{1}{2}}$$

Here $\frac{3}{10}$ is not large enough to allow $\frac{4}{5}$ to be subtracted…

…so you exchange 1 unit from the whole number part to make $\frac{13}{10}$ as shown.

Always check for cancelling opportunities at the end. Here $\frac{5}{10}$ cancels down to $\frac{1}{2}$.

Your GCSE examination will test your ability to manipulate fractions with and without a calculator, so it is important to learn the methods thoroughly. When a calculator is permitted you should use the fraction key. Modern calculators allow you to type in the fractions exactly as you would write them – a highly useful feature to look for when you are buying a new calculator for GCSE work.

The following exercise includes a few calculator questions at the end, to help make sure that you are confident with using the calculator keys on your own calculator. Be aware that in different models the fraction key functions in slightly different ways.

EXERCISE 12.1

Write these fractions in their simplest terms.

1. $\frac{12}{16}$
2. $\frac{14}{18}$
3. $\frac{10}{12}$
4. $\frac{24}{30}$
5. $\frac{24}{32}$

Find the value represented by the symbol * in each of these statements.

6. $\frac{1}{2} = \frac{*}{16}$
7. $\frac{2}{3} = \frac{10}{*}$
8. $\frac{14}{35} = \frac{2}{*}$
9. $\frac{5}{6} = \frac{*}{42}$
10. $\frac{3}{5} = \frac{*}{20}$

Work out the answers to these without using a calculator.

11. $\frac{3}{11} + \frac{4}{11}$
12. $\frac{11}{12} - \frac{5}{12}$
13. $\frac{3}{10} + \frac{1}{5}$
14. $\frac{1}{12} + \frac{1}{2}$
15. $\frac{9}{10} - \frac{1}{5}$
16. $\frac{4}{9} + \frac{1}{3}$
17. $\frac{5}{16} + \frac{1}{4}$
18. $\frac{1}{3} + \frac{1}{2}$
19. $\frac{3}{8} + \frac{1}{6}$
20. $\frac{5}{8} - \frac{1}{4}$
21. $\frac{3}{4} - \frac{1}{10}$
22. $\frac{8}{9} - \frac{2}{3}$
23. $\frac{4}{7} - \frac{1}{4}$
24. $3\frac{2}{3} + 2\frac{1}{2}$
25. $5\frac{7}{9} - 2\frac{1}{3}$

Use pencil and paper to work out the answer to each of these. Then use your calculator fraction key to check your answers.

26. $\frac{7}{12} + \frac{3}{16}$
27. $\frac{11}{36} + \frac{13}{42}$
28. $4\frac{19}{20} + \frac{3}{8}$
29. $10\frac{5}{9} + \frac{3}{8}$
30. $5\frac{1}{8} - 2\frac{6}{7}$
31. $5\frac{3}{4} - 2\frac{1}{8}$
32. $8\frac{1}{2} - 5\frac{9}{10}$
33. $6\frac{1}{4} - 3\frac{1}{2}$
34. $4\frac{2}{3} + 3\frac{5}{6}$
35. $8\frac{1}{4} - 5\frac{1}{10}$

12.2 Multiplying and dividing with fractions

It is often easier to multiply two fractions than to add them! There is no need to worry about establishing the same denominator before you start. Simply multiply the two top numbers (numerators), and multiply the two bottom ones (denominators).

EXAMPLE

Work out $\frac{3}{5} \times \frac{2}{7}$

SOLUTION

$$\frac{3}{5} \times \frac{2}{7} = \frac{3 \times 2}{5 \times 7}$$
$$= \frac{6}{35}$$

In many cases there will be an opportunity for cancelling. The cancelling may be done either before or after the multiplication – but it is much more efficient to do this beforehand, since the numbers you work with are then much smaller. The next example shows how this is done.

EXAMPLE

Work out $\dfrac{4}{9} \times \dfrac{15}{22}$

SOLUTION

$$\dfrac{4}{9} \times \dfrac{15}{22} = \dfrac{\cancel{4}^{\,2}}{9} \times \dfrac{15}{\cancel{22}^{\,11}}$$

$$= \dfrac{\cancel{4}^{\,2}}{\cancel{9}^{\,3}} \times \dfrac{\cancel{15}^{\,5}}{\cancel{22}^{\,11}}$$

$$= \dfrac{2}{3} \times \dfrac{5}{11} = \dfrac{2 \times 5}{3 \times 11}$$

$$= \dfrac{10}{33}$$

> 4 on the top cancels with 22 on the bottom.
> They do not have to be *directly* above/below each other.
> Similarly for 15 on the top and 9 on the bottom.

Division works in a very similar way, with just one extra stage: to divide one fraction by another, turn the second fraction upside down and then multiply them.

EXAMPLE

Work out $\dfrac{5}{8} \div \dfrac{10}{13}$

SOLUTION

$$\dfrac{5}{8} \div \dfrac{10}{13} = \dfrac{5}{8} \times \dfrac{13}{10}$$

$$= \dfrac{\cancel{5}^{\,1}}{8} \times \dfrac{13}{\cancel{10}^{\,2}}$$

$$= \dfrac{13}{16}$$

> Cancelling may take place only once the division has been converted into a multiplication.

> Do not try to cancel the 8 with the 2 – they are both on the bottom (denominator) of the fraction.

To multiply or divide by a whole number, just use the result that the integer n may be written as the fraction $\dfrac{n}{1}$.

EXAMPLE

Work out $\dfrac{5}{24} \times 4$.

SOLUTION

$$\dfrac{5}{24} \times 4 = \dfrac{5}{24} \times \dfrac{4}{1}$$

$$= \dfrac{5}{\cancel{24}^{\,6}} \times \dfrac{\cancel{4}^{\,1}}{1} = \dfrac{5 \times 1}{6 \times 1} = \dfrac{5}{6}$$

> Write the 4 as $\dfrac{4}{1}$ and then proceed as before.

You need to be careful when multiplying or dividing mixed numbers. Unlike addition or subtraction, you cannot process the whole numbers separately from the fractional parts. Instead, you need to use 'top-heavy' or **improper** fractions.

EXAMPLE

Work out $1\frac{3}{4} \times 2\frac{2}{3}$.

SOLUTION

$1\frac{3}{4} = \frac{(1 \times 4) + 3}{4} = \frac{7}{4}$ ← First, convert the mixed fractions to top-heavy fractions.

and $2\frac{2}{3} = \frac{(2 \times 3) + 2}{3} = \frac{8}{3}$

Then:

$1\frac{3}{4} \times 2\frac{2}{3} = \frac{7}{4} \times \frac{8}{3}$

$= \frac{7}{\cancel{4}_1} \times \frac{\cancel{8}^2}{3}$

$= \frac{7 \times 2}{1 \times 3}$

$= \frac{14}{3}$ ← Here the answer is a top-heavy fraction, so you convert it back into mixed fraction form: $\frac{14}{3} = \frac{12 + 2}{3} = \frac{12}{3} + \frac{2}{3} = 4\frac{2}{3}$

$= 4\frac{2}{3}$

EXERCISE 12.2

Work out these multiplications and divisions. Show all your working clearly.

1 $\frac{1}{2} \times \frac{4}{5}$ 2 $\frac{5}{6} \times \frac{2}{3}$ 3 $\frac{3}{4} \times \frac{11}{15}$ 4 $\frac{10}{21} \times \frac{14}{15}$ 5 $\frac{3}{4} \times 20$

6 $\frac{1}{3} \times \frac{1}{5}$ 7 $\frac{2}{7} \times \frac{5}{8}$ 8 $180 \times \frac{2}{3}$ 9 $\frac{4}{9} \div \frac{5}{6}$ 10 $\frac{3}{8} \div \frac{3}{4}$

11 $\frac{5}{6} \div \frac{8}{9}$ 12 $\frac{2}{3} \div 12$ 13 $\frac{3}{8} \div \frac{6}{7}$ 14 $\frac{4}{9} \div 8$ 15 $\frac{1}{12} \div \frac{1}{9}$

16 $\frac{3}{5} \div \frac{3}{5}$ 17 $\frac{15}{16} \times \frac{1}{3}$ 18 $\frac{1}{10} \div \frac{1}{20}$ 19 $\frac{7}{12} \times \frac{27}{28}$ 20 $\frac{5}{7} \div \frac{10}{21}$

Work out the answers to these calculations. Remember to convert mixed numbers into top-heavy fractions before doing the multiplications or divisions.

21 $1\frac{1}{2} \times 2\frac{1}{3}$ 22 $1\frac{1}{3} \times \frac{2}{7}$ 23 $3\frac{1}{3} \times 1\frac{2}{5}$ 24 $3\frac{1}{4} \times \frac{2}{7}$ 25 $1\frac{1}{5} \times 2\frac{1}{2}$

26 $1\frac{1}{2} \div 1\frac{5}{12}$ 27 $\frac{4}{5} \div 1\frac{3}{5}$ 28 $4\frac{1}{2} \div \frac{7}{8}$ 29 $1\frac{1}{5} \div \frac{2}{5}$ 30 $2\frac{1}{4} \div 2\frac{7}{10}$

Use pencil and paper to work out the answer to each of these. Then use your calculator fraction key to check your answers.

31 $3\frac{3}{4} \times 5\frac{1}{2}$ 32 $5\frac{3}{7} \times 1\frac{2}{19}$ 33 $4\frac{3}{8} \times 7\frac{1}{5}$ 34 $18 \div 1\frac{1}{2}$ 35 $66\frac{2}{3} \times 1\frac{1}{2}$ 36 $3\frac{5}{14} \div 6\frac{5}{7}$

12.3 Working with ratios

Many problems on ratios are best thought of as scaling exercises. For example, suppose you have a recipe for 4 people, and you need to adapt the quantities to cater for 10 people. The method is to compute $10 \div 4 = 2.5$. This provides a multiplying **scale factor** that you can use to calculate the required amounts.

EXAMPLE

Here is a recipe for Scotch pancakes:

Plain flour	100 g
Baking power	1 teaspoon
Milk	150 ml
Eggs	3

Serves 4 people

Roz wishes to cook Scotch pancakes for 6 people. Calculate the amount of each ingredient she requires.

SOLUTION

The scale factor is: $6 \div 4 = 1.5$

> Take two matching known amounts: 6 people and 4 people. Divide one by the other to get the scale factor, or multiplier.

Plain flour	$100 \times 1.5 = 150$ g
Baking powder	$1 \times 1.5 = 1.5$ teaspoons
Milk	$150 \times 1.5 = 225$ ml
Eggs	$3 \times 1.5 = 4.5$

Baking powder and milk can be measured in fractional amounts, but the number of eggs used must be an integer, so the solution is:

Plain flour	150 g
Baking powder	1.5 teaspoons
Milk	225 ml
Eggs	5

EXAMPLE

Concrete mix is made by combining 1 part of cement with 2 parts sand and 4 parts gravel (by volume). A builder has 0.6 m³ of sand to use in a concrete mix.
a) Calculate the amount of the other ingredients he uses.
b) Calculate the total volume of the concrete mix.

SOLUTION

a) First, compute the multiplier: $0.6 \div 2 = 0.3$
So the parts of 1, 2, 4 can each be multiplied by 0.3, as follows:
Cement $\quad 1 \times 0.3 = \underline{0.3 \text{ m}^3}$
Sand $\quad\; 2 \times 0.3 = \underline{0.6 \text{ m}^3}$
Gravel $\;\; 4 \times 0.3 = \underline{1.2 \text{ m}^3}$

b) The total is $0.3 + 0.6 + 1.2 = \underline{2.1 \text{ m}^3}$

12 Fractions, ratios and percentages

In the example above, concrete was made by combining 1 part of cement with 2 parts sand and 4 parts gravel. We say that cement, sand and gravel are used **in the ratio** $1:2:4$. Like fractions, ratios can sometimes be cancelled down into simpler equivalent forms.

EXAMPLE

Express these ratios in their simplest terms.
 a) $14:21$
 b) $72:108$
 c) $15:25:45$

SOLUTION

a) $14:21 = 2:3$

14 and 21 are each divisible by 7.

b) $72:108 = 6:9$
   $= 2:3$

*Divide 72 and 108 by 12, to give 6 and 9.
6 and 9 can then be cancelled again, by dividing by 3.*

c) $15:25:45 = 3:5:9$

Triple ratios simplify in exactly the same way.

EXAMPLE

Three brothers are aged 6, 9 and 15 years old. They inherit £630 between them, to be shared in the ratio of their ages. Work out the share that each brother receives.

SOLUTION

The ratio $6:9:15$ may be simplified to $2:3:5$.

$2 + 3 + 5 = 10$ shares

£630 ÷ 10 = 63, so one share is worth £63.

The brothers receive $2 \times £63, 3 \times £63, 5 \times £63$ respectively, that is £126, £189 and £315.

*Check that these final amounts add up correctly:
$126 + 189 + 315 = 630$ ✓*

Although many ratios are expressed using whole numbers, there are some situations where it is desirable to cancel the ratio down until one of the parts is a whole number. Such ratio problems usually require the use of decimals.

EXAMPLE

a) Write the ratio $24:30$ in the ratio $1:n$.
b) Write the ratio $28:40$ in the ratio $n:1$.

SOLUTION

a) Dividing both numbers by 24,
   $24:30 = 1:1.25$
b) Dividing both numbers by 40,
   $28:40 = 0.7:1$

EXERCISE 12.3

Express each of these ratios in its simplest form.

1 4 : 10 **2** 18 : 27 **3** 77 : 121

4 21 : 91 **5** 16 : 20 : 28 **6** 30 : 40 : 60

7 27 : 36 : 63 **8** 144 : 360 **9** 25 : 35 : 40

10 7 : 28 : 35

11 Share £60 in the ratio 3 : 4 : 5.

12 Share 300 in the ratio 3 : 5 : 7.

13 Share £450 in the ratio 1 : 3 : 5.

14 Share $144 in the ratio 2 : 3 : 7.

15 Write 13 : 20 in the form n : 1

16 Write 30 : 42 in the form 1 : n

17 Christie has £216 to spend on a birthday party. She wants to spend this on food, drinks and entertainment in the ratio 4 : 5 : 9. Work out the actual amount she will spend on each of these three things.

18 A computer hard drive has 40 GB of storage space. Za partitions the drive into three sectors. The first, of size 5 GB, is used by the operating system, and the second, of size 10 GB, is used for music files. The third sector is free space. Find the ratio of the sizes of the three sectors. Give your answer in its simplest form.

19 A school's mathematics department spends money on books, photocopying and computer software in the ratio 3 : 5 : 6. The department spends £1200 on photocopying.
   a) Work out how much the department spends on books.
   b) Find the total expenditure on all three things.

20 Food for a wedding reception would cost £640 for 40 guests. Work out the cost of the food if there were to be:
   a) 60 guests   b) 100 guests.

21 Here are the ingredients to make dumplings to accompany a stew.

   100 grams of self-raising flour
   $\frac{1}{4}$ teaspoon salt
   50 grams of suet
   $\frac{1}{3}$ teaspoon dried mixed herbs
   Serves 4 people

   Ginny wants to make dumplings for 6 people. Work out the amounts of each ingredient she needs.

12.4 Percentage increase and decrease

There are two standard ways of increasing an amount by a given percentage. The first method is simply to compute the size of the increase, and add it on to the original amount. This is often a good method in non-calculator examinations.

EXAMPLE

Seamus buys £600 of shares in a new company. One week later, the value of the shares has increased by 15%. Without using a calculator, find the value of the shares one week after Seamus bought them.

SOLUTION

10% of £600 is £60

so 5% of £600 is £30.

10% is easy to compute. Then halve this to give 5%.

Adding, 15% of £600 is £60 + £30 = £90.

Therefore the value of the shares will be £600 + £90 = £690

Exam questions sometimes feature VAT. This is a government tax, and is currently levied at a rate of $17\frac{1}{2}\%$. There is a neat non-calculator way of calculating $17\frac{1}{2}\%$.

EXAMPLE

Jamie buys a new microwave oven for £80 plus VAT at $17\frac{1}{2}\%$. Without using a calculator, find the total cost including VAT.

SOLUTION

10% of £80 is £8

so 5% of £80 is £4

so $2\frac{1}{2}\%$ of £80 is £2

Total: £14

Half of 10% gives 5%. Then halve this again to give $2\frac{1}{2}\%$.

Thus Jamie's total cost is £80 + £14 = £94

If a calculator is available it is far better to acquire the habit of using the **multiplying factor** method. Not only is this quick and elegant, but it is also applicable to a wider variety of other kinds of percentage problems.

The multiplying factor method will underpin most of the ideas encountered in the remainder of this chapter.

EXAMPLE

Martin wins an internet auction. He pays £35 for the goods, but has to add fees of 3% to this. Work out the total amount that Martin has to pay.

SOLUTION

100% + 3% = 103%, so use a multiplying factor of 1.03.

> A multiplying factor *larger* than 1 will *increase* the amount to pay.

Total amount to pay = £35 × 1.03
= £36.05 (by calculator)

The multiplying factor method can be used for percentage decrease problems too.

EXAMPLE

Jeremy pays £35 000 for a new car. One year later it has lost 28% of its initial value. (This is called depreciation.) Find the value of the car one year after Jeremy bought it.

SOLUTION

100% − 28% = 72%, so use a multiplying factor of 0.72.

> Multiplying factors *smaller* than 1 will give a *decrease*, not an increase.

Value after one year = £35 000 × 0.72
= £25 200 (by calculator)

You can also use multiplying factors for multi-stage problems.

EXAMPLE

Pandora buys a new computer for £670. During the first year it loses 30% of its value. After that, its value at the end of each successive year is 25% less than it was at the start of that year.

Find the value of Pandora's computer:

a) after 2 years
b) after 5 years.

SOLUTION

a) 100% − 30% = 70%, so use a multiplying factor of 0.70 for the first year.
100% − 25% = 75%, so use a multiplying factor of 0.75 for each subsequent year.

Value after 2 years = £670 × 0.70 × 0.75
= £351.75

b) Value after 5 years = £670 × 0.70 × 0.75 × 0.75 × 0.75 × 0.75
= £670 × 0.70 × 0.75^4
= £148.39

You can also use multiplying factors to find percentage changes.

EXAMPLE

Anwar bought a house for £250 000. In the first year after he bought it, the value rose by 13%. During the second year it fell by 9%.
a) Calculate the value of Anwar's house after two years.
b) Find the percentage change in value over the two-year period.

SOLUTION

a) The multiplying factors are 1.13 and 0.91.
Value after two years = £250 000 × 1.13 × 0.91
= £257 075 (by calculator)

> You could also use
> % change = $\frac{\text{change}}{\text{original value}} \times 100$
> but the multiplying factor method is more elegant.

b) Divide this by the original price:
$\frac{257\,075}{250\,000} = 1.0283$

The combined multiplying factor is 1.0283.

> You have 102.83% of what you started with, which means there has been a 2.83% increase.

Therefore the house has increased in value by 2.83% overall.

You might have thought that a 13% increase followed by a 9% decrease would give an overall increase of 13 − 9 = 4%, but the above example shows that this is not the case. The reason is that the two percentages are calculated on two different values of the house. This is why the multiplying factor method is so powerful. In fact, you could have obtained the percentage change directly by multiplying 1.13 × 0.91 to give 1.0283.

EXERCISE 12.4

1 Increase 240 by 13%.

2 Decrease 420 by 9%.

3 Increase 1200 by 15%, then by a further 8% of its new value.

4 A kettle costs £29.99 plus VAT at $17\frac{1}{2}$%. Find the total cost of the kettle.

5 Last year the local dance club had 64 members. This year it has 73 members. Calculate the percentage increase in the membership.

6 Lance bought a new car. He paid £14 000. Each year the value of the car depreciated by 18% of its value at the beginning of that year. Work out the value of Lance's car:
a) after one year
b) after five years.

7 Sarah travels by train to visit her grandmother. The train journey used to take $2\frac{1}{2}$ hours, but the track has now been improved, reducing the journey time by 6%. How long does Sarah's journey to her grandmother take now?

8 My salary this year, before tax, is £38 000. Next year I am getting a 4% rise, but 1% of my new salary will be contributed to a savings scheme.
   a) Work out my new salary for next year.
   b) Work out how much I will receive next year after deducting the savings contribution.
   c) The answer to part **b)** could have been found by multiplying £38 000 by a single number. Find the value of that single number.

9 A magazine sold 17 000 copies in June, 23 000 copies in July and 21 000 copies in August.
   a) Calculate the percentage increase in sales between June and July.
   b) Calculate the percentage decrease in sales between July and August.

10 Alan imports a camera from the USA. He has to pay Import Duty and VAT to the UK Customs and Excise authorities. Import Duty at 4.9% is charged on the cost of the camera. VAT at 17.5% is applied to the cost of the camera (including the Import Duty), and to the freight charges. The courier company also charges a non-taxable handling fee.

The cost of the camera (before any taxes) is $1799 and the cost of freight (before any taxes) is $95. The company's handling charge is $15.
   a) Work out the total cost, in $, that Alan has to pay.
   b) Using an exchange rate of $1 = £0.58, work out the total cost in £.

12.5 Reverse percentage problems

Suppose a quantity increases by 10%, and you want to restore it to its original value. If you take off 10% of the new value, you would obtain the wrong answer! This is because you should be taking off 10% of the original value, not 10% of the new value.

An excellent way of solving this type of reverse percentage problem is to turn to multiplying factors. Identify the factor you would have *multiplied* by to make the increase from the original, and then just *divide* by the same factor to reverse the process.

EXAMPLE

The bill in a restaurant comes to £70.20 including a service charge of 8%. Work out the size of the bill before the service charge is included.

SOLUTION

An 8% increase corresponds to a multiplying factor of 1.08.

Original bill × 1.08 = 70.20

So original bill = 70.20 ÷ 1.08

$\qquad\qquad$ = 65

The size of the bill before the service charge was £65

The same method works for percentage decrease problems, too.

EXAMPLE

In a sale, a shop reduces all its prices by 15%. Sarah buys a jacket in the sale. She pays £68. Work out how much she saves by buying it in the sale.

SOLUTION

A 15% reduction corresponds to a multiplying factor of 0.85.

Original price × 0.85 = 68

So original price = 68 ÷ 0.85

= 80

Sarah paid £68, so she saves £80 − £68 = £12

EXERCISE 12.5

This exercise contains a mixture of forwards and reverse percentage problems – so you can train yourself to spot the difference! You should use multiplying factor methods as much as possible.

1 An electrical goods shop reduces all of its prices by 20% in a sale.
   a) Find the sale price of a television originally priced at £350.
   b) Find the original price of a radio that is £68 in the sale.

2 In a board game you can mortgage properties. To redeem them from mortgage you have to pay the mortgage value plus 10%.
   a) Work out the cost of redeeming a property that was mortgaged for £60.
   b) Ed redeems a set of properties, at a total cost of £715. What was the mortgage value of this set of properties?

3 A meal costs £89.30 inclusive of VAT at 17.5%. Work out the cost of the meal before VAT was applied.

4 A bookshop is having a sale. The prices of all books are reduced by 15%.
   a) Work out the sale price of a book that would normally cost £24.
   b) The shop assistant mistakenly reduces the prices by 25% instead. She charges a customer £13.50 for a book in the sale. Work out how much she should have charged if the sale reduction had been applied correctly.

5 I have upgraded my ageing computer, and it can now do tasks in only 70% of the time it used to take. A particular task now takes 630 milliseconds. How long did this take before the upgrade?

6 A year ago I bought a new car. It depreciates at 22% per year. My car is presently worth £7176.
   a) Work out the value of my car when I bought it.
   b) Work out how much my car will be worth three years from now.

7 Joan's diet has been successful, and she has managed to lose 15% of her body weight. She now weighs 136 pounds.
   a) Work out her weight, in pounds, before she began the diet.
   b) Rewrite your answer in stones and pounds. (1 stone = 14 pounds)

8 A galaxy was once thought to be 2.2 million light years away from Earth, but astronomers now believe its actual distance to be 30% greater than this. Calculate the distance at which it is now thought to be.

9 The average attendance at City's soccer ground has fallen by 12% from last year. This year's average is 13 552. What was the average attendance last year?

10 A graphic designer has drawn a rectangle on her computer screen. She resizes the rectangle by making it 20% smaller than it was in both length and width. After resizing, the rectangle measures 960 pixels by 620 pixels.
   a) Work out the dimensions of the rectangle before it was resized.
   b) By what percentage has the area of the rectangle been reduced when resized in this way?

12.6 Simple and compound interest

When money is placed in a savings bank it may earn interest at a given percentage rate per year (*per annum*, or p.a.). If the money is left in the bank for several years, **simple interest** may be calculated by working out the yearly interest, then multiplying this by the number of years.

Some people like to use the formula:

$$I = \frac{PRT}{100}$$

In this formula:
I = total amount of simple interest earned
P = principal (the amount invested)
R = the percentage rate of interest
T = the number of years.

EXAMPLE

£1200 is invested at 4.5% per annum. Calculate the simple interest earned over 5 years.

SOLUTION

Method 1
The interest earned in 1 year

$$= \frac{4.5}{100} \times 1200 = 54$$

Thus the interest in 5 years
$$= 54 \times 5 = \underline{£270}$$

Method 2
Let $P = 1200$, $R = 4.5$ and $T = 5$.
Then, using the simple interest formula:

$$I = \frac{PRT}{100} = \frac{1200 \times 4.5 \times 5}{100} = 270$$

So the interest in 5 years is £270

In reality, interest calculations are usually more complicated than this. The rate of interest might change over time, for example. Perhaps even more importantly, interest is generated on the previous interest as well as the original capital. So, if £100 were invested at 10% per annum, you would earn £10 in the first year. This is added to the principal amount, so in the second year you earn interest on £110, which would be £11. This type of interest is called **compound interest**.

Compound interest problems are best solved using multiplying factors.

EXAMPLE

£1200 is invested at 4.5% per annum. Calculate the compound interest earned over 5 years.

SOLUTION

The multiplying factor for a 4.5% increase is 1.045.

At the end of 5 years, the money invested will have grown to:

$$1200 \times 1.045 \times 1.045 \times 1.045 \times 1.045 \times 1.045 = 1200 \times 1.045^5$$
$$= 1495.42$$

So the compound interest earned is £1495.42 − £1200 = £295.42

EXAMPLE

£800 is invested at $r\%$ per annum. After 6 years it has grown to £955.24. Use a trial and improvement method to find the value of r.

SOLUTION

After 6 years the investment has a value of $800 \times \left(1 + \dfrac{r}{100}\right)^6$.

Try $r = 10$: $800 \times 1.10^6 = 1417.25$ too big

Try $r = 5$: $800 \times 1.05^6 = 1072.08$ too big

Try $r = 2$: $800 \times 1.02^6 = 900.23$ too small

Try $r = 3$: $800 \times 1.03^6 = 955.24$ correct

Hence $r = 3$

> Show full details of all the trials, not just the final one.

EXERCISE 12.6

1. Work out the simple interest on £1800 invested at 6% per annum for 5 years.

2. Work out the compound interest on £450 invested at 3% per annum for 4 years.

3. Work out the simple interest on £90 invested at 2.5% per annum for 6 years.

4. Work out the compound interest on £3000 invested at 5.5% per annum for 8 years.

5. Tina opens a savings account that pays simple interest of 4.6% per annum. She earns £39.10 over 5 years. How much did she invest to start with?

6. Bill invests some money at a compound interest rate of 3.5% per annum. After 6 years his investment is worth £921.94. How much did Bill invest?

7. On his 16th birthday Anu puts £160 in a savings account. The account pays simple interest at 3% per annum. How old will Anu be when his savings have increased to £232?

8   A ten-year savings bond pays 4% interest for the first year, then 5% per annum compound interest after that. Work out the total final value after ten years of an initial investment of £500.

9   Wayne is investing £200 in a long-term savings scheme. He can choose between two savings plans.

   Savings Plan A   **Simple** interest at 4% per annum.
   Savings Plan B   **Compound** interest at 3% per annum.

   a) Which plan gives the better return over 5 years?
   b) Which plan gives the better return over 25 years?

   Justify your answers with numerical calculations.

10 Michelle invests some money in a savings account. It pays compound interest at a rate of 4% per annum. Michelle says, 'My money will double in 25 years.' Michelle is wrong.

   a) Explain how you think Michelle arrived at a figure of 25 years.
   b) Work out the correct figure.

12.7 Using the [ANS] key

Your calculator should have an [ANS] key, probably next to the [=] key, or perhaps as a *second function* of the [=] key. The [ANS] key is used to retrieve the answer to the most recent calculation that the calculator has performed. This makes it a very handy shortcut for repetitive calculations, such as those found in compound interest problems.

EXAMPLE

Marco invests £100 in a savings scheme that pays 5% compound interest per year. Work out how many years Marco has to wait until his investment has grown to £200.

SOLUTION

The long way of doing this question is as follows:

   End of Year 1:   £100 × 1.05 = £105
   End of Year 2:   £105 × 1.05 = £110.25
   End of Year 3:   £110.25 × 1.05 = £115.7625

A multiplying factor of 1.05 is used to make a 5% increase.

…and so on until the total goes past £200.
This is clearly a very tedious method of finding the answer.
A better method, using the [ANS] key, works like this:

Begin by keying [1][0][0][=] (this forces a calculation of 100 into the answer memory).

Now key [ANS][×][1][.][0][5][=] and the display shows 105 (the amount Marco has in the savings scheme at the end of Year 1).

Press [=] again and the display changes to 110.25 (the amount in the savings scheme at the end of Year 2).

Press $\boxed{=}$ again, to obtain 115.7625 (the amount at the end of Year 3).

Repeat, keeping count of how many times you have pressed the $\boxed{=}$ key.

After 14 years, your calculator will display 197.9931599, which is too small an amount for your answer.

After 15 years, 207.8928179 is displayed.

Therefore, Marco has to wait 15 years for his investment to reach £200.

EXERCISE 12.7

1. Andy invests £200 at 6% compound interest.
   Work out how much his investment is worth:
   a) after 1 year
   b) after 2 years
   c) after 15 years.

2. Jenny buys a new car for £18 000.
   At the end of each year, the value of the car has fallen to 75% of its value at the beginning of that year.
   Work out how much Jenny's car is worth:
   a) after 1 year
   b) after 2 years
   c) after 10 years.

3. Adeleke invests £250 at 4% compound interest
   Work out how many years it takes until his investment has reached £400.

4. Tami pays £1200 for a new computer.
   At the end of each year, the computer's value has fallen to 60% of its value at the beginning of that year.
   Tami decides to replace her computer once its value has fallen below £200.
   Work out how many years it takes until Tami replaces her computer.

5. Keith decides to put £250 into a savings scheme.
   The scheme pays 4% compound interest for the first year.
   Then it pays 5% compound interest per annum (each year) after that.
   Work out how much Keith's savings are worth:
   a) after one year
   b) after two years
   c) after 25 years.

6. Here are some instructions for making a number sequence:

   - The first term is 3.
   - To make each new term, multiply the previous one by 3 and subtract 5.

   a) Work out the first three terms of the number sequence.
   b) Use your calculator's $\boxed{\text{ANS}}$ key to help find the value of the 20th term.

REVIEW EXERCISE 12

Solve these problems without using a calculator. Show your working clearly.

1. Write the ratio 18 : 27 in its lowest terms.

2. Write the ratio 12 : 21 in the form $1 : n$.

3. Simplify the ratio 16 : 20 : 30.

4. Write the ratio 14 : 40 in the form $n : 1$.

5. A computer costs £320 plus VAT at $17\frac{1}{2}\%$. Work out the cost of the computer including VAT.

6. Jack buys a box of 20 pens for £3.00. He sells the pens for 21p each. He sells all the pens. Work out his percentage profit. [Edexcel]

7. Brass is made up from copper and zinc. Every 100 grams of brass contains 20 grams of zinc.
   a) Work out the weight of zinc in 60 grams of brass.
   Brass contains 4 parts by weight of copper to 1 part by weight of zinc.
   b) Work out the weight of copper in 350 grams of brass. [Edexcel]

8. There are 800 students at Prestfield School. 45% of these students are girls.
   a) Work out 45% of 800.
   There are 176 students in Year 10.
   b) Write 176 out of 800 as a percentage. [Edexcel]

9. Ben bought a car for £12 000. Each year the car depreciated by 10%. Work out the value of the car 2 years after he bought it. [Edexcel]

10. a) Work out 60% of 5300 kg.
    b) Work out the simple interest on £2500 invested for 2 years at 6% per year. [Edexcel]

You may use a calculator for these remaining questions. Make your methods clear.

11. A photocopier makes copies that are 40% larger than the original.
    a) An original is 12 cm long. Find the length of the copy.
    b) A copy is 35 cm long. Find the length of the original.

12. Calculate the compound interest earned when $360 is invested at 6% per annum for 3 years.

13. This is a list of the ingredients for making a pear & almond crumble for 4 people.

    > Ingredients for 4 people.
    > 80 g plain flour
    > 60 g ground almonds
    > 90 g soft brown sugar
    > 60 g butter
    > 4 ripe pears

    Work out the amount of each ingredient needed to make a pear & almond crumble for **10** people. [Edexcel]

14 In a sale all the prices are reduced by 30%. The sale price of a jacket is £28. Work out the price of the jacket before the sale. [Edexcel]

15 The price of a new television is £423. This price includes Value Added Tax (VAT) at $17\frac{1}{2}\%$.
   a) Work out the cost of the television **before** VAT was added.

   By the end of each year, the value of a television has fallen by 12% of its value at the start of that year. The value of a television was £423 at the start of the first year.
   b) Work out the value of the television at the end of the third year. Give your answer to the nearest penny. [Edexcel]

16 The selling price of a computer is the **list price** plus VAT at $17\frac{1}{2}\%$. The **list price** of a computer is £786.
   a) Work out the selling price of the computer.

   The selling price of another computer is £1292.50.
   b) Work out the **list price** of this computer. [Edexcel]

17 Wayne bought an engagement ring for Tracy. The total cost of the ring was £420 **plus** VAT at $17\frac{1}{2}\%$.
   a) Work out the total cost of the ring.

   Wayne invited 96 people to the engagement party. Only 60 of the 96 people invited came to the party.
   b) Express 60 as a percentage of 96. [Edexcel]

18 Each year the value of a cooker falls by 8% of its value at the beginning of that year. Sally bought a new cooker on 1st January 2001. By 1st January 2002 its value had fallen 8% to £598.
   a) Work out the value of the new cooker on 1st January 2001.
   b) Work out the value of the cooker by 1st January 2005. Give your answer to the nearest penny. [Edexcel]

19 £5000 is invested for 3 years at 4% per annum **compound** interest. Work out the **total interest** earned over the three years.

20 In a sale, all the normal prices are reduced by 15%. The normal price of a jacket is £42. Syreeta buys the jacket in the sale.
   a) Work out the sale price of the jacket.

   In the same sale, Winston pays £15.64 for a shirt.
   b) Calculate the normal price of the shirt. [Edexcel]

21 The price of a telephone is £36.40 plus VAT. VAT is charged at a rate of 17.5%.
   a) Work out the amount of VAT charged.

   In a sale, normal prices are reduced by 12%. The normal price of a camera is £79.
   b) Work out the sale price of the camera. [Edexcel]

22 Wasim opened an account with £650 at the London Bank. After one year the bank paid him interest. He then had £676 in his account.
   a) Work out, as a percentage, London Bank's interest rate.

   Holly opened an account at the Anglia Bank. Anglia Bank's interest rate was 5%. After one year, the bank paid her interest. The total amount in her account was then £1029.
   b) Work out the amount with which she opened her account. [Edexcel]

23 A company bought a van that had a value of £12 000. Each year the value of the van depreciates by 25%.

a) Work out the value of the van at the end of three years.

The company bought a new truck. Each year the value of the truck depreciates by 20%. The value of the new truck can be multiplied by a single number to find its value at the end of four years.

b) Find this single number as a decimal. [Edexcel]

24 Harvey invests £4500 at a compound interest rate of 5% per annum. At the end of n complete years the investment has grown to £5469.78. Find the value of n. [Edexcel]

KEY POINTS

1. Simple ratios may be expressed using whole numbers, such as 4 : 6, or 1 : 2 : 4

2. Ratios may be cancelled down in a similar way to fractions, so 4 : 6 is equivalent to 2 : 3

3. Percentage increase or decrease may be calculated very efficiently using a multiplying factor. This may either be greater than 1 (increase) or less than 1 (decrease). For a 3% increase you would use 1.03; for a 3% decrease, 0.97

4. Reverse percentage problems, such as 'find the price before VAT was applied', are best solved using multiplying factors. To reverse the calculation, simply divide by the multiplying factor instead (1.175 in the case of VAT).

5. Simple interest may be calculated using mental methods in easy cases, or formal written methods. You can also use the formula:

   $$I = \frac{PRT}{100}$$

6. Compound interest requires a fresh calculation to be done for each year. These problems are best solved using multiplying factors.

Internet Challenge 12

Investigating inflation

Each year the price of things goes up, and so does the amount people earn. This is called inflation, and is usually measured using percentages, to give an annual rate of inflation.

Here are some questions about inflation. You will need internet access to help you research the answers.

1 What is the meaning of the Retail Price Index (RPI)?

2 How often is it calculated?

3 What is the value of the present UK yearly rate of inflation, based on the RPI?

4 What is the meaning of the Bank of England base rate?

5 How often is it calculated?

6 What is the present value of the Bank of England base rate?

There was a four-year period in Germany's history when the purchasing power of printed banknotes fell to a purchasing power only one trillionth of what it had been before the inflation set in – in other words, prices soared a trillion times.

7 In which years did this happen?

8 Write the number one trillion in figures. There is an older, imperial definition of a trillion, and a newer, metric one, which are not the same. Give both answers.

> 'In October of 1993 the government created a new currency unit. One new dinar was worth one million of the old dinars. In effect, the government simply removed six zeros from the paper money. This of course did not stop the inflation and between 1 October 1993 and 24 January 1995 prices increased by 5 quadrillion per cent. This number is a 5 with 15 zeros after it.'

9 To which country does this text refer?

10 What name do economists give to excessively high inflation like this?

CHAPTER 13

Algebraic equations

In this chapter you will **revise and extend earlier work on**:
- the language of algebra.

You will **learn how to**:
- solve simple equations
- solve harder linear equations
- solve linear equations involving brackets and fractions
- generate formulae from given information
- change the subject of a formula
- find approximate solutions by trial and improvement.

You will also be **challenged to**:
- investigate the mathematics of Carl Friedrich Gauss.

Starter: Triangular arithmagons

In a triangular arithmagon, the number along each side of the triangle is obtained by adding up the numbers in the adjacent corners. The first arithmagon has been filled in, to show you how this works. See if you can complete the other three arithmagons.

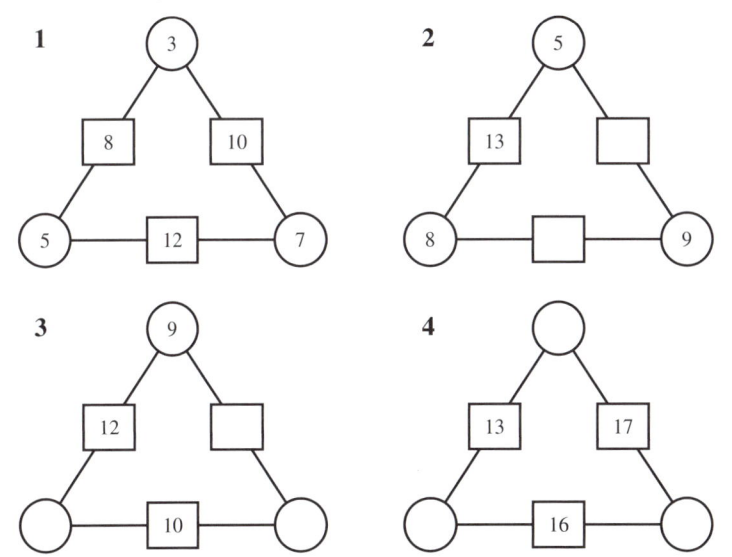

1
Corners: 3 (top), 5 (bottom-left), 7 (bottom-right)
Sides: 8, 10, 12

2
Top corner: 5; bottom-right corner: 9
Sides: 13 (left), 8 (bottom), □ (right)

3
Top corner: 9
Sides: 12 (left), □ (right), 10 (bottom)

4
Sides: 13 (left), 17 (right), 16 (bottom)

Now try devising some arithmagon puzzles of your own.

13.1 Expressions, equations and identities

In your work on algebra, you have met the words *expression*, *equation* and *formula*. They all have similar, but slightly different, meanings.

An **expression** is a piece of algebra usually containing one or more letters.

$\dfrac{x^2 + 7}{4x}$ is an expression.

An **equation** also contains algebraic symbols and numbers, but, in addition, contains an equals sign.

$\dfrac{x^2 + 7}{4x} = 2$ is an equation.

If an equation is designed to solve a problem then it is often called a **formula**. $V = IR$ is a formula used to calculate electrical voltage, V.

You can think of equations as statements that are true for some values of the quantities involved, and false for others. For example, the equation $\dfrac{x^2 + 7}{4x} = 2$ is true when $x = 1$, since $\dfrac{1^2 + 7}{4 \times 1} = \dfrac{8}{4} = 2$ but false when $x = 3$, since $\dfrac{3^2 + 7}{4 \times 3} = \dfrac{16}{12} = 1\tfrac{1}{3}$.

Some equations, however, are true for *all* values of x, and are called identical equations, or **identities**.

$3(x + 5) = 3x + 15$ is an identity.

Strictly speaking, identities should be written with a special symbol $3(x + 5) \equiv 3x + 15$, but in practice this is often overlooked.

EXERCISE 13.1

Look at the various algebraic statements labelled A to J:

A $(1 + x)^3$ B $A = \pi r^2$
C $x^2 + 10x - 3$ D $x(x + 4) = x^2 + 4x$
E $x(x + 4) = 12$ F $x + 5 = 17 - x$
G $(x + 3)(x + 4) = 20$ H $(x + 3)(x + 4) = x^2 + 7x + 12$
I $4x^2 = 9$ J $s = ut + \tfrac{1}{2}at^2$

1 Which ones are expressions?

2 Which ones are equations?

3 Which ones would you call formulae?

4 Pick out any identities, and rewrite them using the identity sign $\equiv$.

13.2 Simple equations

Some simple algebraic equations can be solved in just one step, or even by inspection. For example, if $x + 2 = 9$ you can spot, by inspection, that x must be 7. A more formal approach would be to subtract 2 from both sides, so that $x = 9 - 2 = 7$.

In this section you will be solving simple equations of this kind. Although you may well be able to spot some of the solutions by inspection, it is better to solve them formally, since this equips you with the skills needed for harder equations where the solutions cannot be spotted by inspection.

EXAMPLE

Solve these equations:
a) $3x = 12$ b) $x + 5 = 7$ c) $x - 5 = 1$ d) $\frac{1}{2}x = 12$ e) $\frac{x}{2} = \frac{4}{9}$

SOLUTION

a) $3x = 12$
$x = \frac{12}{3}$ ← Divide both sides by 3 ….
$x = 4$

b) $x + 5 = 7$
$x = 7 - 5$ ← Subtract 5 from both sides …
$x = 2$

c) $x - 5 = 1$
$x = 1 + 5$ ← Add 5 to both sides …
$x = 6$

d) $\frac{1}{2}x = 12$
$x = 12 \times 2$ ← $\frac{1}{2}x$ means 'x divided by 2'. To solve the equation, multiply both sides by 2.
$x = 24$

e) $\frac{x}{2} = \frac{4}{9}$
Cross-multiplying:
$9 \times x = 4 \times 2$ ← Cross-multiplying is a handy technique when two fractions are equal to each other.
$9x = 8$ The top of one fraction gets multiplied by the bottom of the other one, and vice versa.
$x = \frac{8}{9}$

If you need to use the square root process, remember to allow for both positive and negative options. For example, if $x^2 = 9$ then x could be 3 or -3.

EXAMPLE

Solve the equation $4y^2 = 9$.

SOLUTION

$4y^2 = 9$

Square rooting both sides,

$2y = 3$ or -3

$y = \frac{3}{2}$ or $-\frac{3}{2}$

EXERCISE 13.2

Solve these algebraic equations. Use a formal method, and show the steps of your working.

1. $5t = 20$
2. $y + 3 = 10$
3. $x - 2 = 7$
4. $\frac{1}{10}x = 3$
5. $\frac{x}{2} = 6$
6. $2y = 4$
7. $t - 3 = 1$
8. $x + 13 = 4$
9. $\frac{x}{5} = \frac{1}{2}$
10. $\frac{x}{2} = \frac{3}{5}$

Find the values of the letters in each of these equations.

11. $3t = 48$
12. $u + 7 = 4$
13. $7p = 4$
14. $3q = 8$
15. $14 = 20 - r$
16. $13 = 30 - u$
17. $98g = 7$
18. $3 - z = 3$
19. $16x^2 = 25$
20. $y^2 = 144$

13.3 Harder linear equations

Some equation problems contain many stages, not just one or two. You may have to reorganise the equation to collect all the x terms on one side and all the numbers on the other, for example. The like terms are then collected together and simplified, before performing the final step of the solution.

When reorganising the terms, you can move a term from one side of the equation to the other – but it must then change its sign. These examples show you how this works.

EXAMPLE

Solve the equation $5x + 3 = 3x + 17$.

SOLUTION

$5x + 3 = 3x + 17$

$5x - 3x + 3 = 17$ — First, subtract $3x$ from both sides. This causes the $3x$ to disappear from the right-hand side, and appear as $-3x$ on the left-hand side.

$2x + 3 = 17$

$2x = 17 - 3$ — Similarly, subtract 3 from both sides.

$2x = 14$

$x = \dfrac{14}{2}$ — Finally, divide both sides by 2.

$\underline{x = 7}$

Here is another example, this time with some minus signs. The principle is exactly the same.

EXAMPLE

Solve the equation $3x - 11 = 3 - x$.

SOLUTION

$3x - 11 = 3 - x$

$3x + x - 11 = 3$ — First, add x to both sides.

$4x - 11 = 3$

$4x = 3 + 11$ — Next, add 11 to both sides.

$4x = 14$

$x = \dfrac{14}{4}$ — Finally, divide both sides by 4.

$\underline{x = 3\tfrac{1}{2}}$

If the overall coefficient of x looks like being negative, it may be more convenient to collect the x terms on the right-hand side instead, as in this final example.

EXAMPLE

Solve the equation $17 + x = 12 + 5x$.

SOLUTION

$17 + x = 12 + 5x$

$17 = 12 + 5x - x$ — First, take x from both sides.

$17 = 12 + 4x$

$17 - 12 = 4x$ — Next, take 12 from both sides.

$5 = 4x$

$\underline{x = \dfrac{5}{4}}$ — Finally, divide both sides by 4.

EXERCISE 13.3

Solve these algebraic equations, showing the steps of your working clearly. All the answers should be integers, but some may be negative.

1. $4x + 5 = x + 14$
2. $6x + 1 = 8 - x$
3. $10t + 3 = 8t + 11$
4. $x + 3 = 7x + 15$
5. $12m + 5 + m = 44$
6. $15 - 2u = 30 - 5u$
7. $14 + 2x = 9x$
8. $10 + 5k = 3k + 6$
9. $x + 3 = 3 - x$
10. $4x = 55 - x$

Solve these algebraic equations, showing the steps of your working clearly. Answers should be given as top-heavy fractions or mixed numbers, rather than decimals.

11. $6t + 2 = 2t + 5$
12. $4u + 3 = 10 - u$
13. $8p + 13 = 10p + 4$
14. $5q + 7 = 12 - 3q$
15. $10r - 4 = 4r - 7$
16. $10u - 1 = 11u + 1$
17. $3x + 31 = x + 30$
18. $4y - 1 = y + 4$
19. $5x - 4 = 1 + 6x$
20. $10y - 3 = 4 + 7y$

13.4 Equations and brackets

You may encounter brackets in an equation. It is usually a good idea to expand the brackets, so that you can gather together like terms in order to solve the equation.

EXAMPLE

Solve the equation $3(x + 2) + 2(2x - 5) = 5(x - 1) + 9$.

SOLUTION

$$3(x + 2) + 2(2x - 5) = 5(x - 1) + 9$$
$$3x + 6 + 4x - 10 = 5x - 5 + 9$$
$$7x - 4 = 5x + 4$$
$$7x = 5x + 4 + 4$$
$$7x = 5x + 8$$
$$7x - 5x = 8$$
$$2x = 8$$
$$x = 4$$

Some word problems can be formulated using brackets, to obtain an equation that can then be solved.

EXAMPLE

I am thinking of a number. If I add 20 on to my number I get twice as much as if I only add 6. What number am I thinking of?

SOLUTION

Suppose the number I am thinking of is x.

Then $x + 20$ is twice as much as $x + 6$.

$x + 20 = 2(x + 6)$
$x + 20 = 2x + 12$
$ 20 = 2x + 12 - x$
$ 20 = x + 12$
$20 - 12 = x$
$8 = x$

So the number I am thinking of is 8.

EXERCISE 13.4

Multiply out the brackets, and hence solve these equations. Show each step of your working.

1 $5(x + 5) + 3 = 13$
2 $4(x - 1) + 3x = 45$
3 $3(y + 5) + y = 23$

4 $2(n - 4) + 3 = 7$
5 $3(2p + 7) - 38 = 4p + 3$
6 $x + 13 = 6(x - 2) + 5$

7 $5(2x - 1) - 2(3x + 4) = 3$
8 $4(r - 2) - 2(r - 3) = 6$
9 $2(3s + 14) + 11 = 3(s + 9)$

10 $3(2x + 3) = 2(x + 1) + 23$
11 $2d - 9 = 5d - 3(3d + 2)$
12 $5(x + 4) - 2(x - 1) = 43$

Write an equation, involving brackets, to formulate each of the problems below. Then expand your brackets and solve the equation, to obtain the answer to the problem.

13 I think of a number, add 12, and then multiply the new total by 2. I get the same answer as if I had just multiplied the original number by 4. What number did I think of?

14 At the moment Ravi is n years old. He is five years older than his brother. In four years' time, Ravi will be exactly twice as old as his brother is now. Find out how old Ravi is now.

15 Nat and Marina each think of the same number. Nat multiplies the number by 7, and then adds 5. Marina adds 7 to the number, and then multiplies by 5. They both end up with the same answer.
  a) Write this information as an equation.
  b) Solve your equation, to find the number they both thought of.

13.5 Equations with fractional coefficients

Some equations contain fractional coefficients. A good approach is to multiply the whole equation by a positive whole number, to clear the fractions away. You would normally use the lowest common denominator of the various fractions.

EXAMPLE

Solve the equation $\dfrac{3x}{5} = \dfrac{x+1}{10}$.

SOLUTION

The lowest common multiple of 5 and 10 is 10, so multiply both fractions by 10:

$$\frac{10 \times 3x}{5} = \frac{10 \times (x+1)}{10}$$

Cancelling, and then simplifying:

$$\frac{\cancel{10}^{\,2} \times 3x}{\cancel{5}^{\,1}} = \frac{\cancel{10}^{\,1} \times (x+1)}{\cancel{10}^{\,1}}$$

$6x = x + 1$
$6x - x = 1$
$5x = 1$
$x = \tfrac{1}{5}$

Harder examples may involve more terms.

EXAMPLE

Solve $\dfrac{5y+8}{6} - \dfrac{3y+2}{4} = 1$.

SOLUTION

The LCM of 6 and 4 is 12, so multiply all three terms by 12:

$$\frac{12 \times (5y+8)}{6} - \frac{12 \times (3y+2)}{4} = 12 \times 1$$

Cancelling, and then simplifying:

$$\frac{\cancel{12}^{\,2} \times (5y+8)}{\cancel{6}^{\,1}} - \frac{\cancel{12}^{\,3} \times (3y+2)}{\cancel{4}^{\,1}} = 12 \times 1$$

$2(5y+8) - 3(3y+2) = 12$
$10y + 16 - 9y - 6 = 12$
$y + 10 = 12$
$y = 12 - 10$
$y = 2$

It is a good idea to check your answer, by substitution:

$$\frac{5y+8}{6} - \frac{3y+2}{4} = \frac{5 \times 2 + 8}{6} - \frac{3 \times 2 + 2}{4}$$
$$= \frac{18}{6} - \frac{8}{4}$$
$$= 3 - 2$$
$$= 1 \quad \text{as required}$$

EXERCISE 13.5

Solve these equations.

1. $\dfrac{x-1}{2} = \dfrac{x+1}{3}$

2. $\dfrac{7x-5}{10} = \dfrac{x}{2}$

3. $\dfrac{3x+2}{7} = \dfrac{x+2}{3}$

4. $\dfrac{x+8}{2} + \dfrac{x+6}{4} = 7$

5. $\dfrac{7x-5}{10} = \dfrac{3x}{5}$

6. $\dfrac{x+1}{2} + \dfrac{2x+1}{3} = 9$

7. $\dfrac{x+1}{2} = \dfrac{x}{3}$

8. $\dfrac{x+1}{2} + \dfrac{3x-1}{4} = 4$

9. $\dfrac{x+13}{2} - \dfrac{12-3x}{3} = 1$

10. $\dfrac{3x-1}{7} = \dfrac{9-x}{2}$

13.6 Using equations to solve geometry problems

Some examination questions will set problems on triangles or quadrilaterals that lead to simple equations. These may be based on perimeter, or might use the fact that angles in a triangle add up to 180°, or that angles in a quadrilateral add up to 360°. This next example shows a problem based on the angle sum in a quadrilateral.

EXAMPLE

The diagram shows a quadrilateral PQRS. Find the value of x. Hence find the values of the angles.

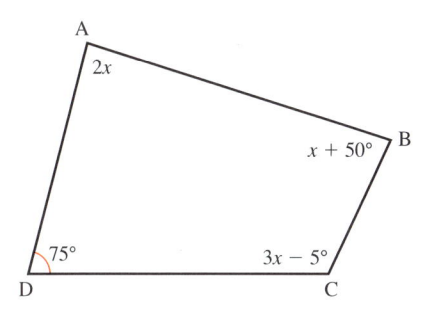

SOLUTION

Since the angles in a quadrilateral add up to 360°:

$2x + x + 50 + 3x - 5 + 75 = 360$

$6x + 120 = 360$

$6x = 360 - 120$

$6x = 240$

$x = \dfrac{240}{6}$

$x = 40°$

Then angle DAB = $2x$ = 80°, angle ABC = $x + 50$ = 90° and angle BCD = $3x - 5$ = 115°

13 Algebraic equations U4

EXERCISE 13.6

1. Find the value of x.
   Hence work out the size of the largest angle.

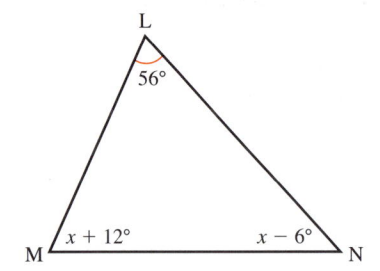

2. Form and solve an equation in y.
   Hence find the sizes of the angles in the triangle.

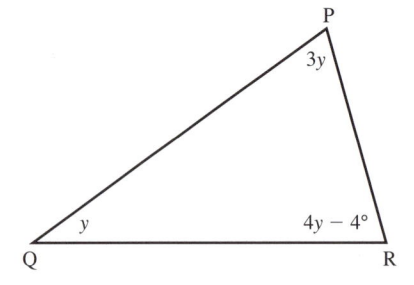

3. A triangle has angles $x + 8°$, $2x - 8°$ and $90°$.
   a) Set up an equation in x.
   b) Solve your equation, to find the value of x.
   c) Work out the sizes of the angles in the triangle.

4. The angles in a triangle are $4c + 4°$, $5c - 7°$ and $7c + 7°$.
   a) Set up an equation in c.
   b) Solve your equation, to find the value of c.
   c) Work out the sizes of the angles in the triangle.
   d) What kind of triangle is this?

5. The diagram shows a quadrilateral. Work out the size of the angle m.

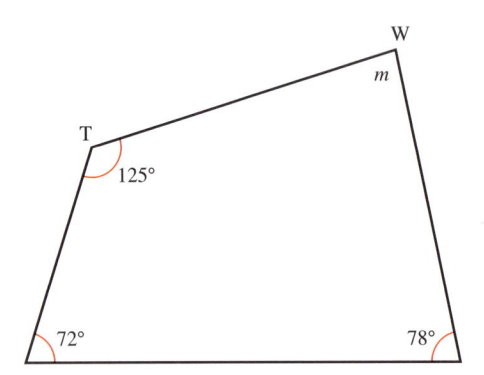

6 **a)** Form and solve an equation in y.
   b) Hence find the sizes of the angles in the quadrilateral.
   c) What do your answers tell you about the line segments PR and QS?

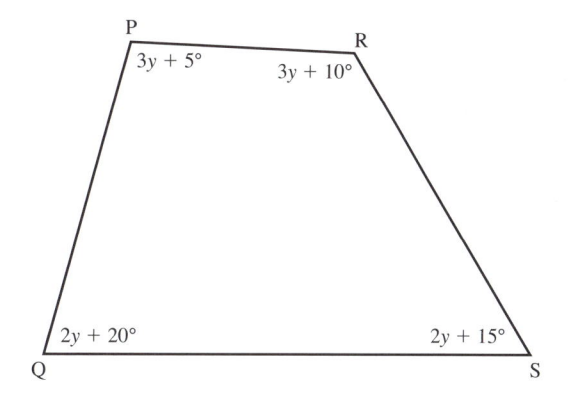

7 Form and solve an equation in k. Hence find the values of the angles in the quadrilateral.

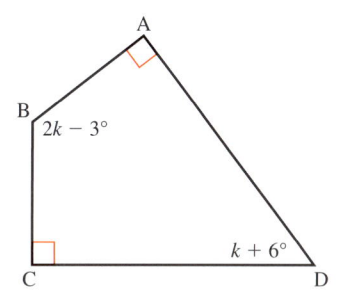

8 The angles in a quadrilateral are $x + 16°$, $2x - 2°$, $3x + 9°$ and $5x - 15°$.
   a) Set up an equation in x.
   b) Solve your equation, to find the value of x.
   c) Work out the sizes of the angles in the quadrilateral.
   d) Check that your four answers add up to $360°$.

13.7 Generating formulae

Formulae can be generated from information given in words. You may also generate them from information given by a diagram, or even another formula.

EXAMPLE

A factory produces handbags by cutting and shaping rectangles of material. To make one bag, a rectangle of material p cm by q cm is needed. The factory finds that an area A of material is just sufficient to make n bags.

Obtain a formula for A in terms of p, q and n.

SOLUTION

The area required for one bag is found by multiplying p and q together: pq.

For n such bags, the area of material must be n times bigger: npq.

Thus the required formula is

$A = npq$

EXAMPLE

A square of side x cm is removed from each corner of a rectangle measuring a cm by b cm.

a) Draw a sketch to show this information.
b) Find a formula for the area, A cm², remaining after the removal of the four squares.
c) The sides are now folded up to make a rectangular tray of depth x cm. Find a formula for the volume, V cm³, of the tray.

SOLUTION

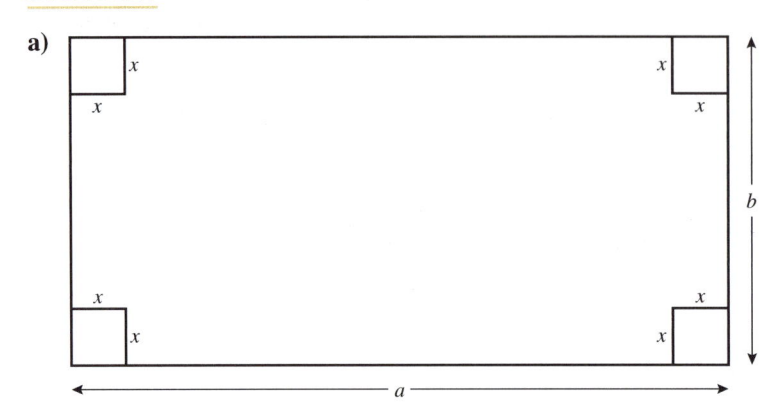

a)

b) The original rectangle has an area of ab.

Each square has an area of x^2, and there are four, giving a total of $4x^2$.

Thus the area remaining is:

$A = ab - 4x^2$

c) Fold up the sides to make a tray:

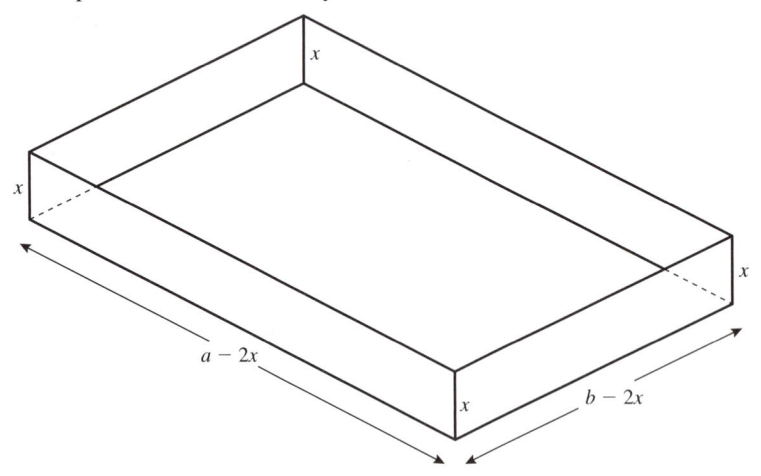

The base is now a rectangle of dimensions $(a - 2x)$ and $(b - 2x)$, so the area of the rectangular base of the tray is $(a - 2x)(b - 2x)$. To obtain the volume, this is multiplied by the depth, x, to give:

$V = x(a - 2x)(b - 2x)$

EXERCISE 13.7

1. An equilateral triangle has sides of length x cm. Obtain a formula for the perimeter P of the triangle.

2. A helicopter consumes n litres of fuel per minute. Obtain a formula for the total number of litres T of fuel consumed during a flight lasting half an hour.

3. Each month I have to pay £x for my house mortgage, and each year I have to pay £y for buildings insurance. Find a formula for the total £T I have to pay in mortgage and buildings insurance over a period of 5 years.

4. Ginny is given £500 on her 18th birthday, which she saves in a building society account. She then adds £10 per month to her savings. Obtain a formula for the amount £P she will have in the account after m months of saving.

5. A rectangle of area A has length l cm. Find a formula for its width, w cm, in terms of A and l.

6. My brother is 11 years older than me.
    a) Denoting my present age as n years, write down my brother's present age.
    b) Obtain a formula for T, the total obtained by adding our two ages together.

7. Pencils cost 15 pence each, and pens 25 pence each.
    a) Write an expression for the cost of x pencils.
    b) Write a formula for the total cost, T pence, of x pencils and y pens.

8. The cost of hiring a bicycle is £5 plus a daily charge of £2 per day.
    a) Find the cost of hiring the bicycle for 5 days.
    b) Obtain a formula for the cost, £C, of hiring the bicycle for n days.

9. Digital photos are stored as files on a memory card. Each photo takes up 0.3 MB of space on the card. The card can hold 128 MB of data.
    a) Find the amount of space occupied by 60 photos.
    b) Obtain a formula for the amount of space S remaining on the card when n photos have been stored on it.
    c) What is the maximum value of n?

10. A rectangle of dimensions a cm by b cm has a 1 cm square cut out from each of its four corners. The sides thus formed are then folded up to make a rectangular tray.
    a) Find an expression for the area of the base of the tray.
    b) Find a formula for the volume, V cm^3, of the rectangular tray.

13.8 Changing the subject of a formula

A formula usually has a single letter term on the left-hand side of the equals sign. This is called the **subject** of the formula. For example, the formula $C = 2\pi r$ has C as its subject.

Sometimes you will want to rearrange the formula so that one of the other letters becomes the subject instead.

EXAMPLE

Make r the subject of $C = 2\pi r$.

SOLUTION

$$C = 2\pi r$$
$$2\pi r = C$$
$$\pi r = \frac{C}{2}$$
$$r = \frac{C}{2\pi}$$

First, rewrite the original equation with the left and right-hand sides swapped over…

… next, divide both sides by 2…

… and finish by dividing both sides by π.

Note that the π goes next to the 2. Do not write $\frac{\frac{C}{2}}{\pi}$.

Some problems require a mixture of addition/subtraction and multiplication/division. You need to think carefully about the appropriate order in which to do these.

EXAMPLE

Make x the subject of $y = mx + c$.

SOLUTION

$$y = mx + c$$
$$mx + c = y$$
$$mx = y - c$$
$$x = \frac{y - c}{m}$$

Again, begin by swapping over the left- and right-hand sides…

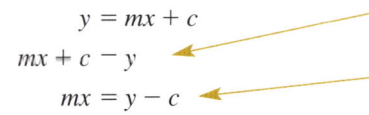

…. next, subtract c from both sides….

… and finish by dividing both sides by m.

The quantity to be made the new subject might appear as a squared term in the initial formula, for example, r^2. In this case, just make r^2 the subject of the new formula, then square root at the end.

EXAMPLE

Make r the subject of $V = \frac{1}{3}\pi r^2 h$.

SOLUTION

$$V = \tfrac{1}{3}\pi r^2 h$$
$$\tfrac{1}{3}\pi r^2 h = V$$
$$\pi r^2 h = 3V$$
$$r^2 = \frac{3V}{\pi h}$$

Start by swapping the left and right-hand sides over …

… then multiply both sides by 3 …

… and divide both sides by πh.

Square rooting both sides, we obtain:

$$r = \sqrt{\frac{3V}{\pi h}}$$

Harder examination questions might be set where the new subject appears twice in the original equation, or the new subject appears as part of an algebraic fraction. You will find some examples of these harder types of problems in Chapter 27 of this book.

EXERCISE 13.8

Rearrange these formulae so that the indicated letter becomes the subject.

1. $A = \pi r l$ (make r the subject)
2. $v = u + at$ (u)
3. $v = u + at$ (a)
4. $V = \frac{1}{3}\pi r^2 h$ (h)
5. $E = mc^2$ (m)
6. $y = 4x + 3$ (x)
7. $y = \frac{x}{5} + 3$ (x)
8. $y = \frac{x + 3}{5}$ (x)
9. $A = \frac{1}{2}bh$ (h)
10. $E = mc^2$ (c)
11. $A = 4xy + x^2$ (y)
12. $P = I^2 R$ (R)
13. $y = m(x - a)$ (x)
14. $v^2 = u^2 + 2as$ (a)
15. $A = 4\pi r^2$ (r)
16. $y = x^2 - 9$ (x)
17. $x^2 = y^2 + z^2$ (y)
18. $V = abc$ (b)
19. $V = \frac{4}{3}\pi r^3$ (r)
20. $v^2 = u^2 + 2as$ (u)

13.9 Trial and improvement

So far, you have been using formal methods to develop the exact solution to an equation. Not all equations can be solved like this, however, so there are ways of using trial and improvement to find an approximate solution.

When using such a method you can find the solution correct to 1 decimal place, or 2, and so on – but you will never find the exact solution. Exam questions will tell you when you must use a trial and improvement method. They will also tell you how accurate your final answer needs to be.

EXAMPLE

The equation $x^2 + 4x = 25$ has a solution between 3 and 4. Use trial and improvement to find this solution correct to 1 decimal place.

SOLUTION

Trial x value	$x^2 + 4x$	25	
3	$3^2 + 4 \times 3 = 21$	21	too small
3.5	$3.5^2 + 4 \times 3.5 = 26.25$	26.25	too big

By looking at these results, you can see that 3 is too low and 3.5 is too high.
Thus the solution lies between 3 and 3.5
For the next trial, try 3.4

Trial x value	$x^2 + 4x$	25	
3	$3^2 + 4 \times 3 = 21$	21	too small
3.5	$3.5^2 + 4 \times 3.5 = 26.25$	26.25	too big
3.4	$3.4^2 + 4 \times 3.4$	25.16	too big

3.4 is too big, but not by much.
For the next trial, try 3.3

Trial x value	$x^2 + 4x$	25	
3	$3^2 + 4 \times 3 = 21$	21	too small
3.5	$3.5^2 + 4 \times 3.5 = 26.25$	26.25	too big
3.4	$3.4^2 + 4 \times 3.4$	25.16	too big
3.3	$3.3^2 + 4 \times 3.3$	24.09	too small

Since 3.3 is too small and 3.4 is too big, the solution must lie between these two values.

To see which one is closest, we *must* make one more calculation, using the mid-value, 3.35

Trial x value	$x^2 + 4x$	25	
3	$3^2 + 4 \times 3 = 21$	21	too small
3.5	$3.5^2 + 4 \times 3.5 = 26.25$	26.25	too big
3.4	$3.4^2 + 4 \times 3.4$	25.16	too big
3.3	$3.3^2 + 4 \times 3.3$	24.09	too small
3.35	$3.35^2 + 4 \times 3.35$	24.6225	too small

So, the solution is $x = 3.4$ correct to 1 d.p.

In the examination it is very important to show the examiner full details of all your trials – even the ones that missed by a long way. Do not forget to do the extra trial to one more decimal place using the mid-value. The examiner will want to see the improvement taking place, not just the final result.

EXERCISE 13.9

1. The equation $x^2 + 7x = 48$ has a solution between $x = 4$ and $x = 5$.
   Use trial and improvement to find this solution correct to 1 decimal place.

2. The equation $x^2 + 5x = 9$ has a solution between $x = 1$ and $x = 2$.
   Use trial and improvement to find this solution correct to 1 decimal place.

3. The equation $x^3 + 2x = 10$ has a solution between $x = 1$ and $x = 2$.
   Use trial and improvement to find this solution correct to 1 decimal place.

4. The equation $x^2 - 2x = 11$ has a solution between $x = 4$ and $x = 5$.
   Use trial and improvement to find this solution correct to 1 decimal place.

5. The equation $x^2 + 7x - 35 = 0$ has a solution between $x = 3$ and $x = 4$.
   Use trial and improvement to find this solution correct to 1 decimal place.

6. The equation $2x^2 + x = 7$ has a solution between $x = 1$ and $x = 2$.
   Use trial and improvement to find this solution correct to 1 decimal place.

7. The equation $x^3 + 2x^2 = 100$ has a solution near $x = 4$.
   Use trial and improvement to find this solution correct to 1 decimal place.

8. The equation $x(x + 1) = 3$ has a solution between $x = 1$ and $x = 2$.
   Use trial and improvement to find this solution correct to 1 decimal place.

9. The equation $x^3 - 10x + 1 = 0$ has a solution between $x = 3$ and $x = 4$.
   Use trial and improvement to find this solution correct to 1 decimal place.

10. a) Show that the equation $3x^2 - x - 1 = 0$ has a solution between $x = 0$ and $x = 1$.
    b) Use trial and improvement to find this solution correct to 2 decimal places.
    c) The same equation has another solution between $x = 0$ and $x = -1$.
       Find this solution, correct to 2 decimal places.

REVIEW EXERCISE 13

1. Insert the best word (expression, equation, formula or identity) into the missing space in each of the following sentences.
   a) The volume of a cuboid may be found by using the ▢▢▢▢▢▢▢ $V = abc$.
   b) My age n years after my 21st birthday is given by the ▢▢▢▢▢▢▢▢▢▢ $21 + n$.
   c) The ▢▢▢▢▢▢▢▢ $3x + 5 = 17$ has a solution at $x = 4$.
   d) The result $x(x + 12) = x^2 + 12x$ is an example of an ▢▢▢▢▢▢▢▢.

Solve these equations. You may solve them by inspection, which means by sight, and write the answer down.

2. $x + 5 = 11$
3. $y + 2 = 0$
4. $x - 5 = 2$
5. $3y = 1$
6. $4x = 7$
7. $25y^2 = 64$
8. $16 - 2x = 8$
9. $x^2 = 81$
10. $\dfrac{z}{4} = 5$

Solve these linear equations. Show all the steps in your working.

11. $4x + 3 = x + 15$
12. $7x - 5 = 2x + 15$
13. $x - 1 = 5 - 2x$
14. $13 + x = 7x + 25$
15. $\dfrac{x}{5} = \dfrac{7}{20}$
16. $2x + 6 = 9x + 13$
17. $10 - x = 15 - 2x$
18. $16 + 3x = 5x + 20$
19. $8 - x = 8 + x$
20. $\dfrac{2x}{3} = \dfrac{10}{9}$

Expand the brackets, and hence solve these equations.

21. $5(y - 1) = 2y + 7$
22. $9z = 4(z - 2) + 3$
23. $2x = 5(12 - x) + 3$
24. $9(x + 7) = 7(x + 9)$
25. $7(2x - 3) = 59 + 4(x - 5)$
26. $15(x - 1) + 3 = 2(x + 1) + 3(x + 2)$

Solve these equations.

27. $\dfrac{3x + 4}{5} = x$
28. $\dfrac{8 - x}{6} = \dfrac{x - 3}{4}$
29. $\dfrac{x}{2} + \dfrac{x}{3} = 5$
30. $\dfrac{x + 1}{3} + \dfrac{x}{4} = 5$

31. A Post Office sells x 26 pence stamps and y 19 pence stamps during one day. The total income from the stamps is T pence. Write a formula expressing T in terms of x and y.

32 A theatre charges £5 for adult tickets and £3 for children. Altogether a group of x adults and y children pays a total of £T.
   a) Find a formula for T in terms of x and y.
   b) What can you say about the values of x and y if the average ticket price for the group turned out to be £4?

33 In a dice game you score either 5 points or 2 points each time you play. Fred plays 10 times, and wins 5 points on n of the 10 games.
   a) Write an expression for the total number of points Fred scores in all 10 games.
   b) Simplify your expression as much as possible.

34 Rearrange the formula $C = 2\pi r$ to make r the subject.

35 Make a the subject of the formula $s = ut + \frac{1}{2}at^2$.

36 Rearrange the formula $A = \pi r^2$ to make r the subject.

37 Make l the subject of the formula $T = 2\pi \sqrt{\dfrac{l}{g}}$.

38 Lisa packs pencils in boxes. She packs 12 pencils in each box. Lisa packs x boxes of pencils.
   a) Write an expression, in terms of x, for the number of pencils Lisa packs.
   Lisa also packs pens in boxes. She packs 10 pens into each box. Lisa packs y boxes of pens.
   b) Write down an expression, in terms of x and y, for the total number of pens and pencils Lisa packs.
   [Edexcel]

39 Sharon earns p pounds per hour. She works for h hours. She also earns a bonus of b pounds. Write down a formula for the total amount she earns, w pounds. [Edexcel]

40 Daniel buys n books at £4 each. He pays for them with a £20 note.
   He receives C pounds change. Write down a formula for C in terms of n. [Edexcel]

41 The equation $x^2 + 10x = 44$ has a solution between $x = 3$ and $x = 4$. Use the method of trial and improvement to find this solution, giving your answer correct to 1 d.p.

42 The equation $x^3 - x = 10$ has a solution between $x = 2$ and $x = 3$. Use the method of trial and improvement to find this solution, giving your answer correct to 1 d.p.

43 The equation $x^2 = 18 + x$ has a solution between $x = 4$ and $x = 5$. Use trial and improvement to find this solution correct to 1 d.p.

44 a) The equation $x^2 - x - 1 = 0$ has a solution between $x = 1$ and $x = 2$. Find its value correct to 1 d.p., using the method of trial and improvement.
   b) The same equation has another solution, between $x = -1$ and $x = 0$.
   Use trial and improvement to find this solution, also correct to 1 d.p.

45 Glenn has done a homework exercise about solving equations. He got 19 of the 20 questions right. Here is the one he got wrong.

$$5(2x - 1) - 2(x + 4) = 19$$
$$10x - 5 - 2x + 8 = 19$$
$$8x + 3 = 19$$
$$8x = 16$$
$$x = 2$$

Look carefully at Glenn's work, and see if you can spot what he has done wrong. Then write out the corrected answer, showing all the lines of working.

46 Marco and Seyi are solving the equation $3(2x - 1) + 4(x + 8) = 19$.

Marco: I reckon that $x = 1$.

Seyi: I reckon that $x = -1$.

Work out which one of them was right.

47 a) Solve $7p + 2 = 5p + 8$.
  b) Solve $7r + 2 = 5(r - 4)$. [Edexcel]

48 Solve the equation $7(x - 1) = 2x - 1$. [Edexcel]

49 a) Solve $7x + 18 = 74$.
  b) Solve $4(2y - 5) = 32$.
  c) Solve $5p + 7 = 3(4 - p)$. [Edexcel]

50 a) Solve the equation $5p - 4 = 11$.
  b) Solve the equation $7(q + 5) = 21$.
  c) Solve the equation $\dfrac{21 + x}{6} = x$. [Edexcel]

51 The equation $x^3 + 3x = 47$ has a solution between 3 and 4. Use a trial and improvement method to find this solution. Give your answer correct to one decimal place. You must show *all* your working. [Edexcel]

52 Nassim thinks of a number. When he multiplies his number by 5 and subtracts 16 from the result he gets the same answer as when he adds 10 to his number and multiplies that result by 3. Find the number Nassim is thinking of. [Edexcel]

53 a) Solve $20y - 16 = 18y - 9$.
  b) Solve $\dfrac{40 - x}{3} = 4 + x$. [Edexcel]

54 The diagram represents a garden in the shape of a rectangle.

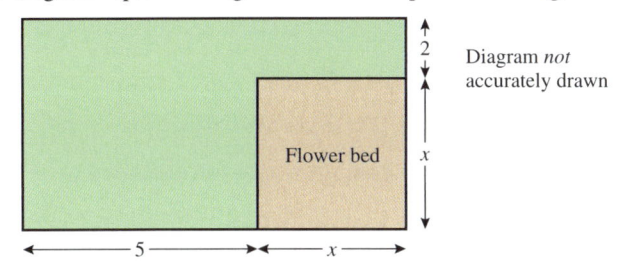

Diagram *not* accurately drawn

All measurements are given in metres.
The garden has a flower bed in one corner.
The flower bed is a square of side x.
  a) Write an expression, in terms of x, for the shortest side of the garden.
  b) Find an expression, in terms of x, for the perimeter of the garden.
     Give your answer in its simplest form.
     The perimeter of the garden is 20 metres.
  c) Find the value of x. [Edexcel]

55 The equation $x^3 - 2x = 67$ has a solution between 4 and 5. Use a trial and improvement method to find this solution. Give your answer correct to one decimal place.
You must show *all* your working. [Edexcel]

KEY POINTS

1. An expression is a mathematical phrase, such as $x^2 + 5x$.
2. An equation is a mathematical sentence, containing an $=$ sign, such as $y = x^2 + 5x$.
3. An equation designed for a purpose, for example to calculate an area, is called a formula.
4. An equation that is always true is called an identity.
5. Simple equations may be solved by inspection. If square rooting, remember to allow for both positive and negative options.
6. Harder equations may include several stages and, possibly, the expansion of brackets. With this kind of problem you should always show each step of your working carefully.
7. Some algebraic equations involve fractions. You can clear the fractions away by multiplying through by the lowest common denominator of the fractions.
8. The GCSE exam will require you to be able to change the subject of a formula, by rearranging. Be sure to practise this technique, as there are many variations in the questions.
9. Some equations, especially those involving powers, may be solved using approximate methods based on trial and improvement. You should always include full details of your trials. You will often be asked to work to one decimal place: if you have established that the solution lies between 2.6 and 2.7, for example, you must remember to perform one further trial at 2.65.

Internet Challenge 13

Carl Friedrich Gauss

Much pioneering work on the theory of equations was done by Gauss. Use the internet to help answer these questions about him:

1. What nationality was Carl Friedrich Gauss?

2. When and where was he born?

3. How long did he live?

4. Gauss solved a difficult geometric construction problem while he was still a teenager. What was this?

5. '*Work out 1 + 2 + 3 + … + 100 in your head.*' How did Gauss do this when he was 9 years old?

6. Which university did Gauss enter in 1795?

7. What astronomical discovery is jointly credited to Gauss and the Italian astronomer Guiseppe Piazzi?

8. '*Every (positive) whole number is the sum of at most three triangular numbers.*'
   Is this statement true or false?

9. What is the Fundamental Theorem of Algebra?

10. It is sometimes necessary to *degauss* a computer's CRT monitor. What does this mean?

11. A central idea in modern statistics is the *Gaussian distribution*, but this name is misleading, as it was not originated by Gauss. Which mathematician was responsible for first introducing this distribution, and by what other name is it often known?

12. What are complex numbers?

13. Gauss allegedly said words to the effect '*Tell her to wait a minute until I've finished*' on what occasion?

14. By what regal nickname is Gauss sometimes known?

15. When and where was Gauss buried?

16. What mathematical shape did Gauss want inscribed on his gravestone? Was this done?

17. What is the significance of the number of questions in this exercise?

CHAPTER 14

Graphs of straight lines

In this chapter you will **learn how to**:
- use gradient and intercept to sketch linear graphs
- recognise the equation of a linear graph by looking at its gradient and intercept
- use properties of parallel lines.

You will also be **challenged to**:
- investigate parallels.

Starter: Number sequences

1 Look at these number sequences. Write down the next two terms in each one.
   a) 1, 2, 3, 4, 5, ...
   b) 1, 2, 4, 8, 16, ...
   c) 1, 2, 4, 7, 11, 16, ...
   d) 9, 13, 17, 21, 25, ...
   e) 20, 18, 16, 14, 12, ...
   f) 20, 10, 5, 2.5, ...
   g) 60, 59, 57, 54, ...
   h) 60, 57, 54, 51, ...
   i) −5, −3, −1, 1, ...
   j) 1, 4, 9, 16, ...

2 Number sequences that go up (or down) in equal steps are called *linear sequences*, because they correspond to straight line graphs. Decide which of the ten sequences above are linear sequences.

14.1 Gradient and intercept of linear functions

In Chapter 6 of this book you were asked to plot the graph of $y = 2x$. Your graph should have looked like this:

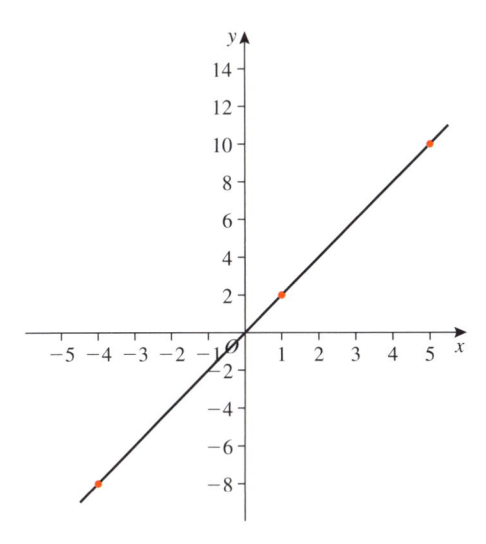

You can measure the *gradient* of the line by constructing a triangle underneath it – the exact size of the triangle is unimportant – and measuring the horizontal and vertical changes. These are sometimes referred to as the 'rise' and 'run'. You can choose any two points on the line.

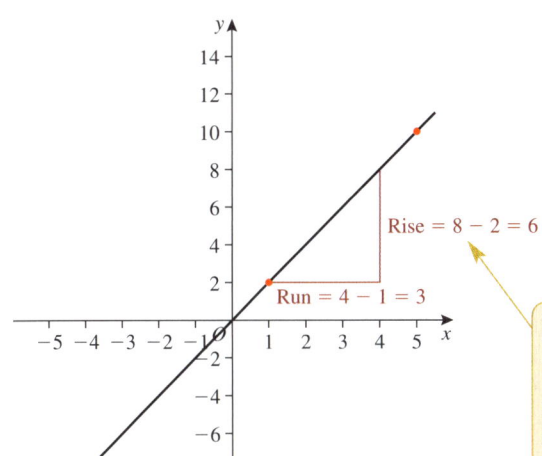

Rise = 8 − 2 = 6
Run = 4 − 1 = 3

> It is dangerous just to count squares.
> You must read the values off the graph carefully: the x and y axes may have different scales, as here.

Then the **gradient** m is defined as:

$$\text{Gradient } m = \frac{\text{rise}}{\text{run}} = \frac{6}{3} = 2$$

14 Graphs of straight lines U4

The diagram below shows a family of three graphs, all with gradient 2. They are distinguished by the fact that each one crosses the y axis at a different position – this point is known as the **intercept** (or y intercept, to give it its full name).

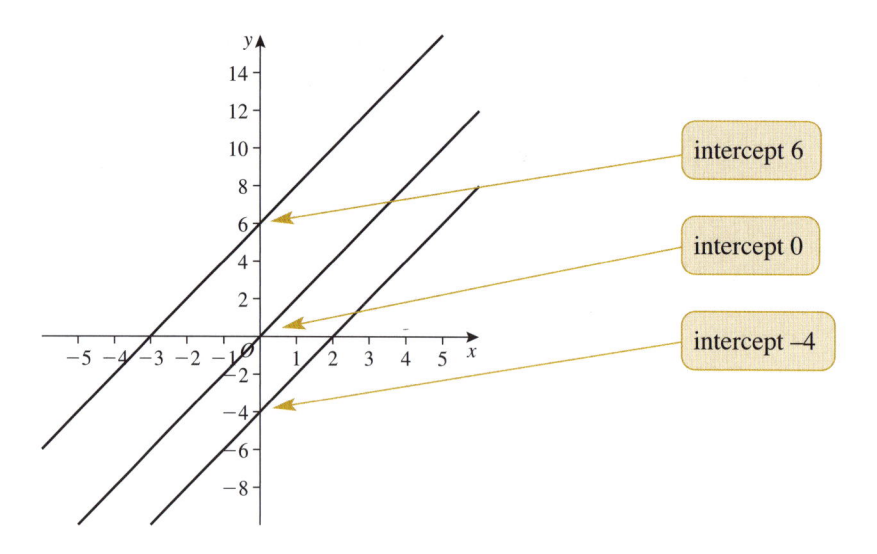

EXAMPLE

A straight line passes through the points (0, 5) and (3, 14). Find its gradient m and intercept c.

SOLUTION

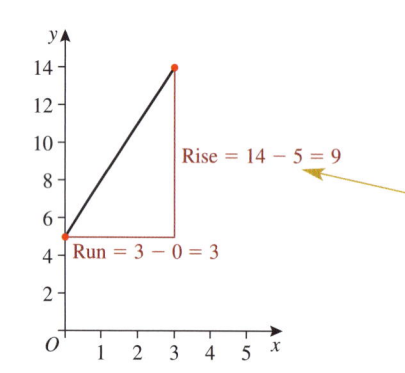

You do not need the graph to be plotted accurately: a sketch to show which numbers are being used is enough.

Gradient = $\dfrac{\text{rise}}{\text{run}} = \dfrac{9}{3} = 3$

Intercept = 5

Thus $m = 3$ and $c = 5$

Some linear graphs have negative gradients. This simply means that the graph slopes *down*, as you move to the right, not up.

EXAMPLE

A straight line passes through the points $(1, 6)$ and $(3, 2)$. Find its gradient m and intercept c.

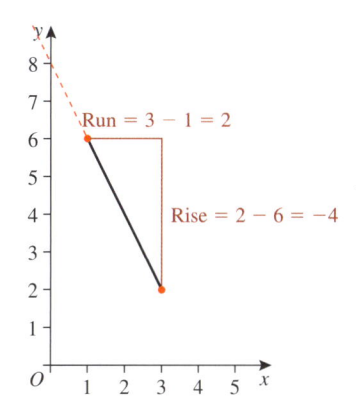

Gradient $= \dfrac{\text{rise}}{\text{run}} = \dfrac{-4}{2} = -2$.

By extending the line segment to the left the intercept may be read from the y axis:

Intercept $= 8$.

Thus $m = -2$ and $c = 8$

EXERCISE 14.1

Find the gradient m and the intercept c for each of the lines marked in questions **1** to **8** below.

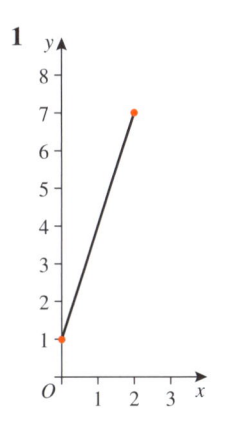

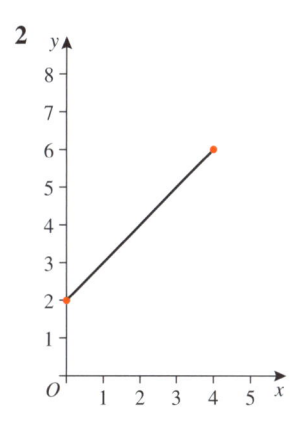

3, **4**, **5**, **6**, **7**, **8**

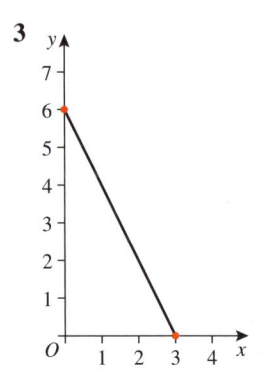

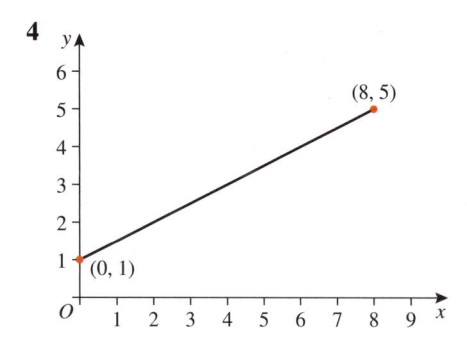

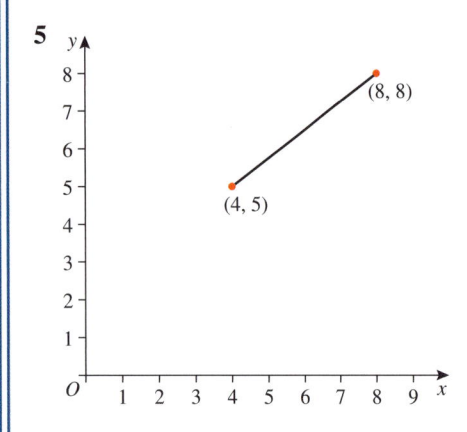

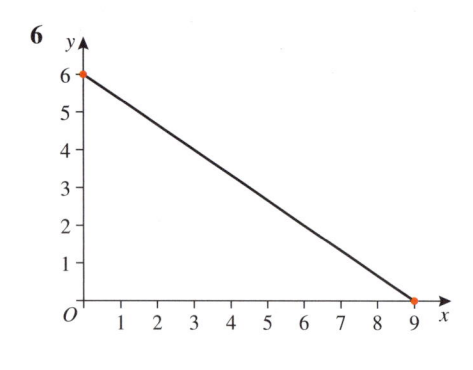

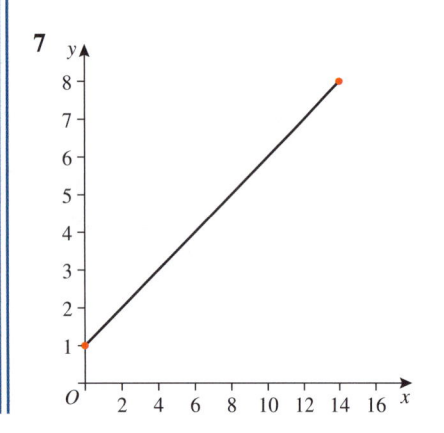

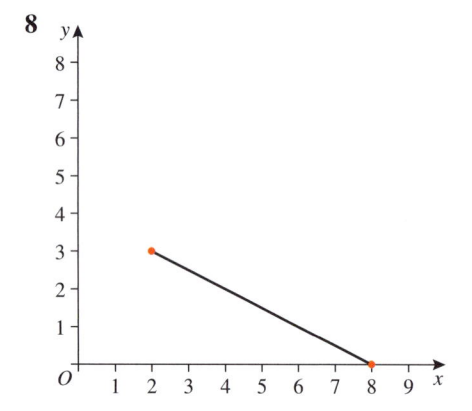

14.2 Equations and graphs

Look again at this graph of $y = 2x + 3$ that was used in Chapter 6.

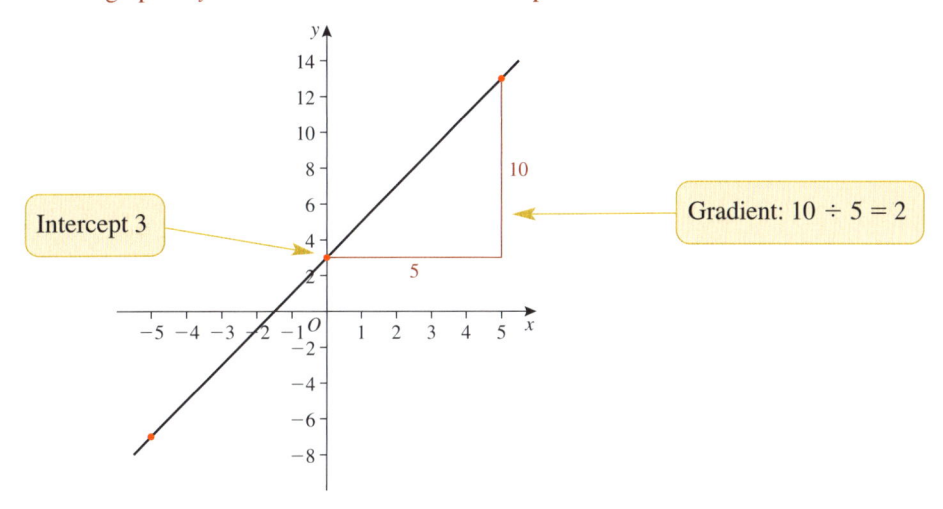

Intercept 3

Gradient: $10 \div 5 = 2$

Notice that the line has gradient 2, and intercept 3, and these also happen to be the values of the two coefficients that appear in the equation of the line.

This illustrates an important general result:

The graph of the function $y = mx + c$ has gradient m and intercept c.

You can use this principle to help sketch graphs of linear functions.

EXAMPLE

Sketch the graph corresponding to the function $y = 3x + 1$.

$y = 3x + 1$
gradient   intercept

Note: the equation must be in the form $y = \ldots$

SOLUTION

The intercept is $c = 1$, so the graph must cross the y axis at $(0, 1)$.
The gradient is $m = 3$, so the graph rises by 3 units for each 1 unit to the right.
Thus the graph will look like this:

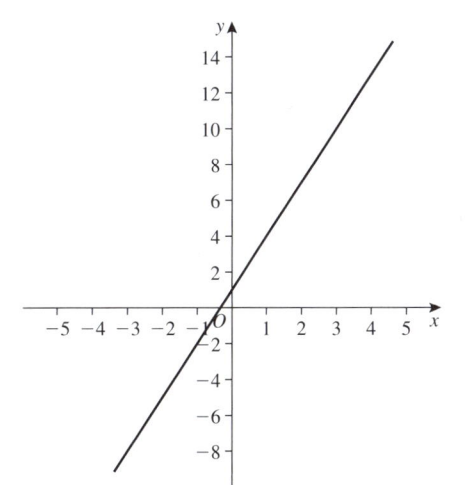

You can use this idea the other way round, to find the equation of a given straight-line graph.

EXAMPLE

Find the equation of this straight line:

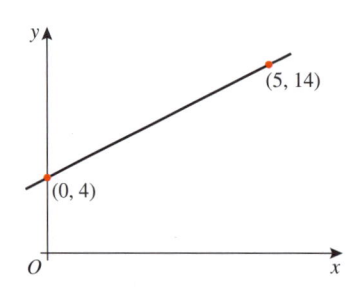

SOLUTION

The intercept is $c = 4$.

The gradient is $\dfrac{14 - 4}{5 - 0} = \dfrac{10}{5} = 2$.

Thus the equation of the line is $\underline{y = 2x + 4}$

EXERCISE 14.2

1 to 8 Write down the equations of the straight lines whose gradients and intercepts you found in Exercise 14.1, questions **1** to **8**.

9 The diagram shows the graph corresponding to a linear function of x.
   a) Write down the coordinates of the points P and Q on the line.
   b) Find the gradient and intercept of the line.
   c) Hence write down the equation of the straight line.

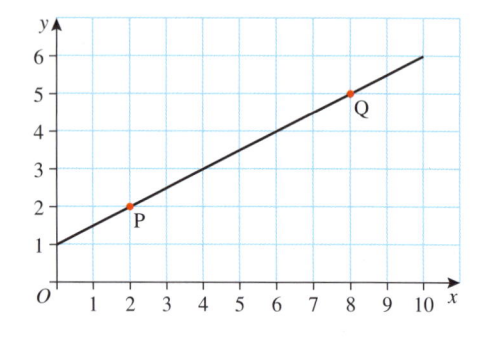

10 The diagram shows the graph of a linear function of x.
   a) Find the gradient and intercept of the line.
   b) Hence write down the equation of the straight line.

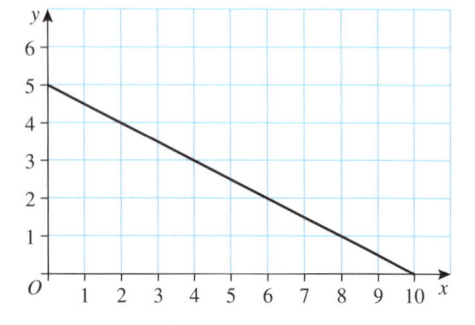

14.3 Parallel lines

Here are the graphs of $y = 2x - 4$, $y = 2x$ and $y = 2x + 6$ from Section 14.1.

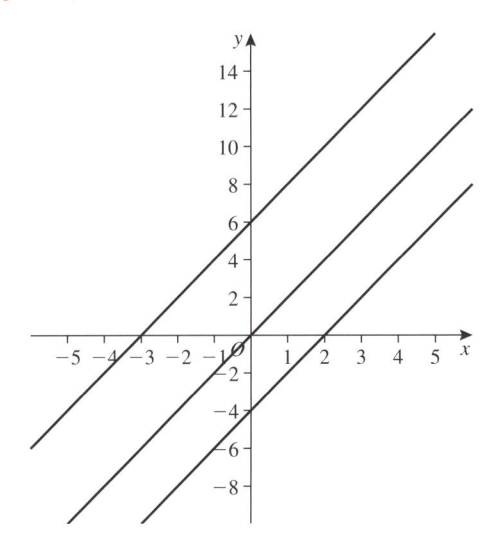

All three graphs have the same gradient, namely 2.

Geometrically, this means that all three lines are parallel.

In general, two lines will be parallel if, and only if, their gradients are equal.

EXAMPLE

Find the equation of the line passing through (5, 13) that is parallel to the line $y = 2x - 4$.

SOLUTION

Suppose the required line has equation $y = mx + c$.

Since it is parallel to $y = 2x - 4$ then the gradient must be 2, that is, $m = 2$.

Thus the required line has equation $y = 2x + c$.

Since it passes through the point (5, 13), we may substitute $x = 5$ and $y = 13$ to obtain:

$13 = (2 \times 5) + c$
$13 = 10 + c$
$c = 3$

Thus the required line has equation $y = 2x + 3$

EXAMPLE

Investigate whether any of these lines is parallel to any of the others:

A $y = 3x + 5$
B $y = 2x + 5$
C $y = x + 5$
D $x - y = 9$
E $2y - 4x = 7$

SOLUTION

Clearly neither A nor B nor C is parallel to another since they have gradients of 3, 2, 1 respectively.

Equations D and E need to be rearranged to make y the subject before any further comparison is possible.

D may be written as $y = x - 9$, which has gradient 1, so C and D are parallel.

E may be written as $y = 2x + 3.5$, which has gradient 2, so B and E are parallel.

EXERCISE 14.3

1 Rearrange each of these equations into the form $y = ax + b$. Then pick out the two that represent a pair of parallel lines.

   a) $x - y = 6$ **b)** $2x + y + 5 = 0$ **c)** $y - 1 = \frac{1}{2}x$ **d)** $x - 2y + 5 = 0$

2 Look at this list of equations. There are four pairs of parallel lines, and one odd one out.

$y = 3x + 2$
$y = 2x + 3$
$y = x + 2$
$y = 4 + 3x$
$2y = 8x - 3$
$y = 2x - 1$
$x + y = 2$
$x - y = 5$
$2y = 8x + 1$

   a) Pick out the four pairs of parallel lines.
   b) Suggest the equation of another line that is parallel to the odd one out.

3 The line $y = ax + b$ is parallel to $y = 5x + 1$, and passes through the point $(1, 0)$.
   a) Write down the value of a.
   b) Work out the value of b, and hence obtain the equation of the line.

4 The line $y = mx + c$ is parallel to the line $y = 4x - 1$, and passes through the point $(0, 3)$.
   a) Find the values of m and c, and write down the equation of the line.
   b) The line also passes through the point $(3, p)$. Find p.

5 A line has equation $\dfrac{y - 2}{3} = x$.
   a) Rearrange the equation into the form $y = mx + c$.
   b) Find the equation of the parallel line that passes through the point $(2, 1)$.

REVIEW EXERCISE 14

1 Work out the gradient and intercept of each of the lines shown below. Hence obtain their equations.

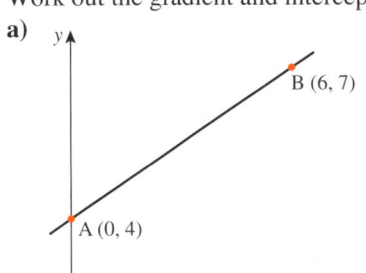

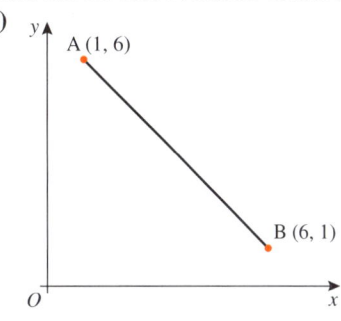

a) [Graph showing line through A(0, 4) and B(6, 7)]

b) [Graph showing line through A(1, 6) and B(6, 1)]

2 The diagram shows six lines, labelled A, B, C, D, E and F.

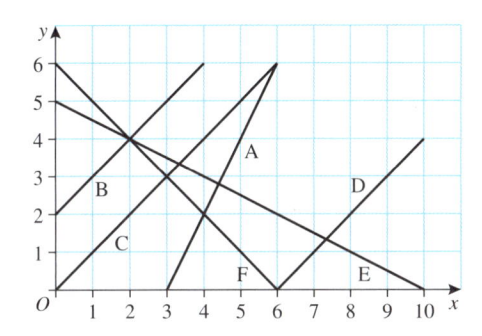

[Graph showing six lines labelled A, B, C, D, E, F on a coordinate grid]

Match each line to one of these equations:
$y = x$ $x + y = 6$ $y = x + 2$
$y = 2x - 6$ $y = -\frac{1}{2}x + 5$ $x = y + 6$

3 Find the equation of a line parallel to $y = 4x + 3$ but with a y-intercept of 7.

4 Find the equation of the line parallel to $y = 3x - 5$ that passes through $(2, 8)$.

5 The diagram shows three points A $(-1, 5)$, B $(2, -1)$ and C $(0, 5)$.

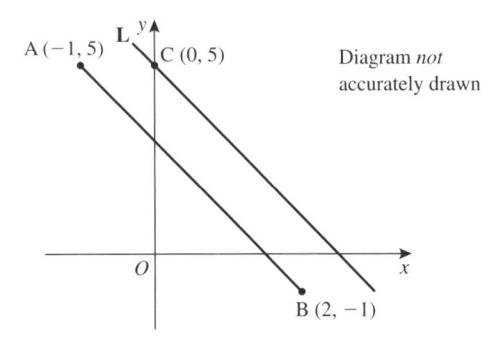

[Diagram showing points A(−1, 5), C(0, 5), B(2, −1) with line L parallel to AB passing through C]

Diagram *not* accurately drawn

The line **L** is parallel to AB and passes through C.
Find the equation of the line **L**.

[Edexcel]

6 A straight line has equation $y = \frac{1}{2}x + 1$. The point P lies on the straight line. P has a y-coordinate of 5.
   a) Find the x-coordinate of P.
   b) Write down the equation of a different straight line that is parallel to $y = \frac{1}{2}x + 1$.
   c) Rearrange $y = \frac{1}{2}x + 1$ to make x the subject. [Edexcel]

7 The line with equation $x + 2y = 6$ has been drawn on the grid below.

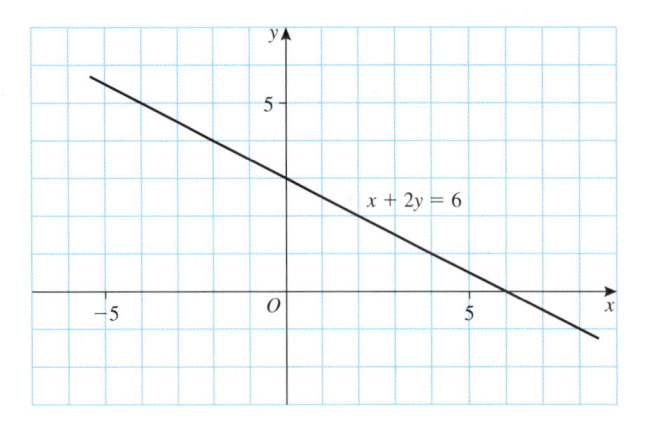

   a) Rearrange the equation $x + 2y = 6$ to make y the subject.
   b) Write down the gradient of the line with equation $x + 2y = 6$.
   c) Write down the equation of the line that is parallel to the line with equation $x + 2y = 6$ and passes through the point with coordinates $(0, 7)$. [Edexcel]

8 ABCD is a rectangle. A is the point $(0, 1)$. C is the point $(0, 6)$.
The equation of the straight line through A and B is $y = 2x + 1$

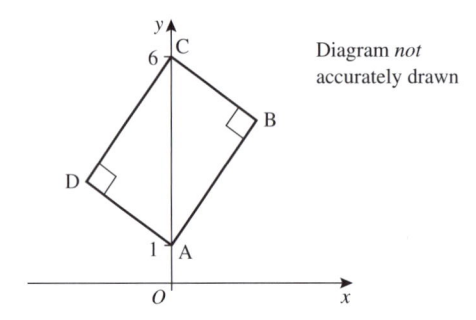

Diagram *not* accurately drawn

Find the equation of the straight line through D and C. [Edexcel]

KEY POINTS

1. The gradient of a linear function is defined as the ratio of the height gained to the horizontal distance covered, or 'rise over run' for short. Graphs that go down as you move to the right will have negative gradients.

2. The intercept (or y intercept) of a linear function tells you where it crosses the y axis.

3. A linear graph with gradient m and y intercept c will have equation $y = mx + c$. This principle allows you to sketch linear functions, and to recognise the equation of a given straight line graph. In order to compare the gradients of two linear functions, it is best to rearrange them (if necessary) into the form $y = mx + c$.

4. Two lines will be parallel if, and only if, their gradients have the same value.

5. Finally, the methods in this chapter apply to linear functions containing both x and y terms. You will occasionally encounter linear graphs that are purely vertical (equation $x =$ a constant) or purely horizontal ($y =$ a constant), like these:

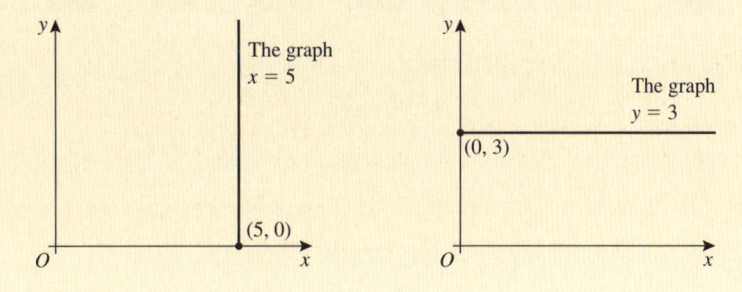

Internet Challenge 14

Parallels

Use the internet to help you answer these questions about parallels.

1. What name is given to a quadrilateral with two sets of parallel sides?

2. What name is given to a quadrilateral with only one set of parallel sides?

3. What is a parallelepiped? How do you draw one?

4. Which iconic rock group recorded the album 'Parallel Lines' in 1978?

5. What is the 49th parallel?

6. What are parallel universes?

7. What is the parallel postulate?

8. Where might you find a parallel port?

9. Where might you make a parallel turn?

10. 'Parallel lines never meet.' True or false?

11. Is it possible for two curves to be parallel?

12. Who might choose to place things in parallel rather than in series?

13. Look at the picture at the top of this page.
    a) How many of the lines running from left to right are parallel? Now check your answer with a ruler or straight edge.
    b) The picture is called 'Café Wall'. Find out the location of the café that inspired this picture, and the name of the mathematician who first described it.

CHAPTER 15

Simultaneous equations

In this chapter you will **learn how to**:
- solve simple simultaneous equations by inspection
- solve harder simultaneous equations by algebraic elimination
- solve simultaneous equations by graphical methods
- solve problems using simultaneous equations.

You will also be **challenged to**:
- investigate magic squares.

Starter: Fruity numbers

Each fruit symbol stands for a missing number – and has the same value each time it occurs.

Work out the value of each fruit.

cherry + cherry + cherry = 15

cherry + lemon + lemon = 11

cherry + lemon + apple = 20

apple − lemon − orange = 1

grapes + grapes + grapes + banana = 25

grapes + grapes + banana + banana = 22

15.1 Solving simultaneous equations by inspection

Sometimes you need to solve a pair of equations such as:

$$5x + 2y = 19$$
$$5x + 3y = 21$$

These are called **simultaneous equations**. The idea is to find a value for x and a matching value for y so that both equations are true together.

The method of **inspection** requires you to look at the two equations and spot any obvious slight differences between them. It should be used only for simple problems.

EXAMPLE

Solve the simultaneous equations:

$$5x + 2y = 19$$
$$5x + 3y = 21$$

SOLUTION

First, label the two equations as (1) and (2). Then compare them.

$$5x + 2y = 19 \quad (1)$$
$$5x + 3y = 21 \quad (2)$$

> You can see that equation (2) has an extra y on the left, and a total of 2 more on the right ($21 - 19$)

By inspection, $y = 2$

Now substitute this value into equation (1):

$$5x + 2 \times 2 = 19$$
$$5x + 4 = 19$$
$$5x = 19 - 4$$
$$5x = 15$$
$$x = 3$$

> Your answer should give values for both x and y.

So the final solution pair is $x = 3$ and $y = 2$

You can check your answer by substituting these values into the other equation, i.e. number (2):

$$5x + 3y = 5 \times 3 + 3 \times 2 = 15 + 6 = 21 \quad \text{as required.}$$

> Checking is a very good habit.

EXAMPLE

Solve the simultaneous equations: $3x + y = 7$
$5x + y = 5$

SOLUTION

$3x + y = 7$ (1)
$5x + y = 5$ (2)

> Equation (2) has an extra $2x$ on the left but is 2 less $(7 - 5)$ on the right, so $2x = -2$.

By inspection, $2x = -2$, so $x = -1$.

Now substitute this value into equation (1) to obtain:

$3 \times (-1) + y = 7$
$-3 + y = 7$
$y = 7 + 3$
$y = 10$

So the final solution pair is $x = -1$ and $y = 10$.

Check by substituting these values into equation (2):
$5x + y = 5 \times (-1) + 10 = -5 + 10 = 5$ as required.

EXERCISE 15.1

Solve these problems using the method of inspection. Write out all the stages clearly, as in the examples above.

1 $3x + 4y = 16$
$3x + 5y = 17$

2 $x + 4y = 15$
$x + 5y = 18$

3 $3x + y = 3$
$4x + y = 2$

4 $4x + 2y = 6$
$5x + 2y = 5$

5 $x + 8y = 4$
$x + 10y = 6$

6 $6x - y = 9$
$5x - y = 7$

7 $5x - 3y = 47$
$7x - 3y = 67$

8 $2x - y = 7$
$4x - y = 13$

9 $x + 2y = 3$
$x + 3y = 1$

10 $5x + 3y = 20$
$5x + 4y = 20$

15.2 Solving simultaneous equations by algebraic elimination

This method is used for most problems, if the answer is not obvious by inspection. The idea is to multiply one, or both, of the equations by a suitable multiplier, until they have a matching number of x's (or y's).

There are two variants of the elimination method, depending on the signs involved.

If the matching terms are the same, but one is positive and the other is negative, then you use the **addition** method. If, however, they are both positive or both negative, then you use the **subtraction** method instead. A useful rule is DASS: Different, Add; Same, Subtract!

EXAMPLE

Solve the simultaneous equations:

$2x - y = 8$

$x + 3y = 11$

SOLUTION

$2x - y = 8$ (1)

$x + 3y = 11$ (2)

> Look at the y terms. If you multiply equation (1) by 3 then they will both contain $3y$.

(1) × 3: $6x - 3y = 24$ (3)

(2) × 1: $x + 3y = 11$ (4)

Adding: $7x = 35$

$x = 35 \div 7$

$x = 5$

> The matching parts are $-3y$ and $+3y$.
> One of these is positive and the other negative, so you use the addition method.
> When you add $-3y$ and $+3y$ together there are no y's left at all.

Now substitute this value into equation (1) to obtain:

$2 \times (5) - y = 8$

$10 - y = 8$

$2 - y = 0$

$y = 2$

So the solution is $x = 5$ and $y = 2$

Check by substituting these values into equation (2):

$x + 3y = (5) + 3 \times (2) = 5 + 6 = 11$ as required.

EXAMPLE

Solve the simultaneous equations:

$7x + 2y = 24$

$5x + 3y = 25$

SOLUTION

$7x + 2y = 24$ (1)

$5x + 3y = 25$ (2)

> Look at the y terms. If you multiply equation (1) by 3 and equation (2) by 2 then they will both contain $6y$.

(1) × 3: $21x + 6y = 72$ (3)

(2) × 2: $10x + 6y = 50$ (4)

Subtracting: $11x = 22$

$x = 22 \div 11$

$x = 2$

> The matching parts are $+6y$ and $+6y$.
> These are both positive, so you use the subtraction method.
> When you subtract $+6y$ from $+6y$ there are no y's left at all.

Now substitute this value into equation (1) to obtain:

$$7 \times (2) + 2y = 24$$
$$14 + 2y = 24$$
$$2y = 24 - 14$$
$$2y = 10$$
$$y = 5$$

So the solution is $x = 2$ and $y = 5$

Check by substituting these values into equation (2):

$$5x + 3y = 5 \times (2) + 3 \times (5) = 10 + 15 = 25 \quad \text{as required.}$$

Take care when subtracting a quantity that is negative to begin with; a double minus generates a plus in this case.

EXAMPLE

Solve the simultaneous equations:

$$x + 2y = 4$$
$$5x - 7y = 3$$

SOLUTION

$$x + 2y = 4 \quad (1)$$
$$5x - 7y = 4 \quad (2)$$

(1) × 5: $\quad 5x + 10y = 20 \quad (3)$

(2): $\quad\quad\quad 5x - 7y = 3 \quad (4)$

Subtracting: $\quad 17y = 17$

$10y - -7y$ gives $10y + 7y = 17y$

$$y = 1$$

Now substitute this value into equation (1) to obtain:

$$x + 2 \times (1) = 4$$
$$x + 2 = 4$$
$$x = 4 - 2$$
$$x = 2$$

So the solution is $x = 2$ and $y = 1$

Check by substituting these values into equation (2):

$$5x - 7y = 5 \times (2) - 7 \times (1) = 10 - 7 = 3 \quad \text{as required.}$$

This final example shows the subtraction method applied again, this time when both the matching terms are negative.

EXAMPLE

Solve the simultaneous equations:

$5x - 2y = 25$

$4x - 3y = 13$

SOLUTION

$5x - 2y = 25$ (1)

$4x - 3y = 13$ (2)

Look at the y terms. If you multiply equation (1) by 3 and equation (2) by 2 then they will both contain $-6y$.

(1) × 3: $15x - 6y = 75$ (3)

(2) × 2: $8x - 6y = 26$ (4)

The matching parts are $-6y$ and $-6y$. These are both negative, so you use the subtraction method. When you subtract $-6y$ from $-6y$ there are no y's left at all.

Subtracting: $7x = 49$

$x = 49 \div 7$

$x = 7$

Now substitute this value into equation (1) to obtain

$5 \times (7) - 2y = 25$

$35 - 2y = 25$

$10 - 2y = 0$

$2y = 10$

$y = 5$

So the solution is $x = 7$ and $y = 5$

Check by substituting these values into equation (2):

$4x - 3y = 4 \times (7) - 3 \times (5) = 28 - 15 = 13$ as required.

EXERCISE 15.2

Solve questions **1** to **8** using the algebraic *addition* method. Write out all the stages clearly, as in the worked examples above.

1 $4x + 2y = 22$
    $3x - 2y = 6$

2 $x - 3y = 4$
    $4x + 3y = 1$

3 $5x - y = 9$
    $3x + 2y = 8$

4 $x + y = 1$
    $4x - 3y = 11$

5 $2x + 5y = 20$
    $x - 2y = 1$

6 $3x + 2y = 5$
    $5x - 4y = 1$

7 $x - 2y = 9$
    $2x + 3y = 4$

8 $3x + 4y = -8$
    $11x - 5y = 10$

Solve questions **9** to **16** using the algebraic *subtraction* method, showing all your working clearly.

9 $2x + y = 6$
    $x + 3y = 13$

10 $2x + 3y = 13$
    $x + 2y = 8$

11 $9x + 2y = 5$
    $3x + y = 1$

12 $4x - 3y = 5$
    $x - y = 1$

13 $3x - 2y = 2$
    $5x - 3y = 3$

14 $x + 4y = 2$
    $2x + 5y = 10$

15 $6x - y = 4$
    $2x - 3y = 28$

16 $x - 4y = 10$
    $2x - 7y = 18$

Solve questions **17** to **32** using algebra. For each question you will have to decide whether the addition method or the subtraction method is appropriate. Remember to show all the stages of your working.

17 $2x + 3y = 9$ $x - y = 2$	**18** $x - y = 5$ $4x - 3y = 19$	**19** $6x + y = 18$ $7x - 2y = 2$	**20** $4x - y = -1$ $3x - 4y = 9$
21 $x + 2y = 5$ $3x - 4y = 10$	**22** $3x - 6y = 9$ $x + 2y = 9$	**23** $x + y = 0$ $x - y = 6$	**24** $2x + y = 10$ $x + 11y = 5$
25 $14x + 3y = 7$ $5x - 2y = 24$	**26** $3x - 4y = 3$ $x + 6y = 12$	**27** $5x + 3y = 1$ $7x + 5y = 1$	**28** $3x - 8y = 22$ $2x - 12y = 23$
29 $3x - 2y = 33$ $2x + 3y = -4$	**30** $x - y = 4$ $4x - 6y = 21$	**31** $5x - 3y = 34$ $7x - 4y = 47$	**32** $x - 4y = 18$ $2x - 5y = 21$

15.3 Solving simultaneous equations by a graphical method

This method is quick and simple – it is particularly effective if the answers are whole numbers. When they are decimals, however, it becomes less accurate than the algebraic method.

EXAMPLE

Solve, graphically, the simultaneous equations:

$$4x + y = 6$$
$$5x - 4y = 18$$

SOLUTION

Consider, first, the equation $4x + y = 6$.

When $x = 0$ then $4x + y = 6$, giving $y = 6$.

Thus the graph passes through $(0, 6)$.

When $y = 0$ then $4x + y = 6$, giving $x = 1.5$.

Thus the graph passes through $(1.5, 0)$.

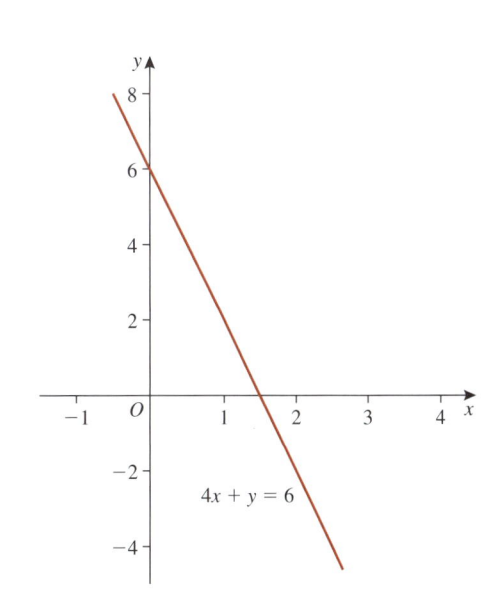

Next, consider the second equation, $5x - 4y = 18$.

When $x = 0$ then $5x - 4y = 18$, giving $y = -4.5$.

Thus the graph passes through $(0, -4.5)$.

When $y = 0$ then $5x - 4y = 18$, giving $x = 3.6$.

Thus the graph passes through $(3.6, 0)$.

Adding this line to the previous graph, we obtain this graph:

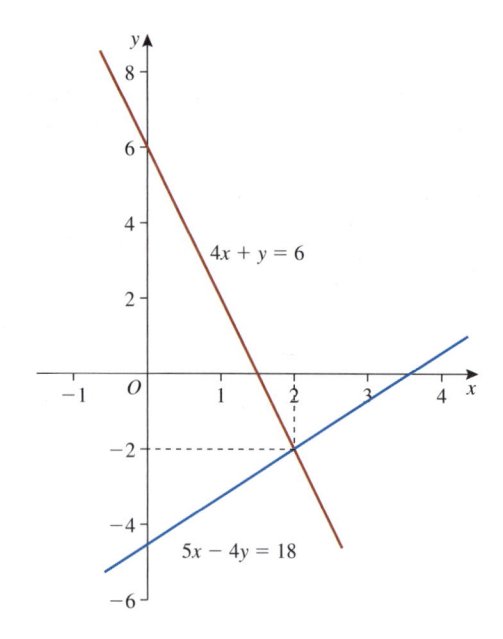

The solution occurs where these two lines cross.

From the graph, this can be read off as $x = 2, y = -2$

EXERCISE 15.3

For each of these questions draw a set of coordinate axes on squared paper (or graph paper). Draw the lines corresponding to each equation, and hence solve the simultaneous equations graphically.

1. $3x + y = 6$
   $x + y = 4$

2. $x + y = 10$
   $y = 2x - 2$

3. $x + 2y = 10$
   $2x + y = 14$

4. $x - y = 6$
   $2x + y = 12$

5. $2x + 3y = 18$
   $x + y = 7$

6. $y = x + 2$
   $x + y = 10$

7. $y = x - 1$
   $x + y = 7$

8. $x + 4y = 14$
   $3x - y = 3$

15.4 Setting up and solving problems using simultaneous equations

Although many exam questions on simultaneous equations will already be set up for you, it is important that you learn how to set them up when needed. This section shows you how to formulate such problems, which can then be solved by the algebraic method.

EXAMPLE

A theatre has two different ticket prices, one for adults and another for children. A party of 6 adults and 10 children has to pay £38, while for 5 adults and 12 children the cost is £39.

a) Write this information as two simultaneous equations.

b) Solve your equations to find the cost of an adult ticket and the cost of a child's ticket.

SOLUTION

a) Let the cost of an adult ticket be £x, and that of a child's ticket, £y.

$6x + 10y = 38$
$5x + 12y = 39$

> Remember to define the symbols you are going to use …
>
> …. then use them to represent the given information.

b) Multiplying the first equation by 6 and the second by 5, we obtain:

$36x + 60y = 228$
$25x + 60y = 195$

Subtracting:

$11x = 33$
$x = 33 \div 11$
$x = 3$

Substituting back into the first equation, we have:

$6 \times (3) + 10y = 38$
$18 + 10y = 38$
$10y = 38 - 18$
$10y = 20$
$y = 2$

Thus an adult ticket costs £3 and a child's ticket costs £2.

EXERCISE 15.4

Use simultaneous equations to help you solve the following problems. Remember to show all your working carefully.

1 A clothes shop is having a sale. All the shirts are reduced to one price. All the jackets are reduced to a single price as well, though they remain more expensive than the shirts. Arthur buys 10 shirts and 3 jackets, and pays £104. Alan buys 4 shirts and one jacket, and pays £38.

   a) Write two simultaneous equations to express this information.

   b) Solve your equations, to find the price of a shirt and the price of a jacket.

2 A hire company has a fleet of coaches and minibuses. Three coaches and four minibuses can carry 180 passengers, while five coaches and two minibuses can carry 230 passengers.

   a) Write two simultaneous equations to express this information.

   b) How many passengers can one coach carry?

3 A mathematics teacher buys some books for her A-level and GCSE students. A-level books cost £10 each, and GCSE books £15 each. She spends a total of £1800, buying a total of 160 books in all.

   a) Write two simultaneous equations to express this information, defining your symbols clearly.

   b) Solve your equations to find how many of each type of book she buys.

4 A shop sells tins of paint in 2 litre and 5 litre cans. The manager checks the amount of paint he has in stock, and finds that there are 500 cans altogether. These cans hold a total of 1420 litres of paint.
   a) Write two simultaneous equations to express this information. Explain the meaning of the symbols you use.
   b) Solve your equations to find the number of each size of can in stock.

5 A plant stall at a school fete sells tomato plants and pepper plants. Martin buys two tomato plants and four pepper plants for £2.50, while Suzy buys five tomato plants and three pepper plants for £3.10. Work out the cost of each type of plant.

REVIEW EXERCISE 15

Solve these simultaneous equations by inspection.

1 $3x + 4y = 24$
   $3x + 5y = 27$

2 $x + 5y = 16$
   $x - 2y = 16$

3 $5x + 2y = 5$
   $3x + 2y = 7$

4 $8x - 3y = 11$
   $8x - 7y = 15$

Solve these by the elimination (addition or subtraction) method.

5 $x + 3y = 7$
   $4x + y = 17$

6 $6x + y = 11$
   $4x + 5y = 3$

7 $3x - 2y = 13$
   $4x + 3y = 6$

8 $3x - 4y = 5$
   $2x - 5y = 8$

9 $x + 2y = 6$
   $x - 2y = 4$

10 $3x - 4y = 8$
   $5x - 6y = 13$

11 $2x - 3y = 13$
   $10x + y = 1$

12 $5x + 4y = 4$
   $x - 2y = 5$

13 The diagram shows part of the graph of $2x + y = 11$.

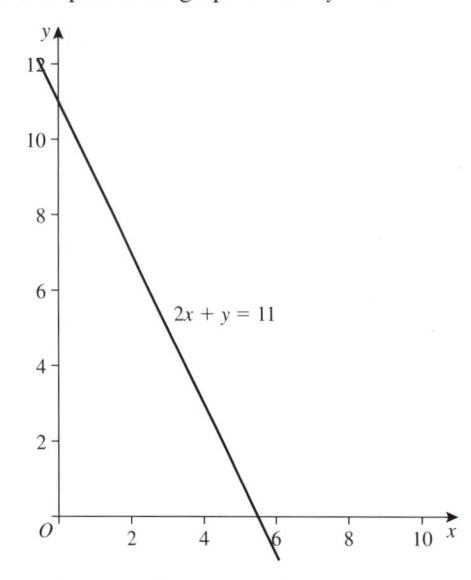

   a) Make a copy of this graph on squared paper or graph paper.
   b) On the same diagram, plot the graph of the line $4x + 5y = 40$.
   c) Hence solve the simultaneous equations $2x + y = 11$, $4x + 5y = 40$.

14 The diagram shows part of the graph of $2x + 3y = 18$.

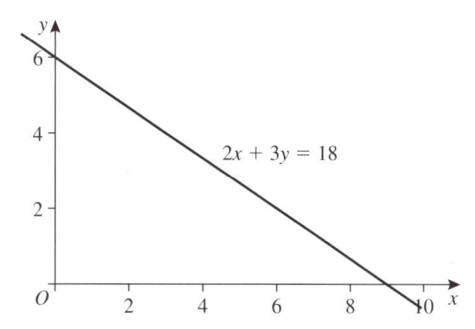

a) Make a copy of this graph on squared paper or graph paper.
b) On the same diagram, plot the graph of the line $y = x + 1$.
c) Hence solve the simultaneous equations $y = x + 1$, $2x + 3y = 18$.

15 Use a graphical method to solve the simultaneous equations:
$$5x + 3y = 30$$
$$y = x - 2$$

16 At a seaside drinks stall you can buy cans of cola and cans or orange drink. Five cans of cola and one can of orange cost £2.07. Two cans of cola and three cans of orange cost £1.66.
a) Using x to represent the cost of a can of cola and y to represent the cost of a can of orange, in pence, write this information as two simultaneous equations.
b) Solve your equations to find the cost of each type of drink.

17 A potter is making cups and saucers. Each cup takes c minutes to produce, and each saucer takes s minutes. The potter can produce three cups and two saucers in 19 minutes, while it would take exactly half an hour to produce four cups and five saucers.
a) Write this information as two simultaneous equations.
b) Solve your equations, to find the values of c and s.
c) How long would it take to produce a set of six cups and six saucers?

18 A phone network charges x pence per minute for telephone calls, and y pence for each text message sent. 100 minutes and 50 texts cost £4, while 150 minutes and 100 texts cost £6.50.
a) Write this information as two simultaneous equations.
b) Solve your equations to find the values of x and y.
c) How much would it cost for 300 minutes and 50 texts?

19 Solve the simultaneous equations:
$$4x + y = 8$$
$$2x - 3y = 11$$
[Edexcel]

20 Solve:
$$2x - 3y = 11$$
$$5x + 2y = 18$$
[Edexcel]

KEY POINTS

1. Simple simultaneous equations may be solved by inspection. This method works well if the two equations are almost the same, and you can then examine the slight differences between them for clues to the values of the unknown quantities.

2. In practice, the most frequently used method is that of algebraic elimination. Multiply one or both of the equations by a suitable scaling factor, so the x (or y) coefficients are numerically the same in both equations. If the matching coefficients are one positive and one negative, then you add the two equations to achieve the elimination. If they are both positive, or both negative, then you must subtract one equation from the other instead. Remember DASS:

   Different signs
   Add

   Same sign
   Subtract

3. The graphical method of solution can be quite neat, but it is not reliable if the solutions are not whole numbers or simple decimals.

Internet Challenge 15

Magic squares

In a magic square each row, column and diagonal adds up to the same total, known as the square constant.

Here is a 3 by 3 magic square, with a square constant of 15.

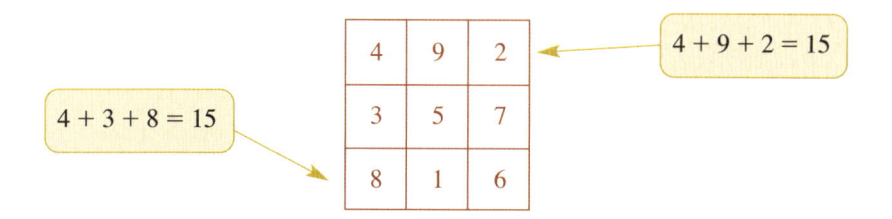

4	9	2
3	5	7
8	1	6

$4 + 9 + 2 = 15$

$4 + 3 + 8 = 15$

1 Try to make a 4 by 4 magic square using the numbers 1 to 16. The square constant will be 34. (This is quite difficult!)

2 Use the internet to find a picture of Albrecht Dürer's engraving *Melancholia*. What do you find in the top right corner of the picture?

3 Magic squares with an odd number of rows/columns are much easier to make than those with an even number of rows. Use the internet to find a procedure for making odd-sized magic squares. Then use the procedure to make:
   a) a 5 by 5 magic square
   b) an 11 by 11 magic square.

4 An 8 by 8 magic square was constructed by Benjamin Franklin in the nineteenth century.
   a) Use the internet to find a copy of Franklin's 8 by 8 square, and print it out.
   b) Using a red pen, join the numbers 1, 2, 3, …, 16 using a set of straight lines. Now do the same for the numbers 17, 18, 19, …, 32. What do you notice?
   c) Using a blue pen, join the numbers 33, 34, 35, …, 48 using a set of straight lines. Now do the same for the numbers 49, 50, 51, …, 64. What do you notice?
   d) Try to find out some other interesting properties of Franklin's square.
   e) Find out a little about the life and achievements of Benjamin Franklin.

5 The image to the right shows the world's oldest known magic square.
   a) By what name is this square known?
   b) Approximately when does it date from?

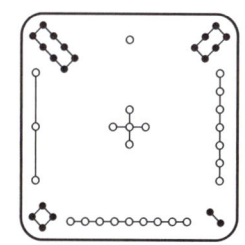

CHAPTER 16

Inequalities

In this chapter you will learn how to:
- solve simple linear inequalities in one variable
- represent solution sets on a number line
- solve linear inequalities in two variables and find the solution set.

You will also be challenged to:
- investigate mathematical symbols.

Starter: Treasure hunt

Here is a map of Treasure Island. The pirates have buried their treasure at a place where the x and y coordinates are whole numbers. Use the clues to work out where the treasure is buried.

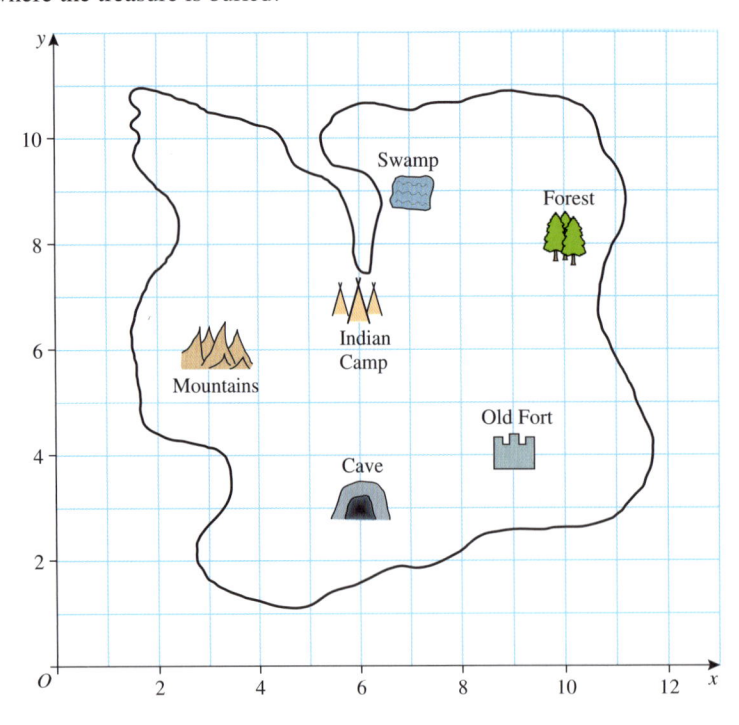

Clue 1: x is greater than 5.
Clue 2: y is greater than 6.
Clue 3: One of x and y is prime, and the other is not.
Clue 4: x and y add up to 16.

16.1 Whole-number solutions to inequalities

Inequalities are similar, in many ways, to equations. Simple inequality problems with whole number (integer) solutions may be solved at sight, but you will need to use algebraic and graphical methods for dealing with harder problems where the solutions need not be integers.

In this chapter you will be working with these four symbols:

$<$ less than
$>$ greater than
$\leqslant$ less than or equal to
$\geqslant$ greater than or equal to

For example, $x < 3$ would be read as 'x is less than 3'. $y \geqslant 6$ would be read as 'y is greater than or equal to 6'. The narrow end of the symbol points to the smaller quantity.

EXAMPLE

Write down whole-number solutions to these inequalities:
a) $x > 5$
b) $y \leqslant 6$
c) $3 \leqslant z < 10$

SOLUTION

a) 6, 7, 8, 9, 10, …
b) …, 2, 3, 4, 5, 6
c) 3, 4, 5, 6, 7, 8, 9

> This means that z lies between 3 and 10.

> Dots indicate that the number pattern continues beyond those written down.

EXAMPLE

Find the whole-number solutions to these inequalities:
a) $2x > 5$
b) $3y \leqslant 6$
c) $3 \leqslant 2z < 10$

SOLUTION

a) $2x > 5$
   Dividing both sides by 2, we obtain $x > 2\frac{1}{2}$.
   Since x has to be a whole number, the possible values are 3, 4, 5, 6, 7, …

b) $3y \leqslant 6$
   Dividing both sides by 3, we obtain $y \leqslant 2$.
   The whole-number solutions are …, −2, −1, 0, 1, 2

c) $3 \leqslant 2z < 10$
   Dividing through by 2, we obtain $1\frac{1}{2} \leqslant z < 5$.
   The integer solutions are 2, 3 and 4

EXERCISE 16.1

Find the whole-number (integer) solutions to each of these inequalities.

1. $x > 3$
2. $2x > 5$
3. $y < 4$
4. $3y < 7$
5. $0 < y \leq 6$
6. $0 \leq 2p \leq 13$
7. $1 < x < 3$
8. $1 \leq 2w \leq 3$
9. $1 < z - 1 < 5$
10. $1 < 2z < 5$
11. $1 \leq z \leq 5$
12. $1 \leq 2z \leq 5$
13. $2x \leq 11$
14. $3x > 10$
15. $7 < 2y + 3 \leq 13$
16. $5 > g \geq 1$
17. $14 \geq 3x > 0$
18. $10 < 2x \leq 20$
19. $98 \leq t + 1 \leq 99$
20. $-3 < u < 3$

16.2 Using algebra to solve linear inequalities

In the previous section you solved inequalities using whole numbers. The solution could be listed as a set of whole numbers, for example 2, 3, 4, 5, 6.

If you are not told that the solution is a whole number, then you must leave your solution as an inequality, covering a range of possible values. When this inequality is in its simplest form, you are said to have solved the inequality.

To solve an inequality, you can use similar methods to those used for solving equations, such as:

- You can add (or subtract) the same number to both sides.
- You can multiply (or divide) both sides by the same positive number.

You should *not*, however, multiply or divide both sides by a *negative* number, as this would cause the direction of the inequality to reverse, and may well introduce a mistake.

EXAMPLE

Solve, algebraically, the inequality $3x - 8 \leq 30 + x$.

SOLUTION

$3x - 8 \leq 30 + x$ First, subtract x from both sides.
$3x - 8 - x \leq 30$
$2x - 8 \leq 30$ Next, add 8 to both sides.
$2x \leq 30 + 8$
$2x \leq 38$ Finally, divide both sides by 2.
$x \leq 19$

Your work will be more accurate, and easier to follow, if you process only a small step at each stage. Also, the lines of working should be aligned at the inequality signs.

Note: Make sure you do **not** use any equals signs (=) anywhere.

EXAMPLE

Solve, algebraically, the inequality $10 - 3x < 30 + 2x$.

SOLUTION

$$10 - 3x < 30 + 2x$$
$$10 < 30 + 2x + 3x$$
$$10 < 30 + 5x$$
$$10 - 30 < 5x$$
$$-20 < 5x$$
$$-4 < x$$

Note the alignment here.

It would be a bad idea to take $2x$ from both sides to begin with, because $10 - 5x < 30$ is leading towards a solution that will require you to divide by a negative number: this is best avoided.

EXERCISE 16.2

Solve, algebraically, these inequalities.

1. $x + 5 \geq 13$
2. $3x - 1 > 14$
3. $10x + 43 < 13$
4. $6 + x < 10 - x$
5. $2x - 5 < x + 1$
6. $3x + 11 \leq 17 + x$
7. $5x \geq x + 20$
8. $32 + x < 12 + 6x$
9. $16 + x \leq 10 + 4x$
10. $3(x + 2) > x + 4$
11. $2x + 13 \geq 41 - 5x$
12. $6x + 1 < 28$
13. $13 - x > 5 + 3x$
14. $x + 15 \leq 7 - x$
15. $3x + 7 \leq x + 7$
16. $16 - x < 2x + 31$
17. $144 \geq 360 - 6x$
18. $4 + 3x < 4 - x$
19. $6(x + 2) \geq x + 7$
20. $3(2x + 3) < 4(x + 4)$

21. Solve the inequality $\dfrac{x}{2} - 3 \leq 4$

22. Solve the inequality $\dfrac{3x - 1}{2} > 7$

23. Solve the inequality $\dfrac{x}{3} + 1 < 10$

24. Solve the inequality $\dfrac{x + 1}{3} \geq 4$

16.3 Illustrating inequalities on a number line

In the first section of this chapter you learned how to list the solution set as a list of whole numbers, but this is not usually possible in more general problems where x is not restricted to being an integer. The solutions may, however, be illustrated graphically by means of a 'thermometer diagram' drawn alongside a number line. The end of the line is left as an open 'bulb' if it is not to be included, or filled in if it is included.

This symbol shows a region not including the end-points:

○────────○ , for example $-2 < x < 5$

This region includes the left-hand end but not the right-hand end:

, for example $-2 \leqslant x < 5$

This region includes both end-points:

, for example $-2 \leqslant x \leqslant 5$

Note: We never combine $<$ and $>$ in one single inequality.

EXAMPLE

Solve the inequality $6 + x < 13$ and illustrate the solution with a number line diagram.

SOLUTION

$6 + x < 13$
$x < 13 - 6$
$x < 7$

The solid line shows that x can take any value below 7 …

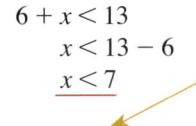

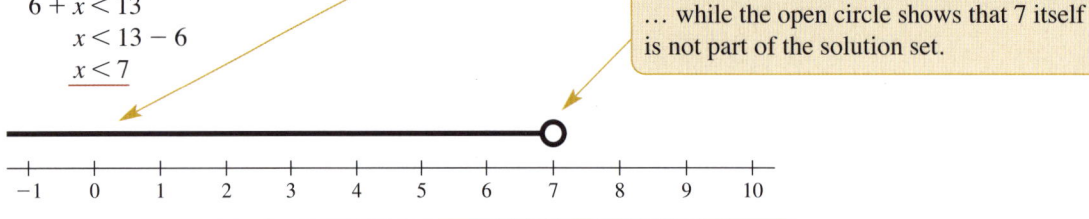

… while the open circle shows that 7 itself is not part of the solution set.

EXAMPLE

Solve the inequality $x - 6 \leqslant 2x - 5$ and illustrate the solution with a diagram.

SOLUTION

$x - 6 \leqslant 2x - 5$
$-6 \leqslant 2x - 5 - x$
$-6 \leqslant x - 5$
$-6 + 5 \leqslant x$
$-1 \leqslant x$

The filled circle shows that -1 is part of the solution.

The solid line shows that all values above -1 are part of the solution.

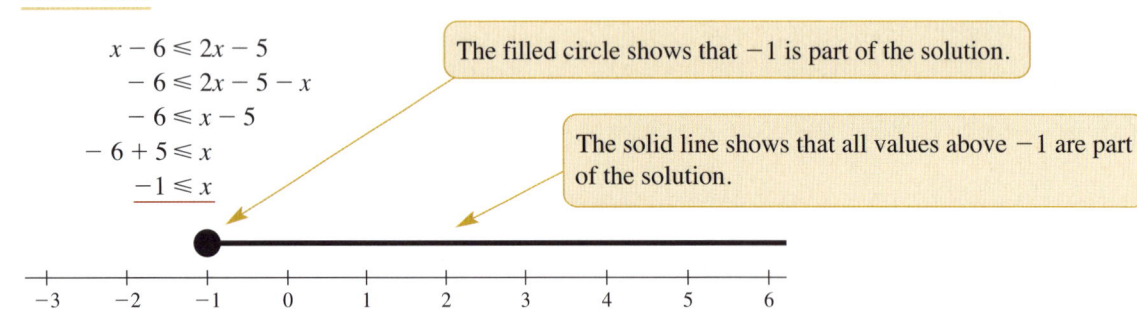

EXERCISE 16.3

In questions **1** to **10** you are given the solution to an inequality. Draw a suitable number line diagram to illustrate the solution in each case.

1 $x < 5$ **2** $x \geqslant 2$ **3** $1 \leqslant x \leqslant 5$ **4** $-2 < x < 2$

5 $x \leqslant 7$ **6** $x < -1$ **7** $-3 < x < 0$ **8** $-4 < x \leqslant -1$

9 $-2 \leqslant x \leqslant 2$ **10** $x > 2.5$

In questions **11** to **20**, solve each inequality and then illustrate it with a line diagram.

11 $5 + x < 19$ **12** $3x - 2 \leq 13$ **13** $20 - x > 10$ **14** $5x + 4 \geq 19$

15 $10 < 2x < 17$ **16** $15 - x < 2x - 3$ **17** $2x + 1 \leq 5x - 11$ **18** $3x - 1 < 11 - x$

19 $20 - x < 6x - 1$ **20** $9x + 1 \leq 2(x - 3)$

16.4 Graphs of linear inequalities in two variables

Suppose two variables x and y are restricted by a rule such as $x + y < 5$. The solution set is the set of all possible combinations of values for x and y so that $x + y$ does not exceed 5. Obviously any (x, y) point on the line $x + y = 5$ will meet this condition, but there are others too, as shown in the diagram below.

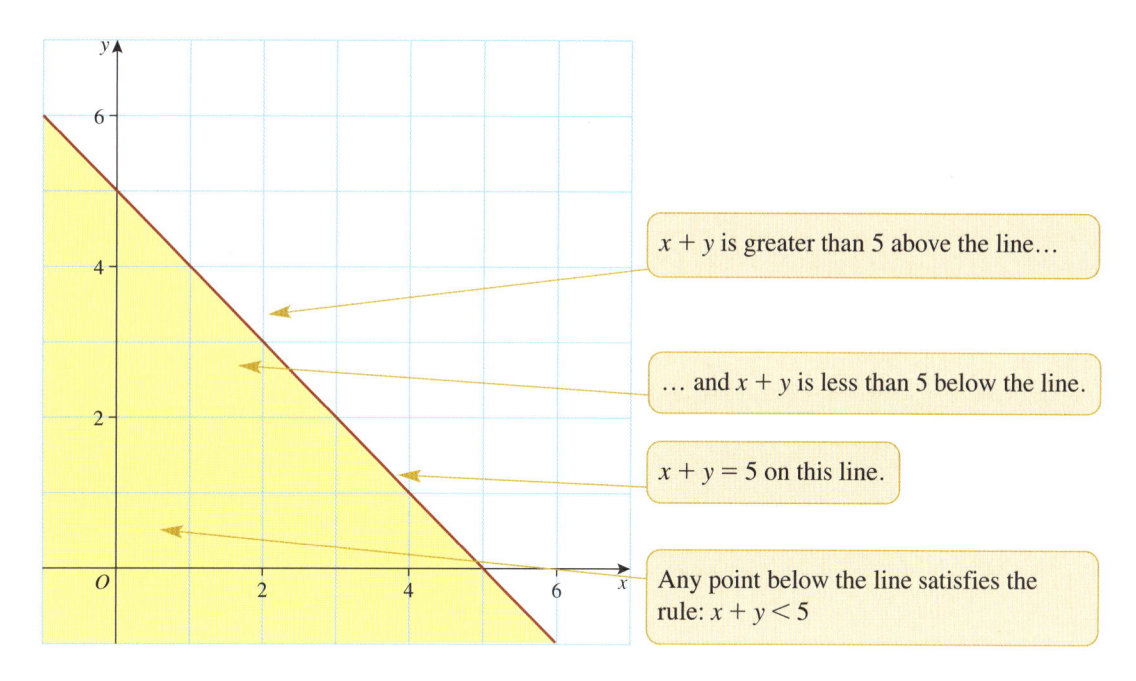

$x + y$ is greater than 5 above the line…

… and $x + y$ is less than 5 below the line.

$x + y = 5$ on this line.

Any point below the line satisfies the rule: $x + y < 5$

Examination questions are likely to include more than one inequality, so the required region is bounded by several straight lines, as in the example below.

EXAMPLE

The point (x, y) satisfies the following inequalities:

$x > 1, x < 3, y < 4, y > x$

a) Illustrate these inequalities on a graph, shading the region that satisfies all four inequalities. Label your region R.
b) The point P lies in the region R. The coordinates of P are integers. Write down the coordinates of P.

SOLUTION

a) First, draw the four straight lines $x = 1$, $x = 3$, $y = 4$ and $y = x$.

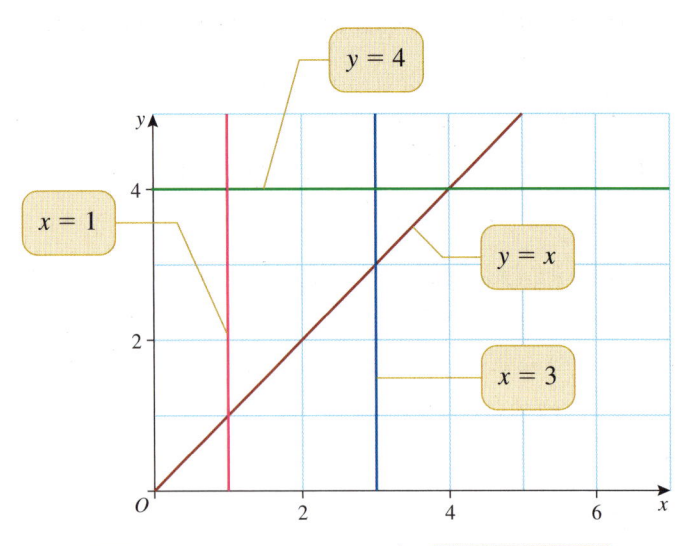

Next, shade the region corresponding to the inequalities.

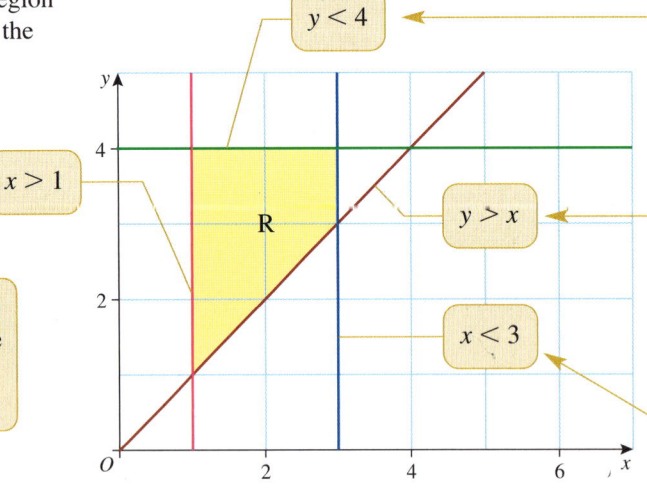

- $y = 4$
- $x = 1$
- $y = x$
- $x = 3$

- $y < 4$
- $y < 4$ means the y coordinates lie *below* the line $y = 4$
- $x > 1$
- $x > 1$ means the x coordinates lie to the *right* of the line $x = 1$
- $y > x$
- $y > x$ means the y coordinates are greater than if they were on the line $y = x$, so the region is *above* the line.
- $x < 3$
- $x < 3$ means the x coordinates lie to the *left* of the line $x = 3$

b) P lies within the region R and has integer coordinates:

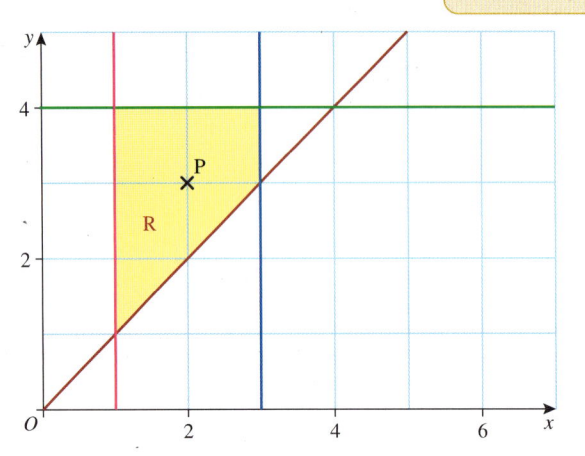

Thus P is at (2, 3)

EXERCISE 16.4

For each of questions **1** to **5**, draw a coordinate grid in which x and y can range from 0 to 10.

1. Draw the graphs of these straight lines:
   $x = 2, x = 5, y = 1, y = x$

   Hence shade the region R corresponding to the inequalities:
   $x \geq 2, x < 5, y > 1, y \leq x$

2. Draw the graphs of these straight lines:
   $x = 2, y = 2, y = 7, y = x - 1$

   Hence shade the region R corresponding to the inequalities:
   $x > 2, y > 2, y < 7, y > x - 1$

3. Draw the graphs of these straight lines:
   $x = 9, y = 7, y = x$

   Hence shade the region R corresponding to the inequalities:
   $x < 9, y > 7, y < x$

4. Shade the region R corresponding to the inequalities:
   $x > 3, x \leq 7, y > 1, x + y \leq 10$

5. Shade the region R corresponding to the inequalities:
   $x > 0, y > 1, y < x + 4, x + y < 8$

6. The diagram shows a region R bounded by three straight lines, L_1, L_2 and L_3.

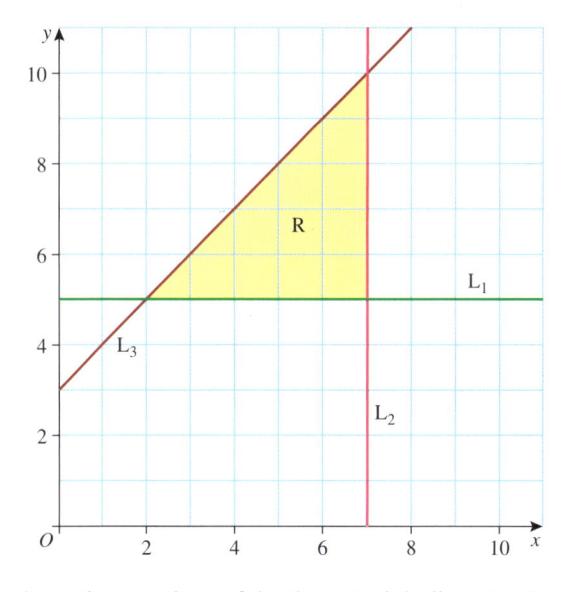

   a) Write down the equations of the three straight lines, L_1, L_2 and L_3. Show clearly which equation applies to which line.
   b) Write down three inequalities that define the region R.

REVIEW EXERCISE 16

Find whole-number solutions to these inequalities:

1. $0 \leqslant 2x \leqslant 7$
2. $1 < 3y < 27$
3. $8 \leqslant 2n < 18$
4. $5 < 2x + 1 < 20$
5. $-3 \leqslant 2t - 1 \leqslant 12$
6. $2 < \frac{1}{2}x < 4$
7. $4 \leqslant 3m + 2 < 9$
8. $5 < 2(x + 1) \leqslant 12$
9. $6 \leqslant 3(x - 2) \leqslant 12$
10. $8 < 5t < 11$

Solve these linear inequalities. Illustrate each one on a number line.

11. $7 \leqslant 2x + 5$
12. $6 < 4 - x$
13. $5x + 3 < 18$
14. $3x - 7 \leqslant 11$
15. $2 \leqslant 2x + 4 < 7$
16. $3 < 4x + 3 \leqslant 11$
17. $5x + 1 < 2x + 7$
18. $2x + 17 < 7x + 2$
19. $3 \leqslant x + 5 < 19 - x$
20. $15 - x < 2x - 3 \leqslant x + 6$

21. The diagram shows the graphs of the lines $y = \frac{1}{2}x + 4$, $y = x - 1$ and $x = 3$.

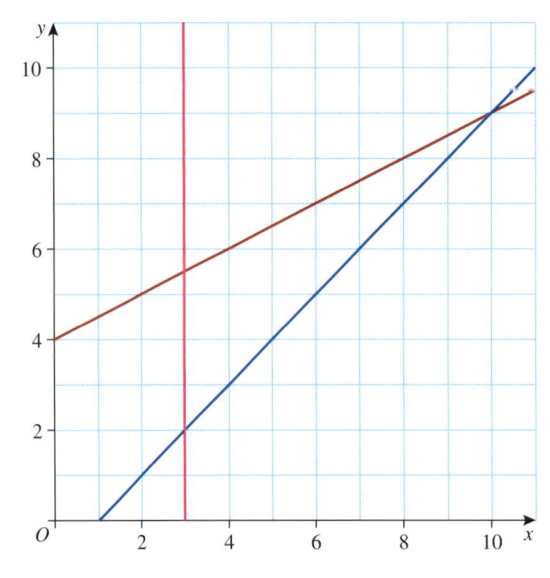

a) Make a copy of this diagram.
The point P(x, y) has integer coordinates. P satisfies the inequalities:
$$y < \tfrac{1}{2}x + 4,\ y > x - 1,\ x > 3$$
b) Mark on your diagram, with a cross, each of the points where P could lie.

22 a) $-2 < x \leq 1$ and x is an integer. Write down all the possible values of x.
   b) $-2 < x \leq 1$, $y > -2$ and $y < x + 1$ and x and y are integers. On a copy of the grid, mark with a cross (×) each of the six points which satisfies *all* these three inequalities.

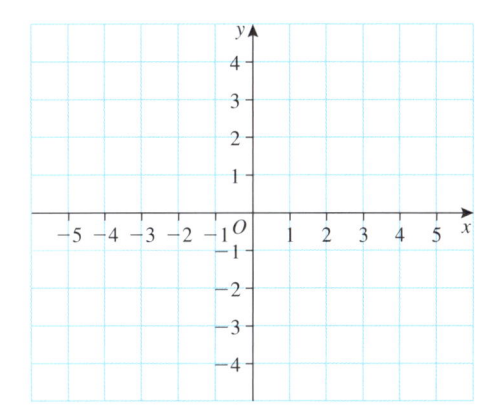

[Edexcel]

23 n is a whole number such that $6 < 2n < 13$. List all the possible values of n. [Edexcel]

24 a) Solve the inequality $4y + 3 \geq 1$.
   b) Write down the smallest **integer** value of y which satisfies the inequality
   $$4y + 3 \geq 1$$
   [Edexcel]

25 The line with equation $6y + 5x = 15$ is drawn on the grid below.

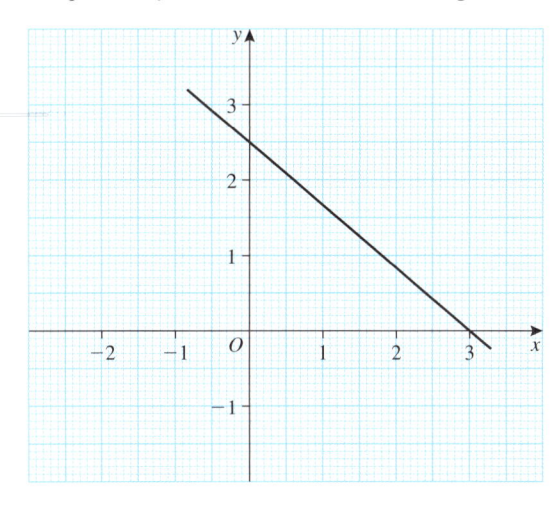

a) Rearrange the equation $6y + 5x = 15$ to make y the subject.
b) The point $(-21, k)$ lies on the line. Find the value of k.
c) (i) On a copy of the grid, shade the region of points whose coordinates satisfy the four inequalities:
   $$y > 0, x > 0, 2x < 3, 6y + 5x < 15$$
   Label this region R.
P is a point in the region R. The coordinates of P are both integers.
(ii) Write down the coordinates of P.

[Edexcel]

16 Inequalities U4 243

26 a) (i) Solve the inequality $5x - 7 < 2x - 1$.
  (ii) Copy this number line, and use it to represent the solution set to part **(i)**.

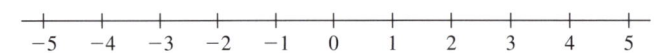

n is an integer such that $-4 \leqslant 2n < 3$.
b) Write down the possible values of n. [Edexcel]

KEY POINTS

1. Inequalities may be manipulated using many of the methods applicable to ordinary equations.

2. The solution to an inequality is usually a range of values, rather than just a single value.

   For example, the solution to $5x + 1 < 16$ is $x < 3$.

3. It is best to avoid multiplying or dividing an inequality by a negative number, since this causes the direction of the inequality to reverse.

4. Solutions to inequalities in one variable may be shown on a number line, using a 'thermometer diagram'. For example, to represent $-1 < x \leqslant 3$ we have:

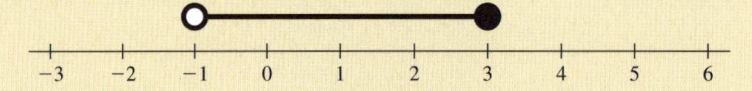

   The open bulb shows that -1 is not to be included. The filled bulb shows that 3 is included.

5. Inequalities in two variables are usually represented on a coordinate grid. Turn the inequalities into equations first, and plot the lines. Then decide which side of the line represents the required solution set.

6. In the examination you will usually have to plot several lines, and find the intersection of the corresponding regions. Integer solutions will often be asked for in both one- and two-variable inequalities.

Internet Challenge 16

Investigating mathematical symbols

The mathematical symbols we use nowadays have evolved over a long period of time, from many different and diverse cultures. In this investigation you will try to uncover the origins of some of the more widely used symbols – some of these symbols will be quite familiar to you, but there may be others that you have not yet encountered.

Here are some mathematical symbols, and some facts about them. Unfortunately the symbols and the facts have become jumbled up. Match the symbols to the corresponding fact.

∞	The Golden Ratio.
$<$	The eighteenth letter of the Greek alphabet, denotes 'the sum of'.
$\sqrt{}$	This 17th century symbol was formerly used in Europe to indicate subtraction.
ϕ	A sculpture of this symbol, by Marta Pan, stands on the A6 roadside in France.
θ	The (not real) square root of -1.
$\div$	First used in Harriot's *Artis Analyticae Praxis* in 1631.
$=$	This originated from Hindu mathematics, where it was known as *sunya*.
i	Invented by Robert Recorde in 1557.
Σ	The eighth letter of the Greek alphabet, used to denote an unknown angle.
0	This 16th century symbol may be a corrupted abbreviation for *radix*.

Try to find out some more facts about each symbol.

CHAPTER 17

Travel and other graphs

In this chapter you will **learn how to**:
- use straight line graphs to model real-life situations
- draw graphs to represent rates of change, such as in containers being filled with water
- solve problems using travel graphs.

You will also be **challenged to**:
- investigate speeds of artificial objects.

Starter: Animal races

Here is some information about the speeds of various animals.

Giant tortoise	Ostrich
0.17 miles per hour	40 miles per hour

Human	Cheetah
28 miles per hour	70 miles per hour

Black mamba snake	Garden snail
20 miles per hour	0.03 miles per hour

1 How many times faster is the ostrich, compared with the giant tortoise?

2 How many times faster is the cheetah, compared with the garden snail?

3 How long would it take a black mamba to travel 100 yards?

4 How far (in yards) can a garden snail travel during one night of 12 hours?

Note: 1 mile = 1760 yards.

17.1 Modelling with straight line graphs

Many real-life situations can be described, or modelled, by linear graphs. The price charged by a carpet shop increases steadily as the length of the carpet increases, for example. Similarly the amount of fuel in a car fuel tank decreases at a steady rate as the car cruises along a motorway at constant speed.

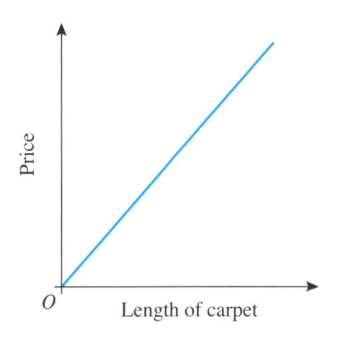

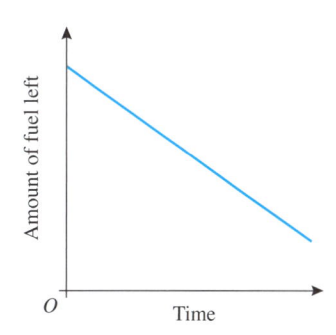

EXAMPLE

Jenny runs a bath. The water from the taps fills the bath at a rate of 12 litres per minute. She runs the bath water for 10 minutes.
a) Work out the amount of water in the bath when Jenny has finished running it.

Jenny stays in the bath for 20 minutes. She then empties it. The bath drains at a rate of 15 litres per minute.
b) Work out how long it takes the bath to empty.
c) Draw a graph to show how the amount of water in the bath changes.

SOLUTION

a) The amount of water is $12 \times 10 = \underline{120 \text{ litres}}$
b) Draining time = $120 \div 15 = \underline{8 \text{ minutes}}$
c)

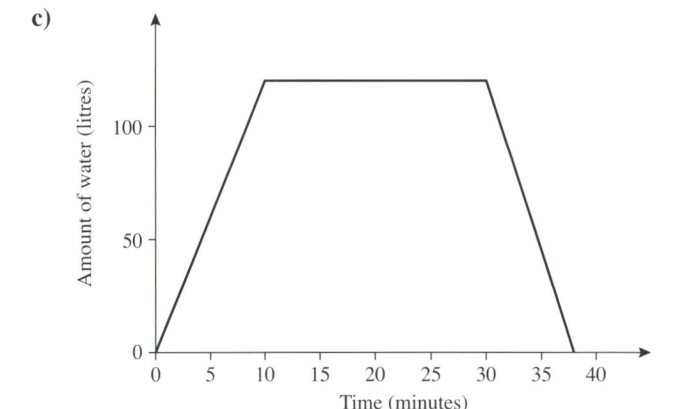

Some graphs can be built up by constructing a table of values first.

EXAMPLE

Jean is marking examination papers. She marks 10 papers on Day 1, and then marks 25 papers every day after that.

Number of days (n)	Total number of papers marked (T)
1	10
2	35
3	
4	
5	

a) Copy and complete the table, to show the total number of papers marked over the first five days.
b) Find a formula for the total number of papers marked, T, in terms of the number of days, n.
c) Draw a graph to show how many papers Jean could mark over 20 days.

In fact, Jean has to mark a total of 410 papers.

d) Use your graph to find out how many days this takes.

SOLUTION

a)

Number of days (n)	Total number of papers marked (T)
1	10
2	35
3	60
4	85
5	110

b) The figures for the first five days are $[-15]$, 10, 35, 60, 85, 110, going up in steps of 25. Thus the required formula is:

$$T = 25n - 15$$

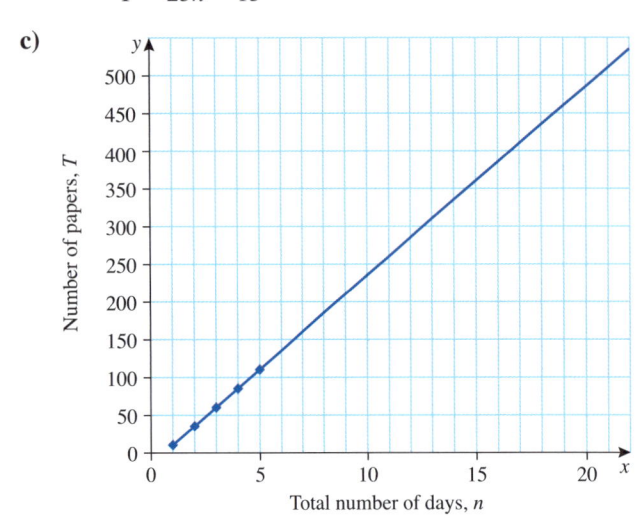

c)

d)

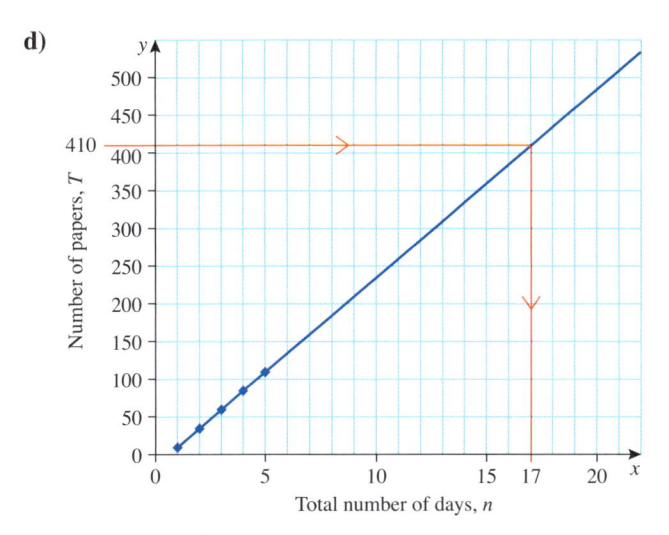

Using the graph, it takes Jean <u>17 days</u> altogether.

> When quantities change at a uniform rate, they can be modelled with straight line graphs. Other quantities may change at a varying rate; the corresponding graphs then become curves. In the GCSE examination you will be expected to recognise the difference between constant and variable rates of change.

EXAMPLE

Water is poured at a steady rate into four different containers A, B, C and D.

The graphs P, Q, R and S show how the depth of water in each container changes over time. Match the shapes to their corresponding graphs. Explain your reasoning.

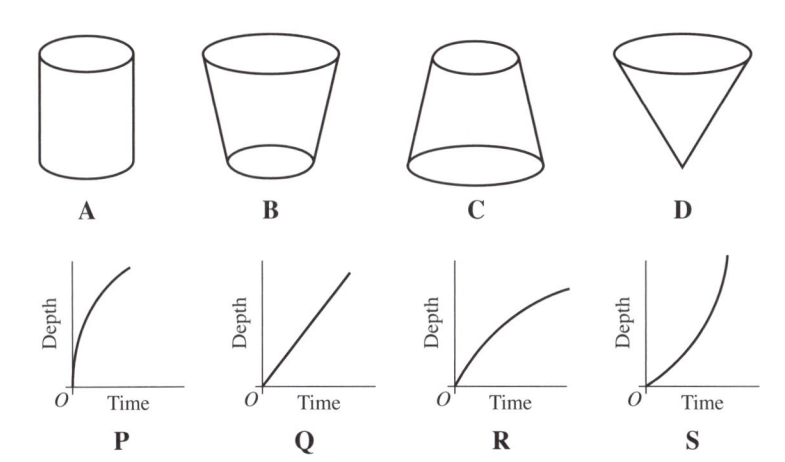

SOLUTION

Shape A has constant cross section as you move upwards, so its depth increases at a uniform rate. Thus shape A must correspond to graph Q.

Shape C becomes narrower near the top, so its depth will rise more quickly as time goes on. Thus shape C must correspond to graph S.

Shapes B and D are both wider at the top, so the rate at which their depth rises will tail off in both cases. Because shape D has a point at the bottom, however, its initial rate of increase of depth is very high, as in graph P. So shape B matches graph P, leaving shape B to match graph R.

The matchings are: A – Q, B – R, C – S and D – P

EXERCISE 17.1

1. John climbs a mountain. He gains height at a rate of 10 metres per minute, and it takes him 45 minutes to reach the top. He then stops for 20 minutes to have lunch. Then he descends at 15 metres per minute.
   a) How high is the mountain?
   b) How long does John's descent take?
   c) Copy and complete the graph below, labelling the scales on both axes.

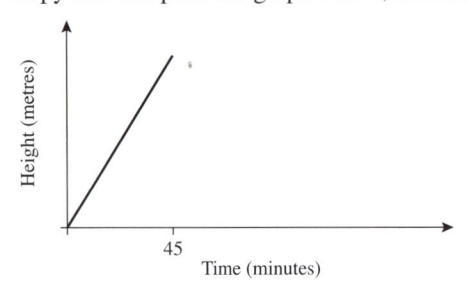

2. The diagram below shows a bowl. It is in the shape of a hemisphere (half a sphere). Water is poured into the bowl at a steady rate.

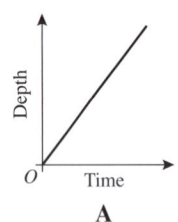

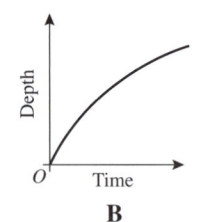

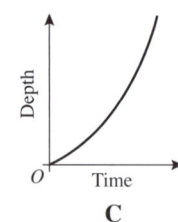

   Say which of graphs A, B or C best describes how the depth of water in the bowl varies over time. Explain your reasoning.

3. Jeremy has a full tank of petrol. It holds 50 litres of fuel. He then drives for 3 hours at a steady speed, during which time the car consumes 1 litre of fuel every 5 minutes. At the end of the 3 hours, Jeremy stops and refills the tank at a service station, which takes 5 minutes. He rests for a further 25 minutes. He completes his journey by travelling at the same steady speed for a further one hour.
   a) Work out how much petrol remains in the tank after 3 hours.
   b) Copy and complete the graph.
   c) Use your graph to find how much fuel is in the tank at the end of the journey.

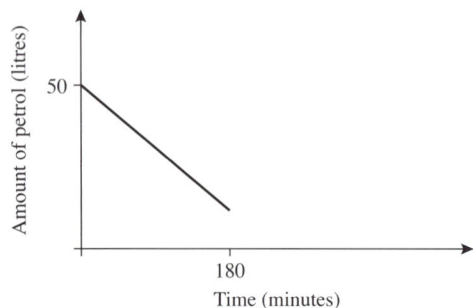

4 Water is poured into a container at a constant rate. The container is in the shape of a cone and a cylinder joined together as shown in the diagram. Sketch a set of depth/time axes, and complete the diagram to show how the depth of water in the container changes over time.

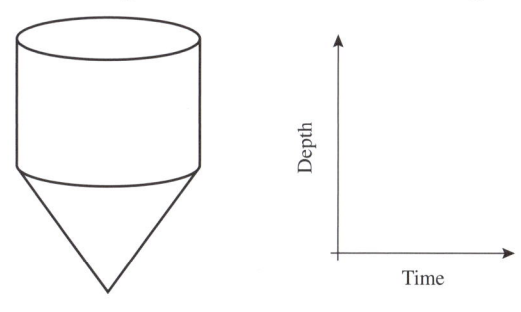

5 Sophie is writing a book. She writes 15 pages on Day 1, and then writes 20 pages a day after that.

Number of days (n)	Total number of pages written (T)
1	15
2	35
3	
4	

a) Copy and complete the table, to show the total number of pages written over the first four days.
b) Find a formula for T in terms of n.
c) Draw a graph to show how many pages Sophie could write over 20 days.

The finished book will contain 595 pages.

d) Use your graph to find out how many days it takes to reach the halfway stage.
e) Use your formula to work out how many days it will take Sophie to finish the book.

6 Water runs out of a hole in the bottom of a container. The water runs out at a steady rate. The diagram below shows how the depth of water in the container varies over time.

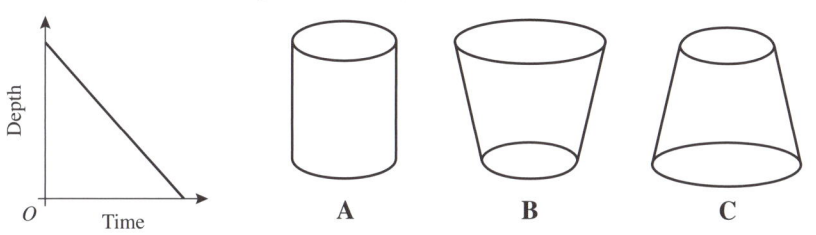

A   B   C

Say which of containers A, B or C best matches this graph. Explain your reasoning.

17.2 Distance–time graphs

Linear graphs are often used to illustrate the movement of an object away from a given point, or back towards it. Distance is plotted up the vertical axis, against time along the horizontal axis, and the result is called a distance–time graph.

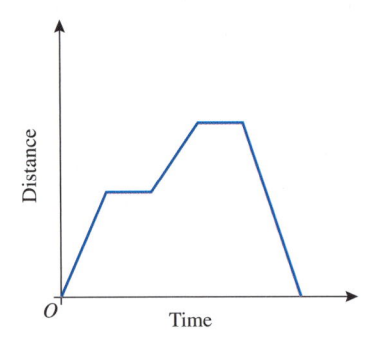

On a distance–time graph:

- *Straight lines* correspond to motion with a *constant speed*.
- The *gradient* of the line indicates the value of the *speed*.
- The *steeper* the gradient, the *faster* the speed.
- Lines with *positive gradient* indicate movement *away* from the starting point.
- Lines with *negative gradient* indicate movement back *towards* the starting point.
- *Horizontal lines* indicate no movement at all, which means that the object is *stationary*.

EXAMPLE

Lance walks from home to the bicycle shop. He spends 20 minutes choosing a new bicycle. He then rides it home, at a constant speed of 9.6 km/h. The distance–time graph below shows part of his journey.

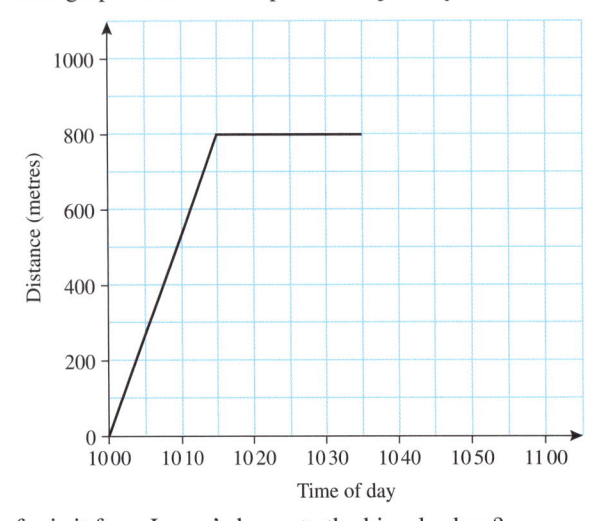

a) How far is it from Lance's home to the bicycle shop?
b) How fast does he walk to the shop?
c) At what time does he arrive back home?
d) Complete the graph, to show his return journey.

SOLUTION

a) From the vertical scale, the distance from home to the shop is <u>800 metres</u>

b) Lance walks 800 m in 15 minutes …
  … which is 1600 m in 30 minutes …
  … which is 3200 m in 60 minutes …
  … which is 3.2 km in 1 hour.

His speed is <u>3.2 km per hour</u>

> This type of simple proportion calculation is usually a very good way of solving distance–time graph calculations …

c) His return speed on the bike is 9.6 km per hour …
  … which is 9600 m in 60 minutes …
  … which is 4800 m in 30 minutes …
  … which is 1600 m in 10 minutes …
  … which is 800 m in 5 minutes.

> … because these questions may well come up on the non-calculator paper.

It takes 5 minutes for the return journey, starting at 1035.

Therefore Lance arrives back home at <u>1040</u>.

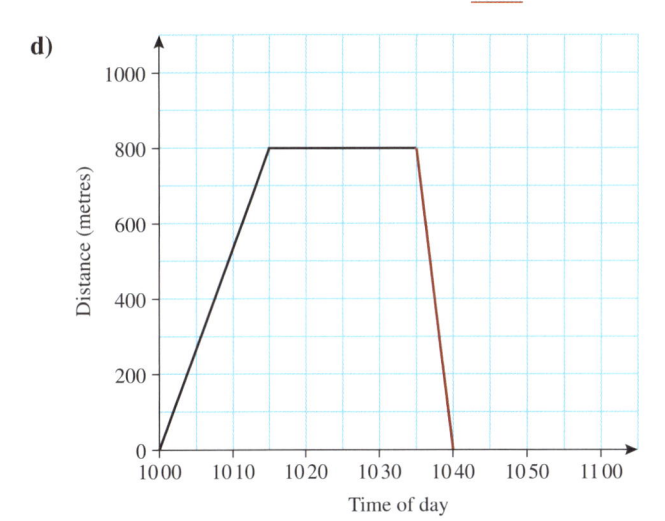

d)

17 Travel and other graphs   U4   253

EXERCISE 17.2

1. Tim cycles from home to his grandmother's for tea. He has a puncture on the way. He fixes the puncture, and is able to complete his journey. After tea, he cycles back home again. The travel graph below shows his journey.
   a) How long did Tim spend at his grandma's house?
   b) Work out his speed, in km per hour, for the journey *home* from his grandma.
   c) Did he cycle at the same speed as this on the *outward* journey?

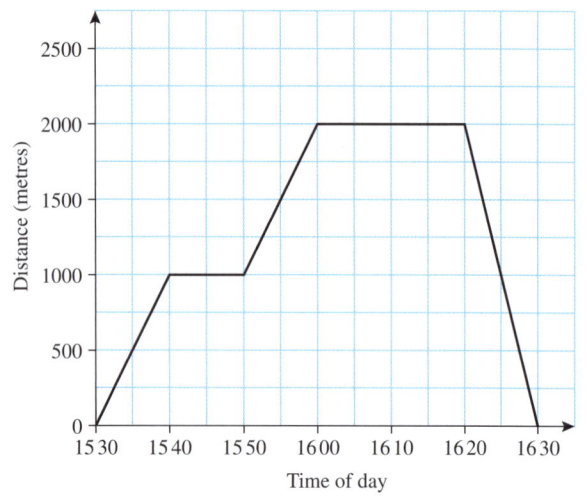

2. The diagram shows a distance–time graph for a train travelling between Ayton and Beesville.

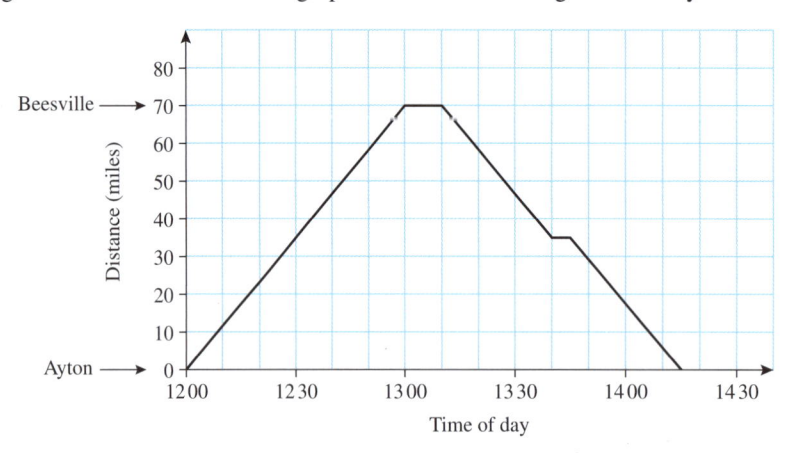

   The train leaves Ayton at 1200 for its outward journey to Beesville.
   a) Work out the speed of the train on its journey from Ayton to Beesville.

   The train leaves Beesville at 1310 for its return journey to Ayton.
   b) State one difference between the outward journey and the return journey.
   c) State one thing that is the same on the outward journey and the return journey.

   At 1210 a second train leaves Beesville. It travels towards Ayton at a constant speed of 60 miles per hour.
   d) Draw the journey of the second train on a copy of the graph.
   e) At what time do the two trains pass each other?

3. Tom is a polar explorer. He is pulling a sledge across the Antarctic icecap. Tom had planned a schedule to travel 16 kilometres every day, but because of poor weather conditions he managed only 6 kilometres on Day 1. Then the weather improved, and he managed to travel 18 kilometres per day from Day 2 onwards.
   a) Copy and complete this table to show the distance travelled by the end of each of the first four days.

Day number (n)	Total distance travelled (D km)
1	6
2	24
3	
4	

b) Construct a graph to show the total distance travelled over the first 10 days.
c) Add a second line to your graph to show his progress if he had travelled at the planned rate of 16 kilometres per day. On which day does Tom manage to get back on schedule?
d) Write down a formula for D in terms of n.

Tom has a resupply depot located 240 kilometres from the start point.

e) Use your formula to work out on which day he arrives at the depot. How does this compare with his original schedule?

4 Some teenagers are doing an outdoor walk. They set off from their base at 0900.
They walk for two hours at 4 km per hour.
Then they rest for one hour.
After their rest, they walk on for a further two hours at 5 km per hour.
Then they rest for one hour again.
Finally, they walk for another two hours at 5 km per hour.

a) On a copy of the grid, complete the travel graph.

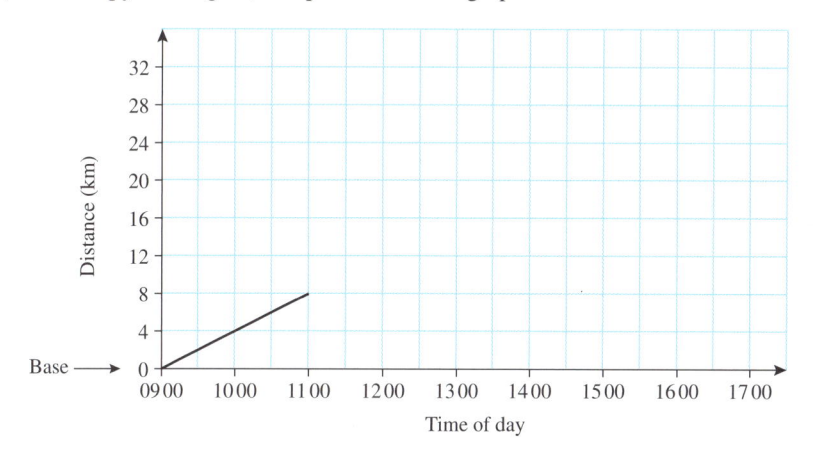

A teacher is camped 20 km from the start point. At 1200 he starts walking towards the group at 4 km per hour. He keeps walking until he meets the group.

b) Add a line on your graph to show the teacher's journey.
c) At what time does the teacher meet the group?

17.3 Velocity–time graphs

Sometimes a travel graph is drawn to show velocity along the *y* axis and time on the *x* axis; this is a **velocity–time** graph. The velocity is often changing, and the rate of change of velocity is called **acceleration**.

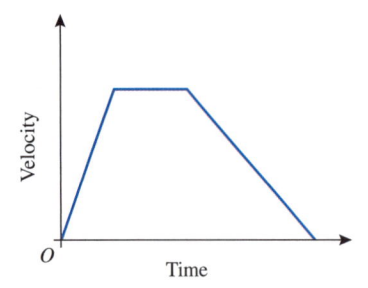

On a velocity–time graph:

- *Straight lines* correspond to motion with a *constant acceleration*.
- The *gradient* of the line indicates the value of the *acceleration*.
- The *steeper* the gradient, the higher the *acceleration*.
- Lines with *positive gradient* indicate that the velocity is *increasing*.
- Lines with *negative gradient* indicate that the velocity is *decreasing*.
- *Horizontal lines* indicate no acceleration at all; the object is moving at *constant velocity*.

EXAMPLE

The velocity–time graph below shows some information about a cyclist's journey.

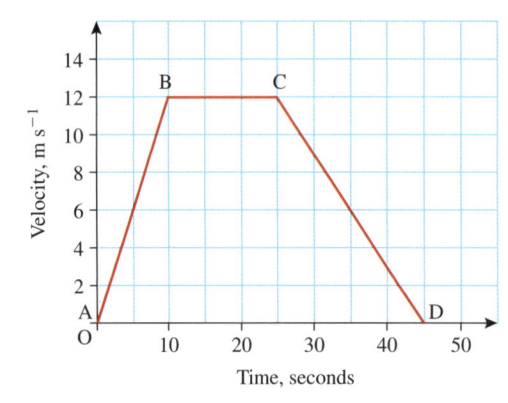

a) Describe what is happening during each of the parts AB, BC and CD on the graph.
b) Work out the cyclist's acceleration during the first 10 seconds.
c) Write down the highest velocity that the cyclist achieves during his journey.
d) Work out the distance travelled while he is travelling at his highest velocity.

SOLUTION

a) AB: the cyclist is accelerating.
   BC: he is cycling at constant velocity.
   CD: the cyclist is decelerating.

b) During the first 10 seconds, his velocity increases from 0 to 6 m s^{-1}.
   Acceleration = 6 ÷ 10
   = 0.6 m s^{-2} ← Acceleration = $\dfrac{\text{velocity}}{\text{time}}$

c) The highest velocity is 12 m s^{-1}

d) BC: constant velocity of 12 m s^{-1} for 30 seconds.
   Thus distance = 12 × 30 ← Distance = $\dfrac{\text{velocity}}{\text{time}}$
   = 360 m

EXERCISE 17.3

1 Raff goes for a ride on his new motorcycle. He accelerates at a constant rate for the first 10 seconds, then travels at a steady velocity for the next 20 seconds. He then sees a speed limit sign ahead, so he slows down at a constant rate until he reaches the speed limit, before continuing at a steady velocity again.

The diagram below shows these parts of his journey, with corresponding line segments PQ, QR, RS and ST.

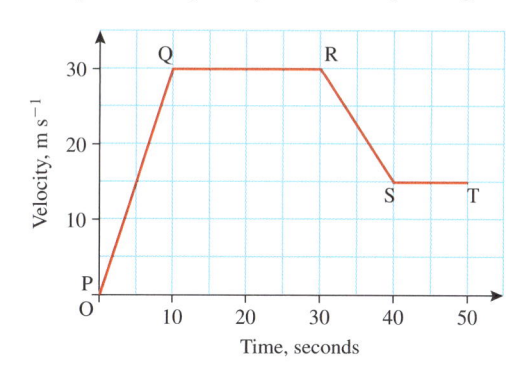

a) Work out Raff's acceleration during the first 10 seconds of his journey.
b) Write down the maximum velocity during his journey.
c) Work out how far Raff travels during the section of the journey marked QR on the diagram.
d) What does the graph suggest about the value of the speed limit?

2 A spacecraft accelerates from rest to a speed of 2700 m s^{-1} in 2 minutes.
a) Convert 2 minutes into seconds.
b) Work out the acceleration of the spacecraft, in m s^{-2}.

3 Steve is running in a 100 metres sprint race. Steve accelerates uniformly from rest to a velocity of 7 m s^{-1}. This takes 2 seconds. Then he maintains a constant velocity of 7 m s^{-1} until he crosses the finish line. The (incomplete) velocity–time graph below shows part of the race.

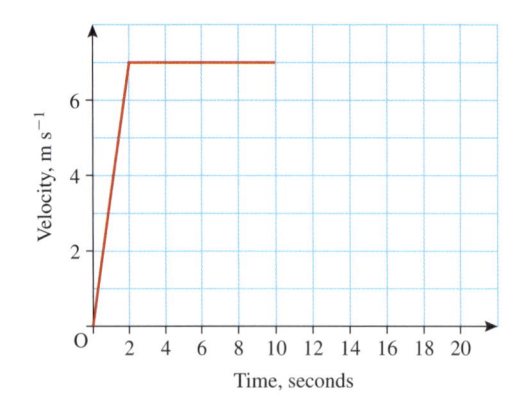

a) Work out the value of Steve's acceleration during the first 2 seconds.

During the first 2 seconds Steve travels 7 metres.
b) Work out the total distance Steve travels during the first 8 seconds.
c) Work out the total time it takes Steve to complete the 100 metres race.

4 A car is travelling at a constant velocity of 25 m s^{-1} when it passes a police car P. It continues at this velocity for 8 seconds until it reaches a point Q. Then it decelerates uniformly over the next five seconds, when it passes a road sign R at 15 m s^{-1}. It continues at this new velocity for 12 seconds, to reach the point S.

a) Illustrate this information on a velocity–time graph. Indicate the points P, Q, R and S on your graph.
b) Work out how far the car travels between points P and Q.
c) Work out how far the car travels between points R and S.

REVIEW EXERCISE 17

1 Anil cycled from his home to the park.
Anil waited in the park.
Then he cycled back home.
Here is a distance–time graph for Anil's complete journey.

a) At what time did Anil leave home?
b) What is the distance from Anil's home to the park?
c) How many minutes did Anil wait in the park?
d) Work out Anil's average speed on his journey home. Give your answer in kilometres per hour. [Edexcel]

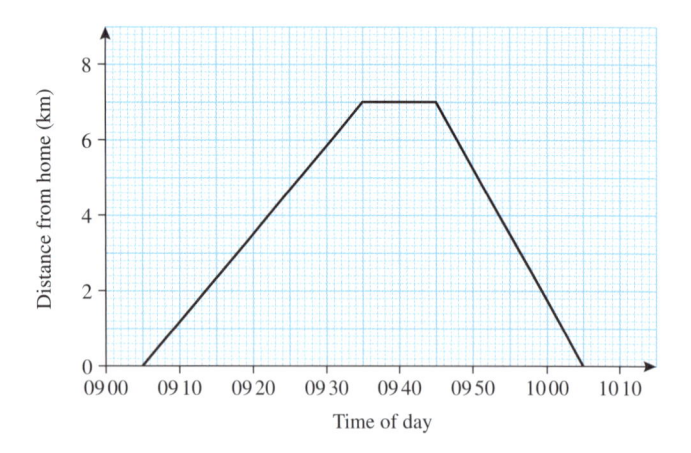

2 Here is a part of a travel graph of Siân's journey from her house to the shops and back.

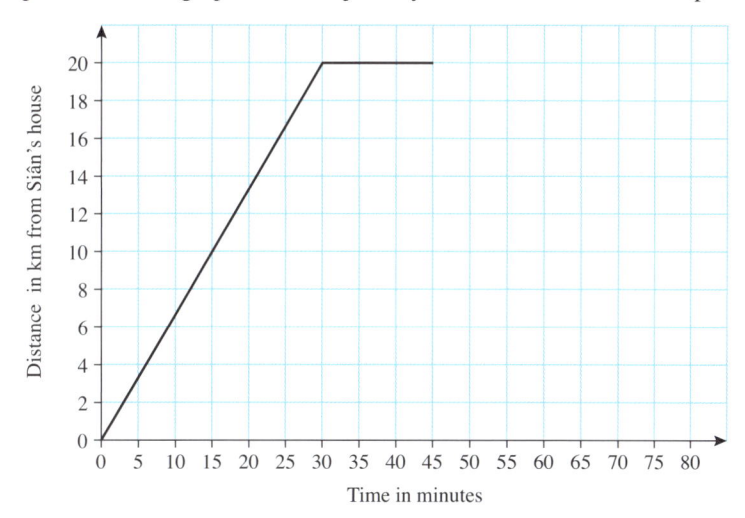

a) Work out Siân's speed for the first 30 minutes of her journey. Give your answer in km/h.
   Siân spends 15 minutes at the shops. She then travels back to her house at 60 km/h.
b) Copy and complete the travel graph. [Edexcel]

3 Elizabeth went for a cycle ride. The distance–time graph shows her ride.

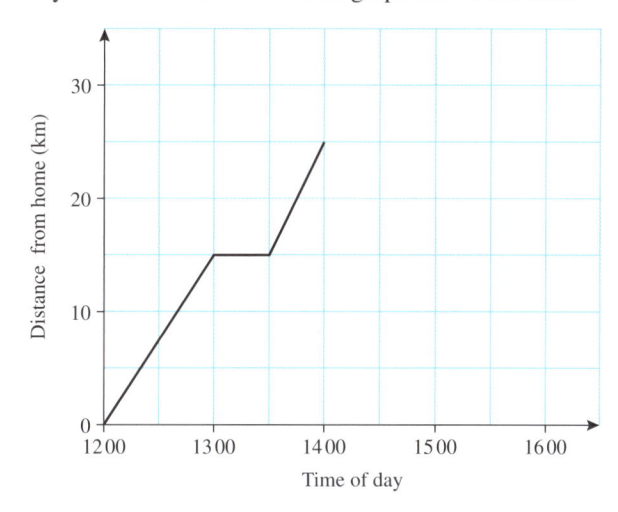

She set off from home at 1200 and had a flat tyre at 1400. During her ride, she stopped for a rest.
a) (i) At what time did she stop for a rest?
   (ii) At what speed did she travel after her rest?
It took Elizabeth 15 minutes to repair the flat tyre. She then cycled home at 25 kilometres per hour.
b) Copy and complete the distance–time graph to show this information. [Edexcel]

4 The diagram shows a water tank. The tank is a hollow cylinder joined to a hollow hemisphere at the top. The tank has a circular base.

The empty tank is slowly filled with water.

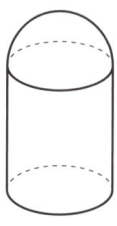

On a copy of the axes, sketch a graph to show the relation between the volume $V\,\text{cm}^3$, of water in the tank and the depth, $d\,\text{cm}$, of water in the tank.

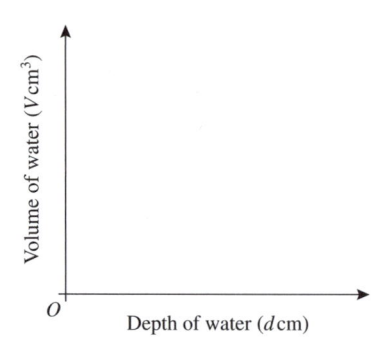

[Edexcel]

5 The diagram shows four empty containers. Water is poured at a constant rate into each of these containers. Each sketch graph shows the relationship between the height of water in a container and the time as the water is poured in.

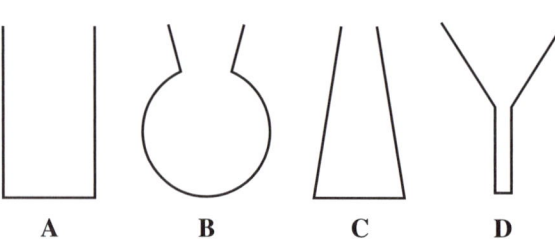

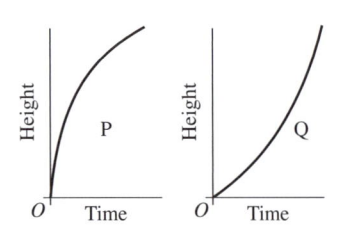

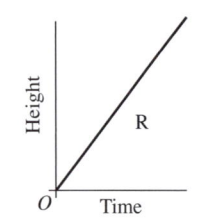

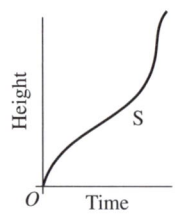

A   B   C   D

Copy this table and write the letter of each graph in the correct place.

Container	Graph
A	
B	
C	
D	

[Edexcel]

6 David went for a ride on his bike.
He rode from his home to the lake.
The travel graph shows this part of his trip.

a) Find David's average speed between 1300 and 1500.
b) What happened to David between 1500 and 1600?

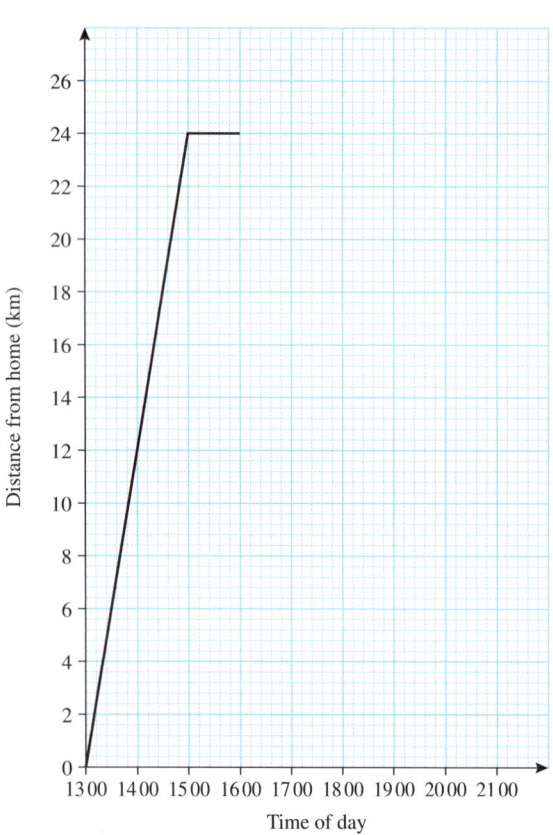

David started to travel back to his home at 1600. He travelled at a speed of 10 miles per hour for half an hour. He remembered he had left his water bottle at the lake. He immediately rode back to the lake at 10 miles per hour. He picked up his water bottle and immediately travelled back home at 20 miles per hour.

c) Copy and complete the travel graph. [Edexcel]

7 A train travelled 430 km from London to Durham. The graph shows the train's journey from London as far as York.

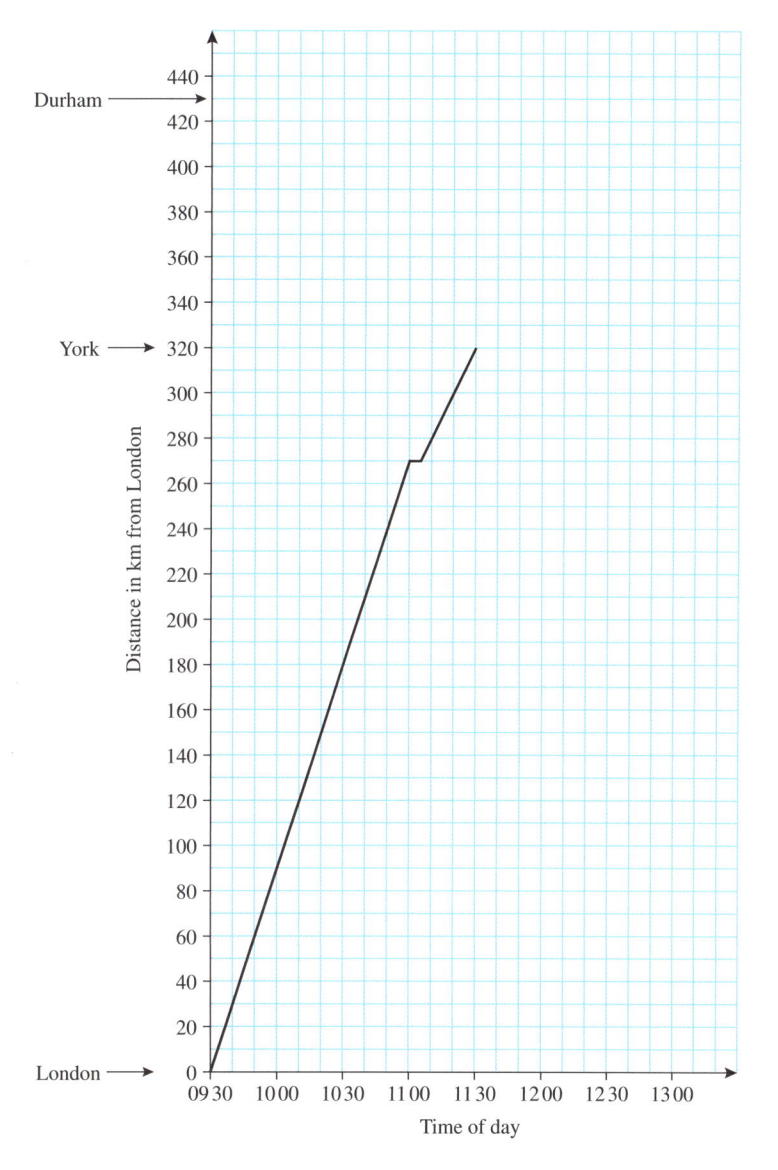

On the way to York, the train stopped at Doncaster.
a) Write down the distance of Doncaster from London.
b) Work out the average speed at which the train travelled from London to Doncaster.

The train stopped at York for 10 minutes. It then went on to Durham at a steady speed. It did not stop between York and Durham. It reached Durham at 1230.

c) On a copy of the grid, complete the graph of the train's journey to Durham. [Edexcel]

8 Ken and Wendy go from home to their caravan site. The caravan site is 50 km from their home. Ken goes on his bike. Wendy drives in her car. The diagram shows information about the journeys they made.

  a) At what time did Wendy pass Ken?
  b) Between which two times was Ken cycling at his greatest speed?
  c) Work out Wendy's average speed for her journey.   [Edexcel]

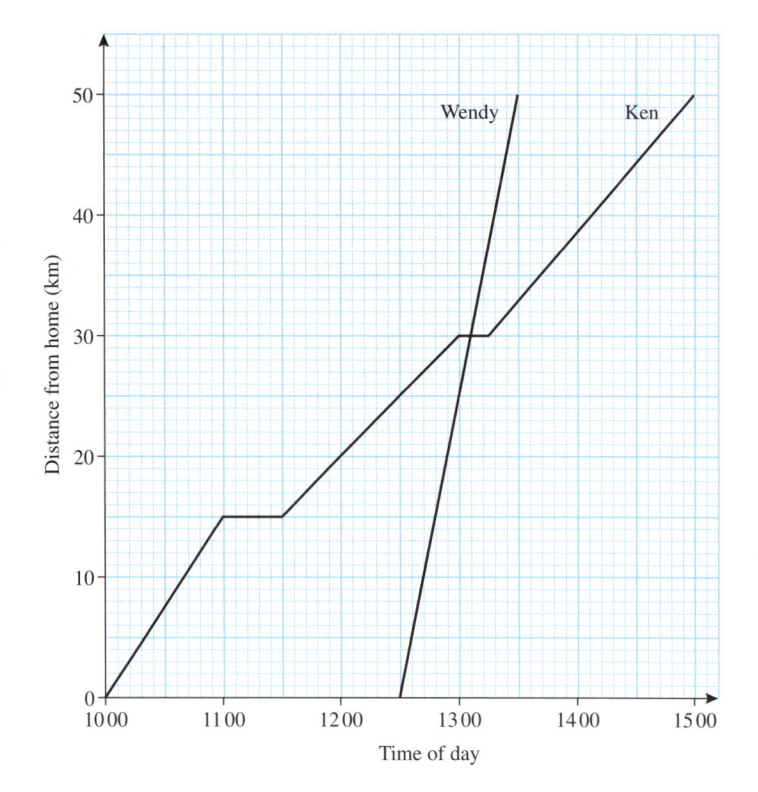

9 P, Q and R are three stations on a railway line.
PQ = 26 miles. QR = 4 miles.
A passenger train leaves P at 1200.
It arrives at Q at 1230.
Information about the journey from P to Q is shown on the travel graph below.

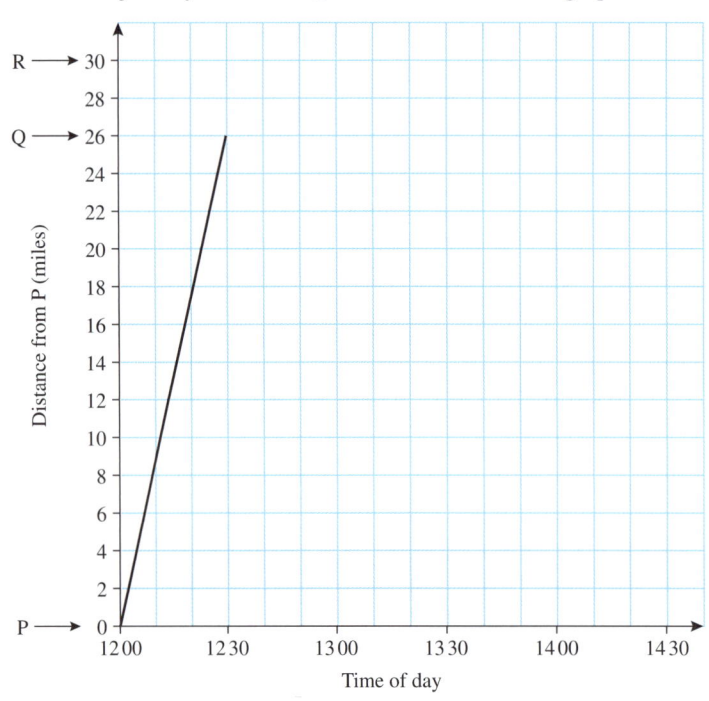

The passenger train stops at Q for 10 minutes. It then returns to P at the same speed as on the journey from P to Q.
a) On a copy of the grid, complete the travel graph for this train.

A goods train leaves R at 1200. It arrives at P at 1300.
b) On the grid, draw the travel graph for the goods train.
c) Write down the distance from P where the goods train passes the passenger train.   [Edexcel]

10 Linford runs in a 100 metres race. The graph shows his speed, in metres per second, during the race.

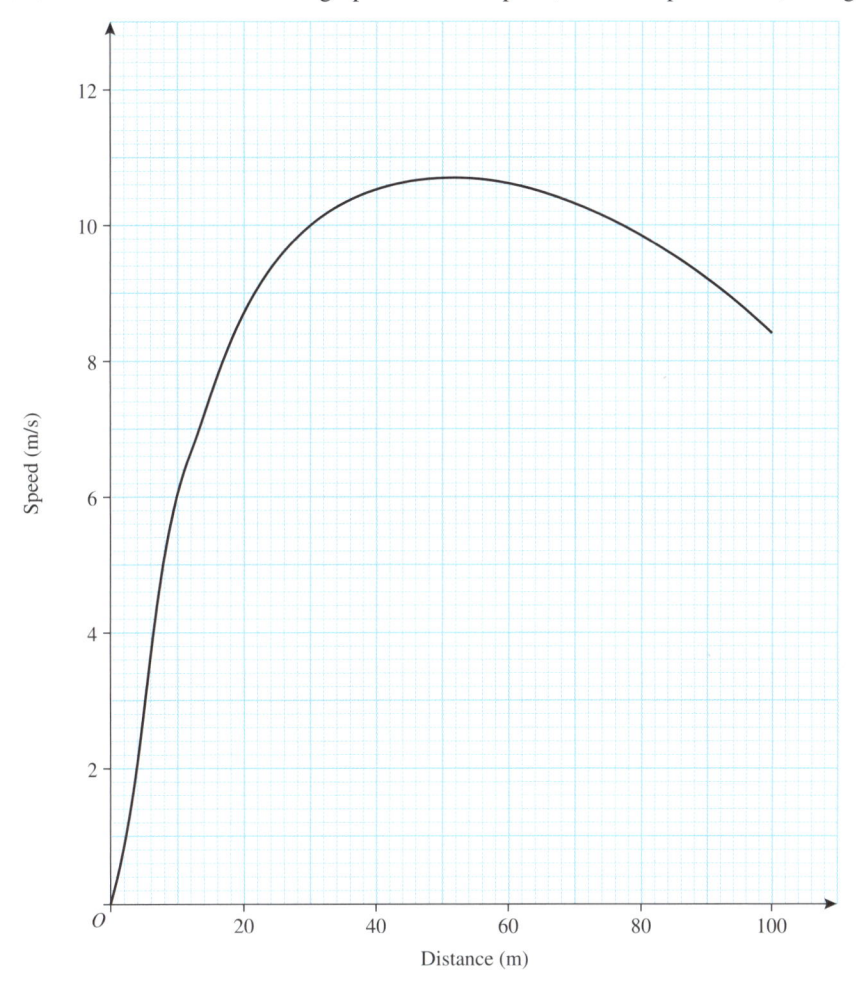

a) Write down Linford's speed, after he has covered a distance of 10 m.
b) Write down Linford's greatest speed.
c) Write down the distance Linford has covered when his speed is 7.4 m/s.   [Edexcel]

KEY POINTS

1. Linear graphs are used to model a variety of real-life situations. They can be constructed from a table, or by looking at start and finish points.

2. If containers such as cylinders and cuboids are filled at a uniform rate, then the graph of depth against time is a straight line. Other shaped containers, such as cones and spheres, will generate curved graphs, and you need to be able to recognise how these are formed.

3. Distance–time graphs show how the position of an object (or person) changes over time. On a distance–time graph:
   - Straight lines correspond to motion with a constant speed.
   - The gradient of the line indicates the value of the speed.
   - Lines with positive gradient indicate movement away from the start point.
   - Lines with negative gradient indicate movement back towards the start point.
   - The steeper the gradient, the faster the speed.
   - Horizontal lines indicate no movement at all (the object is stationary).

4. The gradient of the line corresponds to its speed, but care must be taken with units. For example, some distance–time graphs show distances in metres and times in minutes, but expect speeds to be computed in kilometres per hour. In this case, it is better to work out speeds or distances by a proportional method, rather than using formulae such as speed = distance ÷ time.

5. Distance–time graphs may occur on a non-calculator exam paper, so you should practise solving questions using pencil and paper methods only.

6. Velocity–time graphs have velocity plotted along the y axis. The gradient of the graph indicates the acceleration. On a velocity–time graph:
   - Straight lines correspond to motion with a constant acceleration.
   - The gradient of the line indicates the value of the acceleration.
   - Lines with positive gradient indicate that the velocity is increasing.
   - Lines with negative gradient indicate that the velocity is decreasing.
   - The steeper the gradient, the higher the acceleration.
   - Horizontal lines indicate no acceleration at all (the object is moving at constant velocity).

| Internet Challenge 17 |

Faster and faster

Some artificial objects are capable of travelling at very high speeds.

Use your judgement to arrange these in order of speed, slowest to fastest. Then use the internet to check if your order was correct.

- Intercity 225 train
- Porsche 911 GT3 RS car
- Apollo 11 spacecraft
- Speed of sound (in air)
- Eurofighter *Typhoon* jet aircraft
- Challenger 2 tank
- Disney's *Space Mountain* roller coaster (Paris)
- Orbiting Space Shuttle
- Boeing 747-400 passenger jet aircraft
- The tea clipper *Cutty Sark*

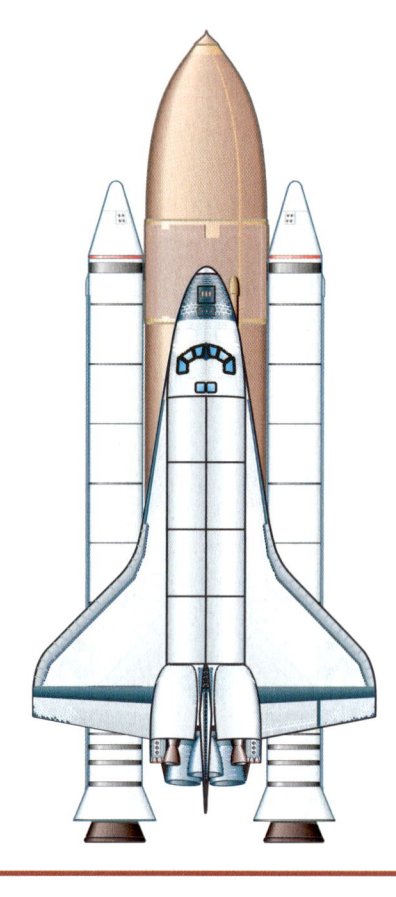

CHAPTER 18

Circles and cylinders

In this chapter you will **learn how to**:

- calculate the circumference and area of a circle
- calculate areas of sectors
- use circle formulae in reverse
- find the surface area and volume of a cylinder
- obtain exact expressions for areas and volumes in terms of π.

You will also be **challenged to**:

- investigate measuring the Earth.

Starter: Three and a bit …

Use your calculator to work out the value of each of these expressions. Write down all the figures on your calculator display. Each answer should be a little over 3.

$$3 + \frac{1}{8}$$

$$\frac{22}{7}$$

$$\sqrt{10}$$

$$3 + \frac{8}{60} + \frac{30}{60^2}$$

$$\frac{333}{106}$$

$$\left(\frac{2143}{22}\right)^{\frac{1}{4}}$$

$$\left(\frac{4}{3}\right)^4$$

$$\frac{88}{\sqrt{785}}$$

$$\sqrt{2} + \sqrt{3}$$

$$\frac{355}{113}$$

These are all approximations to an important mathematical quantity called pi. This is stored on your calculator as a key marked with a π symbol. Use this key to obtain the value of pi correct to as many significant figures as possible, and write it down.

Which one of these approximations is the closest?

18.1 Circumference and area of a circle

The distance all the way around the perimeter of a circle is known as its **circumference**. The circumference of any circle is just over three times its diameter. More precisely, this ratio is 3.141 592 6 ... and is known as **pi** (the Greek letter p), written π. The value of pi will be stored in your calculator, and can be called up at the press of a key.

Circumference of a circle = pi × diameter
$$C = \pi d$$

Sometimes it is more convenient to work with a circle's radius instead. The radius is exactly half the diameter, so it must be doubled in order for this method to work.

Circumference of a circle = two × pi × the radius
$$C = 2\pi r$$

EXAMPLE

Find the circumferences of these two circles:

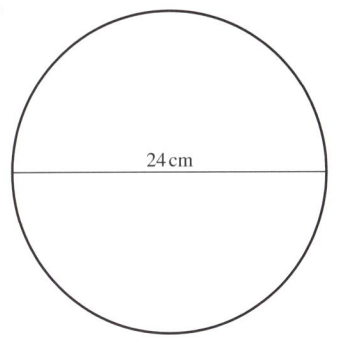

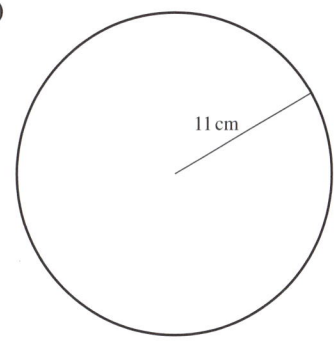

a) [circle with diameter 24 cm]

b) [circle with radius 11 cm]

SOLUTION

a) This circle has diameter $d = 24$.

$C = \pi d$
$= \pi \times 24$
$= 75.398\ 223\ 69$
$= \underline{75.4 \text{ cm}}$ (3 s.f.)

> It is usual to round the answer to 3 significant figures in this kind of question. Make sure you show your unrounded answer too.

b) This circle has radius $r = 11$.

$C = 2\pi r$
$= 2 \times \pi \times 11$
$= 69.115\ 038\ 38$
$= \underline{69.1 \text{ cm}}$ (3 s.f.)

Your calculator makes easy work of finding the area of a circle, too. The area of a circle is found by using this formula.

Area of a circle = pi × the square of the radius
$$A = \pi r^2$$

EXAMPLE

Find the areas of these two circles:

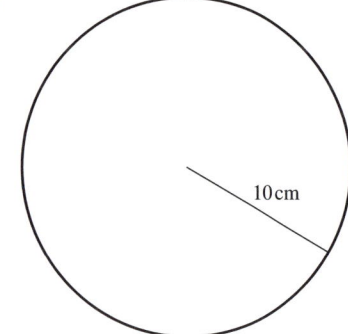

a) [circle with radius 10 cm]

b) [circle with diameter 18 cm]

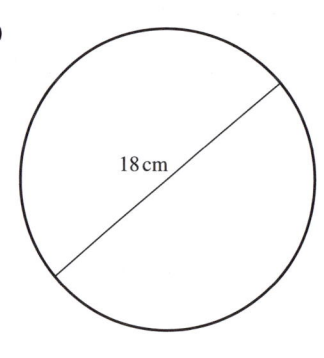

SOLUTION

a) This circle has radius $r = 10$.

$A = \pi r^2$
$= \pi \times 10^2$ — Square the radius *first*, then multiply the result by pi.
$= \pi \times 100$
$= 314.159\,265\,4$
$= \underline{314 \text{ cm}^2}$ (3 s.f.)

b) This circle has radius $r = 18 \div 2 = 9$.

$A = \pi r^2$
$= \pi \times 9^2$ — You can type this expression straight in your calculator – it knows that it must work out the square first.
$= \pi \times 81$
$= 254.469\,004\,9$
$= \underline{254 \text{ cm}^2}$ (3 s.f.)

Take care to choose the right formula when working with circles. It might help to remember that the formula containing a **squared** term – πr^2 – is used for finding **area**, which is measured in **square units**.

Some questions may require you to use these circle formulae in combination with other area or perimeter calculations.

EXAMPLE

The diagram shows an ornamental flowerbed. It is in the shape of a rectangle, with a semicircle at each end. The rectangle is of length 2.8 metres. Each semicircle has a radius of 1.1 metre.

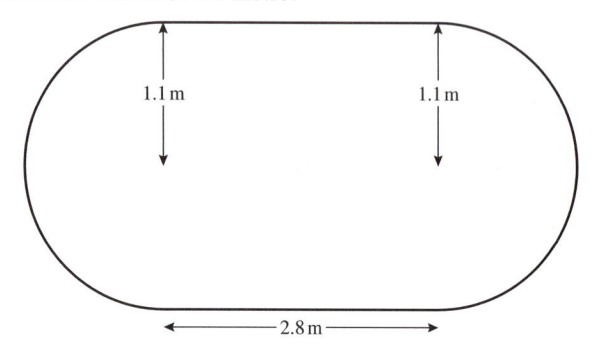

a) Calculate the perimeter of the flowerbed.
b) The gardener is going to put edging around the flowerbed. Edging costs £2.50 per metre. Work out how much the edging will cost.
c) Calculate the area of the flowerbed.
d) The gardener plans to add fertiliser to the flowerbed. One bag of fertiliser will be sufficient for 0.8 square metre of flowerbed. How many bags of fertiliser will the gardener need to buy?

SOLUTION

a) The two semicircles are equivalent to a single circle with radius $r = 1.1$ m.

$C = 2\pi r$
$= 2 \times \pi \times 1.1$
$= 6.911\,503\,838$

The two rectangular edges are 2.8 metres each, so the total perimeter is:

$P = 2.8 + 2.8 + 6.911\,503\,838$
$= 12.511\,503\,838$
$= \underline{12.5 \text{ m}}$ (3 s.f.)

b) Cost of edging $= 12.5 \times £2.50$
$= \underline{£31.25}$

c) The area of the semicircles is equivalent to the area of a single circle with $r = 1.1$ m.

Area of circle $= \pi r^2$
$= \pi \times 1.1^2$
$= 3.801\,327\,111$
$= 3.80 \text{ m}^2$ (3 s.f.)

The rectangular part measures 2.8 m by 2.2 m, so:

Area of rectangle $= 2.8 \times 2.2$
$= 6.16 \text{ m}^2$

The total area is $3.80 + 6.16 = \underline{9.96 \text{ m}^2}$

d) 1 bag of fertiliser is sufficient for 0.8 m².
Therefore the gardener needs $9.96 \div 0.8 = 12.45$ bags.
The gardener needs to buy $\underline{13 \text{ bags}}$.

EXERCISE 18.1

1 A circle has radius 12 mm. Find its circumference, correct to 3 significant figures.

2 A circle has diameter 22 cm. Find its circumference, correct to 3 significant figures.

3 A circle has radius 18 cm. Find its area, correct to 3 significant figures.

4 A circle has diameter 11.5 cm. Find its area, correct to 3 significant figures.

5 Find, correct to 4 significant figures, the circumference of a circle with radius 21.25 cm.

6 Find, correct to 4 significant figures, the area of a circle with diameter 66.25 mm.

7 Find, correct to 4 significant figures, the circumference of a circle with diameter 1.25 cm.

8 Find, correct to 4 significant figures, the area of a circle with radius 0.455 cm.

9 A circle has diameter 11 cm. Find its area, correct to 3 significant figures.

10 A circle has radius 0.85 mm. Find its area, correct to 3 significant figures.

11 A circle has diameter 250 cm. Find its circumference, correct to 3 significant figures.

12 A circle has radius 1.06 m. Find its circumference, correct to 3 significant figures.

13 A tennis ball has a diameter of 66 mm. Calculate its circumference, correct to 2 significant figures.

14 A face of a one euro coin is a circle of diameter of 23.25 mm. Calculate its area, correct to 3 significant figures

15 Emma decides to run around a circular race track. The radius of the track is 25 metres.
   a) Work out the length of one lap of the track, correct to 3 significant figures.
   Emma wants to run at least 5000 metres. She wants to run a whole number of laps.
   b) Work out the minimum number of laps that Emma must run.

16 A circular CD is cut from a plastic square of side 12 cm. A hole of diameter 1.5 cm is then cut from the centre. Calculate the area of the CD, correct to 3 significant figures.

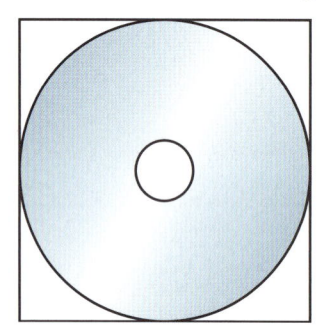

17 The diagram shows a simple 'eclipse viewer' observing aid. The frame is made of cardboard, and comprises a rectangle with two circular holes cut into it. The holes are then filled with a reflective safety film that blocks harmful radiation from the Sun.

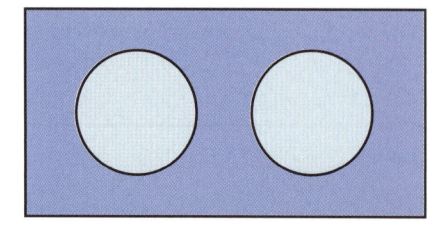

The holes are each of diameter 4 cm. The rectangle measures 15 cm by 6 cm.
   a) Calculate the area of one of the circular holes, correct to the nearest 0.1 cm^2.
   b) Work out the area of the cardboard frame, correct to the nearest 0.1 cm^2.

18 The diagram shows an ornamental stained glass window.

The window is a circle, of radius 30 cm. The rectangle measures 48 cm by 36 cm. The glass inside the rectangle is stained blue; the glass outside the rectangle is stained yellow. There is a boundary, made of lead, indicated by the heavy black line. (The lead is of negligible thickness.) 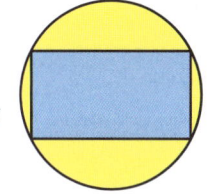
   a) Work out the length of the boundary, correct to the nearest centimetre.
   b) Work out the area of the blue glass, correct to 3 significant figures.
   c) Work out the area of the yellow glass, correct to 3 significant figures.

19 The diagram shows a running track. It is made up of two straight sections, and two semicircular ends. The dimensions are marked on the diagram.

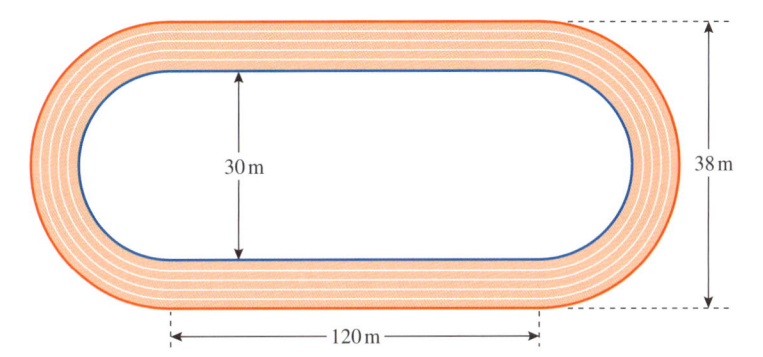

Steve runs around the outside boundary of the track, marked with a red line. Seb runs around the inside boundary, marked in blue. They each run one lap of the track.
   a) Work out the length of the outside boundary of the track.
   b) Work out the length of the inside boundary of the track.
   c) How much longer is the outside boundary, compared with the inside one? Give your answer as a percentage.

20 The diagram shows a metal washer. It is made from a circular sheet of radius 6 mm. A smaller circle of radius 3 mm is then removed from the centre and discarded.

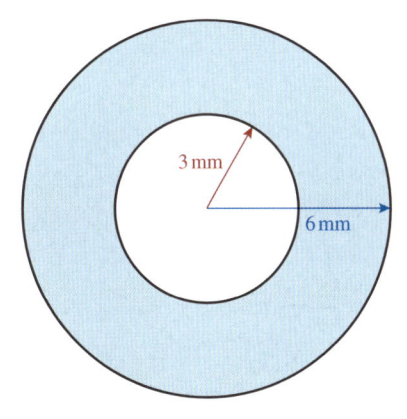

   a) Calculate the area of the large circle.
   b) Calculate the area of the smaller circle.
   c) Hence find the area of the washer.

Fred says 'Since 3 mm is half of 6 mm, then 50% of the metal is wasted by discarding the smaller circle.' Fred is incorrect.
   d) Calculate the correct percentage of metal wasted.

18.2 Sectors of a circle

In some of the previous examples you have worked with **semicircles**. Circles can be sliced into quarters, called **quadrants**, or other parts of a complete circle. These are called **sectors**.

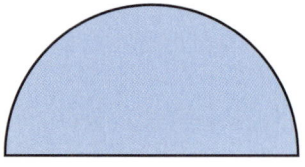

Semicircle   Quadrant   Sector   Arc

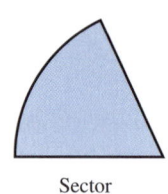

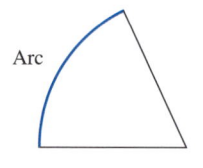

The curved boundary along the edge of a sector is called an **arc**. You can find the length of an arc by calculating the corresponding fraction of a circumference of a circle. The area of a sector can be found in a similar manner.

$$\text{Arc length} = \frac{\text{sector angle}}{360°} \times 2\pi r \qquad \text{Sector area} = \frac{\text{sector angle}}{360°} \times \pi r^2$$

EXAMPLE

Calculate the perimeter and area of each of these sectors of a circle.

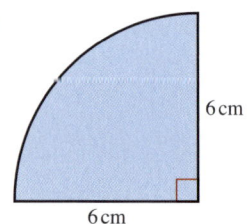

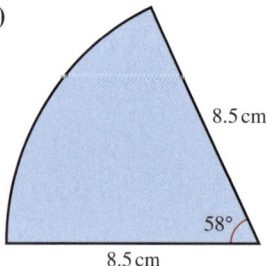

a) 6 cm, 6 cm

b) 8.5 cm, 8.5 cm, 58°

SOLUTION

a) The sector is a quadrant; one-quarter of a circle.
The circumference of the full circle would be $2 \times \pi \times 6 = 37.699\,111\,84$ cm.
The arc length of the quadrant is $\frac{1}{4} \times 37.699\,111\,84 = 9.42$ cm.
Thus the perimeter is $9.42 + 6 + 6 = \underline{21.42 \text{ cm}}$ (4 s.f.)

The area of the full circle would be $\pi \times 6^2 = 113.097\,335\,5$ cm².
The area of the quadrant is $\frac{1}{4} \times 113.097\,335\,5 = \underline{28.27 \text{ cm}^2}$ (4 s.f.)

b) This sector has a central angle of 58°, so it represents $\frac{58}{360}$ of a circle.
The arc length of the sector is $\frac{58}{360} \times 2 \times \pi \times 8.5 = 8.60$ cm.
Thus the perimeter is $8.60 + 8.5 + 8.5 = \underline{25.60 \text{ cm}}$ (4 s.f.)

The area of the sector is $\frac{58}{360} \times \pi \times 8.5^2 = \underline{36.57 \text{ cm}^2}$ (4 s.f.)

EXERCISE 18.2

Calculate the perimeter and area of each sector. Give your answer correct to 3 significant figures.

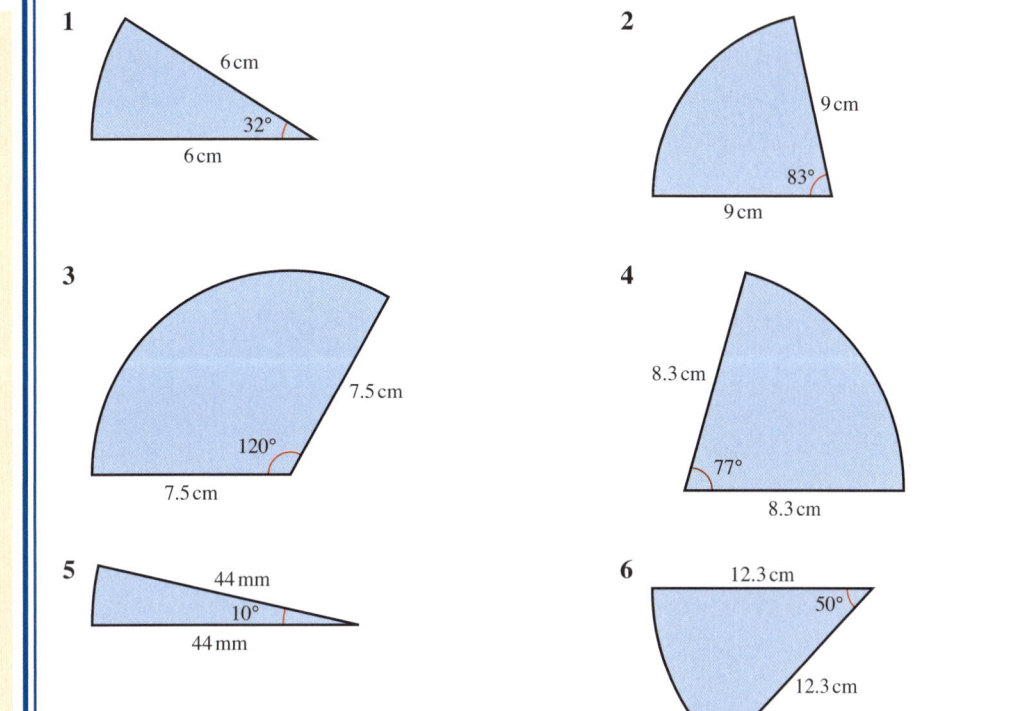

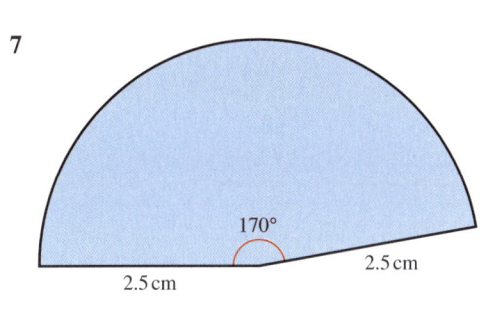

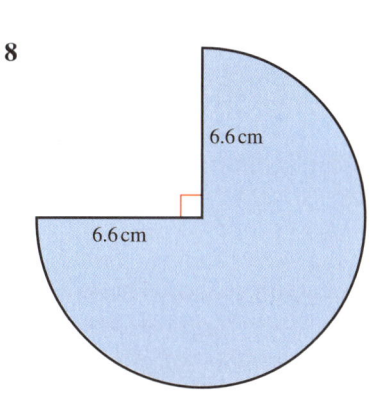

1. 6 cm, 6 cm, 32°

2. 9 cm, 9 cm, 83°

3. 7.5 cm, 7.5 cm, 120°

4. 8.3 cm, 8.3 cm, 77°

5. 44 mm, 44 mm, 10°

6. 12.3 cm, 12.3 cm, 50°

7. 2.5 cm, 2.5 cm, 170°

8. 6.6 cm, 6.6 cm (right angle shown)

9. Bob wants to display some statistical data in a pie chart. The three sectors of the pie chart are to have angles of 160°, 140° and 60°. The radius of the pie chart is to be 10 cm.
   a) Work out the area of each sector of Bob's pie chart, correct to the nearest cm^2.
   b) Work out the perimeter of the smallest sector, correct to 3 significant figures.

10. A pizza of diameter 12 inches is to be shared between five people. It is cut into five equal segments.
    a) Work out the angles at the centre of each segment of pizza.
    b) Work out the area of one segment, correct to 3 significant figures.

18.3 Circumference and area in reverse

Supposing you want to find the dimensions of a circle in order for it to have a given circumference or area. Then it is necessary to apply the circle formulae in reverse.

EXAMPLE

A circular hula-hoop has a circumference of 2.4 metres. Find its diameter in centimetres, correct to the nearest centimetre.

SOLUTION

Let the diameter be d metres.
$$\pi \times d = 2.4$$
So $d = 2.4 \div \pi$
$= 0.763\,943\,726\,8$ m
$= \underline{76 \text{ cm}}$ (nearest cm)

Reverse area problems require a little more care. It is best to find r^2 first, then square root at the end to find r. If the question asks for the diameter, just double the final r value.

EXAMPLE

A coin has an area of 4 cm². Work out its diameter, in millimetres, correct to 3 significant figures.

SOLUTION

Let the radius of the coin be r cm.
Then $\pi r^2 = 4$
$r^2 = 4 \div \pi$
$= 1.273\,239\,545$
$r = \sqrt{1.273\,239\,545}$
$= 1.128\,379\,167$
The diameter is $2r = 2.256\,758\,334$ cm
$= \underline{22.6 \text{ mm}}$ (3 s.f.)

EXERCISE 18.3

Give the answers to each of these problems correct to 3 significant figures.

1. A circle has circumference 15.5 cm. Find its radius.

2. A circle has circumference 12.8 cm. Find its diameter.

3. A circle has area 120 cm². Find its radius.

4. A circle has area 44 cm². Find its diameter.

5. A circle has circumference 1.45 cm. Find its radius.

6. A circle has area 850 cm². Find its diameter.

7. A circle has circumference 6.25 cm. Find its diameter.

8. A circle has area 225 cm². Find its radius.

9. The diagram shows a segment of a circle. The angle at the centre of the segment is 40°.

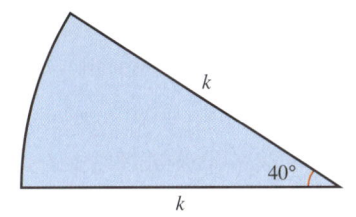

The radius of the segment is k centimetres. The area of the segment is 427.6 cm².
   a) Work out the area of the corresponding complete circle.
   b) Hence find the value of k.
   c) Calculate the perimeter of the segment.

10. The diagram shows the boundary of a running track. The ends are semicircles of radius x metres. The straights are of length 35 metres each. The total distance around the outside of the track is 100 metres.

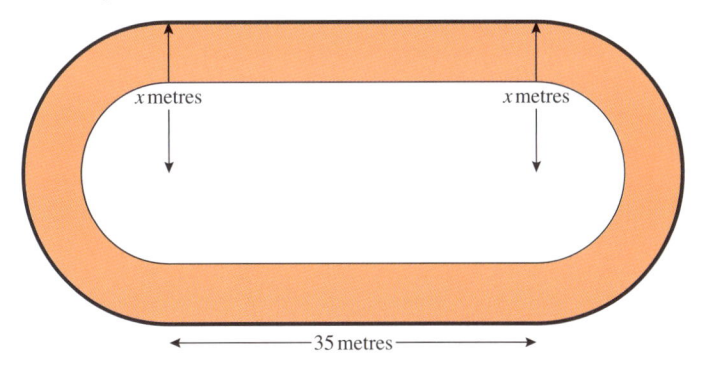

Calculate the value of x.

18.4 Surface area and volume of a cylinder

You can make a hollow cylinder by rolling up a rectangular sheet of paper.

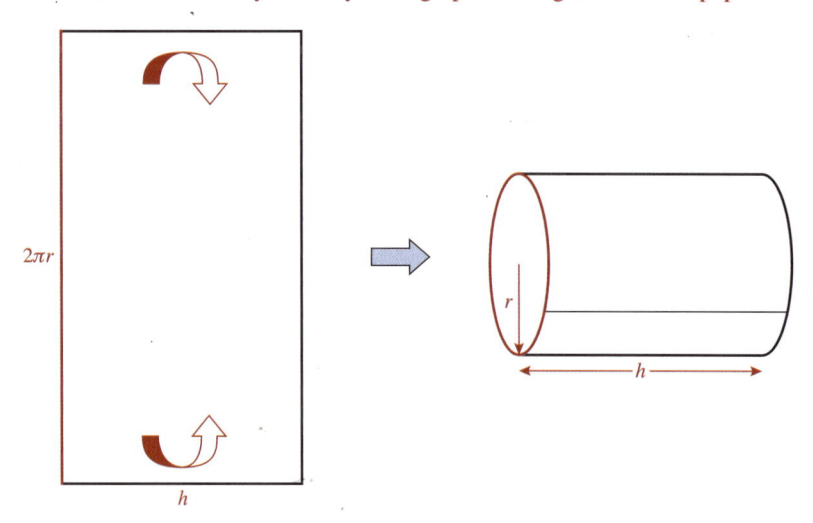

Suppose the cylinder has height h and radius r.

Then the distance marked in red on the diagram is the circumference of the end of the cylinder, which is $2\pi r$.

The cylinder forms a **curved surface area**, which must be equal in area to the original rectangle.

This is $2\pi r$ times h, giving the formula:

Curved surface area of a cylinder $= 2\pi rh$

A cylinder can be thought of as a prism with a circular base. Then its volume is found by multiplying the cross-sectional area (πr^2) by the length (h) to obtain this formula:

Volume of a cylinder $= \pi r^2 h$

EXAMPLE

A metal pipe is in the form of a cylinder, 1.5 metres long and 22 centimetres in diameter.

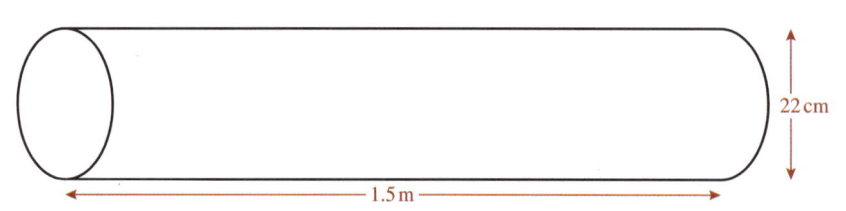

a) Calculate the curved surface area of the pipe, in square centimetres.
b) Work out the volume of the cylindrical pipe, in cubic centimetres.

SOLUTION

Using centimetres as a standard unit, $r = 11$ and $h = 150$.

a) Curved surface area $= 2\pi r h$
$$= 2 \times \pi \times 11 \times 150$$
$$= 10\,367.255\,76$$
$$= \underline{10\,400\text{ cm}^2}\text{ (3 s.f.)}$$

b) Volume $= \pi r^2 h$
$$= \pi \times 11^2 \times 150$$
$$= 57\,019.906\,66$$
$$= \underline{57\,000\text{ cm}^3}\text{ (3 s.f.)}$$

The volume of a solid can be used to work out its mass, if you know the density of the material from which it is made. Density is often measured in grams per cubic centimetre or in kilograms per cubic metre.

Mass = volume × density

EXAMPLE

The diagram shows a steel cylinder. It has a radius of 10 centimetres and is 2 centimetres thick.

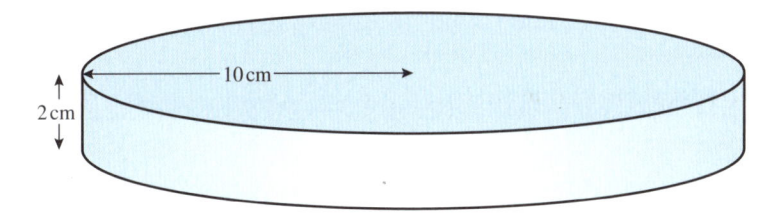

a) Work out the volume of the cylinder.

The steel has a density of 7.6 grams per cubic centimetre.

b) Work out the mass of the cylinder.

SOLUTION

a) The cylinder has $r = 10$ and $h = 2$.
$$\text{Volume} = \pi r^2 h$$
$$= \pi \times 10^2 \times 2$$
$$= 628.3185\,307$$
$$= \underline{629\text{ cm}^3}\text{ (3 s.f.)}$$

b) Mass of cylinder $= 628.3185\,307 \times 7.6$
$$= 4775.220\,833$$
$$= \underline{4780\text{ grams}}$$

EXERCISE 18.4

1. A cylinder has radius 12 cm and height 19 cm. Find its volume, correct to 3 significant figures.

2. A cylinder has radius 5 cm and height 2 cm. Find its curved surface area, correct to 3 significant figures.

3. A cylinder has diameter 22 cm and height 8 cm.
   a) Find its volume, correct to 3 significant figures.
   b) Find its curved surface area, correct to 3 significant figures.

4. A cylinder has radius 6 cm and height 4.5 cm. Find its volume, correct to 3 significant figures.

5. The diagram shows a hollow cylinder.

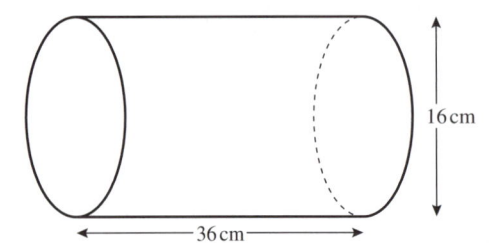

   Work out the curved surface area of the cylinder, correct to 3 significant figures.

6. A hollow cylindrical pipeline has an internal diameter of 15 cm. The pipeline is 120 metres in length.
   a) Work out the volume of the pipeline. Give your answer in cm^3, correct to 3 significant figures.
   b) $1000 \, cm^3 = 1$ litre. Express the volume of the pipeline in litres.

7. A biscuit tin is in the shape of a cylinder. It has radius 9 cm and height 14 cm. Work out the volume of the cylinder. Give your answer to the nearest cm^3.

8. A cylinder of radius 8.5 cm has a volume of $3178 \, cm^3$, correct to 4 significant figures. Work out the height of the cylinder.

9. A sweet packet is in the shape of a hollow cardboard cylinder. The inside diameter of the cylinder is 2.5 cm and it has a height of 15 cm.
   a) Work out the volume of the cylinder, correct to 3 significant figures.
   b) The sweets have a volume of $1.5 \, cm^3$ each. Show that the packet cannot contain as many as 50 sweets.

10. Nick and Alan have been working on an exercise about cylinders. They have to find the volume of a cylinder with diameter 14 cm and height 24 cm.

    Nick: The volume is $3690 \, cm^3$ correct to 3 significant figures.

    Alan: The volume is $14\,800 \, cm^3$ correct to 3 significant figures.

    a) Work out who was right.
    b) Suggest what mistake has been made by the person who was wrong.

18.5 Exact calculations using pi

So far in this chapter you have used the pi key on your calculator. Although this is very convenient, it does introduce a slight inaccuracy in your work.

You can make exact statements about areas and volumes of circles and cylinders, by leaving π in your working and final answer. Some exam questions will instruct you to do this.

EXAMPLE

The diagram shows a circular washer. It is made from a circular sheet of radius 4 mm, with a circular hole of radius 2 mm removed. Work out the area of the washer. Leave your answer in terms of π.

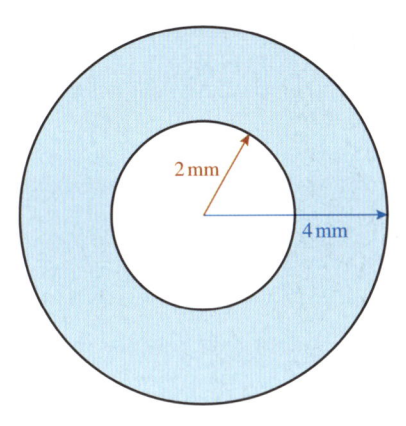

SOLUTION

The area of the larger circle is $\pi r^2 = \pi \times 4^2$
$= \pi \times 16$
$= 16\pi \text{ mm}^2$

The area of the smaller circle is $\pi r^2 = \pi \times 2^2$
$= \pi \times 4$
$= 4\pi \text{ mm}^2$

Thus the area of the washer $= 16\pi - 4\pi$
$= \underline{12\pi \text{ mm}^2}$

EXAMPLE

A cylinder has height 8.5 cm and radius 4 cm. Work out its curved surface area and volume. Leave your answer in terms of π.

SOLUTION

For this cylinder, $h = 8.5$ and $r = 4$.

$$\begin{aligned}\text{Curved surface area} &= 2\pi rh \\ &= 2 \times \pi \times 4 \times 8.5 \\ &= 2 \times \pi \times 34 \\ &= \pi \times 68 \\ &= \underline{68\pi \text{ cm}^2}\end{aligned}$$

$$\begin{aligned}\text{Volume} &= \pi r^2 h \\ &= \pi \times 4^2 \times 8.5 \\ &= \pi \times 16 \times 8.5 \\ &= \pi \times 136 \\ &= \underline{136\pi \text{ cm}^2}\end{aligned}$$

EXERCISE 18.5

1 A circle has diameter 24 cm. Work out its circumference and area. Leave your answer as an exact multiple of π.

2 A circle has radius 11 cm. Work out its circumference and area. Leave your answer in terms of π.

3 A cylinder has radius 12 cm and height 8 cm.
   a) Find the curved surface area of the cylinder.
   b) Find the volume of the cylinder.
   Give your answers as exact multiples of π.

4 A circle has circumference 24π centimetres.
   a) Find the exact radius of the circle.
   b) Find the exact area of the circle. Leave your answer in terms of π.

5 A circle has area 121π square centimetres.
   a) Find the exact radius of the circle.
   b) Find the exact circumference of the circle.

6 A cylinder has volume 300π cm³. It has radius 10 cm. Work out its height.

7 A cylinder has volume 480π cm³. It has diameter 8 cm. Work out its height.

8 The diagram shows a quadrant of a circle. The radius is 16 cm.

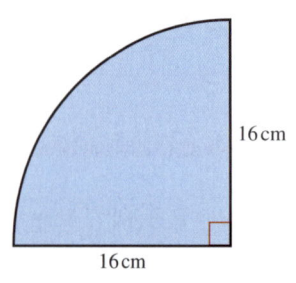

a) Find the area of the quadrant, in terms of π.
b) Find an exact expression for the perimeter of the quadrant.

9 The diagram shows an ornamental design. It is in the shape of a square, with a semicircle on each of the four sides. The square is of side 12 cm.

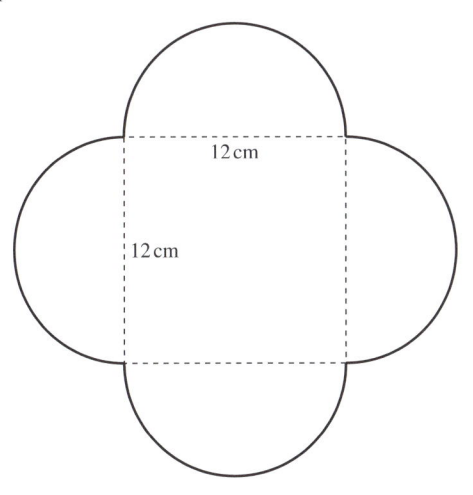

a) Find the area of one of the semicircles, leaving your answer in terms of π.
b) Hence find an exact expression for the area of the ornamental design.

10 The diagram shows two cylinders. Cylinder A has diameter 6 cm and height 8 cm. Cylinder B has diameter 8 cm and height 6 cm.

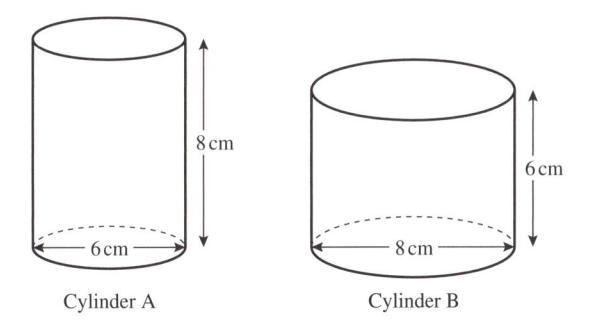

a) Show that both cylinders have exactly the same curved surface area.
b) Work out the volume of each cylinder, leaving your answers in terms of π. Which cylinder has the larger volume?

REVIEW EXERCISE 18

1 A circle has radius 28 cm. Work out its area, correct to 3 significant figures.

2 A circle has diameter 90 mm. Work out its circumference, correct to 3 significant figures.

3 A circle has radius 1.9 cm. Work out its circumference, correct to 4 significant figures.

4 A circle has diameter 64 mm. Work out its area, correct to 4 significant figures.

5 A circle has an area of 64π cm².
  a) Write down its radius.
  b) Find its circumference. Give your answer in terms of π.

6 A closed cylinder has a radius of 10 cm and a height of 15 cm.
   a) Calculate the curved surface area of the cylinder.
   b) Calculate the area of one of its circular ends.
   c) Hence find the total surface area of the cylinder.

7 A circle has a circumference of 15.71 cm, correct to 4 significant figures.
   a) Calculate the radius of this circle.
   b) Hence find the area of the circle. Give your answer to 3 significant figures.

8 The diagram shows a rectangle inscribed in a circle.
   AB = 5 cm, BC = 12 cm, AC = 13 cm.
   The line segment AC is a **diameter** of the circle.
   Work out the size of the shaded area.
   Give your answer to 3 significant figures.

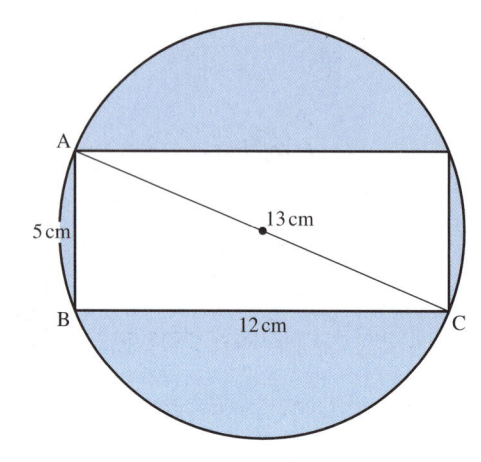

9 The radius of a circle is 5.1 m.

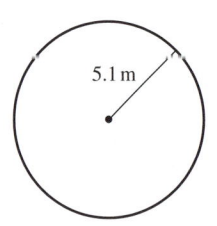

   Work out the area of the circle. State the units of your answer. [Edexcel]

10 A circle has a radius of 3 cm.

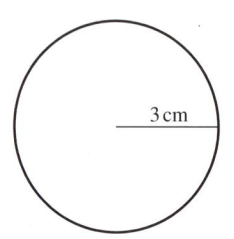

   a) Work out the area of the circle. Give your answer correct to 3 significant figures.
   A semicircle has a diameter of 9 cm.

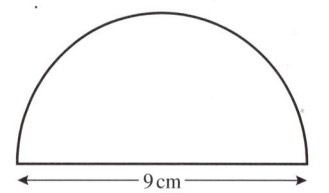

   b) Work out the perimeter of the semicircle. Give your answer correct to
      3 significant figures. [Edexcel]

11 The diagram shows a semicircle.
The diameter of the semicircle is 15 cm.

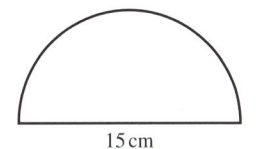

Diagram *not* accurately drawn

15 cm

Calculate the area of the semicircle. Give your answer correct to 3 significant figures. [Edexcel]

12 A circle has a radius of 32 cm. Work out the circumference of the circle. Give your answer correct to the nearest centimetre. [Edexcel]

13 The diagram shows a right-angled triangle ABC and a circle.

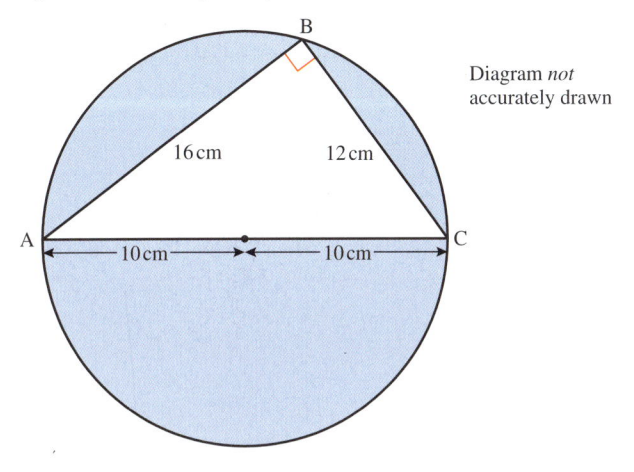

Diagram *not* accurately drawn

A, B and C are points on the circumference of the circle. AC is a diameter of the circle.
The radius of the circle is 10 cm. AB = 16 cm and BC = 12 cm.
Work out the area of the shaded part of the circle. Give your answer correct to the nearest cm^2. [Edexcel]

14 A can of drink is in the shape of a cylinder.
The can has a radius of 4 cm and a height of 15 cm.

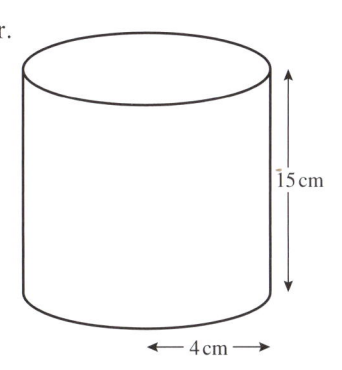

Diagram *not* accurately drawn

Calculate the volume of the cylinder. Give your answer correct to 3 significant figures. [Edexcel]

15 A ten pence coin has a diameter of 2.45 cm.

Work out the circumference of the coin. Give your answer in cm correct to 1 decimal place. [Edexcel]

16 An ice hockey puck is in the shape of a cylinder with a radius of 3.8 cm, and a thickness of 2.5 cm.

It is made out of rubber with a density of 1.5 grams per cm^3.

Work out the mass of the ice hockey puck. Give your answer correct to 3 significant figures.

Diagram *not* accurately drawn

[Edexcel]

17 The diagram shows a shape, made from a semicircle and a rectangle.

The diameter of the semicircle is 12 cm.
The length of the rectangle is 14 cm.
Calculate the **perimeter** of the shape.
Give your answer correct to
3 significant figures.

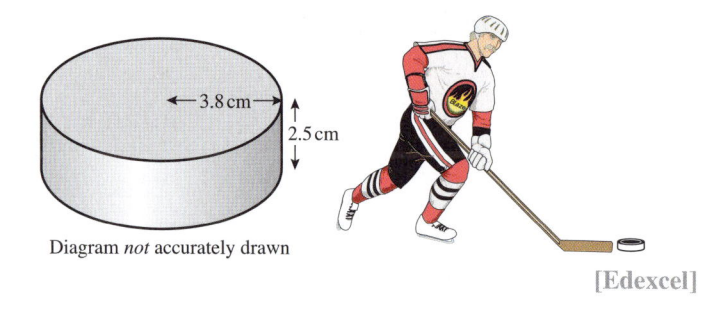

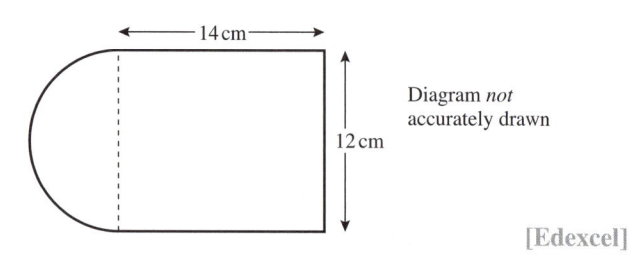

Diagram *not* accurately drawn

[Edexcel]

18 The heaviest stick of rock ever made was in the shape of a cylinder. The cylinder had a length of 503 cm and a radius of 21.6 cm.

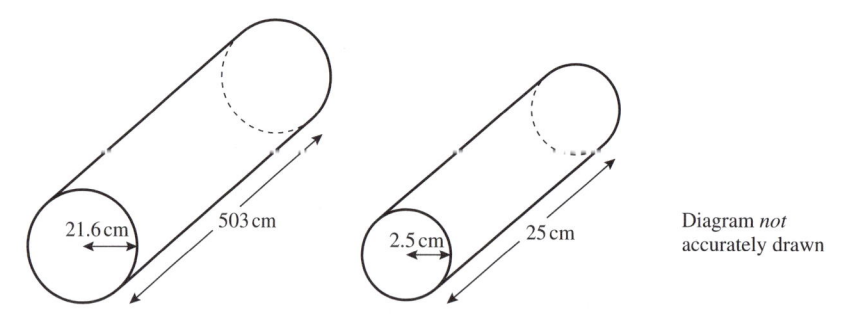

Diagram *not* accurately drawn

a) Work out the volume of the cylinder. Give your answer correct to 3 significant figures.

A small stick of rock, in the shape of a cylinder, has a length of 25 cm and a radius of 2.5 cm. It is made using the same recipe as the heaviest stick of rock. The weight of the heaviest stick of rock ever made was 413.6 kg.

b) Calculate the weight of the small stick of rock. Give your answer, in grams, correct to 3 significant figures.

[Edexcel]

19 The diagram shows a sector of a circle, centre O.

The radius of the circle is 9 cm. The angle at the centre of the circle is 40°.
Find the perimeter of the sector. Leave your answer in terms of π.

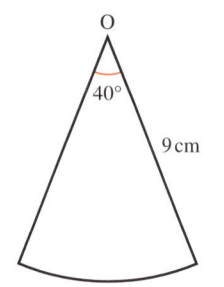

Diagram *not* accurately drawn

[Edexcel]

284 U4 18 Circles and cylinders

20 The diagram shows the shape PQRST.

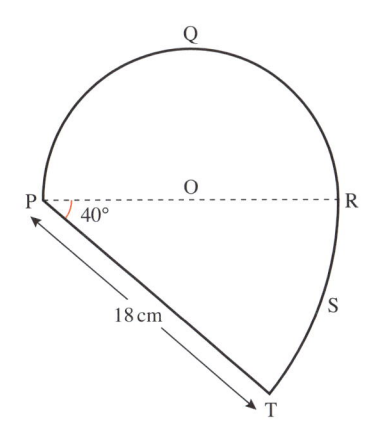

Diagram *not* accurately drawn

RST is a circular arc with centre P and radius 18 cm. Angle RPT = 40°.

a) Calculate the length of the circular arc RST. Give your answer correct to 3 significant figures.

PQR is a semicircle with centre O.

b) Calculate the total area of the shape PQRST. Give your answer correct to 3 significant figures.

[Edexcel]

KEY POINTS

1. The circumference of a circle of radius r is found from the formula $C = 2\pi r$

   Writing the diameter as d, you could also use $C = \pi d$

2. The area of a circle is found from the formula $A = \pi r^2$

3. When reading exam questions, take care to check whether you have been told the radius or the diameter of the circle.

4. A sector of a circle is a slice formed by two radii. To compute the area of a sector, begin by working out the area for the full circle. Then compute the corresponding fraction of this. If the sector forms an angle of x degrees, then its area is $\dfrac{x}{360}$ of the full circle.

5. A sector is bounded by a curved arc and two radii. The arc length of a sector can be found in a similar way, by taking a fraction of the full circumference. If a question asks you to find the perimeter of a sector, remember to include the two radii as well as the curved arc.

6. The volume of a cylinder of radius r and height h is $V = \pi r^2 h$

7. The curved surface area of the cylinder is $A = 2\pi rh$

8. Make sure that you know how to use your calculator's π key correctly. Answers to calculations will normally need to be rounded off: an exam question will tell you how many significant figures or decimal places are required. It is a good idea to show your unrounded answer too.

9. Remember that some exam questions will ask you to leave your answers as exact expressions in terms of π.

Internet Challenge 18

Measuring the Earth

A few hundred years ago, many people thought the Earth was flat. They feared you might fall off the edge if you travelled too far from home!

Most people now accept that the Earth is roughly spherical, with a diameter of roughly 12 800 kilometres.

Use the internet to help research the answers to these questions about the Earth.

1. What observational evidence can you find to support the claim that the Earth is roughly spherical?
2. What organisation claims to have been 'deprogramming the masses since 1547'?
3. Find an accurate value for the Earth's equatorial diameter. Use this figure to calculate the Earth's circumference (around the equator).
4. Find an accurate value for the Earth's polar diameter. Use this figure to calculate the Earth's circumference pole to pole.
5. Find the definition of a Great Circle. Is the equator a Great Circle?
6. Who was the first person to circumnavigate the globe, that is, to travel right around the Earth? How long did the journey take, and when was it completed?
7. Who first circumnavigated the world pole to pole? When?
8. Some adventurous sailors take part in round the world yacht races. How far do they typically travel? Do you think they really do travel around the world, in the strictest sense?
9. What is the origin of our word 'geometry'?
10. The size of the Earth was first measured accurately by Eratosthenes, around 200 BC. Find out as much as you can about Eratosthenes and the methods he used. You might want to collect your findings into a poster for your classroom, or prepare a Powerpoint presentation for your class.

CHAPTER 19

Constructions and loci

In this chapter you will **learn how to**:
- construct triangles from given information
- carry out standard compass constructions on line segments
- solve locus problems, including the use of bearings.

You will also be **challenged to**:
- investigate perspective.

Starter: Round and round in circles

Use a sharp pencil, compasses and straight edge to make this drawing.

You may want to colour the diagram after you have made it.

Here are some ideas:

Now try designing your own circle patterns.

19.1 Constructing triangles from given information

Surveyors often use a method called **triangulation** to measure distances. The idea is to measure some combination of angles and distances, and then use them to reconstruct a triangle whose vertex is at the place being surveyed. In fact, many mountaintops in the UK have concrete blocks, or triangulation points, that have been used in this way.

There are several different ways of constructing triangles, depending on the information you are given about them.

1. **To construct a triangle, given two sides and the angle in between them (SAS, or side–angle–side)**

EXAMPLE

A triangle PQR has sides PQ = 9 cm, PR = 5 cm and angle QPR = 55°. Make an accurate construction of this triangle.

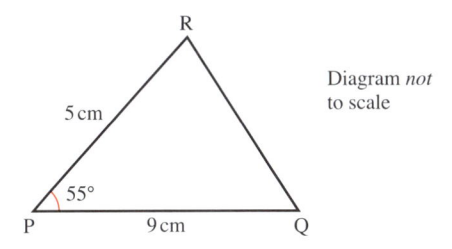

Diagram *not* to scale

SOLUTION

Begin by using your ruler to draw a line segment of length 9 cm, and label the ends P and Q. Then use your protractor to measure an angle of 55° at P.

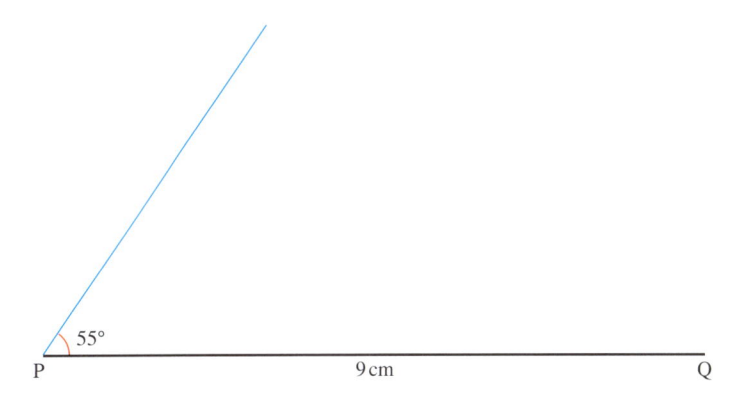

Next, measure a length of 5 cm along the line from P, to locate the point R.

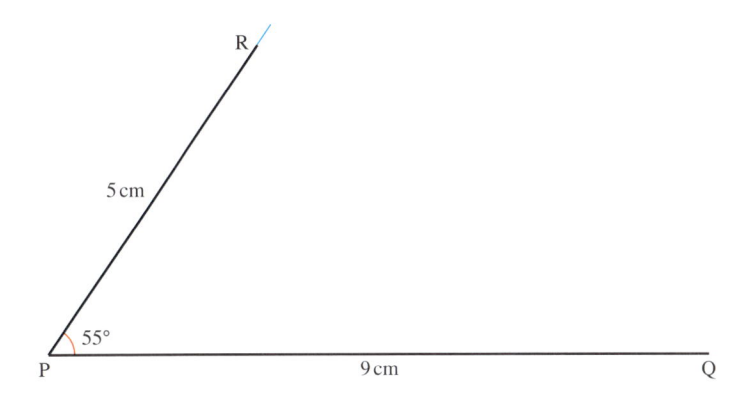

Finally, complete the construction by joining R and Q.

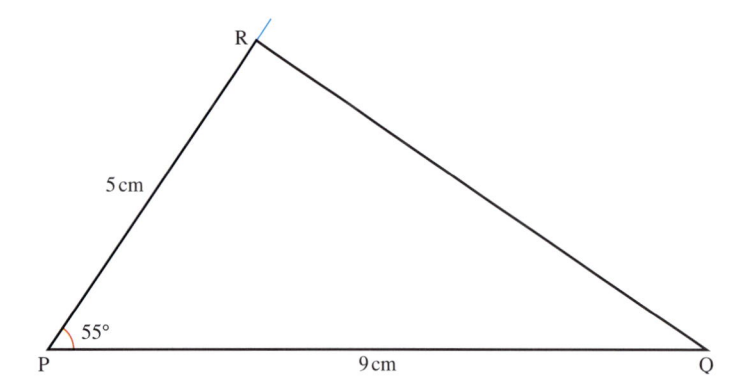

A different procedure is used when you know two angles and an included side.

2. To construct a triangle, given two angles and the side in between them (ASA, or angle–side–angle)

EXAMPLE

A triangle ABC has side AB = 8 cm, angle BAC = 40° and angle ABC = 70°. Make an accurate construction of this triangle.

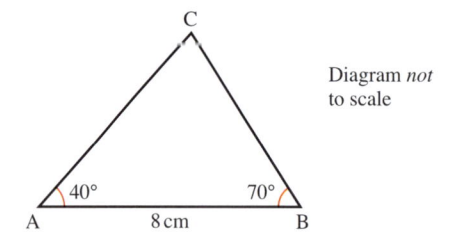

Diagram *not* to scale

SOLUTION

Begin by constructing a line segment AB, of length 8 cm, and add a line from A at an angle of 40°, using your protractor to measure this angle.

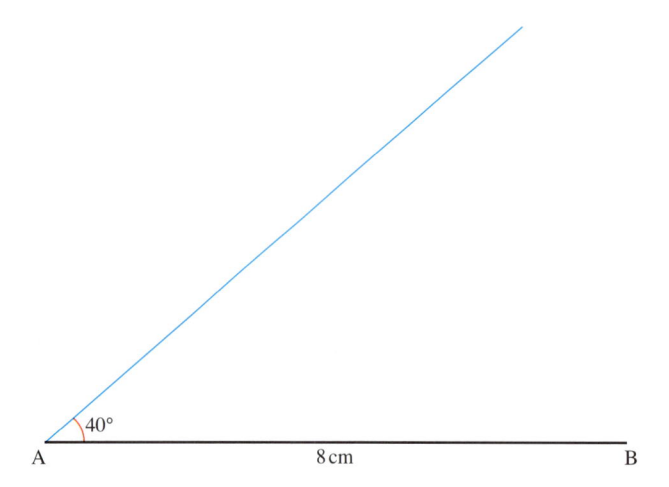

Next, draw a line at an angle of 70° from B.

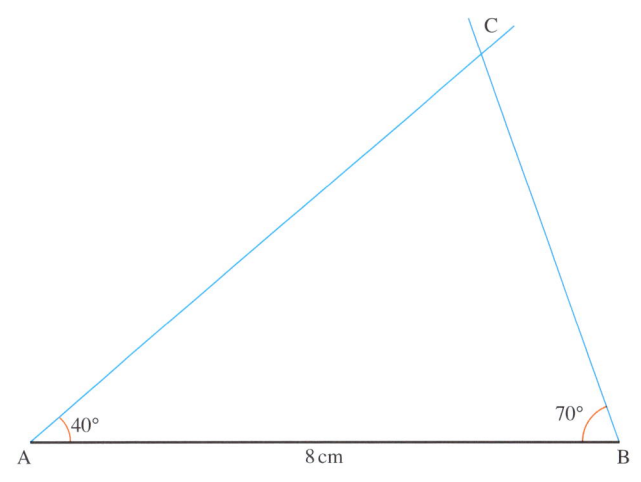

These two lines must intersect at C, so the diagram may be completed:

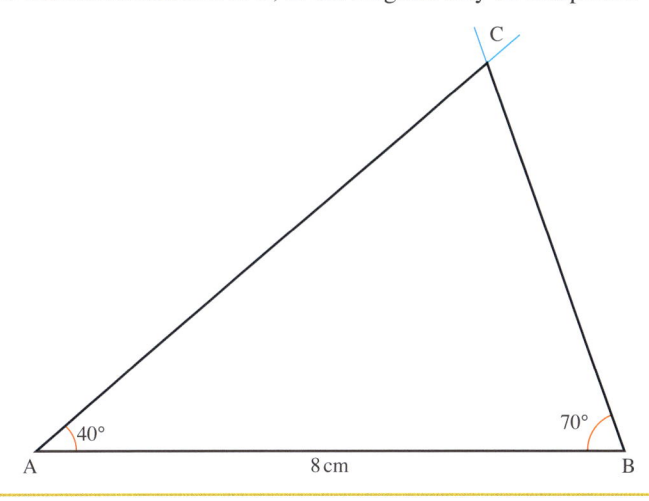

You may be given the values of all three sides but no angles at all. A protractor is now of no use, and you need compasses instead.

3. To construct a triangle, given three sides (SSS, or side–side–side)

EXAMPLE

A triangle LMN has sides LM = 6 cm, LN = 7 cm and MN = 8 cm. Make an accurate construction of this triangle.

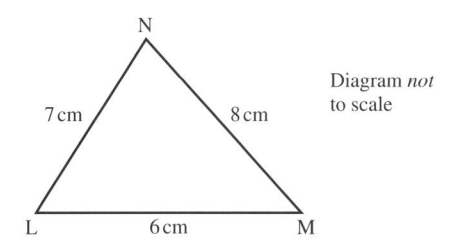

Diagram *not* to scale

SOLUTION

Begin by constructing a line segment LM, of length 6 cm.

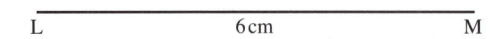

Next, draw an arc of radius 7 cm from L, and another of radius 8 cm from M.

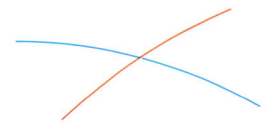

These arcs must intersect at N, so the construction can be completed.

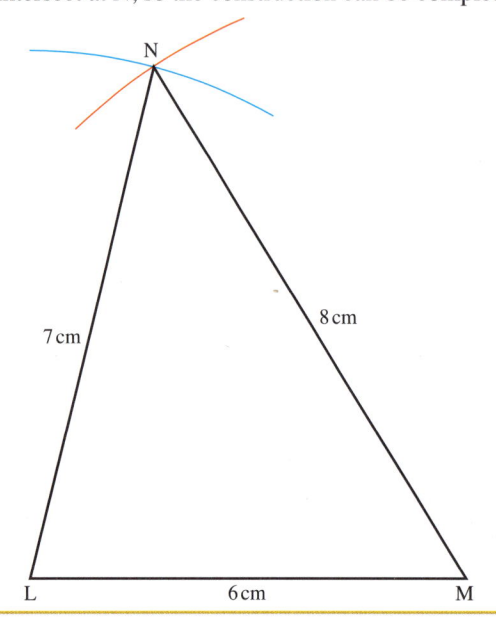

A more confusing scenario is encountered when you are given the values of two sides, and an angle that is *not* included between them. The construction may be *ambiguous*, or even *impossible*!

4. To construct a triangle, given two sides and an angle not between them (SSA, or side–side–angle)

EXAMPLE

In triangle ABC you are given that AB = 7 cm, BC = 5 cm and angle CAB = 40°.

Construct an accurate drawing of this triangle, and show that there are two different solutions based on the given information.

SOLUTION

Begin by drawing a line segment AB of length 7 cm, and construct a line from A at an angle of 40°.

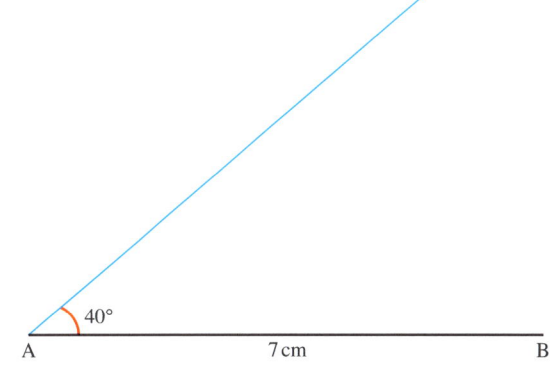

Now open your compasses to a radius of 5 cm, and draw an arc centred on B.

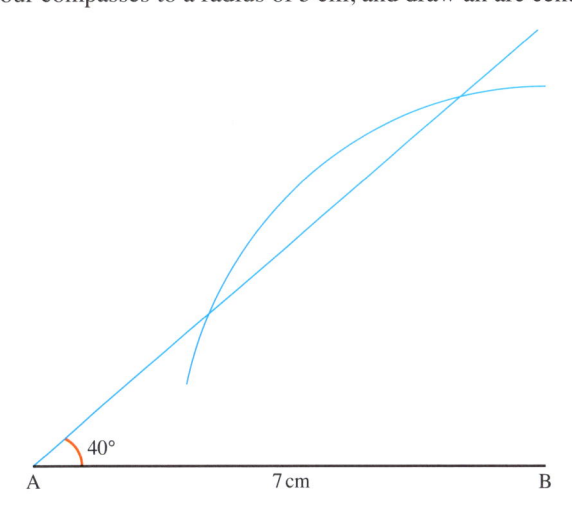

This arc intersects the original line from A in two distinct places, so there are two different ways of completing the construction.

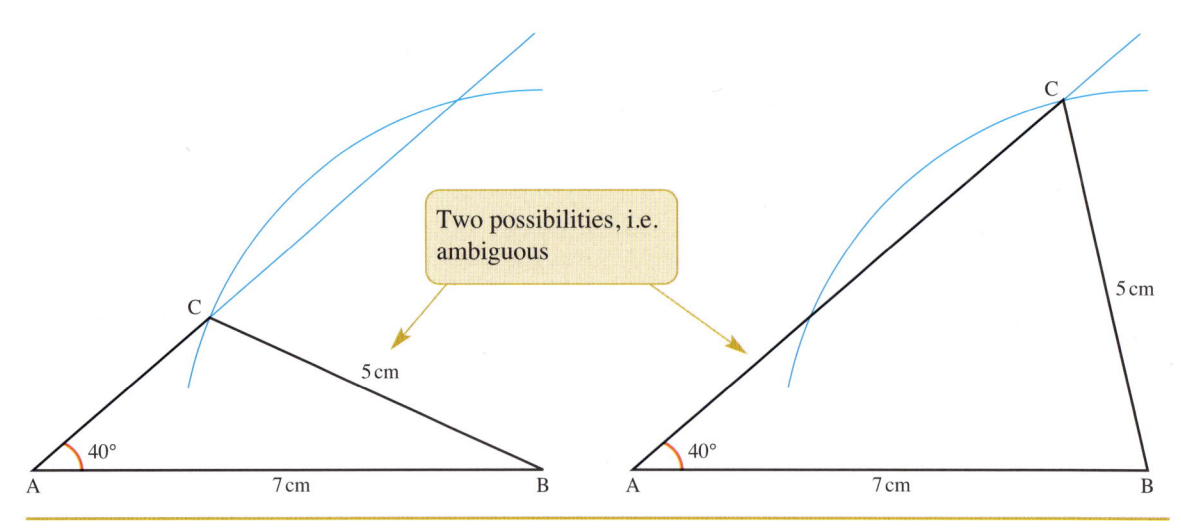

The following exercise gives you some practice at making accurate drawings of triangles. Make sure you leave your construction lines visible, so that your teacher can follow your methods clearly.

EXERCISE 19.1

Make accurate drawings of these triangles, stating which of the various combinations of information you have been given – SAS, ASA, SSS or SSA. If any triangles are ambiguous, draw both possibilities.

1. Draw triangle PQR with PQ = 8 cm, PR = 9 cm, angle QPR = 65°.

2. Draw triangle KLM with KL = 5 cm, angle MKL = 80°, angle KLM = 56°.

3. Draw triangle ABC with AB = 6 cm, AC = 5 cm, angle BAC = 130°.

4. Draw triangle RST with RT = 7.5 cm, RS = 8.5 cm, angle RTS = 90°.

5. Draw triangle PQR with PQ = 8 cm, PR = 7.5 cm, angle PQR = 62°.

6. Draw triangle FGH with HG = 8 cm, HF = 10 cm, FG = 6 cm.

7. The sketch shows a triangle with AB = 85 mm, BC = 55 mm, AC = 70 mm.

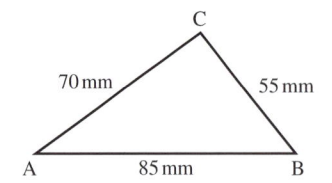

   Diagram *not* accurately drawn

   Make an accurate diagram of the triangle.

8 The sketch shows a triangle with AB = 75 mm, AC = 70 mm and angle ACB = 90°.

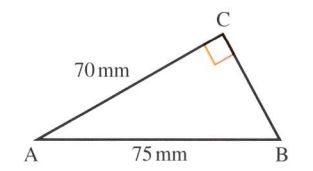

Diagram *not* accurately drawn

Make an accurate diagram of the triangle.

9 Using compasses, try to make an accurate drawing of triangle PQR with sides PQ = 10 cm, QR = 5 cm, RP = 4 cm. What difficulty do you encounter? Explain why this arises.

10 Triangle JKL is to be constructed with JK = 8 cm, KL = 6.5 cm and angle LJK = 45°.
  a) Try making an accurate construction of this triangle.
  b) What difficulty do you encounter?

19.2 Constructions with line segments

There are four fundamental geometrical constructions that you need to master. Exam questions will expect you to do these with compasses and a straight edge, not with measuring equipment, such as protractors, and ruler measurements would not be permitted. You should leave any construction lines plainly visible.

1. To bisect a given angle

EXAMPLE

Use ruler and compasses to construct the angle bisector of the angle Q shown in the diagram.

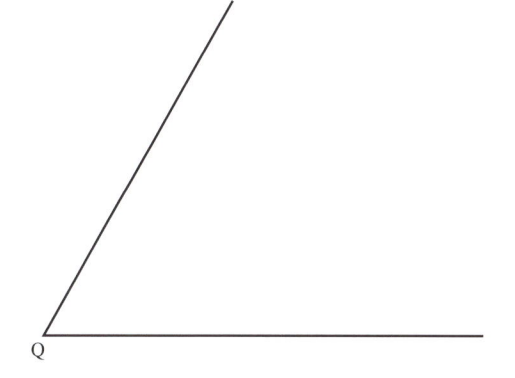

SOLUTION

Using compasses, draw an arc with centre Q, so it cuts one of the original lines. Call this point P.

Without changing the compass setting, construct a second arc with centre Q, to cut the other line at R.

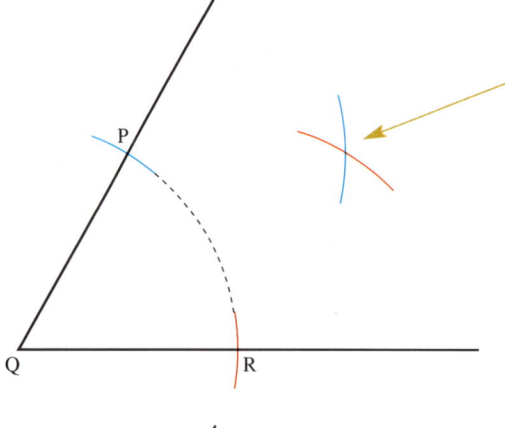

Next, construct two further arcs, centres P and R, to cut here. Once again, do not change the compass setting.

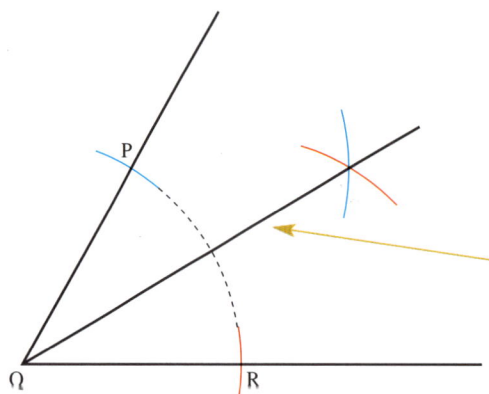

Finally, complete the construction by drawing a straight line from Q to the point of intersection here.

The original angle at Q has now been *divided into two equal parts* – it has been **bisected**.

2. To construct the perpendicular bisector of a given line segment

EXAMPLE

Use straight edge and compasses to construct the perpendicular bisector of the line segment shown in the diagram.

SOLUTION

Open the compasses to more than half the distance from K to L.

From K, construct these two arcs …

… and from L, construct these two.

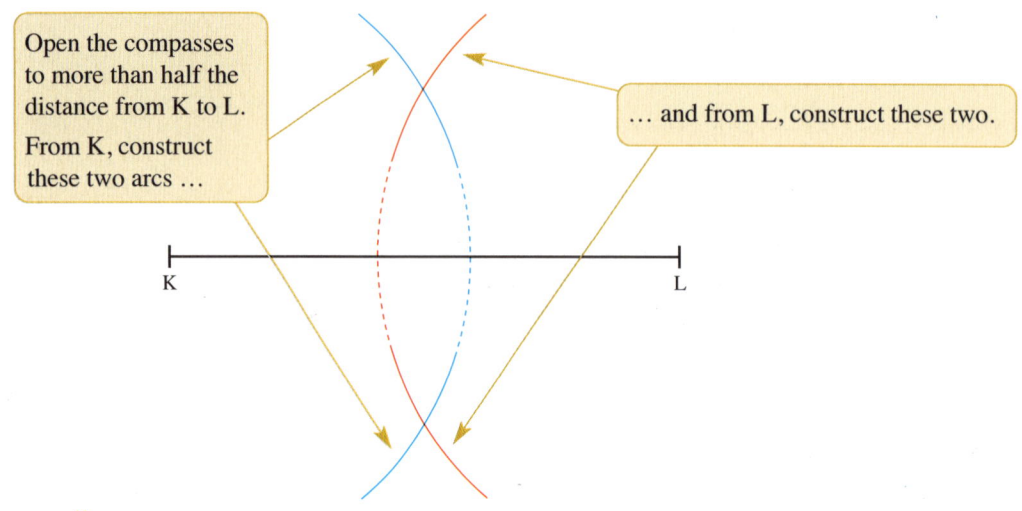

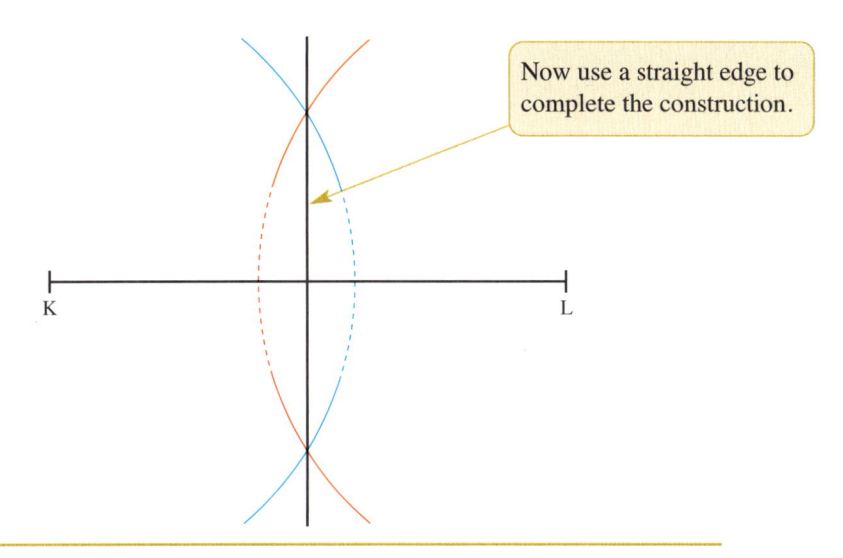

Now use a straight edge to complete the construction.

3. To drop a perpendicular from a point to a given line segment

EXAMPLE

Use straight edge and compasses to draw a line from P perpendicular to the line segment shown in the diagram.

SOLUTION

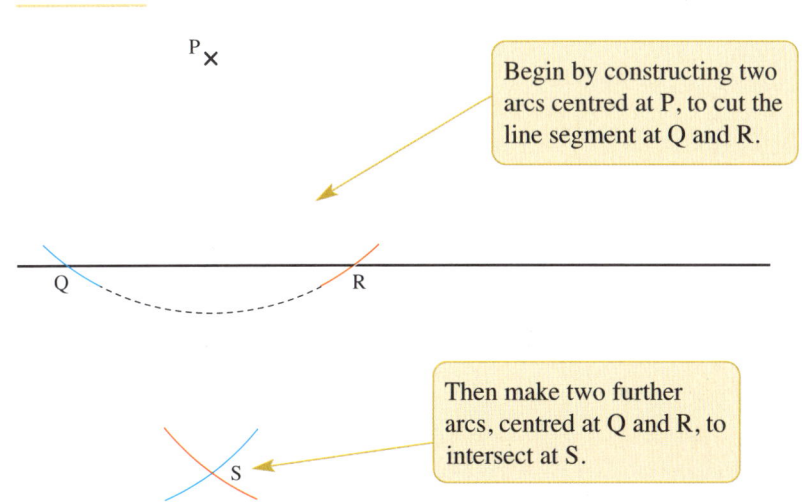

Begin by constructing two arcs centred at P, to cut the line segment at Q and R.

Then make two further arcs, centred at Q and R, to intersect at S.

19 Constructions and loci U4

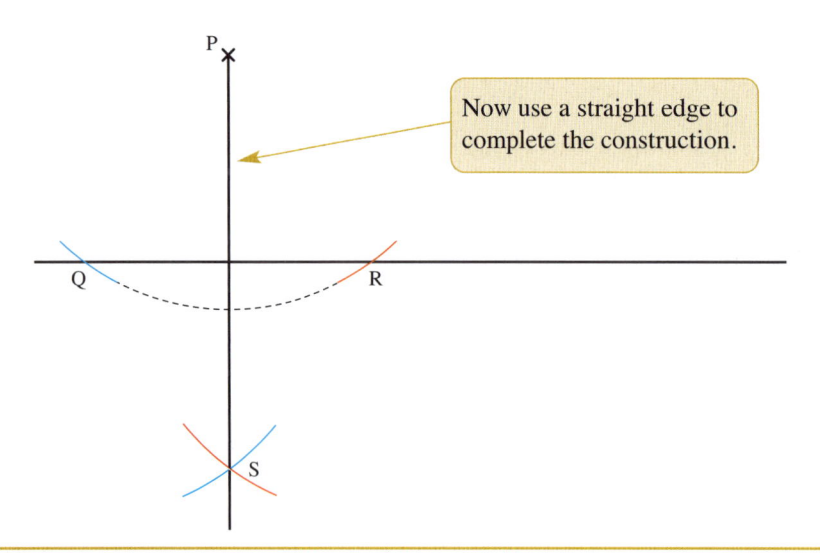

Now use a straight edge to complete the construction.

4. To construct a perpendicular from a point on a given line segment

EXAMPLE

Use straight edge and compasses to draw a line from P perpendicular to the line segment AB shown below.

SOLUTION

First, use compasses to draw two arcs at equal distances on opposite sides of P. Label X and Y where these arcs cut the line AB.

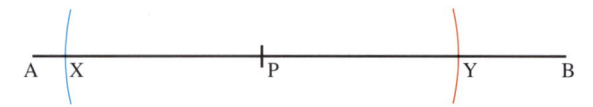

Now complete the solution by constructing the perpendicular bisector of XY, using method 2 from above.

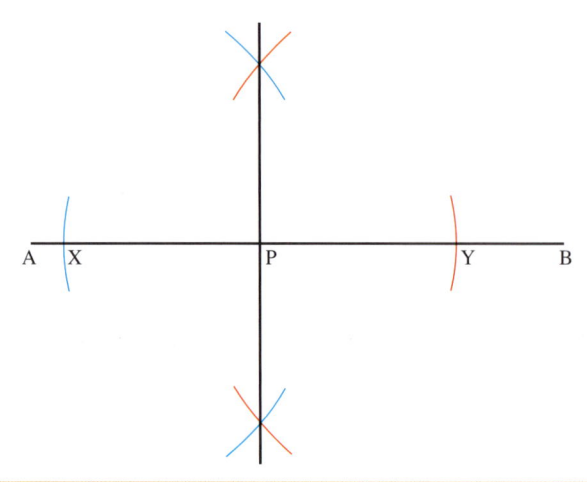

EXERCISE 19.2

Start each of these questions by making a copy of the diagram.

1 Use ruler and compasses to construct the perpendicular bisector of the line segment PQ (PQ is 8 cm long).

P————————————Q

2 Use ruler and compasses to construct the bisector of angle ABC.

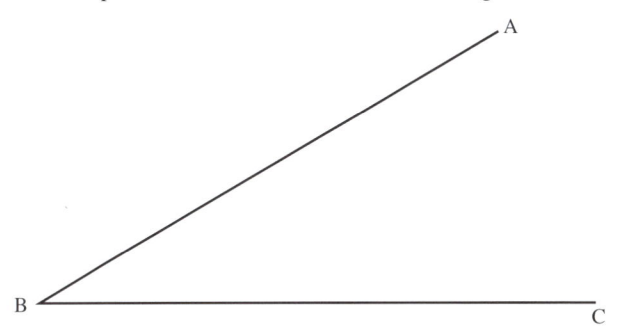

3 Use ruler and compasses to construct the perpendicular from P to the line segment AB.

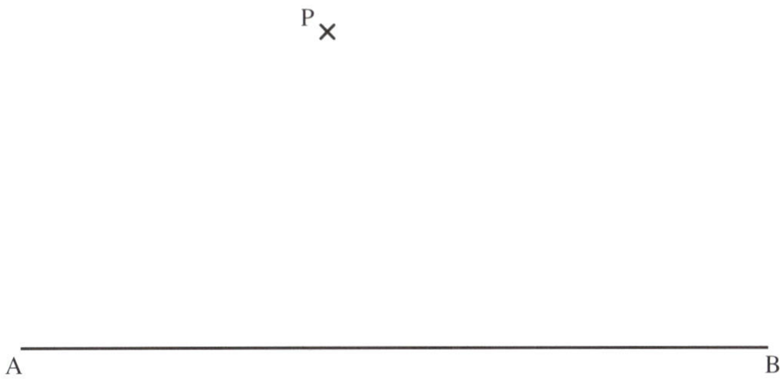

4 Use ruler and compasses to construct a line passing through X, perpendicular to the line PQ.

5 Use ruler and compasses to construct the bisector of angle LMN.

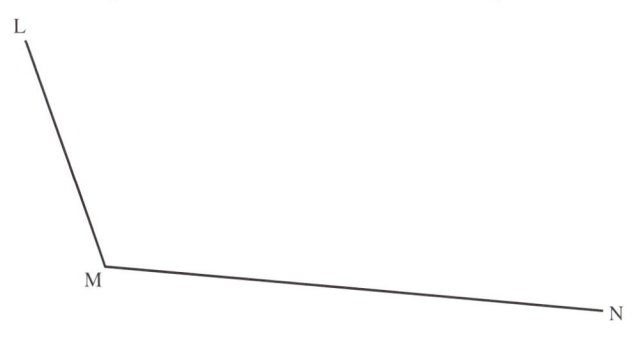

6 Use ruler and compasses to construct the perpendicular bisector of the line segment AB (AB is 6 cm long).

7 Use ruler and compasses to construct a line passing through X, perpendicular to the line PQ.

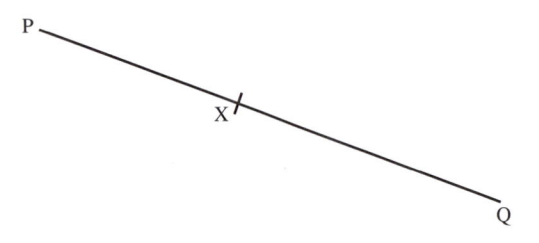

8 Use ruler and compasses to construct the line from P perpendicular to the line segment AB.

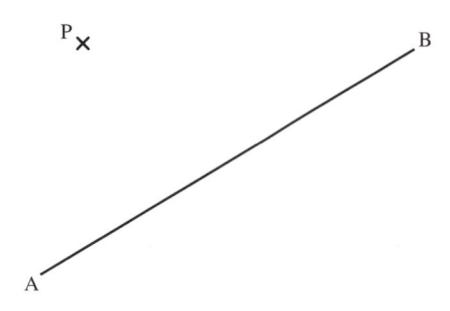

9 Using compasses and a straight edge, construct an angle of exactly 30°.
Hint: Draw a line segment about 7 or 8 centimetres long – the exact length is unimportant. Then use compasses and a straight edge to construct an equilateral triangle, using this segment as one side of the triangle. Finally, take one of the angles and bisect it.

10 Using compasses and a straight edge, construct an angle of exactly 45°.
Hint: Make a right angle (by dropping a perpendicular to a line segment) and then bisect it.

19.3 Locus constructions

When a point P moves in the plane, subject to a certain rule, it traces out a path, known as a **locus** (*plural* **loci**). Here are some loci that you need to know for your GCSE.

P is a fixed distance from a given point, T.

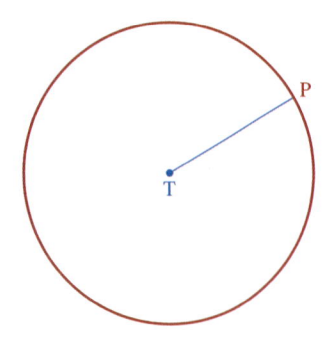

P is a fixed distance from a line segment L.

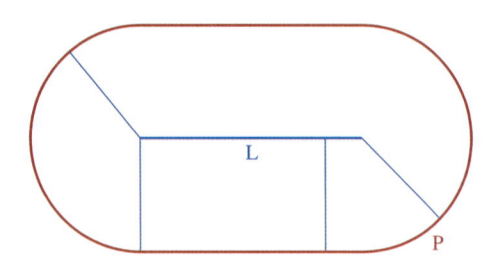

Circle

Rectangle with **semicircular ends**

P is equidistant from two points A and B.

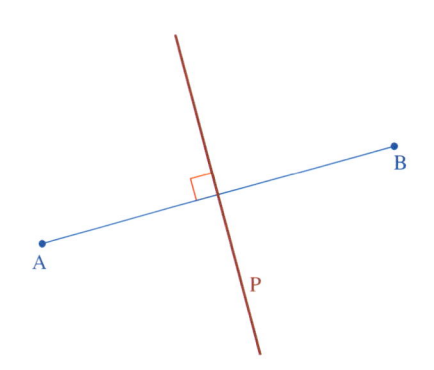

P is equidistant from two line segments L and M.

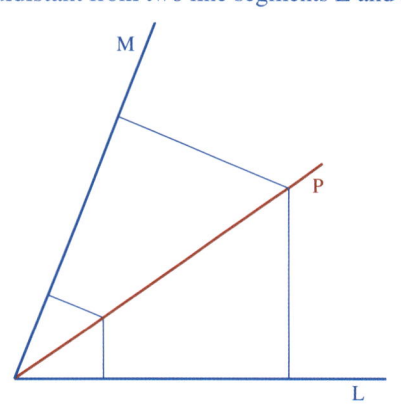

Perpendicular bisector

Angle bisector

P is a fixed distance *inside* a rectangle.

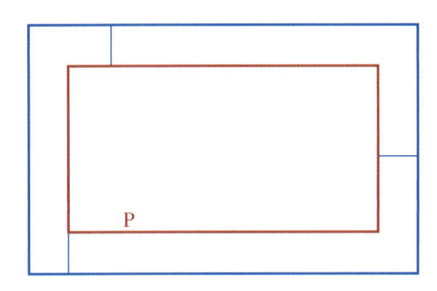

P is a fixed distance *outside* a rectangle.

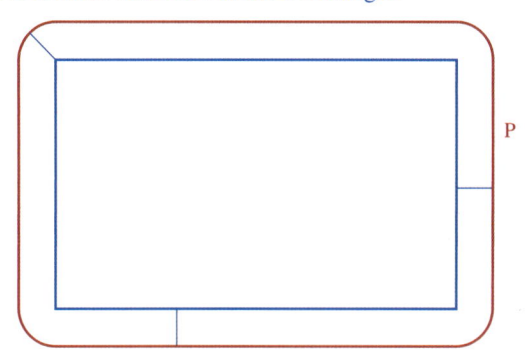

Smaller rectangle

Larger rectangle with **arcs**

EXAMPLE

A ship sails from an island to the mainland. Throughout the journey the ship remains at equal distances from the two lighthouses marked P and Q. Draw the path of the ship's journey.

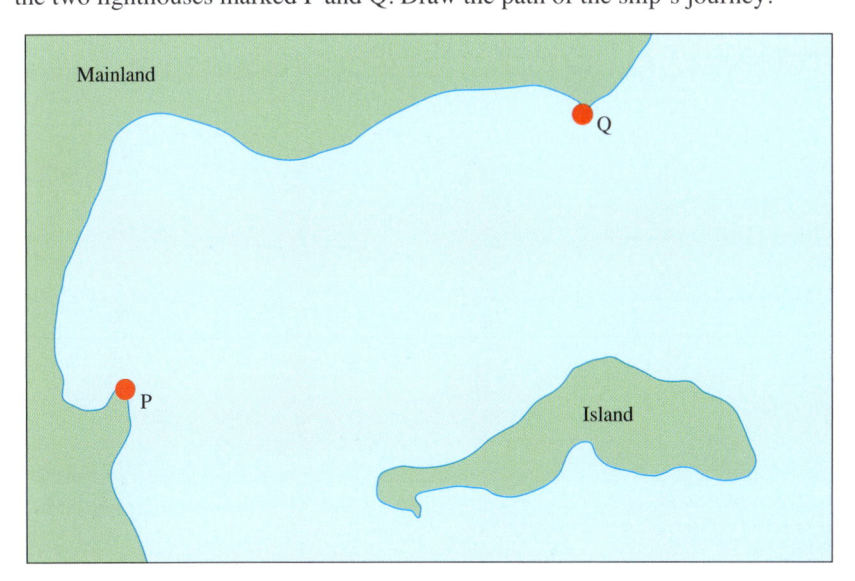

SOLUTION

Using compasses, construct the bisector of PQ:

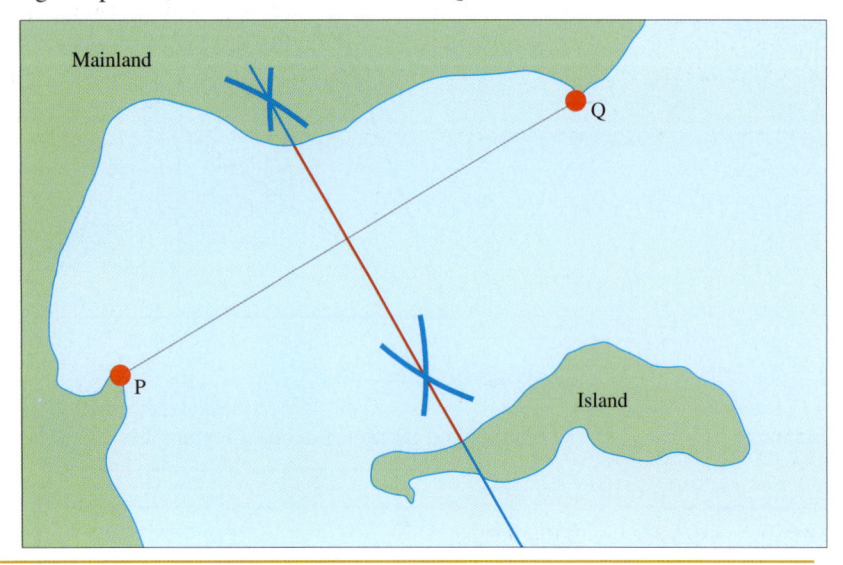

EXAMPLE

The diagram shows a rectangular garden. AB = DC = 3 metres, AD = BC = 6 metres.

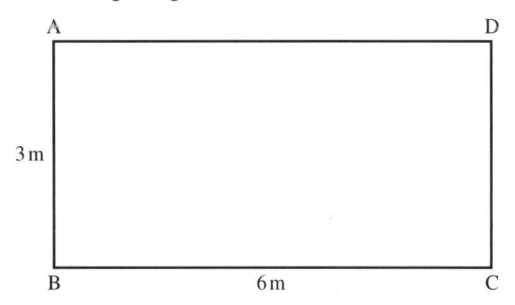

A gardener wishes to plant a tree in the garden. The tree must be the same distance from AB as from BC. The tree must be 3.5 metres from B. Mark the position of the tree on the diagram.

SOLUTION

Construct the bisector of the angle ABC, and also draw an arc of radius 3.5 centred at B. Then the tree must lie on *both* these loci, as indicated.

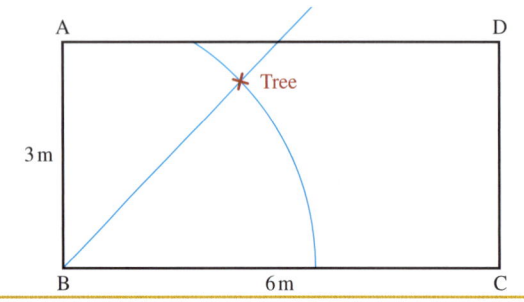

EXERCISE 19.3

1. In the diagram, the rectangle ABCD represents an allotment. It is to be divided up into three regions. The region formed by all points within 3 metres of AD will be planted with potatoes. The region formed by all points within 4 metres of B will be planted with cabbages. The rest of the allotment will be planted with carrots.

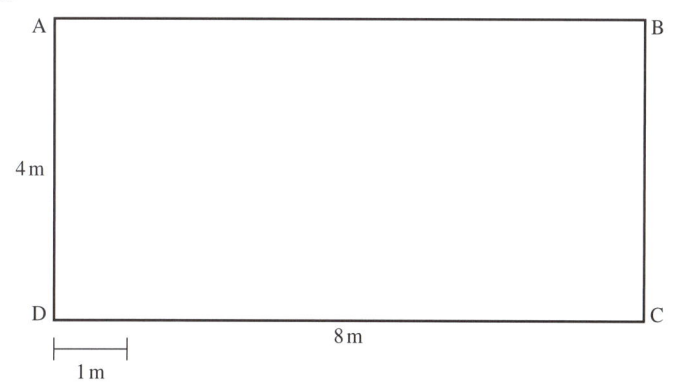

   Indicate each of the three regions on a copy of the diagram.

2. The diagram shows an animal enclosure at a zoo.

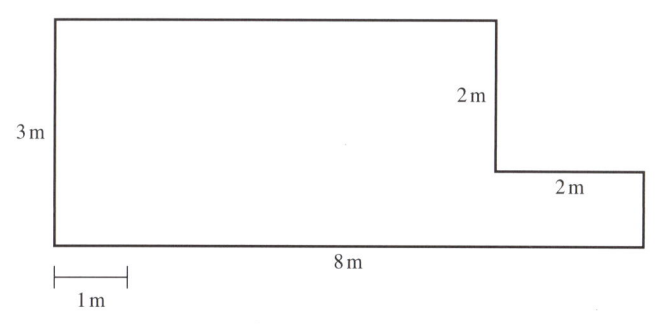

   The zoo management want to erect a safety fence around the outside of the enclosure. They want the public to have a good view of the animals, without getting dangerously close, so they decide that the fence should come to within 1 metre of the nearest point of the enclosure.

   On a copy of the diagram, make a drawing to show the position of the safety fence.

3. The diagram shows a rectangular piece of land. A gravel path is to be laid. The centre line of the path runs diagonally from A to C. All parts of the land within 1 metre of this centre line are to be gravelled.

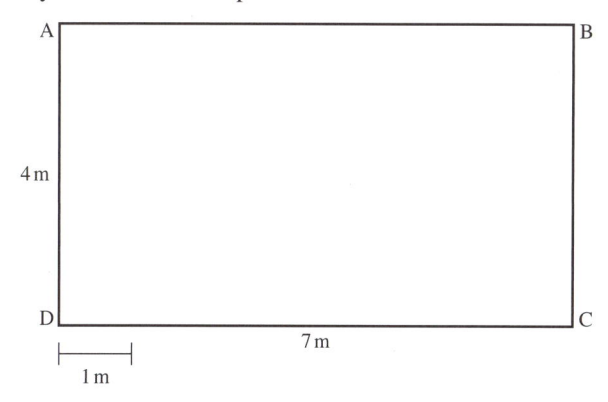

a) On a copy of the diagram, mark the centre line of the path.
b) Shade the region to be gravelled.

A rockery is to be planted in the rectangular plot. The rockery will occupy all points within 1.5 metres of the corner B.

c) Shade the area to be planted as the rockery.

4 In a town there are three mobile phone transmitters, all belonging to the same phone network. When people move around the town, their phones automatically connect to the nearest transmitter. The diagram shows the outline of the town, and the three transmitters, A, B, C.

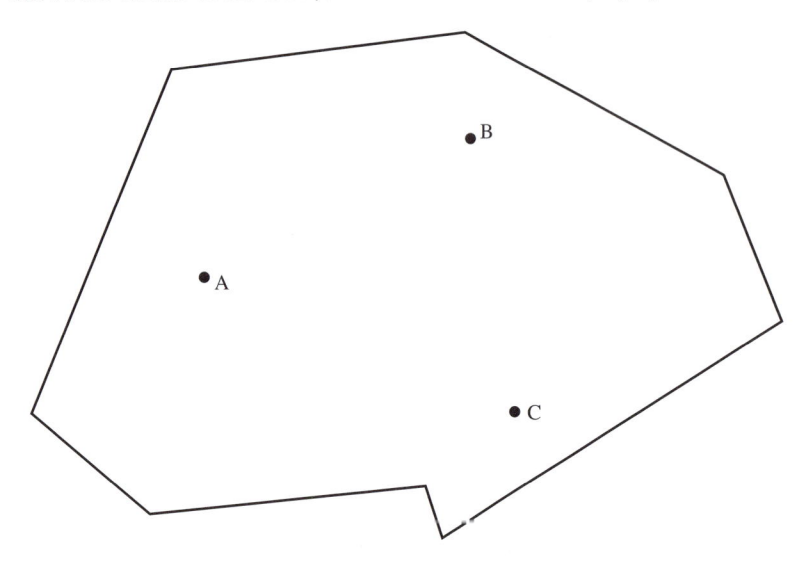

a) Using compasses and a straight edge, construct the locus of all points that are equidistant from A and B.
b) Repeat the construction using B and C, and again, using A and C.
c) Hence divide the town into three service regions, one for each transmitter. Use coloured pencils to mark the regions distinctly.

5 The diagram shows a rectangular flower bed. A gardener is going to add fertiliser to the flower bed. He adds fertiliser to the entire flower bed except those points within 50 cm of its perimeter. The gardener also puts turf around the *outside* of the flower bed. He turfs the region of all points within 50 cm of the *outside* perimeter of the flower bed.

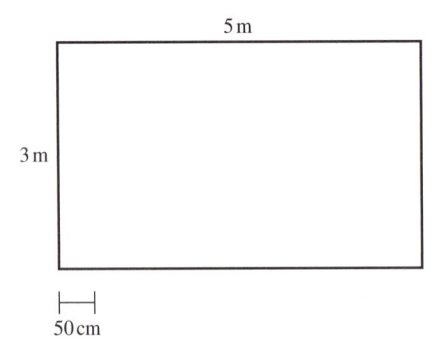

a) Shade the region to which fertiliser is applied.
b) Shade the region that is turfed.

19.4 Bearings

Examination questions may use **bearings** to describe direction.
Here is a reminder of how bearings are used:
- North is taken as the zero angle: 000°.
- Bearings are measured as angles clockwise from North.
  Thus East = 090°, South = 180° and West = 270°.

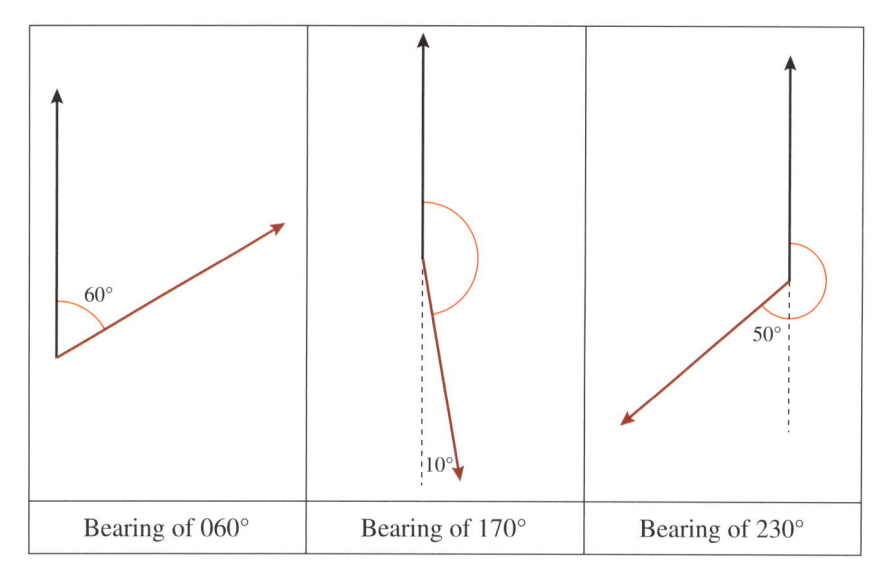

Bearing of 060°	Bearing of 170°	Bearing of 230°

You will have an opportunity to practise using bearings in some of the problems in the Review Exercise.

REVIEW EXERCISE 19

1 Draw the locus of all the points that are 3 cm away from the line AB.

   A   B

   [Edexcel]

2 On a copy of the diagram draw the locus of
   the points, outside the rectangle, that are
   3 centimetres from the edges of this rectangle.

3 Triangle ABC is shown in the diagram.

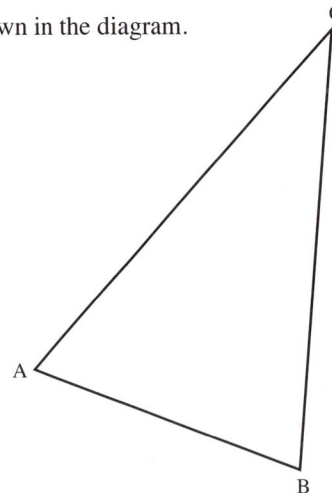

a) On a copy of the diagram, draw accurately the locus of the points which are 3 cm from B.
b) On the diagram, draw accurately the locus of the points which are the same distance from BA as they are from BC.
T is a point inside triangle ABC.
T is 3 cm from B.
T is the same distance from BA as it is from BC.
c) On the diagram, mark the point T clearly with a cross. Label it with the letter T. [Edexcel]

4 B is 5 km North of A.
C is 4 km from B.
C is 7 km from A.

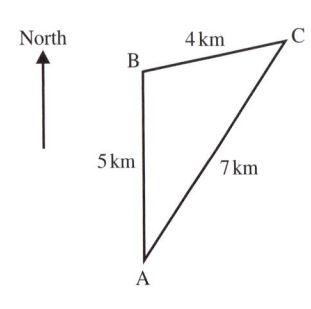

Diagram *not* accurately drawn

a) Make an accurate scale drawing of triangle ABC. Use a scale of 1 cm to 1 km.
b) From your accurate scale drawing, measure the bearing of C from A.
c) Find the bearing of A from C. [Edexcel]

5 ABCD is a quadrilateral.
AB = 6 cm, AC = 9 cm, BC = 5 cm.
Angle BAD = 66°.
AD = 3.5 cm.
Starting with the line AB, make an accurate drawing of the quadrilateral ABCD. [Edexcel]

6

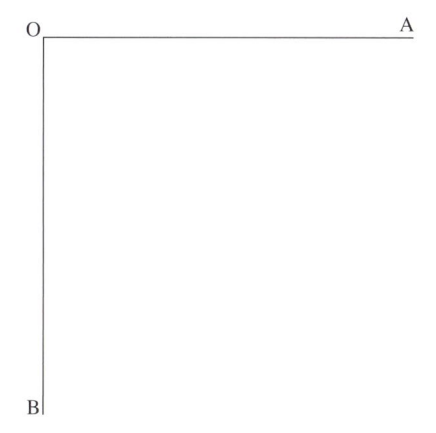

O ─────────────── A
│
│
│
│
│
│
B

a) Draw accurately, on a copy of the diagram above, the locus of points which are the same distance from the line OA and the line OB.

Some points are the same distance from the line OA and the line OB and are also 4 cm from the point B.

b) Mark the positions of these points with crosses. [Edexcel]

7 Here is a sketch of a triangle.

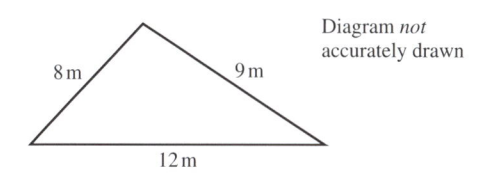

Diagram *not* accurately drawn

Sides: 8 m, 9 m, 12 m

The lengths of the sides of the triangle are 8 m, 9 m and 12 m.
Use a scale of 1 cm to 2 m to make an accurate scale drawing of the triangle. [Edexcel]

8 A map is drawn to a scale of 1 : 25 000
Two schools A and B are 12 centimetres apart on the map.

a) Work out the actual distance from A to B. Give your answer in kilometres.

B is due East of A. C is another school. The bearing of C from A is 064°. The bearing of C from B is 312°.

b) Copy and complete the scale drawing below.
Mark with a cross (✗) the position of the school C.

N ↑

A ──────────────────────────── B [Edexcel]

9 Here is a sketch of a triangle.

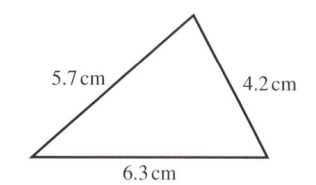

5.7 cm, 4.2 cm, 6.3 cm

Use ruler and compasses to *construct* this triangle accurately.
You must show all construction lines. [Edexcel]

10 The diagram is a plan of a field drawn to a scale of 1 cm to 20 m.

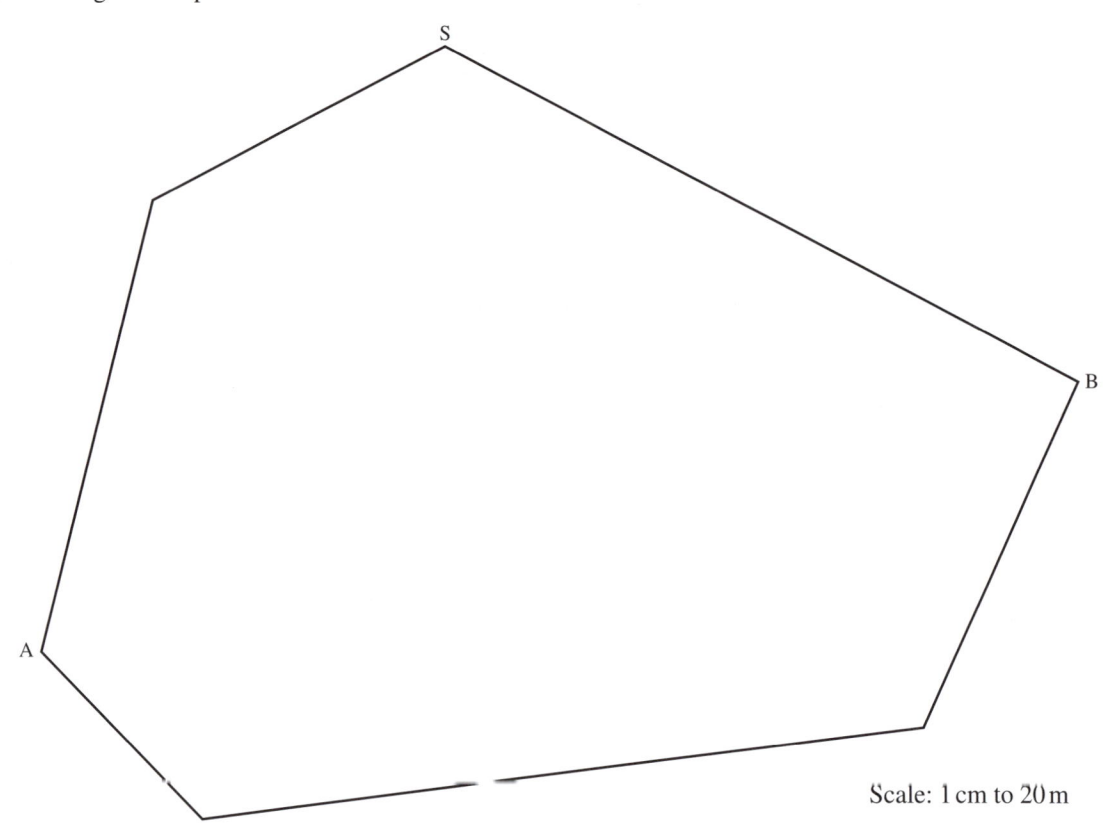

Scale: 1 cm to 20 m

There is a water sprinkler at S. The sprinkler can water the region of the field that is 60 metres or less from the sprinkler.
  a) Shade, on a full size copy of the diagram, the region of the field that is 60 metres or less from the sprinkler.

A farmer is going to lay a pipe to help water the field. A and B are posts that mark the widest part of the field. The pipe will cross the field so that it is always the same distance from A as it is from B.
  b) On the diagram draw a line accurately to show where the pipe should be laid. [Edexcel]

11 Use ruler and compasses to **construct** the perpendicular to the line segment AB that passes through the point P. You must show all construction lines.

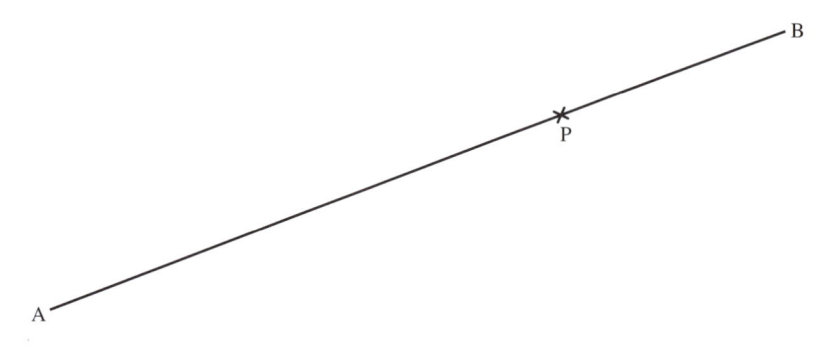

[Edexcel]

12 The diagram shows a sketch of triangle ABC.

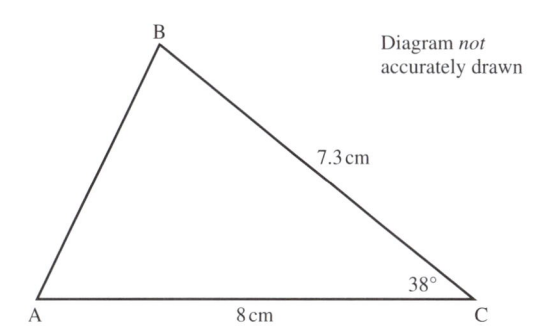

B
Diagram *not* accurately drawn
7.3 cm
38°
A   8 cm   C

a) Make an accurate drawing of triangle ABC.
b) Measure the size of angle A on your diagram. [Edexcel]

13 The diagram represents a triangular garden ABC. The scale of the diagram is 1 cm to 1 m.
A tree is to be planted so that it is:
- nearer to AB than to AC
- within 5 m of point A.

On a copy of the diagram, shade the region where the tree may be planted.

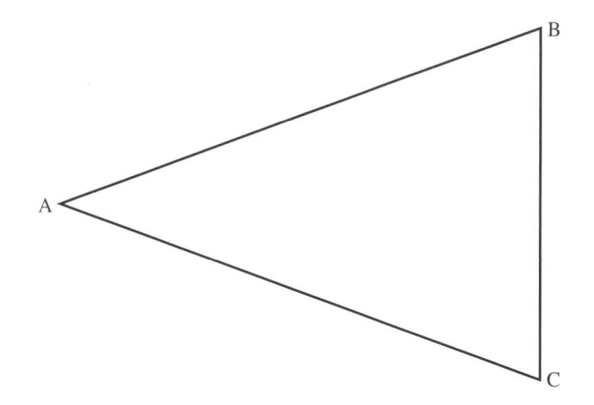

[Edexcel]

14 The diagram shows the position of each of three buildings in a town.

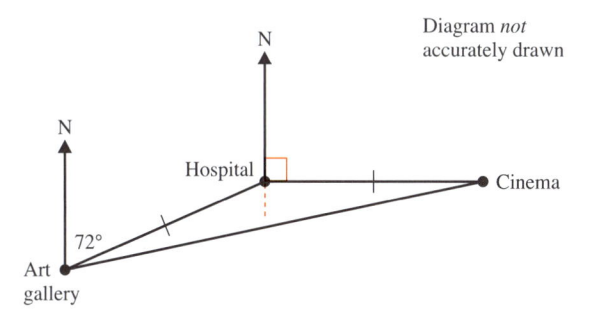

Diagram *not* accurately drawn

The bearing of the Hospital from the Art gallery is 072°.
The Cinema is due East of the Hospital.
The distance from the Hospital to the Art gallery is equal to the distance from the Hospital to the Cinema.
Work out the bearing of the Cinema from the Art gallery. [Edexcel]

KEY POINTS

1. Accurate drawings of triangles may be made with geometrical instruments, provided you are given information about:

   - Two sides and an included angle (SAS)
   - Two angles and an included side (ASA)
   - All three sides (SSS).

2. You can also construct a unique triangle given two sides and a non-included angle, provided the angle is a right angle. If the non-included angle is not a right angle then the information can be ambiguous, which means that two different solutions might be possible (SSA).

3. The examination may ask you to carry out standard geometrical constructions on line segments. In particular you must know how to:

   - Bisect a given angle
   - Bisect a given line
   - Drop a perpendicular from a point to a line segment
   - Construct a perpendicular at a point on a line segment.

4. You might be asked to use these constructions in order to make an angle of 30° (construct an equilateral triangle and then bisect one of its angles) or 45° (construct a right angle and bisect it).

5. Geometrical constructions are also used in locus questions. Loci are sometimes described using three figure bearings: remember that North is 000°, East 090°, South 180° and West 270°, so you start at North and measure the angle in a clockwise direction.

Internet Challenge 19

In perspective

The diagram shows a perspective drawing of two buildings near a crossroads.

Both buildings are cuboids.

Building A is 10 metres tall.

Can you tell whether Building B is taller or less tall than Building A?

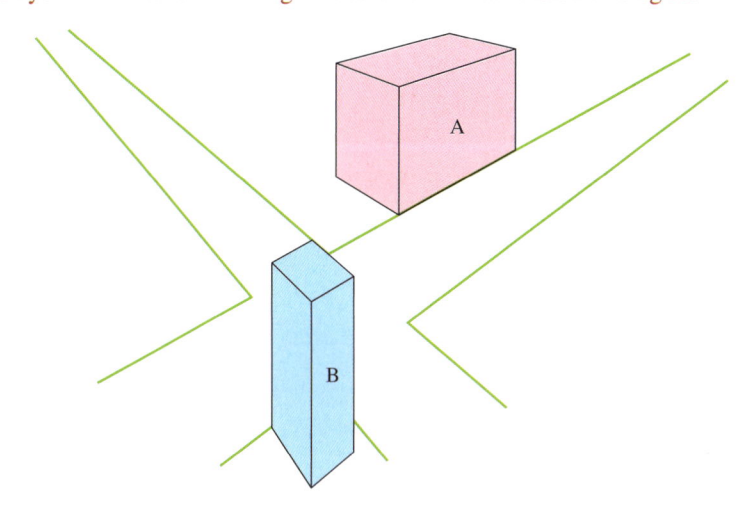

Use the internet to find out how perspective drawings are made. Your search terms might include *horizon*, *vanishing point* and *two dimensions*. Once you understand how vanishing points work, you should be able to add some construction lines to a copy of the diagram. Then use your construction to help you to:

- decide which building is taller
- estimate the height of Building B.

You can find out more about the history of perspective in art by using the internet to search for material about *Brunelleschi*.

CHAPTER 20

Transformation and similarity

In this chapter you will **learn how to**:
- carry out simple reflections, rotations and enlargements
- use combinations of these transformations
- find missing lengths in 2-D problems using similarity
- find areas and volumes of similar shapes.

You will also be **challenged to**:
- investigate geometrical definitions.

Starter: Monkey business

Nine monkeys have fallen out of their tree. They are not all the same shape and size.

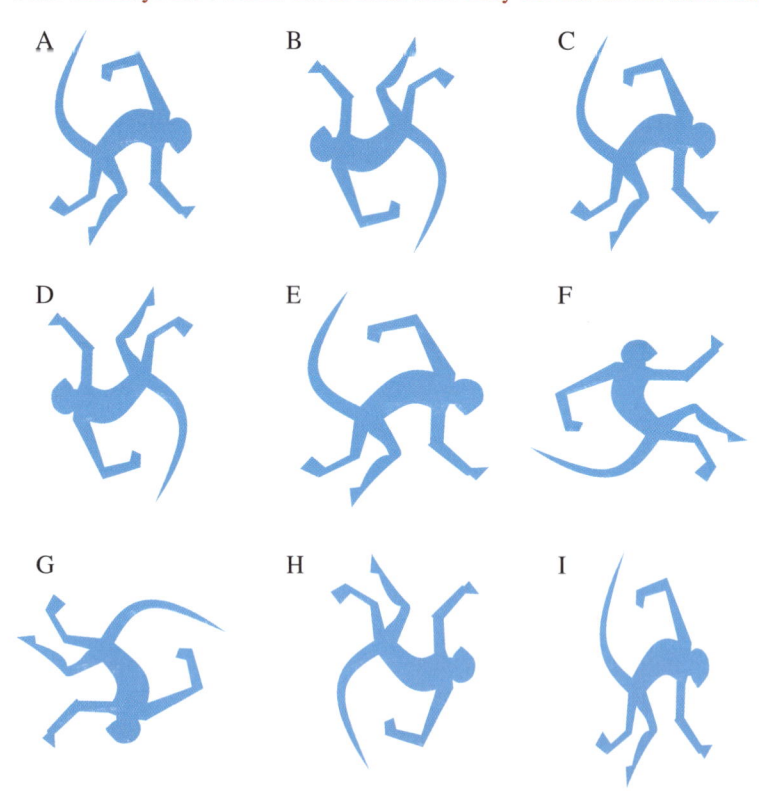

A   B   C

D   E   F

G   H   I

Pick out the monkeys that are not the same shape and size as the rest.

Are there any other differences?

20.1 Reflections

Many objects in mathematics possess **mirror symmetry**, or **reflection symmetry**. 2-D objects will have a mirror line, and this will divide the object into two matching halves, one being a mirror image of the other. The matching halves are **congruent**, i.e. exactly the same shape and size.

3-D objects will have a **plane of symmetry** instead. Again, the object divides into two congruent halves.

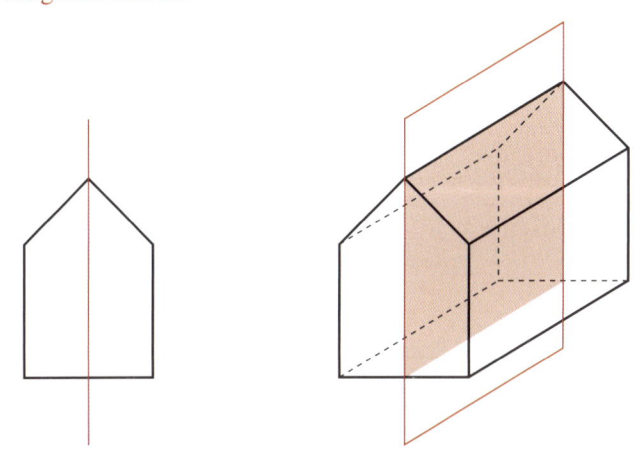

You can make a symmetric 2-D shape by reflecting a given shape in a mirror line. This is usually done using a squared coordinate grid. The mirror line may then be described by a simple linear equation. The mirror line might be horizontal (e.g. $y = 3$), vertical (e.g. $x = -2$) or at a 45° angle (e.g. $y = x$).

EXAMPLE

Reflect the given shape in the line $x = 5$

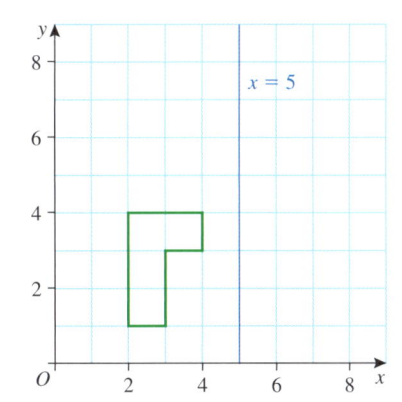

SOLUTION

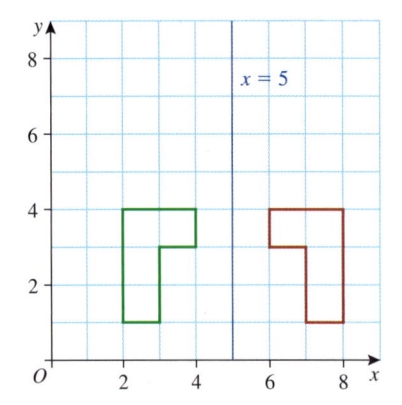

Questions with a diagonal mirror line can be more difficult to visualise. It helps if you rotate your book so that the mirror line is vertical.

EXAMPLE

The diagram shows a triangle P. The triangle has been reflected in a mirror line to form an image Q.
a) Draw the mirror line on the diagram.
b) Write down the equation of the mirror line.

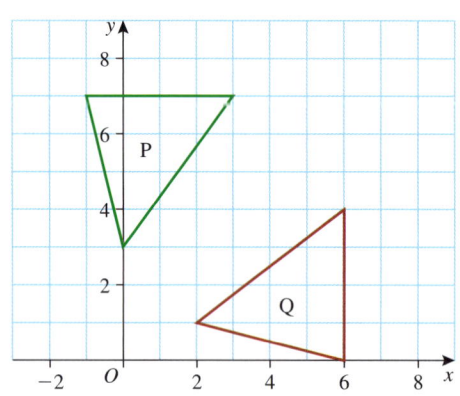

SOLUTION

a)

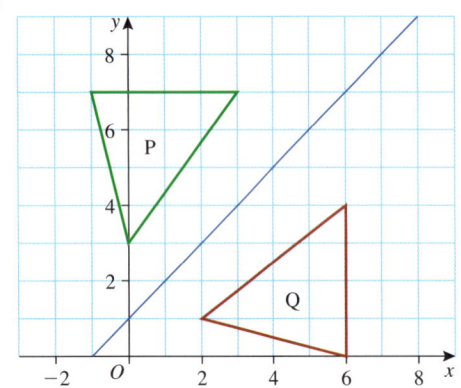

b) The mirror line has equation $y = x + 1$

EXERCISE 20.1

1. Diagram **a)** shows a 2-D shape. Draw a line of symmetry on a copy of this diagram.

   Diagram **b)** shows a sketch of a 3-D object. Indicate a plane of symmetry on a copy of this sketch.

   a)

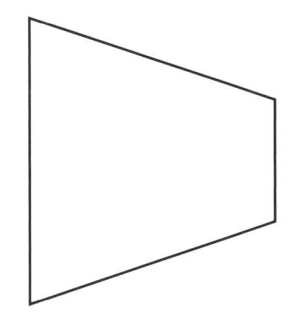

   b)

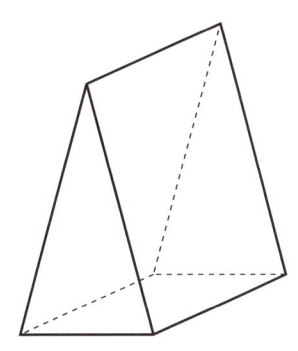

In questions **2** to **5**, on a copy of the grid draw the reflection of the given shape in the mirror line indicated. Label the mirror line with its equation in each case.

2.

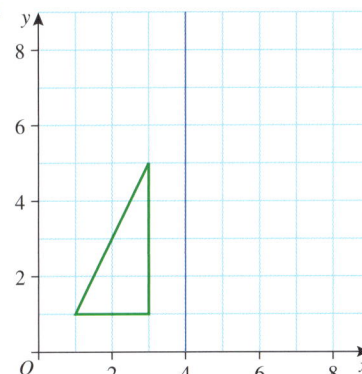

3.

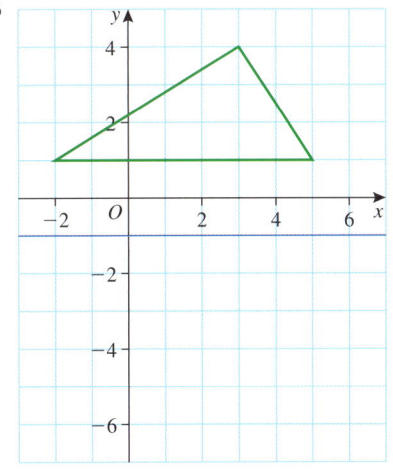

4

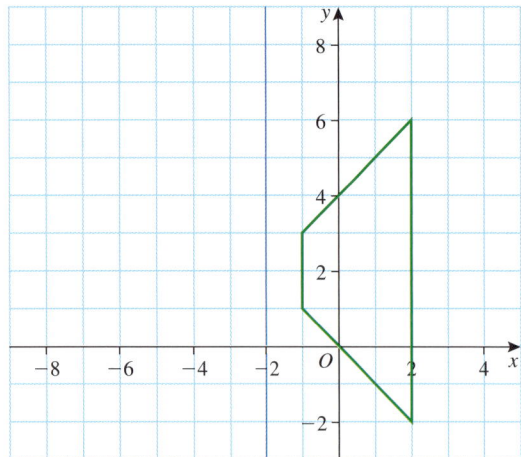

5

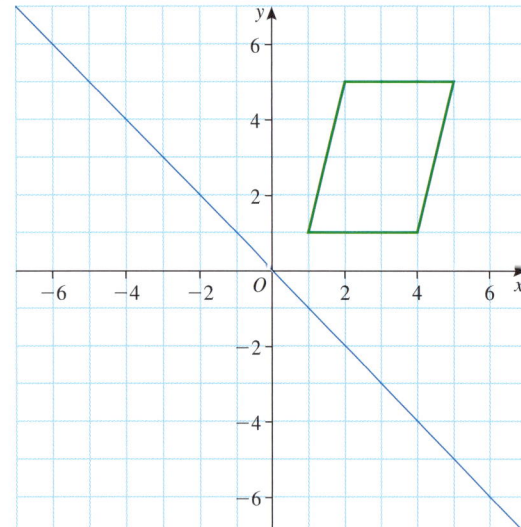

6 The diagram shows a triangle S and its mirror image T.

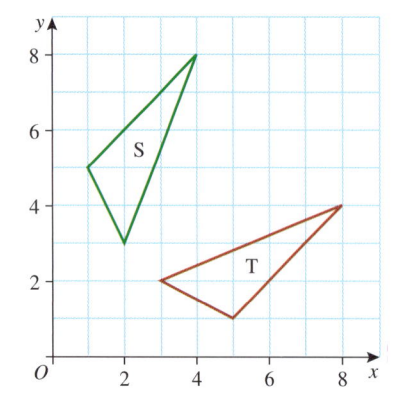

   a) On a copy of the grid, draw the mirror line that has been used for the reflection.
   b) Write down the equation of the mirror line.

7 The diagram shows a triangle S and its mirror image T.

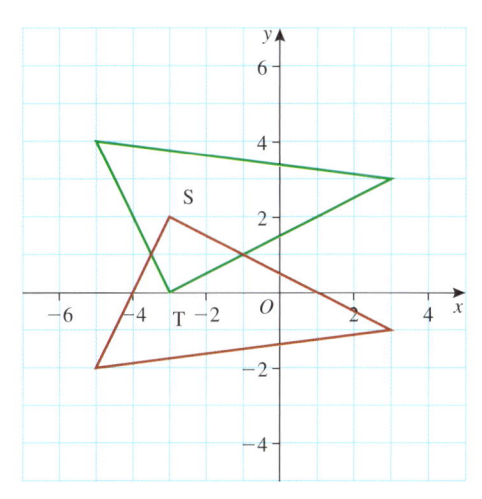

a) On a copy of the grid, draw the mirror line that has been used for the reflection.
b) Write down the equation of the mirror line.

8 The diagram shows a letter L shape, labelled X.
The shape is to be reflected in a mirror line.
Part of the reflection has been drawn on the diagram.

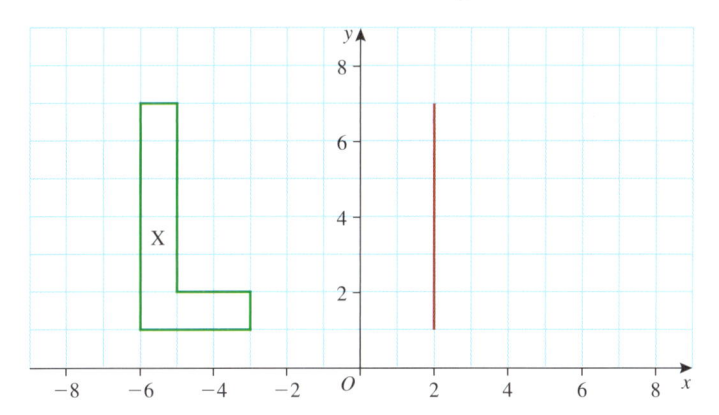

a) Copy and complete the drawing to shown the image. Label it Y.
b) Mark the mirror line, and give its equation.

9 The diagram shows six triangles A, B, C, D, E and F. The six triangles are all congruent to each other.

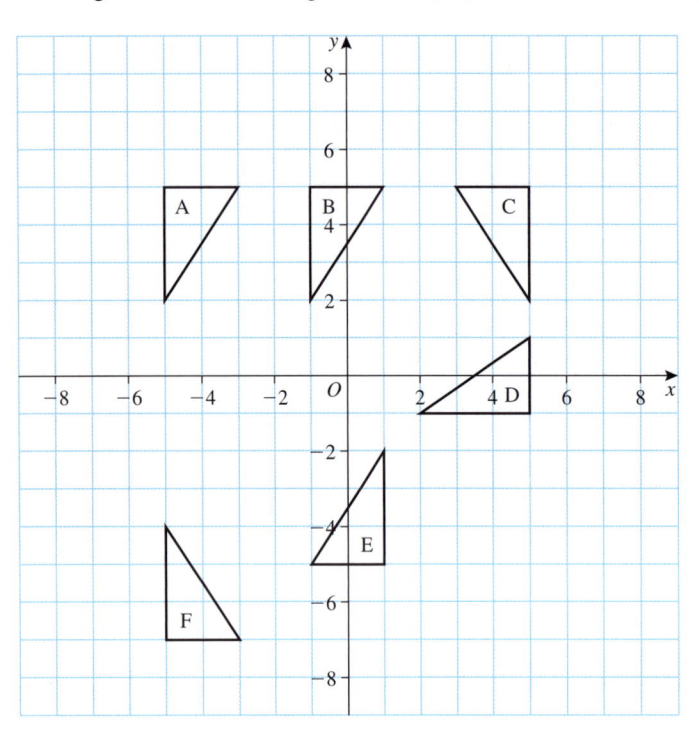

    a) Explain the meaning of the word *congruent*.
    b) Triangle A can be reflected to triangle F.
        State the equation of the mirror line that achieves this.
    c) Triangle C is reflected to another triangle using a mirror line $x = 2$.
        Which one?
    d) Triangle D can be reflected to triangle B using a mirror line.
        Give the equation of this line.
    e) Triangle D can be reflected to triangle E using a mirror line.
        Give the equation of this line.

10 A triangle T is reflected in a mirror line, to form an image, triangle U.
Then triangle U is reflected in the same mirror line, to form an image, triangle V.
What can you deduce about triangle T and triangle V?

20.2 Rotations

A mathematical object may be turned to face in a different direction, while remaining the same shape and size: this is known as **rotation**. An imaginary point acts as a pivot for the rotation: this is the **centre of rotation**. You must remember to specify the size of the turn, or **angle of rotation**, and whether it is **clockwise** or **anticlockwise** as well as specifying the **centre of rotation.**

If you find rotations difficult to visualise, ask your teacher for some tracing paper. (This is also permitted in the GCSE examination.)

EXAMPLE

The diagram shows a rectangle labelled S.
a) Rotate shape S through 90° clockwise, about the origin O.
   Label the resulting shape T.
b) Now rotate the shape T through 180° about O.
   Label the resulting shape U.
c) Describe a single rotation that would take S directly to U.

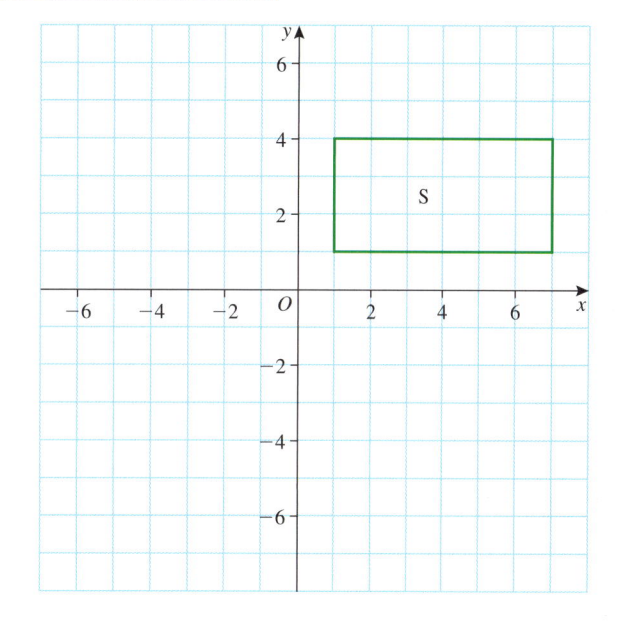

SOLUTION

a)

> Imagine a ray from the centre (O) to a corner of the shape S.
> Rotate this ray to find the new position for the corner.
> Repeat as necessary.

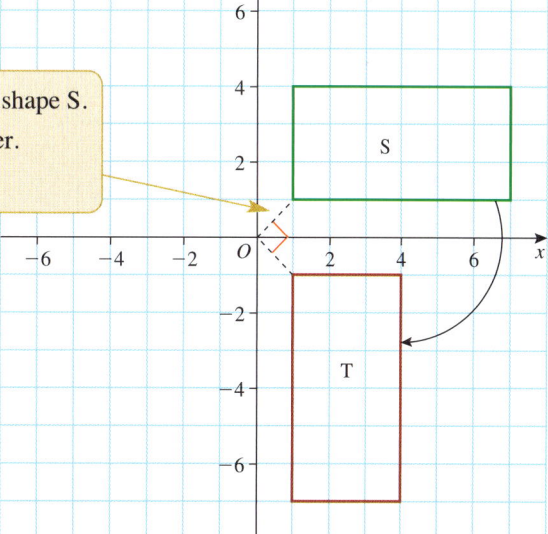

20 Transformation and similarity   U4

b)

The direction of this second rotation was not specified in the question because 180° clockwise and 180° anticlockwise are exactly the same.

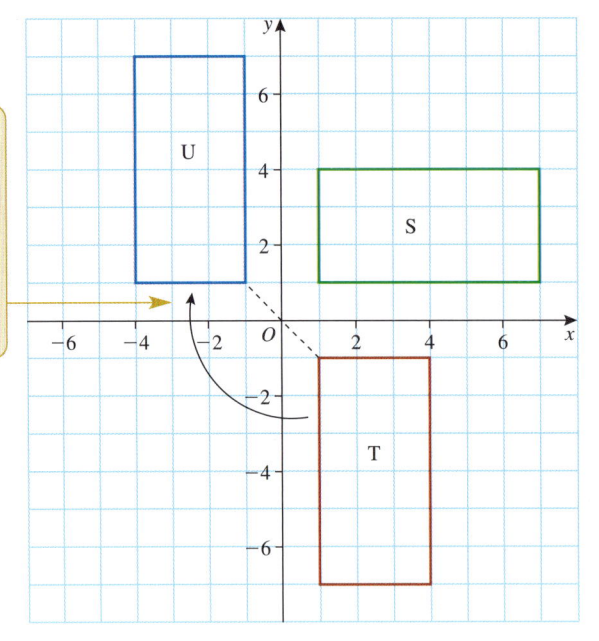

c) U can be obtained directly from S by a 90° rotation anticlockwise about O.

Rotations are often performed with the point (0, 0), called the origin O, as the centre of rotation, but they can be done about other centres.

EXAMPLE

The diagram shows a triangle M drawn on a grid.

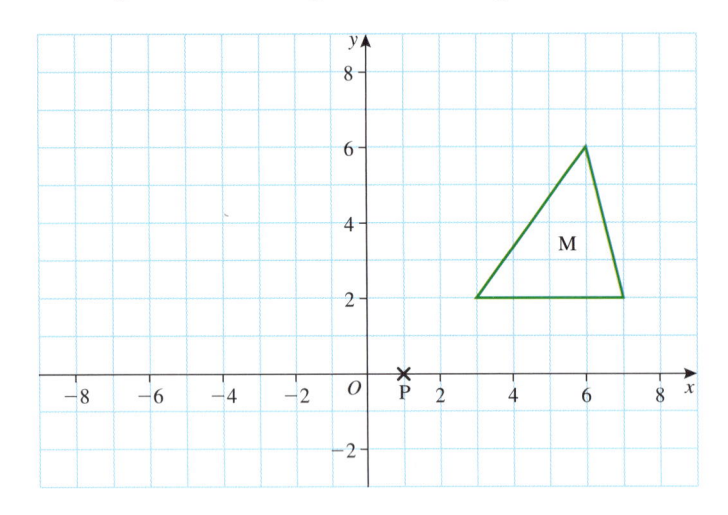

Rotate the triangle M through 90° anticlockwise about the point P (1, 0). Label this new triangle N.

SOLUTION

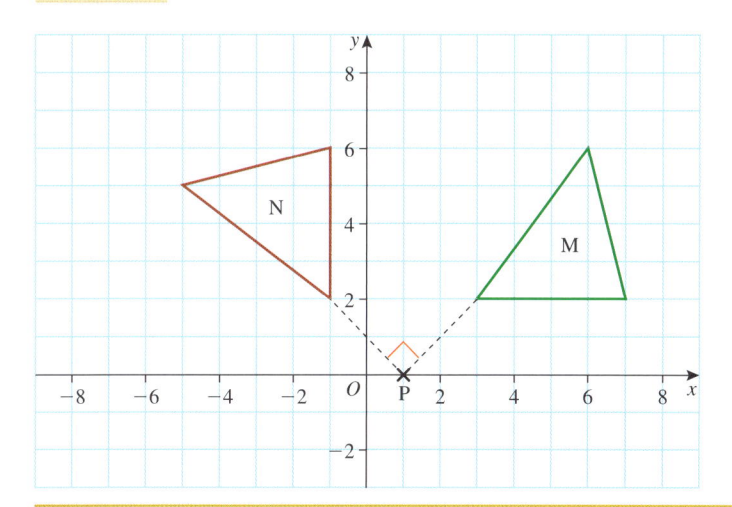

EXERCISE 20.2

Each of these questions requires a coordinate grid in which x and y can range from -8 to 8.

1 Rotate the trapezium shape 90° clockwise, about O.

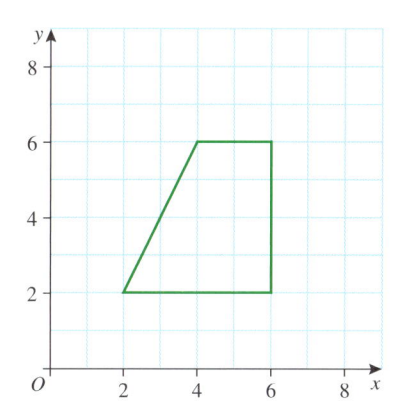

2 Rotate the shape 180°, about O.

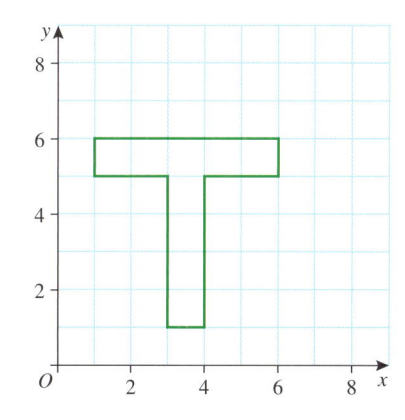

3 a) Rotate the triangle T1 90° anticlockwise about O. Label the result T2.
  b) Rotate T2 180° about O. Label the result T3.
  c) Describe the single rotation that takes T1 directly to T3.

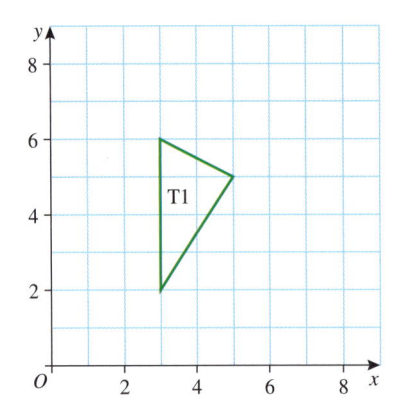

4 a) Rotate shape A 90° anticlockwise about $(1, 0)$. Label the result B.
  b) Rotate shape B 180° about $(0, 0)$. Label the result C.
  c) Describe carefully the single rotation that takes shape C to shape A.

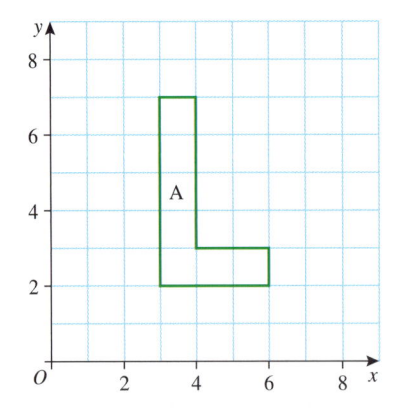

5 a) Rotate shape U 90° anticlockwise about point P $(0, 1)$.
  b) Rotate shape V 90° clockwise about point Q $(-1, -1)$.

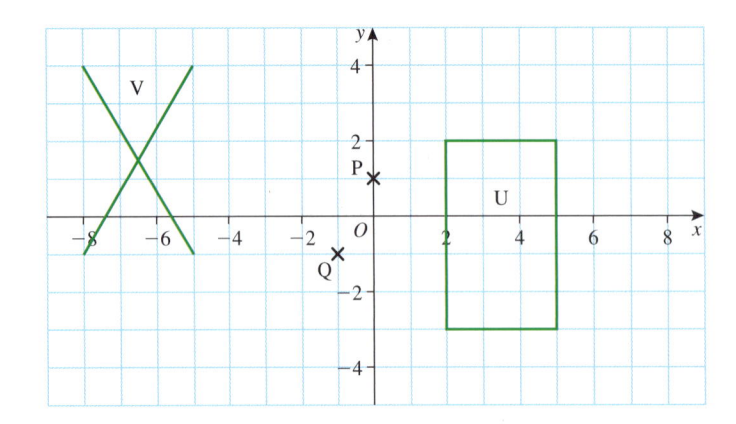

6 a) Rotate the triangle 90° clockwise about (1, 1).
  b) Now rotate both the new triangle and the original one 180° about (1, 1).

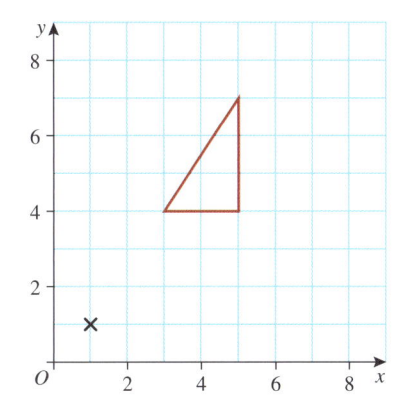

7 The diagram shows an object A and its image B after a rotation.
  a) Write down the size and direction of the angle of rotation.
  b) Write down the coordinates of the centre of rotation.

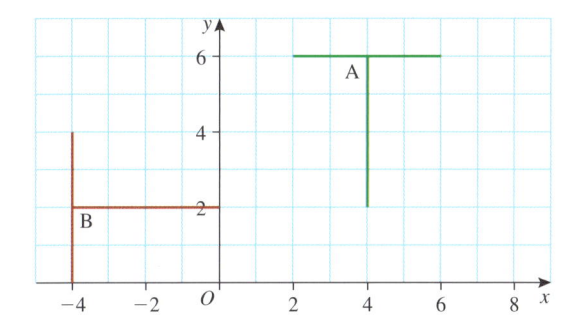

8

Anita: If you rotate a shape and then rotate it again, the result is equivalent to a single rotation.

Bella: If you reflect a shape and then reflect it again, the result is equivalent to a single reflection.

Cat: I'm afraid only one of you is right.

Who is right, and who is wrong?

20.3 Combining transformations

There are three important geometric transformations that preserve congruence – meaning that they do not change the shape or size of an object. These transformations are reflection, rotation and translation.

A **translation** consists simply of sliding an object left/right and/or up/down. You specify a translation by stating how far the object is to be moved in each of the x and y directions, and it can be written as two numbers in a column vector. For example, $\begin{bmatrix} 5 \\ 2 \end{bmatrix}$ indicates a translation of 5 units to the right and 2 units up.

In the GCSE examination you may be required to combine two transformations. Transformations are said to **map** one shape to another, that is, turn one shape into the other.

EXAMPLE

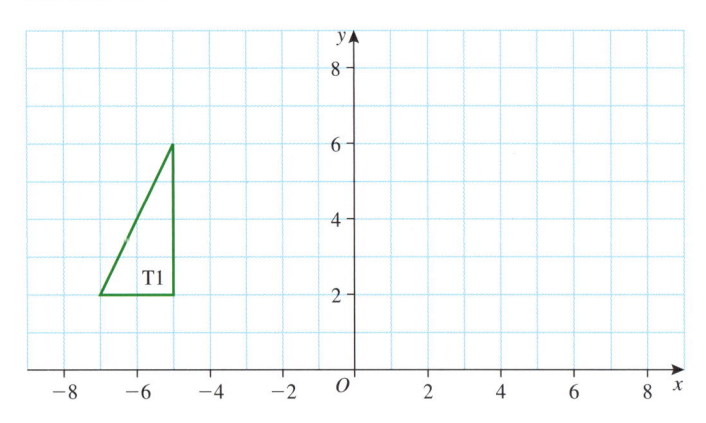

a) Reflect the given triangle T1 in the line $x = -4$, and label the result T2.
b) Reflect T2 in the line $x = 1$, and label the result T3.
c) What single transformation maps T1 directly to T3?

SOLUTION

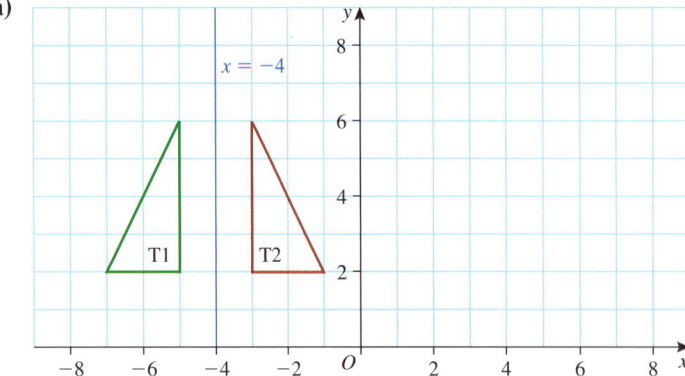

a)

b)

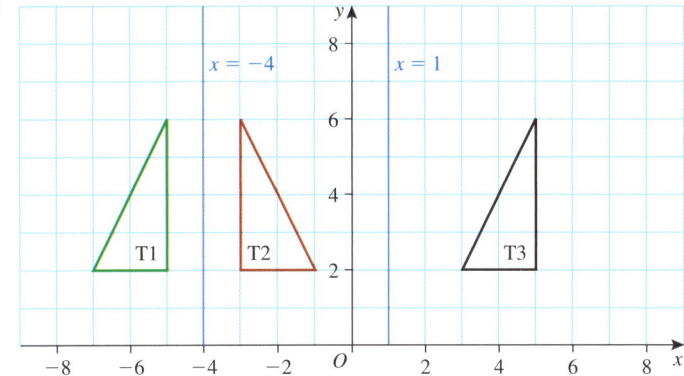

c) T3 is 10 units to the right of T1, so the transformation that maps T1 to T3 is a translation of $\begin{bmatrix} 10 \\ 0 \end{bmatrix}$.

EXERCISE 20.3

Each of questions **1** to **6** requires a coordinate grid in which x and y can range from -8 to 8.

1

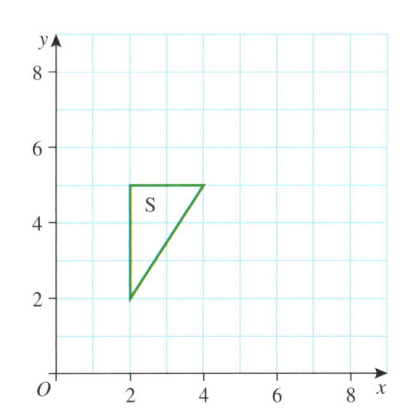

a) Reflect triangle S in the line $x = -1$. Label the new triangle T.
b) Reflect triangle T in the x axis. Label the new triangle U.
c) Describe the *single* transformation that maps S to U.

2 The diagram shows a triangle, T.

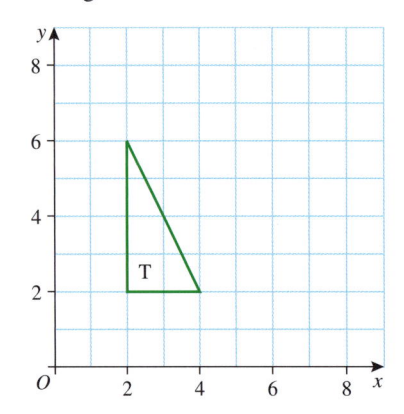

a) Translate triangle T by $\begin{bmatrix} -6 \\ 0 \end{bmatrix}$. Label its image triangle U.
b) Rotate triangle U by 180° about O. Label the result triangle V.
c) Describe the *single* transformation that maps T to V.

3 The diagram shows a triangle, S.

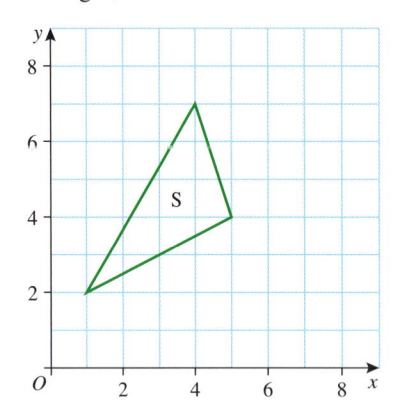

a) Reflect triangle S in the *y* axis. Label this image triangle T.
b) Reflect triangle S in the line $y = 1$. Label this image triangle U.
c) Describe the *single* transformation that maps T directly to U.

4 The diagram shows a set of points that make a letter F shape. The shape is labelled F1.

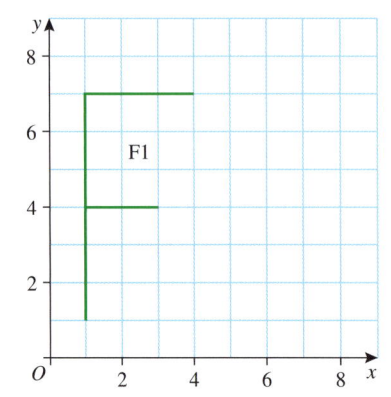

a) Reflect the shape F1 in the x axis. Label the result F2.
b) Reflect F2 in the line $y = x$. Label the result F3.
c) Describe the single transformation that would take shape F3 to shape F1.

5 The diagram shows a quadrilateral F.

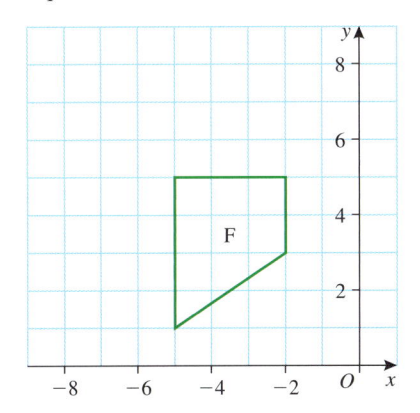

a) Rotate quadrilateral F through 90° anticlockwise about O. Label the result G.
b) Rotate quadrilateral G through 90° clockwise about $(4, -4)$. Label the result H.
c) Describe a single transformation that would take F to H.

6 The diagram shows a triangle A.

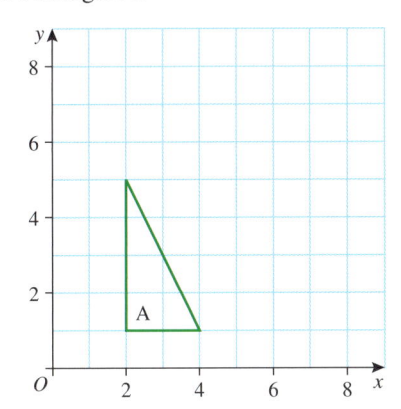

a) Rotate triangle A 90° anticlockwise about $(0, 3)$. Label this image B.
b) Rotate triangle A 180° about the origin O. Label this image C.
c) Describe the *single* transformation that transforms triangle B to triangle C.

20.4 Enlargements

You should already be familiar with the idea of enlarging shapes on grids. At Higher Tier GCSE this should be done in a specific way, using a **centre of enlargement** and a **scale factor**. Rays may be drawn from the centre of enlargement, to show how the transformation is operating.

There are three different scenarios, depending on the value of the scale factor:

- Scale factor *greater than 1*: simple enlargement – the object gets bigger
- Scale factor *between 0 and 1*: the enlargement is a reduction – the object gets smaller
- *Negative* scale factor: the object is enlarged/reduced and inverted.

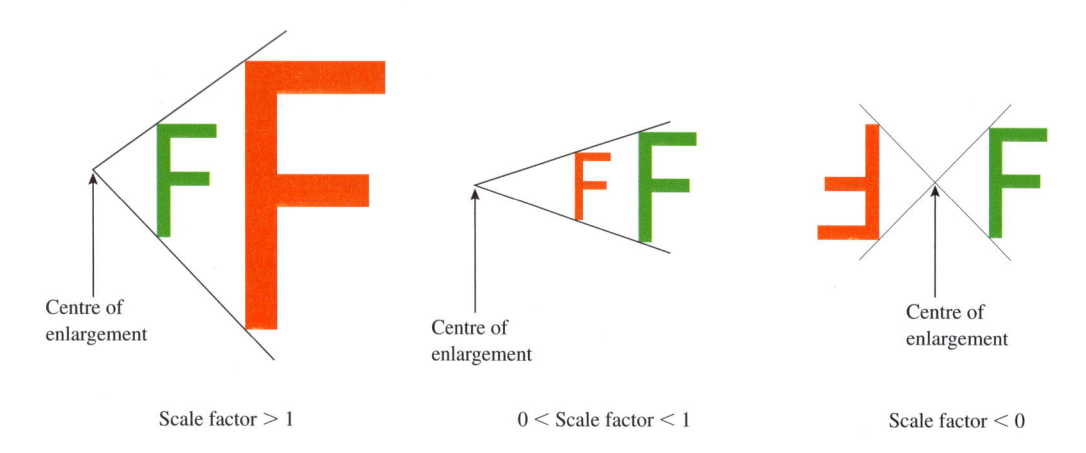

Scale factor > 1   0 < Scale factor < 1   Scale factor < 0

EXAMPLE

The diagram shows a letter F shape and two points, P and Q.

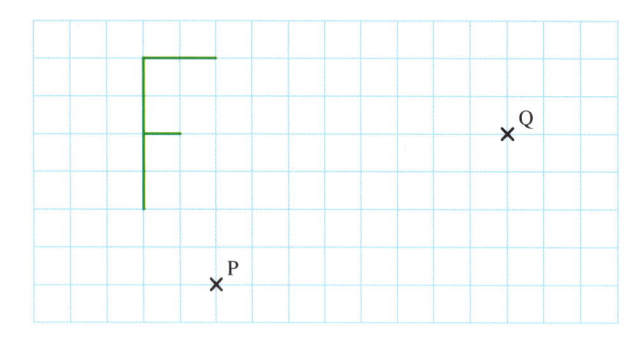

a) Enlarge the letter F by scale factor 2, using P as the centre of enlargement.
b) Enlarge the letter F by scale factor $\frac{1}{2}$, using Q as the centre of enlargement.

SOLUTION

a)

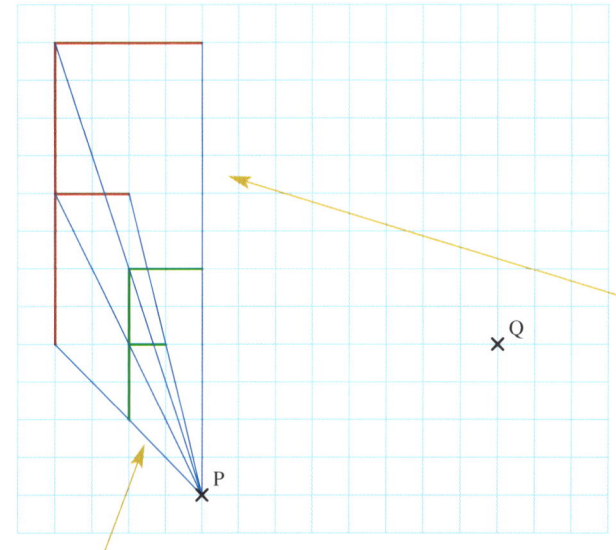

Draw rays from P to each corner of the original F shape. Then extend these rays so they are twice their original length (factor is ×2).

The rays will locate the corners of the enlarged shape.

The final F is not the same size as the original, so the two shapes are not congruent, but they are the same shape. The two shapes are said to be mathematically similar.

b)

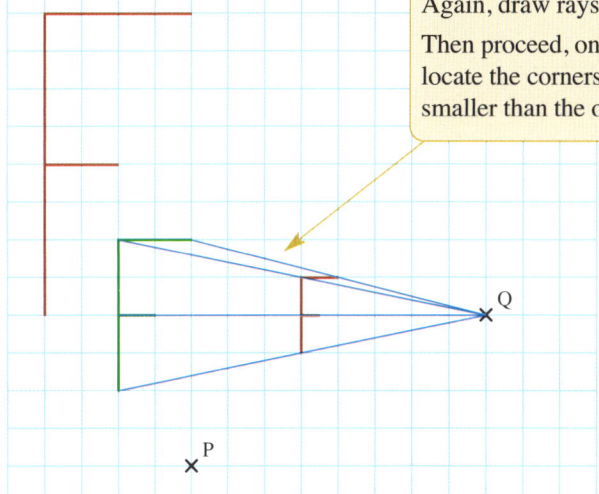

Again, draw rays, from Q to each corner of the original F shape. Then proceed, only half way along the rays (factor is $\times \frac{1}{2}$), to locate the corners of the 'enlarged' shape (which is actually smaller than the original).

For an enlargement with a negative scale factor, simply draw the extended rays in the opposite direction from the original ones. This will turn the shape upside down as well as enlarging it.

EXAMPLE

Enlarge the given shape by scale factor of $-1\frac{1}{2}$, using the indicated centre of enlargement.

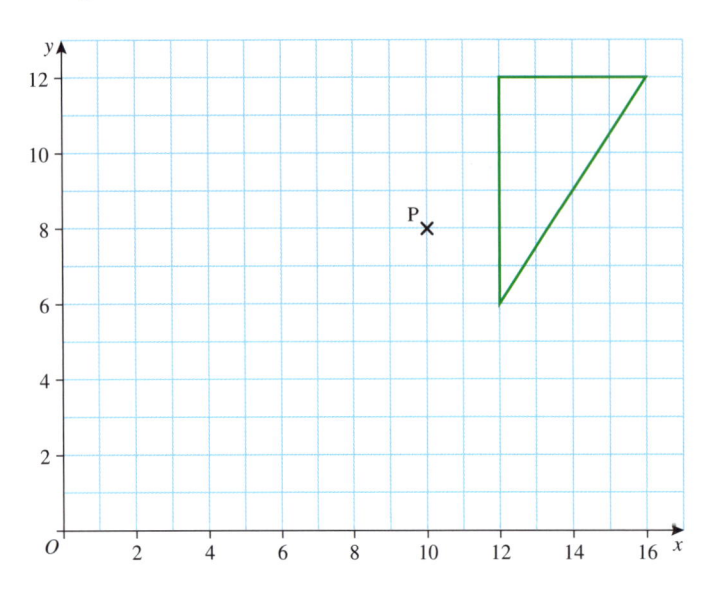

SOLUTION

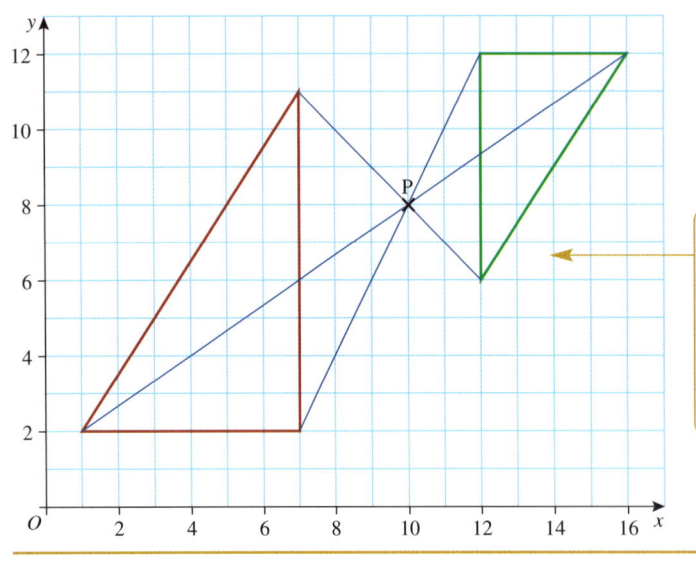

Note that each construction line on the left of the centre of enlargement is $1\frac{1}{2}$ times the corresponding length on the right.

Each new line begins at P but is drawn in the opposite direction from before.

EXERCISE 20.4

1. The diagram shows a shape A.

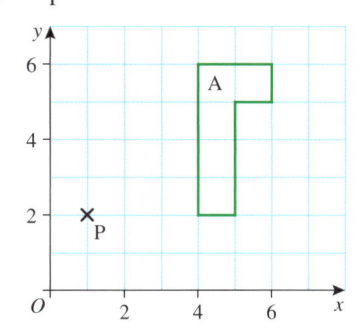

   a) On a copy of the grid, enlarge shape A by scale factor 2, centre P. Label the new shape B.
   b) Enlarge shape A by scale factor 3, centre P. Label the new shape C.
   c) Are shapes B and C congruent? Are they similar?

2. The diagram shows a triangle, and a centre of enlargement, P.

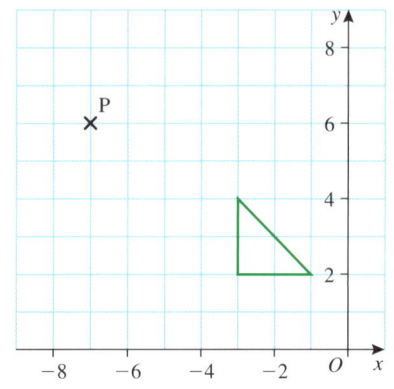

   On a copy of the grid, enlarge the shape by scale factor $2\frac{1}{2}$, centre P.

3. The diagram shows a shape, A, and two centres P and Q marked with crosses.

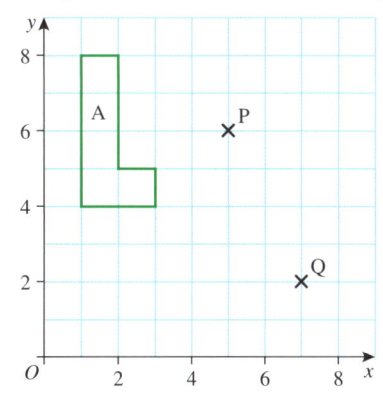

   a) On a copy of the grid, enlarge shape A, with scale factor -2, centre P. Label the result B.
   b) Enlarge shape B, with scale factor $\frac{1}{2}$, centre Q. Label the result C.
   c) Are shapes A and B congruent? Are they similar?
   d) Are shapes A and C congruent?

4 The diagram shows an object, A, and its image B after an enlargement.

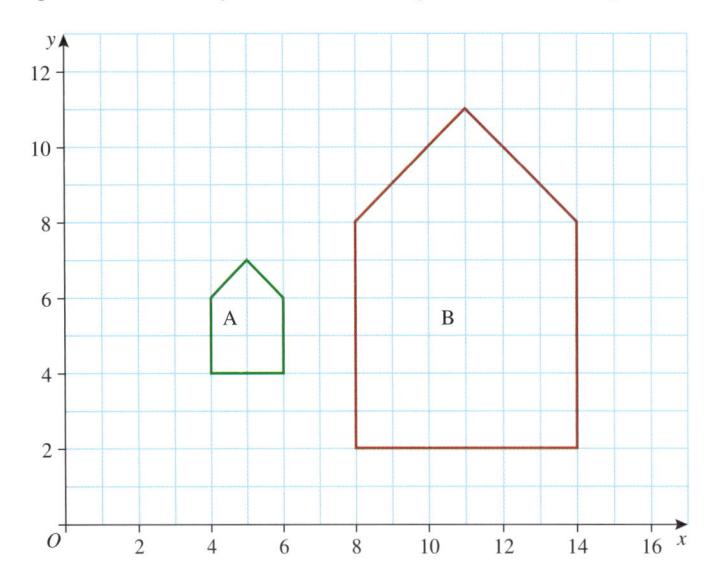

a) State the scale factor for the enlargement.
b) Obtain the coordinates of the centre of enlargement.

5 The diagram shows a triangle, and a centre of enlargement, P.

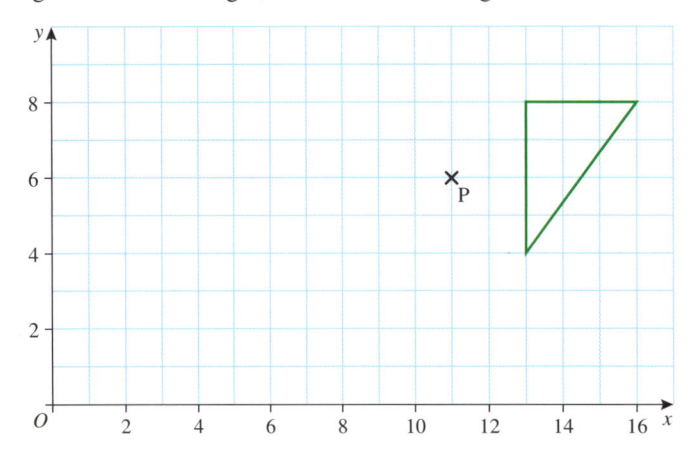

On a copy of the grid, enlarge the triangle by scale factor −2, centre P.

6 Nik draws a triangle and then enlarges it. He notices that the image of the triangle is congruent to the original triangle.
a) What scale factor do you think Nik has used?
b) Is your answer to a) unique (i.e. the only possibility)?

20.5 Similar shapes and solids

If two objects are similar, then they are exactly the same shape, but one of them is an enlargement of the other. If the enlargement factor is n, then:

- corresponding lengths are in the ratio $1 : n$
- corresponding areas are in the ratio $1 : n^2$
- corresponding volumes are in the ratio $1 : n^3$.

EXAMPLE

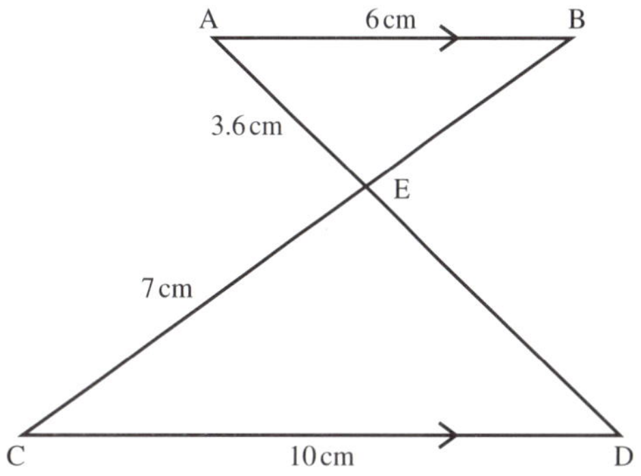

In the diagram, AB and CD are parallel.
AB = 6 cm, CD = 10 cm, AE = 3.6 cm and CE = 7 cm.
a) Explain carefully why triangles AEB and DEC are similar.
b) Calculate the length BE.
c) Work out the length DE.

SOLUTION

a) Angles ABE and DCE are equal (alternate angles).
   Angles BAE and CDE are equal (alternate angles).
   Angles AEB and DEC are equal (vertically opposite).
   Thus <u>both triangles contain exactly the same angles</u>, so they must be similar.

b) Redrawing the similar triangles so that they are the same way up:

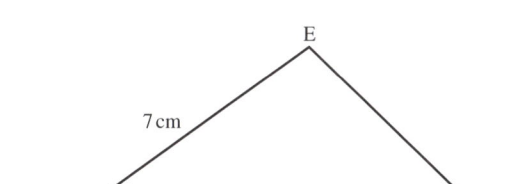

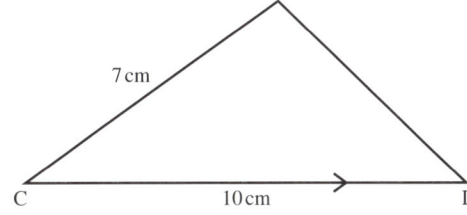

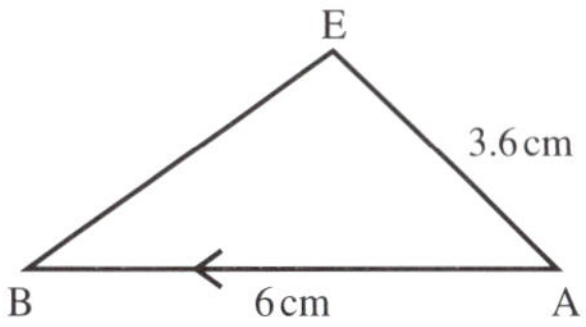

Then, by comparing corresponding sides:
$$\frac{BE}{7} = \frac{6}{10}$$
Thus, cross-multiplying:
$10 \times BE = 6 \times 7$
$10 \times BE = 42$
$BE = \frac{42}{10}$
$BE = \underline{4.2 \text{ cm}}$

c) Likewise:
$$\frac{DE}{3.6} = \frac{10}{6}$$
Thus, cross-multiplying:
$6 \times DE = 10 \times 3.6$
$6 \times DE = 36$
$DE = \frac{36}{6}$
$DE = \underline{6 \text{ cm}}$

EXAMPLE

The diagram shows two solid cones. They are mathematically similar.

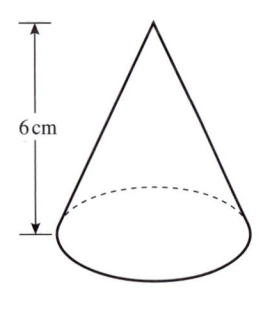

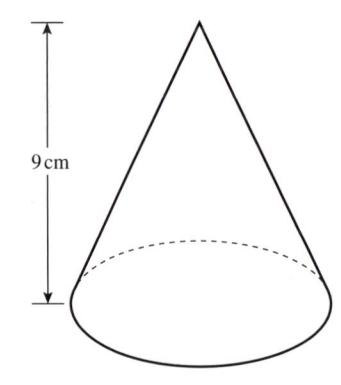

[Diagram: smaller cone with height 6 cm, larger cone with height 9 cm]

The smaller cone has a curved surface area of 64 cm².
a) Work out the curved surface area of the larger cone.

The two cones are made of the same material. The larger cone has a mass of 1080 grams.
b) Work out the mass of the smaller cone.

SOLUTION

The enlargement factor is $9 \div 6 = 1.5$
a) Area of larger cone = $64 \times (1.5^2)$
$= \underline{144 \text{ cm}^2}$

b) Mass of smaller cone = $1080 \div (1.5^3)$
$= \underline{320 \text{ grams}}$

EXERCISE 20.5

1 The diagram shows two rectangles. They are mathematically similar.

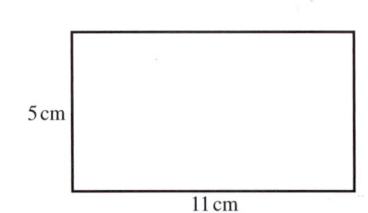

[Diagram: smaller rectangle 5 cm by 11 cm; larger rectangle with height 8 cm]

a) Work out the length of the larger rectangle.
b) Work out the ratio of the perimeters of the rectangles, in the form $1 : n$.
c) Find the ratio of the areas of the rectangles.

2 The diagram shows two similar triangles. The smaller triangle has an area of 24 cm².

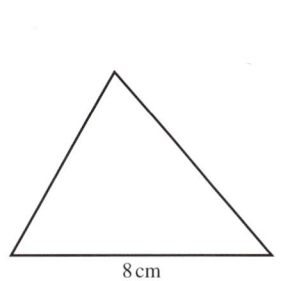

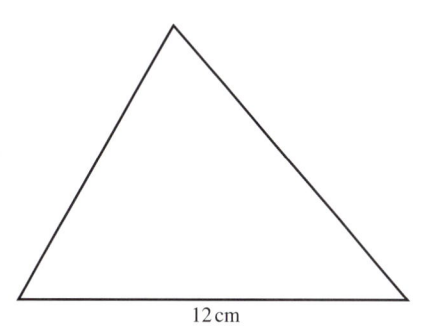

8 cm   12 cm

Work out the area of the larger triangle.

3 The diagram shows two solid cylinders. They are similar. Both cylinders are made of the same material.

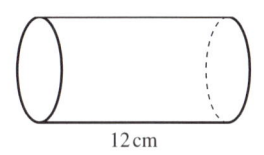

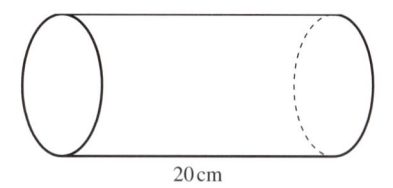

12 cm   20 cm

The larger cylinder has a mass of 40 kg. Work out the mass of the smaller cylinder.

4 The diagram shows five points, P, Q, R, S, T. The line segments PQ and RS are parallel.

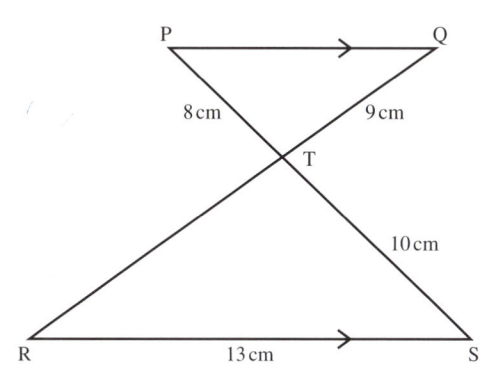

8 cm   9 cm
T
10 cm
13 cm

a) Work out the length RT. Hence find the length RQ.
b) Calculate the length PQ.

5 HMS *Cumberland* is a Type 22 frigate.
This ship has a length of 148 metres and a mass of 5300 tonnes.
A marine architect is thinking of designing a larger version of HMS *Cumberland*.
The new ship would be mathematically similar to the original one, but 25% larger in all dimensions.
a) Calculate the length of the new ship design.

The new ship is to be built using the same materials as the original one.
b) Calculate the mass of the new ship.

6 The diagram shows five points, J, K, L, M and N. The line segments JK and MN are parallel.

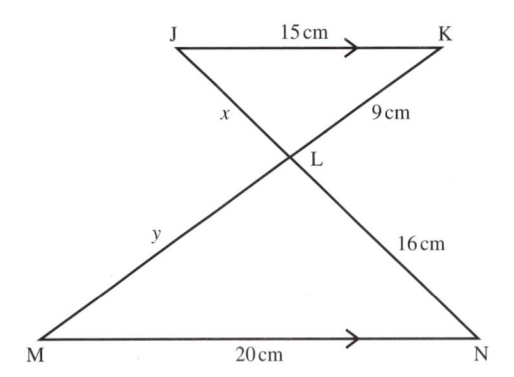

Calculate the lengths x and y.

7 A garden centre sells two similar statues.
The smaller one is 30 cm tall and weighs 5.5 kg.
The larger one is 40 cm tall. Work out its weight.

8 The diagram shows five points, P, Q, R, S and T. The line segments PQ and ST are parallel.
PR = 8 cm, PS = 4 cm, QR = 10 cm, ST = 18 cm.

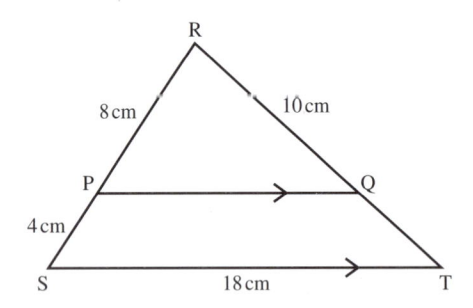

a) Explain fully why triangles RPQ and RST are similar.
b) Work out the length PQ.
c) Work out the length RT.

9 A model aircraft is $\frac{1}{4}$ of full size.
a) The real aircraft is 6.56 metres long. How long is the model?
b) The model has a wing area of 0.925 m². Find the wing area of the real aircraft.

10 Two chocolate bars are mathematically similar. They weigh 250 grams and 500 grams respectively.
The 250 gram bar is 12 cm long. Calculate the length of the 500 gram bar.

REVIEW EXERCISE 20

1 Cylinder **A** and cylinder **B** are mathematically similar.

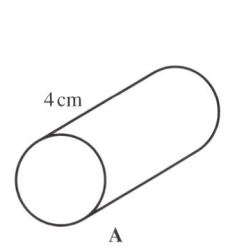

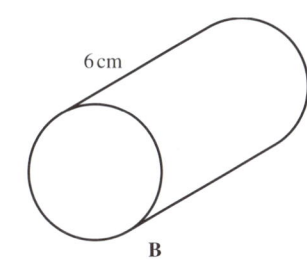

Diagram *not* accurately drawn

The length of cylinder **A** is 4 cm and the length of cylinder **B** is 6 cm.
The volume of cylinder **A** is 80 cm³.
Calculate the volume of cylinder **B**. [Edexcel]

2

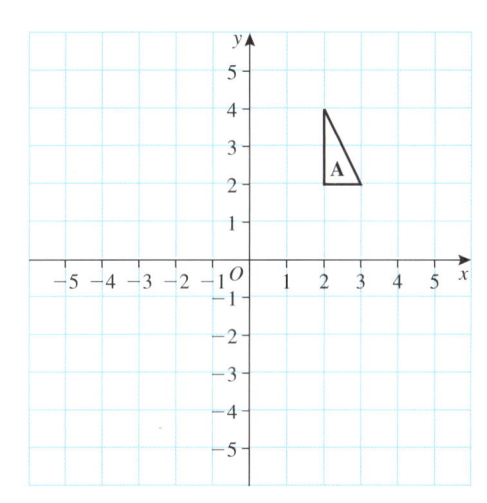

a) On a copy of the grid, rotate triangle **A** 180° about O. Label your new triangle **B**.
b) On the grid, enlarge triangle **A** by scale factor $\frac{1}{2}$, centre O. Label your new triangle **C**. [Edexcel]

3 Shape A is enlarged by scale factor 2 to obtain shape B. Shape B is then enlarged by scale factor 3 to obtain shape C. State the single enlargement factor that would transform shape A to shape C.

4 Two cuboids are mathematically similar. The smaller one has a shortest edge of 5 cm, and its surface area is 400 cm². The larger one has a shortest edge of 8 cm.
Find the surface area of the larger cuboid.

5 On a copy of the grid, enlarge the shaded triangle by a scale factor $1\frac{1}{2}$, centre P.

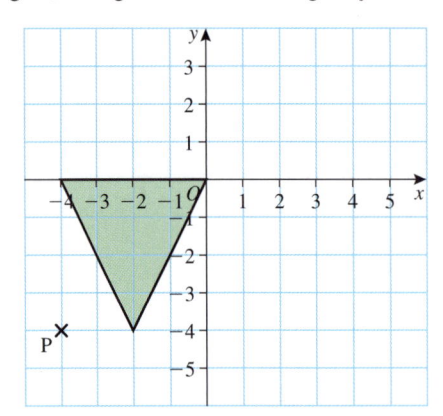

[Edexcel]

6

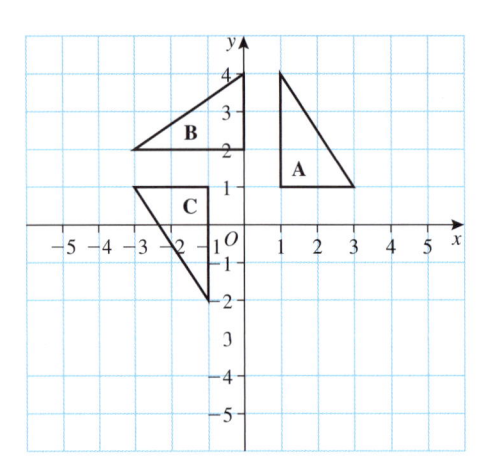

Shape **A** is rotated 90° anticlockwise, centre (0, 1), to shape **B**.
Shape **B** is rotated 90° anticlockwise, centre (0, 1), to shape **C**.
Shape **C** is rotated 90° anticlockwise, centre (0, 1), to shape **D**.
a) On a copy of the grid, mark the position of shape **D**.
b) Describe the single transformation that takes shape **C** to shape **A**.

[Edexcel]

7 Triangle **B** is a reflection of triangle **A**.

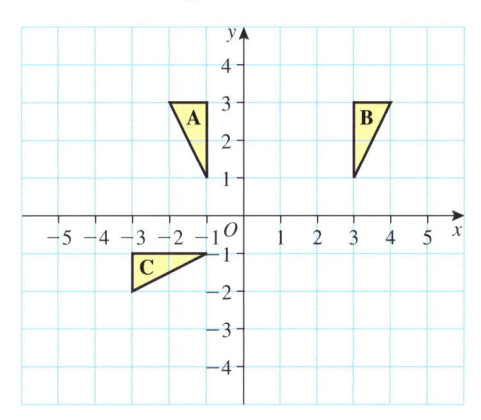

a) (i) On a copy of the grid, draw the mirror line for this reflection.
   (ii) Write down the equation of the mirror line.
b) Describe fully the single transformation that maps triangle **A** onto triangle **C**. [Edexcel]

8

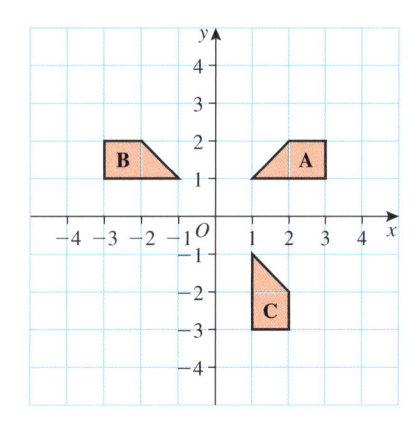

a) Describe fully the single transformation which takes shape **A** onto shape **B**.
b) Describe fully the single transformation which takes shape **A** onto shape **C**. [Edexcel]

9

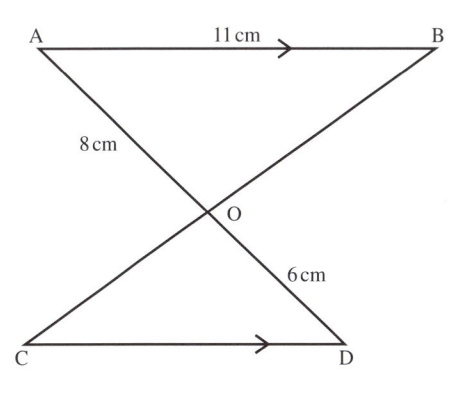

Diagram *not* accurately drawn

AB is parallel to CD.
The lines AD and BC intersect at point O.
AB = 11 cm, AO = 8 cm, OD = 6 cm.
Calculate the length of CD. [Edexcel]

20 Transformation and similarity U4

10

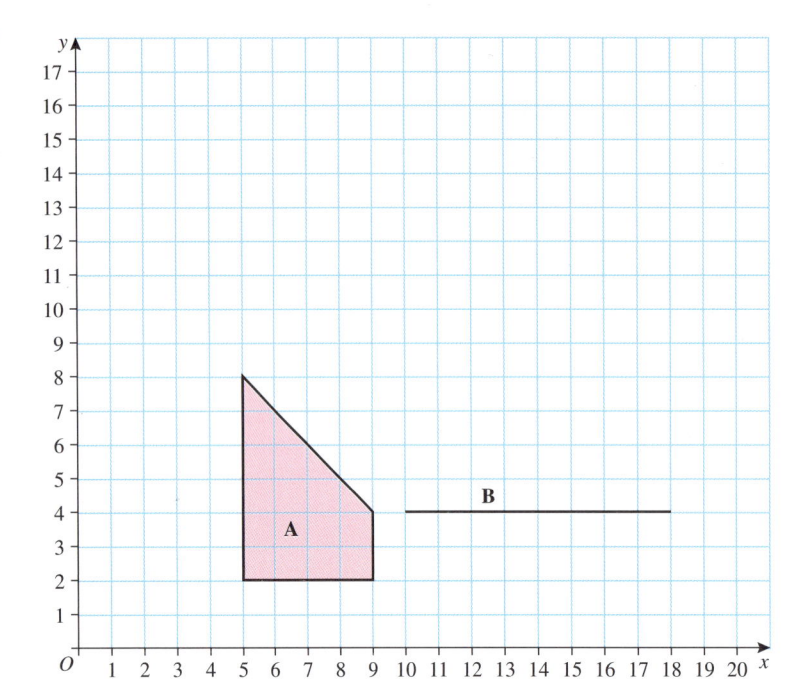

Shape **A** is shown on the grid. Shape **A** is enlarged, centre (0, 0), to obtain shape **B**.
One side of shape **B** has been drawn for you.
a) Write down the scale factor of the enlargement.
b) On a copy of the grid, complete shape **B**.

The shape **A** is enlarged by scale factor $\frac{1}{2}$, centre (5, 16) to give the shape **C**.
c) On the grid, draw shape **C**.

[Edexcel]

11

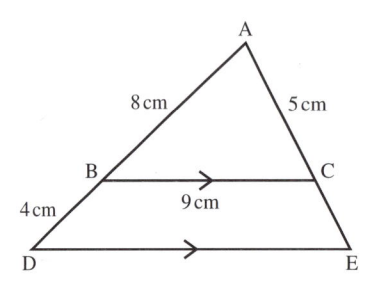

In the triangle ADE, BC is parallel to DE.
AB = 8 cm, AC = 5 cm, BD = 4 cm, BC = 9 cm.
a) Work out the length of DE.
b) Work out the length of CE.

[Edexcel]

12.

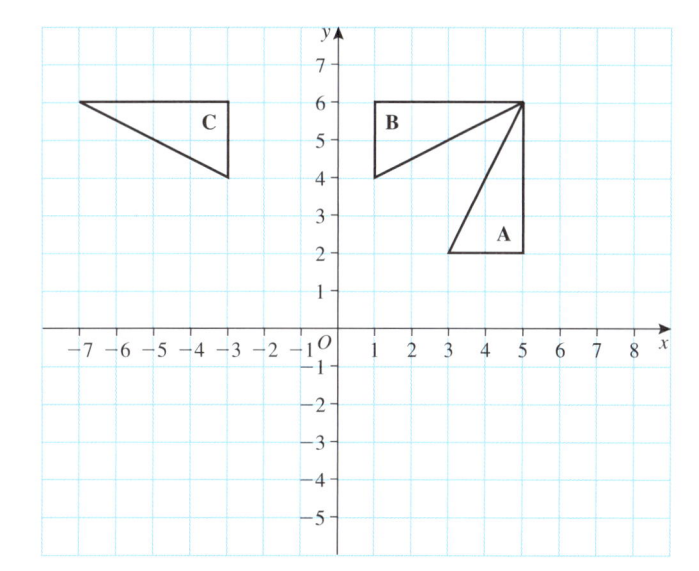

Triangle **B** is a reflection of triangle **A**.
a) (i) Draw the line of reflection.
   (ii) Write down the equation of the line of reflection.
b) Describe fully the single transformation that maps triangle **A** onto triangle **C**.
c) On a copy of the grid, enlarge triangle **C** by scale factor $-1\frac{1}{2}$ from the centre $(-1, 2)$.
   Label the enlargement **D**.
   [Edexcel]

13. A sheet of drawing paper is mathematically similar to a sheet of A5 paper. A sheet of A5 paper is a rectangle 210 mm long and 148 mm wide. The sheet of drawing paper is 450 mm long.
    Calculate the width of the sheet of drawing paper. Give your answer correct to 3 significant figures.
    [Edexcel]

14.

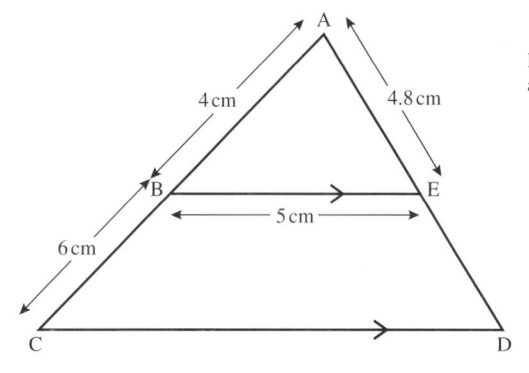

BE is parallel to CD. ABC and AED are straight lines.
AB = 4 cm, BC = 6 cm, BE = 5 cm, AE = 4.8 cm.
a) Calculate the length of CD.
b) Calculate the length of ED.
   [Edexcel]

15. Martin and Nina have made sandcastles on the beach. Martin's is exactly the same shape as Nina's, but is larger in each dimension. Nina's sandcastle is 24 cm high. It took 12 buckets of sand to make. Martin's sandcastle is 30 cm high.
    Work out the number of buckets of sand that Martin needed to make his sandcastle.

KEY POINTS

1. A reflection is specified by a mirror line.

2. A rotation is specified by a centre of rotation, an angle of rotation, and a direction (clockwise or anticlockwise.)

3. A translation can be expressed in vector form, e.g. $\begin{bmatrix} 2 \\ 3 \end{bmatrix}$ means 2 to the right and 3 up.

4. Two shapes are congruent if they are exactly the same shape and size. Reflections, rotations and translations all preserve congruence.

5. An enlargement is specified by a centre of enlargement and a scale factor. Scale factors larger than 1 actually make the image larger, while scale factors between 0 and 1 cause the image to be reduced so it is smaller in size than the original. Negative enlargements turn the object upside-down and move it to the opposite side of the centre of enlargement.

6. Enlargements do not normally preserve congruence. The object and its image will, however, be mathematically similar, i.e. the same shape.

7. When solid objects are enlarged by a scale factor, their perimeters increase by the same ratio. Areas increase according to the square of the scale factor, and volumes by its cube. Exam questions on solid objects sometimes use mass; this also increases as the cube of the scale factor, since mass is dependent on the bulk of material inside an object, i.e. its volume.

Internet Challenge 20

Geometrical definitions

Mathematicians like to attach precise meanings to certain words – these are **definitions**. In the sentences below, the letters of the key words have been replaced with ☐ symbols. Find the missing word in each case. (You will know some of these already, but you may need to look up some of the less well-known ones on the internet.)

1 An ☐☐☐☐☐☐☐☐☐☐☐ is a mathematical solid with 20 faces.

2 A ☐☐☐☐☐☐☐ is the simple name for a circular prism.

3 If two objects are the same shape and size they are said to be ☐☐☐☐☐☐☐☐☐.

4 If two shapes are alike in shape but one is larger than the other, they are said to be mathematically ☐☐☐☐☐☐☐.

5 Z-angles are, more properly, called ☐☐☐☐☐☐☐☐☐ angles.

6 ☐☐☐☐☐☐☐☐ lines never touch; they remain at a constant distance apart.

7 A ☐☐☐☐☐ is a solid object in the form of a perforated ring (like a ring doughnut).

8 The interior angles of an ☐☐☐☐☐☐☐ add up to 1080°.

9 A ☐☐☐☐☐☐☐☐☐☐ is exactly half of a sphere.

10 The highest point of a pyramid is known as its ☐☐☐☐.

11 A pyramid with a triangular base is called a ☐☐☐☐☐☐☐☐☐☐☐.

12 ☐☐☐☐☐☐☐ is the correct mathematical name for a 'diamond' with four equal sides.

13 An angle of one-sixtieth of a degree is called a ☐☐☐☐☐☐ of ☐☐☐.

14 An angle of 57.296° is called one ☐☐☐☐☐☐☐.

15 The diagram below shows a ☐☐☐☐☐☐☐☐ cone. This is also a ☐☐☐☐☐☐☐☐.

CHAPTER 21

Pythagoras' theorem

In this chapter you will **learn how to**:

- use Pythagoras' theorem to test whether triangles are right angled
- use Pythagoras' theorem to find an unknown side in a right-angled triangle
- use Pythagoras' theorem to solve simple three-dimensional problems.

You will also be **challenged to**:

- investigate Pythagorean triples.

Starter: Finding squares and square roots on your calculator

When you multiply a number by itself, you are finding its **square**. For example, 3 squared is 9, because $3 \times 3 = 9$. This is usually written $3^2 = 9$. To find the square of 3.1, you would probably prefer to use a calculator:

3.1 $\boxed{x^2}$ = 9.61

The reverse process of squaring is called **square rooting**, or finding the **square root**. This is much harder than squaring, and usually requires the use of a calculator equipped with a square root $\boxed{\sqrt{}}$ key. You may find your calculator screen fills with decimal figures; if so, it is usual to round the answer to 3 significant figures.

Task 1
Look at these numbers. Work out the square of each one. Several of them can be done without a calculator, but you may use a calculator for the harder ones.

    4   7   2.5   1.2   0.8   13   6   16

Task 2
Look at these numbers. Work out the square root of each one. If the answers are not exact then you should round to 3 significant figures.

    13   10   16   22.5   6.25   49   120   121

Task 3
Use your calculator to find the square roots of these numbers, to 3 significant figures where necessary:

    8   9   10   11   12   13   14   15   16   17

Why is it possible to find the square roots of some whole numbers without the need for a calculator?

21.1 Introducing Pythagoras' theorem

Pythagoras' theorem concerns right-angled triangles. Suppose you have a right-angled triangle with sides of lengths a, b and c, with c being the longest side, or **hypotenuse**. Then Pythagoras' theorem states that:

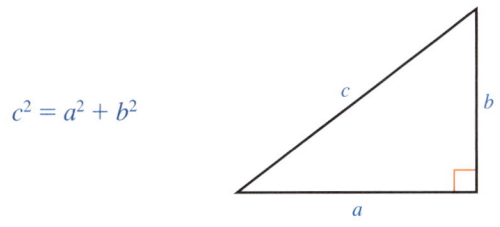

$$c^2 = a^2 + b^2$$

For example, if $a = 4$ cm and $b = 3$ cm then c would be 5 cm, since $5^2 = 25$, $4^2 = 16$, $3^2 = 9$ and $25 = 16 + 9$

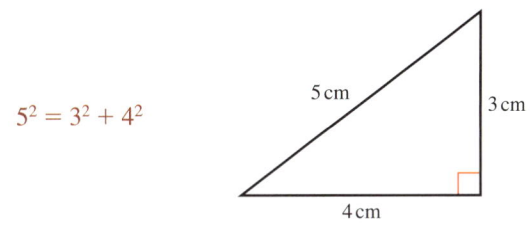

$$5^2 = 3^2 + 4^2$$

There are many ways to prove Pythagoras' theorem; in this book you will find a proof in Chapter 31. In fact, Pythagoras' theorem works only in right-angled triangles, so it may be used to check whether a triangle is right angled or not.

In the examples and exercises that follow, capital letters will be used for the vertices of a triangle, such as ABC or PQR. The simplest way of naming an angle is just to use the capital letter of the point at the angle – angle A for example. You refer to sides by using two capital letters – the side joining points A and B is written as AB.

Regardless of the letters used for naming corners of the triangle, when substituting into Pythagoras' theorem you may find it convenient to use c for the hypotenuse, and a and b for the other two sides.

EXAMPLE

Use Pythagoras' theorem to check whether each of these triangles is right angled or not.

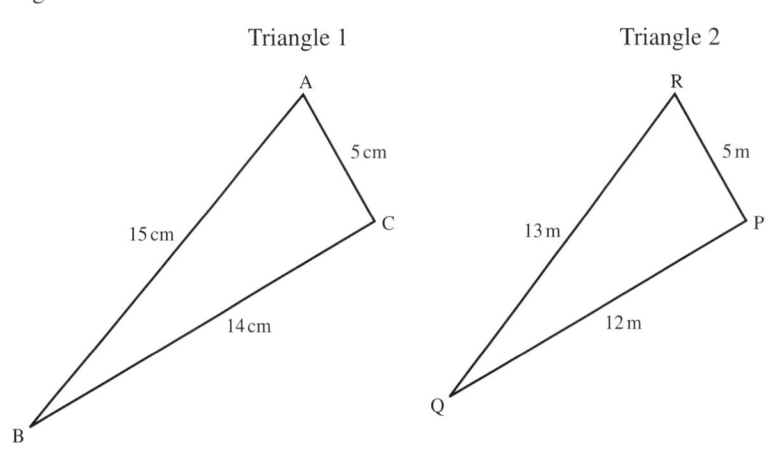

Triangle 1

Triangle 2

SOLUTION

In triangle 1, the longest side is 15 cm, so try $c = 15$, $a = 14$, $b = 5$

Then $c^2 = 225$ and $a^2 + b^2 = 14^2 + 5^2$
$= 196 + 25$
$= 221$

Since $225 \neq 221$, triangle 1 cannot be right angled.

In triangle 2, the longest side is 13 m, so try $c = 13$, $a = 12$, $b = 5$

Then $c^2 = 169$ and $a^2 + b^2 = 12^2 + 5^2$
$= 144 + 25$
$= 169$

Since c^2 and $a^2 + b^2$ are equal ($= 169$), triangle 2 must be right angled.

EXERCISE 21.1

Look at these triangles, and use Pythagoras' theorem to decide whether they are right angled or not.
Note: The diagrams are not drawn to scale.

1 Triangle with AB = 12 cm, BC = 6 cm, CA = 10 cm

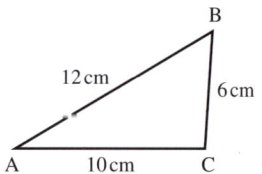

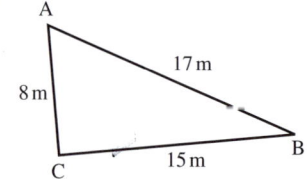

2 Triangle with AC = 8 m, AB = 17 m, CB = 15 m

3 Triangle with BC = 7 mm, BA = 19 mm, CA = 16 mm

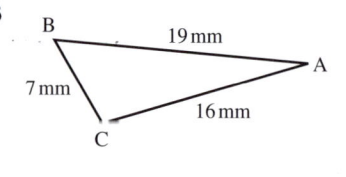

For each of the triangles described below, use Pythagoras' theorem to decide whether it is right angled. If so, name the angle at which the right angle is located.

4 AB = 8 cm, BC = 6 cm, CA = 2.5 cm

5 AB = 7.5 cm, BC = 4.5 cm, CA = 6 cm

6 AB = 12 mm, BC = 12 mm, CA = 5 mm

7 PQ = 10.1 cm, QR = 7.1 cm, RP = 7.2 cm

8 PQ = 12 m, QR = 16 m, RP = 20 m

9 PQ = 3.3 cm, QR = 5.8 cm, RP = 4.5 cm

10 AB = 6 km, BC = 7 km, CA = 8 km

21.2 Using Pythagoras' theorem to find a hypotenuse

In this section, we shall be working with triangles that are known to be right angled, and will use Pythagoras' theorem to find the hypotenuse. This is the longest side, and is always located directly opposite the right angle.

EXAMPLE

Calculate the length of the side AB, marked x, in the triangle below.

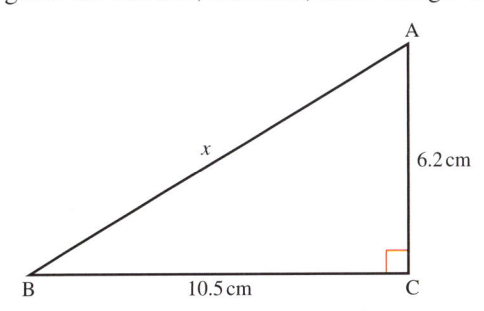

SOLUTION

Pythagoras tells us that:

$x^2 = 6.2^2 + 10.5^2$
  $= 38.44 + 110.25$
  $= 148.69$

Therefore: $x = \sqrt{148.49}$

  $= 12.193\,850\,91$
  $= \underline{12.2\text{ cm}}$ (3 s.f.)

Set out the details of the working clearly…

… and show your full calculator result…

… before finally rounding off to 3 significant figures.

EXERCISE 21.2

Find the length of the hypotenuse represented by the letters a to i below. Give your answers to 3 significant figures where appropriate.

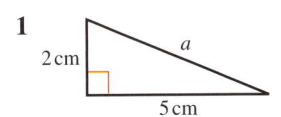

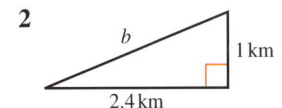

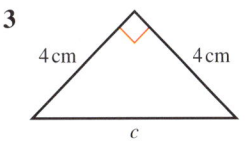

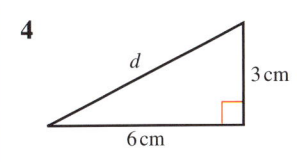

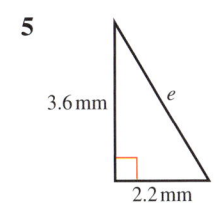

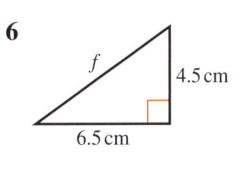

1. 2 cm, 5 cm, a
2. 1 km, 2.4 km, b
3. 4 cm, 4 cm, c
4. d, 3 cm, 6 cm
5. 3.6 mm, 2.2 mm, e
6. f, 4.5 cm, 6.5 cm

7 1.8 m, 2.1 m, g

8 h, 3.8 cm, 2.8 cm

9 0.8 km, i, 0.6 km

Find the length of the diagonal of each rectangle.

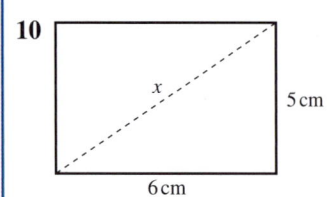

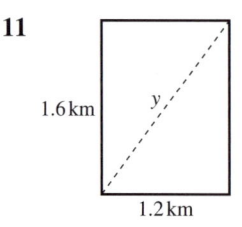

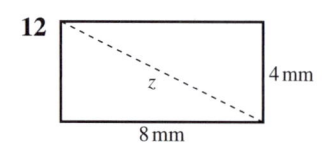

10 x, 5 cm, 6 cm

11 1.6 km, y, 1.2 km

12 z, 4 mm, 8 mm

21.3 Using Pythagoras' theorem to find one of the shorter sides

The method used above may be adapted when the unknown side is not the hypotenuse. In this case, the calculation requires a *subtraction* instead of an *addition*, as shown in the example below.

EXAMPLE

Find the value of y in the right-angled triangle below.

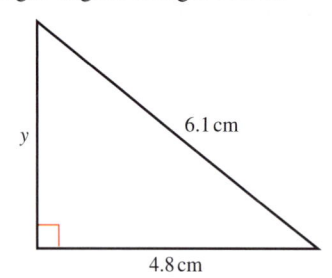

y, 6.1 cm, 4.8 cm

SOLUTION

By Pythagoras:
$6.1^2 = 4.8^2 + y^2$

Begin by writing Pythagoras' theorem in full. (You could start with the rearranged version.)

Rearranging:
$y^2 = 6.1^2 - 4.8^2$
$= 37.21 - 23.04$
$= 14.17$
Therefore: $y = \sqrt{14.17}$

Your numerical answer should be shown:
- as an exact statement ($\sqrt{14.17}$)
- then the full calculator result
- and, finally, the rounded value.

$= 3.764\,306\,045$
$= \underline{3.76\text{ cm}}$ (3 s.f.)

Remember to include units (cm) in your answer.

EXERCISE 21.3

Find the length of the side marked by the letters *a* to *i* below.
Give your answers to 3 significant figures, where appropriate.

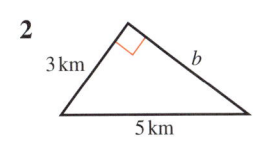

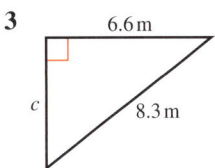

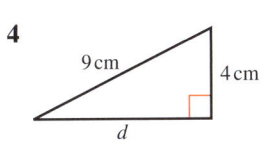

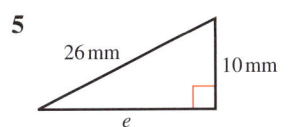

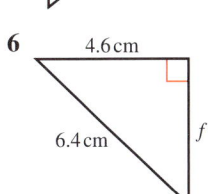

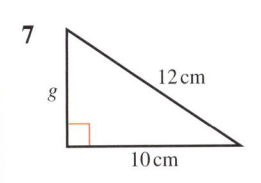

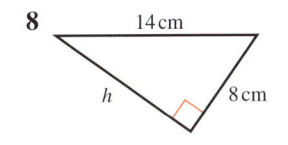

1 Triangle with legs 8 cm and 6 cm, hypotenuse *a*.

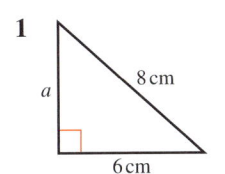

2 Triangle with legs 3 km and *b*, hypotenuse 5 km.

3 Triangle with legs *c* and 6.6 m, hypotenuse 8.3 m.

4 Triangle with legs 4 cm and *d*, hypotenuse 9 cm.

5 Triangle with legs 10 mm and *e*, hypotenuse 26 mm.

6 Triangle with legs 4.6 cm and *f*, hypotenuse 6.4 cm.

7 Triangle with legs *g* and 10 cm, hypotenuse 12 cm.

8 Triangle with legs 8 cm and *h*, hypotenuse 14 cm.

9 Triangle with legs 2 cm and *i*, hypotenuse 3 cm.

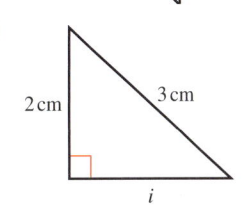

10 A rectangle has length 24 cm and width *x* cm. Its diagonal is of length 25 cm. Find the value of *x*.

11 A ship sails due North for 12 km, then turns and sails due East for *y* km. It ends up 16 km in a direct straight line from its start point. Find the value of *y*.

The last part of this exercise contains a mixture of questions. Remember to square and add when you are finding a hypotenuse, but square and subtract when finding a shorter side. In both cases, remember to square root at the end.

12 Find *x*, correct to 3 significant figures. Triangle with sides *x* cm, 11.5 cm (hypotenuse), and 8 cm.

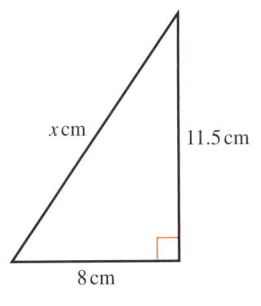

13 Find *y*, correct to 3 significant figures. Triangle with sides *y* cm, 16 cm (hypotenuse), and 6.5 cm.

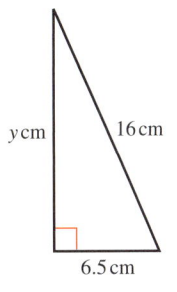

14 Find *z*, correct to 3 significant figures. Triangle with sides 9.2 cm, 15.1 cm (hypotenuse), and *z* cm.

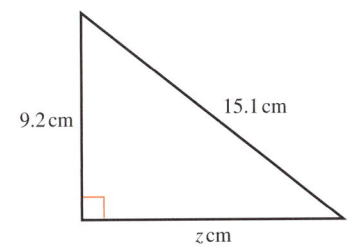

15 Find *s*, correct to 3 significant figures. Triangle with sides *s* cm, 8.8 cm, and 7.8 cm.

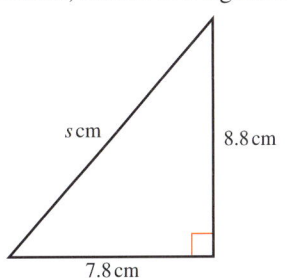

21.4 Pythagoras' theorem in three dimensions

EXAMPLE

A room is in the shape of a cuboid measuring 5 m by 7 m by 2.5 m. A string is stretched diagonally across the room, from bottom corner B to the opposite top corner G. Find the length of the string, correct to 3 significant figures.

SOLUTION

To find the length of the string BG we use Pythagoras' theorem twice.

First, in triangle BCD:

$BD^2 = 5^2 + 7^2$
$= 25 + 49$
$= 74$

Thus $BD = \sqrt{74}$.

Now in triangle BDG:

$BG^2 = BD^2 + DG^2$
$= (\sqrt{74})^2 + 2.5^2$
$= 74 + 6.25$
$= 80.25$

So $BG = \sqrt{80.25}$
$= 8.958\ 2\ldots$
$= \underline{8.96\ m}$ (3 s.f.)

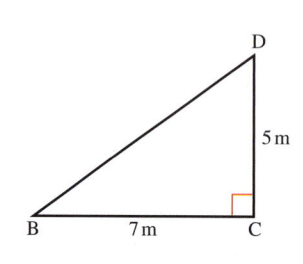

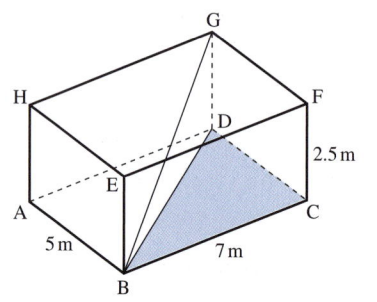

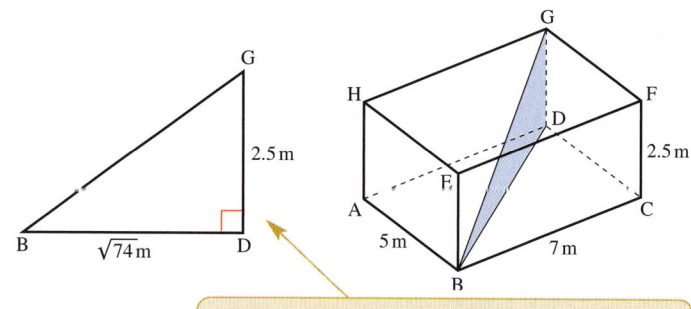

Always make a sketch of the 2-D triangle you have extracted from the 3-D solid object.

EXERCISE 21.4

1. The diagram shows a box in the shape of a cuboid.

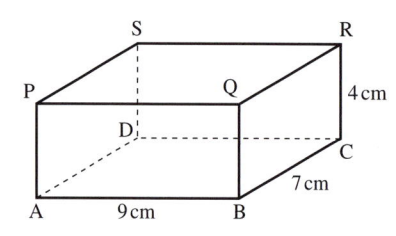

    a) Work out the length AC. Give your answer to 3 significant figures.
    b) Work out the length AR. Give your answer to 3 significant figures.

2 The diagram shows a box in the shape of a cuboid.

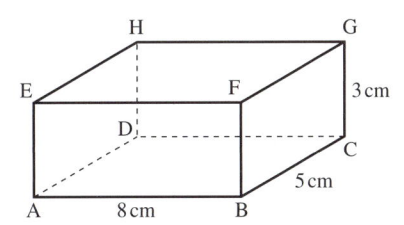

a) Calculate the length BD. Give your answer to 3 significant figures.
b) Calculate the length BH. Give your answer to 3 significant figures.

3 A cuboid measures 4 cm by 10 cm by 12 cm.
a) Make a sketch of the cuboid.
b) Calculate the length of the diagonal, giving your answer correct to 3 significant figures.

4 A postal carton measures 10 cm by 14 cm by 20 cm. Ray wishes to pack a thin brass rod of length 25 cm inside the carton. Use Pythagoras' theorem to explain whether this is possible or not.

5 The diagram shows a wedge. The face ABED is a rectangle, and is at right angles to the face CBEF, which is also a rectangle. AB = 10 cm, BC = 4 cm, BE = 18 cm.

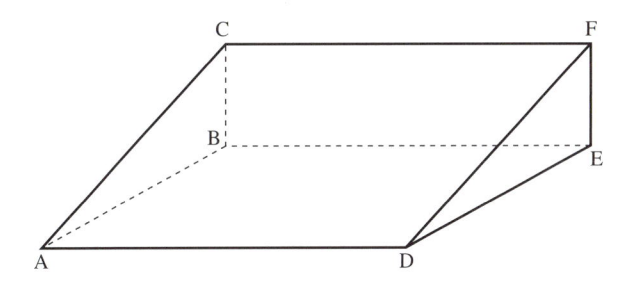

a) Calculate the length AE, correct to 3 significant figures.
b) Calculate the direct distance from A to F, correct to 3 significant figures.

6 A thin straw of length 20.5 cm just fits inside a cylindrical container of length 20 cm.

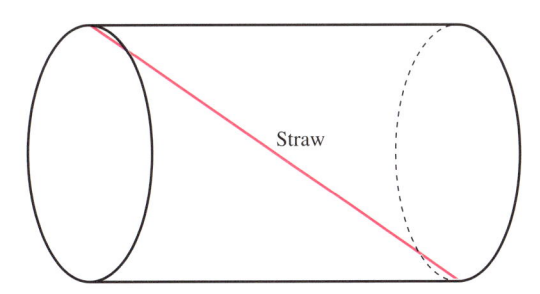

Find the diameter of the cylinder.

7 Find the length of the longest thin rod that will just fit inside a cuboid-shaped box with dimensions 3 cm by 4 cm by 12 cm.

REVIEW EXERCISE 21

Find the missing lengths, denoted by the letters *a* to *f*.
Round your answers to 3 significant figures where appropriate.

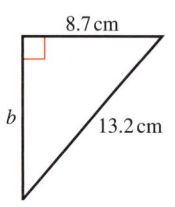

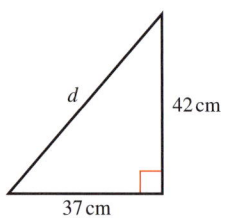

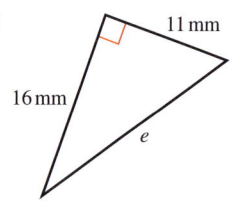

1 Right-angled triangle with legs 3 cm and 2.5 cm, hypotenuse *a*.

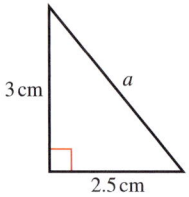

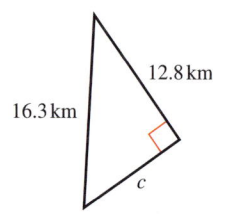

2 Right-angled triangle with legs 8.7 cm and *b*, hypotenuse 13.2 cm.

3 Right-angled triangle with legs 12.8 km and *c*, hypotenuse 16.3 km.

4 Right-angled triangle with legs *d* and 37 cm, hypotenuse 42 cm.

5 Right-angled triangle with legs 11 mm and *e*, hypotenuse 16 mm.

6 Right-angled triangle with legs *f* and 13.3 cm, hypotenuse 17.4 cm.

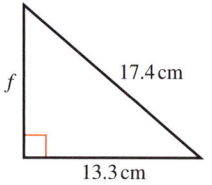

7 The diagram shows two connected right-angled triangles.

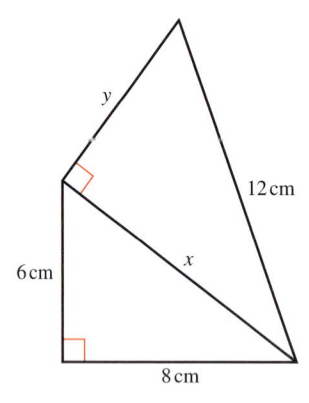

a) Write down the exact value of *x*, without using a calculator.
b) Use your calculator to find the value of *y*, giving your answer correct to 2 significant figures.

8 ABCDEFGH is a cuboid, with AD = 2.5 cm, DC = 6.5 cm and CG = 4.5 cm.

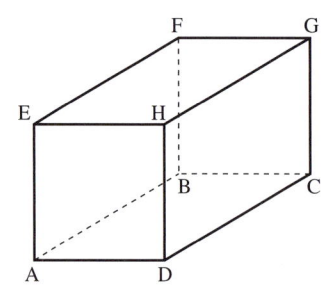

a) Calculate AH, CH and FH, each correct to 3 significant figures.
b) Calculate the distance BH, correct to 3 significant figures.

9 XYZ is a right-angled triangle. XY = 3.2 cm. XZ = 1.7 cm.

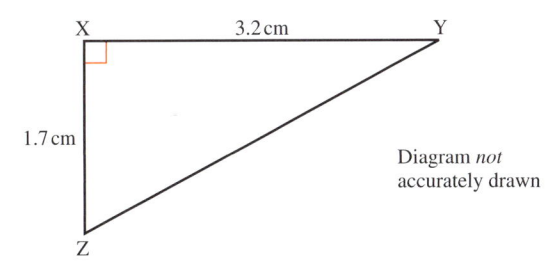

Diagram *not* accurately drawn

Calculate the length of YZ. Give your answer correct to 3 significant figures. [Edexcel]

10 The diagram shows a sketch of a triangle.

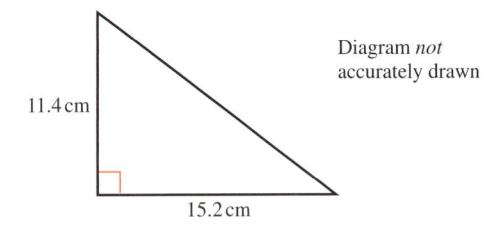

Diagram *not* accurately drawn

a) Work out the area of the triangle. State the units of your answer.
b) Work out the perimeter of the triangle. [Edexcel]

11

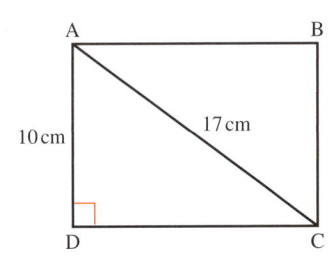

Diagram *not* accurately drawn

ABCD is a rectangle. AC = 17 cm. AD = 10 cm.
Calculate the length of the side CD. Give your answer correct to one decimal place. [Edexcel]

12

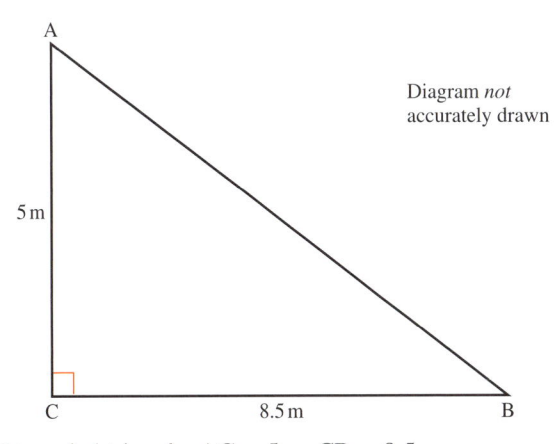

Diagram *not* accurately drawn

ABC is a right-angled triangle. AC = 5 m. CB = 8.5 m.
a) Work out the area of the triangle.
b) Work out the length of AB. Give your answer correct to 2 decimal places. [Edexcel]

13 The diagram represents a cuboid ABCDEFGH. AB = 5 cm. BC = 7 cm. AE = 3 cm.

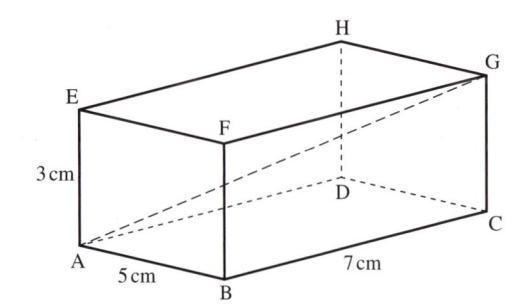

Diagram *not* accurately drawn

Calculate the length of AG. Give your answer correct to 3 significant figures. [Edexcel]

KEY POINTS

1. Suppose a triangle has sides a, b, c, where c is the longest side. If the triangle is right angled, then $c^2 = a^2 + b^2$. This is Pythagoras' theorem.

2. Pythagoras' theorem also works in reverse. Therefore, if $c^2 = a^2 + b^2$ then the triangle must be right angled.

3. To find an unknown hypotenuse, use Pythagoras' theorem in the form $c^2 = a^2 + b^2$

   This can be rearranged to give $c = \sqrt{a^2 + b^2}$

4. To find an unknown shorter side, a, say, use Pythagoras' theorem in the form $a^2 = c^2 - b^2$

   This can be rewritten as $a = \sqrt{c^2 - b^2}$

5. Pythagoras problems sometimes involve two stages, especially if they are in three dimensions. Do not round off answers to multi-stage problems until all the calculations have been completed.

6. It is useful to draw the right-angled triangle you are using at each stage of your calculations.

Internet Challenge 21

Investigating Pythagorean triples

Probably the most well-known right-angled triangle has sides in the ratio of 3 : 4 : 5, and is known as the (3, 4, 5) triangle. The numbers (3, 4, 5) form a **Pythagorean triple**, which means that they are whole numbers satisfying $a^2 + b^2 = c^2$. Another Pythagorean triple is (5, 12, 13).

Here are some questions about Pythagorean triples. You may use the internet to help you research some of the answers.

1   Find c such that (8, 15, c) is a Pythagorean triple.

2   How can we easily see that (6, 8, 10) and (10, 24, 26) are Pythagorean triples without doing any detailed calculations?

3   Find all the Pythagorean triples in which each number does not exceed 25.

4   Are there any patterns or formulae for generating them?

5   Are there infinitely many Pythagorean triples?

6   Are there any **Pythagorean quadruples**, that is, positive whole numbers a, b, c, d such that $a^2 + b^2 + c^2 = d^2$?

7   Find out as much as you can about Fermat's last theorem. Has it been proved yet?

CHAPTER 22

Introducing trigonometry

> In this chapter you will **learn how to**:
> - use sine, cosine and tangent to find unknown lengths in right-angled triangles
> - use inverse functions to find unknown angles in right-angled triangles
> - solve multi-stage problems using sine, cosine and tangent.
>
> You will also be **challenged to**:
> - investigate famous geometers.

Starter: A triangular spiral

Draw a right-angled triangle with two shortest sides of lengths two units and one unit (use a scale of 2 cm to 1 unit), like this:

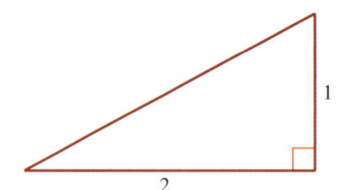

Now construct another right-angled triangle, using the hypotenuse of the first one as one of its short sides, and a length of 1 unit (2 cm) for the other:

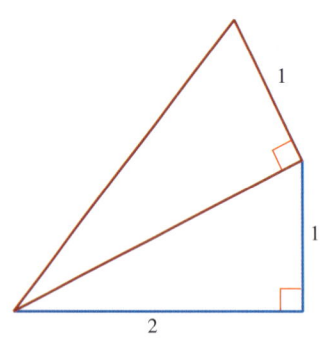

Are these two triangles similar?

Continue the pattern, using a one-unit short side each time.
Measure the hypotenuse of the fifth triangle in the pattern. What do you notice?
Try to make as many triangles in the pattern as you can, to make a spiral pattern.

What do you notice about the angles at the centre of the spiral?

22.1 The sine ratio

Consider these two triangles. They both have angles of 30°, 60° and 90°. The two triangles are mathematically similar.

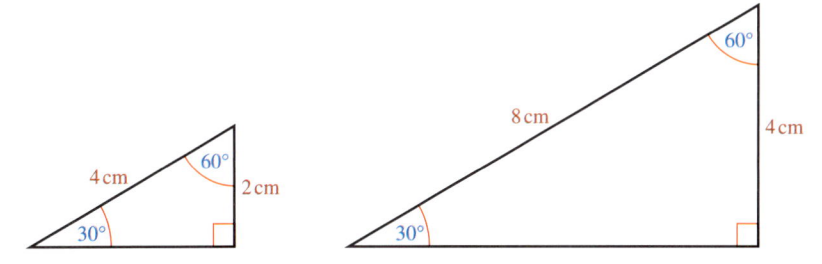

Compare the length of the side opposite the 30° angle, with the length of the hypotenuse. In the smaller triangle this is 2 ÷ 4 = 0.5, and in the larger triangle it is 4 ÷ 8 = 0.5. If you make some other 30° right-angled triangles, you will find the ratio always gives 0.5, regardless of the scale of a particular triangle.

In any right-angled triangle, the answer obtained by dividing the length opposite an angle by the length of the hypotenuse is called the **sine** of that angle. Sines of angles other than 30° do not work out to be such convenient quantities. For example, sin 29° = 0.484 809 620 2, correct to 10 decimal places.

The symbol θ is often used to denote a general angle, so:

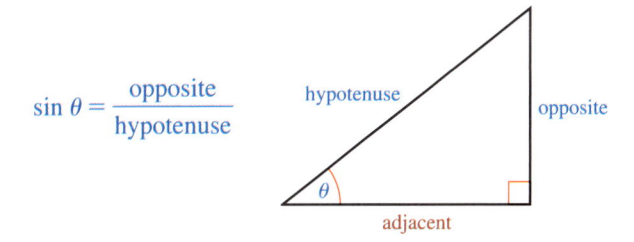

$$\sin \theta = \frac{\text{opposite}}{\text{hypotenuse}}$$

Your calculator should contain a sine function button that enables you to obtain the sine of any angle. Make sure that your calculator is set to DEGree mode (rather than RADian or GRADian mode); ask your teacher to check this if you are not sure.

The equation:

$$\sin \theta = \frac{\text{opposite}}{\text{hypotenuse}}$$

can be rewritten as:

$$\text{opposite} = \text{hypotenuse} \times \sin \theta$$

and this allows you to calculate the missing length of a side opposite a given angle.

EXAMPLE

Find the missing length marked x.

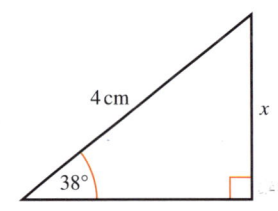

(Right-angled triangle with hypotenuse 4 cm, angle 38°, opposite side x.)

SOLUTION

In this triangle, the side opposite to 38° is x, and the hypotenuse is 4 cm.

$$\text{opposite} = \text{hypotenuse} \times \sin \theta$$
$$x = 4 \times \sin 38°$$
$$= 2.462\,645\,901$$
$$= \underline{2.46 \text{ cm}} \text{ (3 s.f.)}$$

> Calculations should be rounded to a sensible number of figures at the end. Remember to include the units.

You can also find the missing length of a hypotenuse by rearranging the usual equation.

EXAMPLE

Find the missing length marked y.

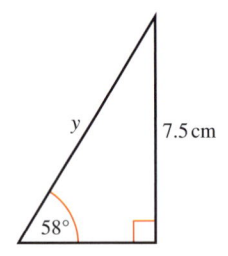

(Right-angled triangle with side 7.5 cm opposite 58°, hypotenuse y.)

SOLUTION

In this triangle, the side opposite to 58° is 7.5 cm, and the hypotenuse is y.

$$\text{opposite} = \text{hypotenuse} \times \sin \theta$$
$$7.5 = y \times \sin 58°$$
$$\text{so } y = \frac{7.5}{\sin 58°}$$
$$= 8.843\,838\,025$$
$$= \underline{8.84 \text{ cm}} \text{ (3 s.f.)}$$

> Show your full calculator value ...

> ... as well as the rounded value.

Examination questions can ask you to do either type of calculation. As a check, remember that the hypotenuse is always the longest side in a right-angled triangle; in the example above you would check that your value for y is larger than 7.5 cm.

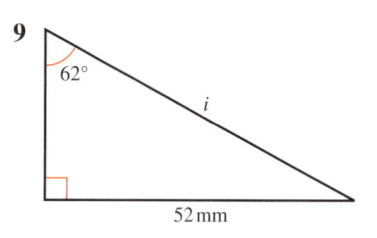

EXERCISE 22.1

Work out the values of the sides represented by letters. Show details of your calculations, and round your final answers correct to 3 significant figures in each case.

1. Right-angled triangle with hypotenuse 9 cm, angle 28°, side a opposite the 28° angle (vertical leg).

2. Right-angled triangle with side 5 cm, angle 47°, side b opposite the right angle (hypotenuse).

3. Right-angled triangle with side 5.6 cm, angle 46°, side c (hypotenuse).

4. Right-angled triangle with side 7.5 cm, angle 74°, side d.

5. Right-angled triangle with side 13 cm, angle 28°, side e.

6. Right-angled triangle with side 5.4 cm, angle 44°, side f.

7. Right-angled triangle with side 4.1 cm, angle 51°, side g (hypotenuse).

8. Right-angled triangle with side 48 mm, angle 37°, side h.

9. Right-angled triangle with side 52 mm, angle 62°, side i (hypotenuse).

10. Right-angled triangle with side 18 cm, angle 32°, side j.

11. In triangle ABC, AB = 12 cm, angle ACB = 90°, angle CAB = 36°. Calculate BC.

12. In triangle PQR, angle PQR = 90°, angle QPR = 29°, PR = 8.8 cm. Calculate QR.

13. In triangle LMN, angle LMN = 90°, angle LNM = 28°, LN = 75 mm. Calculate LM.

14. In triangle ABC, angle CAB = 90°, angle ABC = 44°, AC = 60 mm. Calculate CB.

15. In triangle RST, angle RTS = 90°, angle RST = 17°, RS = 145 mm. Calculate RT.

22.2 The cosine ratio

The **cosine** of an angle is defined in a similar way to the sine function, but using the adjacent side instead of the opposite:

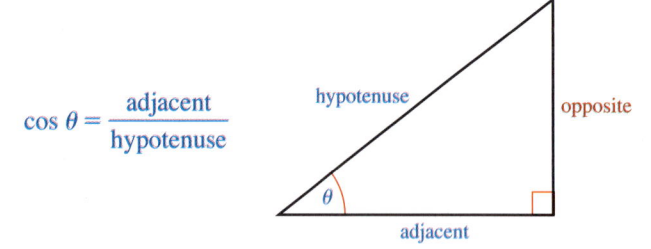

$$\cos \theta = \frac{\text{adjacent}}{\text{hypotenuse}}$$

The equation:

$$\cos \theta = \frac{\text{adjacent}}{\text{hypotenuse}}$$

can be rewritten as:

$$\text{adjacent} = \text{hypotenuse} \times \cos \theta$$

EXAMPLE

Find the missing length marked x.

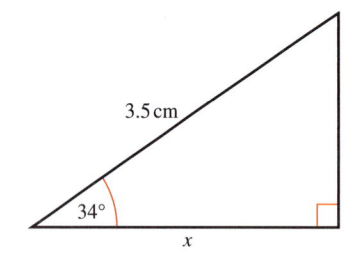

SOLUTION

Labelling the sides as seen from the 34° angle:

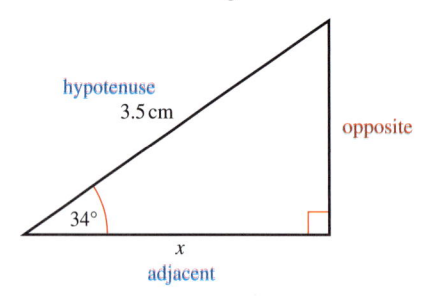

In this triangle, the side adjacent to 34° is x, and the hypotenuse is 3.5 cm.

$$\begin{aligned}
\text{adjacent} &= \text{hypotenuse} \times \cos \theta \\
x &= 3.5 \times \cos 34° \\
&= 2.901\,631\,504 \\
&= \underline{2.90 \text{ cm}} \text{ (3 s.f.)}
\end{aligned}$$

If you need to find the hypotenuse, division will be necessary.

EXAMPLE

Find the missing length marked as *p*.

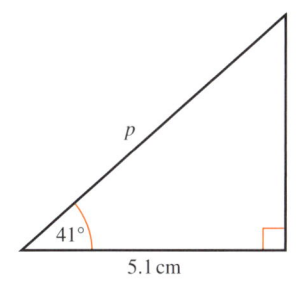

SOLUTION

Labelling the sides as seen from the 41° angle:

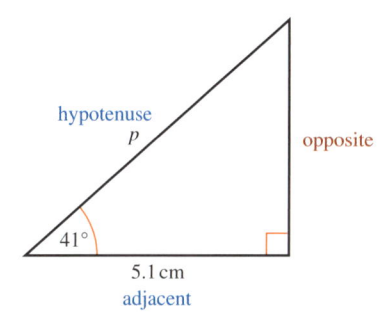

In this triangle, the side adjacent to 41° is 5.1 cm, and the hypotenuse is *p* cm.

$$\text{adjacent} = \text{hypotenuse} \times \cos \theta$$
$$5.1 = p \times \cos 41°$$
$$p = \frac{5.1}{\cos 41°}$$
$$= \underline{6.76 \text{ cm}} \text{ (3 s.f.)}$$

Some questions might require the use of both sine and cosine. Take care to identify the sides correctly.

EXAMPLE

Find the missing lengths marked as *x* and *y*.

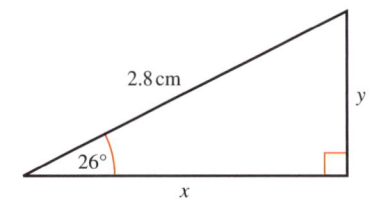

SOLUTION

Labelling the sides as seen from the 26° angle:

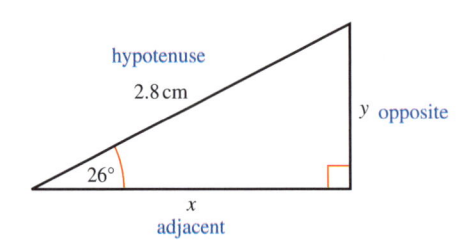

In this triangle, the side *adjacent* to 26° is *x*, and the hypotenuse is 2.8 cm.

$$\text{adjacent} = \text{hypotenuse} \times \cos \theta$$
$$x = 2.8 \times \cos 26°$$
$$= 2.516\,623\,33$$
$$= \underline{2.52 \text{ cm}} \text{ (3 s.f.)}$$

The side *opposite* to 26° is *y*, so:

$$\text{opposite} = \text{hypotenuse} \times \sin \theta$$
$$x = 2.8 \times \sin 26°$$
$$= 1.227\,439\,211$$
$$= \underline{1.23 \text{ cm}} \text{ (3 s.f.)}$$

> You could check these answers by putting them into Pythagoras' theorem:
> $1.232^2 + 2.522^2 = 7.8633$
> then $\sqrt{7.8633} = 2.804$ cm (4 s.f.)
> (This check does not give exactly 2.8 because of the rounding that has been used.)

EXERCISE 22.2

Work out the values of the sides represented by letters, giving your final answers correct to 3 significant figures.

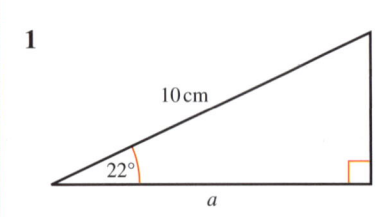

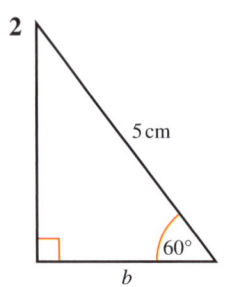

1.

2.

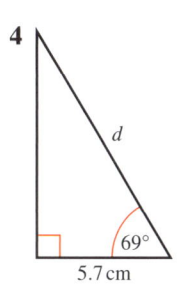

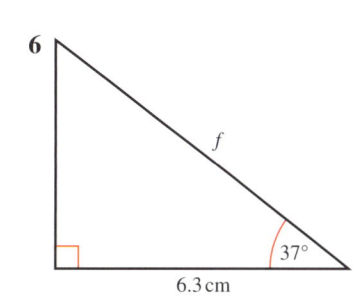

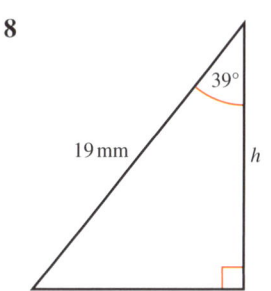

3 Triangle with right angle, 62° at top, hypotenuse 6.5 cm, side c opposite to 6.5 cm along top.

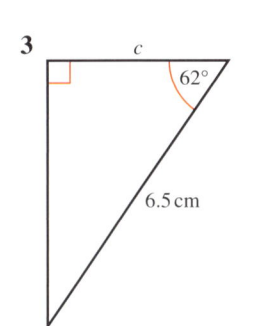

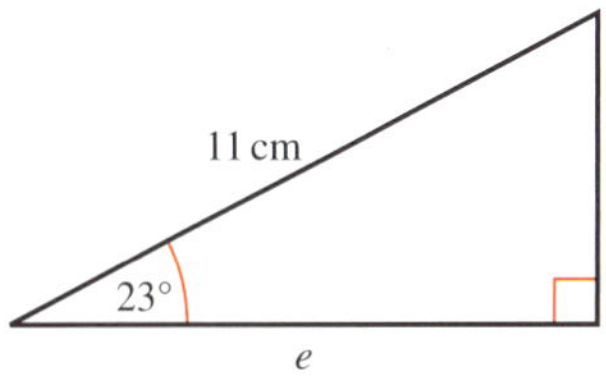

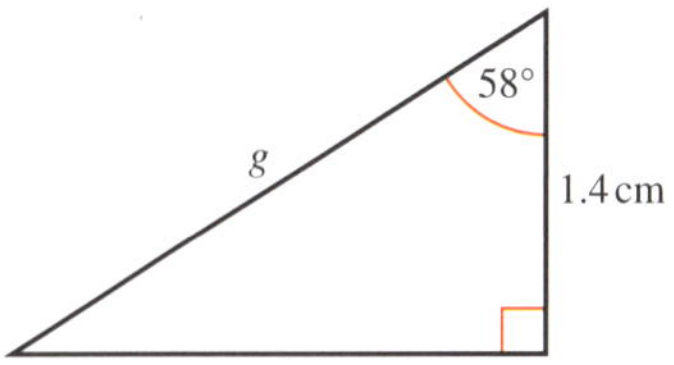

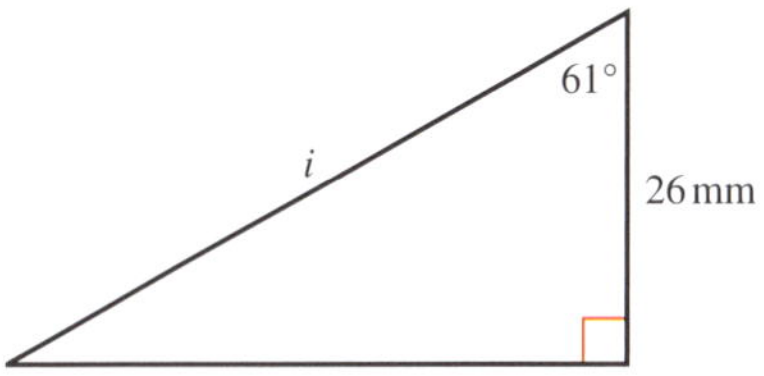

4 Triangle with right angle at bottom left, 69° at bottom right, base 5.7 cm, hypotenuse d.

5 Triangle with 23° at bottom left, right angle at bottom right, hypotenuse 11 cm, base e.

6 Triangle with right angle at bottom left, 37° at bottom right, base 6.3 cm, hypotenuse f.

7 Triangle with 58° at top, right angle at bottom right, side 1.4 cm, hypotenuse g.

8 Triangle with 39° at top, right angle at bottom right, hypotenuse 19 mm, side h.

9 Triangle with 61° at top right, right angle at bottom right, side 26 mm, hypotenuse i.

10 Triangle with 38° at top, right angle at bottom left, hypotenuse 17 cm, side j.

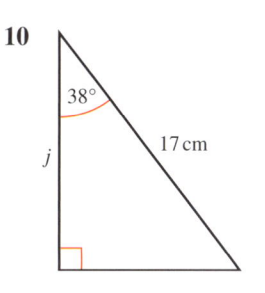

11 In triangle ABC, AB = 9 cm, angle ACB = 90°, angle CBA = 27°. Calculate BC.

12 In triangle PQR, angle PQR = 90°, angle QPR = 41°, PR = 6.5 cm. Calculate PQ.

13 In triangle ABC, angle ABC = 90°, angle BCA = 66°, BC = 44 mm. Calculate AC.

14 In triangle JKL, angle KJL = 90°, angle JKL = 46°, LK = 87 mm. Calculate JK.

15 In triangle EFG, angle EGF = 90°, angle FEG = 33°, EG = 48 cm. Calculate EF.

22.3 The tangent ratio

Sine and cosine are examples of trigonometrical ratios, that is ratios that arise from measuring triangles. There is one further important trigonometrical ratio, namely the **tangent** of an angle, defined as follows:

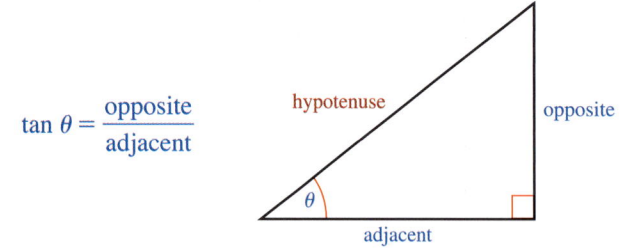

$$\tan \theta = \frac{\text{opposite}}{\text{adjacent}}$$

The equation:

$$\tan \theta = \frac{\text{opposite}}{\text{adjacent}}$$

can be rewritten as:

$$\text{opposite} = \text{adjacent} \times \tan \theta$$

EXAMPLE

Find the missing length marked as x.

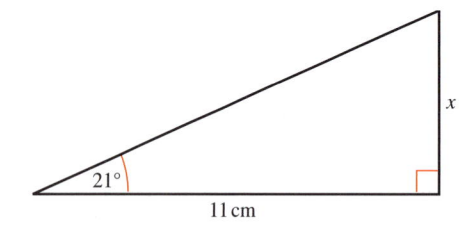

SOLUTION

Labelling the sides as seen from the 21° angle:

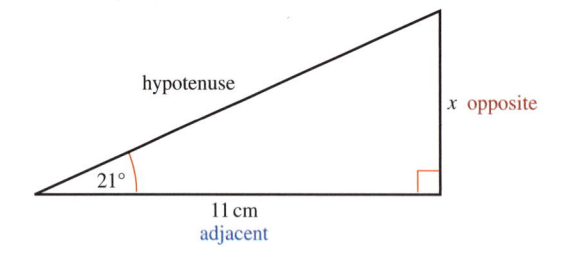

In this triangle, the side opposite to 21° is x, and the adjacent is 11 cm.

$$\text{opposite} = \text{adjacent} \times \tan \theta$$
$$x = 11 \times \tan 21°$$
$$= 4.222\,504\,385$$
$$= \underline{4.22 \text{ cm}} \text{ (3 s.f.)}$$

EXERCISE 22.3

Work out the values of the sides represented by letters, giving your final answers correct to 3 significant figures.

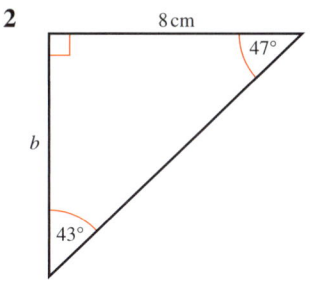

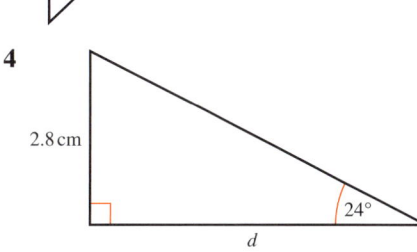

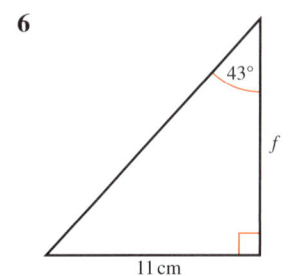

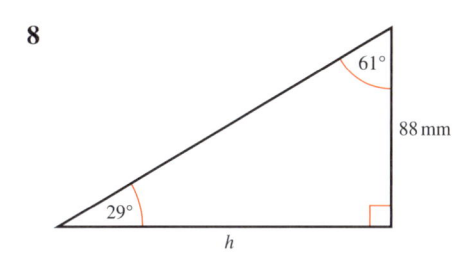

1. Triangle with 32° angle, adjacent side 12 cm, opposite side a (right angle opposite to 32°).

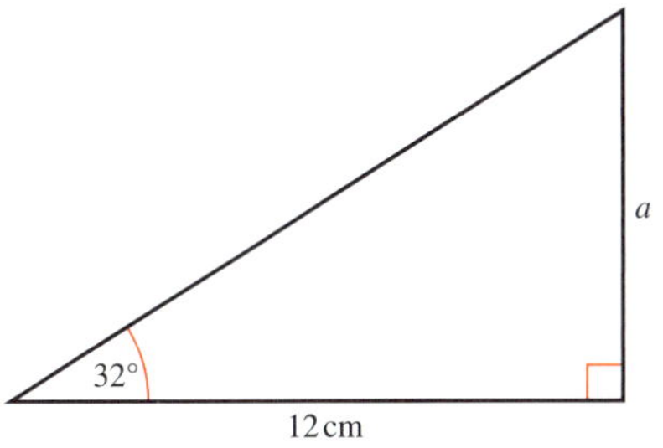

2. Right-angled triangle with top side 8 cm, angle 47° at top right, angle 43° at bottom, side b on the left.

3. Triangle with 53° angle at top, side 5 cm, side c opposite; right angle at bottom right.

4. Right-angled triangle with vertical side 2.8 cm, angle 24° at bottom right, base d.

5. Triangle with 61° angle, base 14 cm, side e.

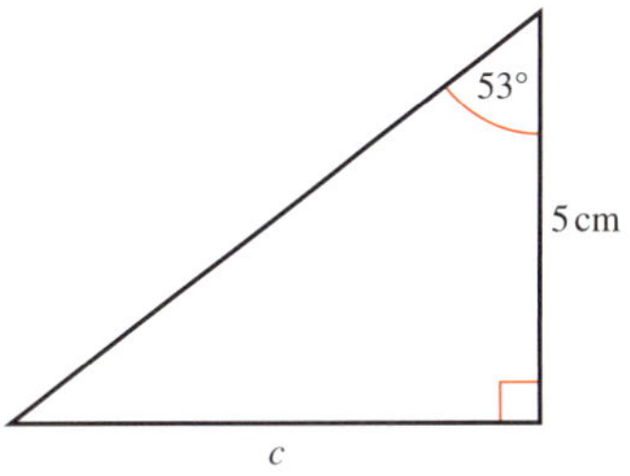

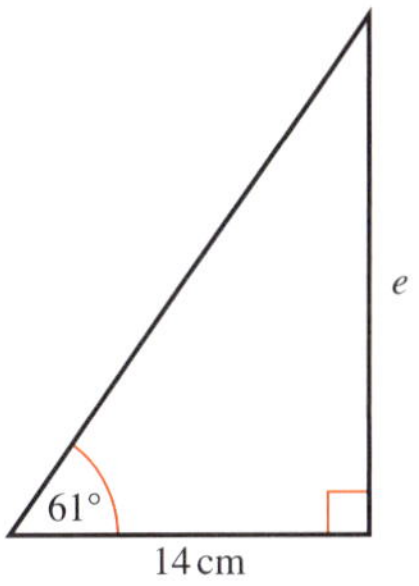

6. Triangle with 43° angle, side f, base 11 cm, right angle at bottom right.

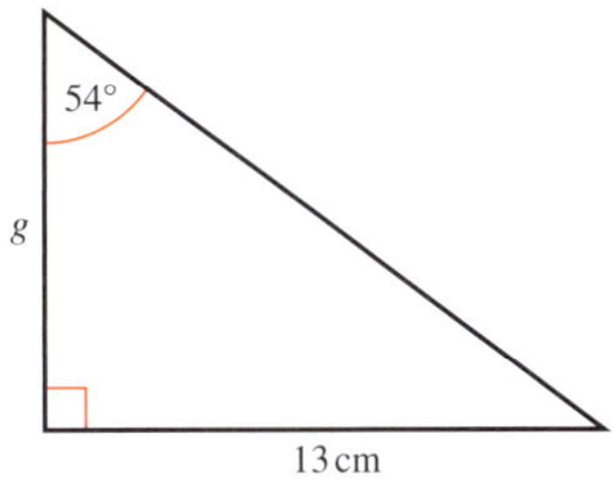

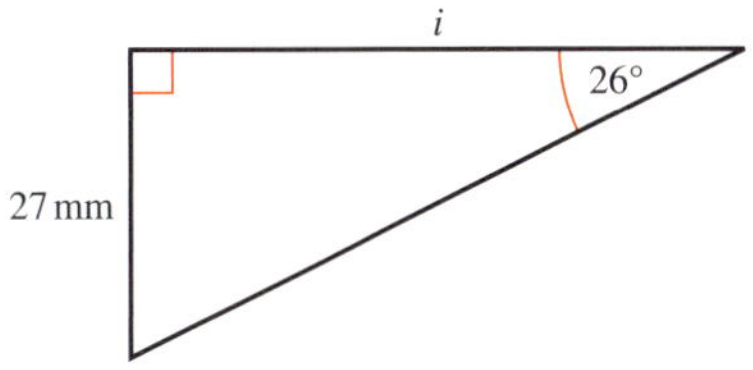

7. Triangle with 54° angle, side g, base 13 cm, right angle at bottom left.

8. Triangle with 61° angle at top, side 88 mm, angle 29° at bottom left, base h, right angle at bottom right.

9. Triangle with right angle at top left, side 27 mm, top side i, angle 26°.

10. Triangle with top side 2.9 cm, angle 38°, right angle at top right, side j.

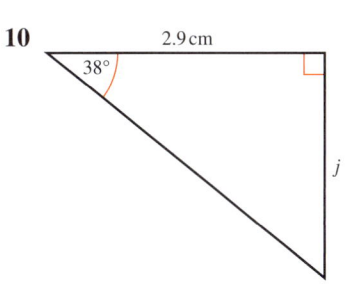

11 In triangle ABC, AB = 21 cm, angle ABC = 90°, angle CAB = 43°. Calculate BC.

12 In triangle PQR, angle PQR = 90°, angle QPR = 17°, QR = 22.5 cm. Calculate PQ.

22.4 Choosing the right trigonometrical function

Exam questions will expect you to recognise which of sine, cosine or tangent is appropriate in a particular setting. To help remember which is which, you might want to use the mathematical 'word' SOHCAHTOA. This is best written across three triangles:

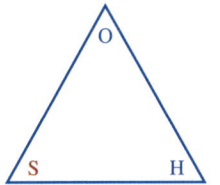

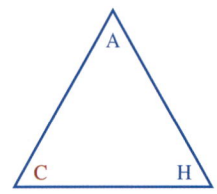

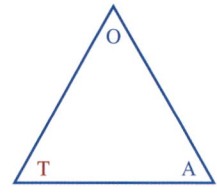

There are two stages to solving a problem. First, decide which of the three ratios is appropriate: for example, if the question refers to the adjacent and the hypotenuse but makes no reference at all to the opposite, then you cannot use either sine or tangent, but you can use cosine. Then cover up the quantity you are looking for, and the triangle tells you whether to multiply or divide the two remaining values. (You may have used a similar technique in a science lesson with distance, speed and time.)

The next two examples will use this method. Do not write a trig ratio such as 'sin' on its own – it must always contain an angle, for example $\sin 42°$ or $\sin x$.

EXAMPLE

Find the missing lengths x and y.

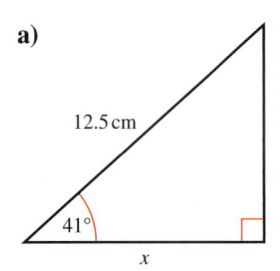

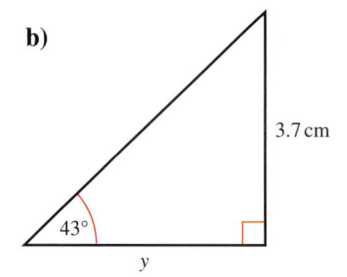

a) 12.5 cm, 41°, x

b) 3.7 cm, 43°, y

SOLUTION

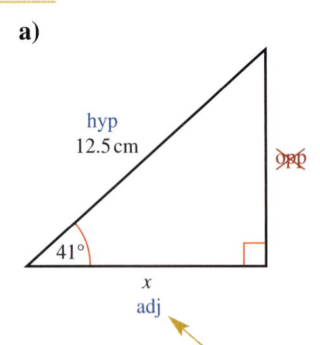

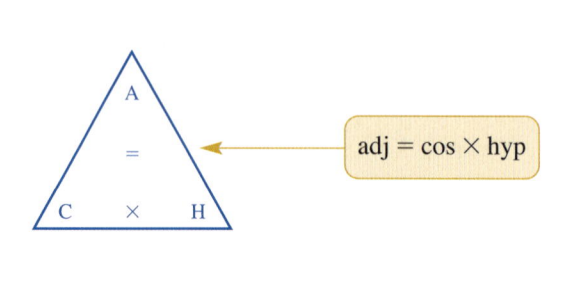

a) hyp 12.5 cm, opp, 41°, x adj

adj = cos × hyp

The adjacent is to be found, and the hypotenuse is known, but the opposite plays no part. Therefore select the cosine function, since it does not use opposite.

adjacent = cos θ × hypotenuse
x = cos 41° × 12.5
  = 9.433 869 753
  = 9.43 cm (3 s.f.)

b)

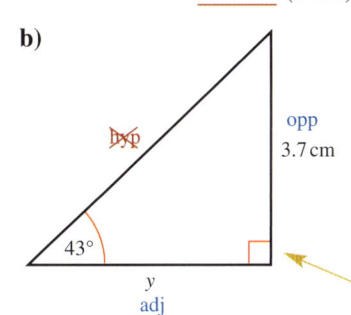

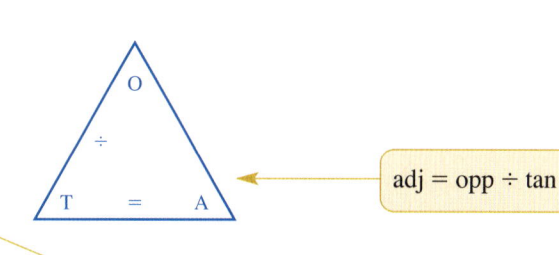

adjacent = opposite ÷ tan θ
y = 3.7 ÷ tan 43°
  = 3.967 764 227
  = 3.97 cm (3 s.f.)

adj = opp ÷ tan

This time the hypotenuse plays no part, so the tangent function is selected: it uses opposite and adjacent.

EXERCISE 22.4

Find the unknown lengths, represented by letters, correct to 3 significant figures.

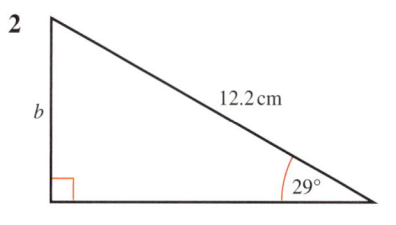

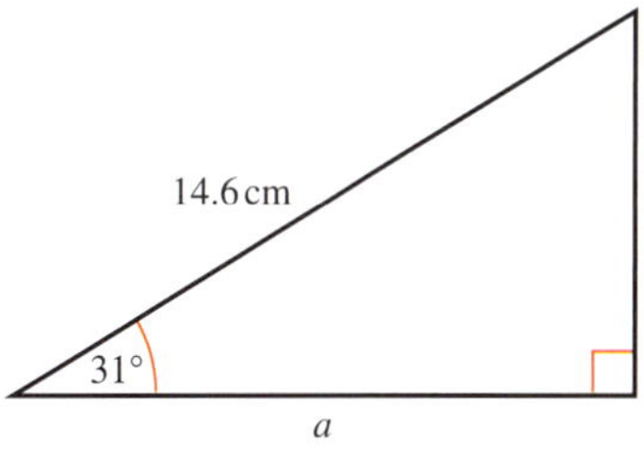

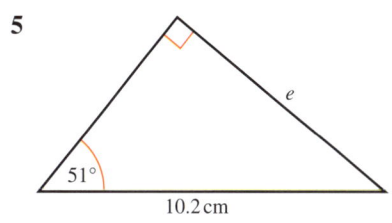

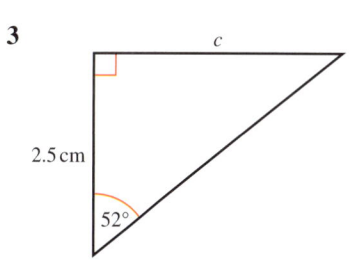

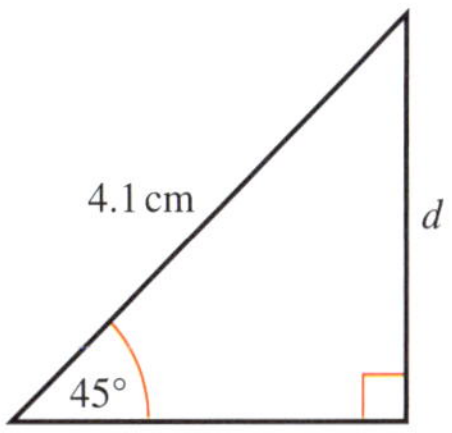

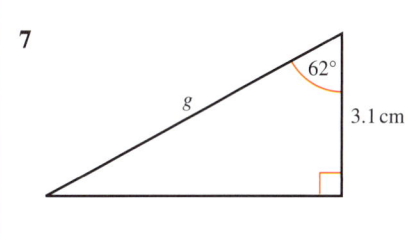

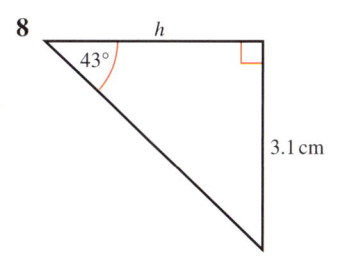

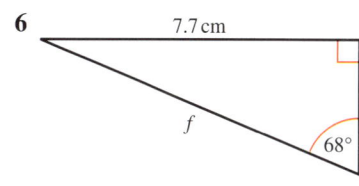

9

(triangle with side 12.4 cm, angle 28°, side i)

10

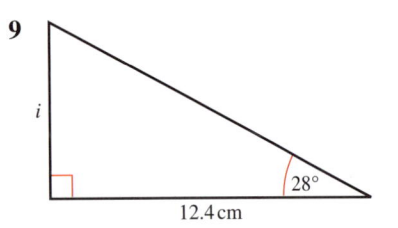

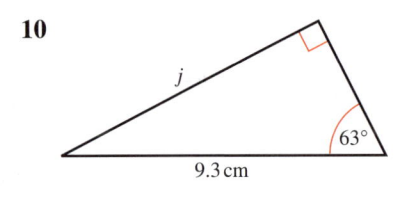

(triangle with side 9.3 cm, angle 63°, side j)

22.5 Finding an unknown angle

So far you have used sine, cosine and tangent to find an unknown side in a right-angled triangle. In such problems you will always be told the value of angle θ – in effect you are using a known angle to help you find an unknown side.

The process can be done in reverse, which means you can use known sides to help you find an unknown angle. When you come to use the sine, cosine or tangent button on your calculator, you must tell the calculator that you are performing the calculation in reverse. This is usually done by pressing the shift or second function key, written as $\sin^{-1}$, $\cos^{-1}$ or $\tan^{-1}$. (You would say *inverse sine*, etc.) Always use these inverse functions when you are expecting the answer to be an angle.

EXAMPLE

A ladder is 4 metres long. It leans against a vertical wall, and reaches 3.5 metres up the wall. Find the angle that the ladder makes with the horizontal ground.

SOLUTION

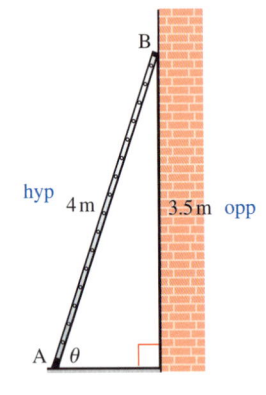

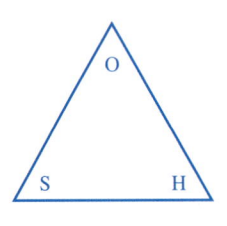

$\sin \theta$ = opposite ÷ hypotenuse
    = 3.5 ÷ 4
    = 0.875
$\theta = \sin^{-1} 0.875$
    = 61.044 975 63
    = 61.0° (nearest 0.1°)

EXERCISE 22.5

Work out the values of the angles represented by letters. Show details of your calculations, and round your final answers correct to 1 decimal place.

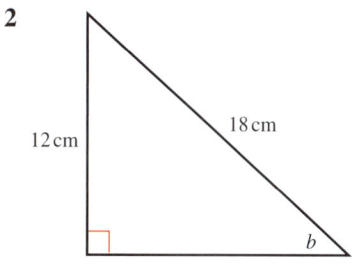

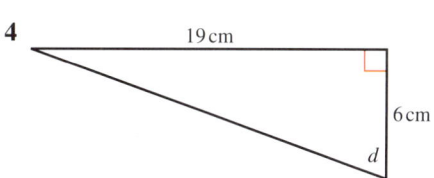

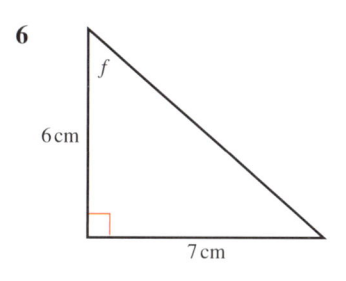

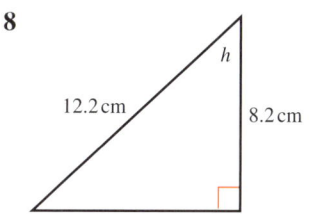

1. Right-angled triangle with legs 4 cm and 3 cm; angle a opposite the 3 cm side.

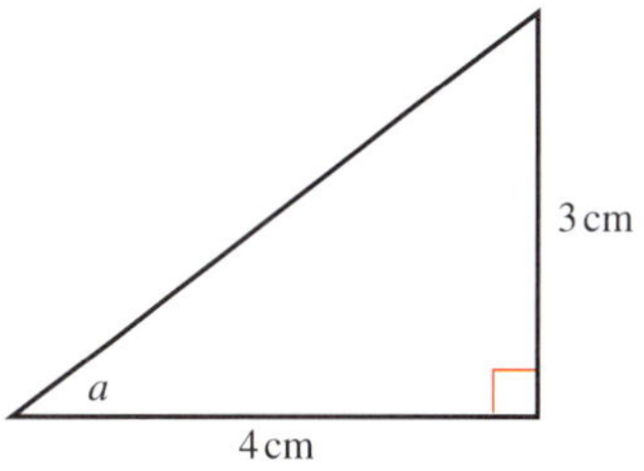

2. Right-angled triangle with one leg 12 cm and hypotenuse 18 cm; angle b opposite the 12 cm side.

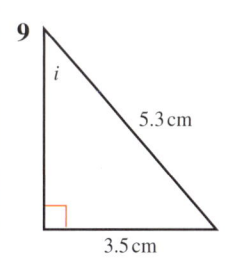

3. Right-angled triangle with hypotenuse 10 cm and vertical side 3 cm; angle c opposite the 3 cm side.

4. Right-angled triangle with hypotenuse 19 cm and one leg 6 cm; angle d opposite the 6 cm side.

5. Right-angled triangle with hypotenuse 14 cm and one leg 7 cm; angle e opposite the 7 cm side.

6. Right-angled triangle with legs 6 cm and 7 cm; angle f at the top.

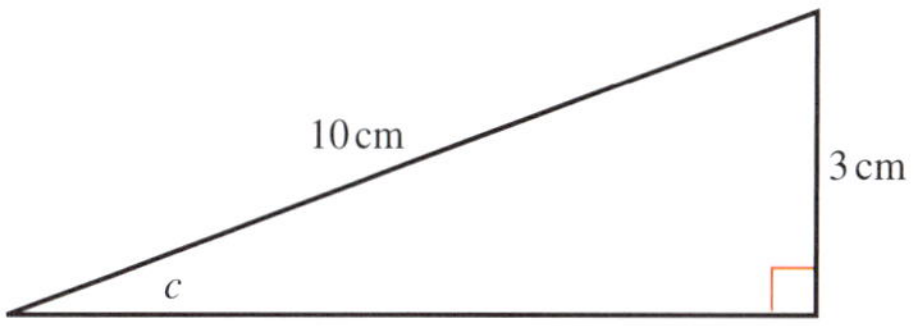

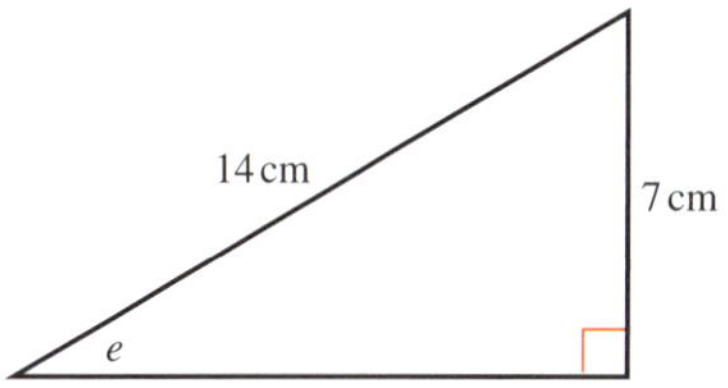

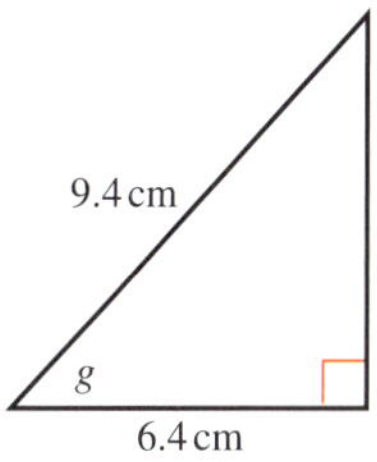

7. Right-angled triangle with hypotenuse 9.4 cm and one leg 6.4 cm; angle g opposite the vertical side.

8. Right-angled triangle with hypotenuse 12.2 cm and one leg 8.2 cm; angle h at the top.

9. Right-angled triangle with hypotenuse 5.3 cm and one leg 3.5 cm; angle i at the top.

10. Right-angled triangle with legs 7.4 cm and 6.4 cm; angle j on the right.

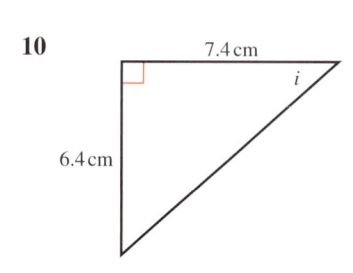

11 In triangle PQR, PQ = 14 cm, QR = 10 cm, angle PQR = 90°. Calculate angle PRQ.

12 In triangle LMN, angle LMN = 90°, MN = 17 cm, LN = 25 cm. Calculate angle LNM.

22.6 Multi-stage problems

Some questions will ask you to find a missing quantity, and then go on to use this to find another, possibly using Pythagoras' theorem as well as trigonometry. *Do not round off too early* – whenever you carry out a new calculation you should use the full calculator value of any previous calculations; otherwise inaccuracies can creep into your work.

EXAMPLE

The diagram shows a flagpole CB. It is supported by a wire, AB, 25 metres long. A is 21 metres from the base C of the flagpole. The flagpole is supported by a second wire, BD, which makes an angle of 65° with the horizontal ground.

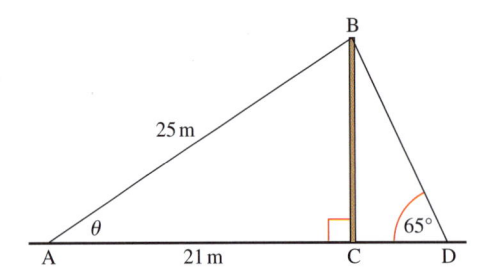

a) Calculate the height BC of the flagpole, correct to 3 significant figures.
b) Calculate the length BD.
c) Work out the value of the angle marked θ on the diagram.

SOLUTION

a) By Pythagoras' theorem, in triangle ABC:

$$BC^2 = 25^2 - 21^2$$
$$= 184$$
$$BC = \sqrt{184}$$
$$= 13.564\,659\,97$$
$$= \underline{13.6 \text{ m}} \text{ (3 s.f.)}$$

b) Now in triangle BCD:

$$\text{hypotenuse} = \frac{\text{opposite}}{\sin \theta}$$

$$BD = \frac{13.564\,659\,97}{\sin 65°}$$
$$= 14.966\,946\,28$$
$$= \underline{15.0 \text{ m}} \text{ (3 s.f.)}$$

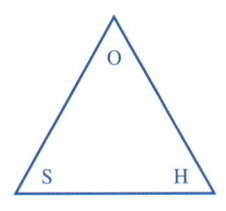

c) For the angle θ, AC = 21 m (adj) and AB = 25 m (hyp), so use cosine:

$$\cos\theta = \frac{\text{adjacent}}{\text{hypotenuse}}$$
$$= \frac{21}{25}$$
$$= 0.84$$
$$\theta = \cos^{-1} 0.84$$
$$= 32.859\,880\,38$$
$$= \underline{32.9°} \text{ (nearest 0.1°)}$$

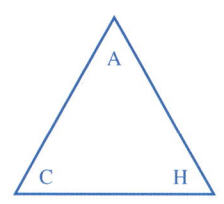

Trigonometry questions can include references to bearings.

EXAMPLE

A ship leaves its harbour and sails due South for 10 km.
It then sails due East for 20 km, then stops.

a) How far is the ship from its harbour?
b) The ship wishes to return directly to its harbour.
   On what bearing must it sail?

SOLUTION

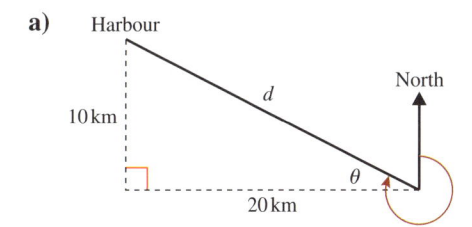

a) By Pythagoras' theorem:

$$d^2 = 10^2 + 20^2$$
$$= 100 + 400$$
$$= 500$$
$$d = \sqrt{500}$$
$$= 22.360\,679\,77$$
$$= \underline{22.4} \text{ km (3 s.f.)}$$

b) The angle θ is found using the tangent function:

$$\tan\theta = \frac{10}{20}$$
$$= 0.5$$
$$\theta = \tan^{-1} 0.5$$
$$= 26.6° \text{ (nearest 0.1°)}$$

The bearing is $270° + 26.6° = \underline{296.6°}$

EXERCISE 22.6

1 A ship sails 30 km due East, then 45 km due North.
   a) Illustrate this information on a sketch.
   b) How far, to the nearest 0.1 km, is the ship from its starting point?
   c) What bearing, to the nearest degree, should it steer to return directly to its start point?

2 In the diagram, PRS is a straight line.
   PQ = 18 cm, PR = 13 cm, QS = 16 cm.
   QR is perpendicular to PS.

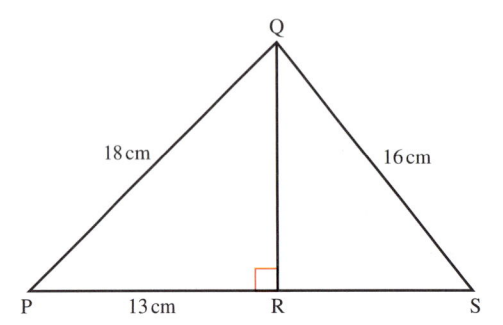

   a) Calculate the length QR. Give your answer to 3 significant figures.
   b) Calculate the area of triangle PQR. Give your answer to 3 significant figures.
   c) Calculate angle RQS. Give your answer to the nearest 0.1°.

3 The diagram shows a cross section of a tent.
   PQ = QR = 1.9 m. PR = 1.6 m.
   M is the midpoint of the line segment PR.

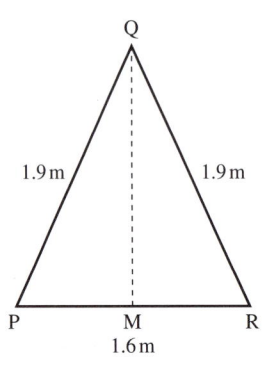

   a) Explain why angle PMQ must be a right angle.
   b) Calculate the angle QPM. Give your answer to the nearest 0.1°.
   c) Calculate the height of the tent. Give your answer to the nearest centimetre.

4 ABCD is a kite.
   AB = AD = 10 cm. BC = DC = 7 cm.
   Angle ABC = angle ADC = 90°.
   a) Illustrate this information on a sketch.
   b) Calculate the length AC, correct to the nearest millimetre.
   c) Find angle BAD, correct to the nearest degree.

5 In the diagram, EHG is a straight line.
Angle EHF = 90°, angle FGH = 34°.
EF = 11 cm, HG = 14 cm.

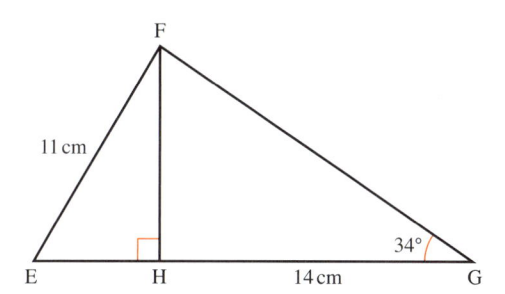

a) Work out the length of FH, correct to 3 significant figures.
b) Work out the value of angle FEH, correct to the nearest 0.1°.

6 A ship leaves port and sails on a bearing of 075° for 20 km.
It then sails on a bearing of 345° for 8 km, before stopping because of engine failure.
a) Draw a sketch to show this information.
b) How far is the ship from port when it stops? Give your answer to 3 significant figures.
c) A helicopter leaves port with spare parts to repair the ship's engines. Calculate the bearing that the helicopter should fly on in order to reach the ship by the shortest route. Give your answer to the nearest degree.

REVIEW EXERCISE 22

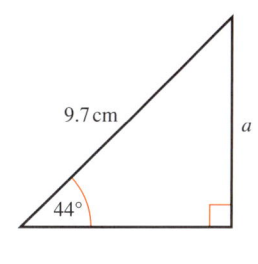

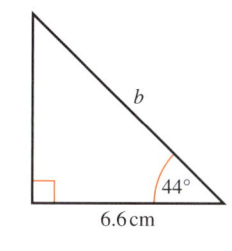

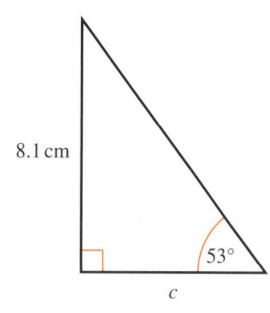

1 Find the unknown lengths, marked with letters. Give your answers correct to 3 significant figures.

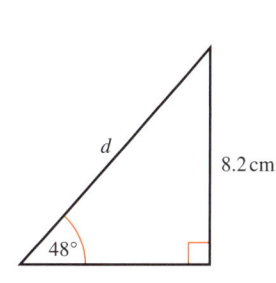

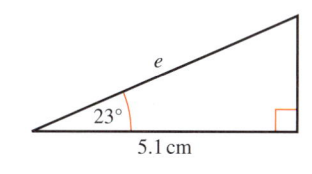

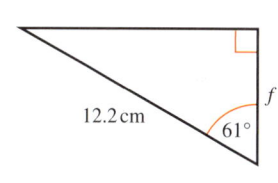

2 Find the unknown angles, marked with letters. Give your answers to the nearest 0.1°.

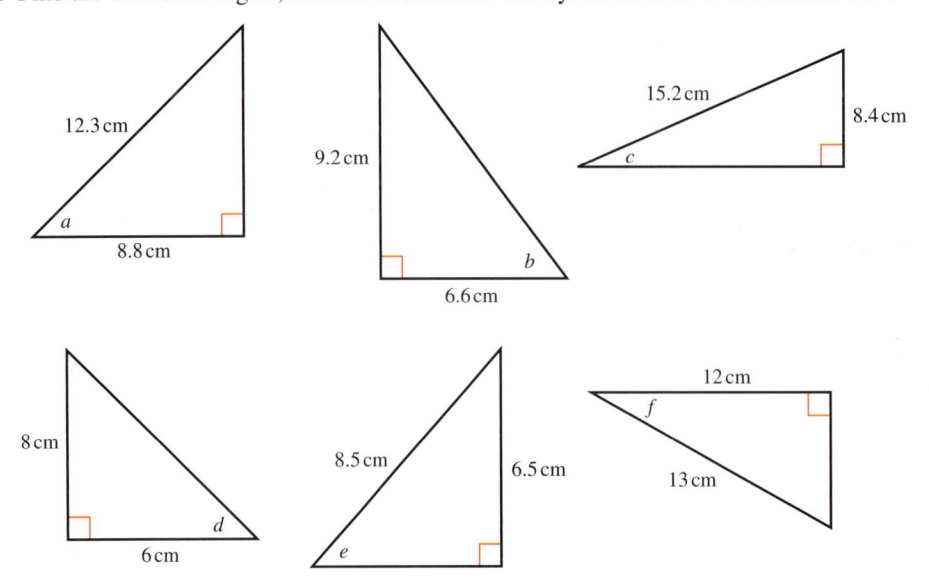

3 Mr Jones puts his ladder against the wall of his house.

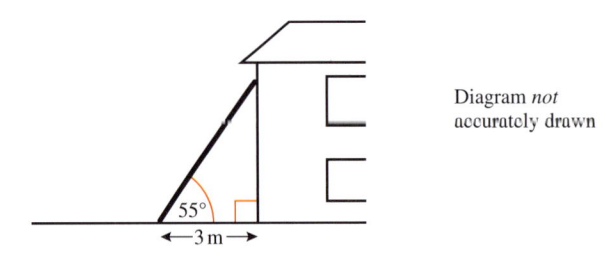

The angle the ladder makes with the ground is 55°. The foot of the ladder is 3 metres from the base of the wall of the house. Work out how far up the wall the ladder reaches. Give your answer, in metres, correct to 3 significant figures.
[Edexcel]

4 ABCD is a quadrilateral.

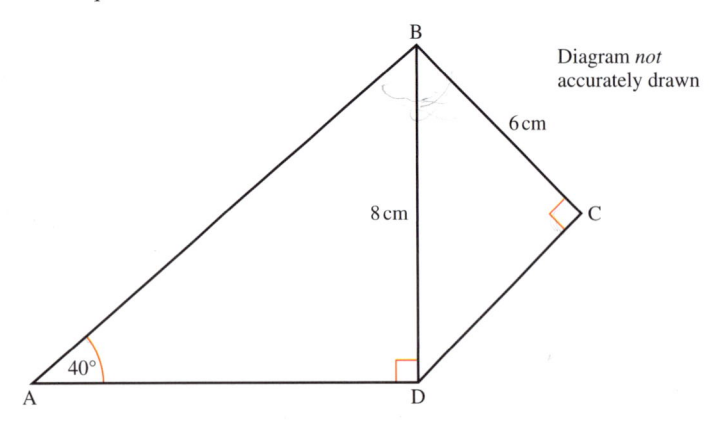

Angle BDA = 90°, angle BCD = 90°, angle BAD = 40°. BC = 6 cm, BD = 8 cm.
 a) Calculate the length of DC. Give your answer correct to 3 significant figures.
 b) Calculate the size of angle DBC. Give your answer correct to 3 significant figures.
 c) Calculate the length of AB. Give your answer correct to 3 significant figures.
[Edexcel]

5 ABD and DBC are two right-angled triangles.
AB = 9 m. Angle ABD = 35°. Angle DBC = 50°.
Calculate the length of DC.
Give your answer correct to 3 significant figures.

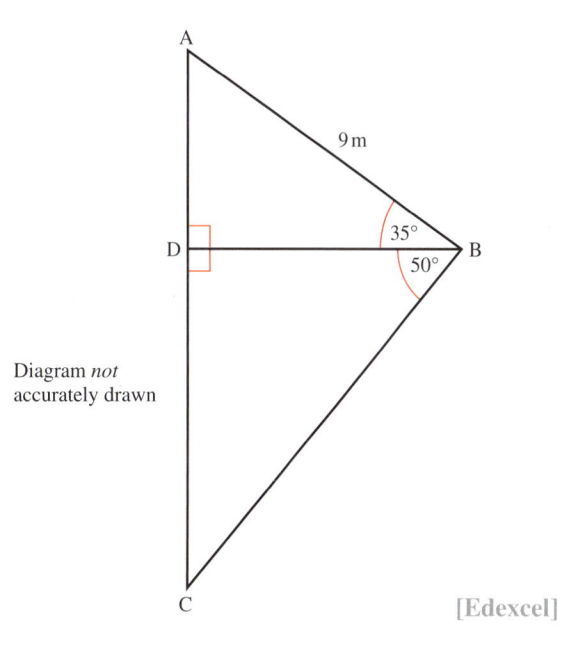

Diagram *not* accurately drawn

[Edexcel]

6 AB and BC are two sides of a rectangle.

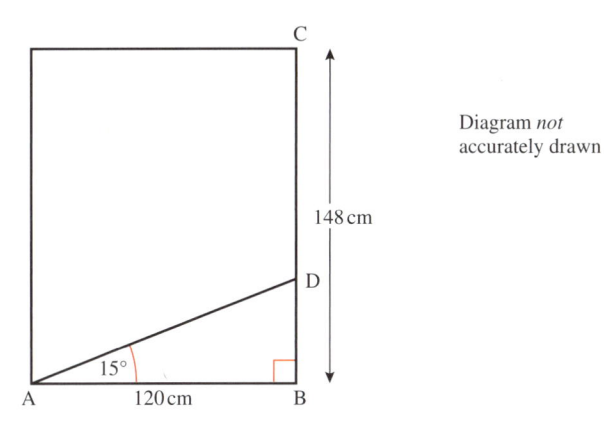

Diagram *not* accurately drawn

AB = 120 cm and BC = 148 cm. D is a point on BC. Angle BAD = 15°.
Work out the length of CD. Give your answer correct to 3 significant figures. [Edexcel]

7 The diagram shows the positions of three schools P, Q and R.
School P is 8 kilometres due West of School Q.
School R is 3 kilometres due North of School Q.

Diagram *not* accurately drawn

a) Calculate the size of the angle marked $x°$. Give your answer correct to one decimal place.

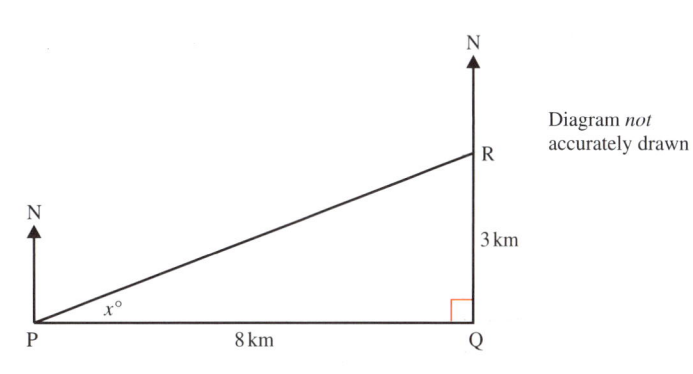

Simon's house is 8 kilometres due East of School Q.
b) Calculate the bearing of Simon's house from School R.

[Edexcel]

8 The diagram shows a trapezium.

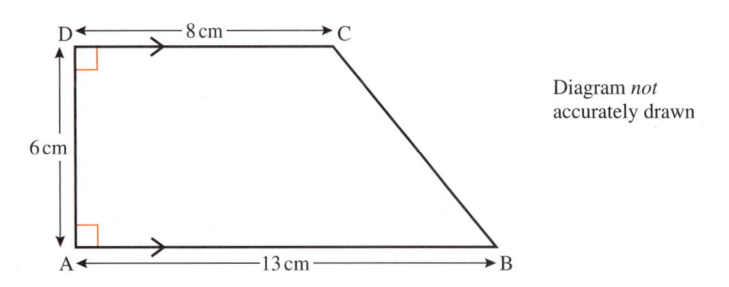

AB is parallel to DC. Angle A = 90°. AB = 13 cm, AD = 6 cm and CD = 8 cm.
Calculate the size of the angle B. Give your answer correct to one decimal place. [Edexcel]

9 The diagram represents a vertical flagpole, AB. The flagpole is supported by two ropes, BC and BD, fixed to the horizontal ground at C and at D.

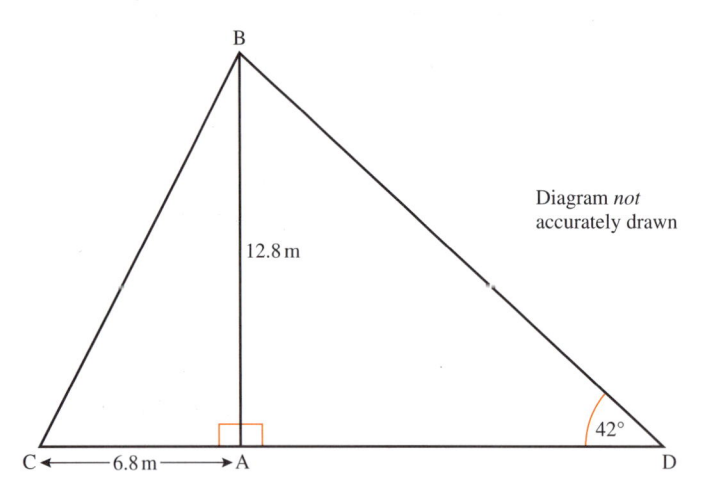

AB = 12.8 m, AC = 6.8 m, angle BDA = 42°.
 a) Calculate the size of angle BCA. Give your answer correct to 3 significant figures.
 b) Calculate the length of the rope BD. Give your answer correct to 3 significant figures. [Edexcel]

10 DE = 6 m. EG = 10 m. FG = 8 m.
Angle DEG = 90°. Angle EFG = 90°.
 a) Calculate the length of DG.
  Give your answer correct to 3 significant figures.
 b) Calculate the size of the angle marked $x°$.
  Give your answer correct to one decimal place.

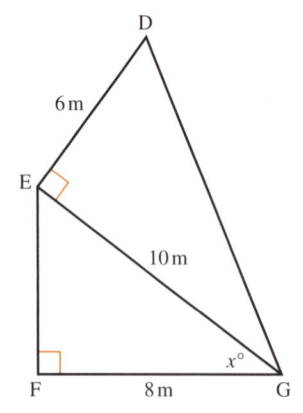

[Edexcel]

KEY POINTS

1. Trigonometry can be used to find unknown lengths or angles in right-angled triangles. Calculators have several different angle modes available: make sure yours is set to 'DEG' mode before doing any trigonometrical calculations.

2. The three basic trigonometrical ratios are sine (sin), cosine (cos) and tangent (tan). Their definitions are readily remembered using SOHCAHTOA, which can be written in triangular form:

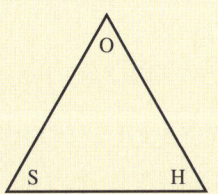

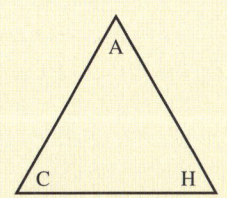

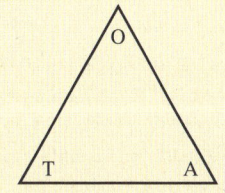

3. When these ratios are used to find missing lengths, the calculator will usually generate large numbers of decimal figures. Examination questions will typically ask you to round off to 3 significant figures.

4. If you are given some sides of a triangle, and asked to find a missing angle, then sin, cos or tan are used in reverse. Remember to press the 'Inv' or 'Second Function' key on your calculator, to tell it that the function is being inverted. Examination questions will typically ask for angles to be rounded to one decimal place of a degree or, sometimes, 3 significant figures.

5. In the examination, you may have to use Pythagoras' theorem in combination with trigonometry. Use your full calculator value throughout any multi-stage calculation, and save all the rounding until the end.

6. The examination might also ask you to use trigonometry to solve problems with bearings. Remember that these are measured using three figures, so that North is 000°, East 090°, South 180° and West 270°.

Internet Challenge 22

Famous geometers

Here are some clues about people who are famous for their work in geometry. Use the internet to find out their names. Try to find some interesting facts about each one.

1 This person wrote a set of 13 geometry books, called 'The Elements', in the third century BC.

2 A famous geometry theorem, named after him, was well known to the ancient Egyptians and Chinese. He was born on the Greek island of Samos.

3 'Clouds are not spheres, mountains are not cones …' said this 20th century mathematician, a pioneering thinker behind the development of fractal geometry.

4 The 'Great geometer', he lived from about 262 BC to 190 BC.

5 This German mathematician and astronomer used geometrical methods to understand the movement of the planets in their orbits. His three laws of planetary motion were published in 1609 and 1619.

6 'If I have seen further, it is by standing on the shoulders of giants' is a quote attributed to this English mathematical genius, who worked in geometry, algebra and calculus.

7 This outstanding Swiss geometer lived from 1707 to 1783.

8 He developed a geometry in which angles in a triangle do not need to add up to 180°. He suffered from poor health throughout his life, dying of tuberculosis in Italy in 1866.

9 The tetrahedron, cube, octahedron, dodecahedron and icosahedron are collectively named after this philosopher/mathematician and pupil of Socrates.

10 This German mathematician had a 'bottle' with no inside named after him.

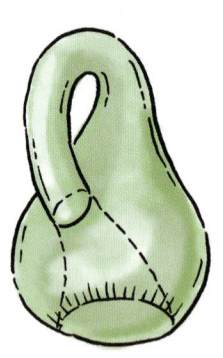

CHAPTER 23

2-D and 3-D objects

> In this chapter you will **learn how to**:
> - calculate interior and exterior angles of polygons
> - draw and construct 3-D objects
> - draw and interpret plans and elevations
> - find areas and volumes of pyramids, cones and spheres
> - convert between systems of units
> - use the method of dimensions to classify expressions
> - work with upper and lower bounds.
>
> You will also be **challenged to**:
> - investigate polyhedra.

Starter: Making cubes

Some of these shapes can be folded up to make a cube, others cannot. Pick out the ones that will work as nets.

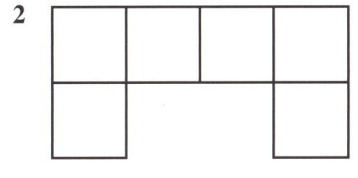

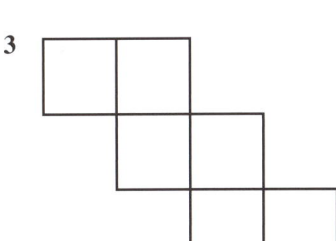

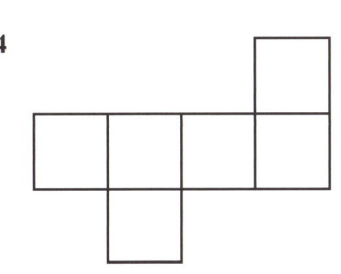

1

2

3

4

5

6

7

8

9

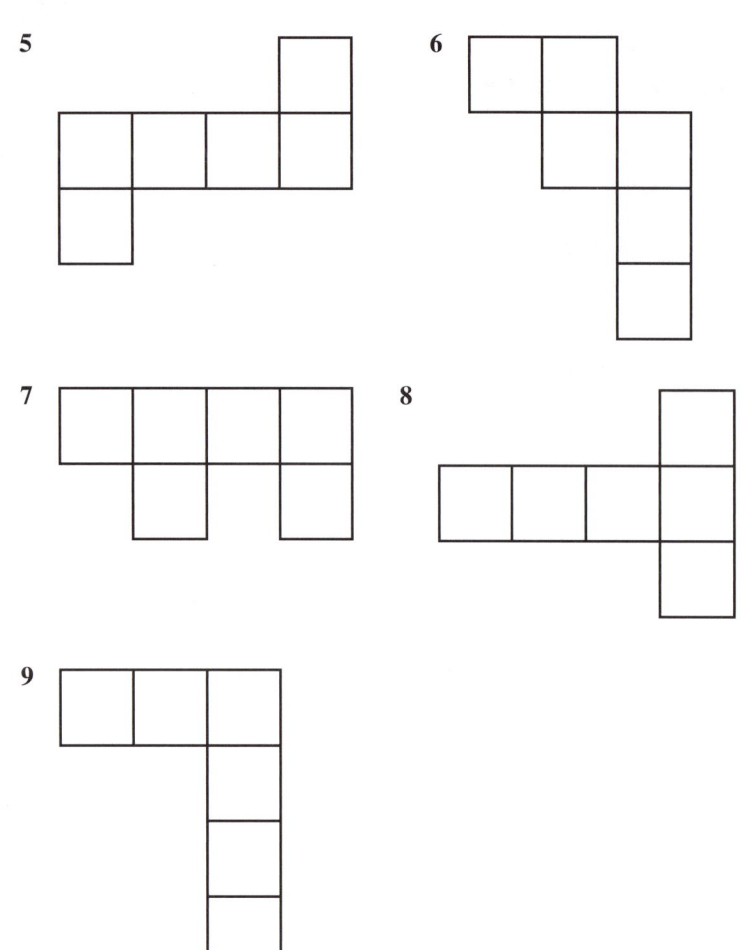

23.1 Angles in polygons

The angles in a triangle add up to 180° and those in a quadrilateral add up to 360°. For polygons with more sides, another 180° is added for each extra side. For example, the angles in a pentagon must add up to 360° + 180° = 540°.

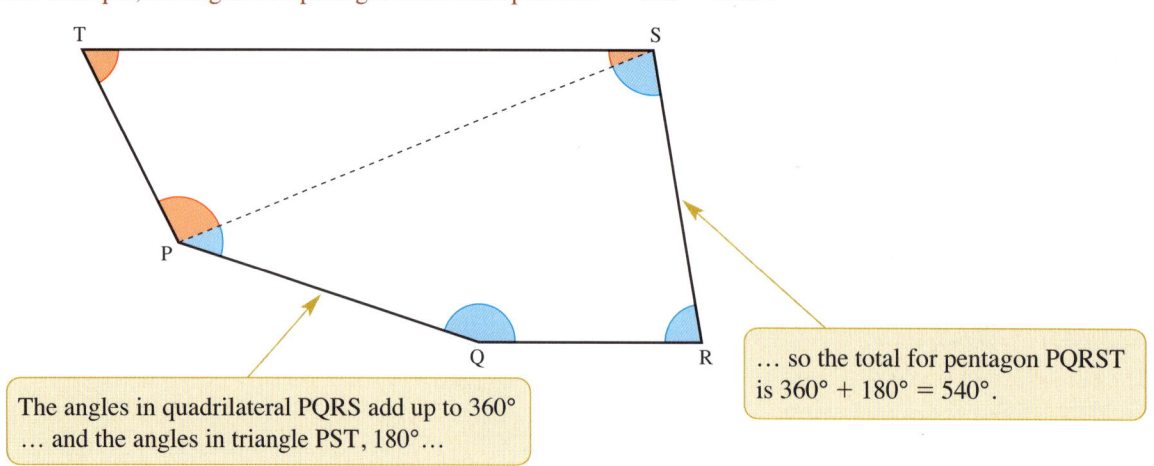

The angles in quadrilateral PQRS add up to 360° … and the angles in triangle PST, 180° …

… so the total for pentagon PQRST is 360° + 180° = 540°.

This can also be expressed as a mathematical formula:

Sum of interior angles of a polygon with n sides $= 180° \times (n - 2)$

EXAMPLE

Find the sum of all the interior angles of:
a) a hexagon
b) a ten-sided polygon.

SOLUTION

a) Since a pentagon has an angle sum of 540°, a hexagon must have an angle sum of $540° + 180° = 720°$.

b) Using the formula with $n = 10$:

$$\begin{aligned}\text{Angle sum} &= 180° \times (n - 2)\\ &= 180° \times (10 - 2)\\ &= 180° \times 8\\ &= \underline{1440°}\end{aligned}$$

EXAMPLE

Six of the angles in a seven-sided polygon are 100°, 110°, 130°, 145°, 145° and 150°. Find the value of the seventh angle.

SOLUTION

The angle sum for a seven-sided polygon is $180° \times (7 - 2) = 900°$.

The given angles have a sum of:

$100 + 110 + 130 + 145 + 145 + 150 = 780°$

Thus the remaining angle is $900 - 780 = \underline{120°}$

If you were to travel all the way around the perimeter of a polygon, you would need to change direction at each corner, or vertex. The angle by which you change direction is called the **exterior angle** at that vertex. To indicate an exterior angle on a diagram, you need to **produce** (extend) each of the sides slightly, in the same sense (clockwise or anti-clockwise) each time. The diagram shows the exterior angles for a pentagon, with each side produced in a clockwise direction.

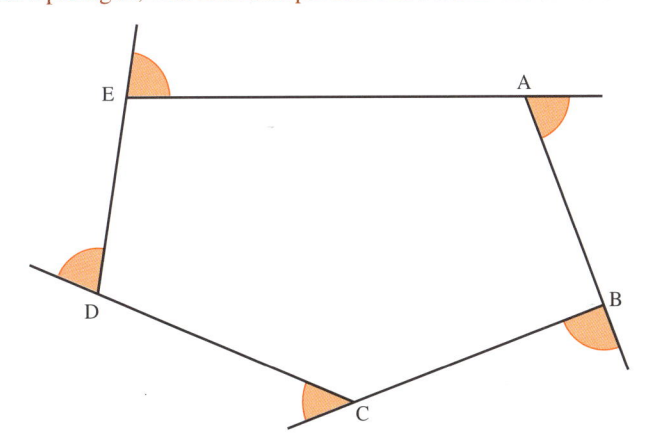

The sum of the exterior angles is simply the total angle you would turn through by travelling all the way around the perimeter. This must be a complete turn, or 360°.

Sum of exterior angles of a polygon with n sides = 360°

Some polygons have all their sides the same length and all their angles equal; these are called **regular polygons**. If a regular polygon has n sides, then each exterior angle must be 360° ÷ n.

EXAMPLE

A regular polygon has 12 sides.
a) Calculate the size of each exterior angle.
b) Hence find the size of each interior angle.

> This kind of question works only for a regular polygon – all the interior (or exterior) angles are the same size.

SOLUTION

a) Exterior angle = 360° ÷ 12 = 30°
b) Interior angle = 180° − 30° = 150°

EXAMPLE

The diagram shows one vertex of a regular polygon with n sides.

144°
X

Calculate the value of n.

SOLUTION

Each exterior angle is 180° − 144° = 36°.

Number of sides is 360° ÷ 36° = 10 sides. So n = 10.

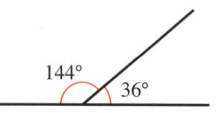

144° 36°

EXERCISE 23.1

1. Find the sum of the interior angles of:
   a) an octagon
   b) a 20-sided polygon.

2. Five of the angles in a hexagon are 102°, 103°, 118°, 125° and 130°. Find the sixth angle.

3. Work out the value of the exterior angle at each vertex of:
   a) a regular hexagon
   b) a regular 15-sided polygon.

4 a) The diagram shows part of a regular polygon.

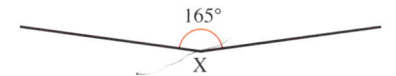

165° X

Work out how many sides the polygon has.

b) Albert draws this diagram. He says it shows part of a regular polygon.

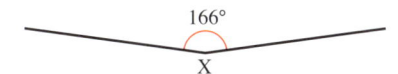

166° X

Explain how you can tell that Albert must have made a mistake.

5 The diagram shows an irregular pentagon. Work out the value of the angle marked y.

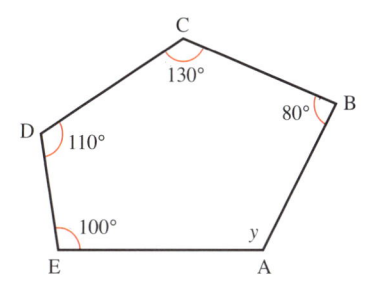

Pentagon with angles: C = 130°, B = 80°, D = 110°, E = 100°, A = y

6 Five of the angles in a hexagon are 100°, 110°, 120°, 145° and 155°.
  a) Write down the sum of the interior angles in a hexagon.
  b) Work out the value of the sixth angle.

7 The diagram shows a hexagon. All the angles marked a are equal. Calculate the value of a.

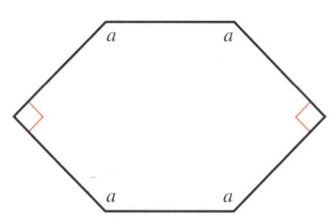

Hexagon with four angles marked a and two right angles.

8 Four of the angles in a pentagon are 85°, 90°, 120° and 135°. Work out the size of the fifth angle.

23.2 Drawing and constructing 3-D objects

If you want to show a 3-D object as a drawing on paper, then you must represent it using some kind of 2-D approach. There are several ways of doing this. For example, a cuboid measuring 3 cm by 4 cm by 6 cm could be shown in these ways:

Sketch of a cuboid

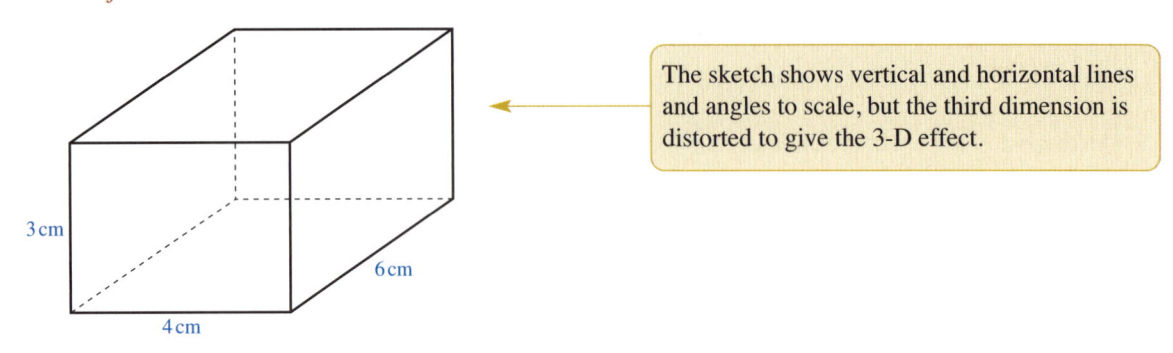

The sketch shows vertical and horizontal lines and angles to scale, but the third dimension is distorted to give the 3-D effect.

Isometric drawing of a cuboid

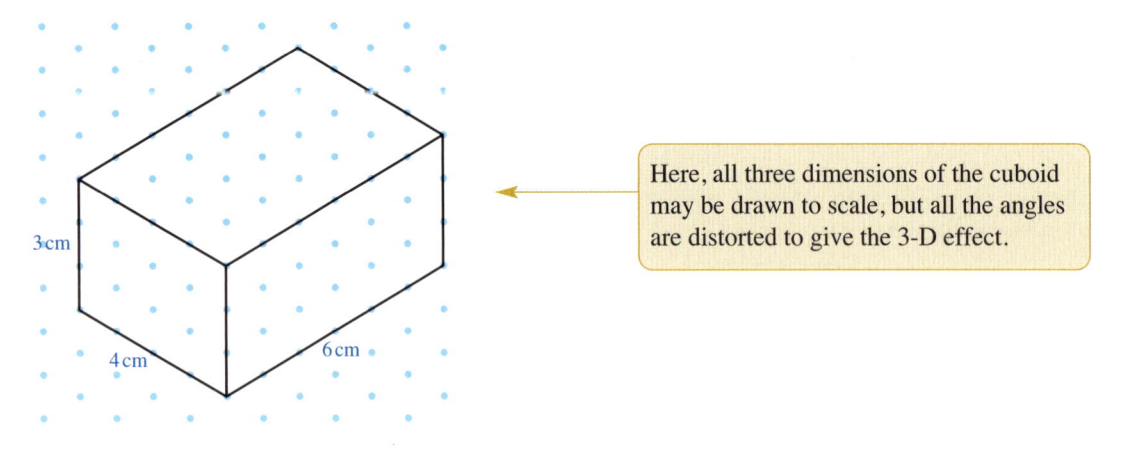

Here, all three dimensions of the cuboid may be drawn to scale, but all the angles are distorted to give the 3-D effect.

Plan and elevation of a cuboid

A **plan** is a bird's-eye view, that is, a projection of the object to show how it looks when viewed from a distance above. So the plan view of a cuboid is a rectangle.

You can make a similar projection from the front or side of the solid, to obtain a **front elevation** or a **side elevation**.

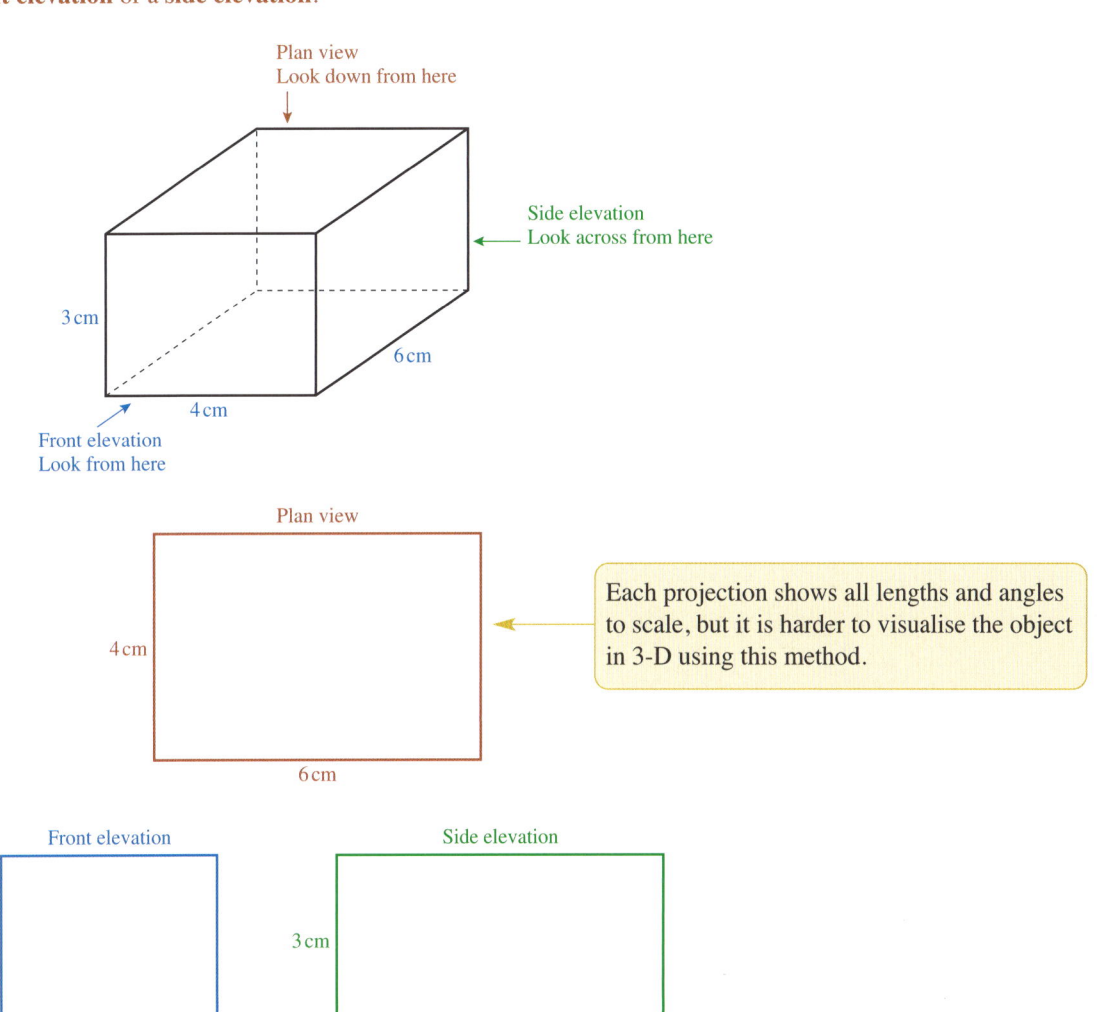

Each projection shows all lengths and angles to scale, but it is harder to visualise the object in 3-D using this method.

For a more complicated shape, there may be some edges running across the projections (plan, front or side). Visible edges are shown as solid lines; invisible edges (such as those round the back) are shown as dotted lines.

EXAMPLE

The isometric drawing shows some cubes forming an L shape. Draw:
a) a plan view as seen from A
b) a front elevation as seen from B
c) a side elevation as seen from C.

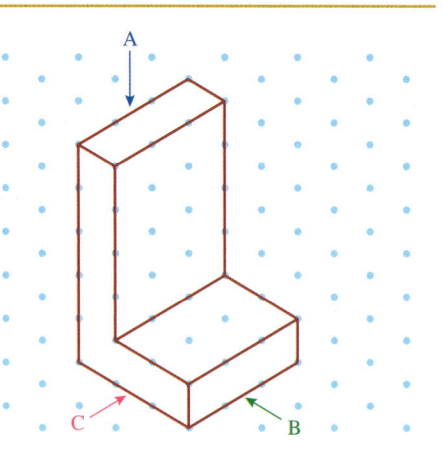

SOLUTION

a) From A, these two faces may be seen.

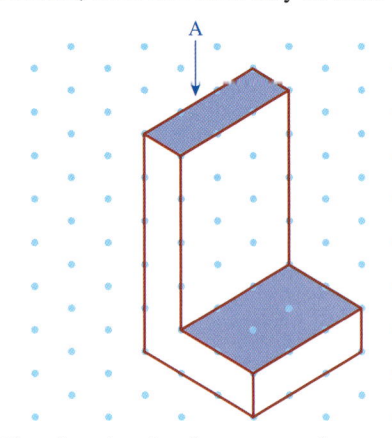

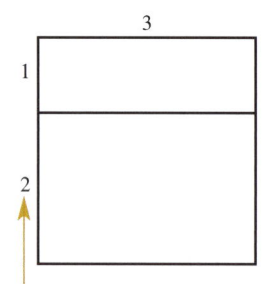

The plan view is of two rectangles.

These numbers indicate the dimensions of each side.

b) From B, these two faces may be seen.

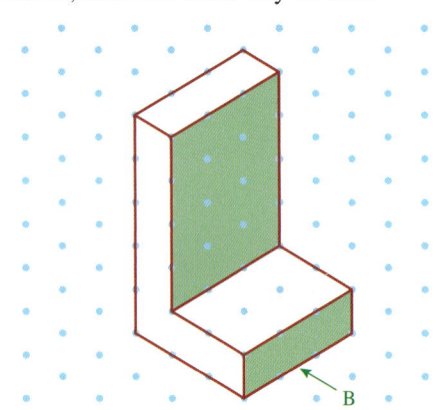

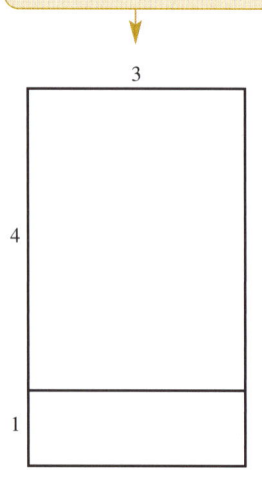

The front elevation is of two rectangles.

c) From C, a single L-shaped face may be seen.

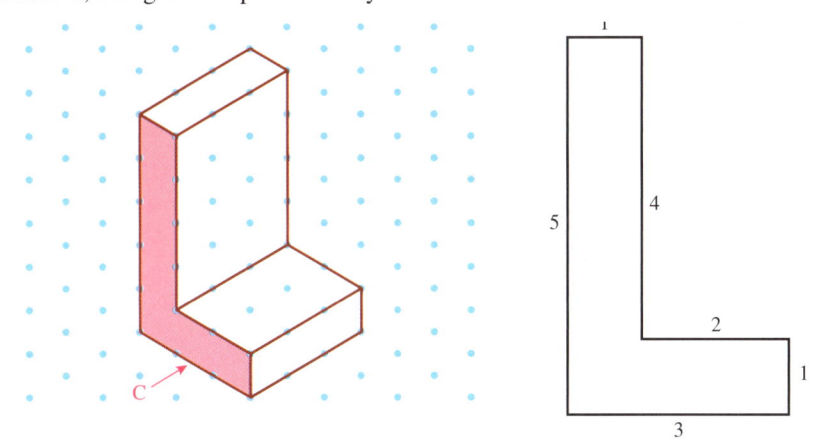

The side elevation is the single face shown.

Nets

If you want to make a model of a 3-D object, you could draw its various faces on a flat surface, or plane, then cut them out. A **net** is a drawing of this kind, with each face connected to at least one other face, so the cut-out will fold up to make the 3-D solid.

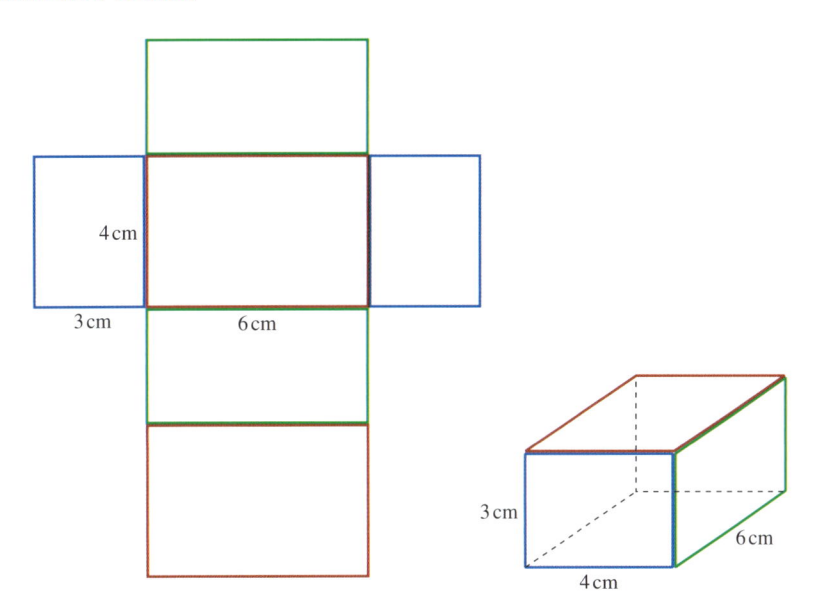

EXAMPLE

A pyramid has a square base whose sides are 6 cm long. The triangular faces have sides 5 cm, 5 cm, 6 cm.
a) Draw a sketch of the pyramid.
b) Draw a plan view of the pyramid.
c) Draw a net for the pyramid.

SOLUTION

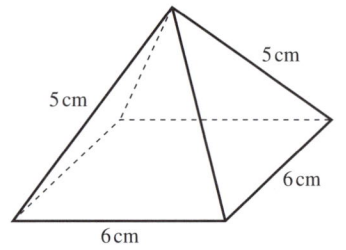

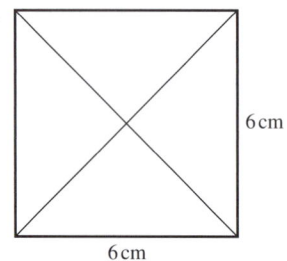

a)

b)

c)

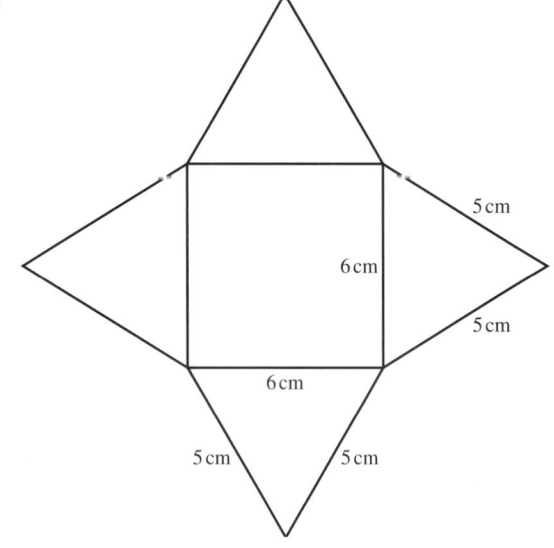

EXERCISE 23.2

1. A cuboid measures 3 cm by 4 cm by 7 cm.
   a) Draw a sketch of the cuboid.
   b) Make an isometric drawing of the cuboid.
   c) Draw a net for the cuboid.

2. A pyramid is drawn on a rectangular base. The base is 6 cm by 8 cm. The pyramid is 10 cm tall.
   a) Draw a sketch of the pyramid.
   b) Draw a plan view, a front elevation and a side elevation.

3 A triangular prism is 10 cm long. Its ends are equilateral triangles of side 4 cm.
   a) Draw a sketch of the prism.
   b) Draw an accurate net for the prism.

4 The diagram shows a sketch of a 3-D object. It is made from six cubes, each of side 1 cm.

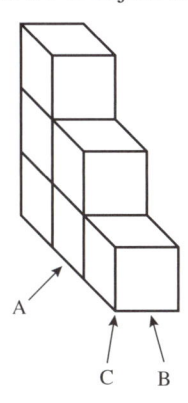

   a) Draw
      (i) a side elevation to show the object as viewed along the direction of arrow A,
      (ii) a front elevation as viewed along the direction of arrow B,
      (iii) a plan view.
   b) Draw an isometric representation to show how the object looks along the direction of arrow C.

5 Damini and Jonty have been building shapes with centimetre cubes on a square grid. The diagrams show plan views of their shapes. The numbers 1, 2, 3 tell you how many cubes are stacked on top of each square.

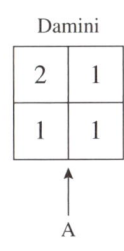

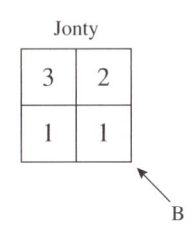

   a) Draw a front elevation to show how Damini's shape appears seen from direction A.
   b) Make an isometric drawing of Jonty's shape, viewed from direction B.

6 Here are three projections of a solid object.

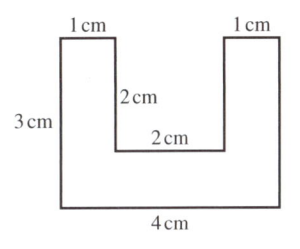

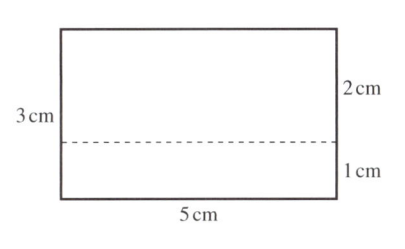

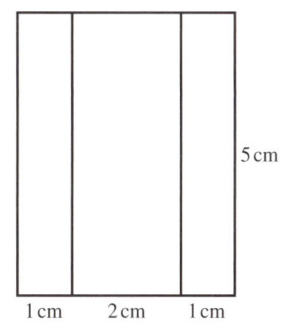

   Side elevation   Front elevation   Plan view

   a) Make a sketch of the solid object.
   b) Make an isometric drawing of the solid object.

7 *This is a practical question, requiring thin card and scissors.*
A hexagonal prism is to be made. The prism is to be 10 cm long. Each end is to be a regular hexagon of sides 8 cm.
   a) Construct an accurate net for the prism.
   b) Copy your net on to thin card, and add some tabs. Then cut it out and assemble the prism.
   c) Draw a sketch to show what the prism looks like in 3-D.

23.3 Volume and surface area of pyramids, cones and spheres

A **pyramid** has a **base** and an **apex**, or point. Rays drawn from the edge of the base converge at the apex. Pyramids may have square or triangular bases, but other polygons can be bases as well. A **cone** is like a pyramid with a circular base.

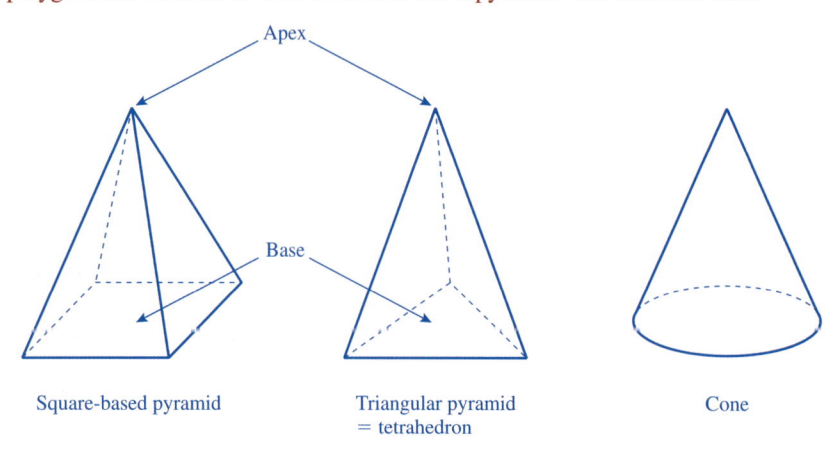

Square-based pyramid   Triangular pyramid = tetrahedron   Cone

A remarkable property of these shapes is that they fill exactly *one-third* of the enveloping prism (or cylinder) that would just contain them:

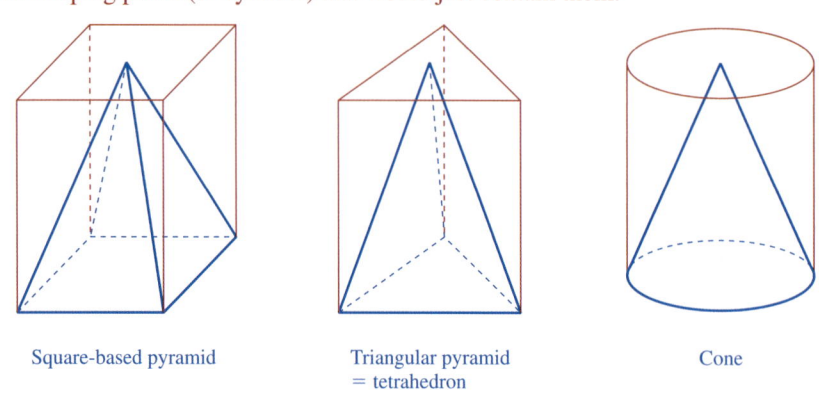

Square-based pyramid   Triangular pyramid = tetrahedron   Cone

Therefore, the **volume of a pyramid** is:

$V = \frac{1}{3} \times$ area of the base $\times$ (perpendicular) height

In the case of a complex polygon, the area of the base is not always easy to work out. For a cone of base radius r and height h, however, the base area will be πr^2, so the **volume of a cone** is given by the formula:

$V = \frac{1}{3}\pi r^2 h$

U4 23 2-D and 3-D objects

EXAMPLE

Find the volume of these two shapes.

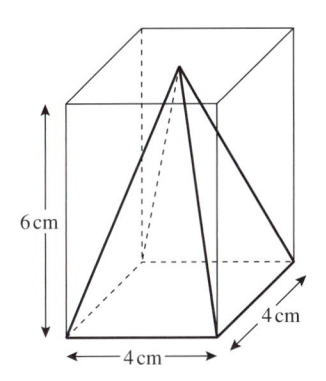

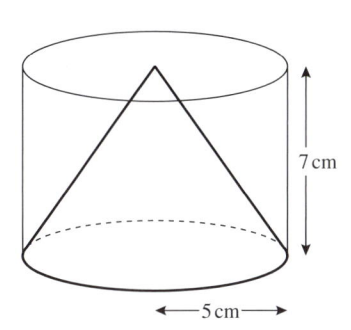

SOLUTION

For the pyramid:

    area of base = 4 × 4 = 16 cm²

Therefore the volume V is:

    $V = \frac{1}{3} \times$ area of base × height

       $= \frac{1}{3} \times 16 \times 6$

       $= \underline{32 \text{ cm}^3}$

For the cone:

    radius $r = 5$ and height $h = 7$

So the volume V is:

    $V = \frac{1}{3} \pi r^2 h$

       $= \frac{1}{3} \times \pi \times 5^2 \times 7$

       $= 183.259\,571\,5$

       $= \underline{183 \text{ cm}^3}$ (3 s.f.)

> Remember to include units with the answers, e.g. mm³ or cm³ for volumes and mm² or cm² for areas.

To find the **volume of a sphere**, radius r, you may use this formula:

$$V = \tfrac{4}{3}\pi r^3$$

EXAMPLE

A spherical ball bearing has a diameter of 6 mm. Find its volume.

SOLUTION

Since $d = 6$ we have $r = 3$ mm, so the volume V is:

$V = \frac{4}{3}\pi r^3$

  $= \frac{4}{3} \times \pi \times 3^3$

  $= 113.097\,335\,5$

  $= \underline{113 \text{ mm}^3}$ (3 s.f.)

Finally, you may need to calculate the surface area of one of these shapes. For a pyramid, there is no short cut: you simply find the area of each face and add them up. For a sphere or a cone, these formulae may be used:

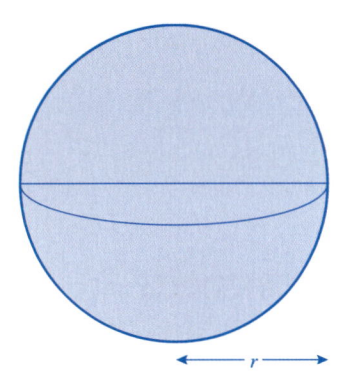

Surface area of a sphere
$A = 4\pi r^2$

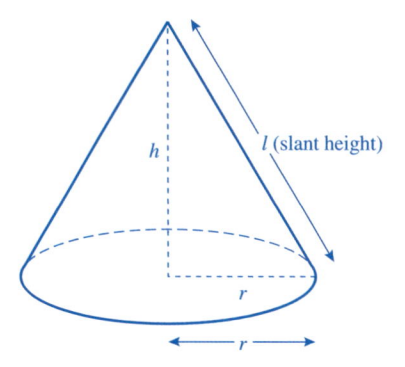

(Curved) Surface area of a cone
$A = \pi r l$

EXAMPLE

Find the total surface area of each of these shapes, giving your answers exactly in terms of π.

a)

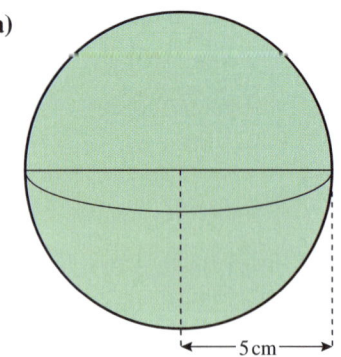

b)

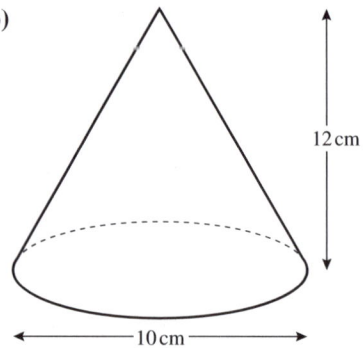

SOLUTION

a) For the sphere, $r = 5$ cm, so:

$A = 4\pi r^2$
$= 4 \times \pi \times 5^2$
$= 4 \times \pi \times 25$
$= 100\pi \, \text{cm}^2$

b) For the cone, $r = 5$ cm and $h = 12$ cm, but the slant height h is needed.

By Pythagoras' theorem:

$l^2 = r^2 + h^2$
$= 25 + 144$
$= 169$
$l = 13$ cm

Then the curved surface area:

CSA = $\pi r l$
    = $\pi \times 5 \times 13$
    = $65\pi \, cm^2$

The circular base has area:

$\pi r^2 = \pi \times 5^2$
     = $25\pi \, cm^2$

Thus the total surface area is:

$65\pi + 25\pi = \underline{90\pi \, cm^2}$

EXERCISE 23.3

Find the volume and total surface area of each of these solids. Give your answers correct to 3 significant figures.

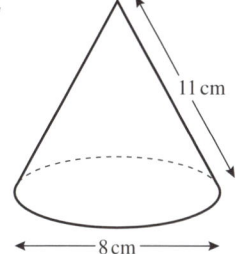

1 Sphere, diameter 9 cm

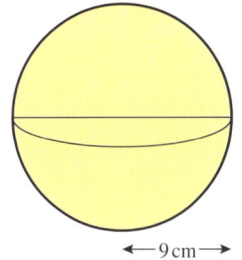

2 Cone, slant height 11 cm, base diameter 8 cm

3 Cone, slant height 12 cm, base diameter 10 cm

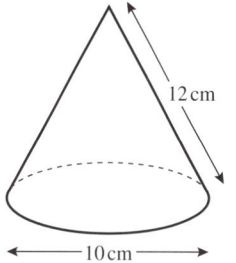

Find the volume and surface area of each of these solids, in terms of π.

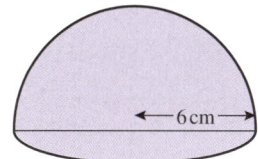

4 Sphere, diameter 12 cm

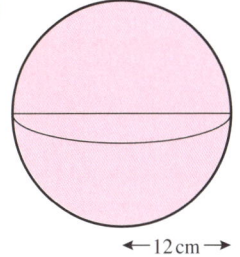

5 Hemisphere, radius 6 cm

6 Cone, vertical height 4 cm, base diameter 6 cm

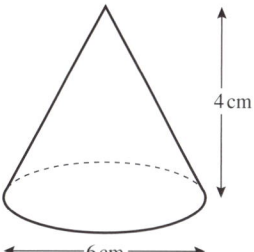

7 A pyramid has a square base of side 6 cm and a vertical height of 12 cm. Find its volume.

8 A square-based pyramid has a volume of 960 cm³. Its height is 45 cm. Find the dimensions of the base.

9 A sphere has surface area $900\pi \, cm^2$. Find its volume in terms of π.

10 A cone of slant height 7 cm has curved surface area of $28\pi \, cm^2$. Find the area of its base in terms of π.

23.4 Converting between units of area and volume

Sometimes you may want to convert an area or a volume from one set of units to another. This needs to be done carefully!

There are, for example, 10 millimetres in 1 centimetre, but there are **not** 10 square millimetres in 1 square centimetre. The diagram shows why:

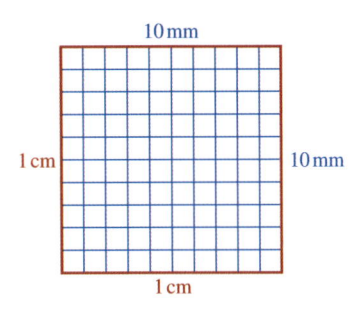

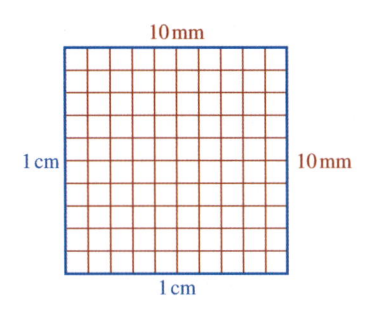

Area = 1 cm × 1 cm = 1 cm²   Area = 10 mm × 10 mm = 100 mm²

Thus we have:

$1 \text{ cm} = 10 \text{ mm}$
$1 \text{ cm}^2 = 10 \times 10 = 100 \text{ mm}^2$
$1 \text{ cm}^3 = 10 \times 10 \times 10 = 1000 \text{ mm}^3$

These results illustrate a general principle, that **areas** must be multiplied by the **square** of the conversion factor, and **volumes** by its **cube**.

EXAMPLE

a) Convert 2 m² into cm².

b) Convert 5000 cm³ into m³.

SOLUTION

a) $2 \text{ m}^2 = 2 \times 100^2 \text{ cm}^2$
$= \underline{20\,000 \text{ cm}^2}$

b) $5000 \text{ cm}^3 = 5000 \div 100^3 \text{ m}^3$
$= 5000 \div 1\,000\,000 \text{ m}^3$
$= \underline{0.005 \text{ m}^3}$

EXERCISE 23.4

1. Convert 2 m³ into cm³.

2. Convert 5000 cm² into m².

3. Convert 3 000 000 m² into km².

4. Convert 660 mm² into cm².

5. Convert 1 m³ into mm³.

6. A sphere has a volume of 35 000 cm³. Express its volume in m³.

7 A cone has a surface area of 2.4 m². Express its area in cm².

For the next three questions, you may use the information that 1 litre = 1000 cm³.

8 A bucket contains 20 litres of water.
   a) Convert 20 litres into cm³.
   b) Hence find the amount of water in the bucket in m³.

9 A water tank in the shape of a cuboid measures 1.4 m by 1.5 m by 2 m.
   a) Find the volume of the tank, in m³.
   b) Convert this answer into cm³.
   c) How many litres of water can the tank hold?

10 A tank in the shape of a cube has a capacity of 512 litres.
   a) Express this capacity in cm³.
   b) Convert your answer to a) into m³.
   c) Find the dimensions of the tank, in metres.

23.5 Dimensional analysis

Suppose you have a mathematical formula that might represent a length, an area or a volume, and you need to decide which one it could be. You can use a method based on **dimensions**.

For example, the expression πr^2 contains three parts multiplied together: π, times r, times another r. The π is just a number (it is dimensionless) but r is a length, so the expression πr^2 has dimensions of:

(dimensionless) × (length) × (length)

which is (length)², which is an area.

So πr^2 could represent an area, but it certainly cannot represent a length or a volume.

EXAMPLE

Paul has been reading a book about cones. He remembers seeing an expression $\frac{1}{3}\pi r^2 h$, where r and h are lengths in centimetres. Paul cannot remember whether $\frac{1}{3}\pi r^2 h$ represents the area of the cone or its volume. Use the method of dimensions to decide which one it could be.

SOLUTION

The expression contains $\frac{1}{3}$ and π, both of which are dimensionless, so, in effect, they may be ignored.

The rest of the formula contains $r^2 h$, which has dimensions of:

(length)² × (length) = (length)³

So the expression $\frac{1}{3}\pi r^2 h$ could represent a volume (but definitely not an area).

EXAMPLE

In the table below, the letters a, b, c represent lengths. Put a tick in each column, to show whether each expression could represent a length, an area, a volume, or none of these.

	πab	$\dfrac{(a^2 + b^2)c}{4\pi}$	$\dfrac{b^3}{2a}$	$3a^2 + 2b$
Length				
Area				
Volume				
None of these				

SOLUTION

Since the numbers 2, 3, 4 and π are dimensionless, the expressions have dimensions determined just by a, b, c as follows:

πab length × length = (length)^2 = area

$\dfrac{(a^2 + b^2)c}{4\pi}$ $(a^2 + b^2)$ has dimensions of (length)^2 + (length)^2
= area + area = another area
then multiplying this by c gives area × length = volume

$\dfrac{b^3}{2a}$ $\dfrac{\text{length}^3}{\text{length}}$ = (length)^2 = area

$3a^2 + 2b$ (length)^2 + length = area + length
which does not give a meaningful answer.

	πab	$\dfrac{(a^2 + b^2)c}{4\pi}$	$\dfrac{b^3}{2a}$	$3a^2 + 2b$
Length				
Area	✓		✓	
Volume		✓		
None of these				✓

EXERCISE 23.5

1. The table shows six expressions. a, b and c are lengths. 2 and 3 are numbers and have no dimension.

$2a + 3b$	$3ab$	$a + b + c$	$2a^2c$	$2a^2 + bc$	$ab(b + 2c)$

a) Copy the table and put the letter **A** in the box underneath each of the **two** expressions that could represent an **area**.
b) Put the letter **V** in the box underneath each of the **two** expressions that could represent a **volume**.

[Edexcel]

2 Here are three expressions.

Expression	Length	Area	Volume	None of these
$\pi a^2 b$				
$\pi b^2 + 2h$				
$2ah$				

a, b and h are lengths. π and 2 are numbers and have no dimensions.
Put a tick (✓) in the correct column to show whether the expression can be used for length, area, volume or none of these. [Edexcel]

3 The expressions below can be used to calculate lengths, areas or volumes of some shapes.
The letters p, q and r represent lengths. π and 2 are numbers and have no dimension.
Pick out the **three** expressions that can be used to calculate an **area**.

$\pi(p + q)$ $\dfrac{pq}{r}$ $rq(p + q)$ πpq $\dfrac{p^2 r}{2}$

$2r$ $\dfrac{qr}{2}$ $r(p + q)$ $\dfrac{p^2 \pi}{r}$ $\dfrac{\pi pqr}{2}$ [Edexcel]

4 Here are three expressions.

Expression	Length	Area	Volume	None of these
$3rl$				
$\dfrac{2(r + l)^2}{h}$				
$\dfrac{4\pi r^4}{3l}$				

r, l and h are lengths. π, 2, 3 and 4 are numbers and have no dimensions.
Put a tick (✓) in the correct column to show whether the expression can be used for length, area, volume or none of these. [Edexcel]

5 Here are some expressions. The letters a, b, c and h represent lengths. π and 2 are numbers that have no dimensions. Three of the expressions could represent areas.
Copy the grid and tick (✓) boxes underneath the three expressions that could represent areas.

$\dfrac{ab}{h}$	$2\pi b^2$	$(a + b)ch$	$2\pi a^3$	πab	$2(a^2 + b^2)$	$\pi a^2 b$

23.6 Upper and lower bounds

Suppose you are asked to find the perimeter of a rectangle that measures 12 cm by 15 cm, both measurements being correct to the nearest centimetre. A reasonable calculation for finding the perimeter is:

$$12 + 15 + 12 + 15 = 54 \text{ cm}$$

The true perimeter is unlikely to be *exactly* 54 cm, however, as the dimensions are probably not exactly 12 cm and 15 cm, since they are only correct to the nearest centimetre.

It can be helpful to establish an **upper bound** and a **lower bound** for the perimeter. These are the limits between which the true perimeter must lie.

The length of the rectangle is 15 cm to the nearest centimetre, which means it could lie anywhere between 14.5 cm and 15.5 cm. Similarly, the width given as 12 cm to the nearest centimetre could actually lie anywhere between 11.5 cm and 12.5 cm.

The upper bound for the perimeter is therefore $12.5 + 15.5 + 12.5 + 15.5 = 56$ cm, and the lower bound is $11.5 + 14.5 + 11.5 + 14.5 = 52$ cm. This could be written as:

$$52 \text{ cm} \leq \text{true perimeter} < 56 \text{ cm}$$

Note the different inequality signs at each end of the above statement. The length of the perimeter cannot actually be as high as 56 cm, since the rectangle is smaller than 12.5 by 15.5 cm – those numbers would be 13 and 16 cm correct to the nearest centimetre. You cannot, however, use a smaller limit like 12.4 or 12.49, because such values are inevitably too small. If this sounds confusing, remember that the upper bound is the same as finding the boundary for the number, even though it can never quite equal it.

EXAMPLE

A rectangle measures 18 cm by 12 cm. Find the upper and lower bound for
a) its perimeter and **b)** its area.

SOLUTION

a) Upper bounds for the dimensions are 18.5 cm and 12.5 cm, so the upper bound for the perimeter is $18.5 + 12.5 + 18.5 + 12.5 =$ 62 cm

Lower bounds for the dimensions are 17.5 cm and 11.5 cm, so the lower bound for the perimeter is $17.5 + 11.5 + 17.5 + 11.5 =$ 58 cm

b) Upper bounds for the dimensions are 18.5 cm and 12.5 cm, so the upper bound for the area is $18.5 \times 12.5 =$ 231.25 cm^2

Lower bounds for the dimensions are 17.5 cm and 11.5 cm, so the lower bound for the area is $17.5 \times 11.5 =$ 201.25 cm^2

In the examination you may be asked for the least value and the greatest value:

Least value   = lower bound
Greatest value = upper bound

If your calculator has a replay function, you can edit the first calculation rather than keying the expression in again.

In the previous example you simply performed the calculation once, using all the upper bounds for the measurements involved, and then a second time, using all the lower bounds. Sometimes the procedure is less straightforward, as, for example, when working with compound measures involving division.

EXAMPLE

Anita sprints along an athletics track.
The track is 100 metres long, correct to the nearest 1 metre.
Her time is measured as 12.5 seconds, to the nearest half second.
a) Treating these as exact values, work out her average speed for the sprint.
b) Calculate the upper and lower bounds for her average speed.

SOLUTION

a) Average speed $= \dfrac{\text{distance}}{\text{time}}$

$= \dfrac{100}{12.5}$

$= 8$ metres per second

For the *highest* answer, divide the *highest* top by the *lowest* bottom…

b) Upper bound $= \dfrac{100.5}{12.25}$

$= 8.204$ metres per second (4 s.f.)

…and for the *lowest* answer, divide the *lowest* top by the *highest* bottom.

Lower bound $= \dfrac{99.5}{12.75}$

$= 7.804$ metres per second (4 s.f.)

EXERCISE 23.6

1 A square has sides of length 12 cm, correct to the nearest centimetre.
   a) Calculate the upper and lower bounds for the perimeter of the square.
   b) Calculate the upper and lower bounds for the area of the square.

2 A rectangle has a length of 10 cm and a width of 6 cm. Both these measurements are correct to the nearest centimetre.
   a) Calculate an upper bound for the perimeter of the rectangle.
   b) Calculate a lower bound for the area of the rectangle.

3 To the nearest centimetre, $x = 4$ cm and $y = 6$ cm.
   a) Calculate the upper bound for the value of xy.
   b) Calculate the lower bound for the value of $\dfrac{x}{y}$.
   Give your answer correct to 3 significant figures.   [Edexcel]

4 A car travels a distance of 150 miles in 2.5 hours.
   a) Taking these as exact values, work out its average speed, in miles per hour.

   In fact, the distance is correct to the nearest 10 miles and the time is correct to the nearest 0.1 hour.
   b) Work out a lower bound for the speed of the car.
   c) Work out an upper bound for the speed of the car.

5 Bill has a rectangular sheet of metal.
The length of the rectangle is **exactly** 12.5 cm.
The width of the rectangle is **exactly** 10 cm.

Bill cuts out a trapezium. Its dimensions,
shown in the diagram, are correct to the nearest millimetre.
He throws away the rest of the metal sheet.

Calculate the greatest possible area of the rectangular
sheet that he throws away.

[Edexcel]

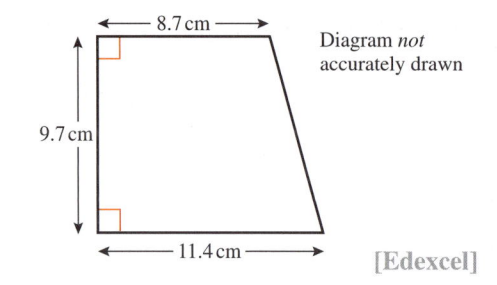

REVIEW EXERCISE 23

1 Work out the size of the exterior angle of a regular 12-sided polygon. Hence find the size of each interior angle.

2 The angles inside a certain polygon add up to 1980°. How many sides has it?

3 A regular polygon has interior angles of size 176°. How many sides has it?

4 Triangle ABC is isosceles, with AC = BC. Angle ACD = 62°.
BCD is a straight line.

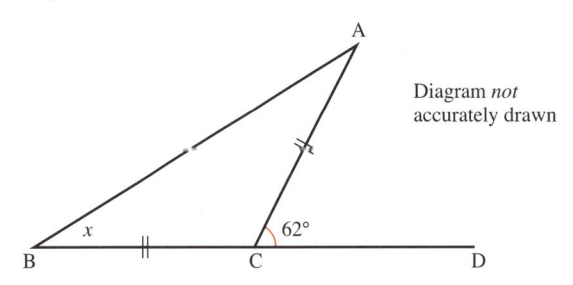

a) Work out the size of angle x.

b) The diagram shows part of a **regular** octagon.

Work out the size of angle x.

[Edexcel]

5 The diagram shows a regular hexagon.

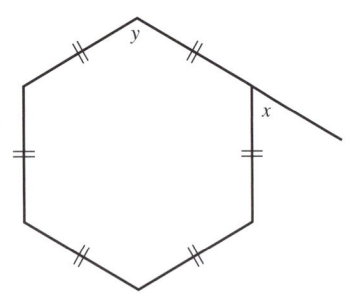

a) Work out the value of x.
b) Work out the value of y.

[Edexcel]

6 The diagram shows a pentagon. AB = AE, and BC = CD = DE.

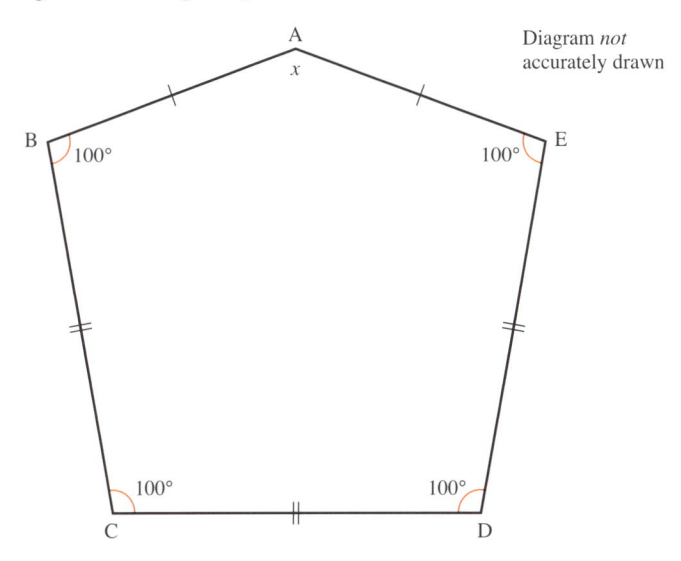

Diagram *not* accurately drawn

Find the size of the angle marked $x°$. [Edexcel]

7 This is part of the design of a pattern found at the theatre of Diana at Alexandria. It is made up of a regular hexagon, squares and equilateral triangles.

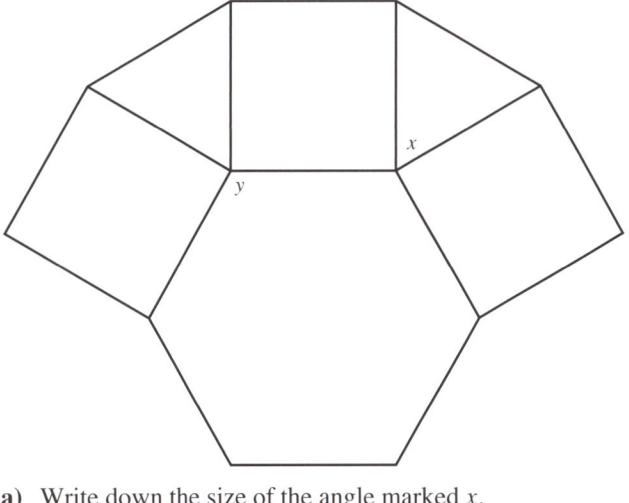

Diagram *not* accurately drawn

a) Write down the size of the angle marked x.
b) Work out the size of the angle marked y.
The area of each equilateral triangle is 2 cm².
c) Work out the area of the regular hexagon. [Edexcel]

8 A cuboid measures 3 cm by 4 cm by 8 cm. Draw an accurate net for this cuboid.

9 $x = 3$, correct to 1 significant figure. $y = 0.06$, correct to 1 significant figure.
Calculate the greatest possible value of:

$$y - \frac{x-7}{x}$$

[Edexcel]

10 a) Convert 3500 mm² into cm².
   b) Convert 2.5 m³ into cm³.

11 a) A sphere has radius 1.1 m. Calculate its volume, in m³. Give your answer to 3 significant figures.
   b) Convert your answer from **a)** into cm³.
   c) Calculate the surface area of the sphere, in m². Give your answer to 3 significant figures.
   d) Convert your answer from **c)** into cm².

12 A cone has a volume of 10 m³. The vertical height of the cone is 1.5 m.
   Calculate the radius of the base of the cone. Give your answer correct to 3 significant figures. [Edexcel]

13 Here are the plan and front elevation of a prism. The front elevation shows the cross section of the prism.

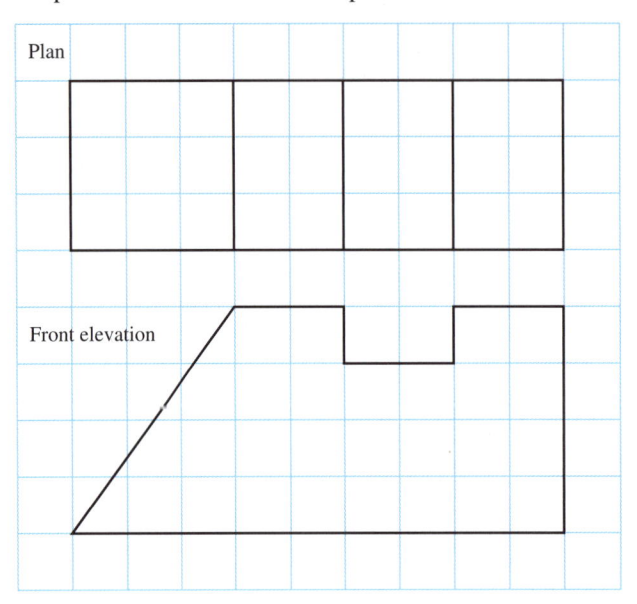

   a) On squared paper, draw a side elevation of the prism.
   b) Draw a 3-D sketch of the prism. [Edexcel]

14 The boxes A, B, C and D show four expressions. The letters p and q represent lengths. 2 and 3 are numbers which have no dimensions.

A	B	C	D
$p^3 + 3q^2$	$p^2 + 2q$	$2p + 3q$	$3p^2 + 2pq$

   a) Write **one** of the letters **A, B, C** or **D** for the expression which represents:
      (i) an area   (ii) a length.

   The box **X** shows an expression.
   The letters p and q represent lengths. n is a number.
   The expression represents a volume.

   X: $p^n(p + q)$

   b) Find the value of n. [Edexcel]

15 Here are some expressions.

$\dfrac{\pi r^2}{x}$	$\pi(r+x)$	$\pi r + r$	$\dfrac{\pi r^3}{x}$	$\pi r^2 + rx$	$\dfrac{r^2}{\pi x}$

The letters r and x represent lengths. π is a number which has no dimension. Two of the expressions could represent areas.

a) Copy the grid and tick the boxes (✓) underneath the two expressions which could represent areas.

Here are four more expressions.

πr^3	$\pi r^4 + \pi x$	$\dfrac{\pi r^4}{x}$	$\pi r^2 + \pi rx$

One of these four expressions cannot represent a length or an area or a volume.

b) Copy the grid and put a cross in the box (✗) underneath the one expression which cannot represent a length or an area or a volume. [Edexcel]

16 Peter transports metal bars in his van. The van has a safety notice *Maximum Load 1200 kg*. Each metal bar has a label *Weight 60 kg*.

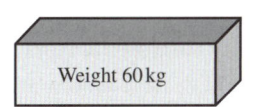

MAXIMUM LOAD 1200 kg

Weight 60 kg

For safety reasons Peter assumes that:

1200 is rounded correct to 2 significant figures
60 is rounded correct to 1 significant figure.

Calculate the greatest number of bars that Peter can *safely* put into the van if his assumptions are correct. [Edexcel]

17 The time period, T seconds, of a pendulum is calculated using the formula:

$$T = 6.283 \times \sqrt{\dfrac{L}{g}}$$

where L metres is the length of the pendulum, and g m/s² is the acceleration due to gravity.

$L = 1.36$ correct to 2 decimal places
$G = 9.8$ correct to 1 decimal place.

Find the difference between the lower bound of T and the upper bound of T. [Edexcel]

18 The diagram shows a water tank.
    The tank is a hollow cylinder joined to a hollow
    hemisphere at the top. The tank has a circular base.
    Both the cylinder and the hemisphere have a
    diameter of 46 cm. The height of the tank is 90 cm.
    Work out the volume of water which the tank
    holds when it is full. Give your answer, in cm³,
    correct to 3 significant figures.

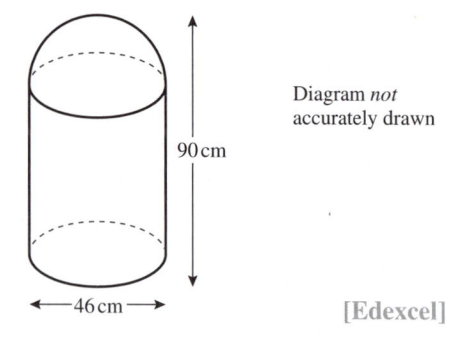

    Diagram *not* accurately drawn

    [Edexcel]

19 A sphere has a radius of 5.4 cm. A cone has a height of 8 cm. The volume of the sphere is equal
    to the volume of the cone. Calculate the radius of the base of the cone. Give your answer,
    in centimetres, correct to 2 significant figures. [Edexcel]

20 A cone fits exactly on top of a hemisphere to form a solid toy.
    The radius, CA, of the base of the cone is 3 cm. AB = 5 cm.
    Show that the total surface area of the toy is 33π cm².

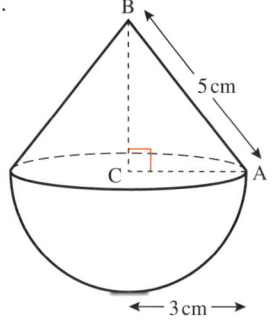

    Diagram *not* accurately drawn

    [Edexcel]

21

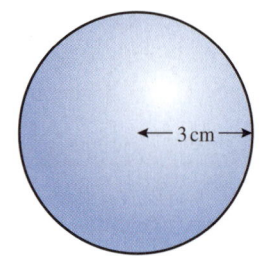

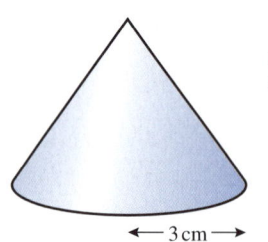

    Diagram *not* accurately drawn

    The radius of a sphere is 3 cm. The radius of the base of a cone is also 3 cm. The volume of the
    sphere is three times the volume of the cone.
    Work out the curved surface area of the cone. Give your answer as a multiple of π. [Edexcel]

KEY POINTS

1. For a polygon with n sides, the interior angles will sum to $180° \times (n - 2)$
2. The exterior angles of any polygon add up to $360°$.
3. If the polygon has equal sides and equal angles, it is regular.
4. Each exterior angle of an n-sided regular polygon is $360° \div n$.
5. 3-D objects may be portrayed using sketches, isometric drawings and plan/elevation views.
6. Volumes and surface areas of pyramids, cones and spheres may be found using these formulae:

   Volume of a pyramid: $\quad V = \frac{1}{3} \times$ area of the base $\times$ (perpendicular) height

   Volume of a cone, radius r, height h: $\quad V = \frac{1}{3}\pi r^2 h$

   Volume of a sphere, radius r: $\quad V = \frac{4}{3}\pi r^3$

   Surface area of a sphere, radius r: $\quad A = 4\pi r^2$

   Curved surface area of a cone, radius r, slant height l: $\quad A = \pi r l$

7. When converting between different units of area, remember to square the ordinary linear conversion factor. For example, 100 cm $= 1$ m, but $10\,000$ cm$^2 = 1$ m^2
   In a similar way, for volumes the factor must be cubed: $1\,000\,000$ cm$^3 = 1$ m^3

8. Expressions for length, area and volume may be distinguished by the method of dimensions.

   For example, an expression such as $\dfrac{3abc}{\pi r}$ has dimensions:

   $$\frac{(\text{length})^3}{\text{length}} = (\text{length})^2$$

   and thus could represent an area.

9. Upper and lower bounds may be computed for quantities that have been rounded to a given level of accuracy:

   Lower bound = stated value minus half a 'step'
   Upper bound = stated value plus half a 'step'

10. In the examination, lower bounds may be referred to as least (or minimum) values, and upper bounds may be referred to as greatest (or maximum) values.

    There is a subtle difference between the concepts of maximum and upper bound, but the examiner will expect you to treat them identically. Thus, if a length has been recorded as 18 cm to the nearest centimetre, and the examiner asks for the greatest possible value, you should write 18.5 cm, not 18.4 cm or 18.49 cm.

Internet Challenge 23

Investigating polyhedra

Polyhedra are 3-D mathematical shapes made up of a number of 2-D plane faces. Many polyhedra exhibit geometrical symmetries of various kinds. The tetrahedron and the cube are simple examples, but many more exotic polyhedra exist. Constructing models of them can be quite challenging!

Use an internet search engine, such as Google, to look for information about **Platonic solids**. Then answer these questions:

1. How many Platonic solids are known? Are we ever likely to find any more?

2. Why are they called Platonic solids?

3. Design nets for each of the Platonic solids, and trace them on to thin card. Then cut them out, and make some models for your classroom. Remember to include tabs in suitable places.

Modern footballs are assembled from a net of pentagons and hexagons.

4. Find out how this net is made.

5. Is such a football an example of a Platonic solid?

The diagram shows a **stellated octahedron**. It is based on an octahedral core, though it also happens to look like two interlocking tetrahedra.

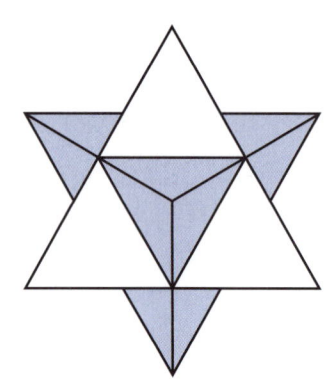

6. Design a net for, and hence build, a model of a stellated octahedron.

7. Use the internet to find examples of other stellated polyhedra.

8. How many different fully symmetric stellations of an icosahedron are known?

9. Find images of Escher's prints *Double Planet* and *Gravity*. On which polyhedra are they based?

10. Use the internet to find out about **fractal polyhedra**. You should be able to find some animated models; add the best ones to your computer's bookmarks.

CHAPTER 24

Circle theorems

In this chapter you will **learn how to**:

- use Pythagoras' theorem inside and outside circles
- prove and use various theorems about angle properties inside a circle
- prove and use the alternate segment (intersecting tangent and chord) theorem.

You will also be **challenged to**:

- investigate the nine-point circle theorem.

Starter: Scrambled words

Here are three basic properties of circles that you met earlier in the book. The letters of the *key words* have been scrambled up. See if you can unscramble them.

A *neli stegmen* drawn from the centre of a circle to the *mindipot* of a chord will intersect the chord at *girth langes*.

A *gnatnet* and *darius* meet at right angles.

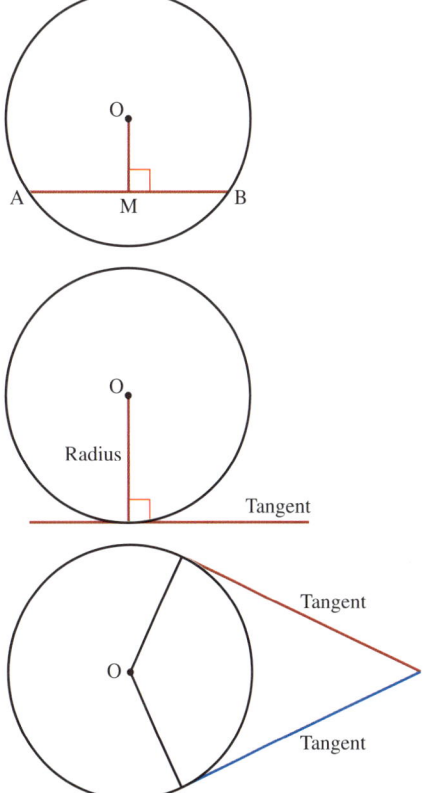

The two tangents from a given point to a circle are *laque* in *ghentl*.

You may need to use these basic properties, as well as the new ones developed in this chapter, to solve GCSE exam problems.

24.1 Pythagoras' theorem and circles

Since a tangent meets a radius at right angles, some circle problems may be solved using Pythagoras' theorem.

EXAMPLE

In the diagram, AT is a tangent to the circle, centre O. The radius OA is 2.5 cm and the length of AT is 6 cm. Calculate the length OT.

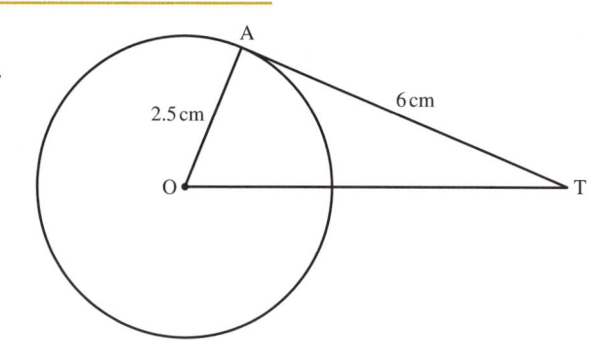

SOLUTION

Since a tangent and radius meet at right angles, OAT is a right-angled triangle.
By Pythagoras' theorem,
$$OT^2 = OA^2 + AT^2$$
$$= 2.5^2 + 6^2$$
$$= 6.25 + 36$$
$$= 42.5$$
So, $OT = \sqrt{42.5}$
$$= 6.519\ 202\ 41$$
$$= \underline{6.5 \text{ cm}} \text{ (1 d.p.)}$$

Since a radius bisects a chord at right angles, there are also opportunities to use Pythagoras' theorem inside a circle, as in the next example.

EXAMPLE

The diagram shows a radius OT that bisects the chord AB at M. MB = 12 cm. The radius of the circle is 13 cm.
Work out the length MT.

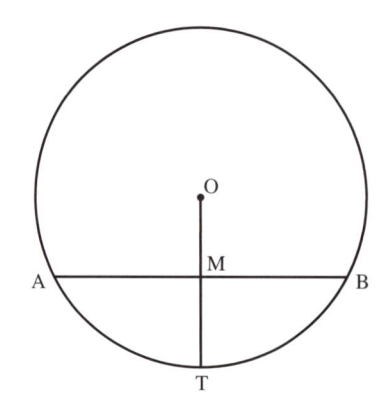

SOLUTION

First join OB:

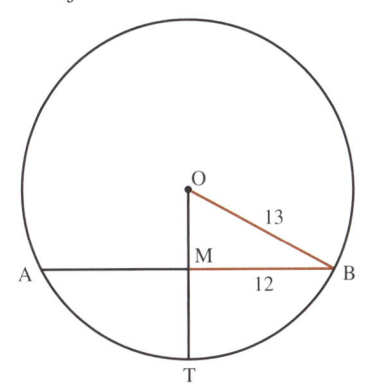

Now apply Pythagoras' theorem to triangle OBM:

$$OM^2 = 13^2 - 12^2$$
$$= 169 - 144$$
$$= 25$$
$$OM = \sqrt{25}$$
$$= 5 \text{ cm}$$

The distance OT is a radius, that is, 13 cm.
Thus MT = 13 − 5
= **8 cm**

EXERCISE 24.1

1 PQ is a tangent to the circle, centre O. OP = 3.5 cm, PQ = 12 cm.

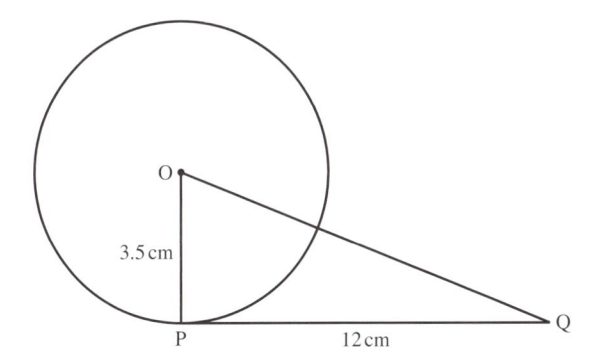

a) State the value of angle OPQ.
b) Calculate the length of OQ.

2 PT is a tangent to the circle, centre O. PT = 24 cm. OP = 7 cm.

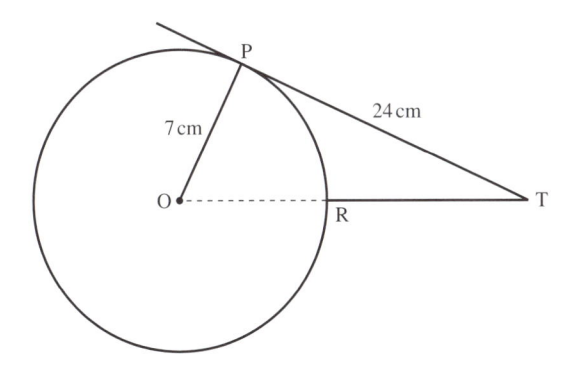

The line OT intersects the circle at R, as shown. Work out the length of RT.

3 The diagram shows a circle, centre O.
The radius of the circle is 5 cm.
M is the midpoint of EF. OM = 3 cm.

Calculate the length of EF.

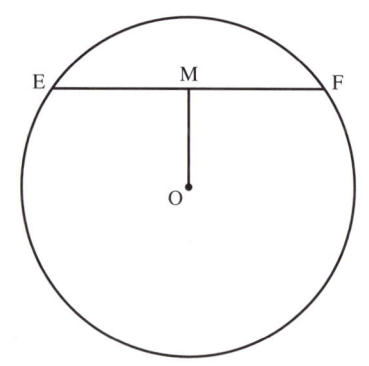

4 The diagram shows a circle, centre O. AB = 34 cm.
M is the midpoint of AB.
OM = 8 cm.

Work out the radius of the circle.

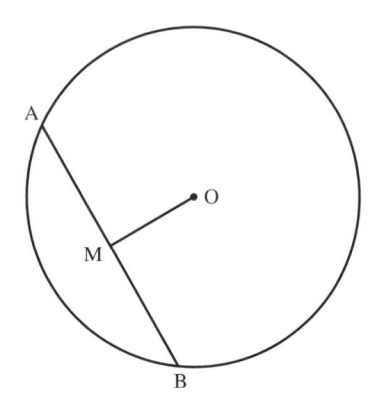

5 The diagram shows a circle, centre O.
AB and CD are chords.
The radius OT passes through the midpoints M and N of the chords.
OM = 8 cm, NT = 3 cm, AB = 30 cm.

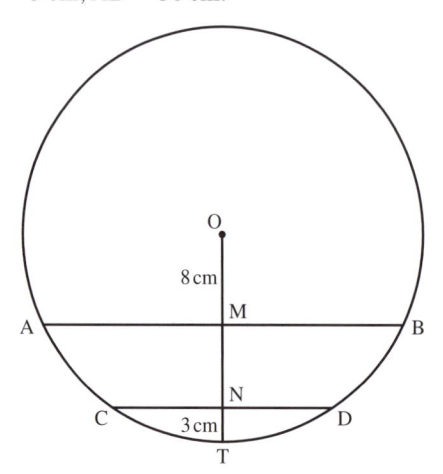

a) Explain why angle AMO = 90°.
b) Use Pythagoras' theorem to calculate the distance AO.
   Show your working.
c) Calculate the distance MN.
d) Calculate the length of the chord CD.

24.2 Angle properties inside a circle

There are several important theorems about angles inside a circle.
You will need to learn these, and use them to solve numerical problems.
You may also be asked to prove why they are true.

Consider two points, A and B say, on the circumference of a circle.
The angle subtended by the arc AB at the centre is angle AOB.

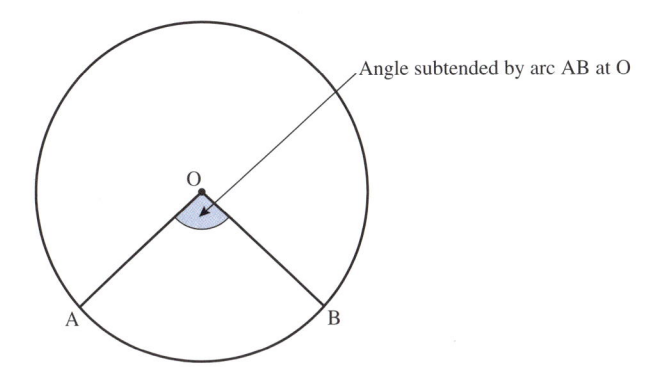

Angle subtended by arc AB at O

The angle subtended by the arc AB at a point X on the circumference is angle AXB.

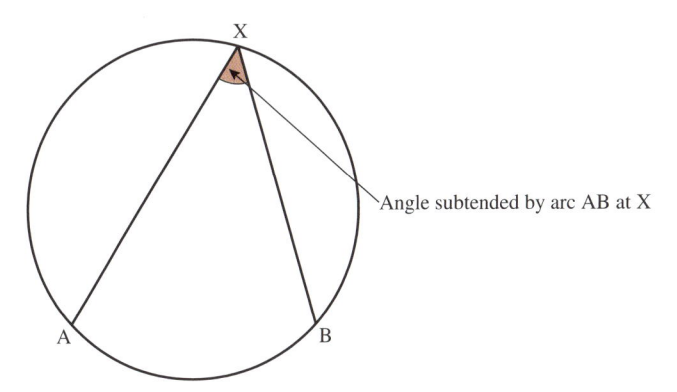

Angle subtended by arc AB at X

There is a theorem in circle geometry which states that angle AOB is exactly twice angle AXB.

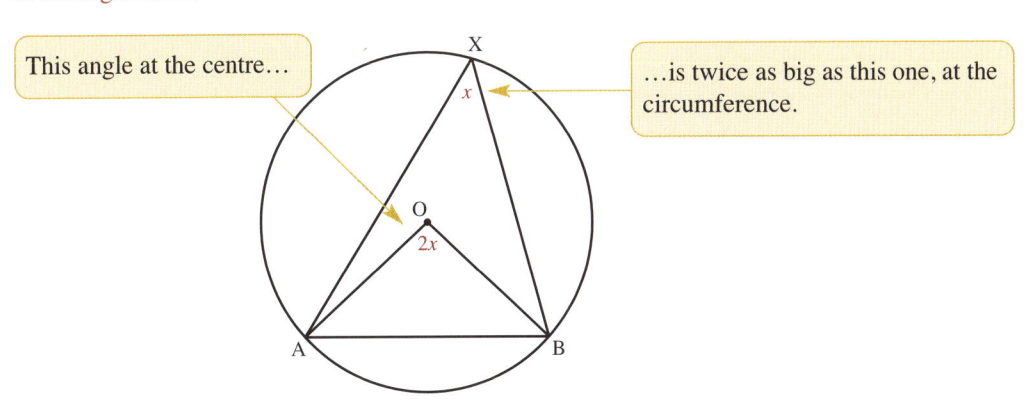

This angle at the centre…

…is twice as big as this one, at the circumference.

This result is quite easy to prove, and is the basic theorem upon which several other circle theorems are built.

24 Circle theorems   U4   411

THEOREM

The angle subtended by an arc at the centre of a circle is twice the angle subtended by the same arc at the circumference of the circle.

PROOF

Make a diagram to show the arc AB, the centre O, and the point X on the circumference of the circle:

From X, draw a radius to O, and produce it, which means extend it slightly:

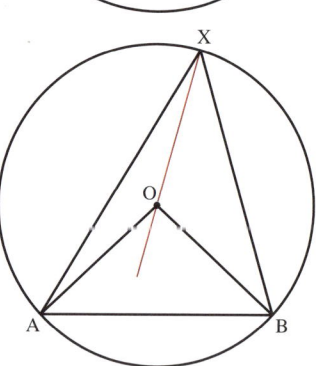

Triangle AOX is isosceles, since both OA and OX are radii of the same circle. Therefore angles OAX and OXA are equal. These are marked on the diagram with a letter a:

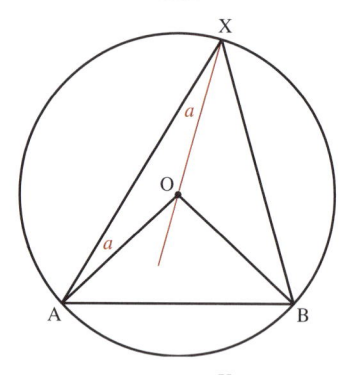

Likewise the triangle BOX is isosceles, since both OB and OX are radii of the same circle. Therefore angles OBX and OXB are equal. These are marked on the diagram with a letter b:

The angle at the circumference is angle AXB = $a + b$.

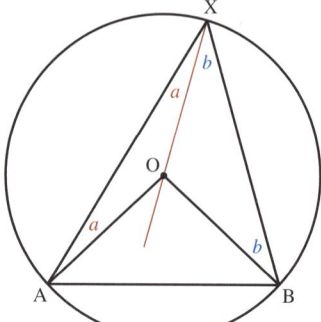

To obtain an expression for the angle at the centre, look at this magnified copy of the diagram:

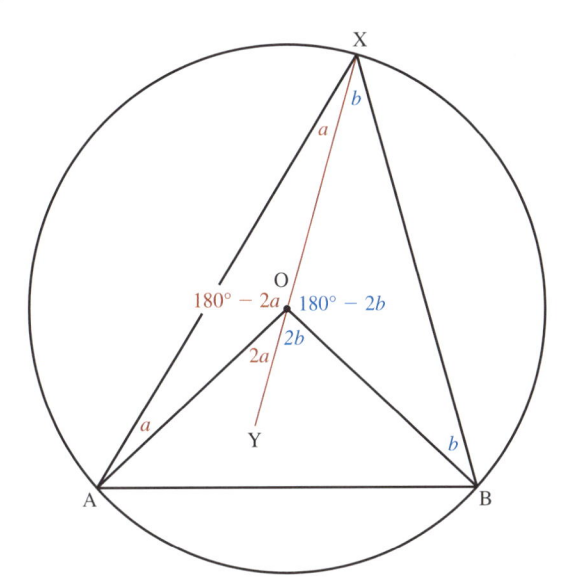

Angle AOX = $180 - a - a = 180 - 2a$

So: angle AOY = $180 - (180 - 2a) = 2a$

Likewise:
angle BOX = $180 - b - b = 180 - 2b$

So: angle BOY = $180 - (180 - 2b) = 2b$

Thus the angle at the centre is:

Angle AOB = $2a + 2b$
$= 2(a + b)$

But angle AXB = $a + b$, from above.

Therefore angle AOB = $2 \times$ angle AXB.

Thus, the angle subtended by an arc at the centre of a circle is twice the angle subtended by the same arc at the circumference of the circle.

Two further theorems can be deduced immediately from this first one.
You can quote the previous theorem to justify these proofs.

THEOREM

Angles subtended by an arc in the same segment of a circle are equal.

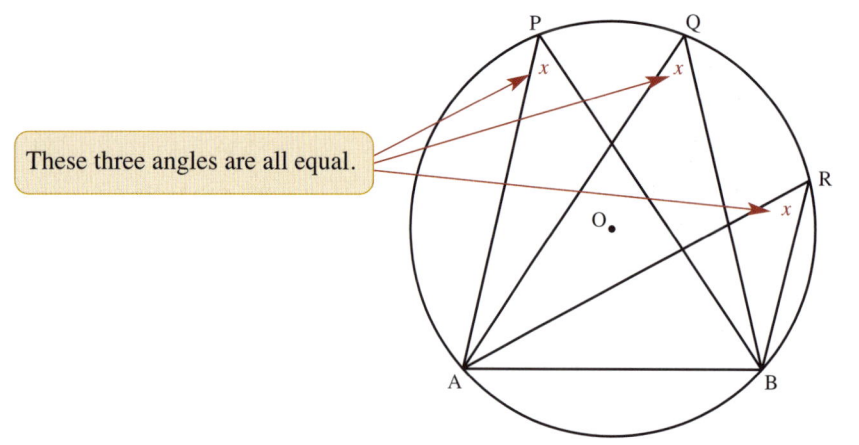

These three angles are all equal.

PROOF

Join AO and OB so that they form an angle at the centre:

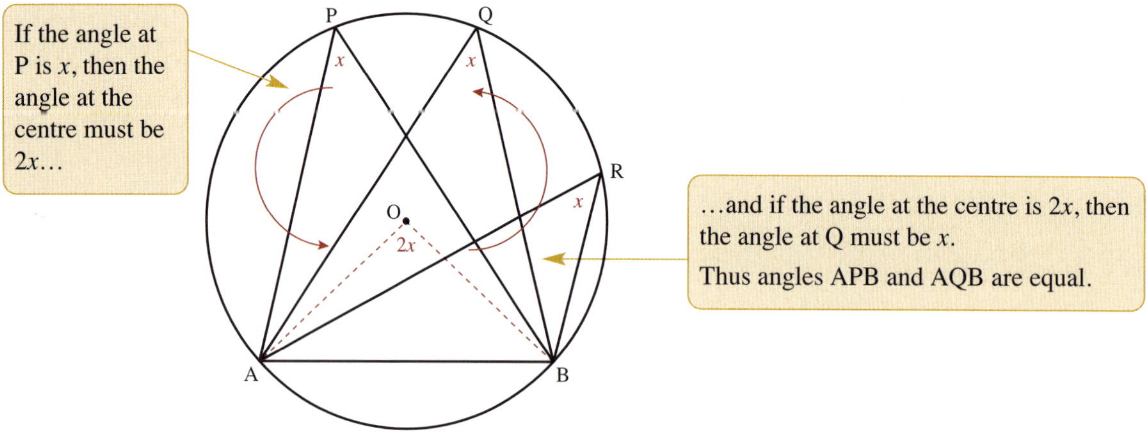

If the angle at P is x, then the angle at the centre must be $2x$…

…and if the angle at the centre is $2x$, then the angle at Q must be x.

Thus angles APB and AQB are equal.

THEOREM

The angle subtended in a semicircle is a right angle.

PROOF

Since AB is a diameter, AOB is a straight line.

Thus angle AOB = 180°.

Using the result that the angle at the circumference is half that at the centre:

Angle APB = 180° ÷ 2 = <u>90°</u>

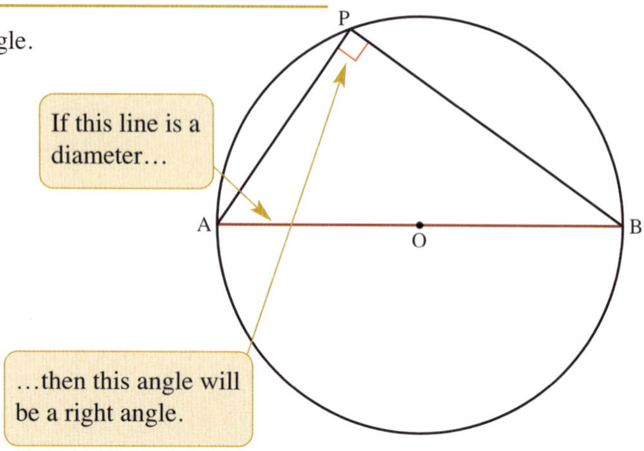

If this line is a diameter…

…then this angle will be a right angle.

EXAMPLE

Find the values of the angles marked x and y. Explain your reasoning in both cases.

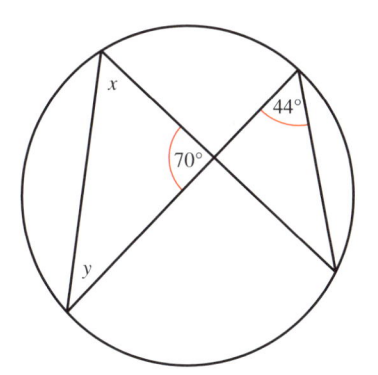

Diagram *not* to scale

SOLUTION

Angle $x = 44°$ (angles in the same segment are equal).

$x + 70° + y = 180°$ (angles in a triangle add up to 180°) and $x = 44°$, so:

$$44° + 70° + y = 180°$$
$$114° + y = 180°$$
$$y = 180° - 114°$$
$$y = 66°$$

EXAMPLE

Find the values of the angles marked x and y. Explain your reasoning in both cases.

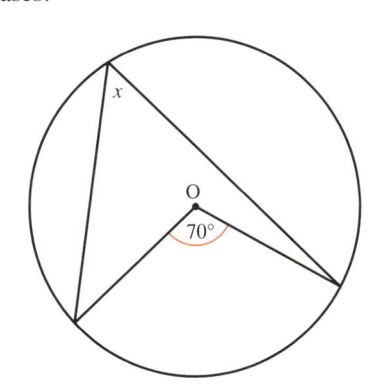

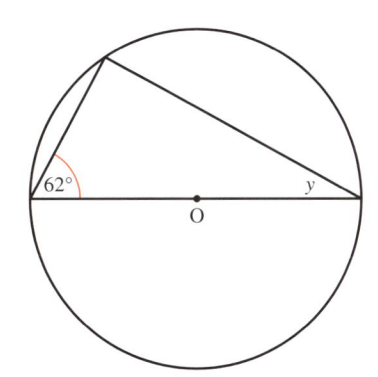

SOLUTION

$x = 70 \div 2 = \underline{35°}$ (angle at centre = 2 × angle at circumference)
$y = 180 - 90 - 62 = \underline{28°}$ (angle in a semicircle is a right angle and angles in a triangle add up to 180°)

EXERCISE 24.2

Find the missing angles in these diagrams, which are not drawn to scale. Explain your reasoning in each case.

24.3 Further circle theorems

THEOREM

The angles subtended in opposite segments add up to 180°.

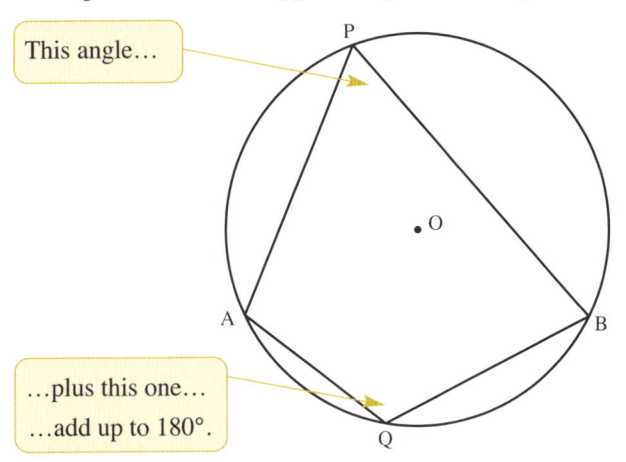

This angle…

…plus this one…

…add up to 180°.

PROOF

Denote the angles APB and AQB as p and q respectively.

Then the angles at the centre are twice these, that is, $2p$ and $2q$.

Angles at point O add up to 360°, so:

$2p + 2q = 360°$

Thus $2(p + q) = 360°$

So $p + q = 180°$

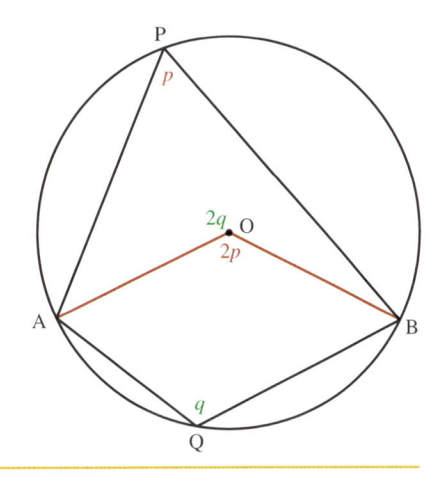

The points A, P, B and Q form a quadrilateral whose vertices lie around a circle; it is known as a **cyclic quadrilateral**. Thus the theorem may also be stated as:

Opposite angles of a cyclic quadrilateral add up to 180°

EXAMPLE

Find the angles x and y.

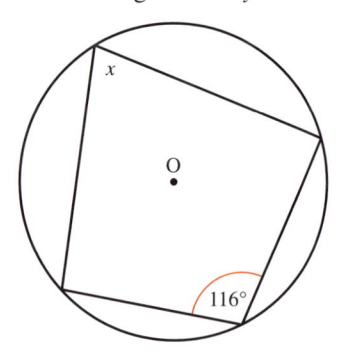

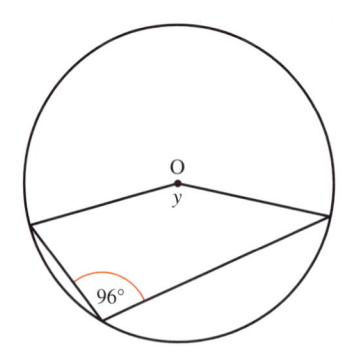

Diagram *not* to scale

SOLUTION

For angle x, we have $x + 116° = 180°$ (angles in opposite segments)

Thus $x = 180° - 116°$
$= \underline{64°}$

For angle y, two construction lines are needed:

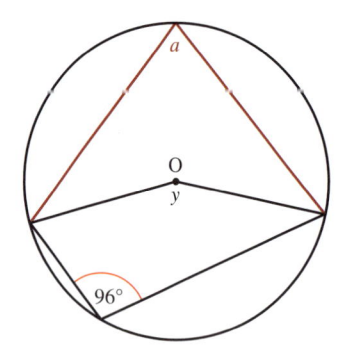

Using angles in opposite segments, $a = 180 - 96 = 84°$.

Using the angle at centre is twice the angle at circumference:

$y = 84 \times 2 = \underline{168°}$

THEOREM

The angle between a tangent and chord is equal to the angle subtended in the opposite segment. (This is often called the **alternate segment** theorem.)

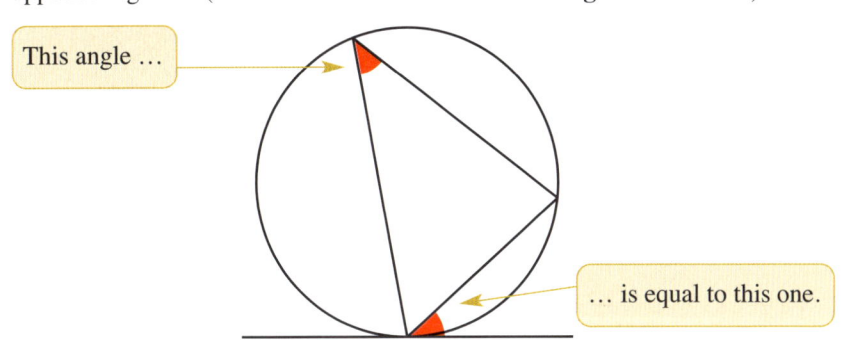

This angle …

… is equal to this one.

PROOF

First, consider the special case of a tangent meeting a diameter:

Since the angle in a semicircle is 90°, the other two angles in the triangle add up to 90°.

Hence $y + z = 90°$.

Since a radius and tangent meet at 90°:

$x + z = 90°$

Hence $x + z = y + z$.
From which it follows that $x = y$.

Now move P around the circle to Q, say, so that it is no longer on the end of a diameter. The angle at Q is equal to the angle at P, as they are angles in the same segment.
Thus the theorem is proved.

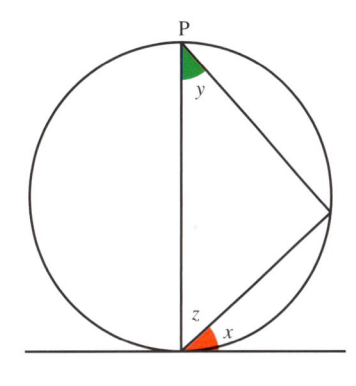

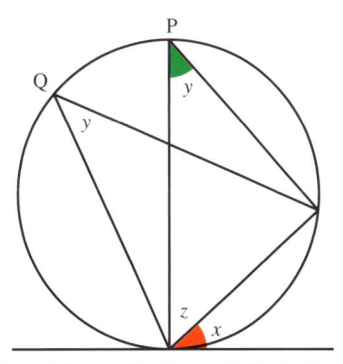

24 Circle theorems   U4

EXERCISE 24.3

Find the missing angles in these diagrams, which are not drawn to scale.
Explain your reasoning in each case.

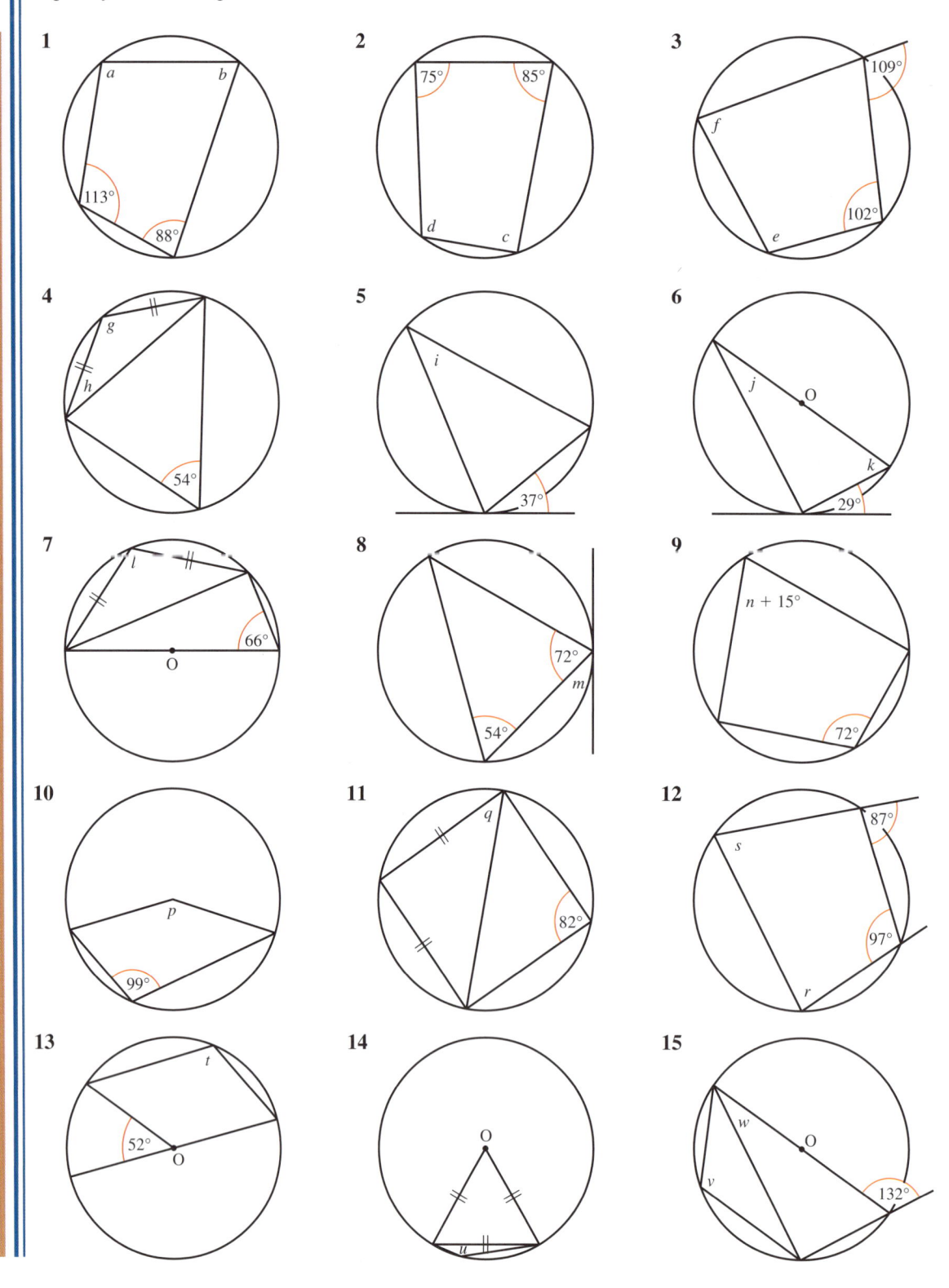

REVIEW EXERCISE 24

1 A circle of diameter 10 cm has a chord drawn inside it. The chord is 7 cm long.
   a) Make a sketch to show this information.
   b) Calculate the distance from the midpoint of the chord to the centre of the circle. Give your answer correct to 3 significant figures.

2 The diagram shows a circle, centre O.
PT and RT are tangents to the circle. Angle POR = 144°.

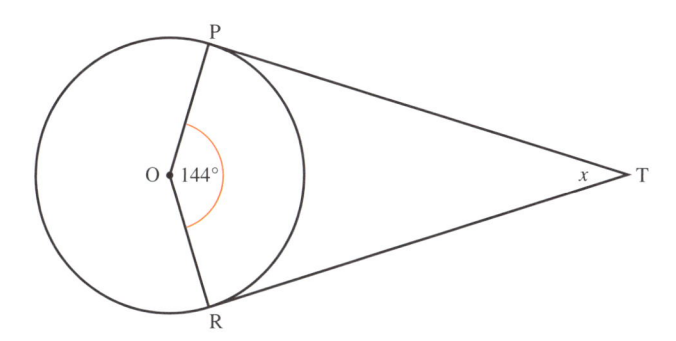

   a) Work out the size of angle PTR, marked x.
   b) Is it possible to draw a circle that passes through the four points P, O, R and T? Give reasons for your answer.

3 The diagram shows a circle, centre O.
PT and RT are tangents to the circle. Angle PTR = 32°.

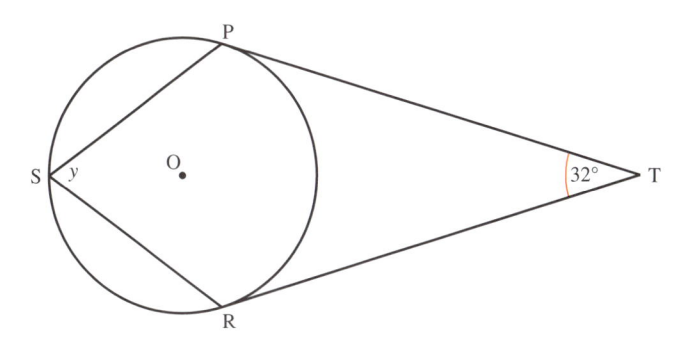

   a) Work out the size of angle PSR, marked y.
   Hint: Draw in OP and OR.
   b) Is it possible to draw a circle that passes through the four points P, S, R and T? Give reasons for your answer.

4 In the diagram, A, B and C are points on the circle, centre O.
Angle BCE = 63°. FE is a tangent to the circle at point C.

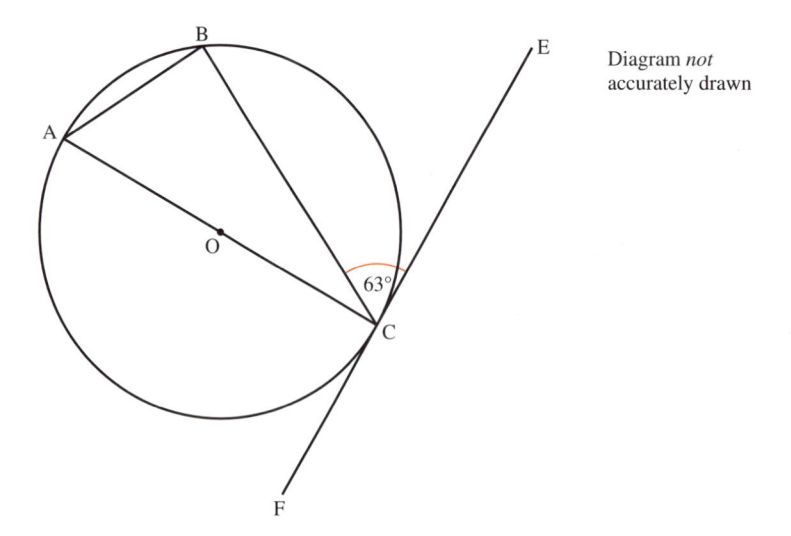

Diagram *not* accurately drawn

a) Calculate the size of angle ACB. Give reasons for your answer.
b) Calculate the size of angle BAC. Give reasons for your answer. [Edexcel]

5 P, Q, R and S are points on the circumference of a circle, centre O.
PR is a diameter of the circle. Angle PSQ = 56°.

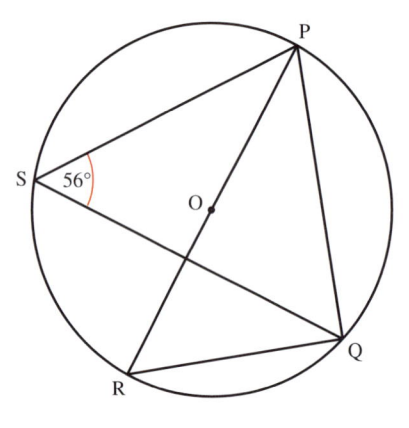

Diagram *not* accurately drawn

a) Find the size of angle PQR. Give a reason for your answer.
b) Find the size of angle PRQ. Give a reason for your answer.
c) Find the size of angle POQ. Give a reason for your answer. [Edexcel]

6 A, B, C and D are four points on the circumference of a circle.
ABE and DCE are straight lines. Angle BAC = 25°. Angle EBC = 60°.
   a) Find the size of angle ADC.
   b) Find the size of angle ADB.

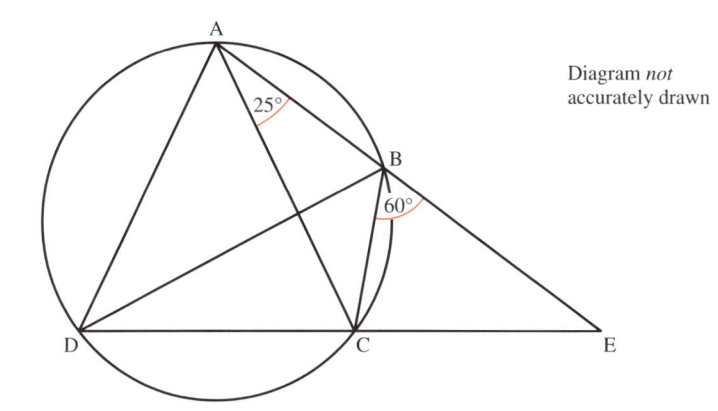

Diagram *not* accurately drawn

Angle CAD = 65°. Ben says that BD is a diameter of the circle.
   c) Is Ben correct? You must explain your answer. [Edexcel]

7 The diagram shows a circle, centre O. AC is a diameter. Angle BAC = 35°.
D is the point on AC such that angle BDA is a right angle.

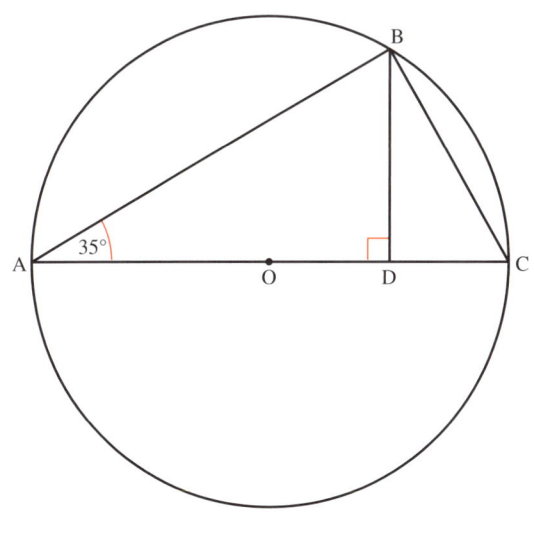

Diagram *not* accurately drawn

   a) Work out the size of angle BCA. Give reasons for your answer.
   b) Calculate the size of angle DBC.
   c) Calculate the size of angle BOA. [Edexcel]

8 A, B, C and D are four points on the circumference of a circle.
TA is the tangent to the circle at A. Angle DAT = 30°. Angle ADC = 132°.

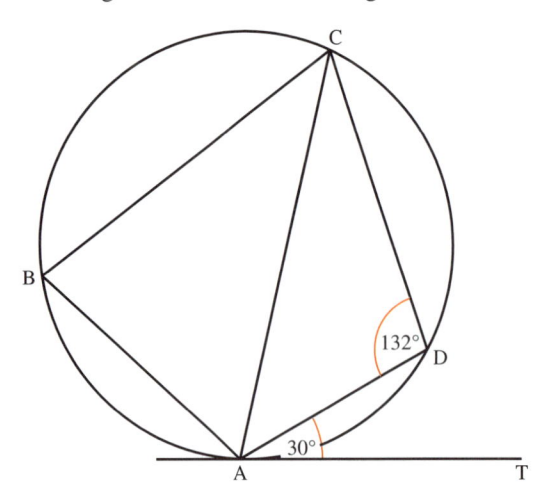

Diagram *not* accurately drawn

  a) Calculate the size of angle ABC. Explain your method.
  b) Calculate the size of angle CBD. Explain your method.
  c) Explain why AC cannot be a diameter of the circle. [Edexcel]

9 Points A, B and C lie on the circumference of a circle with centre O.
DA is the tangent to the circle at A. BCD is a straight line. OC and AB intersect at E.

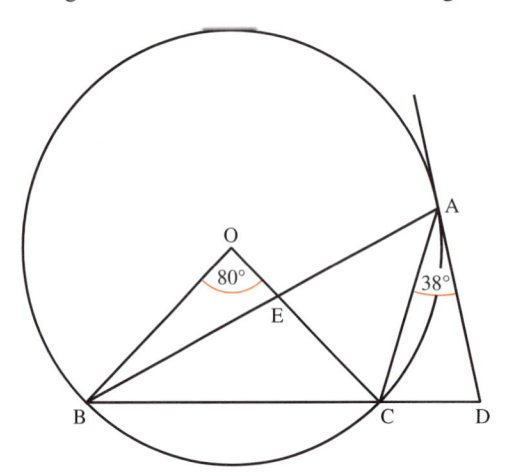

Diagram *not* accurately drawn

Angle BOC = 80°. Angle CAD = 38°.
  a) Calculate the size of angle BAC.
  b) Calculate the size of angle OBA.
  c) Give a reason why it is not possible to draw a circle with diameter ED through the point A. [Edexcel]

10 A, B, C and D are points on the circumference of a circle centre O.
A tangent is drawn from E to touch the circle at C.
Angle AEC = 36°. EAO is a straight line.

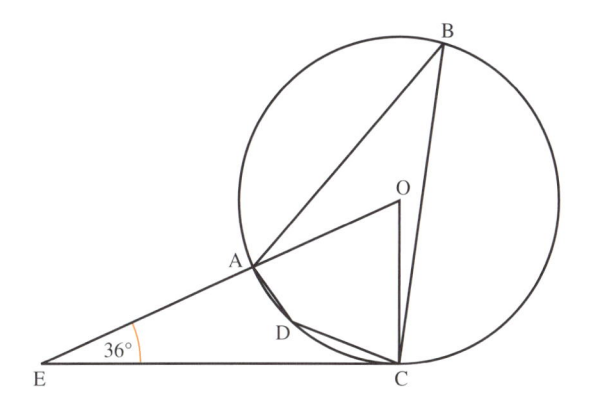

Diagram *not* accurately drawn

a) Calculate the size of angle ABC. Give reasons for your answer.
b) Calculate the size of angle ADC. Give reasons for your answer. [Edexcel]

11 P, Q and R are points on a circle. O is the centre of the circle.
RT is the tangent to the circle at R. Angle QRT = 56°.

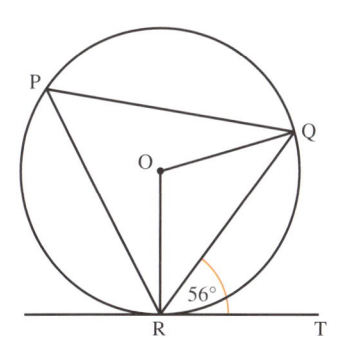

Diagram *not* accurately drawn

a) Find (i) the size of angle RPQ and (ii) the size of angle ROQ.

A, B, C and D are points on a circle. AC is a diameter of the circle.
Angle CAD = 25° and angle BCD = 132°.

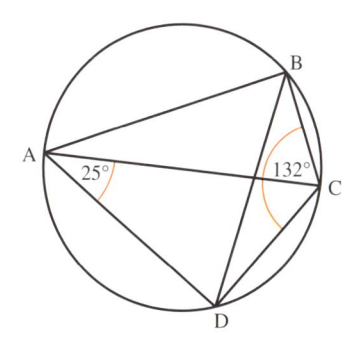

Diagram *not* accurately drawn

b) Calculate (i) the size of angle BAC and (ii) the size of angle ABD. [Edexcel]

KEY POINTS

Basic circle properties

A line segment drawn from the centre of a circle to the midpoint of a chord will intersect the chord at right angles.	A tangent and radius meet at right angles.	The two tangents from a given point to a circle are equal in length.

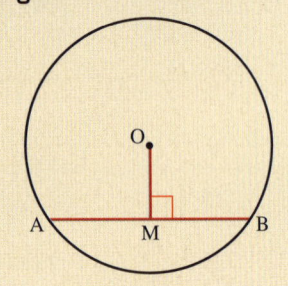

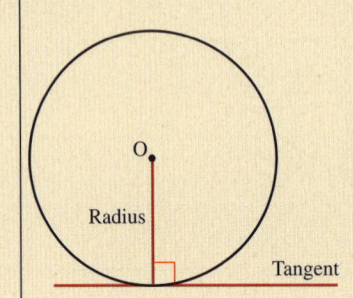

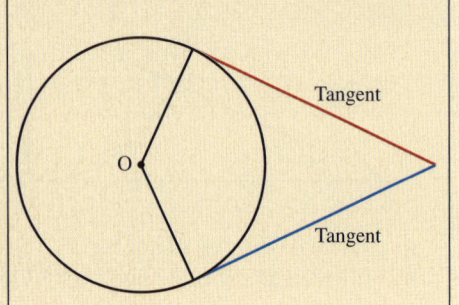

Circle theorems

The angle subtended by an arc at the centre of a circle is twice the angle subtended by the same arc at the circumference of the circle.	Angles subtended by an arc in the same segment of a circle are equal.	The angle subtended in a semicircle is a right angle.

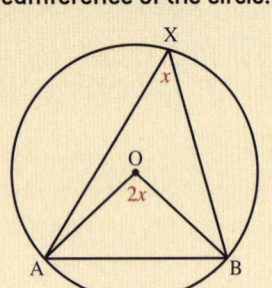

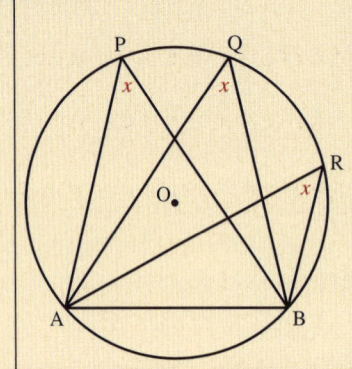

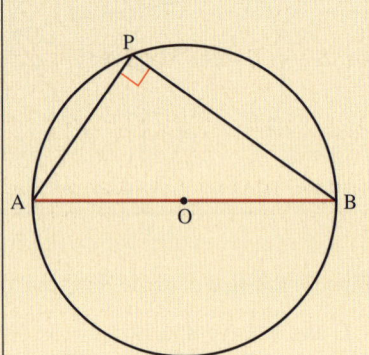

The angles subtended in opposite segments add up to 180°. $x + y = 180°$	The angle between a tangent and chord is equal to the angle subtended in the opposite segment.

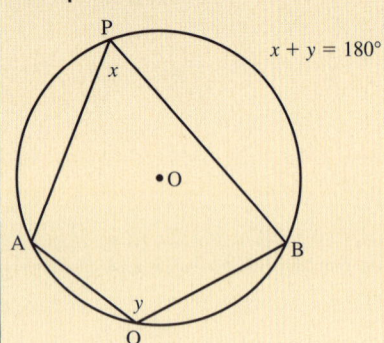

Internet Challenge 24

The nine-point circle theorem

This diagram shows the nine-point circle. Here are the instructions to make it.

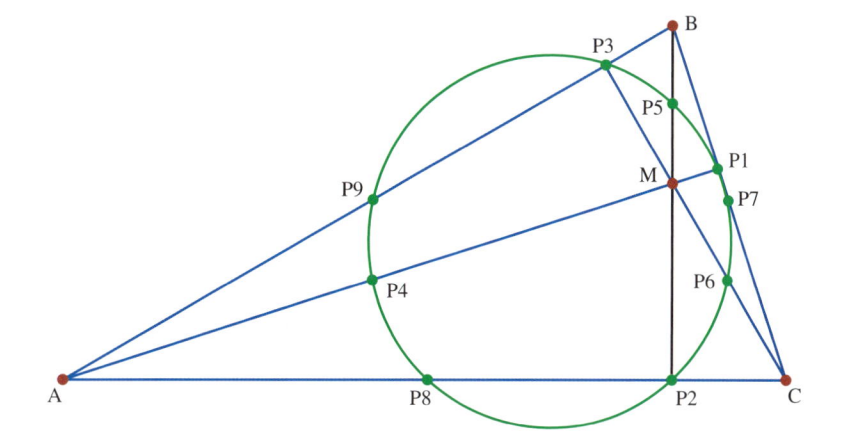

Start with any general triangle, whose vertices are A, B and C.

Construct points P1, P2, P3. Can you see what rule is used to locate them?

Construct the point M. Can you see how P1, P2, P3 are used to do this?

Construct points P4, P5, P6. Can you see what rule is used to locate them?

Construct points P7, P8, P9. Can you see what rule is used to locate them?

Then it should be possible to draw a circle that passes through all nine of the points: P1, P2, P3, P4, P5, P6, P7, P8 and P9.

1. Look at the diagram, and see if you can figure out how the various points are constructed. Use the internet to check that your deductions are correct.

2. Try to make a nine-point circle of your own, using compass constructions. You might also try to do this using computer graphics software.

3. Which mathematician is thought to have first made a nine-point circle?

4. Can you find a proof that these nine points all lie on the same circle?

CHAPTER 25

Direct and inverse proportion

In this chapter you will **learn how to**:

- construct formulae and solve problems using direct proportion
- construct formulae and solve problems using inverse proportion
- understand graphical representations of proportion.

You will also be **challenged to**:

- investigate the planets and their orbits.

Starter: A sense of proportion

Puzzle 1
In a biology experiment, a bean shoot grows by 35 mm in 5 days. How much would it be expected to grow in 7 days?

Puzzle 2
For a high altitude expedition to the Himalayas, a group of eight mountaineers plan to take bottled oxygen to breathe while they are sleeping. Their oxygen supply is enough to last them for 12 nights. But before they start, two are ill and leave the expedition. How many nights will the oxygen last the remaining mountaineers?

Puzzle 3
Nine lumberjacks can chop 6 piles of logs in 20 minutes. How long would it take for 18 lumberjacks to chop 15 piles of logs?

Puzzle 4
A farmer sees 10 crows perched on a fence. He shoots one. How many remain?

Puzzle 5
It takes 10 monkeys 10 minutes to eat 10 bananas. How long does it take 1 monkey to eat 1 banana?

25.1 Direct proportion

Suppose two variables are related in such a way that one of them is a constant multiple of the other, for example $y = 3x$.
Then y is said to be **directly proportional** to x.
The constant multiplier, in this case 3, is the **constant of proportionality**.

Direct proportion can be indicated by the symbol $\propto$, so $y \propto x$ is simply a short way of writing 'y is directly proportional to x'. Algebraically, you would write $y = kx$, where k represents the constant of proportionality.

EXAMPLE

Two quantities, x and y, are such that $y \propto x$.
a) Write an algebraic formula for y in terms of x.
b) When $x = 4$, $y = 10$. Find the constant of proportionality.
c) Using your formula, work out (i) the value of y when $x = 6$ and (ii) the value of x when $y = 8$.

SOLUTION

a) $y = kx$

b) Using $x = 4$ and $y = 10$:
$$10 = 4k$$
$$k = \frac{10}{4}$$
$$k = 2.5$$
Thus $y = 2.5x$

c) (i) When $x = 6$:
$$y = 2.5x$$
$$= 2.5 \times 6$$
$$= 15$$

(ii) When $y = 8$:
$$8 = 2.5x$$
$$x = \frac{8}{2.5}$$
$$= 3.2$$

Sometimes one variable is directly proportional to the *square* of another. This situation can be developed in the same way, though the relationship between the original variables is in this case no longer linear.

EXAMPLE

y is directly proportional to the square of x. When x is 10, y is 300.
a) Obtain a formula for y in terms of x.
b) Use your formula to find the value of y when x is 20.
c) Use your formula to find the value of x when y is 675.

SOLUTION

a) y is directly proportional to the square of x, that is, $y = kx^2$
When x is 10, y is 300, so:
$$300 = k \times 10^2$$
$$300 = 100k$$
$$k = \frac{300}{100} = 3$$
Therefore $y = 3x^2$

> Substitute $x = 10$ and $y = 300$ into the equation $y = kx^2$ in order to find the value of k.

b) When $x = 20$:
$y = 3x^2$
$ = 3 \times 20^2$
$ = 3 \times 400$
$ = \underline{1200}$

c) When $y = 675$:
$675 = 3x^2$
$x^2 = \dfrac{675}{3}$
$ = 225$
$x = \pm\sqrt{225}$
$ = \underline{15 \text{ or } -15}$

Some questions will ask you to formulate the proportional equation from information given in words. You might also find that the constant of proportionality is a fractional amount: in that case, use a fraction rather than a decimal approximation. The next example demonstrates how this works.

EXAMPLE

The weight, W kg, of a spherical garden ornament is directly proportional to the cube of its diameter, d cm. An ornament of diameter 20 cm weighs 2 kg.
a) Find a formula for W in terms of d.
b) Find the weight of an ornament of diameter 15 cm.
c) Tony struggles to lift an ornament weighing 30 kg. Work out the diameter of this ornament. Give your answer correct to the nearest centimetre.

SOLUTION

a) Since W is directly proportional to the cube of d:
$W = kd^3$
When $d = 20$, $W = 2$
$2 = k \times 20^3$
$2 = 8000k$
$k = \dfrac{2}{8000}$
$k = \dfrac{1}{4000}$
so $W = \underline{\dfrac{d^3}{4000}}$

b) When $d = 15$:
$W = \dfrac{15^3}{4000}$
$ = \dfrac{3375}{4000}$
$ = 0.84375$

So weight of a 15 cm ornament
$= \underline{0.84 \text{ kg (2 d.p.)}}$

c) When $W = 30$:
$30 = \dfrac{d^3}{4000}$
$d^3 = 30 \times 4000$
$ = 120\,000$
$d = \sqrt[3]{120\,000}$
$ = 49.324\,241\,48$

So diameter of the ornament
$= \underline{49 \text{ cm (to nearest cm)}}$

EXERCISE 25.1

1. y is directly proportional to x, and $y = 21$ when $x = 7$. Find the value of y when $x = 13$.

2. y is directly proportional to x, and $y = 15$ when $x = 6$. Find x when $y = 40$.

3. Each of the tables below shows a set of matching x and y values, where y is directly proportional to x. Find a formula for y in terms of x, and work out the missing values in each case.

   a)
x	1	2	3
y	2	4	

   b)
x	1	3		30
y		12	18	120

   c)
x	12	18		102
y		3	7	

   d)
x	2	8	
y		5	35

4. y is directly proportional to x, and it is known that $y = 10$ when $x = 15$.
   a) Obtain an equation for y in terms of x.
   b) Use your equation to find the values of:
      (i) y, when $x = 60$ (ii) x, when $y = 25$.

5. y is directly proportional to x^2, and it is known that $y = 20$ when $x = 10$.
   a) Obtain an equation for y in terms of x.
   b) Use your equation to find the values of:
      (i) y, when $x = 30$ (ii) x, when $y = 125$.

6. y is directly proportional to the square of x, and $y = 16$ when $x = 2$. Find y when $x = 3$.

7. y is directly proportional to the cube of x, and $y = 50$ when $x = 5$. Find y when $x = 8$.

8. Dave is working out different ways of travelling round Europe during his gap year. He is making maps showing the cities he might visit. The time, T minutes, that it takes Dave to draw a map is directly proportional to the square of the number of cities, c, he puts on the map. A map with 8 cities takes 10 minutes to draw.
   a) Find a formula for T in terms of c.
   b) Work out how long it would take to draw a map with 12 cities.
   c) Dave eventually spent an hour and a half making his map. How many cities did he decide to include?

9. My computer has a program that can work out the decimal value of π to a large numbers of digits. You can specify the number of digits required. The time it takes is directly proportional to the square of the number of digits specified.

   The computer can work out π to 5000 significant figures in exactly half a second.
   a) Find a formula for the number of digits, n, that the computer can work out in t seconds.
   b) Use the formula to find out how long it would take to calculate π to one million digits.
   c) How many digits can the computer work out in 10 minutes?

10. Square carpet tiles are sold in three sizes – small, medium and large. The cost of a carpet tile is directly proportional to the square of the diagonal dimension of the tile.

    Small tiles cost £2.70 each and have a diagonal of length 15 cm.
    a) A medium tile has diagonal of length 20 cm. Work out its cost.
    b) A large tile costs £10.80. Work out the length of its diagonal dimension.

25.2 Inverse proportion

Consider a rectangle whose area is fixed at 20 cm². Here are some possible dimensions for the rectangle:

20 cm
20 × 1 = 20
1 cm

5 cm
5 × 4 = 20
4 cm

10 cm
10 × 2 = 20
2 cm

Notice that, as one dimension goes down in size, the other one increases. The **product** of the two dimensions remains **constant**, that is, $xy = 20$, where x and y are the length and breadth of the rectangle respectively.

You could also write this as $y = \dfrac{20}{x}$. This type of relation is called **inverse proportion**.

You could write $y \propto \dfrac{1}{x}$. More formally, you would write $y = \dfrac{k}{x}$, where k is the constant of proportionality.

EXAMPLE

Two quantities x and y are such that y is inversely proportional to x.
When $x = 20$, $y = 6$.
a) Find a formula connecting x and y.
b) Work out the value of y when $x = 40$.
c) What is the value of x when y is 2?

SOLUTION

a) Let $y = \dfrac{k}{x}$. Substitute $x = 20$, $y = 6$ into this to obtain:

$6 = \dfrac{k}{20}$

$k = 20 \times 6$

$k = 120$

Thus the required formula is $y = \dfrac{120}{x}$

b) When $x = 40$:

$y = \dfrac{120}{x}$

$= \dfrac{120}{40}$

$y = 3$

c) When y is 2:

$y = \dfrac{120}{x}$

$2 = \dfrac{120}{x}$

$2x = 120$

$x = \dfrac{120}{2}$

$x = 60$

As with direct proportion, some inverse proportion problems can involve powers such as squares.

EXAMPLE

A scientist has squirted a droplet of oil on to the surface of a container of water. The oil has formed a circular patch, and is slowly expanding. The thickness of the circular patch of oil is inversely proportional to the square of its radius.

When the patch has radius 3 cm, its thickness is 60 microns (1 micron = 1×10^{-6} m). At any time, the radius is r cm and the thickness is d microns.
a) Write down a formula connecting d and r.
b) Find the thickness of the patch when the radius is 6 cm.
c) The scientist hopes to end up with an oil patch that is exactly 1 micron thick. What will the radius of the circular patch become if she can achieve this aim?

SOLUTION

a) Since d is inversely proportional to r squared, we have $d = \dfrac{k}{r^2}$

With $r = 3$ and $d = 60$:
$$d = \frac{k}{r^2}$$
$$60 = \frac{k}{9}$$
$$k = 9 \times 60$$
$$k = 540$$

Therefore the required formula is $d = \dfrac{540}{r^2}$

b) When $r = 6$,
$$d = \frac{540}{6^2}$$
$$= \frac{540}{36}$$
$$= 15 \text{ microns}$$

c) When $d = 1$:
$$1 = \frac{540}{r^2}$$
$$r^2 = 540$$
$$r = \sqrt{540}$$
$$= 23.2 \text{ cm (correct to 3 s.f.)}$$

EXERCISE 25.2

1. y is inversely proportional to x, and $y = 20$ when $x = 5$. Find the value of y when $x = 4$.

2. y is inversely proportional to x, and $y = 12$ when $x = 1$. Find x when $y = 4$.

3. Each of the tables below shows a set of matching x and y values, where y is inversely proportional to x. Find a formula for y in terms of x, and work out the missing values in each case.

   a)
x	1		30
y	60	12	

   b)
x		10	40
y	45		9

   c)
x	1	5	
y	1		4

   d)
x		4	10
y	5	1	

4. r is inversely proportional to t, and $r = 7$ when $t = 42$.
   a) Obtain an equation for r in terms of t.
   b) Use your equation to find the values of (i) t, when $r = 14$, (ii) r, when $t = 49$.

5. p is inversely proportional to s, and it is known that $p = 12$ when $s = 15$.
   a) Obtain an equation for p in terms of s.
   b) Use your equation to find the values of (i) p, when $s = 9$, (ii) s, when $p = 60$.

6. y is inversely proportional to the square of x, and $y = 9$ when $x = 16$. Find y when $x = 8$.

7. y is inversely proportional to the cube of x, and $y = 1$ when $x = 4$. Find x when $y = 8$.

8. Light intensity follows an inverse square law, that is, the intensity of light is inversely proportional to the square of the distance to the source of the light.

   A lamp is at a distance of 10 metres from a light detector, and it produces an intensity reading of 300 units.
   a) Find the intensity reading for a similar lamp, at a distance of 16 metres.
   b) How distant would the lamp need to be to in order to produce an intensity reading of 500 units?

9. A bowling machine is able to simulate the action of a fast bowler at cricket. The machine can project cricket balls at a batsman. The velocity, v km/h, at which a ball is projected is inversely proportional to the mass, m kg, of the ball.

   A regular cricket ball has a mass of 0.156 kg. The machine can project it at 54 km/h.
   a) Write a formula to express v in terms of m.
   b) A lightweight ball has a mass of 0.144 kg. How fast can the machine project the lightweight ball?

10. During the run-up to an election, a statistician is trying to forecast what percentage of the votes will be cast for each party. She takes a sample of voters, and uses their responses to make her forecast. The statistician knows that her forecast will only be accurate to within a certain amount, known as the standard error. The size of the standard error is inversely proportional to the square root of the number of voters in the sample.

    When a sample of 1067 voters is taken, the standard error is 3%.
    The statistician wants to improve her accuracy.
    Work out the number of voters to be sampled if the standard error is to be reduced to:
    a) 2%
    b) 1%.

25.3 Graphical representation of direct and inverse proportion

Look at the three graphs below.
Do you think any of them indicate that x and y are in direct proportion?

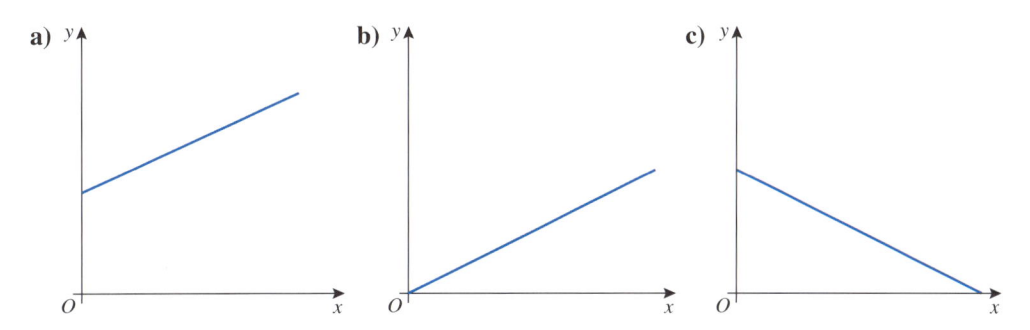

a) b) c)

All three graphs are linear, but only **b)** shows direct proportion, since the other two do not pass through the origin.

If y is **directly proportional** to x, then the graph of y against x *must* be a **straight line passing through the origin**.

Now look at the three graphs below.

Do you think any of them indicates that x and y are in inverse proportion?

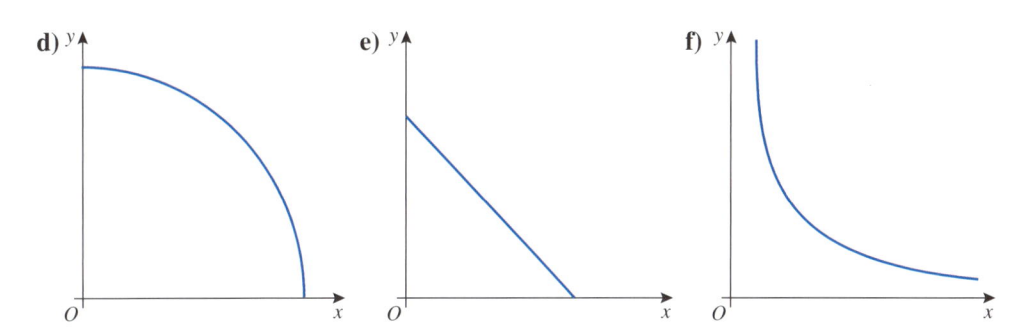

d) e) f)

All three graphs show that y decreases as x increases, but only **f)** does so in a way that matches the graph of $y = \dfrac{1}{x}$.

This distinctively shaped graph is called a **hyperbola**.

Note that **e)** shows a constant rate of decrease of y as x increases, but this is **not** the same as inverse proportion.

EXAMPLE

Look at the graphs and equations below. Only one of them is an example of y being directly proportional to x. Decide which one it is, giving a graphical explanation for your choice.

a) $y = 3x^2$

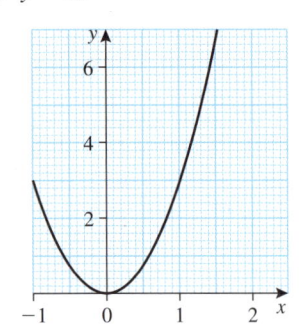

b) $y = 10 - x$

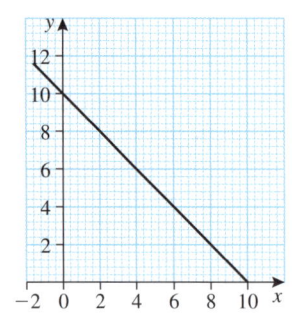

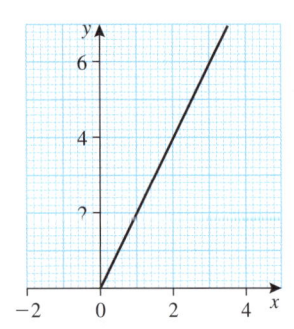

c) $y = 2x$

d) $y = x + 2$

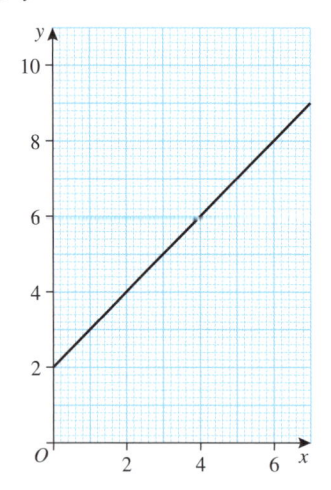

SOLUTION

For direct proportion, the graph of the equation must be a straight line through the origin.

a) $y = 3x^2$ — ✗ This passes through the origin but is not a straight line, due to the square term.

b) $y = 10 - x$ — ✗ This is a straight line but does not pass through the origin – it has a y intercept of 10.

c) $y = 2x$ — ✓ $y = 2x$ is of the form $y = kx$, so it indicates direct proportion. Its graph is a straight line through the origin.

d) $y = x + 2$ — ✗ This is a straight line but does not pass through the origin – it has a y intercept of 2.

Thus $y = 2x$ is the case where y is proportional to x

EXERCISE 25.3

Make a copy these six sketch graphs.
Alongside each, write 'Direct proportion', 'Inverse proportion' or 'Neither'.

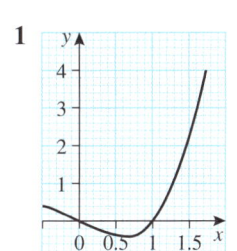

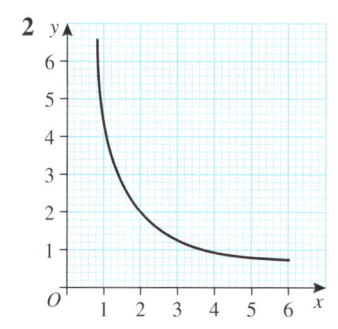

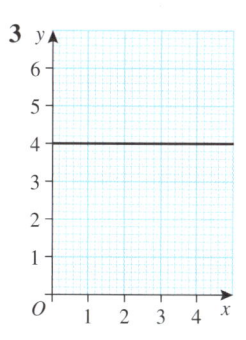

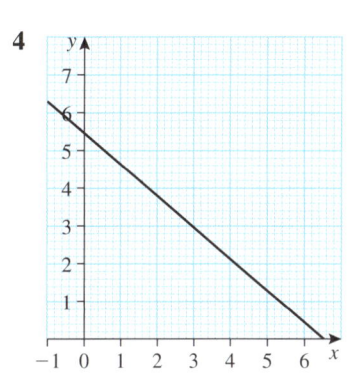

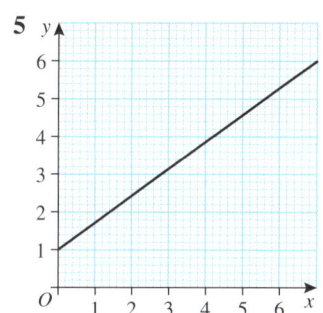

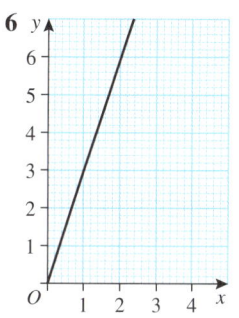

1.

2.

3.

4.

5.

6.

REVIEW EXERCISE 25

1. y is directly proportional to x, and $y = 21$ when $x = 7$. Find the value of y when $x = 13$.

2. y is inversely proportional to x, and $y = 8$ when $x = 4$. Find the value of y when $x = 16$.

3. y is directly proportional to x^2, and $y = 1$ when $x = 5$. Find the value of y when $x = 15$.

4. y is inversely proportional to x^3, and $y = 40$ when $x = 2$. Find the value of y when $x = 1$.

5. Hooke's Law says that the tension, T, in a stretched string is directly proportional to its extension, x.
   A certain string has a tension of 20 units when its extension is 30 units.
   a) Write down a formula to express T in terms of x.
   b) Find the tension T when the extension is 36 units.
   c) Work out the extension x when the tension is 48 units.

6. The periodic time, T seconds, that it takes a pendulum to complete one swing is directly proportional to the square root of the pendulum's length, l cm. A pendulum of length 25 cm has a periodic time of 1 second.
   a) Write a formula for T in terms of l.
   b) Find the periodic time for a pendulum of length 35 cm.

7 A weight is hung at the end of a beam of length L.
This causes the end of the beam to drop a distance d. d is directly proportional to the cube of L.
$d = 20$ when $L = 150$.

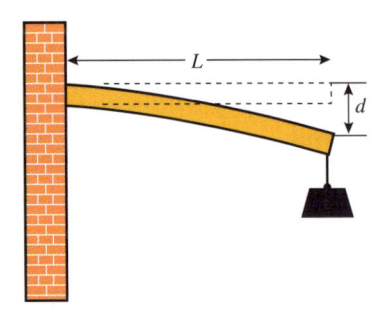

   a) Find a formula for d in terms of L.
   b) Calculate the value of L when $d = 15$. [Edexcel]

8 y is inversely proportional to x^2. $y = 3$ when $x = 4$.
   a) Write y in terms of x.
   b) Calculate the value of y when $x = 5$. [Edexcel]

9 y is directly proportional to x^2. When $x = 2$, $y = 36$.
   a) Express y in terms of x.

   z is inversely proportional to x. When $x = 3$, $z = 2$.
   b) Show that $z = cy^n$, where c and n are numbers and $c > 0$.
   (You must find the values of c and n.) [Edexcel]

10 y is inversely proportional to x. When $x = 3$, $y = 24$.
   a) Write a formula for y in terms of x.

   Hence, or otherwise,
   b) (i) calculate the value of y when $x = 6$
   (ii) calculate the value of x when $y = 4.8$. [Edexcel]

11 d is directly proportional to the square of t. $d = 80$ when $t = 4$.
   a) Express d in terms of t.
   b) Work out the value of d when $t = 7$.
   c) Work out the positive value of t when $d = 45$. [Edexcel]

12 The force, F, between two magnets is inversely proportional to the square of the distance, x, between them. When $x = 3$, $F = 4$.
   a) Find an expression for F in terms of x.
   b) Calculate F when $x = 2$.
   c) Calculate x when $F = 64$. [Edexcel]

13 A car travelling at a speed of V metres per second has a stopping distance of d metres.
The straight-line graph of $\frac{d}{V}$ against V has been drawn on the grid.

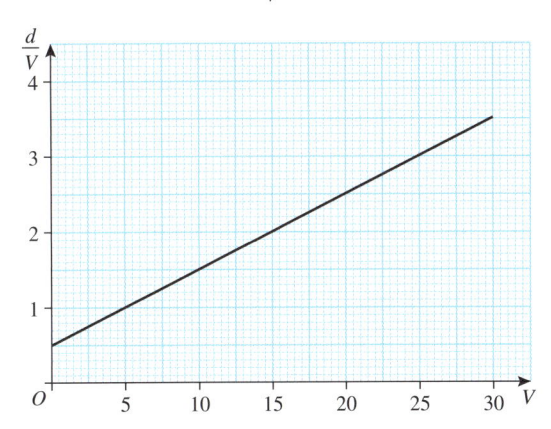

The car travels at a speed of 18 m s^{-1}.
a) Use the straight-line graph to find the stopping distance of the car.
b) By first finding the equation of the line, obtain a formula for d in terms of V.

14 The shutter speed, S, of a camera varies inversely as the square of the aperture setting, f.
When $f = 8$, $S = 125$.
a) Find a formula for S in terms of f.
b) Hence, or otherwise, calculate the value of S when $f = 4$. [Edexcel]

KEY POINTS

1. When y is directly proportional to x, we can write $y = kx$ where k is a constant.

   The graph of y against x will then be a straight line through the origin:

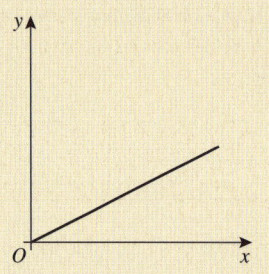

2. When y is inversely proportional to x, we can write $y = \dfrac{k}{x}$ where k is a constant.

   The graph of y against x will then be a curve (more particularly, a hyperbola):

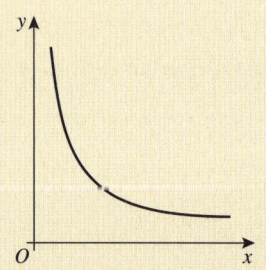

3. GCSE questions will often tell you that y is directly (or inversely) proportional to some power of x, and will give you an x value and a corresponding y value. You should set up an equation using k (e.g. $y = kx^2$) and then use the given x and y values to determine the value of k. This formula can then be used to answer the rest of the question.

Internet Challenge 25

The planets and their orbits

The table shows information about the orbits of the eight planets in our Solar System.

The time T years it takes for a planet to complete one orbit around the Sun is directly proportional to the 1.5th power of its mean distance d from the Sun. For simplicity, the distances have been scaled so that the Earth–Sun distance is 1 unit. The orbital period of the Earth is 1 year.

Planet	Mean distance, d, from the Sun (Earth–Sun = 1 unit)	Orbital period, T (years)
Mercury	0.387	
Venus	0.723	
Earth	1	1
Mars	1.524	
Jupiter	5.203	
Saturn	9.529	
Uranus	19.19	
Neptune	30.06	

1. Use the fact that $T \propto d^{1.5}$ to show that Mars has an orbital period of 1.88 years.

2. Copy and complete the table to include the orbital periods for all the outer planets, namely Mars to Neptune.

3. In a similar way, work out the orbital periods for the inner planets, Mercury and Venus. These should each be less than 1 year, so give your answer in days.

4. Now use the internet to check that you have worked out these orbital periods correctly.

5. The $T \propto d^{1.5}$ law was one of three published by the astronomer Johannes Kepler. Use the internet to find out about Kepler's other laws.

6. In 2003, a remote object named Sedna was discovered far beyond Neptune. Sedna's mean distance from the Sun is approximately 510 times the Sun–Earth distance. Use Kepler's laws to calculate the orbital period for Sedna. Give your answer to the nearest 100 years.

7. Is Sedna really a planet? Is Pluto? Use the internet to help you decide.

CHAPTER 26

Quadratic equations

In this chapter you will **learn how to**:

- solve quadratic equations by factorising
- solve quadratics by the general formula
- set up and solve problems using quadratics
- sketch the graphs of quadratics, using the completing the square method.

You will also be **challenged to**:

- investigate conic sections.

Starter: Solutions of equations

Here are some equations, and some suggested solutions.

Substitute the suggested values into each equation to discover which are correct.

Equation	Suggested solutions
$5x + 3 = 18$	$x = 1, x = 2, x = 3, x = 4, x = 5$
$5x^2 + 4 = 9$	$x = -1, x = 0, x = 1, x = 2, x = 3$
$x^2 = 7x - 10$	$x = 1, x = 2, x = 3, x = 4, x = 5$
$12x - 3 = 45$	$x = 1, x = 2, x = 3, x = 4$
$x^2 = 1$	$x = -2, x = -1, x = 0, x = 1, x = 2$
$x + 4 = 10 - x$	$x = 0, x = 1, x = 2, x = 3, x = 4$
$x(x + 1) = 2$	$x = -2, x = -1, x = 0, x = 1, x = 2$
$x^2 = 36$	$x = -6, x = -3, x = 0, x = 3, x = 6$
$4x^2 = 100$	$x = -5, x = -3, x = 0, x = 1, x = 5$
$x^3 - 6x^2 + 11x - 6 = 0$	$x = 1, x = 2, x = 3, x = 4, x = 5$

Here is an extract from an old mathematics book:

> *Linear equations like $3x + 5 = 21$ have only one solution. Equations containing an x^2 term often have two solutions, however, and equations containing x^3 terms may have as many as three solutions.*

Do your results support this extract?

26.1 Solving quadratic equations – factorising

An equation like $x^2 + 4x + 3 = 0$ is called a **quadratic equation**. Quadratic equations must contain a square term (such as the x^2 in this example), with no higher power of x, such as x^3. You may be able to spot a solution of a quadratic equation by inspection (i.e. by guesswork), but this is not a reliable method because quadratics may have two solutions. **Factorising** (see Chapter 5) is a method of making sure that all of the solutions to a quadratic equation are found.

EXAMPLE

Solve the equation $x^2 + 4x + 3 = 0$

SOLUTION

$x^2 + 4x + 3 = 0$
$(x + 1)(x + 3) = 0$ ← If $(x + 1)(x + 3) = 0$ then one of the brackets must be equal to 0.
$x + 1 = 0$ or $x + 3 = 0$
So, $x = -1$ or $x = -3$

Factorisation can be more difficult, especially if the coefficient of x^2 is greater than 1.

EXAMPLE

Solve the equation $2x^2 - 9x - 5 = 0$

SOLUTION

$2x^2 - 9x - 5 = 0$
$(2x + 1)(x - 5) = 0$
$2x + 1 = 0$ or $x - 5 = 0$
So, $x = -\frac{1}{2}$ or $x = 5$

Some quadratics contain only two terms, not three. If the constant term at the end is missing, then all you need to do is take out a common factor of x.

EXAMPLE

Solve the equation $10x^2 - 4x = 0$

SOLUTION

$10x^2 - 4x = 0$
$2x(5x - 2) = 0$
$2x = 0$ or $5x - 2 = 0$
So, $x = 0$ or $x = \frac{2}{5}$

If, instead, the middle term is missing, then you can simply solve to find x^2. Then take the square root of both sides to find x. Remember to allow for both positive and negative answers.

EXAMPLE

Solve the equation $5x^2 - 80 = 0$

SOLUTION

$5x^2 - 80 = 0$
$5x^2 = 80$
$x^2 = \dfrac{80}{5}$
$x^2 = 16$
Square rooting both sides gives:
$x = 4$ or $x = -4$

Alternatively, by factorising:
$5x^2 - 80 = 0$
$5(x^2 - 16) = 0$
$5(x - 4)(x + 4) = 0$
and so $x = 4$ or $x = -4$

EXERCISE 26.1

Solve each of these quadratic equations by using the factorisation method.

1 $x^2 + 3x + 2 = 0$
2 $x^2 + 6x + 5 = 0$
3 $x^2 + 7x - 8 = 0$
4 $x^2 + x - 2 = 0$
5 $x^2 + 2x - 8 = 0$
6 $x^2 + 4x - 12 = 0$
7 $x^2 - 7x + 12 = 0$
8 $x^2 - 8x + 15 = 0$
9 $x^2 - 2x - 8 = 0$
10 $x^2 - 4x + 4 = 0$
11 $2x^2 + 3x + 1 = 0$
12 $2x^2 + 5x - 3 = 0$
13 $3x^2 + 7x + 2 = 0$
14 $2x^2 + x - 3 = 0$
15 $3x^2 + 8x + 4 = 0$
16 $2x^2 - 9x + 9 = 0$
17 $3x^2 + 8x + 5 = 0$
18 $2x^2 - 9x + 10 = 0$
19 $5x^2 + 26x + 5 = 0$
20 $4x^2 + 4x + 1 = 0$

Here are some more difficult quadratic equations. Solve them by the factorisation method.

21 $6x^2 + x - 1 = 0$
22 $5x^2 - x = 0$
23 $4x^2 - 1 = 0$
24 $3x^2 - 3x = 0$
25 $12x^2 - 7x + 1 = 0$
26 $10x^2 - x = 0$
27 $8x^2 - 10x + 3 = 0$
28 $8x^2 - 11x + 3 = 0$
29 $4x^2 + 12x + 9 = 0$
30 $4x^2 - 9 = 0$

Rearrange these quadratic equations so that the right-hand side is zero. Then solve them, by factorisation.

31 $x^2 - 6x = 7$
32 $x^2 + 40 = 13x$
33 $x^2 + 20x = 7x - 30$
34 $x^2 + 10x = 3x + 44$
35 $2x^2 = 11x + 6$
36 $8 - 23x = 3x^2$
37 $2 = x + 3x^2$
38 $4x^2 = 8x - 3$
39 $6x^2 + 6x = x + 6$
40 $5x^2 + 30 = x^2 + 55$

26.2 Solving quadratic equations – formula

A quadratic equation contains three **coefficients**. For example,

$x^2 + 4x + 3 = 0$

has an x^2 coefficient of 1, an x coefficient of 4 and a constant term of 3.

$2x^2 - 4x - 1 = 0$ has an x^2 coefficient of 2, an x coefficient of -4 and a constant term of -1.

Similarly, $4x^2 - 1 = 0$ has an x^2 coefficient of 4, an x coefficient of 0 and a constant term of -1.

There is a formula that can be used to find solutions to a quadratic equation. If $ax^2 + bx + c = 0$ is a quadratic equation, then the solutions are given by the formula:

$$x = \frac{-b \pm \sqrt{b^2 - 4ac}}{2a}$$

The sign $\pm$ is read as 'plus or minus'.

You obtain one of the solutions of the quadratic by using $x = \dfrac{-b + \sqrt{b^2 - 4ac}}{2a}$

and the other one by using $x = \dfrac{-b - \sqrt{b^2 - 4ac}}{2a}$.

The formula method can be applied to a much wider range of quadratic equations than the factorising method. You would normally use the formula if the equation cannot be factorised in an obvious way. The quadratic formula will be given to you in a GCSE exam. It will be on the formula sheet.

EXAMPLE

Solve the equation $2x^2 - 4x - 1 = 0$. Give your answers to 3 decimal places.

SOLUTION

There is no obvious factorisation, so use the formula.
Inspecting the equation, $a = 2$, $b = -4$ and $c = -1$.
Then substituting these values into the formula:

$$x = \frac{-b \pm \sqrt{b^2 - 4ac}}{2a}$$

gives

$$x = \frac{-(-4) \pm \sqrt{(-4)^2 - 4(2)(-1)}}{2(2)}$$

$$= \frac{4 \pm \sqrt{16 + 8}}{4}$$

$$= \frac{4 \pm \sqrt{24}}{4}$$

$= 2.224\,744\,871$ or $-0.224\,744\,871$

$= \underline{2.225}$ or $\underline{-0.225}$ (3 d.p.)

If you are asked to solve a quadratic equation in an exam, and the number that you calculate under the square root sign is negative, for example $\sqrt{-25}$, then you know you must have made an error.

EXERCISE 26.2

Solve these equations using the quadratic equation formula. Give your answers correct to 3 decimal places.

1 $x^2 + 5x + 2 = 0$
2 $x^2 + 10x + 7 = 0$
3 $2x^2 - 14x + 13 = 0$
4 $2x^2 + 11x - 5 = 0$
5 $x^2 - 7x + 1 = 0$
6 $3x^2 + 2x - 3 = 0$
7 $x^2 + 5x - 1 = 0$
8 $2x^2 - 3x - 4 = 0$
9 $5x^2 - x - 1 = 0$
10 $2x^2 + 9x - 2 = 0$

Rearrange the equations below so that they are in the form $ax^2 + bx + c = 0$. Then solve them using the formula method. Give your answers correct to 3 significant figures.

11 $x^2 + 5x = 7$
12 $2x^2 = 3x + 1$
13 $3x^2 = 5 + 4x$
14 $x^2 + x = 2 - 9x$
15 $11x = 1 - 2x^2$
16 $3x^2 = 12x + 1$
17 $2x = 5x^2 - 4$
18 $21x + 1 = 7x^2$
19 $20x + 4 = 3x - 6x^2$
20 $9x^2 = 2 + x$

26.3 Problems leading to quadratic equations

At Higher Tier GCSE you may be expected to set up a problem that leads to a solution involving a quadratic equation. You will then need to solve the quadratic equation to complete the problem.

EXAMPLE

A rectangular flower bed measures $2x + 5$ metres by $x + 3$ metres.
It has an area of 45 square metres.
a) Draw a sketch to show this information.
b) Show that x must satisfy the equation $2x^2 + 11x - 30 = 0$.
c) Solve this equation, to find the value of x. Hence find the dimensions of the flower bed.

SOLUTION

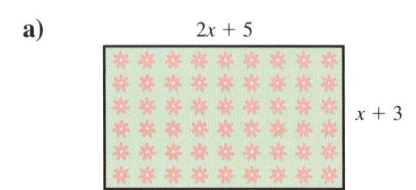

a) [sketch of rectangle with width $2x + 5$ and height $x + 3$]

b) $(2x + 5)(x + 3) = 45$
    $2x^2 + 5x + 6x + 15 = 45$
    $2x^2 + 11x + 15 = 45$
    $2x^2 + 11x - 30 = 0$

c) Factorising $2x^2 + 11x - 30 = 0$ gives:
$$(2x + 15)(x - 2) = 0$$
So, $2x + 15 = 0$ or $x - 2 = 0$

Therefore $x = -7\frac{1}{2}$ or $x = 2$

But $x = -7\frac{1}{2}$ will lead to negative dimensions for the flower bed, so it must be rejected.
Therefore $x = 2$

We know that the dimensions of the flower bed are:
$$2x + 5 \text{ metres by } x + 3 \text{ metres}$$

Substituting $x = 2$ gives dimensions of 9 metres by 5 metres

EXERCISE 26.3

1 Two whole numbers x and $x + 7$ are multiplied together. The result is 144.
   a) Write down an equation in x.
   b) Show that this equation can be expressed as $x^2 + 7x - 144 = 0$.
   c) Solve the equation, to find the values of the two whole numbers (there are two possible sets of answers, and you should give both).

2 A rectangular playing field is x metres wide and $2x - 5$ metres long. Its area is 3000 m².
   a) Write down an equation in x.
   b) Show that this equation can be expressed as $2x^2 - 5x = 3000$
   c) Solve the equation, to find the value of x. Hence find the dimensions of the playing field.

3 Hannah and Jamal each thought of a positive whole number. Jamal's number was 3 more than Hannah's number. Let Hannah's number be represented by x.
   a) Their two numbers multiply together to make 180. Write down an equation in x.
   b) Show that this equation can be expressed as $x^2 + 3x - 180 = 0$
   c) Solve the equation, and hence find the numbers that Hannah and Jamal thought of.

4 A square measures x cm along each side, and a rectangle measures x cm by $2x + 1$ cm. The total area of the square and the rectangle is 114 cm².
   a) Write down an equation in x.
   b) Show that this equation can be expressed as $3x^2 + x - 114 = 0$
   c) Solve the equation, to find the value of x.

5 A rectangle measures $3x + 1$ cm by $2x + 5$ cm. Two squares, each of side x cm, are removed from it. The remaining shape has an area of 55 cm².
   a) Express this information as an equation in x.
   b) Show that this equation can be expressed as $4x^2 + 17x - 50 = 0$
   c) Solve your equation, and hence find the dimensions of the rectangle.

6 A rectangle measures x cm by $2x + 3$ cm. A second rectangle measures $x + 3$ cm by $x + 4$ cm.
   a) Write down expressions for the areas of the two rectangles.

   Both rectangles have the same area.
   b) Write an equation in x.
   c) Solve this equation. Hence determine the dimensions of each rectangle.

26.4 Completing the square

If a quadratic expression can be factorised into two identical brackets then it is called a **perfect square**. For example, $x^2 + 6x + 9$ is a perfect square, because it can be factorised into $(x + 3)(x + 3)$. You would write $x^2 + 6x + 9 = (x + 3)^2$, or, more correctly, $x^2 + 6x + 9 \equiv (x + 3)^2$ since this is an *identity*, not just an equation.

Other quadratics can be factorised into two identical brackets plus an extra part. For example, if you were given $x^2 + 6x + 13$, you could write it as $x^2 + 6x + 9 + 4$, which could then be factorised to give the result $x^2 + 6x + 9 + 4 \equiv (x + 3)^2 + 4$. This method is called **completing the square**.

EXAMPLE

Write the following quadratics in the form $(x + a)^2 + b$, stating the values of a and b.
a) $x^2 + 10x + 21$
b) $x^2 - 6x + 17$

SOLUTION

a) $x^2 + 10x + 21$
The coefficient of x is 10, and half of this is 5.
Consider $(x + 5)^2 = x^2 + 10x + 25$
Therefore $x^2 + 10x + 21 = x^2 + 10x + 25 - 4$
$= (x + 5)^2 - 4$
So, $a = 5$ and $b = -4$

> In each case, finding half the value of the original x coefficient will allow you to choose a suitable value for a.

b) $x^2 - 6x + 17$
The coefficient of x is -6, and half of this is -3.
Consider $(x - 3)^2 = x^2 - 6x + 9$
Therefore $x^2 - 6x + 17 = x^2 - 6x + 9 + 8$
$= (x - 3)^2 + 8$
So, $a = -3$ and $b = 8$

> (This will work for all such problems, but if you go on to study A Level Mathematics you will need to adapt the method when the x^2 coefficient is not 1.)

The graph of a quadratic function will always give a distinctive curve called a **parabola**. The parabola will look like a trough if the x^2 coefficient of the quadratic is positive, with a minimum point at the base of the trough. If the x^2 coefficient is negative, the trough will be inverted, with a maximum point at the top of the parabola.

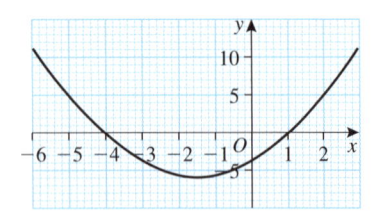

$y = x^2 + 3x - 4$
Positive x^2 coefficient → trough
Minimum point

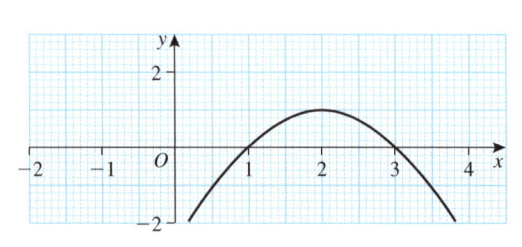

$y = -x^2 + 4x - 3$
Negative x^2 coefficient → inverted trough
Maximum point

The method of completing the square into $(x + a)^2 + b$ can give you useful information that will help to make a sketch of the curve. Since $(x + a)^2 + b$ has a positive x^2 coefficient, the parabola will have a minimum point, rather than a maximum. This will occur when the $(x + a)^2$ term is zero. This means that the corresponding y coordinate is then simply b.

The graph of $y = (x + a)^2 + b$ will be a parabola with a minimum at the point $(-a, b)$ and a line of symmetry at $x = -a$.

EXAMPLE

a) Write the expression $x^2 + 8x + 19$ in the form $(x + a)^2 + b$, giving the values of a and b.
b) Write down the minimum value of $x^2 + 8x + 19$. Then write down the value of x when this occurs.
c) Write down the coordinates at the point where the curve crosses the y axis.
d) Hence sketch the graph of $y = x^2 + 8x + 19$.

SOLUTION

a) $x^2 + 8x + 19$
The coefficient of x is 8, and half of this is 4.
Consider $(x + 4)^2 = x^2 + 8x + 16$
Therefore $x^2 + 8x + 19 = x^2 + 8x + 16 + 3$
$= (x + 4)^2 + 3$

b) The graph will have a minimum when $x + 4 = 0$, giving $y = 3$
The corresponding x value is given by $x + 4 = 0$. So, $x = -4$

c) The curve crosses the y axis when
$x = 0$.
$y = 0^2 + 8 \times 0 + 19$
$y = 19$
So the coordinates are $(0, 19)$

d) Therefore the graph will look like this:

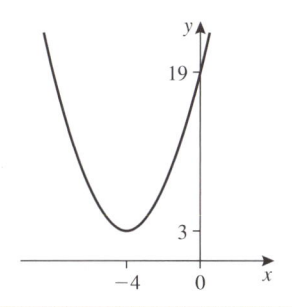

EXERCISE 26.4

1 Write the following expressions in the form $(x + a)^2 + b$, giving the values of a and b:
   a) $x^2 + 4x + 15$
   b) $x^2 + 10x + 2$

2 Write the expression $x^2 - 6x + 10$ in the form $(x - p)^2 + q$, giving the values of p and q.

3 Write the expression $x^2 - 14x + 50$ in the form $(x - f)^2 + g$, giving the values of f and g.

4 Write the expression $x^2 - 12x + 30$ in the form $(x + a)^2 + b$, giving the values of a and b.

5 a) Write the expression $x^2 + 16x + 39$ in the form $(x + a)^2 + b$, giving the values of a and b.
   b) Sketch the graph of $y = x^2 + 16x + 39$, marking the coordinates of the minimum point on the curve.

6 a) Write the expression $x^2 + 20x + 90$ in the form $(x + a)^2 + b$, giving the values of a and b.
   b) Sketch the graph of $y = x^2 + 20x + 90$, marking the coordinates of the minimum point on the curve.

7 a) Write the expression $x^2 + 2x + 5$ in the form $(x + a)^2 + b$, giving the values of a and b.
   b) Sketch the graph of $y = x^2 + 2x + 5$, marking the coordinates of the minimum point on the curve.

8 a) Write the expression $x^2 + 24x + 150$ in the form $(x + a)^2 + b$, giving the values of a and b.
   b) Sketch the graph of $y = x^2 + 24x + 150$, marking the coordinates of the minimum point on the curve.

9 a) Use the method of completing the square to help you sketch the graph of the function:
   $y = x^2 + 12x + 36$.
   b) The graph has a vertical line of symmetry. Give the equation of this line.

REVIEW EXERCISE 26

1 a) Factorise $x^2 - 6x + 8$.   **b)** Solve the equation $x^2 - 6x + 8 = 0$.   [Edexcel]

2 Solve the equation $(2x - 3)^2 = 100$.   [Edexcel]

3 Find the solutions of the equation $x^2 - 4x - 1 = 0$.
Give your solutions correct to three decimal places.   [Edexcel]

4 $(x + 3)(x - 2) = 1$.
   a) Show that $x^2 + x - 7 = 0$.
   b) Solve the equation $x^2 + x - 7 = 0$.
   Give your answers correct to 3 significant figures.   [Edexcel]

5 The length of a rectangle is $(x + 4)$ cm.
The width is $(x - 3)$ cm.
The area of the rectangle is 78 cm².
   a) Use this information to write down an equation in terms of x.
   b) (i) Show that your equation in part **a)** can be written as $x^2 + x - 90 = 0$.
       (ii) Find the values of x which are solutions of the equation $x^2 + x - 90 = 0$.
       (iii) Write down the length and the width of the rectangle.   [Edexcel]

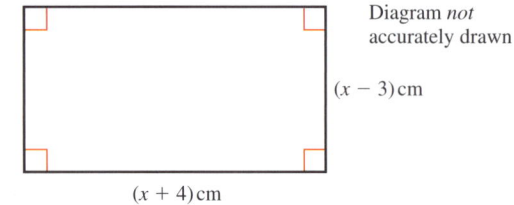

Diagram *not* accurately drawn

6 AT is a tangent to a circle, centre O. OT = x cm, AT = $(x + 5)$ cm and OA = $(x + 8)$ cm.

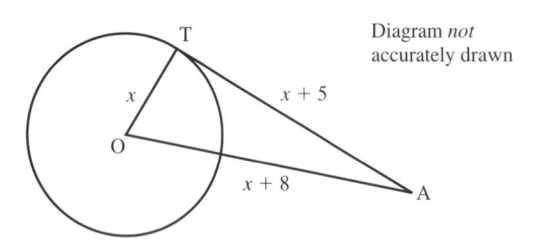

Diagram *not* accurately drawn

   a) Show that $x^2 - 6x - 39 = 0$.
   b) Solve the equation $x^2 - 6x - 39 = 0$ to find the radius of the circle.
   Give your answer correct to 3 significant figures.   [Edexcel]

7 The diagram shows a prism.
   The cross section of the prism is a right-angled triangle.
   The lengths of the sides of the triangle are $3x$ cm, $4x$ cm and $5x$ cm.
   The total length of all the edges of the prism is E cm.
   a) Show that the length, L cm, of the prism is given by the formula $L = \frac{1}{3}(E - 24x)$.
   The surface area, A cm^2, of the prism is given by the formula $A = 12x^2 + 12Lx$. $E = 98$ cm and $A = 448$ cm.
   b) Substitute these values into the formulae of L and A to show that x satisfies the equation $3x^2 - 14x + 16 = 0$. Make the stages in your working clear.
   c) Solve the equation $3x^2 - 14x + 16 = 0$. [Edexcel]

8 The diagram shows a trapezium.
   The measurements on the diagram are in centimetres.
   The lengths of the parallel sides are x cm and 20 cm. The height of the trapezium is $2x$ cm.
   The area of the trapezium is 400 cm^2.
   a) Show that $x^2 + 20x = 400$.
   b) Find the value of x. Give your answer correct to 3 decimal places. [Edexcel]

9 You are given that $x^2 + 8x - 5 \equiv (x + a)^2 + b$, where a and b are integers.
   a) Explain the meaning of the symbol $\equiv$.
   b) Determine the values of a and b.

10 a) Express $x^2 - 10x + 32$ in the form $(x + a)^2 + b$, giving the values of a and b.
   b) Sketch the graph of $y = x^2 - 10x + 32$, marking the coordinates of the minimum point on the curve.

11 For all values of x and m, $x^2 - 2mx = (x - m)^2 - k$.
   a) Express k in terms of m.
   The expression $x^2 - 2mx$ has a minimum value as x varies.
   b) (i) Find the minimum value of $x^2 - 2mx$. Give your answer in terms of m.
      (ii) State the value of x for which this minimum occurs.
           Give your answer in terms of m. [Edexcel]

12 a) (i) Factorise $2x^2 - 35x + 98$.
      (ii) Solve the equation $2x^2 - 35x + 98 = 0$.
   A bag contains $(n + 7)$ tennis balls. n of the balls are yellow. The other seven balls are white.
   John will take a ball at random from the bag. He will look at its colour and then put it back in the bag.
   b) (i) Write down an expression, in terms of n, for the probability that John will take a white ball.
           Bill states that the probability that John will take a white ball is $\frac{2}{5}$.
      (ii) Prove that Bill's statement cannot be correct.
   After John has put the ball back into the bag, Mary will then take at random a ball from the bag.
   She will note its colour.
   c) Given that the probability that John and Mary will take balls with different colours is $\frac{4}{9}$, prove that $2n^2 - 35n + 98 = 0$.
   d) Using your answer to part a) ii), or otherwise, calculate the probability that John and Mary will both take white balls. [Edexcel]

KEY POINTS

1. Quadratic equations contain a term in x^2, and are often written in the form $ax^2 + bx + c = 0$. Sometimes a solution may seem obvious, but you should always use formal methods to solve the equation fully since quadratics can have two solutions.

2. If the factors of a quadratic are easy to spot, then the factorising method is best.

   Otherwise, use the quadratic equation formula:
   $$x = \frac{-b \pm \sqrt{b^2 - 4ac}}{2a}$$

3. If an exam question asks you to solve a quadratic correct to 3 significant figures, this is a clue that the quadratic formula will be required.

4. The graph of any quadratic expression will always follow a distinctive curve called a parabola. There will be one minimum (or maximum) point, and the curve will have mirror symmetry.

5. Completing the square is a method whereby a quadratic is rewritten into the form $(x + a)^2 + b$. This enables you to locate the minimum point at $(-a, b)$, which is helpful when drawing a sketch graph of the curve.

Internet Challenge 26

Conic sections

In this chapter you have been sketching graphs of quadratic equations, using the fact that such graphs always take the shape of a parabola. The parabola belongs to a family of curves called conic sections.

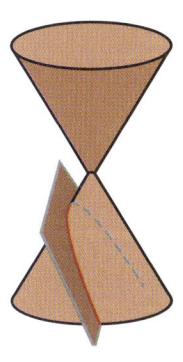

1 The diagram above shows a plane slice through a cone. The slice is parallel to one edge of the cone. What shape is the curve (marked in red) where the plane cuts the cone?

2 The parabola is one of four conic sections. Use the internet to find out the names of the other three.

3 Draw up a set of coordinate axes on squared paper. Then draw some line segments like this:

   Join the point (10, 0) to the origin (0, 0)
   Join (9, 0) to (0, 1)
   Join (8, 0) to (0, 2), etc.

   You should see a curve forming inside these lines. Is it a conic section? If so, which one?

4 When a body such as a planet or a comet moves through the Solar System, it traces out a path known as its orbit. The Earth's orbit, for example, is an ellipse. What shapes are the orbits followed by other bodies in the Solar System?

5 Use the internet to find a method for drawing an ellipse using a string and two drawing pins. Then use the method to draw some ellipses. Is this a good method?

CHAPTER 27

Advanced algebra

In this chapter you will **revise earlier work on**:
- adding algebraic fractions.

You will **learn how to**:
- manipulate and simplify surds
- add algebraic fractions, and solve equations containing them
- solve simultaneously one linear and one quadratic equation
- change the subject of an equation when the symbol occurs twice
- work with exponential growth and decay.

You will also be **challenged to**:
- investigate well-known mathematical formulae.

Starter: How many shapes?

Count the squares and rectangles in this 2 by 2 grid. You should be able to find nine.

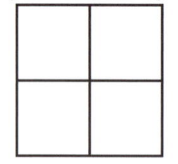

Now count the number of squares and rectangles in these grids. Try to work systematically.

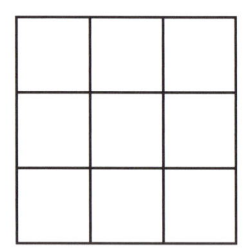

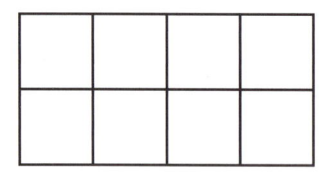

It is suggested that the number of squares or rectangles contained within a grid measuring m by n is given by an expression of the form:

$$\frac{m(m+1)n(n+1)}{k}$$

where k is a fixed number.

Assuming this expression is correct, use your results to work out the value of k.

Now try to prove that this expression is correct, using algebra.

27.1 Working with surds

Some quantities in mathematics can only be written exactly using a square root symbol.

For example, if $x^2 = 5$, then the exact value of x is $\sqrt{5}$ (or $-\sqrt{5}$).

Quantities like these, written using roots, are called **surds**.
Note that $\sqrt{5} \times \sqrt{5} = 5$.

Some surds can be simplified by writing them in terms of simpler surds. You should look for roots of perfect squares (4, 9, 16, 25, etc.) to help achieve this.

EXAMPLE

Simplify $\sqrt{48}$

SOLUTION

Since $48 = 16 \times 3$
$$\begin{aligned}\sqrt{48} &= \sqrt{16 \times 3} \\ &= \sqrt{16} \times \sqrt{3} \\ &= \underline{4\sqrt{3}}\end{aligned}$$

EXAMPLE

Write $\sqrt{48} + \sqrt{27}$ as a single surd term.

SOLUTION

$$\begin{aligned}\sqrt{48} + \sqrt{27} &= \sqrt{16 \times 3} + \sqrt{9 \times 3} \\ &= \sqrt{16} \times \sqrt{3} + \sqrt{9} \times \sqrt{3} \\ &= 4\sqrt{3} + 3\sqrt{3} \\ &= \underline{7\sqrt{3}}\end{aligned}$$

If you need to multiply two surd expressions together, just follow the ordinary rules for multiplying algebraic expressions.

EXAMPLE

A rectangle has a length of $(2 + \sqrt{5})$ cm and a width of $(3 - \sqrt{5})$ cm.
a) Show this information on a sketch.
b) Find the perimeter of the rectangle.
c) Find the area of the rectangle.

SOLUTION

a)

$(2 + \sqrt{5})$

$(3 - \sqrt{5})$

b) Perimeter $= (2 + \sqrt{5}) + (3 - \sqrt{5}) + (2 + \sqrt{5}) + (3 - \sqrt{5})$
$= \underline{10 \text{ cm}}$

c) Area $= (2 + \sqrt{5})(3 - \sqrt{5})$
$= 2 \times 3 - 2 \times \sqrt{5} + \sqrt{5} \times 3 - \sqrt{5} \times \sqrt{5}$
$= 6 - 2\sqrt{5} + 3\sqrt{5} - 5$
$= \underline{1 + \sqrt{5} \text{ cm}^2}$

Sometimes you might meet a fraction with a single surd in the denominator (bottom). It is usually a good idea to multiply the top and the bottom of the fraction by this surd, so that the bottom becomes a simple whole number instead. This process is called **rationalising the denominator**.

EXAMPLE

Write $\dfrac{3 + 2\sqrt{2}}{\sqrt{2}}$ in a form that does not have surds in the denominator.

SOLUTION

$\dfrac{3 + 2\sqrt{2}}{\sqrt{2}} = \dfrac{(3 + 2\sqrt{2})}{\sqrt{2}} \times \dfrac{\sqrt{2}}{\sqrt{2}}$

$= \dfrac{3\sqrt{2} + 2\sqrt{2}\sqrt{2}}{\sqrt{2}\sqrt{2}}$

$= \dfrac{3\sqrt{2} + 4}{2}$

When you solve a quadratic equation by the formula, you will end up with a result containing a square root sign. Instead of using a calculator to work out the answer to 3 or 4 significant figures, you could instead be asked to give an exact answer using surds.

EXAMPLE

Solve the equation $x^2 - 10x + 3 = 0$ using the quadratic equation formula. Leave your answer in surd form.

SOLUTION

For the equation $x^2 - 10x + 3 = 0$ we have $a = 1, b = -10, c = 3$.

$$x = \frac{-b \pm \sqrt{b^2 - 4ac}}{2a}$$

$$= \frac{-(-10) \pm \sqrt{(-10)^2 - 4 \times 1 \times 3}}{2 \times 1}$$

$$= \frac{10 \pm \sqrt{100 - 12}}{2} = \frac{10 \pm \sqrt{88}}{2}$$

$$= \frac{10 \pm 2\sqrt{22}}{2} = \underline{5 \pm \sqrt{22}}$$

EXERCISE 27.1

Simplify the following surds.

1 $\sqrt{18}$ 2 $\sqrt{32}$ 3 $\sqrt{50}$ 4 $\sqrt{45}$ 5 $\sqrt{150}$ 6 $\sqrt{24}$ 7 $\sqrt{99}$ 8 $\sqrt{108}$

Write each of these as a single surd term.

9 $\sqrt{48} + \sqrt{12}$ 10 $\sqrt{8} + \sqrt{50}$ 11 $\sqrt{75} - \sqrt{12}$

12 $\sqrt{18} + \sqrt{32}$ 13 $\sqrt{11} + \sqrt{99}$ 14 $\sqrt{98} - \sqrt{18}$

15 Simplify $\sqrt{3}(4 + 2\sqrt{12})$ 16 Simplify $(6 + \sqrt{2})(1 + \sqrt{2})$ 17 Simplify $(5 - \sqrt{3})(5 + \sqrt{3})$

18 Simplify $(4 + \sqrt{5})(3 + 2\sqrt{5})$ 19 Simplify $\dfrac{3 + 2\sqrt{5}}{\sqrt{5}}$

20 A rectangle measures $4 + \sqrt{28}$ cm long by $5 - \sqrt{7}$ cm wide.
   a) Write the length of the rectangle in its simplest form.
   b) Work out the perimeter of the rectangle. Give your answer as an exact surd, in its simplest form.
   c) Work out the area of the rectangle. Give your answer as an exact surd, in its simplest form.

Solve each of the following quadratic equations, using the quadratic formula. Leave your answers in surd form.

21 $x^2 + 4x - 7 = 0$ 22 $x^2 + x - 1 = 0$ 23 $x^2 + 3x - 1 = 0$

24 $2x^2 + 8x + 3 = 0$ 25 $x^2 - 5x + 2 = 0$

27.2 Algebraic fractions and equations

In Chapter 5 you were introduced to the idea of adding two algebraic fractions. This technique is revised and extended here, to deal with algebraic fractions in equations.

Algebraic fractions should be treated in just the same way as numerical fractions. In order to add (or subtract) two fractions, you need to write them with the same denominator.

EXAMPLE

Write as a single fraction $\dfrac{x+1}{4} + \dfrac{3x+2}{6}$

SOLUTION

The fractions have denominators of 4 and 6. These can be written with a common denominator of 12:

$$\dfrac{x+1}{4} + \dfrac{3x+2}{6} = \dfrac{\mathbf{3} \times (x+1)}{\mathbf{3} \times 4} + \dfrac{\mathbf{2} \times (3x+2)}{\mathbf{2} \times 6}$$

$$= \dfrac{3x+3}{12} + \dfrac{6x+4}{12}$$

$$= \dfrac{3x+3+6x+4}{12}$$

$$= \dfrac{9x+7}{12}$$

EXAMPLE

Write as a single fraction $\dfrac{3}{x+1} - \dfrac{2}{x+5}$

SOLUTION

The fractions have denominators of $(x+1)$ and $(x+5)$. These can be written with a common denominator of $(x+1)(x+5)$. The top and bottom of the first fraction must be multiplied by $(x+5)$, and similarly $(x+1)$ for the second fraction:

$$\dfrac{3}{x+1} - \dfrac{2}{x+5} = \dfrac{3}{(x+1)} \times \dfrac{\mathbf{(x+5)}}{\mathbf{(x+5)}} - \dfrac{2}{(x+5)} \times \dfrac{\mathbf{(x+1)}}{\mathbf{(x+1)}}$$

$$= \dfrac{3(x+5)}{(x+1)(x+5)} - \dfrac{2(x+1)}{(x+1)(x+5)}$$

$$= \dfrac{3(x+5) - 2(x+1)}{(x+1)(x+5)}$$

$$= \dfrac{3x+15-2x-2}{(x+1)(x+5)}$$

$$= \dfrac{x+13}{(x+1)(x+5)}$$

> Note carefully how the subtraction affects the signs with the second bracket here.

Sometimes you may meet an equation containing algebraic fractions. You could simplify the equation to end up with a single fraction on each side, and then cross-multiply.

An alternative method is to multiply both sides by a factor large enough to clear the fractions away. The next example shows you both approaches.

EXAMPLE

Solve the equation $\dfrac{5x-9}{3} + \dfrac{2x+1}{12} = \dfrac{3}{4}$

SOLUTION

Method 1

$$\dfrac{5x-9}{3} + \dfrac{2x+1}{12} = \dfrac{3}{4}$$

$$\dfrac{4\times(5x-9)}{4\times 3} + \dfrac{2x+1}{12} = \dfrac{3}{4}$$

$$\dfrac{20x-36}{12} + \dfrac{2x+1}{12} = \dfrac{3}{4}$$

$$\dfrac{20x-36+12+2x+1}{12} = \dfrac{3}{4}$$

$$\dfrac{22x-35}{12} = \dfrac{3}{4}$$

$$4\times(22x-35) = 3\times 12$$

$$4(22x-35) = 36$$

$$22x - 35 = 9$$

$$22x = 9 + 35$$

$$22x = 44$$

$$x = 2$$

> Express the two fractions on the left-hand side so that they both have denominator 12. Then you can add them together.

> Cross-multiply at this stage.

Method 2

$$\dfrac{5x-9}{3} + \dfrac{2x+1}{12} = \dfrac{3}{4}$$

$$\dfrac{12\times(5x-9)}{3} + \dfrac{12\times(2x+1)}{12} = \dfrac{12\times 3}{4}$$

$$\dfrac{\cancel{12}^{4}\times(5x-9)}{\cancel{3}} + \dfrac{\cancel{12}\times(2x+1)}{\cancel{12}} = \dfrac{\cancel{12}^{3}\times 3}{\cancel{4}}$$

$$4(5x-9) + (2x+1) = 3\times 3$$

$$20x - 36 + 2x + 1 = 9$$

$$22x - 35 = 9$$

$$22x = 44$$

$$x = 2$$

> Here, all three fractions are made 12 times larger. This clears the fractions away entirely.

EXERCISE 27.2

Express these as a single fraction.

1. $\dfrac{x}{3} + \dfrac{x+1}{5}$
2. $\dfrac{x+2}{8} + \dfrac{x-1}{6}$
3. $\dfrac{x+1}{5} + \dfrac{3x}{10}$
4. $\dfrac{3x+2}{2} - \dfrac{2x+3}{3}$
5. $\dfrac{x}{4} + \dfrac{2x+1}{5}$
6. $\dfrac{3x}{4} + \dfrac{x+1}{6}$
7. $\dfrac{5}{x} - \dfrac{3}{x+1}$
8. $\dfrac{2}{x+1} + \dfrac{3}{x+2}$
9. $\dfrac{2}{x+3} + \dfrac{1}{2x+1}$
10. $\dfrac{2}{x+4} + \dfrac{1}{x+3}$
11. $\dfrac{3}{x-2} - \dfrac{2}{x+5}$
12. $\dfrac{5}{(x+1)(x+2)} + \dfrac{4}{x+2}$

Solve these equations involving algebraic fractions.

13. $\dfrac{x-2}{5} + \dfrac{x}{10} = \dfrac{1}{2}$
14. $\dfrac{x+2}{8} + \dfrac{x-1}{4} = \dfrac{3}{4}$
15. $\dfrac{x-2}{10} + \dfrac{x}{20} = \dfrac{1}{4}$
16. $\dfrac{x+3}{5} + \dfrac{x+4}{15} = \dfrac{1}{3}$
17. $\dfrac{1}{12} + \dfrac{x+1}{6} = \dfrac{x}{4}$
18. $\dfrac{1}{x} + \dfrac{2}{3x} = \dfrac{1}{3}$
19. $\dfrac{1}{x-2} + \dfrac{1}{x} = \dfrac{3}{4}$
20. $\dfrac{1}{x} + \dfrac{1}{2x+1} = \dfrac{7}{10}$

27.3 Simultaneous equations, one linear and one quadratic

In Chapter 15 you solved simultaneous equations using the elimination method. This approach can also be used when one of the equations is quadratic. Since quadratics often have two solutions, you should be prepared to find two different solutions to the simultaneous equations.

EXAMPLE

Solve the equations:
$y = x + 1$
$y = x^2 - 1$

SOLUTION

Since both equations are of the form $y = ...$, then the two right-hand sides must be equal.

$x^2 - 1 = x + 1$
$x^2 - x - 2 = 0$
$(x - 2)(x + 1) = 0$
$x = 2$ or $x = -1$

If $x = 2$:
$y = x + 1$
$= 2 + 1$
$= 3$

If $x = -1$:
$y = x + 1$
$= -1 + 1$
$= 0$

Check: If $x = 2$ and $y = 3$, then $y = x + 1 \rightarrow 3 = 2 + 1$ ✓

Check: If $x = -1$ and $y = 0$, then $y = x + 1 \rightarrow 0 = -1 + 1$ ✓

Thus the solutions are $x = 2, y = 3$ or $x = -1, y = 0$.

If both x and y appear in square form in the second equation, the elimination is done by substituting.

EXAMPLE

Solve the equations:
$$y = x - 5$$
$$x^2 + y^2 = 17$$

SOLUTION

$$y = x - 5$$
$$x^2 + y^2 = 17$$

Replace y with $x - 5$ in the second equation:
$$x^2 + (x - 5)^2 = 17$$
$$x^2 + x^2 - 10x + 25 = 17$$
$$2x^2 - 10x + 25 = 17$$
$$2x^2 - 10x + 8 = 0$$
$$x^2 - 5x + 4 = 0$$
$$(x - 4)(x - 1) = 0$$

Thus $x = 4$ or $x = 1$.
If $x = 4$, then $y = x - 5 = 4 - 5 = -1$.
If $x = 1$, then $y = x - 5 = 1 - 5 = -4$.

Thus the solutions are $x = 4, y = -1$ or $x = 1, y = -4$

Check: If $x = 4$ and $y = -1$, then
$y = x - 5 \rightarrow -1 = 4 - 5$ ✓
$x^2 + y^2 = 17 \rightarrow (4)^2 + (-1)^2 = 17$ ✓

Check: if $x = 1$ and $y = -4$,
then $y = x - 5 \rightarrow -4 = 1 - 5$ ✓
$x^2 + y^2 = 17 \rightarrow (1)^2 + (-4)^2 = 17$ ✓

EXERCISE 27.3

Solve these simultaneous equations.

1 $y = x$
    $y = x^2 - 2$

2 $y = x + 7$
    $y = x^2 + 1$

3 $y = 4x + 7$
    $y = 2x^2 + 1$

4 $y = 11x - 2$
    $y = 5x^2$

5 $x^2 = y - 1$
    $y = 4x + 1$

6 $x = y + 2$
    $y = x^2 - 4$

Solve these simultaneous equations.

7 $y = x - 2$
    $x^2 + y^2 = 10$

8 $y = 2x - 2$
    $x^2 + y^2 = 8$

9 $x = y + 4$
    $x^2 + y^2 = 10$

10 $y + 7 = x$
    $x^2 + y^2 = 37$

Solve these simultaneous equations.

11 $y = 2x + 3$
    $y = x^2 - 12$

12 $x - y = 5$
    $y = x^2 - 35$

13 $y = 2x$
    $y = x^2 - x + 2$

14 $y = x^2 - 3x - 1$
    $y = 2x - 7$

15 $y = 2x - 7$
    $x^2 + y^2 = 34$

16 $y - x = 1$
    $x^2 + y^2 = 5$

27.4 Changing the subject of an equation where the symbol occurs twice

Sometimes you need to change the subject of an equation where the required symbol appears twice. It is necessary to collect all the terms containing that symbol on to one side of the equation, and then take the symbol out as a common factor.

EXAMPLE

Make x the subject of the equation $3x + 5 = y - ax$

SOLUTION

$$3x + 5 = y - ax$$
$$3x + 5 + ax = y$$
$$3x + ax = y - 5$$
$$x(3 + a) = y - 5$$
$$x = \frac{y - 5}{3 + a}$$

Sometimes you might need to clear away a fraction first.

EXAMPLE

Make x the subject of the equation:
$$10 = \frac{ax + 12}{bx + 1}$$

SOLUTION

$$10 = \frac{ax + 12}{bx + 1}$$
$$10(bx + 1) = ax + 12$$
$$10bx + 10 = ax + 12$$
$$10bx - ax = 12 - 10$$
$$x(10b - a) = 2$$
$$x = \frac{2}{10b - a}$$

EXERCISE 27.4

1. Make x the subject of the equation $3x - 5 = mx$

2. Make x the subject of the equation $ax + b = cx + d$

3. Make x the subject of the equation $2x = k(2 + x)$

4. Make y the subject of the equation $d = \dfrac{y + 1}{y + 2}$

5. Make t the subject of the equation $\dfrac{t + a}{t + b} = c$

6. Make x the subject of the equation $3x - n = kx + 2$

7 Make x the subject of the equation
$$5x + a = \frac{x}{b}$$

8 Make x the subject of the equation
$$\frac{ax - 3}{x} = 2$$

9 Make x the subject of the equation
$$k = \frac{x}{x + a}$$

10 Make u the subject of the equation
$$\frac{1}{u} + \frac{1}{v} = \frac{1}{f}$$

[Hint: Multiply through by uvf first.]

27.5 Exponential growth and decay

When you studied compound interest in Chapter 12, you used multiplying factors. For example, the value of an investment of £100, after 5 years of earning compound interest at 8%, would be £100 × 1.08^5.

Quantities that increase in this multiplicative way are said to show **exponential growth**. If the multiplying factor is less than 1, you get **exponential decay** instead.

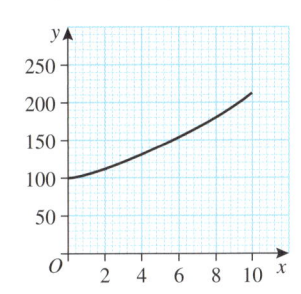

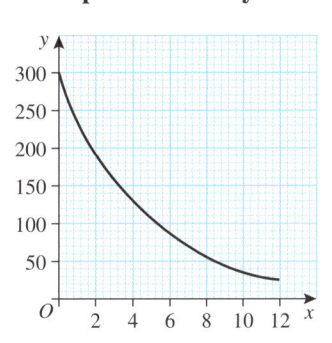

Exponential growth

Exponential decay

Examples
- Growth of capital with compound interest
- Population growth

Examples
- Radioactive decay
- Reduction in value of a used car

EXAMPLE

Bacteria are being grown in a dish in a laboratory. Initially there are 500 bacteria. The number of bacteria doubles every hour.
a) Find the number of bacteria in the dish after **(i)** 1 hour; **(ii)** 3 hours.
b) Write an expression for the number of bacteria after n hours.
c) Work out the number of bacteria in the dish after 24 hours.
   Give your answer in standard form correct to 3 significant figures.

SOLUTION

a) i) After 1 hour, there are 500 × 2 = 1000 bacteria
    ii) After 3 hours, there are 500 × 2^3 = 4000 bacteria

b) After n hours, the number of bacteria will be 500 × 2^n

c) After 24 hours, the number of bacteria will be:
   500 × 2^{24} = 8 388 608 000
   $\phantom{500 \times 2^{24}}$ = 8.39 × 10^9 (3 s.f.)

EXAMPLE

The strength W of a signal from a radioactive device at time t is described by the relationship:

$$W = a \times b^t$$

where a and b are constant numbers.
Initially the strength of the signal is 2000. At time $t = 3$, the strength falls to 1024.
a) Find the value of the constant a.
b) Work out the value of the constant b.
c) Use your results to work out the strength of the signal when $t = 6$.
Give your answer to the nearest whole number.

SOLUTION

a) Initially, $t = 0$, hence:
$$a \times b^0 = 2000$$
$$a = 2000$$

b) The relation is therefore
$$W = 2000 \times b^t$$
When $t = 3$, $W = 1024$, so:
$$2000 \times b^3 = 1024$$
$$b^3 = \frac{1024}{2000}$$
$$= \frac{64}{125}$$
$$b = \sqrt[3]{\frac{64}{125}}$$
$$= \underline{0.8}$$

c) Thus the relation is $W = 2000 \times 0.8^t$
When $t = 6$:
$$W = 2000 \times 0.8^6$$
$$= 524.288$$
$$= \underline{524} \quad \text{(nearest whole number)}$$

EXERCISE 27.5

1 The graph shows the number of bacteria living in a colony.
The number N of bacteria in the colony at time t is given by the relation:

$$N = a \times b^t$$

The curve passes through the point $(0, 500)$.
a) Use this information to show that $a = 500$.
The curve also passes through $(2, 1125)$.
b) Use this information to find the value of b.
c) Work out the number of bacteria in the colony at time $t = 3$.

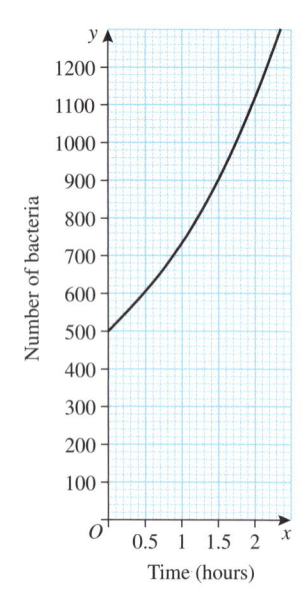

2. Marina buys a car for £12 000. Each year it falls in value by 30% of its value at the beginning of that year. Marina uses a mathematical equation to describe the value £X of her car t years after she bought it. Her equation is of the form $X = a \times b^t$ where a is a whole number and b is a decimal less than 1.
   a) Write down the values of a and b.
   b) Use Marina's equation, with your values from part **a)**, to find the value of her car after 8 years.

3. A company employed 85 000 people in 1989. It decided to reduce the number of employees by 10% per year for each year after 1989.
   a) Write down the number of employees in **(i)** 1990, **(ii)** 1991.
   The number of employees n years after 1989 is given by an expression of the form $p \times q^n$.
   b) Write down the values of p and q.
   c) Hence find the number of employees in 1999.

4. A house had an initial value when it was built. Each year after that, its value increased by a fixed percentage of its value at the start of that year. When the house is n years old its value is £165 000 $\times$ 1.06^n.
   a) Write down the initial value of the house when it was built.
   b) Write down the percentage increase in value each year.
   c) Work out the value of the house when it is 100 years old.

5. A hot drink was poured into a cup and left in a room to cool. The temperature $T\,°C$ of the drink t minutes after it was poured into the cup is given by $T = 22 + 78 \times 0.5^t$.
   a) Find the temperature of the drink when it was first poured into the cup.
   b) Work out the temperature of the drink 3 minutes after it was poured.
   c) Suggest a value for the background temperature of the room.

REVIEW EXERCISE 27

1. a) Find the value of $\sqrt{5} \times \sqrt{20}$
   $\sqrt{5} + \sqrt{20} = k\sqrt{5}$, where k is an integer.
   b) Find the value of k.
   c) Find the value of $\dfrac{\sqrt{5} + \sqrt{45}}{\sqrt{20}}$ [Edexcel]

2. Work out $\dfrac{(5 + \sqrt{3})(5 - \sqrt{3})}{\sqrt{22}}$. Give your answer in its simplest form. [Edexcel]

3. a) Find the value of:
   (i) m when $\sqrt{128} = 2^m$
   (ii) n when $(\sqrt{8} - \sqrt{2})^2 = 2^n$
   A rectangle has a length of 2^t cm and a width of $(\sqrt{8} - \sqrt{2})$ cm.
   The area of the rectangle is $\sqrt{128}$ cm².
   b) Find t. [Edexcel]

4 a) Find the value of $16^{\frac{1}{2}}$.

 b) Given that $\sqrt{40} = k\sqrt{10}$, find the value of k.

A large rectangular piece of card is $(\sqrt{5} + \sqrt{20})$ cm long and $\sqrt{8}$ cm wide.
A small rectangle $\sqrt{2}$ cm long and $\sqrt{5}$ cm wide is cut out of the piece of card.

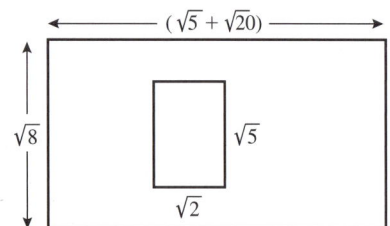

Diagram *not* accurately drawn

 c) Express the area of the card that is left as a percentage of the area of the large rectangle. [Edexcel]

5 a) Express $\dfrac{1}{x-2} + \dfrac{2}{x+4}$ as a single algebraic fraction.

 b) Hence, or otherwise, solve $\dfrac{1}{x-2} + \dfrac{2}{x+4} = \dfrac{1}{3}$ [Edexcel]

6 Solve $\dfrac{2}{x} + \dfrac{3}{2x} = \dfrac{1}{3}$ [Edexcel]

7 a) Factorise $2x^2 + 7x + 5$

 b) Write as a single fraction in its simplest form: $\dfrac{3}{x+1} + \dfrac{5x}{2x^2 + 7x + 5}$ [Edexcel]

8 Simplify fully:
 a) $2(3x + 4) - 3(4x - 5)$
 b) $(2xy^3)^5$
 c) $\dfrac{n^2 - 1}{n + 1} \times \dfrac{2}{n - 2}$ [Edexcel]

You may use a calculator in the remaining questions.

9 a) Solve $\dfrac{40 - x}{3} = 4 + x$ **b)** Simplify fully $\dfrac{4x^2 - 6x}{4x^2 - 9}$ [Edexcel]

10 Rearrange $4y = k(2 - 3y)$ to write y in terms of k. [Edexcel]

11 Make x the subject of the formula $y = \dfrac{x}{a - x}$ [Edexcel]

12 Solve the simultaneous equations:
$$y = 3x - 1$$
$$x^2 + y^2 = 29$$

13 Bill said that the line $y = 6$ cuts the curve $x^2 + y^2 = 25$ at two points.
 a) By eliminating y, show that Bill is incorrect.
 b) By eliminating y, find the solutions to the simultaneous equations:
$$x^2 + y^2 = 25$$
$$y = 2x - 2$$
[Edexcel]

14 Mr Patel has a car.
The value of the car on January 1st 2000 was £1600.
The value of the car on January 1st 2002 was £400.
The sketch graph shows how the value, £V, of the car changes with time. The equation of the sketch graph is $V = pq^t$ where t is the number of years after January 1st 2000.
p and q are positive constants.
a) Use the information on the graph to find the value of p and the value of q.
b) Using your values of p and q in the formula $V = pq^t$, find the value of the car on January 1st 1998. [Edexcel]

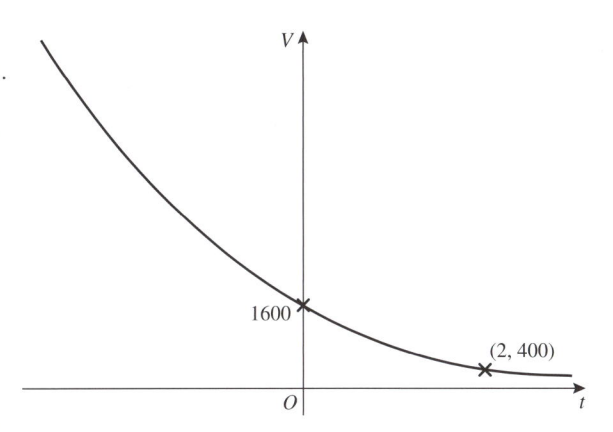

KEY POINTS

1. A surd is an expression containing a root, like $\sqrt{45}$. You can often simplify a surd without using a calculator, by looking for a perfect square inside the root; for example:

   $\sqrt{45} = \sqrt{9 \times 5} = \sqrt{9} \times \sqrt{5} = 3\sqrt{5}$

2. You can rationalise a fraction like $\dfrac{6 + \sqrt{3}}{\sqrt{3}}$ to clear the surd from the bottom; for example:

   $\dfrac{6 + \sqrt{3}}{\sqrt{3}} = \dfrac{(6 + \sqrt{3}) \times \sqrt{3}}{\sqrt{3} \times \sqrt{3}} = \dfrac{6\sqrt{3} + 3}{3} = 2\sqrt{3} + 1$

3. Algebraic fractions can be added to ordinary numerical fractions in a similar way. You must rewrite the fractions to have the same bottom (common denominator) first.

4. Algebraic fractions involving quadratic expressions can sometimes be simplified by cancelling common factors. You may need to factorise the top and bottom separately first.

5. Some GCSE problems on simultaneous equations may give you one linear and one quadratic equation. Use an elimination method to obtain a quadratic equation, and remember to look for both solutions to the quadratic. Pair the matching answers up at the end, e.g.

   $x = 2$ and $y = 3$ or $x = -1$ and $y = 0$

6. Some GCSE problems on changing the subject of an equation will have the new symbol occurring twice. You must isolate the terms containing this symbol on one side of the equation, then extract the symbol as a common factor.

7. Exponential growth is driven by a relation of the form $y = a \times b^x$, where a and b are fixed numbers, or constants. The value of a gives the initial value of y, and the value of b determines the rate of growth, provided $b > 1$. If b lies between 0 and 1 then the result is exponential decay instead.

Internet Challenge 27

Famous formulae

Here are some famous mathematical formulae. Use the internet to help you find out what each one represents. You should know some of them already.

1. $c^2 = a^2 + b^2$
2. $C = 2\pi r$
3. $A = \dfrac{(a+b)h}{2}$
4. $V = IR$
5. $V = \frac{1}{3}\pi r^2 h$
6. $x = \dfrac{-b \pm \sqrt{b^2 - 4ac}}{2a}$
7. $E = mc^2$
8. $A = 4\pi r^2$
9. $s = ut + \frac{1}{2}at^2$
10. $T = 2\pi \sqrt{\dfrac{l}{g}}$
11. $F - E + V = 1$
12. $C = \frac{5}{9}(F - 32)$
13. $E = \frac{1}{2}mv^2$
14. $E = mgh$
15. $\dfrac{1}{u} + \dfrac{1}{v} = \dfrac{1}{f}$
16. $\dfrac{1}{R} = \dfrac{1}{R_1} + \dfrac{1}{R_2}$
17. $I = \dfrac{PRT}{100}$
18. $A = \frac{1}{2}ab \sin C$
19. $F = \dfrac{Gm_1 m_2}{d^2}$
20. $W = Fd$

CHAPTER 28

Further trigonometry

In this chapter you will **learn how to**:

- solve trigonometry problems using the sine and cosine rules
- find the area of a triangle using $\frac{1}{2}ab \sin C$
- find the area of a segment of a circle
- calculate distances and angles in 3-D
- work with frustums.

You will also be **challenged to**:

- investigate Heron's formula.

Starter: How tall is the church?

A mathematically-minded vicar wants to work out the height of the spire on his parish church. He notices that from a point, A, the spire has an angle of elevation of 32°. When he walks 25 metres nearer the spire, to point B, the angle increases to 65°.

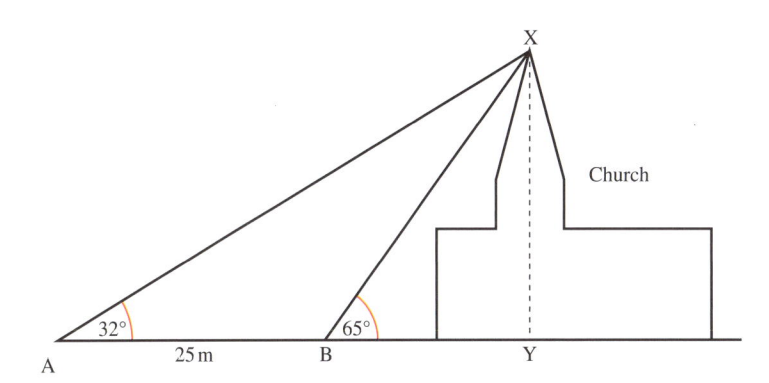

Make a scale drawing, and measure the height of the spire.
A scale of 1 cm = 5 metres should work well.

In this chapter you will meet methods for calculating sides and angles in a non-right-angled triangle. You will meet this question again in the Review exercise, and you will be able to calculate the answer, to see how accurate your scale drawing is.

28.1 The sine rule

In your earlier work on trigonometry you used the sine ratio in a right-angled triangle. It is also possible to use the sine ratio in a non-right-angled triangle. The triangle ABC below has no right angles. The line CX is the perpendicular height, that is, angle CXB = 90°.

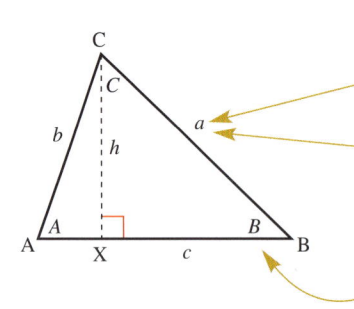

The lengths of the sides are labelled a, b, c using italic small letters.

Notice that side a is opposite angle A, and so on.

The angles are labelled A, B, C using italic capital letters.

The triangle AXC is right angled, so you can use ordinary trigonometry to obtain:

$$h = b \times \sin A$$

The triangle BXC is also right angled, so you can use trigonometry in this triangle, to obtain:

$$h = a \times \sin B$$

Since both these equations refer to the same height h, then the expressions on the right-hand sides must be equal:

$$a \times \sin B = b \times \sin A$$

This may be rearranged into the following form:

$$\frac{a}{\sin A} = \frac{b}{\sin B}$$

By drawing a perpendicular from A on to side BC, or from B on to side AC, it is possible to obtain a similar result including side c and $\sin C$. Putting this altogether, the result is the **sine rule**:

$$\frac{a}{\sin A} = \frac{b}{\sin B} = \frac{c}{\sin C}$$

EXAMPLE

Find the missing lengths, x cm and y cm, in this triangle. Give your answers to 3 significant figures.

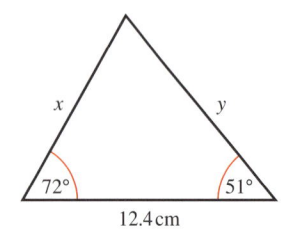

SOLUTION

Labelling the sides and angles we have:

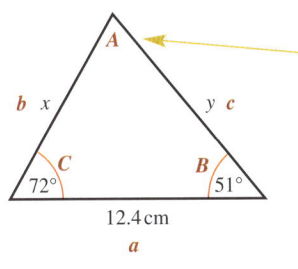

> Since $A + B + C = 180°$, then $A = 180° - (51° + 72°)$
> $= 57°$

The sine rule gives: $\dfrac{a}{\sin A} = \dfrac{b}{\sin B} = \dfrac{c}{\sin C}$

For x: $\dfrac{x}{\sin 51°} = \dfrac{12.4}{\sin 57°}$

$$x = \dfrac{\sin 51° \times 12.4}{\sin 57°}$$

$= 11.490\,339\,94$

$= \underline{11.5\text{ cm}}$ (3 s.f.)

For y: $\dfrac{y}{\sin 72°} = \dfrac{12.4}{\sin 57°}$

$$y = \dfrac{\sin 72° \times 12.4}{\sin 57°}$$

$= 14.061\,660\,51$

$= \underline{14.1\text{ cm}}$ (3 s.f.)

You can also use the sine rule to find an unknown angle in a triangle. Sometimes the sine rule can generate two possible solutions (see the next section, on the ambiguous case of the sine rule), but for the questions that follow in this section each has a unique solution.

EXAMPLE

Find the size of the angle, marked x, in the triangle.

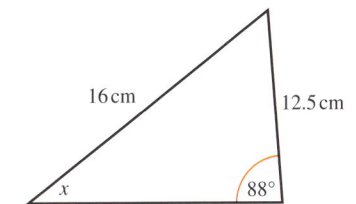

SOLUTION

By the sine rule, we have:

$$\dfrac{16}{\sin 88°} = \dfrac{12.5}{\sin x}$$

Cross-multiplying:

$16 \times \sin x = 12.5 \times \sin 88°$

$\sin x = \dfrac{12.5 \times \sin 88°}{16}$

$= 0.780\,774\,084$

$x = 51.331\,504\,51$

$= \underline{51.3°}$ (nearest 0.1°)

EXERCISE 28.1

Find the lengths of the sides represented by letters. Give your answers to 3 significant figures.

1

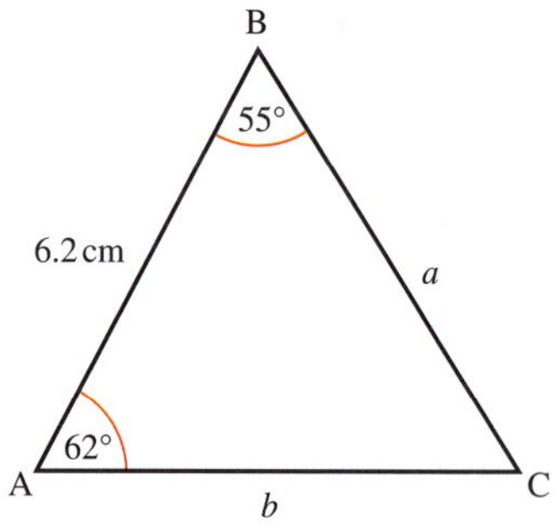
B
55°
6.2 cm
a
62°
A
C
b

2

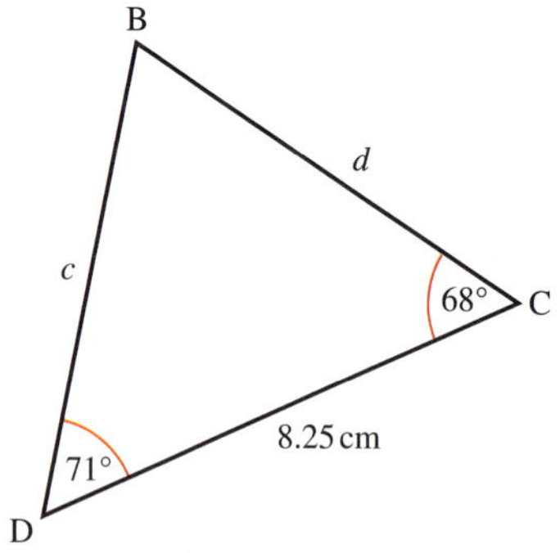
B
d
c
68°
C
71°
8.25 cm
D

3

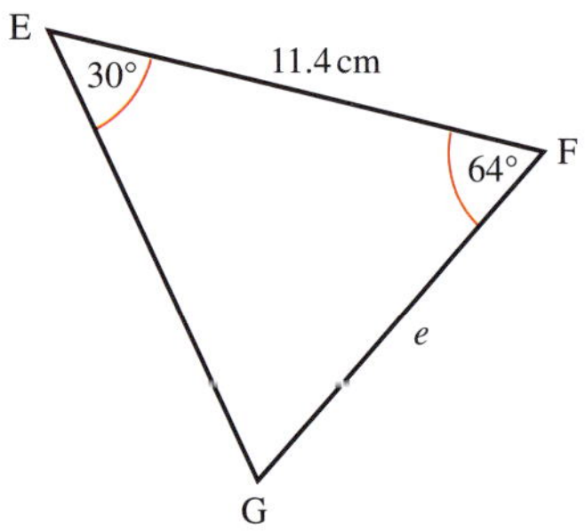
E
30°
11.4 cm
64°
F
e
G

4

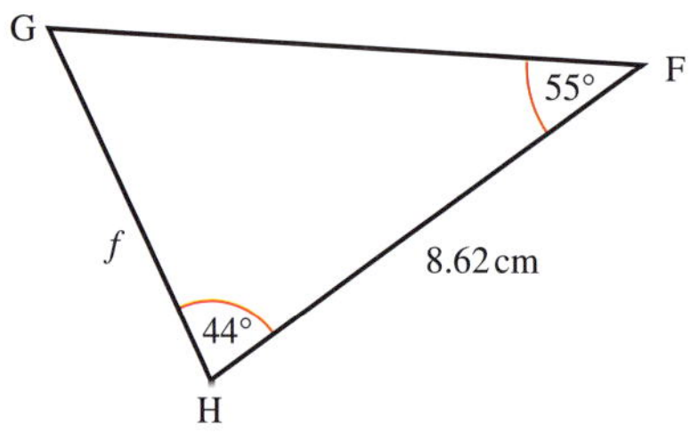
G
55°
F
f
8.62 cm
44°
H

5

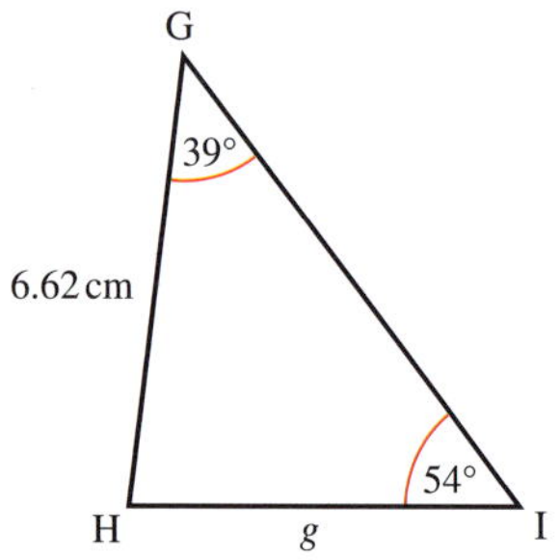
G
39°
6.62 cm
54°
H
g
I

6

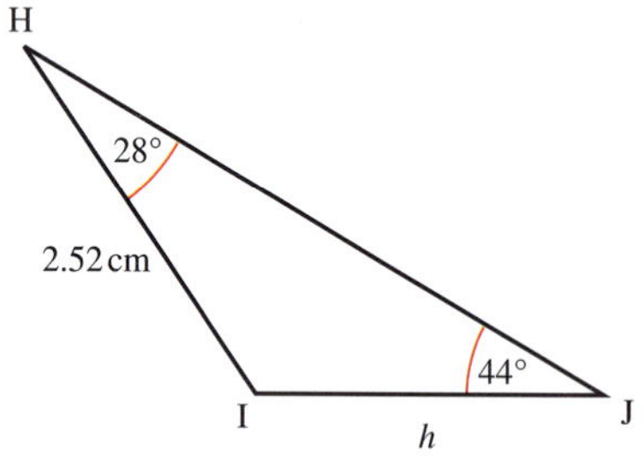
H
28°
2.52 cm
44°
I
h
J

7

Triangle JIK with angle J = 33°, angle at I = 125°, side IK = 4.5 cm, side JK = i.

8

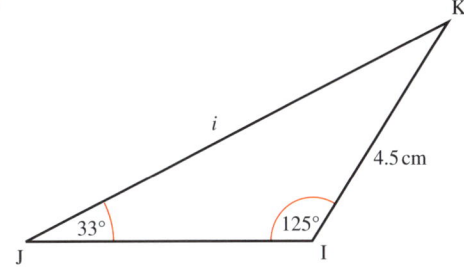

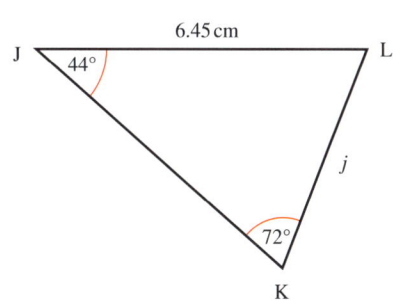

Triangle JLK with angle J = 44°, side JL = 6.45 cm, angle K = 72°, side LK = j.

Find the angles represented by letters. Give your answers to the nearest 0.1°.

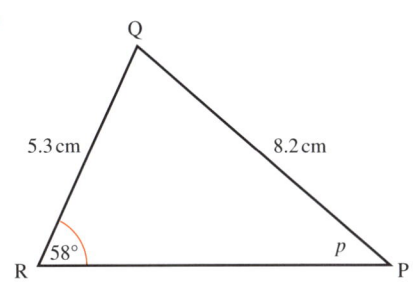

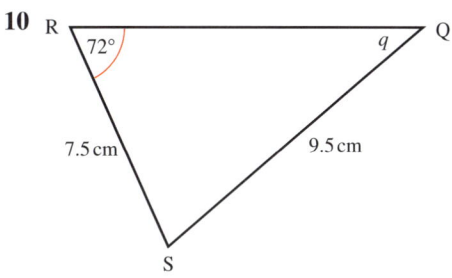

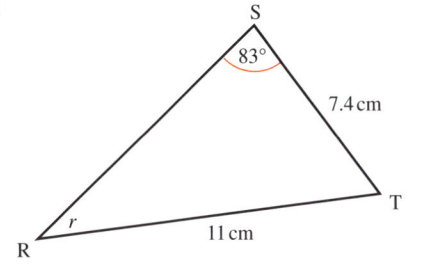

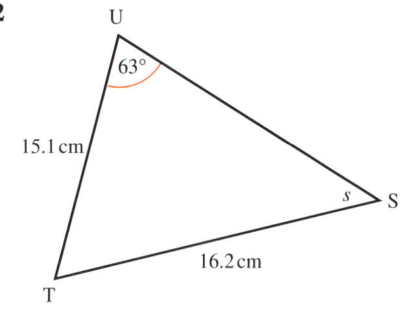

9

Triangle QRP with QR = 5.3 cm, QP = 8.2 cm, angle R = 58°, angle P = p.

10

Triangle RQS with angle R = 72°, RS = 7.5 cm, SQ = 9.5 cm, angle Q = q.

11

Triangle STR with angle S = 83°, ST = 7.4 cm, RT = 11 cm, angle R = r.

12

Triangle UST with angle U = 63°, UT = 15.1 cm, TS = 16.2 cm, angle S = s.

28.2 The ambiguous case of the sine rule

If you are trying to construct a triangle from given information, it is sometimes possible to find more than one triangle that would work.

For example, suppose you want to construct a triangle ABC with AB = 8 cm, AC = 7 cm and angle ABC = 50°. You would begin by drawing a long baseline with one end at B, then measure a 50° angle, and then measure 8 cm to locate point A, like this:

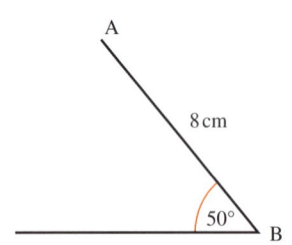

To complete the construction, draw an arc of radius 7 cm from A. This intersects the base line in two places, showing that there are two different possible triangles that satisfy the given information.

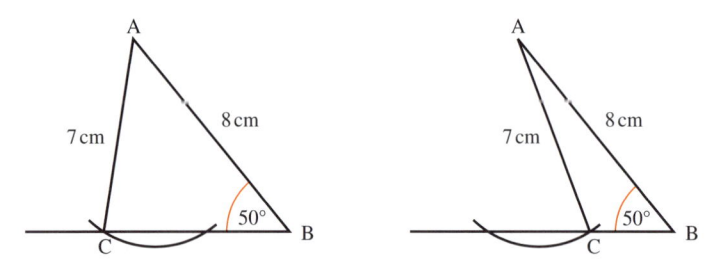

If you use the sine rule to find the angle at C, your calculator will report an acute angle, $\theta°$ say, as in the left-hand diagram above. It turns out that an angle of $180° - \theta°$ also has the same sine, as in the right-hand diagram. Thus there are two feasible alternative solutions to the triangle, so that the value of the angle at C is not uniquely defined. This is the **ambiguous case** of the sine rule.

When using the sine rule to find an unknown angle, you must always be alert for the possibility of two solutions.

EXAMPLE

In triangle ABC, AB = 8 cm, AC = 7 cm and angle ABC = 50°.
Use the sine rule to find angle ACB = C.
Give your answer correct to the nearest 0.1°.

SOLUTION

By the sine rule:

$$\frac{7}{\sin 50°} = \frac{8}{\sin C}$$

Rearranging:

$$\sin C = \frac{8 \times \sin 50°}{7}$$

$$= 0.875\,479$$

$$C = 61.101\,76°$$

$$= 61.1° \text{ (nearest } 0.1°)$$

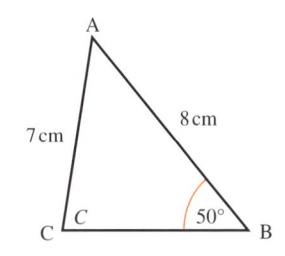

Although the calculator reports 61.1°, another possibility is:
$180° - 61.1° = 118.9°$, so:

Angle ACB = 61.1° or 118.9°

Not all such problems are ambiguous, however. Sometimes there may be other information in the question that allows you to eliminate one of the two possibilities. Remember that:

- the shortest side of a triangle is always opposite the smallest angle
- the longest side of a triangle is always opposite the largest angle.

EXAMPLE

Find the size of the angle marked x.

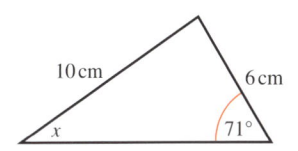

SOLUTION

By the sine rule:

$$\frac{10}{\sin 71°} = \frac{6}{\sin x}$$

Rearranging:

$$\sin x = \frac{6 \times \sin 71°}{10}$$

$$= 0.603\,237$$

$$x = 34.562\,94°$$

$$= 34.6° \text{ (nearest } 0.1°)$$

> Also, since 10 cm is greater than 6 cm, the angle 71° (opposite 10 cm) must be greater than x (opposite 6 cm), so ruling out 145.4°

The alternative $180° - 34.6° = 145.4°$ is not possible, because x and 71° would then add up to more than 180°. Thus there is only one possible value, namely $x = 34.6°$

EXERCISE 28.2

Find the angles represented by letters. Give your answers to the nearest 0.1°. If any are ambiguous, give both possibilities.

1

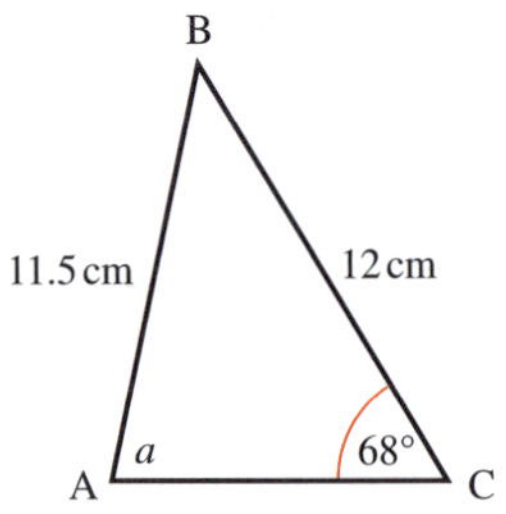

2

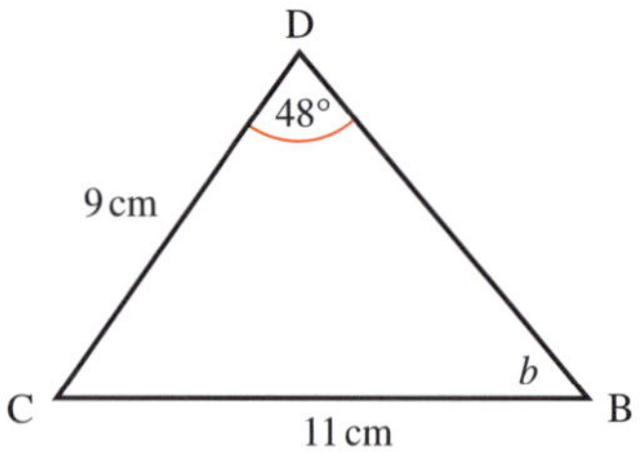

3

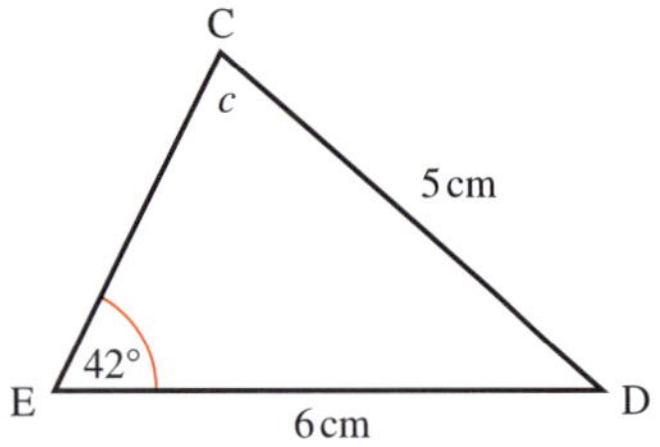

4

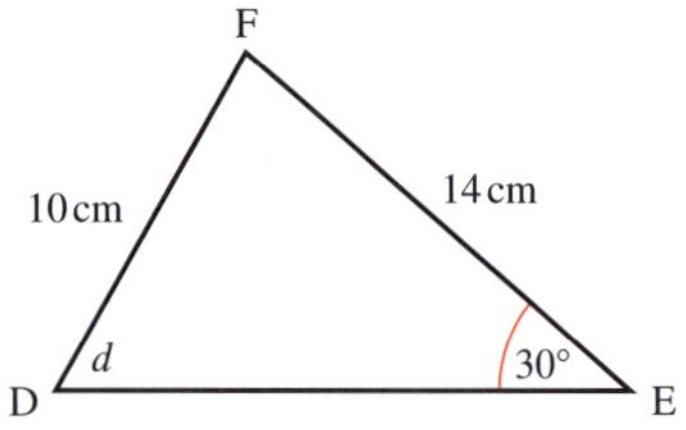

5

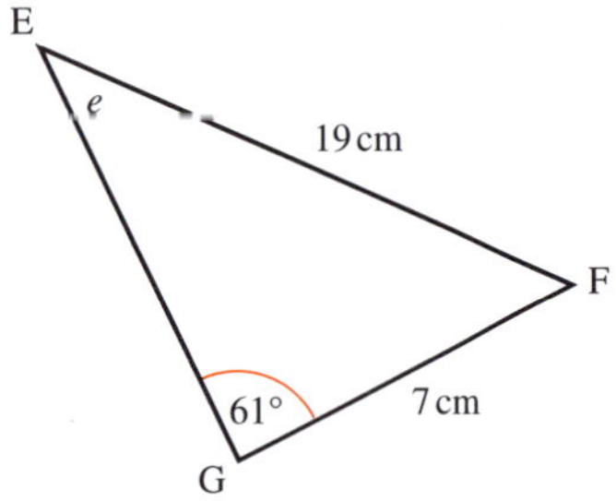

6

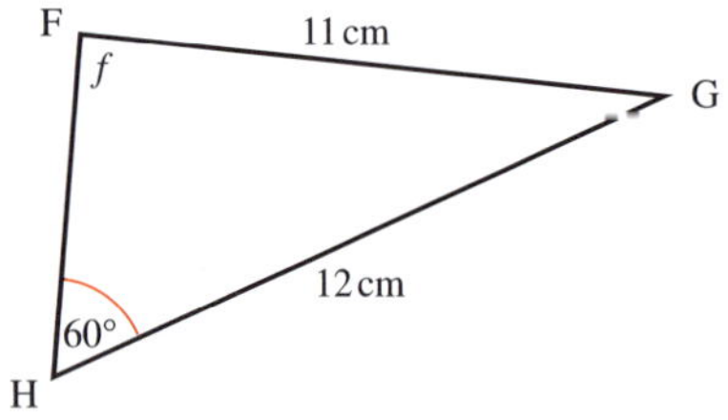

7

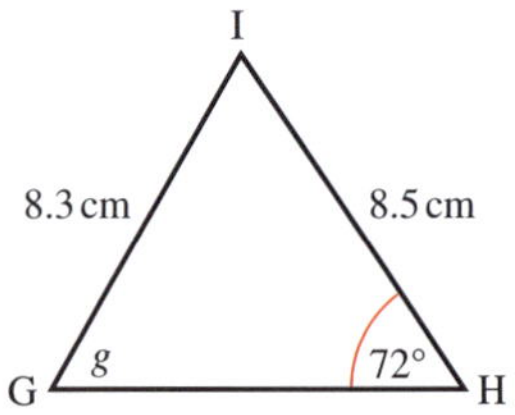

8

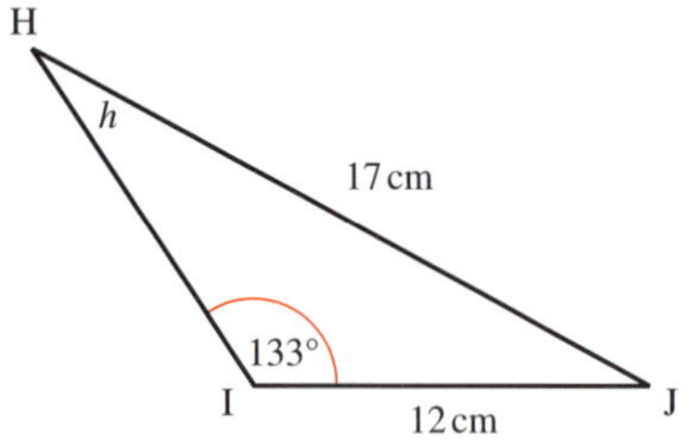

28.3 The cosine rule

The diagram shows a general triangle ABC, labelled so that the sides of length a, b and c are opposite the angles A, B and C.

For all triangles labelled in this way, it may be proved that:

$$c^2 = a^2 + b^2 - 2ab \cos C$$

This is the **cosine rule**. At GCSE you will need to use the cosine rule to find unknown sides or angles, but you do not need to know how to prove it.

Notice that if the angle C were to be a right angle, then $\cos C$ becomes $\cos 90°$, which is zero, and the cosine rule reduces to $c^2 = a^2 + b^2 - \cancel{2ab \cos C}$, that is, $c^2 = a^2 + b^2$. Thus you can think of the cosine rule as being a more general version of Pythagoras' theorem that may be used in triangles when they do not have right angles.

The cosine rule contains one angle and all three sides. The version above has been written from the point of view of angle C. There are two other, equivalent forms based on each of the other two angles. So, for any triangle ABC, the cosine rule states that:

$$a^2 = b^2 + c^2 - 2bc \cos A$$
$$b^2 = a^2 + c^2 - 2ac \cos B$$
$$c^2 = a^2 + b^2 - 2ab \cos C$$

> Notice that the side forming the subject of the equation corresponds with the angle in the cosine expression, for example: $a^2 = b^2 + c^2 - 2bc \cos A$

EXAMPLE

In triangle ABC, AB = 10 cm, BC = 12 cm and angle ABC = 55°.
a) Make a sketch of the triangle, and mark this information on the sketch.
b) Calculate the length of AC. Give your answer correct to 3 significant figures.

SOLUTION

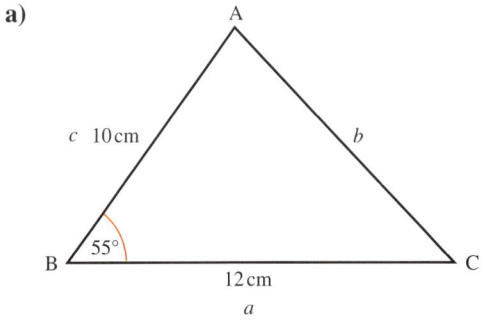

a)

b) Using the cosine rule in the form $b^2 = a^2 + c^2 - 2ac \cos B$, we have:

$b^2 = 12^2 + 10^2 - 2 \times 12 \times 10 \times \cos 55°$
$ = 144 + 100 - 240 \cos 55°$
$ = 106.341\,655\,3$
$b = \sqrt{106.341\,655\,3}$
$ = 10.312\,209\,04$

Thus AC = <u>10.3 cm</u> (3 s.f.)

You can also use the cosine rule to find an unknown angle. If the unknown angle lies between 0° and 90°, its cosine will be *positive*, while if it is between 90° and 180° its cosine will be *negative*. This means that the unknown angle can always be found uniquely – there is no ambiguous case for the cosine rule.

EXAMPLE

Find the angles x and y indicated on these sketch diagrams.
Give your answers to the nearest 0.1°.

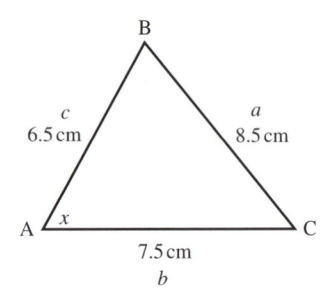

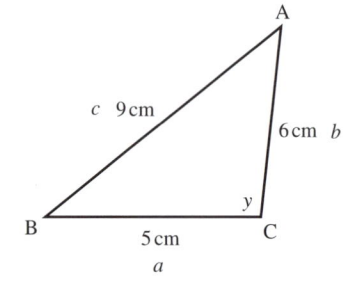

SOLUTION

To find x, use the cosine rule in the form $a^2 = b^2 + c^2 - 2bc \cos A$:

$$8.5^2 = 7.5^2 + 6.5^2 - 2 \times 7.5 \times 6.5 \times \cos x$$

Rearranging:

$$2 \times 7.5 \times 6.5 \times \cos x = 7.5^2 + 6.5^2 - 8.5^2$$

$$\cos x = \frac{7.5^2 + 6.5^2 - 8.5^2}{2 \times 7.5 \times 6.5}$$

$$= \frac{26.25}{97.5}$$

$$= 0.269\,230\,769$$

$$x = \cos^{-1}(0.269\,230\,769)$$

$$= 74.381\,501\,72$$

$$= \underline{74.4°} \text{ (nearest 0.1°)}$$

To find y, use the cosine rule in the form $c^2 = a^2 + b^2 - 2ab \cos C$:

$$9^2 = 5^2 + 6^2 - 2 \times 5 \times 6 \times \cos y$$

Rearranging:

$$2 \times 5 \times 6 \times \cos y = 5^2 + 6^2 - 9^2$$

$$\cos y = \frac{5^2 + 6^2 - 9^2}{2 \times 5 \times 6}$$

$$= \frac{-20}{60}$$

$$= -0.333\,333\,333$$

$$y = \cos^{-1}(-0.333\,333\,333)$$

$$= 109.471\,220\,6$$

$$= \underline{109.5°} \text{ (nearest 0.1°)}$$

> The negative sign here indicates that the angle is more than 90°; in other words, it is obtuse.

$$a^2 = b^2 + c^2 - 2bc \cos A \quad \text{rearranges to give} \quad \cos A = \frac{b^2 + c^2 - a^2}{2bc}$$

$$b^2 = a^2 + c^2 - 2ac \cos B \quad \text{rearranges to give} \quad \cos B = \frac{a^2 + c^2 - b^2}{2ac}$$

$$c^2 = a^2 + b^2 - 2ab \cos C \quad \text{rearranges to give} \quad \cos C = \frac{a^2 + b^2 - c^2}{2ab}$$

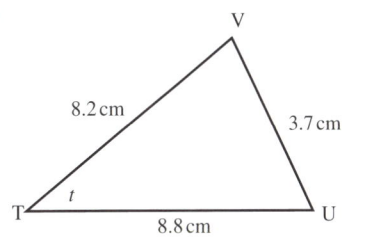

EXERCISE 28.3A

Use the cosine rule to find the unknown sides indicated by letters in these triangles.

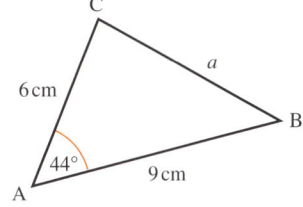

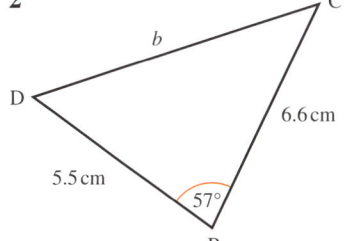

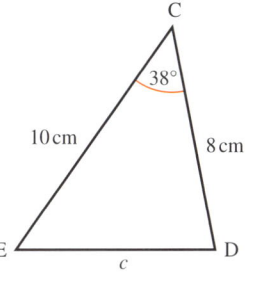

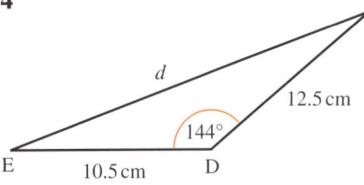

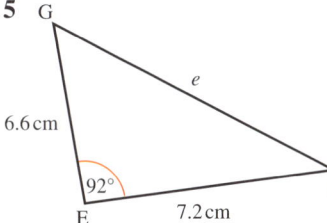

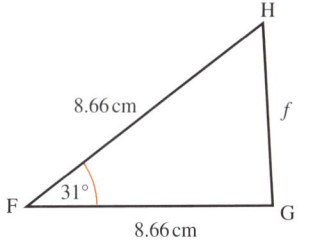

1 Triangle ABC with AC = 6 cm, AB = 9 cm, angle A = 44°, side a = BC.

2 Triangle BCD with BD = 5.5 cm, BC = 6.6 cm, angle B = 57°, side b = CD.

3 Triangle CDE with CE = 10 cm, CD = 8 cm, angle C = 38°, side c = ED.

4 Triangle DEF with ED = 10.5 cm, DF = 12.5 cm, angle D = 144°, side d = EF.

5 Triangle EFG with EG = 6.6 cm, EF = 7.2 cm, angle E = 92°, side e = GF.

6 Triangle FGH with FH = 8.66 cm, FG = 8.66 cm, angle G = 31°, side f = HG.

Use the cosine rule to find the unknown angles indicated by letters in these triangles.

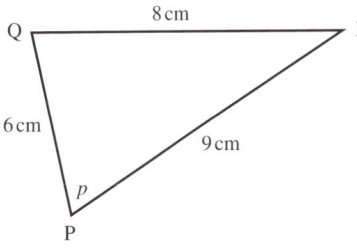

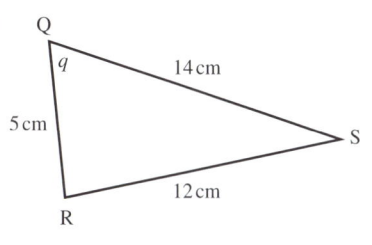

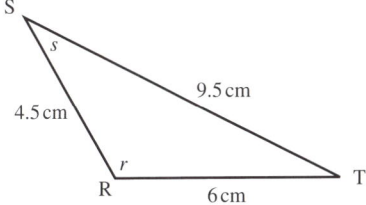

7 Triangle PQR with QR = 8 cm, QP = 6 cm, PR = 9 cm, angle p at P.

8 Triangle QRS with QR = 5 cm, QS = 14 cm, RS = 12 cm, angle q at Q.

9 Triangle RST with SR = 4.5 cm, ST = 9.5 cm, RT = 6 cm, angle s at S, angle r at R.

10 Triangle TUV with TV = 8.2 cm, VU = 3.7 cm, TU = 8.8 cm, angle t at T.

EXERCISE 28.3B

These are mixed questions on the sine and cosine rules.

Find the missing sides represented by letters. Give your answers correct to 3 significant figures.

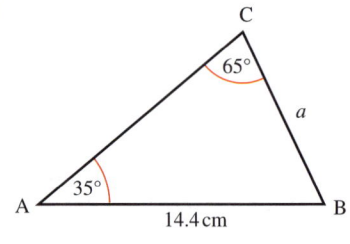

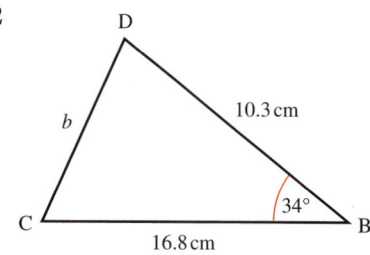

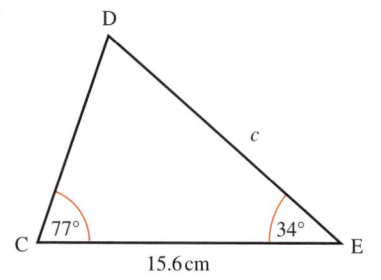

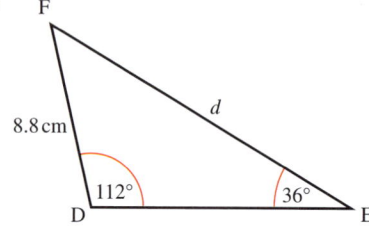

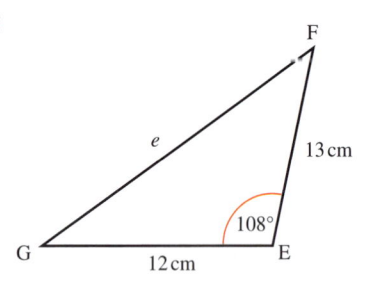

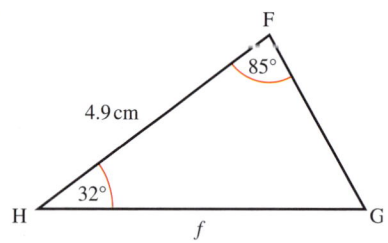

1 Triangle ABC with angle A = 35°, angle C = 65°, AB = 14.4 cm, side a = CB.

2 Triangle BCD with angle B = 34°, DB = 10.3 cm, CB = 16.8 cm, side b = CD.

3 Triangle CDE with angle C = 77°, angle E = 34°, CE = 15.6 cm, side c = DE.

4 Triangle DEF with angle D = 112°, angle E = 36°, DF = 8.8 cm, side d = FE.

5 Triangle EFG with angle E = 108°, EF = 13 cm, GE = 12 cm, side e = GF.

6 Triangle FGH with angle F = 85°, angle H = 32°, FH = 4.9 cm, side f = HG.

Find the unknown angles indicated by letters. Give your answers to the nearest 0.1°.

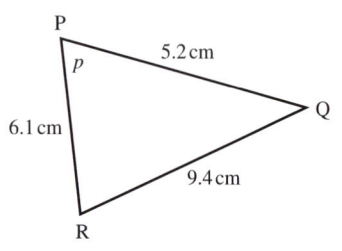

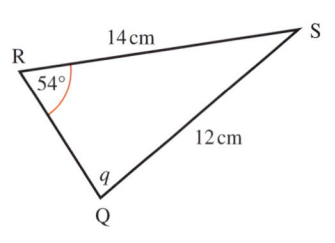

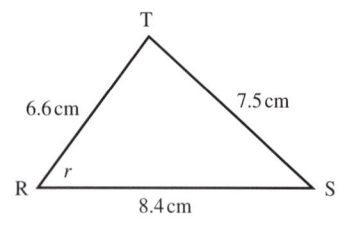

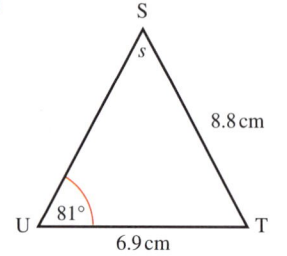

7 Triangle PQR with PQ = 5.2 cm, PR = 6.1 cm, QR = 9.4 cm, angle p at P.

8 Triangle RQS with angle R = 54°, RS = 14 cm, QS = 12 cm, angle q at Q.

9 Triangle RST with RT = 6.6 cm, TS = 7.5 cm, RS = 8.4 cm, angle r at R.

10 Triangle STU with ST = 8.8 cm, UT = 6.9 cm, angle U = 81°, angle s at S.

28.4 Area of a triangle using $\frac{1}{2}ab \sin C$, and segments of circles

Suppose you are given two sides of a non-right-angled triangle, say a and b, and the *included* angle between them, C. This information can be used to find the area of the triangle.

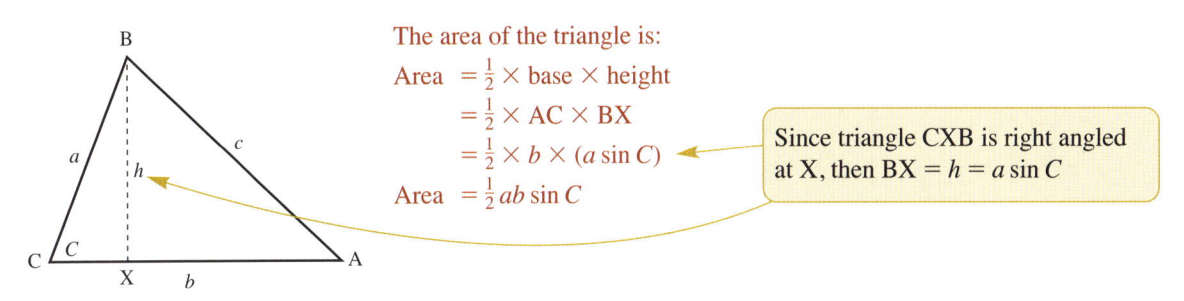

The area of the triangle is:

$$\text{Area} = \tfrac{1}{2} \times \text{base} \times \text{height}$$
$$= \tfrac{1}{2} \times AC \times BX$$
$$= \tfrac{1}{2} \times b \times (a \sin C)$$
$$\text{Area} = \tfrac{1}{2} ab \sin C$$

Since triangle CXB is right angled at X, then $BX = h = a \sin C$

As with the cosine rule, you may wish to learn this formula in three versions, according to which angle you have been given. In each case, in order to use the formula, you must have SAS, meaning 'two Sides and the included Angle'.

$$\text{Area of triangle} = \tfrac{1}{2}ab \sin C = \tfrac{1}{2}bc \sin A = \tfrac{1}{2}ac \sin B$$

EXAMPLE

Find the area of this triangle, correct to 3 significant figures.

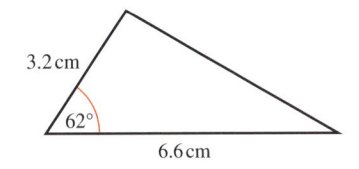

SOLUTION

$$\begin{aligned} \text{Area of triangle} &= \tfrac{1}{2} ab \sin C \\ &= \tfrac{1}{2} \times 3.2 \times 6.6 \times \sin 62° \\ &= 9.323\,926\,581 \\ &= \underline{9.32 \text{ cm}^2} \text{ (3 s.f.)} \end{aligned}$$

You might need to use the formula for the area of a triangle in reverse.

EXAMPLE

The diagram shows a triangle PQR in which PQ = 8 cm and QR = 10 cm. The triangle has an area of 20 cm². Angle PQR is acute.

a) Calculate the size of angle PQR.
b) Calculate the length of PR.
   Give your answer to 3 significant figures.

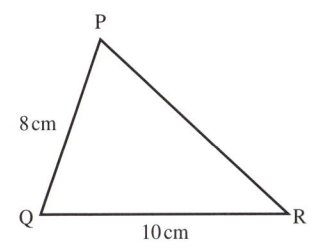

SOLUTION

a) Since the area of the triangle is 20 cm²:

$\frac{1}{2} ab \sin C$ = area of triangle

$\frac{1}{2} \times 8 \times 10 \times \sin Q = 20$

$40 \sin Q = 20$

$\sin Q = \frac{20}{40}$

$\sin Q = 20$

$Q = \sin^{-1}(0.5)$

$Q = 30°$

Thus angle PQR = 30°.

> Since the sine rule has been used, another possibility might be $Q = 180 - 30 = 150°$, but you are told that angle PQR is acute, so 150° may be discounted.

b) The length of PR may now be found, using the cosine rule:

$PR^2 = 8^2 + 10^2 - 2 \times 8 \times 10 \times \cos 30$

$ = 64 + 100 - 160 \cos 30°$

$ = 25.435\,935\,39$

$PR = \sqrt{25.435\,935\,39}$

$ = 5.04$ cm (3 s.f.)

Finally, you can use $\frac{1}{2} ab \sin C$ to help find the area of a segment of a circle. The next example illustrates the method.

EXAMPLE

Find the area of the segment shaded in the diagram below.
Give your answer to 3 significant figures.

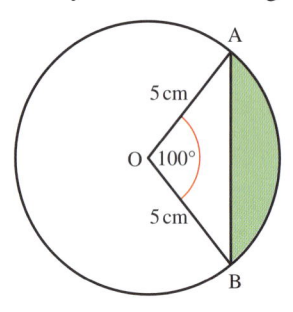

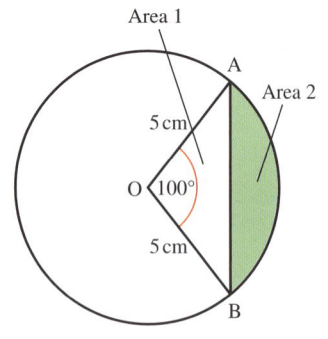

SOLUTION

Area 1 + Area 2 form a sector of angle 100°.
The area of the sector is:

$\frac{100}{360} \times \pi \times 5^2 = 21.816\,6$ cm²

Area 1 on its own forms a triangle.
Its area is:

$\frac{1}{2} \times 5 \times 5 \times \sin 100° = 12.310\,1$ cm²

Thus the area of the segment, Area 2, is:

$21.816\,6 - 12.310\,1 = 9.506\,5$ cm²

$ = 9.51$ cm² (3 s.f.)

EXERCISE 28.4

1. In triangle ABC, AB = 15 cm and BC = 18 cm.
   Angle ABC = 40°.

   Calculate the area of triangle ABC.
   Give your answer correct to 3 significant figures.

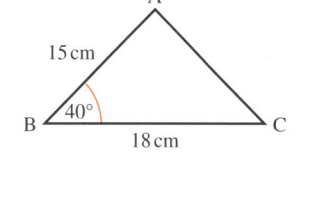

2. In triangle PQR, PQ = 9 cm and QR = 11.4 cm.
   Angle PQR = 142°.

   Calculate the area of triangle PQR.
   Give your answer correct to 3 significant figures.

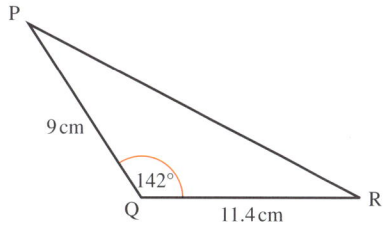

3. In triangle ABC, AB = 5 cm and BC = 8 cm.
   The area of triangle ABC = 15 m^2.
   Angle ABC is acute.
   a) Calculate the size of angle ABC.
      Give your answer correct to the nearest 0.1°
   b) Calculate the perimeter of triangle ABC.
      Give your answer correct to 3 significant figures.

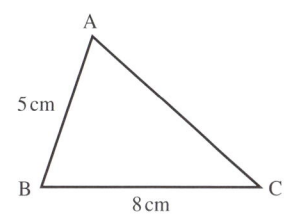

4. In triangle LMN, LM = 6 cm, MN = 8 cm and LN = 12 cm.
   a) Calculate the size of angle LMN.
      Give your answer correct to the nearest 0.1°.
   b) Calculate the area of triangle LMN.
      Give your answer correct to 3 significant figures.

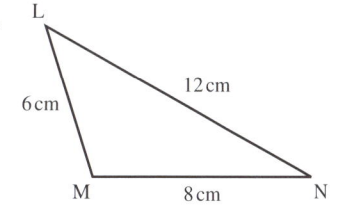

5. A chord AB is drawn across a circle of radius 10 cm.
   The chord AB is of length 15 cm.
   a) Use the cosine rule to find angle AOB.
      Give your answer to the nearest 0.1°.
   b) Hence find the area of the segment shaded in the diagram.

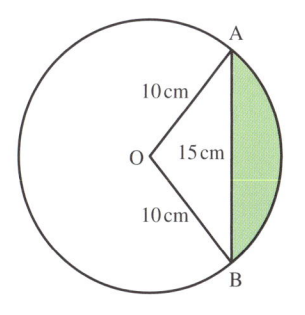

6. In triangle PQR, PQ = 6 cm and PR = 7 cm.
   The area of triangle PQR is 11 cm^2.
   a) Calculate the size of angle QPR.
      Give your answer correct to the nearest 0.1°.
   b) Calculate the perimeter of triangle QPR.
      Give your answer correct to 3 significant figures.

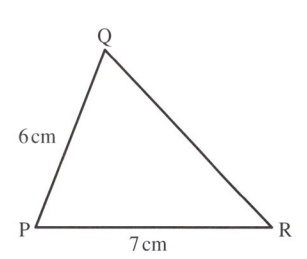

7 The diagram shows a regular hexagon inscribed inside a circle of radius 12 cm.
   a) Work out the area of the circle.
   b) Work out the area of the segment shaded on the diagram.
   c) Hence work out the area of the hexagon.
   Give all your answers correct to 3 significant figures.

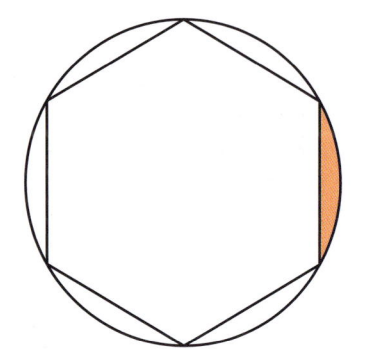

8 An isosceles triangle has sides of length 12 cm, 12 cm and 8 cm. Work out the area of this triangle.

28.5 Trigonometry in 3-D

You have already met the idea of using Pythagoras' theorem in 3-D. The approach is to break the problem down into two or more 2-D triangles, and solve them using the regular Pythagorean methods.

The same principle can be used for sines and cosines, to find unknown angles and lengths.

EXAMPLE

The diagram shows a wedge.
The base of the wedge is a horizontal rectangle measuring 60 cm by 80 cm.
The sloping face ABPQ is inclined at 25° to the horizontal.

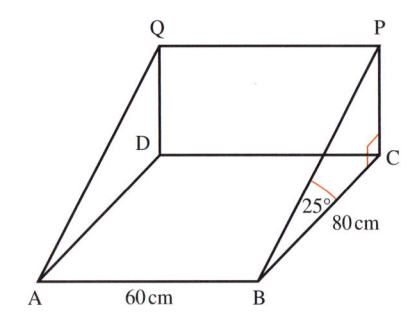

a) Calculate the lengths AC and PC.
b) Calculate the length AP.
c) Calculate the angle that AP makes with the horizontal plane ABCD.

SOLUTION

a) By Pythagoras' theorem:
$$x^2 = 60^2 + 80^2$$
$$= 3600 + 6400$$
$$= 10\,000$$
$$x = \sqrt{10\,000}$$
$$= 100 \text{ cm}$$

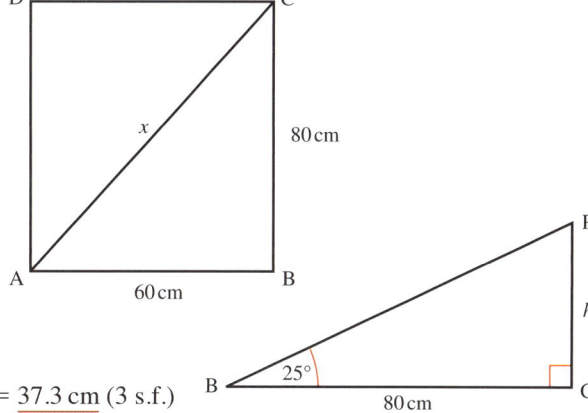

$h = 80 \times \tan 25°$
$= 37.3$ cm (3 s.f.)

Thus AC = 100 cm and PC = 37.3 cm (3 s.f.)

b) From the prism, pick out triangle ACP.

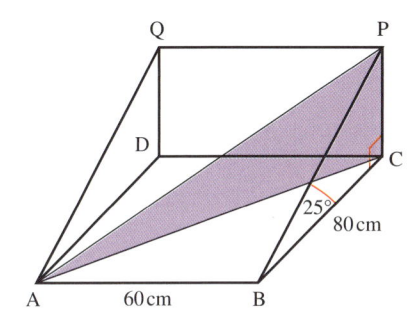

This triangle may be turned flat:

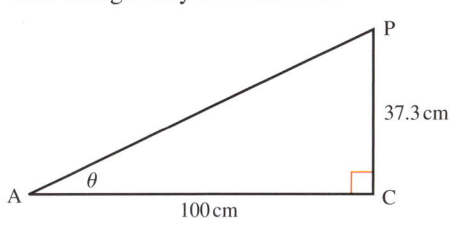

By Pythagoras' theorem:
$$AP^2 = 100^2 + 37.3^2$$
$$= 10\,000 + 1391.6$$
$$= 11\,391.6$$
$$AP = \sqrt{11\,391.6}$$
$$= 106.7315\ldots$$
$$= 106.7 \text{ cm (4 s.f.)}$$

c) Using the same triangle as above:
$$\tan \theta = \frac{37.3}{100}$$
$$= 0.373$$
$$\theta = \tan^{-1}(0.373)$$
$$= 20.5°$$

28 Further trigonometry U4

EXERCISE 28.5

1. The diagram shows a box in the shape of a cuboid ABCDEFGH. AB = 20 cm, BC = 30 cm, AE = 25 cm. A string runs diagonally across the box from C to E.

   a) Calculate the length of the string CE.
      Give your answer correct to 3 significant figures.
   b) Work out the angle between the string CE and the horizontal plane ABCD.
      Give your answer correct to the nearest 0.1°.

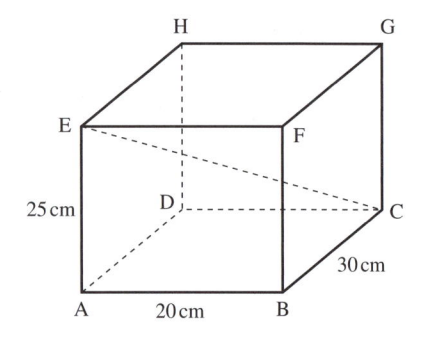

2. The diagram shows a square-based pyramid ABCDX. AB = BC = 20 cm. The point M is the centre of the square base ABCD. XM = 25 cm.

   a) Calculate the length of AC. Give your answer correct to 3 significant figures.
   b) Work out the length of the slanting edge AX.
      Give your answer correct to 3 significant figures.
   c) Work out the angle between the edge AX and the horizontal plane ABCD.
      Give your answer correct to the nearest 0.1°.

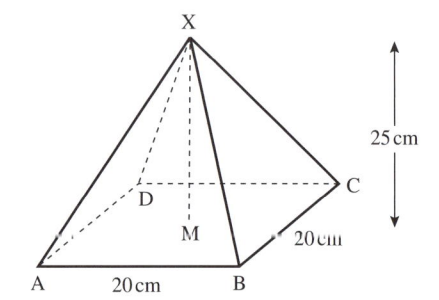

3. The diagram shows a wedge in the shape of a prism PQRSUV. PQ = 40 cm, QR = 90 cm, UR = 10 cm.

   a) Calculate the angle UQR.
      Give your answer correct to the nearest 0.1°.
   b) Calculate the length PU.
      Give your answer correct to 3 significant figures.
   c) Work out the angle between PU and the horizontal plane PQRS.
      Give your answer correct to the nearest 0.1°.

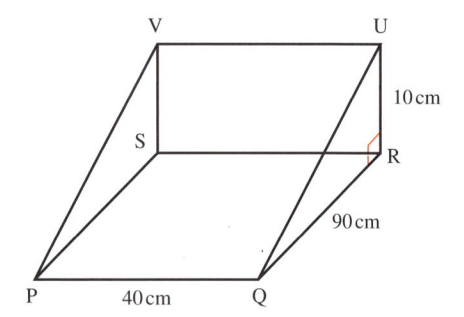

4. The diagram shows a cuboid ABCDEFGH. AB = 16 cm, BC = 18 cm, EC = 34 cm.

   a) Calculate the length AE.
   b) Work out the angle between CE and the horizontal plane ABCD.
      Give your answer correct to the nearest 0.1°.

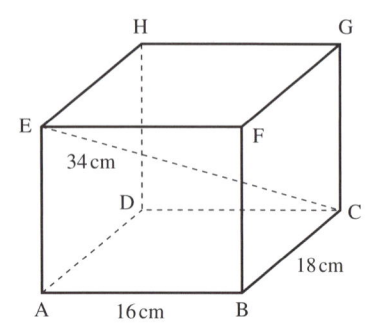

5 The cuboid ABCDEFGH has a square base ABCD.
AB = BC = 25 cm, EA = 8 cm.
   a) Calculate the length BD. Give your answer correct to 3 significant figures.
   b) Calculate the length BH. Give your answer correct to 3 significant figures.
   c) Work out the angle between BH and the horizontal plane EFGH. Give your answer correct to the nearest 0.1°.

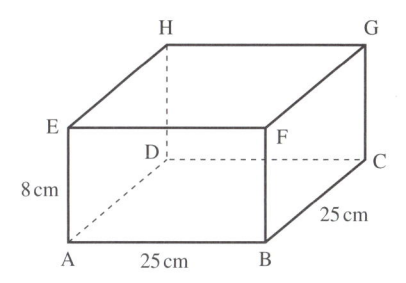

28.6 Frustums

A **frustum** is the shape formed when a small cone is removed from a larger one. Problems about frustums can usually be solved by similarity, because the smaller cone will be mathematically similar to the original larger cone. A frustum is sometimes called a **truncated cone**.

EXAMPLE

The diagram shows a cone of height 24 cm and base radius 18 cm. A smaller cone of height 6 cm is removed to form a frustum.

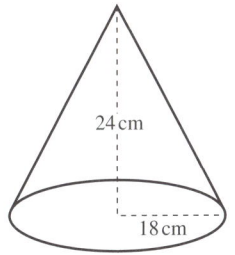

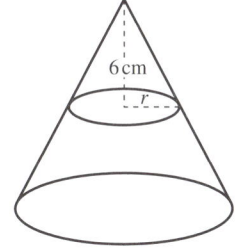

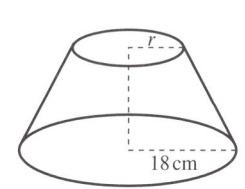

a) Work out the radius r of the base of the smaller cone.

Calculate, correct to the nearest cm³:
b) the volume of the larger cone
c) the volume of the smaller cone
d) the volume of the frustum.

SOLUTION

a) The ratio of the heights of the cones is 24 : 6 = 4 : 1, so the smaller cone is $\frac{1}{4}$ the height of the larger one. Therefore the radius $r = \frac{1}{4} \times 18 = \underline{4.5 \text{ cm}}$

b) The volume of a cone is $V = \frac{1}{3}\pi r^2 h$. For the larger cone, $r = 18$ cm and $h = 24$ cm, so:
$V = \frac{1}{3}\pi \times 18^2 \times 24$
$= \underline{8143 \text{ cm}^3}$

c) For the smaller cone, $r = 4.5$ cm and $h = 6$ cm, so:
$V = \frac{1}{3}\pi \times 4.5^2 \times 6$
$= \underline{127 \text{ cm}^3}$

d) The volume of the frustum is $8143 - 127 = \underline{8015 \text{ cm}^3}$

EXERCISE 28.6

1 A cone of height 12 cm has a base radius of 15 cm.
   a) Work out the volume of the cone.

   A smaller cone of height 4 cm is removed from the top of this cone to make a frustum.
   b) Work out the base radius of the smaller cone.
   c) Work out the volume of the frustum.

2 The diagram shows a cone of height 8 cm.
   The slant height of the cone, indicated on the diagram, is 17 cm.
   a) Work out the radius of the base of the cone.
   b) Hence work out the volume of the cone.

   The cone is cut by removing a smaller cone of height 4 cm, to leave a frustum.
   c) Work out the volume of the frustum.

3 Find the volume of this frustum of a cone.

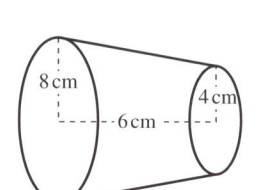

REVIEW EXERCISE 28

1 AB = 11.7 cm, BC = 28.3 cm, angle ABC = 67°.

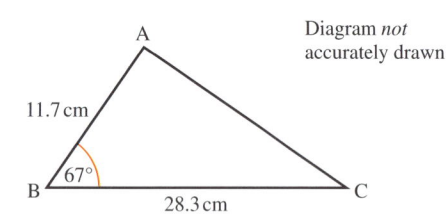

   Diagram *not* accurately drawn

   Calculate the area of triangle ABC.

2 The diagram shows triangle ABC.
   AC = 7.2 cm. BC = 8.35 cm.
   Angle ACB = 74°.

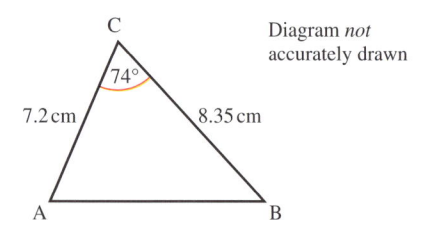

   Diagram *not* accurately drawn

   a) Calculate the area of triangle ABC.
      Give your answer correct to 3 significant figures. Give the units with your answer.
   b) Calculate the length of AB. Give your answer correct to 3 significant figures.   [Edexcel]

3

Diagram not accurately drawn

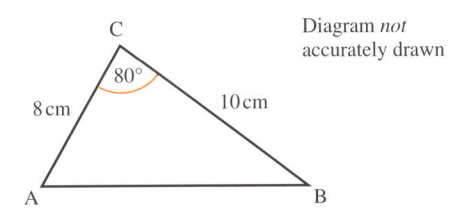

Triangle with C at top, angle 80°, CA = 8 cm, CB = 10 cm, A and B at base.

a) Calculate the length of AB.
   Give your answer, in centimetres, correct to 3 significant figures.
b) Calculate the size of angle ABC.
   Give your answer correct to 3 significant figures. [Edexcel]

4 AB = 3.2 cm. BC = 8.4 cm.
The area of triangle ABC is 10 cm².

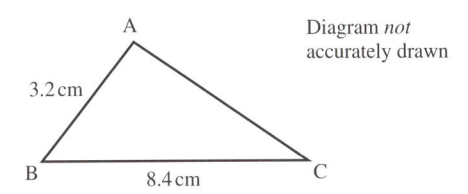

Diagram not accurately drawn

Triangle with A at top, BA = 3.2 cm, BC = 8.4 cm.

Calculate the perimeter of triangle ABC.
Give your answer correct to 3 significant figures. [Edexcel]

5 Angle ACB = 150°. BC = 60 m.
The area of triangle ABC is 450 m².

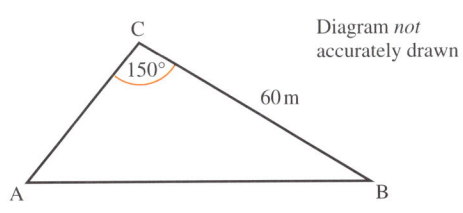

Diagram not accurately drawn

Triangle with C at top, angle 150°, CB = 60 m, A and B at base.

Calculate the perimeter of triangle ABC.
Give your answer correct to 3 significant figures. [Edexcel]

6 In triangle ABC, AC = 8 cm, CB = 15 cm, angle ACB = 70°.

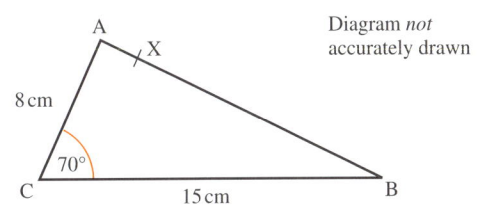

Diagram not accurately drawn

Triangle with A at top, X on AB, CA = 8 cm, angle C = 70°, CB = 15 cm.

a) Calculate the area of triangle ABC.
   Give your answer correct to 3 significant figures.

X is the point on AB such that angle CXB = 90°.
b) Calculate the length of CX.
   Give your answer correct to 3 significant figures. [Edexcel]

7 This question relates to the Starter exercise at the beginning of this chapter.
The diagram shows a triangle ABX. AB = 25 m.
Angle XAB = 32°. Angle XBY = 65°.
The aim is to find the height of the church steeple, XY.
Follow these steps.
  a) Make a copy of triangle ABX. Mark the values of angles ABX and AXB.
  b) Use the sine rule to work out the length AX.
  c) Now look at triangle AXY. Use trigonometry to calculate the height XY.
  How closely does your answer agree with your scale drawing from the Starter?

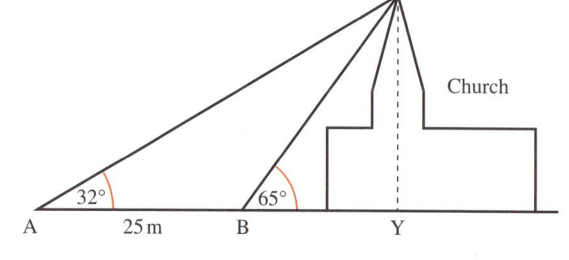

8 The diagram represents a cuboid ABCDEFGH.
AB = 5 cm. BC = 7 cm. AE = 3 cm.
  a) Calculate the length of AG.
     Give your answer correct to 3 significant figures.
  b) Calculate the size of the angle between AG and the face ABCD.
     Give your answer correct to 1 decimal place.

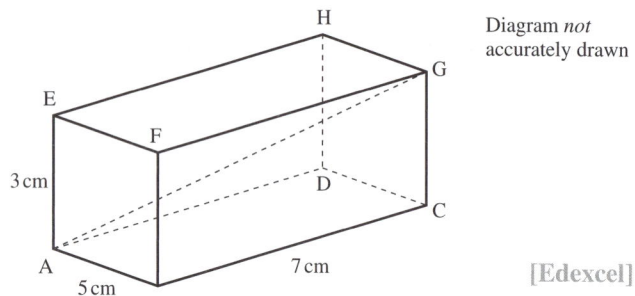

[Edexcel]

9 The diagram represents a prism. AEFD is a rectangle. ABCD is a square.
EB and FC are perpendicular to plane ABCD.
AB = 60 cm. AD = 60 cm. Angle ABE = 90°.
Angle BAE = 30°.
Calculate the size of the angle that the line DE makes with the plane ABCD.
Give your answer correct to 1 decimal place.

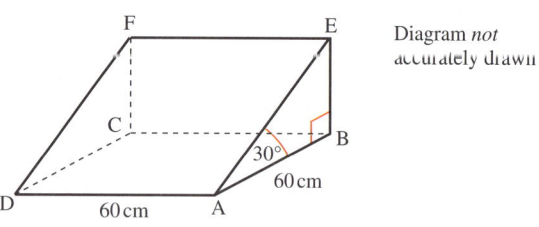

[Edexcel]

10 The left diagram represents a large cone of height 30 cm and base diameter 15 cm.

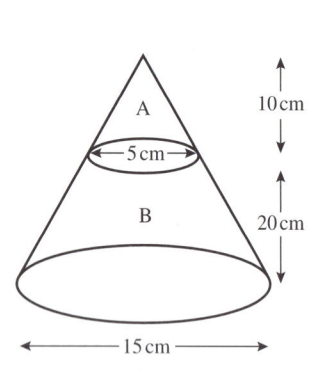

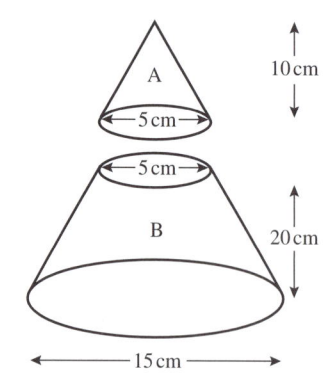

The large cone is made by placing a small cone A of height 10 cm and base diameter 5 cm on top of a frustum B.
  a) Calculate the volume of the frustum B.
     Give your answer correct to 3 significant figures.

The diagram shows a frustum. The diameter of the base is $3d$ cm and the diameter of the top is d cm. The height of the frustum is h cm.

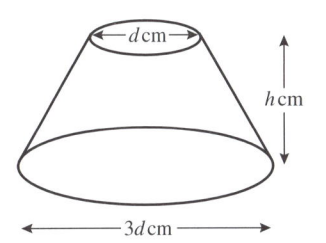

Diagram *not* accurately drawn

The formula for the curved surface area, S cm², of the frustum is:
$$S = 2\pi d\sqrt{h^2 + d^2}$$

b) Rearrange the formula to make h the subject.

Two mathematically similar frustums have heights of 20 cm and 30 cm.
The surface area of the smaller frustum is 450 cm².
c) Calculate the surface area of the larger frustum.

[Edexcel]

> **KEY POINTS**
>
> 1. Unknown sides and angles in triangles may be found by using the sine rule or the cosine rule.
>
> 2. The sine rule is generally used to relate two sides and two angles.
>   The examination formula book gives you the sine rule in this form:
> $$\frac{a}{\sin A} = \frac{b}{\sin B} = \frac{c}{\sin C}$$
>
> 3. The cosine rule is generally used to relate three sides and one angle.
>   The examination formula book gives you the cosine rule in this form:
> $$a^2 = b^2 + c^2 - 2bc \cos A$$
>
> 4. If you know two sides of a triangle, and the included angle (i.e. the angle between the two given sides) then the area can be computed using this result, which is also in the examination formula book:
> $$\text{Area of a triangle} = \tfrac{1}{2}ab \sin C$$
>   This is also a helpful formula for problems about finding the area of a segment of a circle.
>
> 5. For the GCSE examination you will be expected to know how to solve trigonometry problems in three dimensions. The approach is to form right-angled triangles inside the given 3-D object. Such triangles should be drawn out flat to help you see what calculations to do.
>
> 6. A frustum is a cone with a smaller cone removed (many lamp shades are shaped like a frustum). To find the volume of a frustum, work out the volumes of the larger and smaller cones separately, then subtract one from the other.

Internet Challenge 28

Heron's formula

Look at this triangle. How might you work out its area?

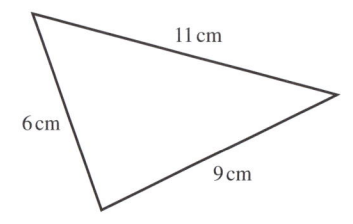

A rather tedious method is to use the cosine rule to find one of the angles. Then use $\frac{1}{2}ab \sin C$ to compute the area.

A much quicker way is to use Heron's formula. You start by working out the **semiperimeter** s of the triangle. For this example:

$$s = \tfrac{1}{2}(6 + 9 + 11) = 13$$

1. Use the internet to find Heron's formula. Write it in your book.

2. Use Heron's formula to find the area of the triangle above.

Here are three more triangles. Their areas are almost the same.

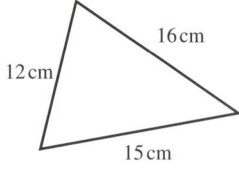

Triangle A 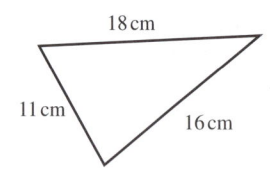   Triangle B 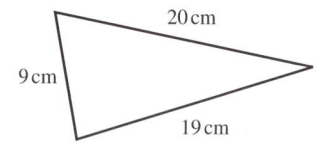   Triangle C

3. Use Heron's formula to work out the area of each triangle. Which of A, B or C has the largest area?

4. Use the internet to find out when Heron's formula was first used.

5. Try to find out how to prove Heron's formula.

CHAPTER 29

Graphs of curves

> In this chapter you will **learn how to**:
> - draw graphs of quadratics and cubics, and use them to solve equations
> - draw graphs of trigonometric functions for any angle
> - apply transformations to standard graphs.
>
> You will also be **challenged to**:
> - investigate famous curves.

Starter: Making waves

Make sure your calculator is in DEG (degree) mode. Then copy and complete this table of values for $\sin x$.

x	0	30	45	60	90	120	135	150	180
$\sin x$	0	0.5			1			0.5	

x	210	225	240	270	300	315	330	360	390
$\sin x$								0	

Now plot your results on graph paper, or a copy of the grid below.

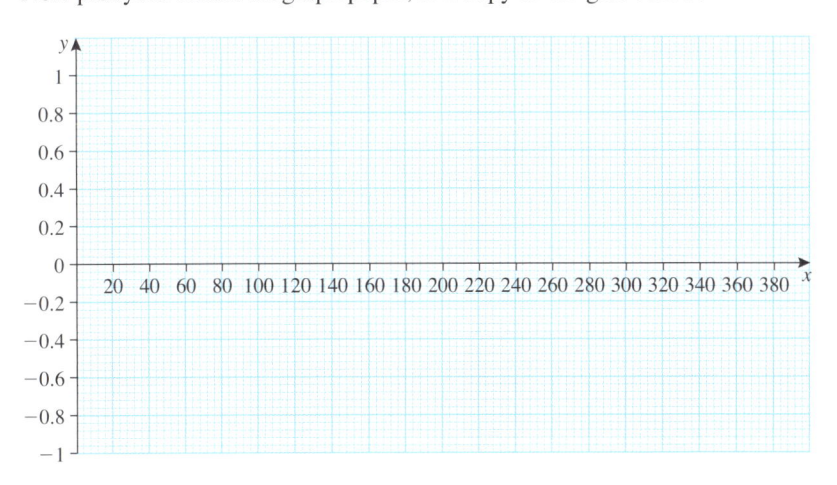

What do you notice?

Do you get a similar result if you use cosine instead of sine?

29.1 Tables of functions

In this chapter you will be working with functions like these:

$y = x^2 - 3$ a **quadratic** function

$y = x^3 + x$ a **cubic** function

$y = 2^x$ a **power** function or **exponential** function

$y = \dfrac{1}{x}$ a **reciprocal** function

You will need to be able to draw up tables of values for such functions. You will be given the x values and be asked to work out corresponding y values.

EXAMPLE

Draw up a table of values of the function $y = x^2 + 2x$ for $x = -3, -2, -1, 0, 1, 2, 3$.

SOLUTION

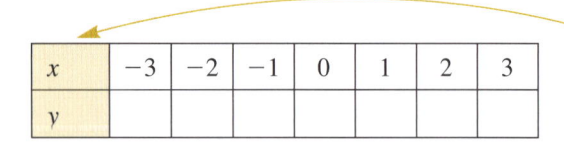

x	-3	-2	-1	0	1	2	3
y							

Begin by listing the x values you are going to work with.

x	-3	-2	-1	0	1	2	3
y	3						

Now work out $(-3)^2 + 2 \times (-3) = 9 - 6 = 3$
Write the result in the table.

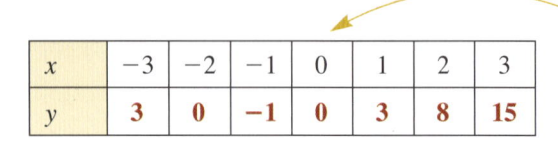

x	-3	-2	-1	0	1	2	3
y	3	0	-1	0	3	8	15

Continue until the table is complete.

A reciprocal function like $y = \dfrac{1}{x}$ can be tabulated in a similar way, but there cannot be an entry for $x = 0$ because you cannot divide by 0. We say this function is **not defined** when $x = 0$.

EXAMPLE

Complete the table of values for the function $y = \dfrac{1}{x}$.

x	-4	-2	-1	-0.5	0	0.5	1	2	4
y					not defined				

SOLUTION

As before, begin with $\frac{1}{-4} = -0.25$, then $\frac{1}{-2} = -0.5$, and so on.

Here is the final table:

x	-4	-2	-1	-0.5	0	0.5	1	2	4
y	-0.25	-0.5	-1	-2	not defined	2	1	0.5	0.25

EXERCISE 29.1

1 Complete the table of values for the function $y = x^2 - 5$.
One value has been filled in for you.

x	-3	-2	-1	0	1	2	3
y		-1					

2 Complete the table of values for the function $y = x^3 + x$.
Two values have been filled in for you.

x	-2	-1	0	1	2	3
y		-2			10	

3 Complete the table of values for the function $y = 2x^2 + 3$.
Two values have been filled in for you.

x	-2	-1	0	1	2	3
y		5			11	

4 Complete the table of values for the function $y = 3x^2 + x$.

x	-2	-1	0	1	2	3
y						

5 Complete the table of values for the function $y = x^2 - 4x$.

x	-1	0	1	2	3	4	5
y							

6 Complete the table of values for the function $y = 2^x$.
Two values have been filled in for you.

x	-2	-1	0	1	2	3
y	0.25				4	

7 Complete the table of values for the function $y = x + \dfrac{1}{x}$.

x	−2	−1	−0.5	0	0.5	1	2
y				not defined			

8 Complete the table of values for the function $y = 10^x$. One value has been filled in for you.

x	−1	0	1	2	3
y		1			

29.2 Plotting and using graphs of curves

Once you have made a table of values, the points can be plotted on graph paper to make a graph of the function. You should join the points using a *smooth* curve. Use a pencil, so that you can easily change your graph if it is not quite right at the first attempt.

EXAMPLE

The table shows values of the function $y = x^2 + 2x$ for $x = −4, −3, −2, −1, 0, 1, 2, 3$.

x	−4	−3	−2	−1	0	1	2	3
y	8	3	0	−1	0	3	8	15

a) Draw a set of axes so that x can range from −4 to 3 and y from −5 to 20, and plot these points on your axes.
b) Join your points with a smooth curve.
c) Use your graph to find: (i) the value of y when $x = 2.5$ (ii) the values of x when $y = 5$.

SOLUTION

a)

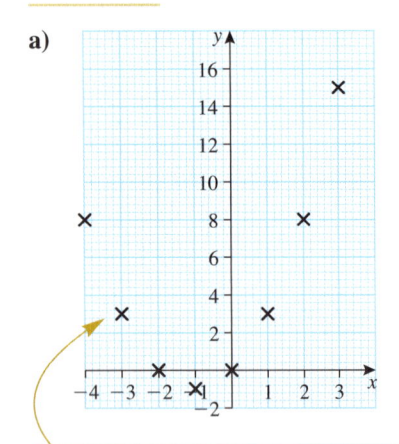

Plot the points carefully, using a neat cross or dot. Use pencil so that errors can be corrected.

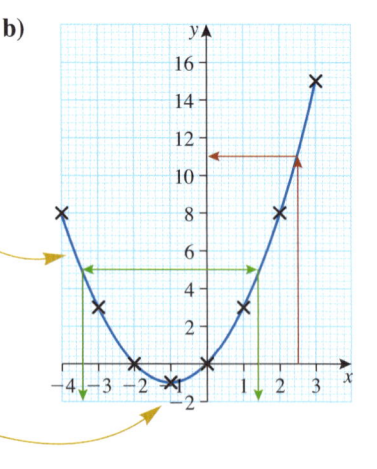

Draw a smooth curve, not a set of straight-line segments.

Take extra care here, where the graph curves rapidly.

b)

c) (i) When $x = 2.5$, $y = 11.3$ (1 d.p.)
(ii) When $y = 5$, $x = −3.4$ or 1.4

Note that whenever you plot the graph of a quadratic function, the curve will always have a distinctive bowl shape: it is a **parabola**.

The graph of a cubic function may be plotted in a similar way. The shape of a cubic function is not a parabola. The graph is now S-shaped, like these examples:

Graph of $y = x^3$

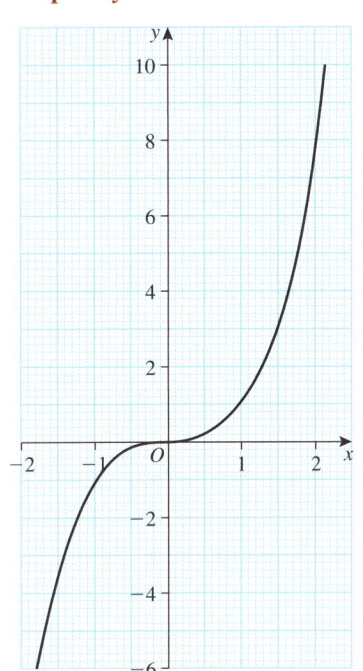

Graph of $y = x^3 - 3x$

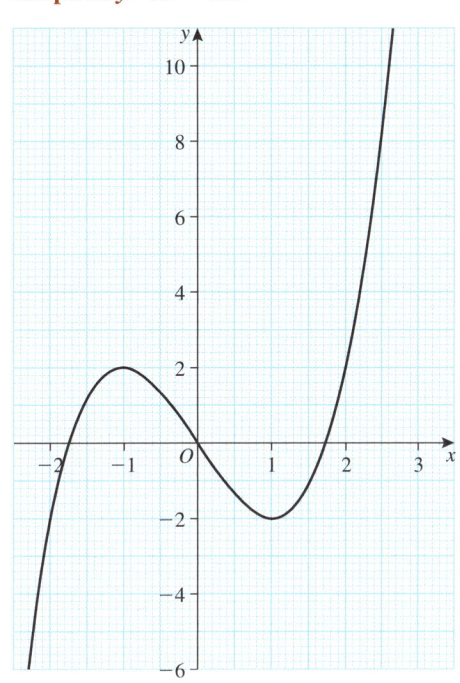

You can use graphs to find approximate solutions to equations. For example, the graph of $y = x^3 - 3x$ can be used to solve the equations $x^3 - 3x = 0$, $x^3 - 3x = 5$, and so on.

The next example shows you how.

EXAMPLE

The table shows some values for the function $y = x^3 - 3x$.

x	−2	−1	0	1	2	3
y	−2					18

a) Complete the missing values of y in the table.
b) Plot the points on a graph and join them with a smooth curve.
c) Use your graph to find all the solutions to the equation $x^3 - 3x = 0$.
d) By adding a horizontal line to your graph, solve the equation $x^3 - 3x = 8$.

SOLUTION

a)

x	−2	−1	0	1	2	3
y	−2	**2**	**0**	**−2**	**2**	18

b)

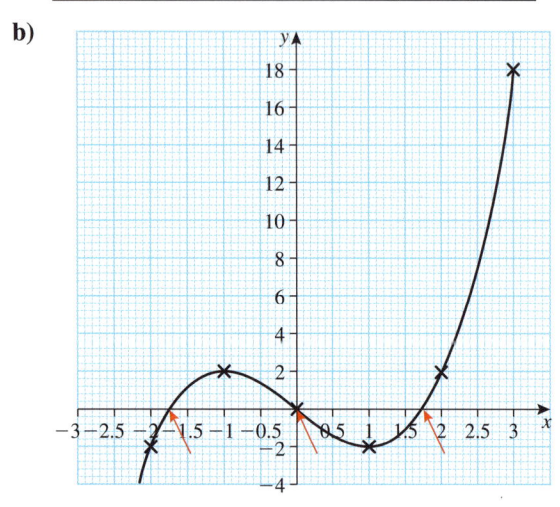

c) The solutions to the equation $x^3 - 3x = 0$ occur when $y = 0$, marked with arrows on the diagram above. Thus $x = \underline{-1.7}$, $x = \underline{0}$ or $x = \underline{1.7}$ (1 d.p.)

d) To solve the equation $x^3 - 3x = 8$, it is necessary to draw a horizontal line representing $y = 8$ on the graph, and see where this crosses $y = x^3 - 3x$:

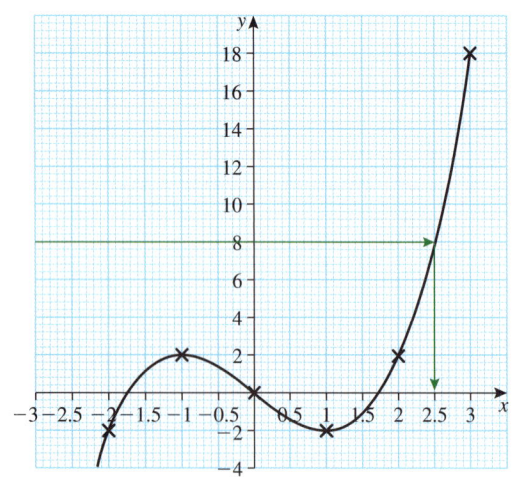

So, the solution is $\underline{x = 2.5}$ (1 d.p.)

EXERCISE 29.2

1. The table shows values of the function $y = x^2 - 3$ for $x = -3, -2, -1, 0, 1, 2, 3$.

x	-3	-2	-1	0	1	2	3
y	6	1	-2	-3	-2	1	6

   a) Draw a set of axes so that x can range from -3 to 3 and y from -5 to 10, and plot these points on your axes.
   b) Join your points with a smooth curve.
   c) Use your graph to find the value of y when $x = 1.5$.
   d) Find the coordinates of the lowest point on the curve.

2. The table shows some values of the function $y = x^2 + 4x$.

x	-3	-2	-1	0	1	2	3
y			-3			12	

   a) Copy and complete the table.
   b) Draw a set of coordinate axes on squared paper, so that x can run from -3 to 3 and y from -5 to 22. Plot these points on your graph, and join them with a smooth curve.
   c) Give the coordinates of the lowest point on the graph.

3. The table shows some values of the function $y = 2x^2 - 3$.

x	-3	-2	-1	0	1	2	3
y		5			-1		

   a) Copy and complete the table.
   b) Draw a set of coordinate axes on squared paper, so that x can run from -3 to 3 and y from -5 to 20. Plot these points on your graph, and join them with a smooth curve.
   c) Use your graph to find all the solutions to the equation $2x^2 - 3 = 0$.

4. The table shows some values for the function $y = x^3 - 4x$.

x	-3	-2	-1	0	1	2	3
y	-15				-3		

   a) Copy and complete the table.
   b) Draw a set of coordinate axes on squared paper, so that x can run from -3 to 3 and y from -15 to 15. Plot these points on your graph, and join them with a smooth curve.
   c) Use your graph to solve the equation $x^3 - 4x = 0$.
   d) Use your graph to solve the equation $x^3 - 4x = 5$.

5. The table shows some values of the function $y = 2^x$.

x	-1	0	1	2	3	4
y		1				16

   a) Copy and complete the table.

b) Draw a set of coordinate axes on squared paper, so that x can run from -1 to 4 and y from 0 to 20. Plot these points on your graph, and join them with a smooth curve.
c) Use your graph to solve the equation $2^x = 12$.

6 The table shows some values of the function $y = 8 - x^2$.

x	-3	-2	-1	0	1	2	3
y		4		8			-1

a) Copy and complete the table.
b) Draw a set of coordinate axes on squared paper, so that x can run from -3 to 3 and y from -5 to 10. Plot these points on your graph, and join them with a smooth curve.
c) State the coordinates of the point on the curve where y takes its maximum value.
d) Use your graph to find the two solutions to the equation $8 - x^2 = 0$.

7 The table shows some values of the function $y = \dfrac{12}{x}$. The function is not defined when $x = 0$.

x	-3	-2	-1	0	1	2	3	4
y	-4			not defined		6		

a) Copy and complete the table.
b) Draw a set of coordinate axes on squared paper, so that x can run from -3 to 4 and y from -15 to 15. Plot these points on your graph.
c) Join the first three points with a smooth curve.
d) Join the last four points with another smooth curve.
e) Use your graph to solve the equation $\dfrac{12}{x} = 9$.

8 The table shows some x values for the function $y = x^2 - x - 6$.

x	-3	-2	-1	0	1	2	3	4
y	6			-6			0	

a) Copy and complete the table.
b) Draw a set of coordinate axes on squared paper, so that x can run from -3 to 4 and y from -8 to 8. Plot these points on your graph, and join them with a smooth curve.
c) Write down the solutions to the equation $x^2 - x - 6 = 0$.
d) Give the coordinates of the minimum point on the curve.

9 The diagram shows part of the graph of the function $y = x^2 - 7x + 9$.
a) Use the graph to find the two solutions to the equation $x^2 - 7x + 9 = 0$.
b) Use the graph to find the two solutions to the equation $x^2 - 7x + 9 = 5$.

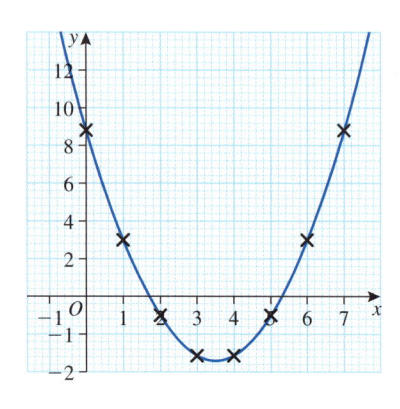

10 The diagram below shows part of the graph of $y = \dfrac{1}{x}$.

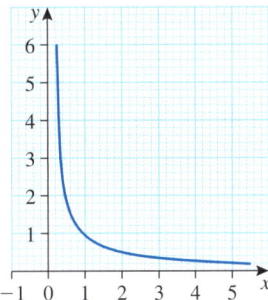

Use the graph to find a solution to the equation $\dfrac{1}{x} = 0.8$.

29.3 Graphs of sine, cosine and tangent functions

The starter for this chapter, Making waves, shows you that you can work out the value of sin x for *any* angle, not just those between 0 and 90°. A graph helps you visualise what is happening.

Here is the graph of $y = \sin x$ for values of x between 0 and 90°.

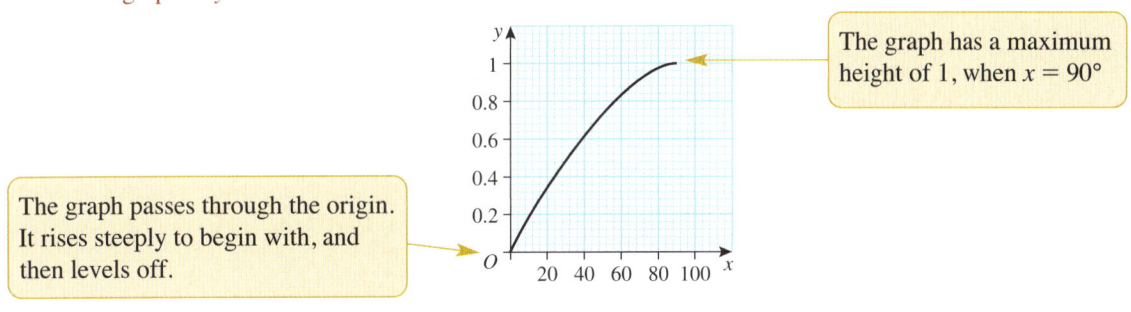

The graph has a maximum height of 1, when $x = 90°$

The graph passes through the origin. It rises steeply to begin with, and then levels off.

By extending the x axis up to 360° we obtain a **sine wave**:

Graph of $y = \sin x$ from 0° to 360°

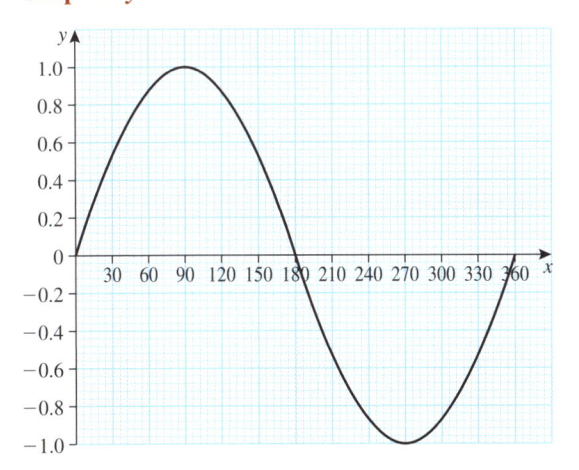

The wave repeats regularly every 360°; we say sin x is a **periodic** function.

Graph of $y = \sin x$ from $-180°$ to $720°$

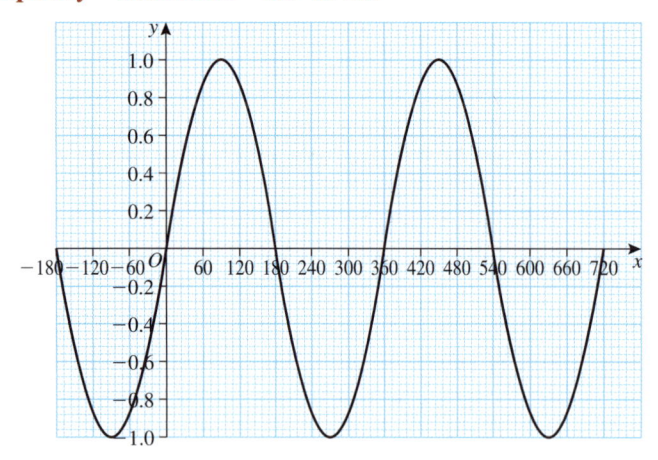

The graph of cos x behaves in a very similar way. The graph of $y = \cos x$ does not pass through the origin, however. Instead, it has a **maximum value** (of 1) when $x = 0°$:

Graph of $y = \cos x$ from $-180°$ to $720°$

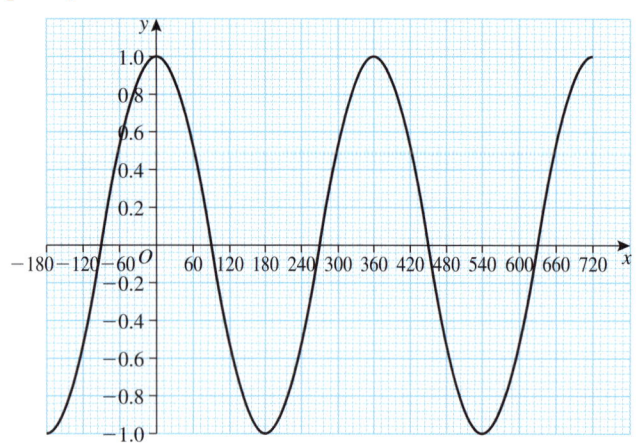

This table summarises some properties of the sine and cosine functions. Study it carefully – there are some obvious similarities, but also subtle differences between the two.

	$y = \sin x$	$y = \cos x$
Behaviour at $x = 0$	Passes through the origin	Has a maximum at (0, 1)
Type of symmetry	Rotation symmetry of order 2 about the origin	Reflection symmetry in the y axis
Range of values	-1 to $+1$	-1 to $+1$

The function $y = \tan x$ behaves in a completely different way from $y = \sin x$ and $y = \cos x$. Unlike sine and cosine, the tangent function does not have a maximum value of 1. You can use your calculator to verify that $\tan 45° = 1$, $\tan 50° = 1.1918$, $\tan 60° = 1.7321$, and so on. By the time you get to 89°, you will find that $\tan 89° = 57.2890$. As the value of x gets closer and closer to 90°, the value of $\tan x$ increases without limit!

Here is the graph of $y = \tan x$ for values of x between 0 and 90°.

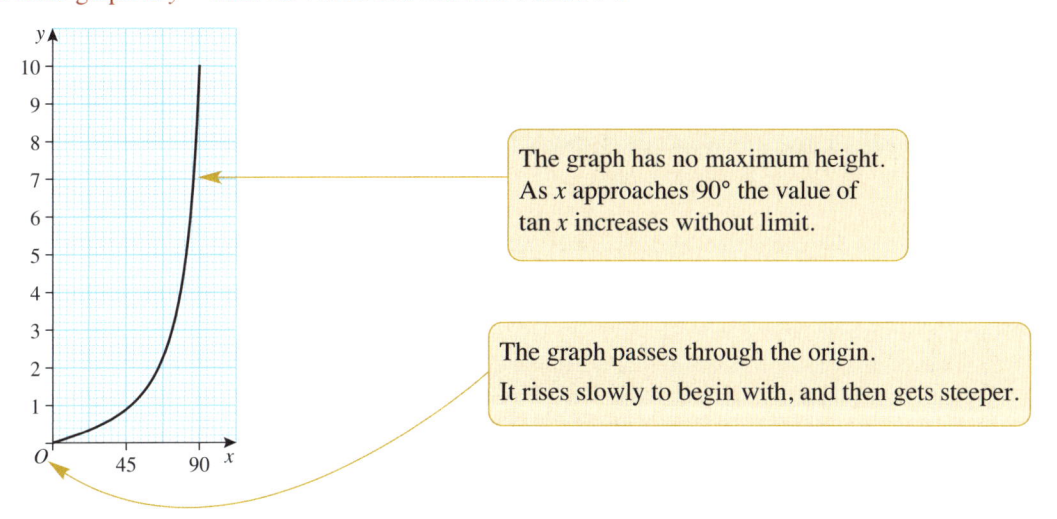

> The graph has no maximum height. As x approaches 90° the value of $\tan x$ increases without limit.

> The graph passes through the origin. It rises slowly to begin with, and then gets steeper.

Here is the graph of $y = \tan x$ over a wider range of x values:

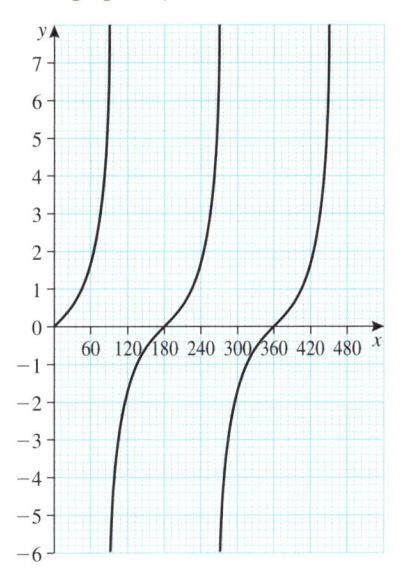

Like the sine function, the graph of $y = \tan x$ passes through the origin, and has rotational symmetry of order 2 about the origin. The curve is disconnected at 90°, 270° and so on.

You will use the properties of these graphs in the next section, **Transformations of graphs**. Before doing so, re-read this section, and then try the following exercise to make sure you have understood the properties of the three graphs.

EXERCISE 29.3

1 Draw three sketch graphs to show:
   a) $y = \sin x$
   b) $y = \cos x$,
   c) $y = \tan x$,
   as x ranges from 0 to 450°.

2 Here are some statements about trigonometric functions. Decide whether each one is true or false. Try to deduce the answer from graphical considerations rather than using a calculator.
 a) sin 30° and sin 150° have the same value.
 b) cos 30° and cos 150° have the same value.
 c) tan x always lies between 0 and 1.
 d) cos x cannot be negative provided x lies between 0° and 180°.
 e) sin 10° and sin 370° have the same value.

3 Here are some clues about trigonometric functions. For each one, decide whether it is referring to $y = \sin x$, $y = \cos x$ or $y = \tan x$.
 a) This function has a maximum when $x = 0$.
 b) This function is not defined when $x = 90°$.
 c) The graph of this function passes through the point (90°, 1).
 d) The graph of this function has reflection symmetry in the y axis.
 e) This function has a minimum when $x = 270°$.

29.4 Transformations of graphs

It is possible to **transform** a graph by moving it vertically or horizontally. For example, the graph $y = x^2$ can be **translated** 5 units **vertically** (in the y direction) to form the graph $y = x^2 + 5$.

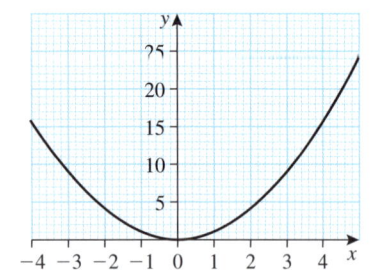

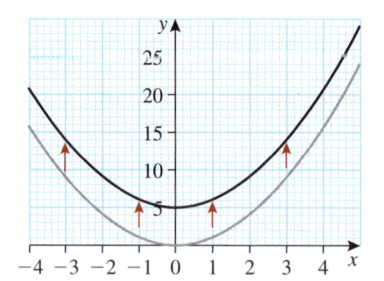

In this topic it is convenient to use function notation f(x). So if the left-hand graph represents the function $y = $ f(x), then the right-hand graph represents the function $y = $ f(x) + 5. In general terms, we would say that:

$$f(x) \rightarrow f(x) + 5$$
moves the graph 5 units **up**

$$f(x) \rightarrow f(x) - 3$$
moves the graph 3 units **down**.

The graph $y = x^2$ could also be translated **horizontally**, by 2 units, for example. The equation of the new graph would then turn out to be $y = (x - 2)^2$.

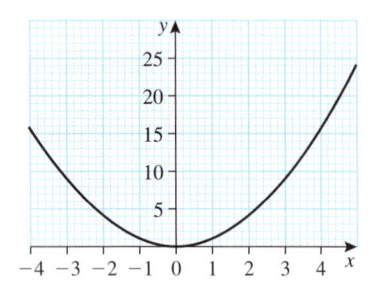

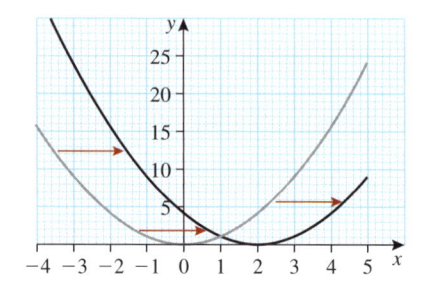

Now, if the left-hand graph represents the function $y = f(x)$, then the right-hand graph represents the function $y = f(x - 2)$. In general terms, we would say that:

$$f(x) \rightarrow f(x - 2)$$
moves the graph 2 units **right**

$$f(x) \rightarrow f(x + 4)$$
moves the graph 4 units **left**.

The translation might be in the opposite direction to that which you were expecting: when the number after the x is negative you move right, not left.

EXAMPLE

The diagram shows a sketch of the graph of $y = f(x)$. On the same axes, draw the graphs of:
a) $y = f(x) + 2$
b) $y = f(x + 1)$

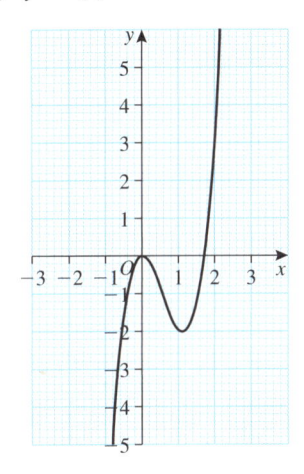

SOLUTION

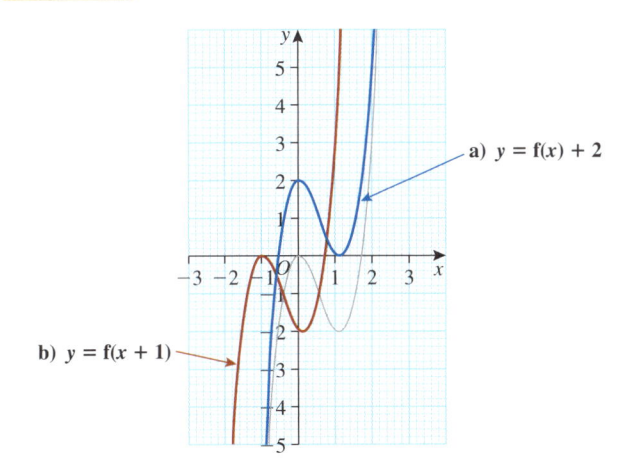

You can also **stretch** (or **compress**) graphs horizontally or vertically. Here is the graph of $y = x^2$ again, compared with the graph of $y = 2x^2$.

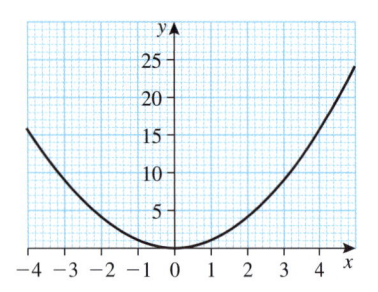

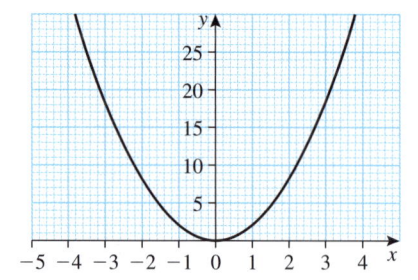

$$f(x) \rightarrow 2f(x)$$
Each y value is doubled; x stays where it is.

If you apply the transformation $f(x) \rightarrow 2f(x)$ to a sine or cosine graph, the y values will now range from -2 to 2 instead of -1 to 1.

EXAMPLE

The diagram below shows part of the graph of $y = \sin x$.
On two copies of this diagram, draw the graphs of:
a) $y = 3 \sin x$ b) $y = 2 \sin x - 1$

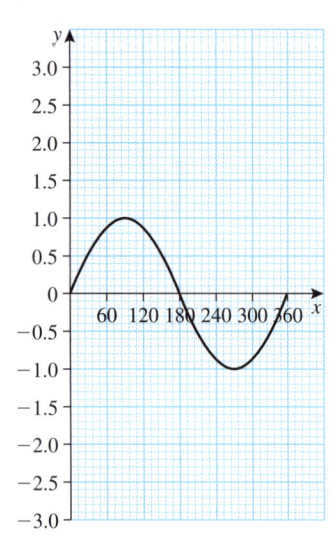

SOLUTION

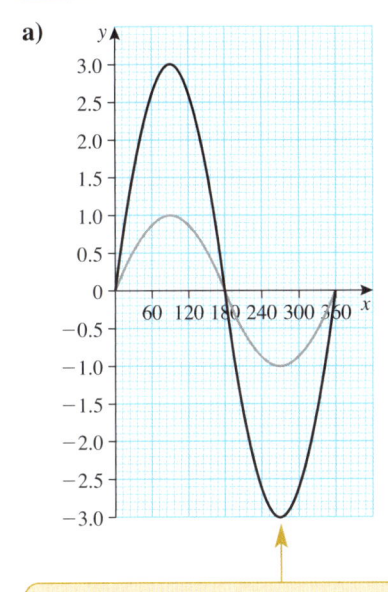

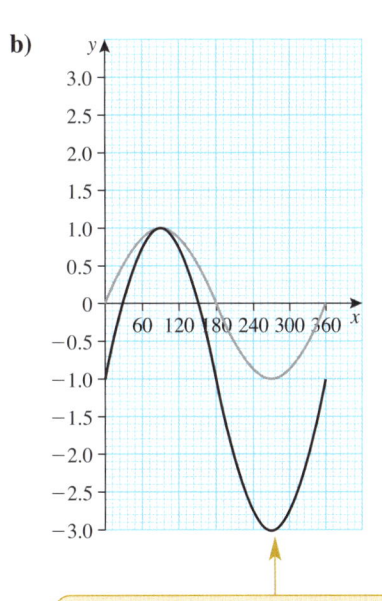

a)

b)

$y = 3 \sin x$ is a vertical stretch of the graph $y = \sin x$ with stretch factor 3, so the new curve ranges from -3 to $+3$.

Changing $\sin x \to 2 \sin x$ will give a vertical stretch with factor 2, so the graph ranges from -2 to $+2$.
Changing $2 \sin x \to 2 \sin x - 1$ will move the resulting graph 1 unit downwards, so the new range is -3 to $+1$.

Graphs can also be stretched (or compressed) horizontally. This is often done with sine or cosine waves, by attaching a numerical scale factor inside the sine or cosine function.

$$f(x) \to f(2x)$$

Each x value is doubled, and y stays where it is.

For example, the function $y = \sin(2x)$ will complete a full wave **twice** in $360°$.

Graph of $y = \sin x$

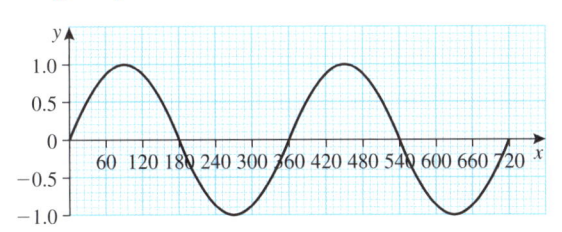

Graph of $y = \sin(2x)$: contains twice as many waves

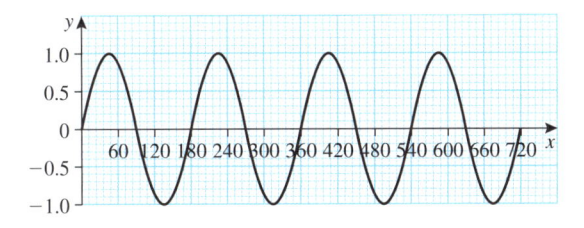

Finally, graphs can be reflected in the *x* axis or the *y* axis:

$$f(x) \to -f(x)$$
Reflection in the *x* axis

$$f(x) \to f(-x)$$
Reflection in the *y* axis

Note that examination questions may well combine several of these transformations.

EXERCISE 29.4

1 The diagram shows part of the graph of $y = f(x)$.

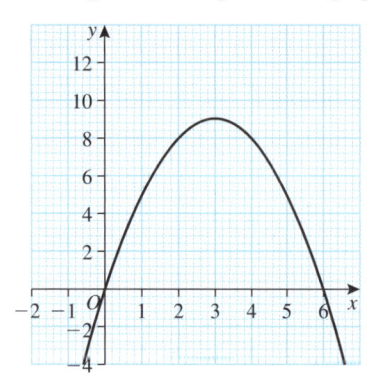

On a copy of this diagram, draw the graphs of:
a) $y = f(x) + 3$ **b)** $y = f(x + 1)$ **c)** $y = f(2x)$
Label your three graphs clearly.

2 The diagram shows part of the graph of $y = f(x)$.

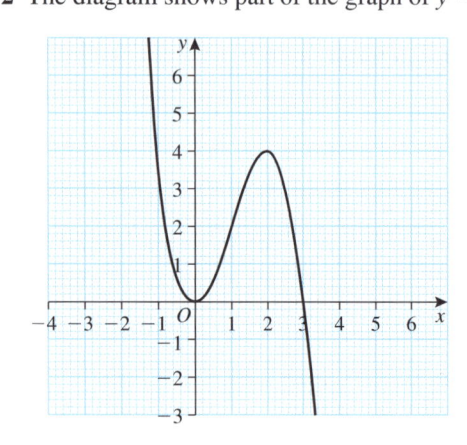

On a copy of this diagram, draw the graphs of:
a) $y = f(x) + 1$ **b)** $y = f(x - 2)$ **c)** $y = f(x) - 2$
Label your three graphs clearly.

3 The diagram shows part of the graph of $y = f(x)$.

On a copy of this diagram, draw the graphs of:
a) $y = f(x + 1)$
b) $y = f(x + 1) + 2$

Label your two graphs clearly.

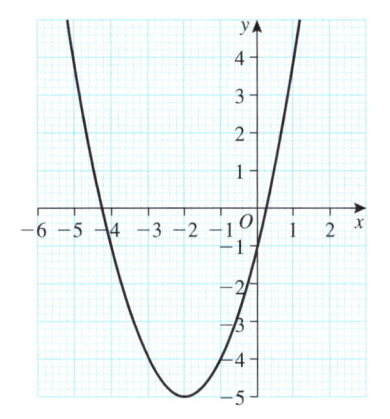

4 The diagram shows part of the graph of $y = f(x)$.

On a copy of the diagram, draw the graphs of:
a) $y = -f(x)$
b) $y = f(-x)$

Label your two graphs clearly.

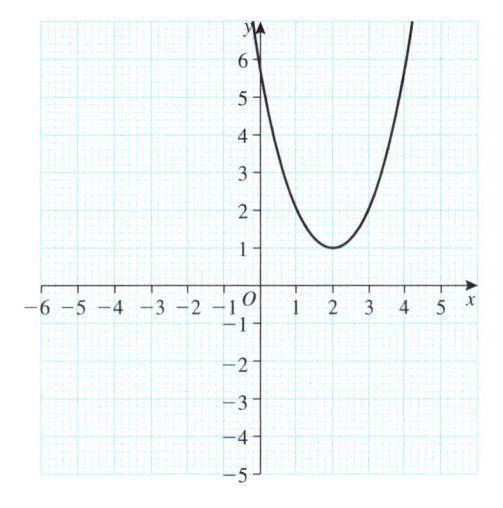

5 The diagram shows part of the graph of $y = a \sin(bx°)$, where a and b are constants.

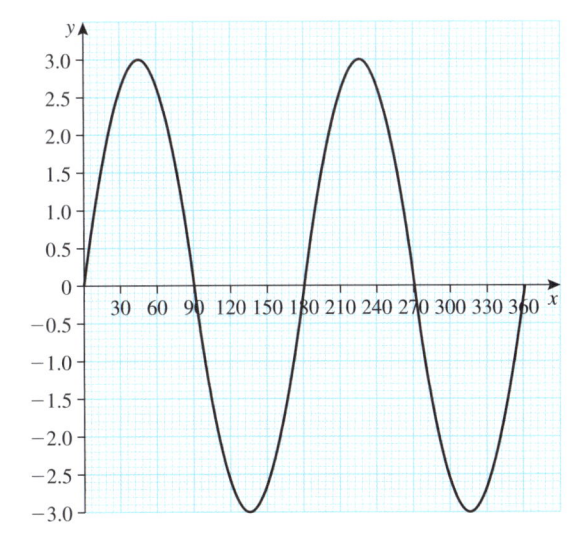

Work out the values of a and b. Explain your reasoning.

6 The diagram shows part of the graphs of $y = f(x)$ and $y = f(x + a) + b$.

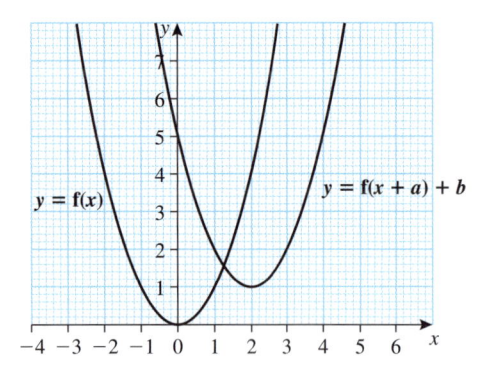

Work out the values of a and b. Explain your reasoning.

7 The diagram below shows part of the graph of $y = a \sin (bx°)$.

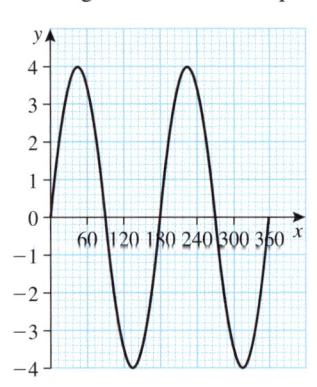

Work out the values of a and b. Explain your reasoning.

8 The diagram below shows part of the graph of $y = a \cos (x°) + b$.

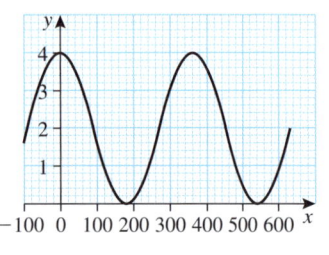

Work out the values of a and b. Explain your reasoning.

REVIEW EXERCISE 29

1 a) Copy and complete the table of values for $y = 2x^2$.

x	−3	−2	−1	0	1	2	3
y	18				2	8	

b) On a copy of the grid below, draw the graph of $y = 2x^2$.

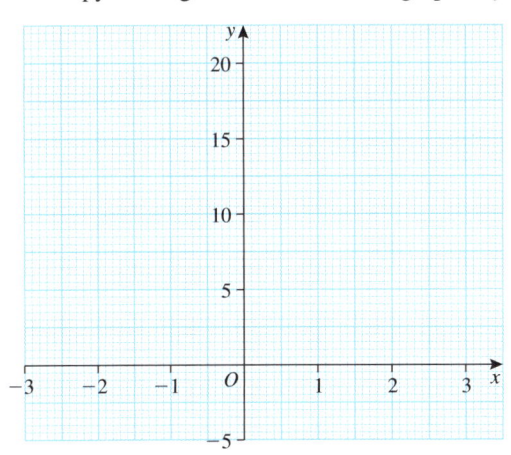

c) Use your graph to find:
   (i) the value of y when $x = 2.5$
   (ii) the values of x when $y = 12$.
   [Edexcel]

2 a) Copy and complete the table of values for the graph $y = x^3 + 2$.

x	-3	-2	-1	0	1	2
$y = x^3 + 2$	-25					10

b) On a copy of the grid, draw the graph of $y = x^3 + 2$.

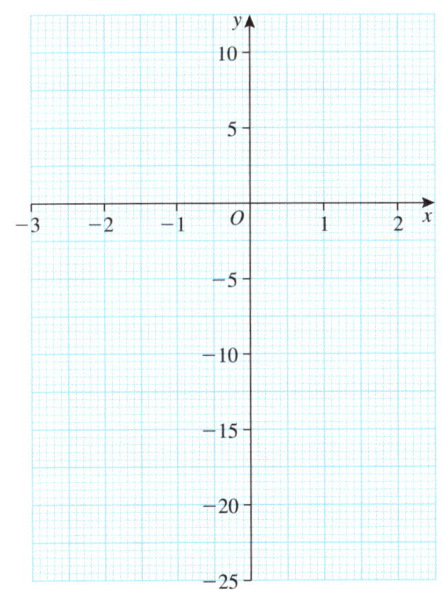

c) Use your graph to find:
   (i) an estimate of the solution of the equation $x^3 + 2 = 0$
   (ii) an estimate of the solution of the equation $x^3 + 2 = 8$
   [Edexcel]

3 This is a sketch of the curve with equation $y = f(x)$. It passes through the origin O.

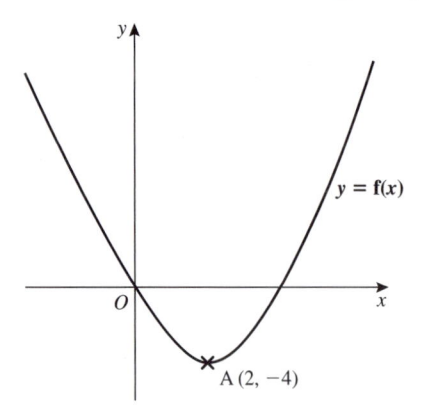

The only vertex of the curve is at A $(2, -4)$.
a) Write down the coordinates of the vertex of the curve with equation:
  (i) $y = f(x - 3)$
  (ii) $y = f(x) - 5$
  (iii) $y = -f(x)$
  (iv) $y = f(2x)$

The curve with equation $y = x^2$ has been translated to give the curve $y = f(x)$.
b) Find $f(x)$ in terms of x. [Edexcel]

4 This is a sketch of the graph of $y = \sin x°$ for values of x between 0 and 360.

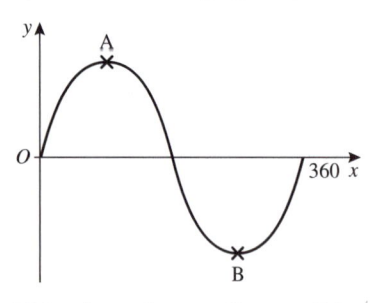

a) Write down the coordinates of the points:
  (i) A   **(ii)** B
b) On a copy of the same axes, sketch the graph of $y = \sin 2x°$ for values of x between 0 and 360. [Edexcel]

5 This is a sketch of the curve with equation $y = f(x)$.

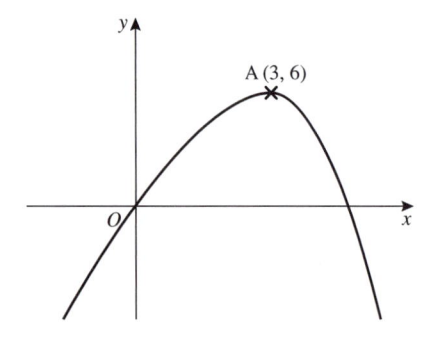

The only maximum point of the curve $y = f(x)$ is A $(3, 6)$.
Write down the coordinates of the maximum point for curves with each of the following equations:
a) $y = f(x + 2)$ **b)** $y = f(x) + 4$ **c)** $y = f(-x)$ [Edexcel]

6 A sketch of the curve $y = \sin x°$ for $0 \leqslant x \leqslant 360$ is shown below.

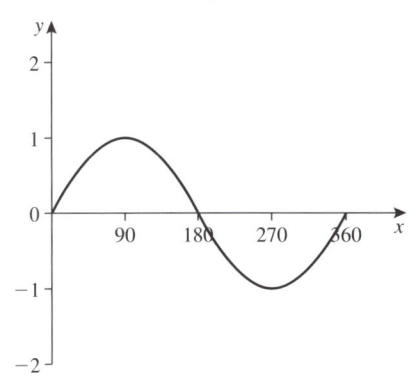

a) Using the sketch above, or otherwise, find the equation of each of the following two curves.
   (i)
   (ii)

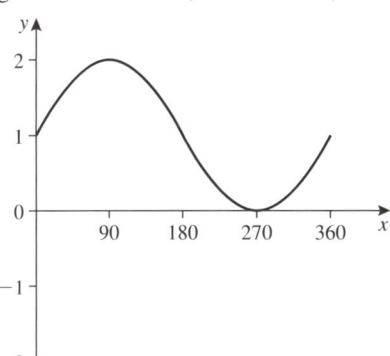

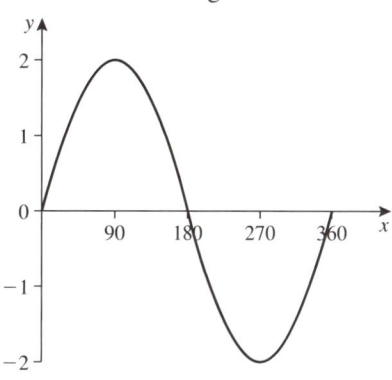

b) Describe fully the sequence of two transformations that maps the graph of $y = \sin x°$ onto the graph of $y = 3 \sin 2x°$. [Edexcel]

7 A transformation has been applied to the graph of $y = x^2$ to give the graph of $y = -x^2$.
   a) Describe fully the transformation.

For all values of x, $x^2 + 4x = (x + p)^2 + q$
   b) Find the values of p and q.

A transformation has been applied to the graph of $y = x^2$ to give the graph of $y = x^2 + 4x$.
   c) Using your answer to part b), or otherwise, describe fully the transformation. [Edexcel]

8 The graph of $y = f(x)$ is sketched in the diagram below.

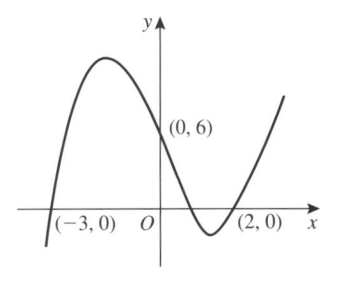

a) On a copy of the graph, sketch the graph of $y = f(x - 3)$.
b) On another copy of the graph, sketch the graph of $y = f(x) - 4$. [Edexcel]

9 The graph of $y = a - b\cos(kt)$, for values of t between $0°$ and $120°$, is drawn on the grid.

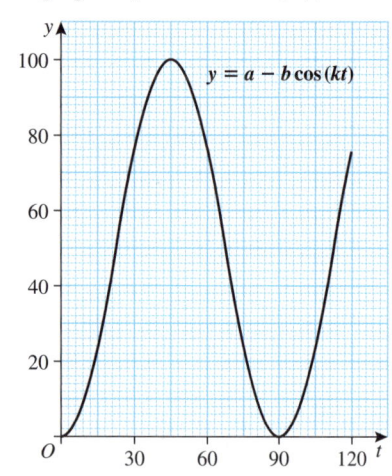

Use the graph to find an estimate for the value of:
a) a **b)** b **c)** k [Edexcel]

10 The diagram shows part of two graphs.
The diagram is **not** accurately drawn.

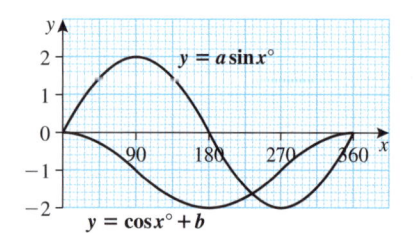

Diagram *not* accurately drawn

The equation of one graph is $y = a\sin x°$. The equation of the other graph is $y = \cos x° + b$.
a) Use the graphs to find the value of a and the value of b.
b) Use the graphs to find the values of x in the range $0° \leq x \leq 720°$ when $a\sin x° = \cos x° + b$.
c) Use the graphs to find the value of $a\sin x° - (\cos x° + b)$ when $x = 450°$.   [Edexcel]

KEY POINTS

1. Graphs of quadratics and cubics may be plotted by drawing up a table of values.

2. Reciprocal graphs such as $y = \dfrac{1}{x}$ may be constructed in a similar way, but will have one point where the curve is not defined (you cannot divide by zero) and this causes the curve to break into two disconnected parts.

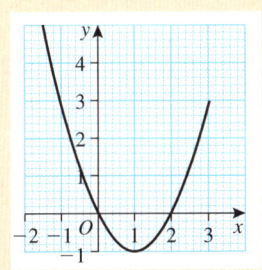

A typical quadratic curve $y = x^2 - 2x$

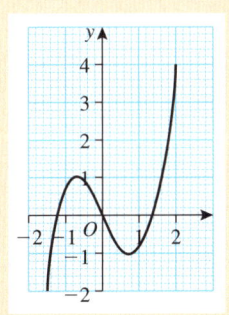

A typical cubic curve $y = x^3 - 2x$

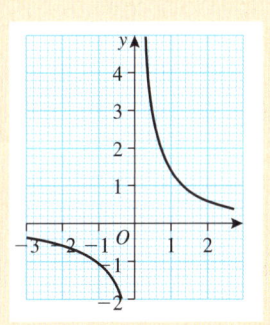

A typical reciprocal curve $y = \dfrac{1}{x}$

3. You can solve equations graphically by finding out where a curve crosses the x axis, or another horizontal straight line.

4. In the examination you will be expected to recognise and distinguish between the graphs of $y = \sin x$, $y = \cos x$, and $y = \tan x$. Make sure that you learn these thoroughly.

5. You will also need to recall the following transformations:

$f(x) \rightarrow f(x) + 5$	move the graph 5 units **up**
$f(x) \rightarrow f(x) - 3$	move the graph 3 units **down**
$f(x) \rightarrow f(x - 2)$	move the graph 2 units **right**
$f(x) \rightarrow f(x + 4)$	move the graph 4 units **left**
$f(x) \rightarrow 2f(x)$	each y value is doubled, x stays where it is
$f(x) \rightarrow f(2x)$	each x value is doubled, y stays where it is
$f(x) \rightarrow -f(x)$	**reflection** in the **x axis**
$f(x) \rightarrow f(-x)$	**reflection** in the **y axis**

Internet Challenge 29

Famous curves

Here are nine famous curves in mathematics.

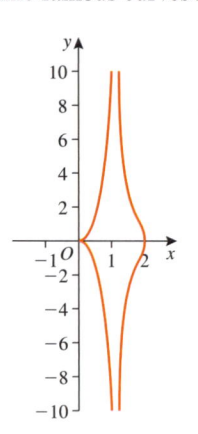

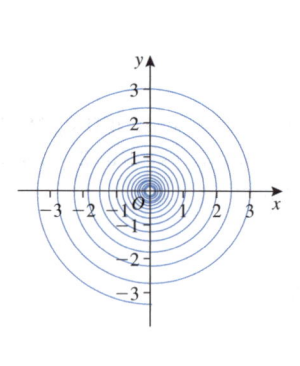

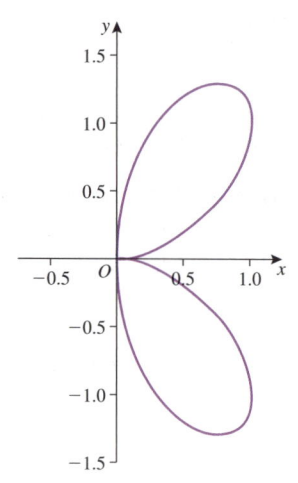

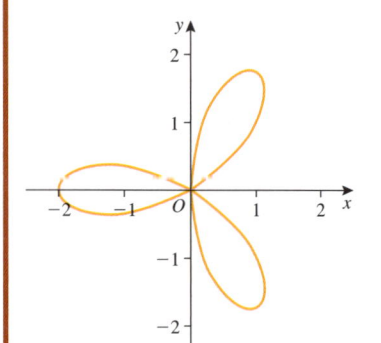

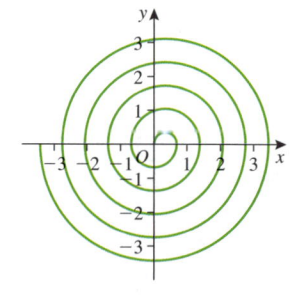

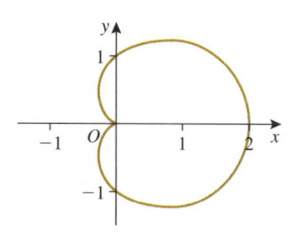

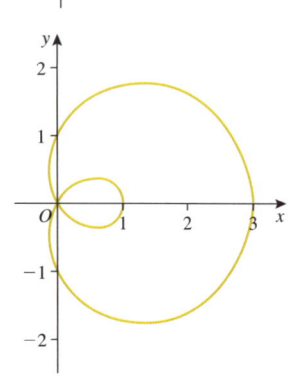

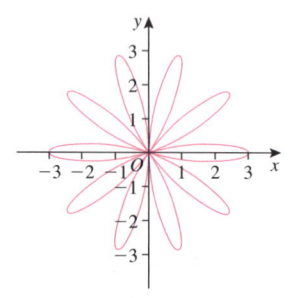

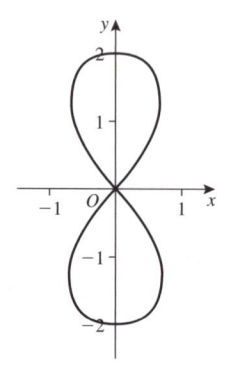

In dictionary order, these curves are:

Archimedean spiral   cardioid   conchoid   double folium   equiangular spiral
lemniscate   limaçon of Pascal   rose curve   trifolium

Use the internet to help you match the names to the right curves. Try to find one interesting fact about each curve.

CHAPTER 30

Vectors

> In this chapter you will **learn how to**:
> - write vectors as column vectors, and find their magnitudes
> - add and subtract vectors, and multiply a vector by a number
> - use vectors to prove geometric theorems.
>
> You will also be **challenged to**:
> - investigate queens on a chessboard.

Starter: Knight's tours

When a knight moves on a chessboard, it can move two squares in a straight line and one square at right angles, like this:

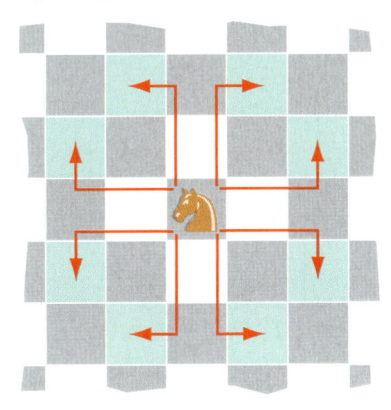

A knight can also move one square in a straight line and two squares at right angles.

See if you can work out how to move a knight around a chessboard so that it visits all 64 squares. The first three moves have been done to start you off.

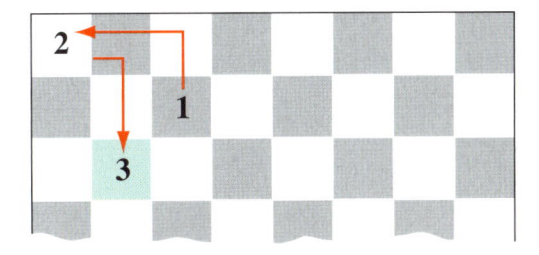

If possible, try to find a route so that the 64th square is a knight's hop away from the first square; this will close the tour so that the knight can get back to its starting position.

30.1 Introducing vectors

A **vector** is a quantity that has a magnitude (length) and a direction. Vectors are often described using **column vector** notation such as $\begin{bmatrix} 3 \\ 5 \end{bmatrix}$. You have already met column vector notation in Chapter 20. Here are some diagrams to remind you how the notation works:

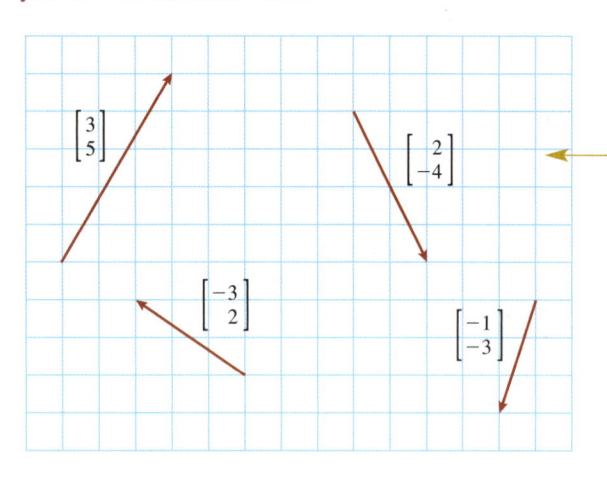

The column vector $\begin{bmatrix} x \\ y \end{bmatrix}$ means that the vector can be drawn by going x units to the *right* and y units *up*.
(*Negative* values indicate *left* or *down*.)

EXERCISE 30.1

1 The diagram below shows some vectors drawn on a grid of unit squares. Write down column vectors to describe each one.

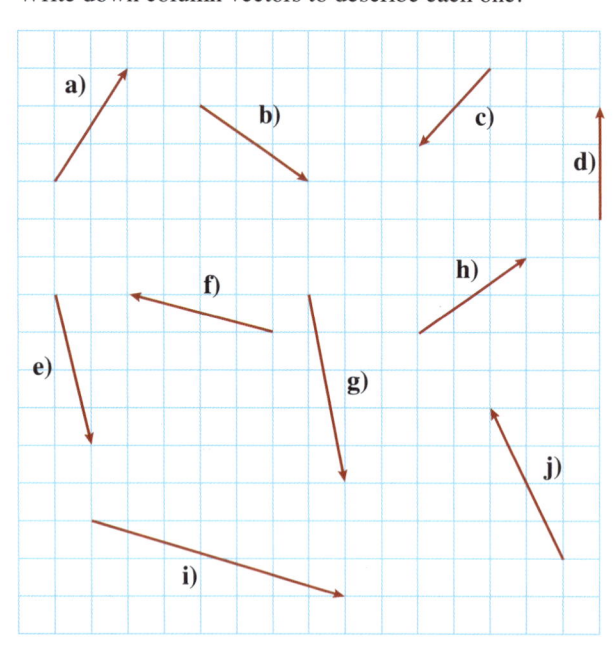

2 Draw a sketch of each of these vectors on squared paper.

a) $\begin{bmatrix} 7 \\ 1 \end{bmatrix}$ b) $\begin{bmatrix} -5 \\ 5 \end{bmatrix}$ c) $\begin{bmatrix} 4 \\ -6 \end{bmatrix}$ d) $\begin{bmatrix} -3 \\ -2 \end{bmatrix}$

30.2 Adding and subtracting vectors

You can add two vectors using simple arithmetic. For example:

$$\begin{bmatrix} 7 \\ 1 \end{bmatrix} + \begin{bmatrix} 5 \\ 3 \end{bmatrix} = \begin{bmatrix} 7+5 \\ 1+3 \end{bmatrix} = \begin{bmatrix} 12 \\ 4 \end{bmatrix}$$

Subtraction is done in a similar way. For example:

$$\begin{bmatrix} 8 \\ 4 \end{bmatrix} - \begin{bmatrix} 2 \\ -3 \end{bmatrix} = \begin{bmatrix} 8-2 \\ 4--3 \end{bmatrix} = \begin{bmatrix} 6 \\ 7 \end{bmatrix}$$

Geometrically, addition corresponds to placing the two vectors head to tail like this:

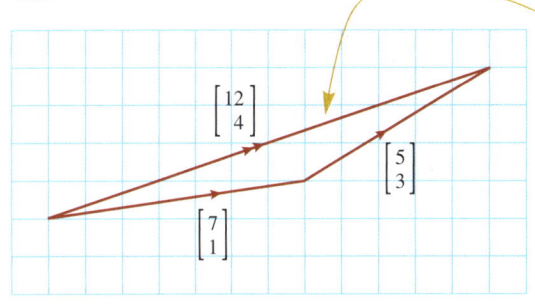

The sum of the two vectors is called the **resultant**.

Vectors are often named using letters **a**, **b**, **c**, etc. The letters are usually underlined if written by hand, but they are in **bold type** in examination papers and textbooks.

EXAMPLE

The vectors **a**, **b** and **c** are given by $\mathbf{a} = \begin{bmatrix} 6 \\ 1 \end{bmatrix}$, $\mathbf{b} = \begin{bmatrix} 2 \\ -3 \end{bmatrix}$ and $\mathbf{c} = \begin{bmatrix} 4 \\ 2 \end{bmatrix}$

Work out: a) **a** + **b**   b) **a** − **c**   c) **a** − **b** + **c**

SOLUTION

a) $\mathbf{a} + \mathbf{b} = \begin{bmatrix} 6 \\ 1 \end{bmatrix} + \begin{bmatrix} 2 \\ -3 \end{bmatrix} = \begin{bmatrix} 6+2 \\ 1+-3 \end{bmatrix} = \begin{bmatrix} 8 \\ -2 \end{bmatrix}$

b) $\mathbf{a} - \mathbf{c} = \begin{bmatrix} 6 \\ 1 \end{bmatrix} - \begin{bmatrix} 4 \\ 2 \end{bmatrix} = \begin{bmatrix} 6-4 \\ 1-2 \end{bmatrix} = \begin{bmatrix} 2 \\ -1 \end{bmatrix}$

c) $\mathbf{a} - \mathbf{b} + \mathbf{c} = \begin{bmatrix} 6 \\ 1 \end{bmatrix} - \begin{bmatrix} 2 \\ -3 \end{bmatrix} + \begin{bmatrix} 4 \\ 2 \end{bmatrix} = \begin{bmatrix} 6-2+4 \\ 1--3+2 \end{bmatrix} = \begin{bmatrix} 8 \\ 0 \end{bmatrix}$

To find the negative of a vector, just reverse the signs of the numbers.

For example, if $\mathbf{a} = \begin{bmatrix} 5 \\ 2 \end{bmatrix}$ then $-\mathbf{a} = \begin{bmatrix} -5 \\ -2 \end{bmatrix}$

When drawn on a grid, the vector $-\mathbf{a}$ will be *parallel* to the vector $\mathbf{a}$, but will point in the *opposite direction*.

EXAMPLE

Given that $\mathbf{p} = \begin{bmatrix} 6 \\ 1 \end{bmatrix}$ and $\mathbf{q} = \begin{bmatrix} 3 \\ -1 \end{bmatrix}$, work out:

a) $\mathbf{p} + \mathbf{q}$ b) $\mathbf{p} - \mathbf{q}$

Illustrate your answers graphically.

SOLUTION

a) $\mathbf{p} + \mathbf{q} = \begin{bmatrix} 6 \\ 1 \end{bmatrix} + \begin{bmatrix} 3 \\ -1 \end{bmatrix} = \begin{bmatrix} 9 \\ 0 \end{bmatrix}$

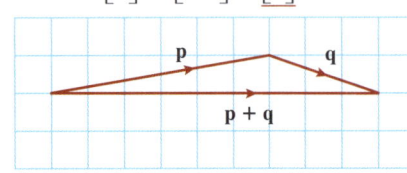

b) $\mathbf{p} - \mathbf{q} = \begin{bmatrix} 6 \\ 1 \end{bmatrix} - \begin{bmatrix} 3 \\ -1 \end{bmatrix} = \begin{bmatrix} 3 \\ 2 \end{bmatrix}$

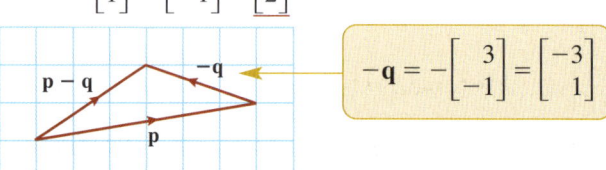

$-\mathbf{q} = -\begin{bmatrix} 3 \\ -1 \end{bmatrix} = \begin{bmatrix} -3 \\ 1 \end{bmatrix}$

EXERCISE 30.2

The vectors **a**, **b** and **c** are given by $\mathbf{a} = \begin{bmatrix} 2 \\ 5 \end{bmatrix}$, $\mathbf{b} = \begin{bmatrix} -3 \\ 8 \end{bmatrix}$ and $\mathbf{c} = \begin{bmatrix} 2 \\ -2 \end{bmatrix}$.

Work out each of these as a column vector. Illustrate your answer with a diagram.

1 $\mathbf{a} + \mathbf{b}$ **2** $\mathbf{b} - \mathbf{c}$ **3** $\mathbf{a} + \mathbf{c}$ **4** $\mathbf{c} - \mathbf{b}$

5 Work out $\mathbf{a} - \mathbf{c} + \mathbf{b}$ **6** Work out $\mathbf{b} - \mathbf{a} + \mathbf{c}$

6 The vectors **p**, **q** and **r** are given by $\mathbf{p} = \begin{bmatrix} 2 \\ -1 \end{bmatrix}$, $\mathbf{q} = \begin{bmatrix} 5 \\ 4 \end{bmatrix}$ and $\mathbf{r} = \begin{bmatrix} 8 \\ 5 \end{bmatrix}$.

Work out each of these as a column vector. Illustrate your answer with a diagram.

7 $\mathbf{p} - \mathbf{q}$ **8** $\mathbf{q} + \mathbf{r}$ **9** $\mathbf{r} - \mathbf{p}$ **10** $\mathbf{r} - \mathbf{q}$

11 Work out $\mathbf{p} + \mathbf{q} + \mathbf{r}$ **12** Work out $\mathbf{p} - \mathbf{r} + \mathbf{q}$

13 You are given that $\begin{bmatrix} 5 \\ 6 \end{bmatrix} + \begin{bmatrix} 1 \\ x \end{bmatrix} = \begin{bmatrix} 6 \\ 9 \end{bmatrix}$. Find the value of x.

14 You are given that $\begin{bmatrix} x \\ 6 \end{bmatrix} - \begin{bmatrix} 7 \\ -1 \end{bmatrix} = \begin{bmatrix} 2 \\ y \end{bmatrix}$. Find the values of x and y.

15 You are given that $\begin{bmatrix} 5 \\ y \end{bmatrix} + \begin{bmatrix} x \\ -3 \end{bmatrix} = \begin{bmatrix} 2 \\ 12 \end{bmatrix}$. Find the values of x and y.

30.3 Multiplying a vector by a number (scalar multiplication)

You can **multiply** a vector by an ordinary number, say k. The direction of the vector remains unaltered, but the magnitude is changed by factor k.

For example, $3\begin{bmatrix} 2 \\ 1 \end{bmatrix} = \begin{bmatrix} 3 \times 2 \\ 3 \times 1 \end{bmatrix} = \begin{bmatrix} 6 \\ 3 \end{bmatrix}$

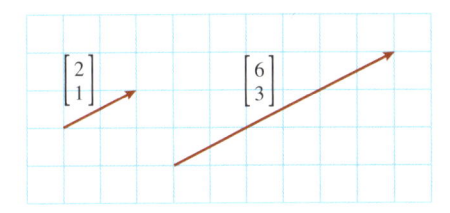

Questions about multiplication are often combined with addition and subtraction.

EXAMPLE

The vectors **a**, **b** and **c** are given by $\mathbf{a} = \begin{bmatrix} 3 \\ -1 \end{bmatrix}$, $\mathbf{b} = \begin{bmatrix} 4 \\ 2 \end{bmatrix}$ and $\mathbf{c} = \begin{bmatrix} 1 \\ 5 \end{bmatrix}$

a) Work out 3**a**. Give your answer as a column vector.
b) Work out 2**a** − **c**. Give your answer as a column vector. Illustrate with a diagram.
c) Work out 4**a** − 3**b** + 2**c**.

SOLUTION

a) $3\mathbf{a} = 3\begin{bmatrix} 3 \\ -1 \end{bmatrix} = \begin{bmatrix} 3 \times 3 \\ 3 \times -1 \end{bmatrix} = \begin{bmatrix} 9 \\ -3 \end{bmatrix}$

b) $2\mathbf{a} - \mathbf{c} = 2\begin{bmatrix} 3 \\ -1 \end{bmatrix} - \begin{bmatrix} 1 \\ 5 \end{bmatrix} = \begin{bmatrix} 6 \\ -2 \end{bmatrix} - \begin{bmatrix} 1 \\ 5 \end{bmatrix} = \begin{bmatrix} 5 \\ -7 \end{bmatrix}$

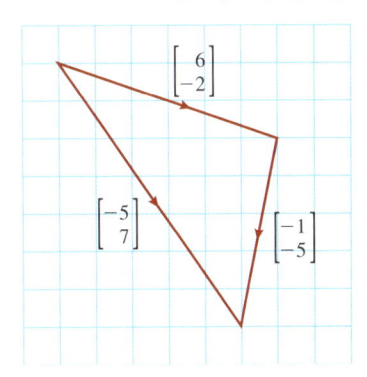

c) $4\mathbf{a} - 3\mathbf{b} + 2\mathbf{c} = 4\begin{bmatrix} 3 \\ -1 \end{bmatrix} - 3\begin{bmatrix} 4 \\ 2 \end{bmatrix} + 2\begin{bmatrix} 1 \\ 5 \end{bmatrix} = \begin{bmatrix} 12 \\ -4 \end{bmatrix} - \begin{bmatrix} 12 \\ 6 \end{bmatrix} + \begin{bmatrix} 2 \\ 10 \end{bmatrix} = \begin{bmatrix} 2 \\ 0 \end{bmatrix}$

EXERCISE 30.3

The vectors **a**, **b** and **c** are given by $\mathbf{a} = \begin{bmatrix} 4 \\ -2 \end{bmatrix}$, $\mathbf{b} = \begin{bmatrix} 1 \\ 5 \end{bmatrix}$ and $\mathbf{c} = \begin{bmatrix} -1 \\ 1 \end{bmatrix}$

Work out:

1 3**a**

2 2**b** + **c**

3 **a** + 3**c**

4 3**c** − 5**b**

5 4**a** + 5**b**

6 2**a** − 4**c**

The vectors **p**, **q** and **r** are given by $\mathbf{p} = \begin{bmatrix} -2 \\ 5 \end{bmatrix}$, $\mathbf{q} = \begin{bmatrix} 0 \\ 4 \end{bmatrix}$ and $\mathbf{r} = \begin{bmatrix} 3 \\ -1 \end{bmatrix}$

Work out:

7 5**p**

8 −3**r**

9 2**r** − 3**p**

10 4**p** + 2**q** + **r**

11 5**r** − 3**q**

12 2**p** − 3**r** + **q**

13 You are given that $3\begin{bmatrix} 2 \\ 3 \end{bmatrix} + \begin{bmatrix} 1 \\ x \end{bmatrix} = \begin{bmatrix} 7 \\ 6 \end{bmatrix}$. Find the value of x.

14 You are given that $3\begin{bmatrix} 1 \\ 4 \end{bmatrix} - 2\begin{bmatrix} 1 \\ -5 \end{bmatrix} = \begin{bmatrix} x \\ y \end{bmatrix}$. Find the values of x and y.

15 You are given that $4\begin{bmatrix} x \\ 5 \end{bmatrix} + 2\begin{bmatrix} 4 \\ y \end{bmatrix} = \begin{bmatrix} 20 \\ 18 \end{bmatrix}$. Find the values of x and y.

30.4 Using vectors

You can use vectors to solve geometric problems, and to prove some theorems about parallel lines. If one vector is a (scalar) multiple of another, then the two vectors must be parallel. The size of the multiple will tell you the scale factor.

In these problems it is often helpful to use $\overrightarrow{AB}$, for example to represent the vector that would translate you from A to B. You can always rewrite the vector if you need to travel via an intermediate point P:

$$\overrightarrow{AB} = \overrightarrow{AP} + \overrightarrow{PB}$$

EXAMPLE

ABCD is a parallelogram. $\vec{AB} = \mathbf{p}$, $\vec{BC} = \mathbf{q}$.

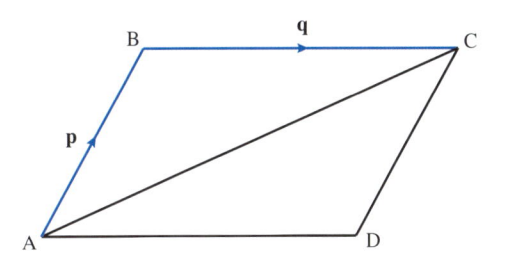

Find, in terms of $\mathbf{p}$ and $\mathbf{q}$, expressions for:

a) $\vec{BA}$　　　　　b) $\vec{AC}$　　　　　c) $\vec{BD}$

SOLUTION

a) $\vec{BA} = -\vec{AB}$　　b) $\vec{AC} = \vec{AB} + \vec{BC}$　　c) $\vec{BD} = \vec{BA} + \vec{AD}$
　　　　$= \underline{-\mathbf{p}}$　　　　　　　$= \underline{\mathbf{p} + \mathbf{q}}$　　　　　　　$= \underline{-\mathbf{p} + \mathbf{q}}$

EXAMPLE

The diagram shows a triangle ABC. M is the midpoint of AB and N is the midpoint of AC.

$\vec{AM} = \mathbf{p}$ and $\vec{AN} = \mathbf{q}$.

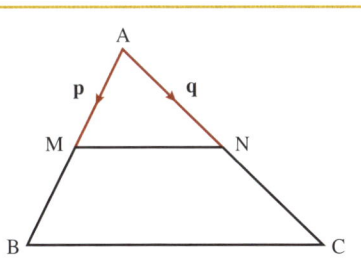

a) Find an expression for $\vec{MN}$ in terms of $\mathbf{p}$ and $\mathbf{q}$.
b) Find an expression for $\vec{BC}$ in terms of $\mathbf{p}$ and $\mathbf{q}$.
c) Use your results from a) and b) to prove that MN is parallel to BC.

SOLUTION

a) $\vec{MN} = \vec{MA} + \vec{AM}$　　← To get $\vec{MN}$ in terms of $\mathbf{p}$ and $\mathbf{q}$, go from M to N via the point A.
　　　$= -\vec{AM} + \vec{AN}$
　　　$= (-\mathbf{p}) + \mathbf{q}$　　← $\vec{MA}$ has the same length as $\vec{AM}$ but points in the opposite direction, so $\vec{MA} = -\vec{AM}$
　　　$= \underline{-\mathbf{p} + \mathbf{q}}$

b) $\vec{BC} = \vec{BA} + \vec{AC}$
　　　$= (-2\mathbf{p}) + 2\mathbf{q}$
　　　$= \underline{-2\mathbf{p} + 2\mathbf{q}}$

c) $\vec{BC} = -2\mathbf{p} + 2\mathbf{q}$
　　　$= 2(-\mathbf{p} + \mathbf{q})$
　　　$= 2 \times \vec{MN}$
　　Therefore <u>BC is parallel to MN</u>

Some exam questions might refer to a line being divided in a certain *ratio*. For example, you might be told that X is the point on AB for which AX : XB = 2 : 1. This simply means that AX is twice as long as XB, so that X is two-thirds of the way along AB.

EXAMPLE

The diagram shows a parallelogram ABCD. $\overrightarrow{AB} = 6\mathbf{p}$ and $\overrightarrow{BC} = 6\mathbf{q}$.

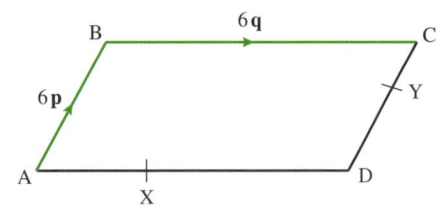

X is the point on AD for which AX : XD = 1 : 2
Y is the point on DC for which DY : YC = 2 : 1

Find, in terms of **p** and **q**, expressions for:
a) $\overrightarrow{AC}$ b) $\overrightarrow{AD}$ c) $\overrightarrow{DC}$
d) $\overrightarrow{XD}$ e) $\overrightarrow{DY}$ f) $\overrightarrow{XY}$

Hence prove that AC is parallel to XY.

SOLUTION

a) $\overrightarrow{AC} = \overrightarrow{AB} + \overrightarrow{BC}$
   $= 6\mathbf{p} + 6\mathbf{q}$

b) $\overrightarrow{AD} = \overrightarrow{BC}$ since they are opposite sides of the parallelogram
   $= 6\mathbf{q}$

c) $\overrightarrow{DC} = \overrightarrow{AB}$ since they are opposite sides of the parallelogram
   $= 6\mathbf{p}$

d) $\overrightarrow{XD} = \frac{2}{3} \times \overrightarrow{AD}$
   $= \frac{2}{3} \times 6\mathbf{q}$
   $= 4\mathbf{q}$

e) $\overrightarrow{DY} = \frac{2}{3} \times \overrightarrow{DC}$
   $= \frac{2}{3} \times 6\mathbf{p}$
   $= 4\mathbf{p}$

f) $\overrightarrow{XY} = \overrightarrow{XD} + \overrightarrow{DY}$
   $= 4\mathbf{q} + 4\mathbf{p}$
   $= 4\mathbf{p} + 4\mathbf{q}$

Now $\overrightarrow{AC} = 6\mathbf{p} + 6\mathbf{q} = 6(\mathbf{p} + \mathbf{q})$

and $\overrightarrow{XY} = 4\mathbf{p} + 4\mathbf{q} = 4(\mathbf{p} + \mathbf{q})$

Thus $\overrightarrow{AC} = 1.5 \times \overrightarrow{XY}$, and therefore AC is parallel to XY

EXERCISE 30.4

1 The diagram shows two squares ABXY and CDYX.
$\overrightarrow{AB} = \mathbf{p}$ and $\overrightarrow{AY} = \mathbf{q}$.

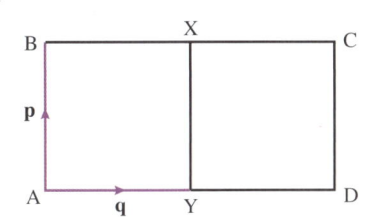

Find, in terms of **p** and **q**, expressions for:
a) $\overrightarrow{BX}$ b) $\overrightarrow{AX}$ c) $\overrightarrow{AD}$ d) $\overrightarrow{AC}$

2 The diagram shows a trapezium PQRS.
$\overrightarrow{PQ} = \mathbf{a}$ and $\overrightarrow{QR} = \mathbf{b}$.
PS is twice the length of QR.

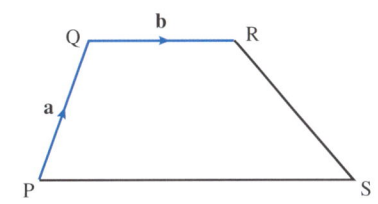

Find, in terms of **p** and **q**, expressions for:
a) $\overrightarrow{QP}$ b) $\overrightarrow{PR}$ c) $\overrightarrow{PS}$ d) $\overrightarrow{QS}$

3 The diagram shows a triangle ABC. $AP = \tfrac{1}{3}AB$, and $AQ = \tfrac{1}{3}AC$.
$\overrightarrow{AP} = \mathbf{p}$ and $\overrightarrow{AQ} = \mathbf{q}$.

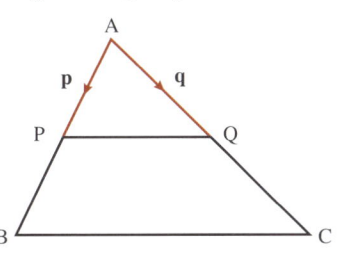

a) Find, in terms of **p** and **q**, expressions for:
  (i) $\overrightarrow{PQ}$ (ii) $\overrightarrow{AB}$ (iii) $\overrightarrow{AC}$ (iv) $\overrightarrow{BC}$

b) Use your results from **a)** to prove that PQ is parallel to BC.

4 A quadrilateral ABCD is made by joining points A (1, 1), B (5, 8), C (11, 11) and D (7, 4).
a) Write column vectors for:
  (i) $\overrightarrow{AB}$ (ii) $\overrightarrow{DC}$
b) What do your answers to part **a)** tell you about AB and DC?
c) Write column vectors for:
  (i) $\overrightarrow{BC}$ (ii) $\overrightarrow{AD}$
d) What kind of quadrilateral is ABCD?

5 The diagram shows a parallelogram PQRS.
$\vec{PQ} = \mathbf{a}$ and $\vec{PS} = \mathbf{b}$.
E is the midpoint of QS.

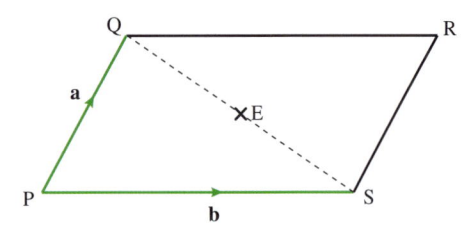

a) Find, in terms of **a** and **b**:
   (i) $\vec{QS}$ 　　　　(ii) $\vec{QE}$ 　　　　(iii) $\vec{PE}$
b) Explain why $\vec{SR} = \mathbf{a}$.
c) Find $\vec{PR}$ in terms of **a** and **b**.
d) What can you deduce about the diagonals of a parallelogram?

6 A quadrilateral ABCD is made by joining A $(-3, -3)$, B $(9, 3)$, C $(3, 7)$ and D $(-1, 5)$.
a) Write column vectors for:
   (i) $\vec{AB}$ 　　　　(ii) $\vec{DC}$
b) What do your answers to part a) tell you about AB and DC?
c) What kind of quadrilateral is ABCD?

7 The diagram shows a quadrilateral PQRS.
$\vec{PQ} = 2\mathbf{a}, \vec{PS} = 2\mathbf{b}$ and $\vec{SR} = 2\mathbf{c}$.
E, F, G and H are the midpoints of PQ, PS, SR and QR respectively.

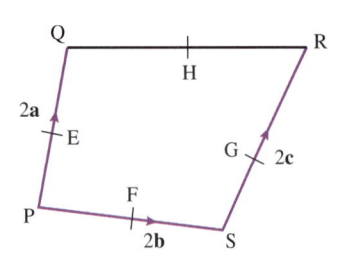

a) Explain why $\vec{QR} = -2\mathbf{a} + 2\mathbf{b} + 2\mathbf{c}$.
b) Find $\vec{EH}$ in terms of **a**, **b** and **c**.
c) Find $\vec{FG}$ in terms of **a**, **b** and **c**.
d) What can you deduce about the line segments EH and FG?
e) What type of quadrilateral is EFGH?

REVIEW EXERCISE 30

1 Given that $3\begin{bmatrix} x \\ 5 \end{bmatrix} - \begin{bmatrix} 2 \\ 4 \end{bmatrix} = \begin{bmatrix} 16 \\ y \end{bmatrix}$, find the values of x and y.

2 P is the point $(5, 4)$ and Q is the point $(-1, 12)$.
 a) Write $\overrightarrow{PQ}$ and $\overrightarrow{QP}$ as column vectors.
 b) Work out the length of the vector $\overrightarrow{PQ}$.

3 A is the point $(2, 3)$ and B is the point $(-2, 0)$.
 a) (i) Write $\overrightarrow{AB}$ as a column vector.
    (ii) Find the length of the vector $\overrightarrow{AB}$.

D is the point such that $\overrightarrow{BD}$ is parallel to $\begin{bmatrix} 0 \\ 1 \end{bmatrix}$ and the length of $\overrightarrow{AD}$ = the length of $\overrightarrow{AB}$.

O is the point $(0, 0)$.

 b) Find $\overrightarrow{OD}$ as a column vector.

C is a point such that ABCD is a rhombus. AC is a diagonal of the rhombus.
 c) Find the coordinates of C.   [Edexcel]

4 OPQ is a triangle.
R is the midpoint of OP.
S is the midpoint of PQ.
$\overrightarrow{OP} = \mathbf{p}$ and $\overrightarrow{OQ} = \mathbf{q}$.

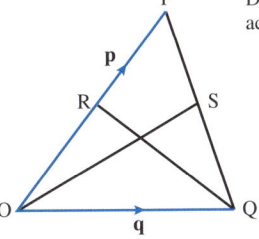

 a) Find $\overrightarrow{OS}$ in terms of $\mathbf{p}$ and $\mathbf{q}$.
 b) Show that RS is parallel to OQ.   [Edexcel]

5 OPQ is a triangle.
T is the point on PQ for which PT : TQ = 2 : 1.
$\overrightarrow{OP} = \mathbf{a}$ and $\overrightarrow{OQ} = \mathbf{b}$.

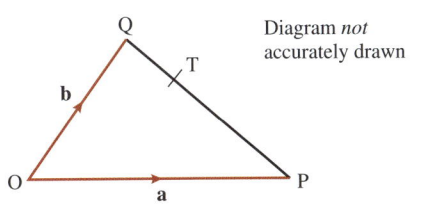

 a) Write down, in terms of $\mathbf{a}$ and $\mathbf{b}$, an expression for $\overrightarrow{PQ}$.
 b) Express $\overrightarrow{OT}$ in terms of $\mathbf{a}$ and $\mathbf{b}$. Give your answer in its simplest form.   [Edexcel]

6 OABC is a parallelogram.
P is the point on AC such that AP = $\frac{2}{3}$AC.
$\overrightarrow{OA}$ = 6**a** and $\overrightarrow{OC}$ = 6**c**.

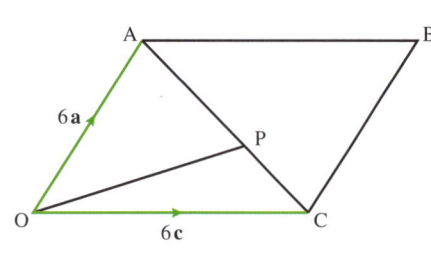

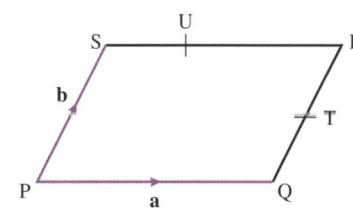

Diagram *not* accurately drawn

a) Find the vector $\overrightarrow{OP}$. Give your answer in terms of **a** and **c**.

The midpoint of CB is M.
b) Prove that OPM is a straight line. [Edexcel]

7 PQRS is a parallelogram.
T is the midpoint of QR.
U is the point on SR for which SU : UR = 1 : 2.
$\overrightarrow{PQ}$ = **a** and $\overrightarrow{PS}$ = **b**.

Diagram *not* accurately drawn

Write down, in terms of **a** and **b**, expressions for:
a) $\overrightarrow{PT}$
b) $\overrightarrow{TU}$ [Edexcel]

8 ABCD is a quadrilateral.

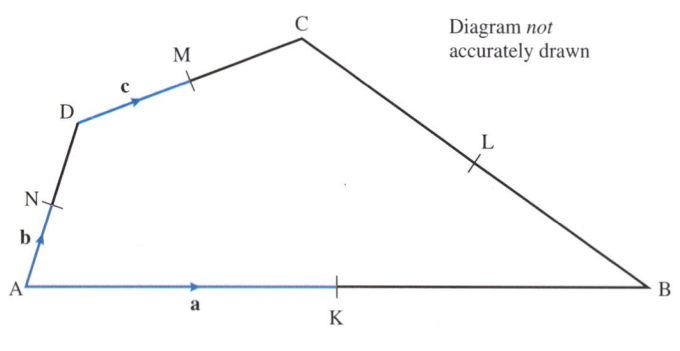

Diagram *not* accurately drawn

K is the midpoint of AB. L is the midpoint of BC.
M is the midpoint of CD. N is the midpoint of AD.
$\overrightarrow{AK}$ = **a**, $\overrightarrow{AN}$ = **b** and $\overrightarrow{DM}$ = **c**.

a) Find, in terms of **a**, **b** and **c**, the vectors:
  (i) $\overrightarrow{KN}$ (ii) $\overrightarrow{AC}$ (iii) $\overrightarrow{BC}$ (iv) $\overrightarrow{LM}$

b) Write down two geometrical facts about the lines KN and LM which could be deduced from your answers to part **a)**. [Edexcel]

9 The diagram shows a regular hexagon ABCDEF with centre O.

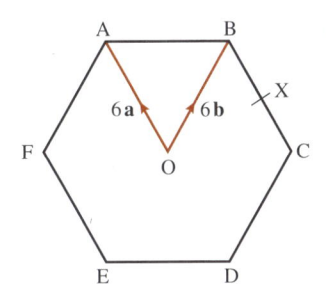

Diagram *not* accurately drawn

$\vec{OA} = 6\mathbf{a}$ and $\vec{OB} = 6\mathbf{b}$.

a) Express in terms of **a** and/or **b**.
   (i) $\vec{AB}$ (ii) $\vec{EF}$

X is the midpoint of BC.

b) Express $\vec{EX}$ in terms of **a** and/or **b**.

Y is the point on AB extended, such that AB : BY = 3 : 2.

c) Prove that E, X and Y lie on the same straight line. [Edexcel]

10 OPQR is a trapezium. PQ is parallel to OR. $\vec{OP} = \mathbf{b}$, $\vec{PQ} = 2\mathbf{a}$, $\vec{OR} = 6\mathbf{a}$.
M is the midpoint of PQ. N is the midpoint of OR.

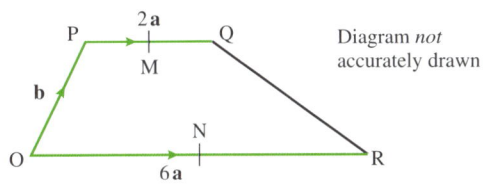

Diagram *not* accurately drawn

a) Find, in terms of **a** and **b**, the vectors:
   (i) $\vec{OM}$ (ii) $\vec{MN}$

X is the midpoint of MN.

b) Find, in terms of **a** and **b**, the vector $\vec{OX}$.

The lines OX and PQ are extended to meet at the point Y.

c) Find, in terms of **a** and **b**, the vector $\vec{NY}$. [Edexcel]

KEY POINTS

1. A vector has a direction and a length, or magnitude. Vectors are usually written in column form, such as $\begin{bmatrix} 4 \\ 6 \end{bmatrix}$, which represents a translation of 4 units in the x direction and 6 in the y direction.

2. Vectors are often used in examination questions to prove geometric theorems. The method is to use given base vectors **a**, **b**, **c**, etc. and then express other lines in terms of these, for example 2**a** + **b**.

3. Two vectors will be parallel if one is a scalar multiple of the other. For example, 6**a** + 3**b** is parallel to 2**a** + **b**, since 6**a** + 3**b** = 3 × (2**a** + **b**)

Internet Challenge 30

Queens on a chessboard

Here is another chessboard problem.

The queen is the most powerful piece on a chessboard. A queen can attack any squares in a straight line from it, forwards, backwards, left, right or diagonally. The diagram below shows this in green for one position of the queen:

Place eight queens on a chessboard so that no two queens can attack each other.
You may want to use squared paper to record your attempts. This problem does have more than one solution. Once you have solved it, you might want to use the internet to help answer the following questions.

1 How many different distinct solutions does this problem have?

2 How many solutions are there in which no three queens lie on an oblique line?

3 What is a Latin square? Is this a Latin square problem?

4 How many knights can be placed on a chessboard so that no knight attacks any other?

5 How about bishops?

Obviously it is not possible to place nine queens on a board without at least two queens attacking each other. (Why not?) There is, however, a 'nine queens' problem:

Place nine queens and one pawn on a chessboard so that no two queens can attack each other.

6 Try to solve the nine queens problem. Use the internet if you get stuck.

CHAPTER 31

Mathematical proof

In this chapter you will **learn how to**:

- prove that triangles are congruent, using:
  - side–side–side (SSS)
  - side–angle–side (SAS)
  - angle–side–angle (ASA)
  - right angle–hypotenuse–side (RHS)
- use algebra to prove results about properties of numbers
- use counter-examples to disprove conjectures.

You will also be **challenged to investigate**:

- famous theorems.

Starter: 1 = 2

Study this piece of algebra carefully. It appears to prove that $1 = 2$!

Step 1	Let a and b be numbers such that a is twice as big as b.	$a = 2b$
Step 2	Multiply both sides by $2b$.	$2ab = 4b^2$
Step 3	Subtract a^2 from both sides.	$2ab - a^2 = 4b^2 - a^2$
Step 4	Take out a common factor of a on the left-hand side.	$a(2b - a) = 4b^2 - a^2$
Step 5	Factorise the right-hand side into two brackets.	$a(2b - a) = (2b + a)(2b - a)$
Step 6	Divide both sides by $(2b - a)$.	$a = 2b + a$
Step 7	Use the fact that $a = 2b$.	$a = a + a$
Step 8	Simplify the right-hand side.	$a = 2a$
Step 9	Divide both sides by a.	$1 = 2$

Where does this 'proof' go wrong?

31.1 Congruent triangles

You will recall that two triangles are **congruent** if they are the **same shape and size**. Two triangles will always be congruent provided one of the following sets of corresponding values agree:

    All three sides   SSS
    Two sides and an included angle   SAS
    Two angles and a corresponding side   ASA or AAS
    A right angle, hypotenuse and a side   RHS

EXAMPLE

Two of these triangles are congruent. State which ones are congruent, and give a reason.

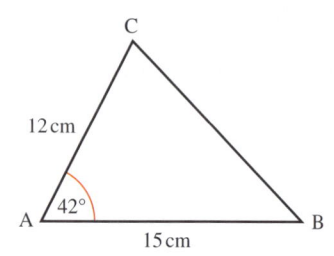

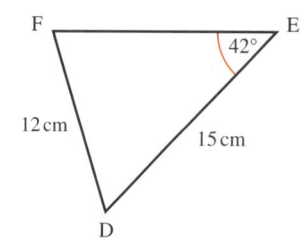

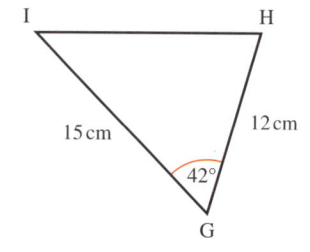

SOLUTION

Triangles ABC and GHI both have sides of 12 cm and 15 cm with an included angle of 42°, so they are congruent. Triangle DEF is not congruent to either of these triangles, since the 42° angle is *not* included between the 12 cm and 15 cm sides.

Angle A corresponds to angle G (both are 42°), angle B corresponds to angle I (they are both at the end of a 15 cm side) and angle C corresponds to angle H (they are both at the end of a 12 cm side). Therefore you can write:

    triangle ABC is congruent to triangle GIH (SAS)

You can also write:

    triangles $\dfrac{ABC}{GIH}$ are congruent (SAS)

Note how the matching vertices were written one underneath the other in this second statement.

You can also use congruent triangles to prove theorems in geometry.

EXAMPLE

The diagram shows two tangents TP, TQ to a circle, centre O.
Prove that TP = TQ.

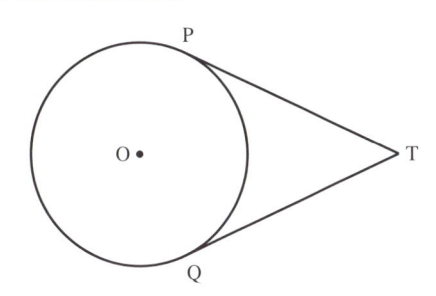

PROOF

Join OP, OQ and OT, as shown on the right.

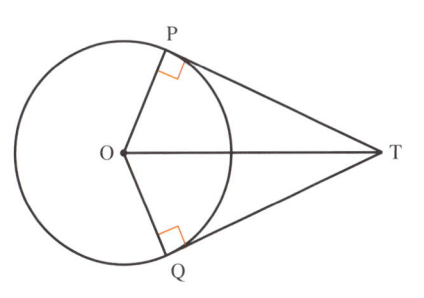

Now, consider the triangles POT and QOT.

OP	= OQ	(radii of the same circle)
angle OPT	= angle OQT	(radii meet tangents at 90°)
OT	= OT	(OT is in both triangles)

Therefore, triangles OPT / OQT are congruent (RHS).

So, TP = TQ

EXERCISE 31.1

1 Look at these pairs of triangles. In each case, decide whether the triangles are congruent or not. If they are congruent, explain why.

a) 14 cm, 18 cm, 72° ; 72°, 14 cm, 18 cm

b) 10 cm, 15 cm, 28° ; 15 cm, 10 cm, 28°

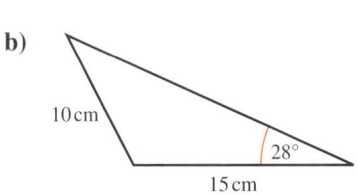

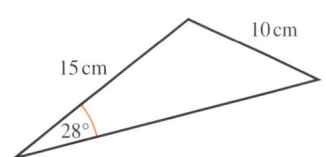

c) 10 cm, 25 cm (right angle) ; 10 cm, 25 cm (right angle)

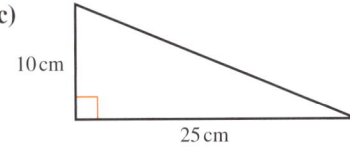

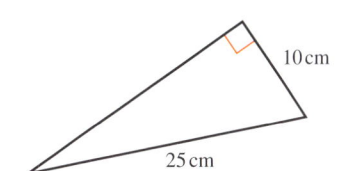

d)

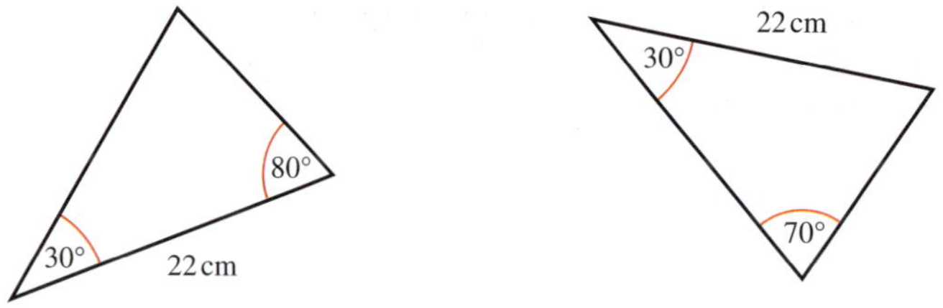

e)

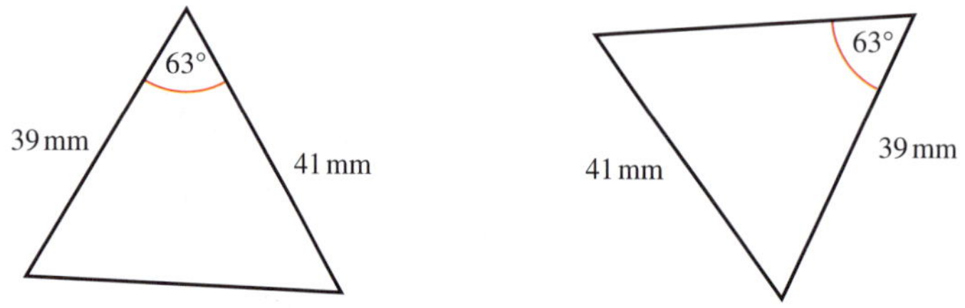

f)

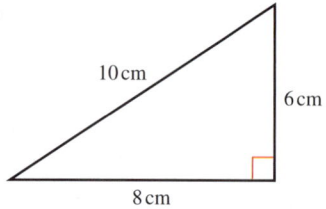

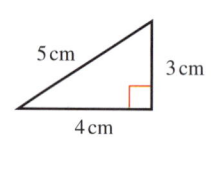

g)

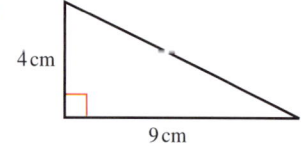

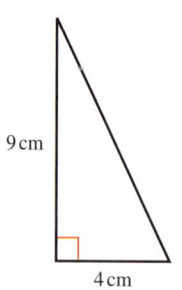

h)

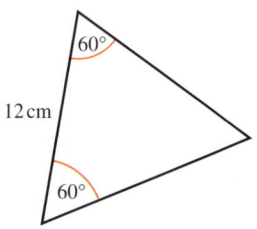

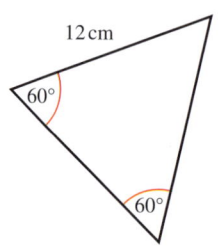

2 The diagram shows two tangents TP and TQ to a circle, centre O.
  a) Show that the line segment OT bisects angle PTQ.
     [Hint: Join OT and consider triangles OPT and OQT.]
  b) Prove that OPTQ is a cyclic quadrilateral.

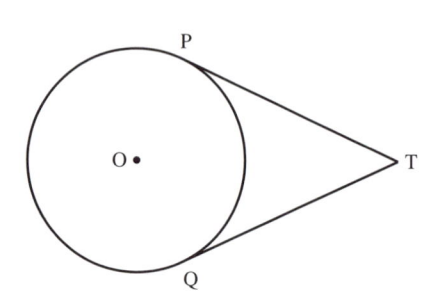

3 The diagram shows five points, P, Q, R, S and T.
PQ is parallel to ST. R is the midpoint of QS.
  a) Prove that triangles PQR and TSR are congruent.
  b) Hence prove that PQ = ST and PR = RT.
  c) What does this tell you about the diagonals of a parallelogram?

4 The diagram shows a circle, centre O. AB is a chord. M is the midpoint of AB.

Prove that angle AMO is a right angle.

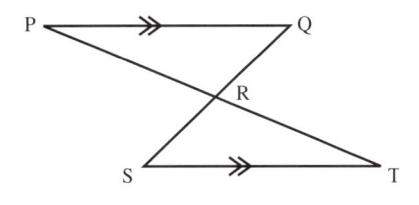

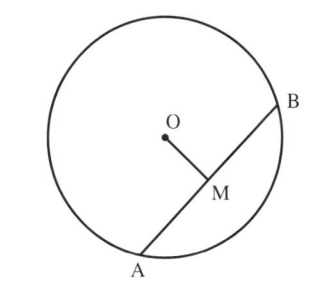

5 Q is the midpoint of the line segment PR. QS is parallel to RT, and QS = RT.

Prove that triangles PQS and QRT are congruent.

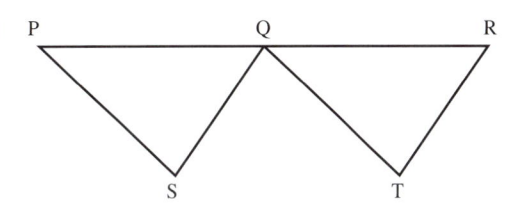

31.2 Algebraic proofs

In this section, a number of general results about properties of numbers will be proved using algebra.

EXAMPLE

Prove that the sum of the squares of two consecutive integers is always odd.

PROOF

Let the two consecutive integers be n and $n + 1$.

The sum of the squares of these numbers is:
$n^2 + (n + 1)^2 = n^2 + n^2 + 2n + 1$
$= 2n^2 + 2n + 1$
$= 2(n^2 + n) + 1$
$=$ an even number $+ 1$
$=$ an odd number

Consecutive integers are integers that are next to each other on a number line, e.g. 9 and 10. Algebraically we write consecutive integers as n and $n + 1$.

In the last example, n and $n + 1$ were used to represent consecutive integers. Some problems will ask about even or odd numbers. $2n$ can be used to represent an even number, and $2n + 1$ can be used to represent an odd number (where n is an integer). If you are using two unrelated even or odd numbers, you must use different variables for each.

Consecutive numbers follow each other in number order:
$3, 4, 5,$ $n, n + 1, n + 2$
$2 \times$ any integer is **even**:
2×3 $2n$
$2 \times$ (any integer) $+ 1$ is **odd**:
$2 \times 3 + 1$ $2n + 1$

EXAMPLE

Prove that the product of an even number and an odd number is always even.

PROOF

Let the even number be $2n$ and the odd number be $2m + 1$.
Then the product of these two numbers is:

$$2n \times (2m + 1) = 4mn + 2n$$
$$= 2(2mn + n)$$
$$= 2(2mn + n)$$
$$= 2k \quad \text{(where } k = 2mn + n\text{)}$$
$$= \text{an even number}$$

EXERCISE 31.2

1. Prove that the sum of two consecutive integers is always odd.

2. Prove that the product of any two even numbers is always even.

3. Prove that the product of any two odd numbers is always odd.

4. Prove that the sum of three consecutive integers is always a multiple of three.

5. Prove that the difference between the squares of any two odd integers is always divisible by four.

6. The diagram shows a square measuring $(a + b)$ along each side.
   A smaller square, of side c, is inscribed inside the larger square.

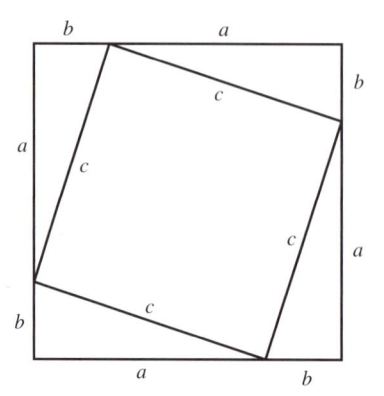

a) Show that the total area of the four triangles is $2ab$.
b) Obtain expressions for the total area of the shape in two ways:
  (i) by adding together the areas of the four triangles and the inner square
  (ii) by expanding $(a + b)^2$.
c) Use your results from part **b)** to prove that $c^2 = a^2 + b^2$.
d) What well-known theorem have you just proved?

7 a) Show that $(100x + 1)(100x - 1) = 10\,000x^2 - 1$.
b) Hence show that 89 999 is not prime.

8 By writing the nth term of the sequence $1, 3, 5, 7, \ldots$ as $(2n - 1)$, or otherwise, show that the difference between the squares of any two consecutive odd numbers is a multiple of 8. [Edexcel]

31.3 Use of counter-examples

Sometimes you may meet a **conjecture** – that is, an unproven claim. If a conjecture turns out to be true, it may be quite difficult to prove for all possible cases. On the other hand, if a conjecture is false, you only need to find *one* case where it fails in order to demonstrate its falsehood. Such a failure case is called a **counter-example**.

EXAMPLE

Didier says, 'All prime numbers are odd.' Show that Didier is wrong.

SOLUTION

The first prime numbers are $2, 3, 5, 7, 11, \ldots$
So, Didier is wrong because 2 is a prime number, and 2 is not odd.

The example above was quite easy, because the counter-example (namely 2) occurred right at the beginning of the list of prime numbers. Other false conjectures might be harder to disprove, because they seem to work for a while.

EXAMPLE

Christie says, 'If x is a positive integer, then $x^2 + x + 1$ is always prime.'
Show that Christie is wrong.

SOLUTION

The conjecture holds for the cases $x = 1$ (3), $x = 2$ (7) and $x = 3$ (13), but fails when $x = 4$ (21).
So, Christie is wrong because $4^2 + 4 + 1 = 16 + 4 + 1 = 21$ and 21 is not a prime.

EXERCISE 31.3

1. Chico says, 'If you add two prime numbers together you will always get another prime number.'
   Show that Chico is wrong.

2. Gill says, 'If a quadrilateral has four equal sides then it must be a square.'
   Show that this statement is false.

3. Paula says, 'When you list the factors of any integer, you will always get an even number of factors.'
   Show that Paula's statement is wrong.

4. Balvinder says, 'You can find the lowest common multiple (LCM) of two numbers just by multiplying the two numbers together.'
   Show that this statement is false.

5. Katia says, 'If the six sides of a hexagon all have the same length, then the six internal angles must all be equal.'
   Draw a diagram to show that Katia is wrong.

6. The perfect squares are 1, 4, 9, ... which are numbers of the form n^2, where n is an integer.
   The perfect cubes are 1, 8, 27, ... which are numbers of the form n^3, where n is an integer.
   David says, 'Apart from 1, there is no other number which is a perfect square and also a perfect cube.'
   Find a counter-example to show that David is wrong.

7. 'If x is positive, then $1 + 10x - x^2$ is also positive.'
   Show that this statement is false.

8. Antonia says, 'If x is less than 1, then x^2 is also less than 1.'
   Show that Antonia is wrong.

9. Pat says, 'If you draw any quadrilateral, its diagonals will always cross inside the quadrilateral.'
   Draw a counter-example to show that Pat is wrong.

10. Petra says 'If n is a positive integer, then the value of $n^2 + n + 41$ is always prime.'
    Show that Petra is wrong.

REVIEW EXERCISE 31

1. PQRS is a quadrilateral.

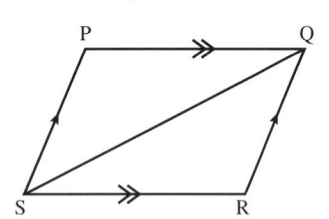

   PQ is parallel to SR. SP is parallel to RQ.
   a) Prove that triangle PQS is congruent to triangle RSQ.
   b) In quadrilateral PQRS, angle SPQ is obtuse. Explain why PQRS cannot be a cyclic quadrilateral.

   [Edexcel]

2 a) Write down an expression, in terms of n, for the nth multiple of 5.
  b) Hence, or otherwise:
  (i) prove that the sum of two consecutive multiples of 5 is always an odd number,
  (ii) prove that the product of two consecutive multiples of 5 is always an even number. [Edexcel]

3 ABCD and DEFG are squares.

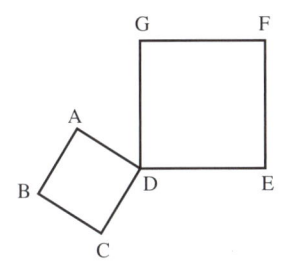

Diagram *not* accurately drawn

Prove that triangle CDG and triangle ADE are congruent. [Edexcel]

4 Prove that $(n+1)^2 - (n-1)^2$ is a multiple of 4, for all positive integer values of n. [Edexcel]

5 A, B and C are three points on the circumference of a circle.
Angle ABC = Angle ACB.
PB and PC are tangents to the circle from the point P.
  a) Prove that triangle APB and triangle APC are congruent.
Angle BPA = 10°.
  b) Find the size of angle ABC. [Edexcel]

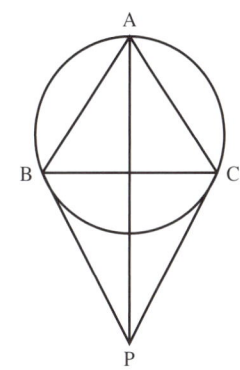

6 a) Show that $(2a-1)^2 - (2b-1)^2 = 4(a-b)(a+b-1)$.
  b) Prove that the difference between the squares of any two odd numbers is a multiple of 8.
(You may assume that any odd number can be written in the form $2r-1$, where r is an integer.) [Edexcel]

7 X and Y are points on the circle, centre O.
M is the point where the perpendicular from O meets the chord XY.
Prove that M is the midpoint of the chord XY. [Edexcel]

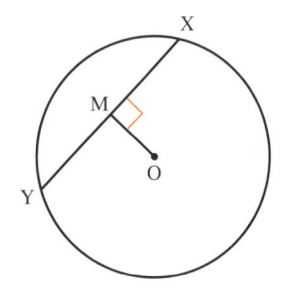

8 John says, 'For all prime numbers, n, the value of $n^2 + 3$ is always an even number.'
Give an example to show that John is **not** correct. [Edexcel]

...gle PQR, PQ = 10 cm, QR = 12 cm, angle PQR = 45°.
...ulate the area of triangle PQR.
...ive your answer correct to 3 significant figures.

The diagram shows triangle ABC and triangle ACD.
BCD is a straight line.
The perpendicular distance from A to the line BCD is h cm.

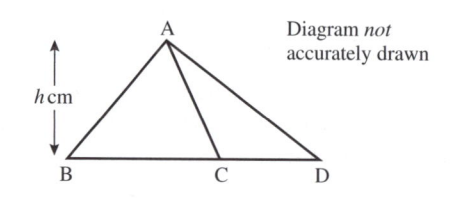

Diagram *not* accurately drawn

b) Explain why $\dfrac{\text{area of triangle ABC}}{\text{area of triangle ACD}} = \dfrac{BC}{CD}$.

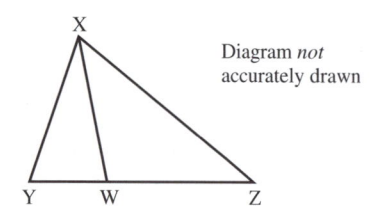

Diagram *not* accurately drawn

The diagram shows triangle XYZ.
W is the point on YZ such that angle YXW = angle WXZ.

c) Using expressions for the area of triangle YXW and the area of triangle WXZ, or otherwise, show that:
$$\dfrac{XY}{XZ} = \dfrac{YW}{WZ}$$

[Edexcel]

KEY POINTS

1. Many of the questions covering proof at GCSE concern congruent triangles or algebraic proofs.

2. Two triangles are congruent if they are the same shape and size. To prove that two triangles are congruent you need to establish that one of the following sets of corresponding values agree:

   All three sides — SSS
   Two sides and an included angle — SAS
   Two angles and a corresponding side — ASA or AAS
   A right angle, the hypotenuse and a side — RHS

3. Algebraic proofs are often about even and odd numbers. You can write any even number in the form $2m$, whilst any odd number has the form $2n + 1$, where m and n are integers.

4. You may also meet questions about consecutive integers, that is, integers that are next to each other on a number line. You can represent two consecutive integers as n and $n + 1$. Two consecutive odd numbers would be $2n - 1$ and $2n + 1$.

5. You may be asked to disprove a claim, or conjecture. This is often done using a counter-example, that is, you find one case where the conjecture breaks down.

6. For example, to disprove the statement, 'If x is any positive integer, then $x^2 + x + 5$ is prime', you can take the case $x = 4$, to give $16 + 4 + 5 = 25$, which is clearly not prime.

Internet Challenge 31

Proofs and theories

Here are some statements about proofs, with the name of a mathematician blotted out. Write out the statements, with the correct mathematician's name inserted. You may know some of these, but you should check them all using the internet.

1. 'There are infinitely many prime numbers.'
   This was proved around 300 BC by the mathematician ☐☐☐☐☐☐.

2. In 1687 ☐☐☐☐☐☐ published his theories of gravitation and motion in a book known as the *Principia*.

3. The year 2005 marked the 100th anniversary of the publication of ☐☐☐☐☐☐☐☐'s theory of special relativity.

4. 'Every even number (greater than 2) may be written as the sum of two primes.'
   This (as yet unproven) result is the ☐☐☐☐☐☐☐☐ conjecture.

5. 'I have a truly marvellous demonstration of this proposition…'
   This dubious claim was made by ☐☐☐☐☐☐ in about 1637.

6. ☐☐☐☐☐'s Law states that when a string is stretched, its extension is proportional to the tension in the string. This 'Law' is only *approximately* true.

7. The theoretical study of genetics began with experiments by the Austrian monk ☐☐☐☐☐☐, who studied heredity in peas.

8. ☐☐☐☐☐☐☐'s rule is a method for estimating the area under a curve, based on quadratic approximations.

9. In 1931 the Czech mathematician ☐☐☐☐☐ announced his Incompleteness Theorem: 'Any logical mathematical system will always contain statements which can neither be proved nor disproved.'

10. The ☐☐☐☐☐☐☐ hypothesis, first proposed in 1859, is claimed to be the most important unproved result in mathematics. A $1 million cash prize awaits the first person to prove it!

CHAPTER 32

Introducing coordinate geometry

In this chapter you will **learn how to**:

- use Pythagoras' theorem to find the distance between two points on a coordinate grid
- write the equation of a circle in the form $x^2 + y^2 = r^2$
- find the point, or points, of intersection of a circle with a straight line
- find the equations of lines parallel or perpendicular to a given line.

You will also be **challenged to**:

- investigate shapes on spotty paper.

Starter: Coded message

The following message has been coded using A = Z, B = Y, and so on. Decode this message:

XLLIWRMZGV TVLNVGIB RH GSV HGFWB LU HSZKVH WIZDM LM TIRWH.

BLF DROO FHV ZOTVYIZ GL WVHXIRYV HGIZRTSG ORMVH ZMW XRIXOVH.

VCZN JFVHGRLMH LM GSRH GLKRX ZKKVZI HXZIB, YFG GSVB ZIV VZHRVI GSZM GSVB OLLP ZG URIHG.

TLLW OFXP DRGS GSV IVHG LU GSRH XSZKGVI!

32.1 Pythagoras' theorem on a coordinate grid

Suppose you want to calculate the distance between two points plotted on a coordinate grid. One way of doing this is to use Pythagoras' theorem.

EXAMPLE

Find the distance between the points A $(-2, 1)$ and B $(10, 6)$.

SOLUTION

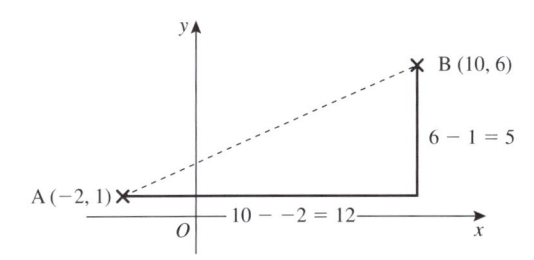

The difference between the x coordinates is $10 - (-2) = 12$.

The difference between the y coordinates is $6 - 1 = 5$.

By Pythagoras' theorem:
$$AB^2 = 12^2 + 5^2$$
$$= 144 + 25$$
$$= 169$$
$$AB = \sqrt{169}$$
$$= 13$$

It is not necessary to draw a diagram for every problem of this type. You could simply use the formula:

$$\text{Distance} = \sqrt{(\text{difference between } x \text{ coordinates})^2 + (\text{difference between } y \text{ coordinates})^2}$$

Generalising, if (x_1, y_1) and (x_2, y_2) are the two coordinates, the formula is written as:

$$\text{Distance} = \sqrt{(x_2 - x_1)^2 + (y_2 - y_1)^2}$$

EXAMPLE

A triangle has vertices A $(2, 7)$, B $(7, -3)$ and C $(-8, 2)$.

a) Find the lengths of:
   (i) AB **(ii)** BC **(iii)** AC
   Give exact answers in surd form.

b) What kind of triangle is ABC?

SOLUTION

a) (i) $AB = \sqrt{(7-2)^2 + (-3-7)^2} = \sqrt{25 + 100} = \sqrt{125} = \sqrt{25 \times 5} = \sqrt{25} \times \sqrt{5} = \underline{5\sqrt{5}}$

(ii) $BC = \sqrt{(-8-7)^2 + (2--3)^2} = \sqrt{225 + 25} = \sqrt{250} = \sqrt{25 \times 10} = \sqrt{25} \times \sqrt{10} = \underline{10\sqrt{5}}$

(iii) $AC = \sqrt{(-8-2)^2 + (2-7)^2} = \sqrt{100 + 25} = \sqrt{125} = \sqrt{25 \times 5} = \sqrt{25} \times \sqrt{5} = \underline{5\sqrt{5}}$

b) These results show that $AB = AC$ but that BC has a different length.
Therefore the triangle ABC is isosceles.

A similar method can be used for problems with 3-D coordinates. Pythagoras' theorem is now adapted as follows:

$$\text{Distance} = \sqrt{(\text{difference of } x \text{ coords})^2 + (\text{difference of } y \text{ coords})^2 + (\text{difference of } z \text{ coords})^2}$$

Generalising, if (x_1, y_1, z_1) and (x_2, y_2, z_2) are the two coordinates, the formula is written as:

$$\text{Distance} = \sqrt{(x_2 - x_1)^2 + (y_2 - y_1)^2 + (z_2 - z_1)^2}$$

EXAMPLE

Find the distance between the points A $(5, -2, 4)$ and B $(8, 3, -2)$. Give an exact answer in surd form.

SOLUTION

$$\begin{aligned} AB &= \sqrt{(8-5)^2 + (3--2)^2 + (-2-4)^2} \\ &= \sqrt{3^2 + 5^2 + (-6)^2} \\ &= \sqrt{9 + 25 + 36} \\ &= \sqrt{70} \end{aligned}$$

EXERCISE 32.1

1. Use Pythagoras' theorem to calculate the distance from:
   a) A $(4, 1)$ to B $(1, 5)$
   b) P $(-5, 5)$ to Q $(3, 20)$
   c) M $(-2, 1)$ to N $(6, -3)$

2. A triangle ABC has vertices A $(-2, -2)$, B $(4, -1)$ and C $(1, 3)$.
   Dee makes a sketch of the triangle. Dee says that the triangle is isosceles.
   a) Use Pythagoras' theorem to find the lengths of AB, BC and CA.
      Give exact answers in surd form.
   b) Use your answers to decide whether Dee is right or wrong.

3. A quadrilateral PQRS has vertices P $(3, 1)$, Q $(7, 2)$, R $(8, 6)$ and S $(4, 5)$.
   a) Make a rough sketch of the quadrilateral.
   b) Use Pythagoras' theorem to find the length of the sides PQ, QR, RS and SP.
      Give exact answers in surd form.
   c) What type of quadrilateral is PQRS?

4. Three points have coordinates A $(5, 2, -1)$, B $(12, -4, -7)$ and C $(-1, 3, -2)$.
   Use the 3-D form of Pythagoras' theorem to find, as exact surds, the lengths of:
   a) AB
   b) BC
   c) CA
   Which side of triangle ABC is the longest?

32.2 Coordinate geometry of a circle

Consider a point P, with coordinates (x, y), moving on a coordinate grid so that it is always 4 units from the origin.

Since P is always 4 units from the origin, it must trace out a circle with centre O.

By Pythagoras' theorem, we know that $x^2 + y^2 = 4^2$. In other words, $x^2 + y^2 = 16$. More generally we can state that:

The **equation of a circle** centred on the origin, with radius r, is given by the formula:

$$x^2 + y^2 = r^2$$

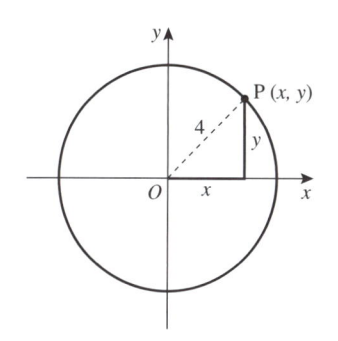

EXAMPLE

Write down the equation of a circle, centre O, with radius 5 units.

SOLUTION

The equation is:

$$x^2 + y^2 = 5^2$$

So, $x^2 + y^2 = 25$

Since the equation of a circle contains the variables x^2 and y^2, questions about circles often lead to quadratic equations.

In particular, for the GCSE examination you need to know how to solve the quadratic equation that arises when a straight line intersects a circle (this is a skill that you have already begun to practise in Chapter 27). There are three different situations that might arise:

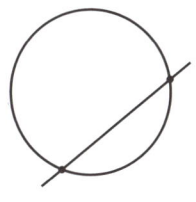

Case 1
The line intersects the circle twice

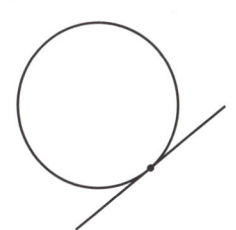

Case 2
The line intersects the circle once

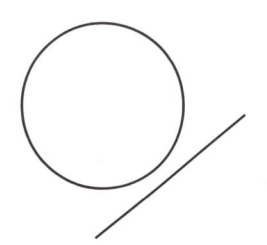

Case 3
The line does not intersect the circle

You can tell the difference between each of these cases by solving (or attempting to solve) the corresponding quadratic equation.

EXAMPLE

The circle C has equation $x^2 + y^2 = 17$.
a) State the radius of the circle C. Give your answer in exact form.
b) Show that the line $y = 2x + 10$ does not meet the circle C at all.
c) Find the coordinates of the points where the line $x + y = 3$ meets the circle C.

SOLUTION

a) Since the general equation of a circle is $x^2 + y^2 = r^2$, then $r^2 = 17$.
Therefore, the radius, r, of the circle C is $\sqrt{17}$

b) Suppose the circle $x^2 + y^2 = 17$ meets the line $y = 2x + 10$.
Substituting $2x + 10$ for y gives:
$$x^2 + (2x + 10)^2 = 17$$
Now, expanding the brackets:
$$x^2 + (2x + 10)(2x + 10) = 17$$
$$x^2 + 4x^2 + 20x + 20x + 100 = 17$$
$$5x^2 + 40x + 100 = 17$$
$$5x^2 + 40x + 83 = 0$$
Using the quadratic formula, $a = 5, b = 40$ and $c = 83$:
$$x = \frac{-b \pm \sqrt{b^2 - 4ac}}{2a}$$
$$= \frac{-40 \pm \sqrt{40^2 - 4 \times 5 \times 83}}{2 \times 5}$$
$$= \frac{-40 \pm \sqrt{1600 - 1660}}{10}$$
$$= \frac{-40 \pm \sqrt{-60}}{10}$$

A negative number cannot have a square root, so this quadratic has no solutions. Therefore the line $y = 2x + 10$ does not meet the circle C

c) Now let the circle $x^2 + y^2 = 17$ meet the line $x + y = 3$.
The line $x + y = 3$ can be rearranged as $y = 3 - x$.
Solving simultaneously:
$$x^2 + (3 - x)^2 = 17$$
$$x^2 + (3 - x)(3 - x) = 17$$
$$x^2 + 9 - 3x - 3x + x^2 = 17$$
$$2x^2 - 6x + 9 = 17$$
$$2x^2 - 6x - 8 = 0$$
$$x^2 - 3x - 4 = 0$$
$$(x - 4)(x + 1) = 0$$
So, $x - 4 = 0$ or $x + 1 = 0$. Therefore $x = 4$ or $x = -1$.
Substituting these values for x back into $y = 3 - x$ gives:
When $x = 4$, then $y = 3 - 4 = -1$.
When $x = -1$, then $y = 3 - (-1) = 4$.
The solutions are $x = 4$ and $y = -1$ or $x = -1$ and $y = 4$

EXERCISE 32.2

1 A circle, centre O, has equation $x^2 + y^2 = 36$.
Write down the radius of the circle.

2 A circle, centre O, has radius 5.
Write down the equation of the circle.

3 A circle, centre O, has equation $x^2 + y^2 = 64$.
Work out the diameter of the circle.

4 A circle, centre O, has diameter 14.
Write down the equation of the circle.

5 A circle, centre O, passes through the point $(2, 5)$.
  a) Work out the radius of the circle. Give your answer as a surd.
  b) Write down the equation of the circle.

6 A circle has equation $x^2 + y^2 = 25$.
  a) State the radius of the circle.
  b) Find the coordinates of the two points on the circle for which $y = 3$.

7 Find the coordinates of the two points where the graph of the line $y = x + 2$ meets the circle with equation $x^2 + y^2 = 52$.

8 A circle C is given by the equation $x^2 + y^2 = 18$.
A line L is given by the equation $y = x + 6$.
  a) Prove that the line L cuts the circle C in exactly one place.
  b) What name is given to such a line?

9 Here are the equations of three graphs.
      Graph A $y = x^2 + 3$
      Graph B $x^2 + y^2 = 21$
      Graph C $y = 10 - x$
  a) Which one of these is a circle?
  b) Describe the shapes of the other two graphs.

10 A circle C, with centre at the origin O, has diameter $\sqrt{136}$.
  a) Write this diameter in the form $2\sqrt{k}$, where k is an integer to be found.
  b) Hence find the equation of the circle C.

  A straight line has equation $x + y = 8$.
  c) Find the coordinates of the points where this straight line meets the circle C.

32.3 Gradients of parallel and perpendicular lines

If two lines are **parallel** then they must have the **same gradient**. Remember that the gradient is the value of m when the straight line is written in the form $y = mx + c$.

$y = 3x + 5$ and $y = 3x - 2$ are parallel. They both have gradient 3.

EXAMPLE

The straight line L_1 has the equation $y = 3x + 5$.
The straight line L_2 is parallel to L_1.
L_2 passes through the point (2, 5).
Find the equation of the line L_2.

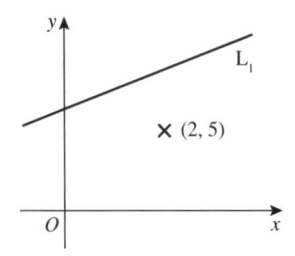

SOLUTION

Let the equation of L_2 be $y = mx + c$.
Since L_2 is parallel to $y = 3x + 5$, it has the same gradient.
So $m = 3$
Therefore the equation of L_2 is $y = 3x + c$.
Since L_2 passes through (2, 5), the values $x = 2$ and $y = 5$ must satisfy the equation $y = 3x + c$.
Substituting these values into the equation gives:

$5 = 3 \times 2 + c$
$5 = 6 + c$

So: $c = -1$
Therefore, the equation of L_2 is:

$y = 3x - 1$

If two lines are **perpendicular**, then one of them will have a positive gradient and the other a negative gradient. The two gradients must **multiply together** to make -1.

$y = 3x + 5$ and $y = -\frac{1}{3}x - 2$ are perpendicular, because $3 \times -\frac{1}{3} = -1$

EXAMPLE

A straight line has equation $y = 2x + 3$. A second line is perpendicular to this line, and passes through the point $(4, 5)$. Find the equation of this second line.

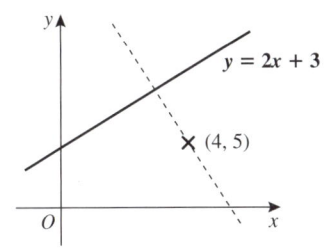

SOLUTION

Let the equation of the second line be $y = mx + c$.

Since it is perpendicular to $y = 2x + 3$, the gradient must be $-\frac{1}{2}$ since $2 \times -\frac{1}{2} = -1$.

Therefore the equation of the line is of the form $y = -\frac{1}{2}x + c$.

The line passes through the point $(4, 5)$, so substituting the values of x and y into the equation gives:

$$5 = -\frac{1}{2} \times 4 + c$$
$$5 = -2 + c$$

So: $c = 7$

Therefore the equation of the second line is:

$$y = -\frac{1}{2}x + 7$$

EXERCISE 32.3

1. For each of the following lines, write down:
   a) the gradient of a line parallel to the given line, and
   b) the gradient of a line perpendicular to the given line.

   (i) $y = 3x + 2$ (ii) $y = \frac{1}{2}x$ (iii) $y = -5x - 2$ (iv) $3y = -7x + 1$

2. Find the equation of the straight line, parallel to $y = 3x - 5$, that passes through the point P $(2, 3)$.

3. Find the equation of the straight line, parallel to $y = -2x + 1$, that passes through the point Q $(3, 4)$.

4. Find the equation of the straight line, perpendicular to $y = 4x + 1$, that passes through the point P $(8, 1)$.

5. Find the equation of the straight line, perpendicular to $y = \frac{1}{2}x + 3$, that passes through the point Q $(3, -1)$.

6. Here are the equations of four straight lines.

   Line A $y = 5x + 2$
   Line B $y = -5x - 3$
   Line C $y = 5x - 4$
   Line D $y = \frac{1}{5}x + 7$

   a) Write down the names of the two lines that are **parallel**.
   b) Write down the names of the two lines that are **perpendicular**.

7 A line L_1 passes through the points A (5, 2) and B (7, 1).
   a) Work out the gradient of the line L_1.
   b) Work out the equation of the line L_1. Give your answer in the form $y = mx + c$.

   A second line L_2 is perpendicular to L_1. L_2 passes through the point A.
   c) Write down the gradient of L_2.
   d) Work out the equation of the line L_2. Give your answer in the form $y = mx + c$.

8 Find the equation of the straight line, parallel to $y = 5x + 1$, that passes through the point P (2, 7).

9 Find the equation of the straight line, perpendicular to $y = x + 7$, that passes through the point P (4, 5).

10 The lines $y = 2x + 3$ and $y = ax + 5$ are perpendicular. Find the value of a.

REVIEW EXERCISE 32

1 Calculate the distance from the point A (2, −1) to the point B (8, 7).

2 Calculate the distance from the point P (5, −7, −2) to the point Q (3, 1, −1).

3 A trapezium PQRS is made by joining points P (1, 2), Q (9, 10), R (7, 9) and S (3, 5).
   a) Make a sketch of the trapezium.
   b) Work out the lengths of PQ and RS.
   c) Hence give the ratio PQ : RS in its simplest form.
   d) Work out the lengths QR and PS.
   e) Explain whether or not the trapezium is isosceles.

4 The diagram shows a cuboid drawn on a set of coordinate axes.

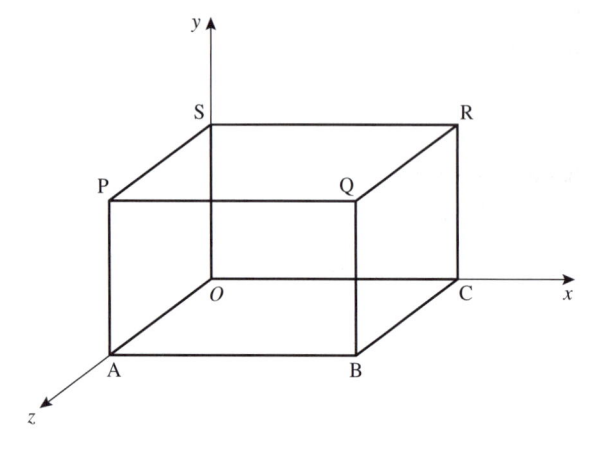

Q is the point (8, 5, 3).
   a) Write down the coordinates of: **(i)** A   **(ii)** C   **(iii)** R.
   b) Calculate the length of AQ.
   c) Calculate the length of AR.

5 A circle C has equation $x^2 + y^2 = 20$.
   a) State the radius of the circle. Give your answer as an exact surd.

   A straight line L has equation $y = x - 6$.
   b) Find the coordinates of the points where the line L meets the circle C.

6 A circle passes through the points P (8, 15) and Q (−8, −15). PQ is a diameter.
   a) Explain why the centre of the circle must be at O (0, 0).
   b) Work out the radius of the circle.
   c) Hence write the equation of the circle in the form $x^2 + y^2 = r^2$.

7 The straight line L_1 has equation $y = 2x + 3$. The straight line L_2 is parallel to the straight line L_1.
   The straight line L_2 passes through the point (3, 2). Find an equation of the straight line L_2. [Edexcel]

8 A straight line, L, passes through the point with coordinates (4, 7) and is perpendicular to the line with equation $y = 2x + 3$. Find an equation of the straight line L. [Edexcel]

9 Solve the simultaneous equations:

   $x^2 + y^2 = 29$
   $y - x = 3$ [Edexcel]

10 ABCD is a rectangle. A is the point (0, 1). C is the point (0, 6).

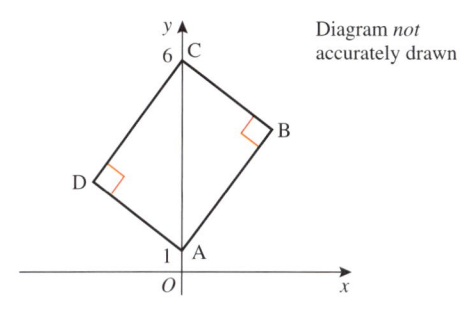

   Diagram *not* accurately drawn

   The equation of the straight line through A and B is $y = 2x + 1$.
   a) Find the equation of the straight line through D and C.
   b) Find the equation of the straight line through B and C.
   c) It is always possible to draw a circle which passes through all four vertices of a rectangle.
      Explain why. [Edexcel]

11 A circle has equation $x^2 + y^2 = 9$. A straight line has equation $y = x + 5$.
   Use elimination to prove that the straight line never crosses the circle.

12 The diagram shows a sketch of a curve. The point P(x, y) lies on the curve.

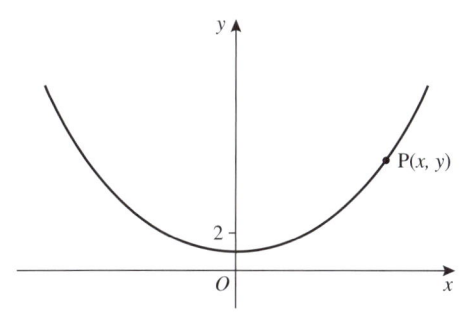

   The locus of P has the following property:
   The distance of P from the point (0, 2) is the same as the distance of the point P from the x axis.
   Show that $y = \frac{1}{4}x^2 + 1$. [Edexcel]

KEY POINTS

1. Coordinate geometry is the study of shapes drawn on coordinate grids. You will meet a wider range of coordinate geometry techniques if you go on to study mathematics at A level.

2. In 2-D, the distance between two points (x_1, y_1) and (x_2, y_2) can be found using Pythagoras' theorem:

   Distance $= \sqrt{(x_2 - x_1)^2 + (y_2 - y_1)^2}$

   This can be remembered in words as:

   Distance $= \sqrt{(\text{difference between } x \text{ coordinates})^2 + (\text{difference between } y \text{ coordinates})^2}$

   The corresponding result for 3-D is:

   Distance $= \sqrt{(x_2 - x_1)^2 + (y_2 - y_1)^2 + (z_2 - z_1)^2}$

   In words:

   Distance $= \sqrt{(\text{difference of } x \text{ coords})^2 + (\text{difference of } y \text{ coords})^2 + (\text{difference of } z \text{ coords})^2}$

3. The equation of a circle centred at the origin may be written as $x^2 + y^2 = r^2$, where r is the radius of the circle. For example, the circle $x^2 + y^2 = 25$ has radius 5.

4. You may be asked to work out the points where a circle meets a straight line. Use substitution to set up a quadratic equation, and then use factorising or the quadratic formula to complete the solution. If the formula method leads to a square root of a negative number, then this tells you that the given line does not cross the circle.

5. Two straight lines will be parallel if they have the same gradient.

   For example, $y = 4x + 1$ and $y = 4x - 5$ are parallel. They both have gradient 4.

6. Two lines will be perpendicular if their gradients multiplied together make -1.

   For example, $y = 2x + 3$ and $y = -\frac{1}{2}x - 2$ are perpendicular, since $2 \times -\frac{1}{2} = -1$

Internet Challenge 32

Shapes on spotty paper

The diagrams show two shapes drawn on spotty paper.

Area: The number of **unit squares** inside the shape.
Internal points: The number of points **inside** the shape.
Boundary points: The number of points **on the boundary** of each shape.

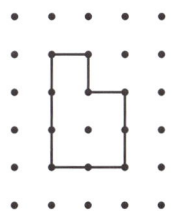

Area: 5 square units
Internal points: 1
Boundary points: 10

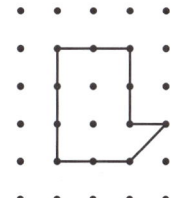

Area: $6\frac{1}{2}$ square units
Internal points: 2
Boundary points: 11

Area A	Internal points L	Boundary points B	$L + \frac{1}{2}B - 1$
5	1	10	
$6\frac{1}{2}$	2	11	

1. Copy the table and fill in the missing values in the fourth column.

2. Now draw some shapes of your own on spotty paper. Count the values of A, L and B for your shapes, and enter this information into the table.

3. Do you notice any pattern in your results?

4. This activity is based on a theorem discovered by a mathematician who lived from 1859 to 1942. Use the internet to find out his name.

5. This theorem can be used to prove that it is not possible to draw an equilateral triangle by connecting three points on spotty paper. Think about this, and then use the internet to find out how the proof is done.

Index

3-D/3-D objects
  coordinates in 86, 544
  drawing and constructing 384–8
  plane of symmetry in 313
  and Pythagoras' theorem 350, 484–5
  trigonometry in 484–5
  see also shapes
AAS (angle-angle-side) 532
acceleration 256, 257
addition 2–3
  decimals in 23
  fractions in 164–5
  and Roman numerals 42
  in standard form 53
  of vectors 519–20
algebra 59–78, 454–68
  and inequalities 236–7
  for perimeters 117
  in proofs 535–6
algebraic equations 185–207
algebraic fractions 60, 73–4, 458–9
allied angles 106
alternate angles 105–6
alternate segment theorem 419
angle–angle–side (AAS) 532
angle of elevation 469
angle of rotation 319
angles 104–11
  allied 106
  alternate 105–6
  and bearings 145–6, 305
  bisectors 295–6, 301, 302
  in circles 131–3, 411–15, 419
  co–interior 106
  corresponding 105–6
  in polygons 135, 380–2
  in quadrilaterals 108, 110–11, 193, 380
  in triangles 108–9, 357–71, 380
    and cosine rule 477–9
    and sine rule 470–1, 474–5
  vertically opposite 106
  see also trigonometry
angle–side–angle (ASA) 290–1, 532
angles in opposite segments 417–18

angles in the same segment are equal 414
angles in a semicircle 414
angles subtended by an arc 411–14
ans key (calculators) 179–80
apexes (pyramids and cones) 390
approximation 29–31
arcs 272
  angles subtended by 411–14
areas 115–17
  of circles 267–9, 274, 279
  of circle segments 482
  converting between units 394
  dimensions of 395–6
  of sectors 272
  and similar shapes 333, 334
  of triangles 115, 481–2, 492
  see also surface area
arithmagons 185
arithmetic sequences 96–9
arrowhead 114
ASA (angle-side-angle) 290–1, 532
astronomical numbers 58

bases (pyramids and cones) 390
bearings 145–6, 305
  and trigonometric problems 371
BIDMAS 60
big numbers 151
bisectors
  of angles 295–6, 301, 302
  perpendicular 296–7, 301–2
brackets
  and calculators 154–5
  in equations 190–1
  expanding and simplifying 63, 64–6
  and factorising 68–70
  multiplying together 66–7
  and substituting into formulae 60

calculators 151–9
  ans key 179–80
  and circles 267, 268
  and fractions 154, 156, 165
  and negative numbers 9
  and powers 43–6, 152
    squares 43–4, 152, 154, 344
  and roots 43–6, 152–3
    square roots 43–4, 152–3, 154, 344
  and standard form 54
  for trigonometry 357, 368
    sine 357, 368, 474, 475
cancelling down 21–2, 167
  in algebraic fractions 74
  ratios 170
Cartesian coordinates 80
  see also coordinates
centre of enlargement 328
centre of rotation 319
chessboard problems 517, 530
chords 131, 133, 408–9
circles 91, 130–8
  area 267–9, 274, 279
  circumference 267–9, 274
  and constructions 135, 287–8
  coordinate geometry of 545–6
  equation of 545–6
  as loci 300
  nine-point circle 427
  sectors of 135, 272
  segments 482
  tangents to 131–3, 533
  theorems 131–3, 407–27
circumference 267–9, 274
coefficients 62–3, 445
co-interior angles 106
column vectors 324, 518
common difference 96–9
common factors 12–14, 68–9, 74
common multiples 14
compound interest 177–8, 179–80
compound measures 142–4, 399
compressing graphs 506–7
computing 159

cones 390, 391, 392–3
  as similar shapes 334, 487
congruence 313, 324
  and triangles 532–3
conic sections 453
conjecture 537
consecutive integers 535–6
constant of proportionality 429, 430, 432
constructing 3–D objects 387–8
constructions
  in circles 135
  with line segments 295–8
  loci 300–2
  triangles 288–94
  see also diagrams; drawings
coordinate geometry 542–53
coordinates 80–4, 542–9
  in 3–D 86, 544
  and maps 90
corresponding angles 105–6
cosine 360–2, 366–7, 368, 371
  cosine rule 477–9
  graphs of 502, 506, 507
cosine rule 477–9
counter-examples 537
cube roots 43, 44, 152
cubes 43, 44, 62–3
  sequences of 92
cubes (shape), nets for 379–80
cubic functions 494, 497–8
  translation 505
cuboids 120–1
  drawing 311, 384–5
  net for 387
  and Pythagoras' theorem 350
curves, graphs of 493–516
cyclic quadrilaterals 417–18
cylinders 276–7, 280

deceleration 257
decimal places (d.p.) 29
decimals 23–8
denominators 21
  and algebraic fractions 73–4, 459
  rationalising 456
density 142, 143, 277
Descartes, René 81

diagrams, vector 518, 519, 520, 521
  see also drawings; graphs
diameter 267, 274
difference of two squares 71–2
dimensional analysis 395–6
direct proportion 429–30
  graphs of 435, 436
distance 142, 143–4
  between points 542–4
  on travel graphs 143–4, 252–3
    velocity–time 257
  triangulation measures 288
  units of 140, 141
distance–time graphs 143–4, 252–3
dividend 7
division 7–8
  and calculators 154, 155
  decimals in 24, 25
  fractions in 166–8
  with indices 51
    in algebra 62–3
  with negative numbers 10
  in standard form 54, 55
  and substituting into formulae 60
divisor 7–8
d.p. (decimal places) 29
drawings
  of 3-D objects 384–8
  perspective 311
  see also constructions; diagrams

Earth, measuring 286
elevation 385, 386–7
elevation, angle of 469
elimination method 223–6, 460–1
ellipses 453
enlargement factors 333
  see also scale factors
enlargements 328–30, 333
equations 186, 187–93
  algebraic 185–207
  algebraic fractions in 459
  brackets in 190–1
  of circles 545–6
  cubic functions 497–8, 505
  fractional coefficients in 191–2
  of lines 83–4, 213–16, 460–1
  quadratic 442–53, 457, 504–5, 506
    and circles 545–6

  and simultaneous equations 460–1
  simultaneous 221–32, 460–1
  subject of, changing 462
  trial and improvement for 200–1
  see also formulae; identities
equivalent fractions 21–2, 163
estimation 23–4
Euclid's method 14
even numbers
  representing algebraically 536
  sequences of 92
exponential functions 494
exponential growth and decay 463–4
expressions 186
  simplifying 62–3
  substituting into 59–61
exterior angles 108, 318–12
  triangles 109

factorising 11–12
  algebraic expressions 68–70
    quadratics 69–70, 71–2, 443–4
  prime factorisation 13–15, 16
factors 11
  common factors 12–14, 68–9, 74
  highest common factors 12–14, 15–16
factor trees 11–12
Fibonacci numbers 103
formulae 186, 468
  changing subject 197–9
  generating 195–6
  and modelling 248–9
  and proportionality 429, 430, 432, 433
  for quadratic equations 445–6, 457
  substituting into 59–61
four-colour theorem 129
fractions 20–2, 26–8, 35, 163–8
  algebraic 60, 73–4, 458–9
  and calculators 154, 156, 165
  and decimals 26–8
  in equations 191–2
  equivalent 21–2, 163
  mixed 156, 165, 168
  and percentages 36–7

  as powers/indices 45–7, 48–9
  reciprocals of 48–9
  with surds 456
front elevation 385, 386
fruity numbers 221
frustums 487
function notation 504
functions, tables of 494–5

Gauss, Carl Friedrich 207
geometers, famous 378
geometry, coordinate 542–53
geometry problems
  equations for 193
  vectors for 522–4
gradient 209–11
  of parallel lines 215–16, 548
  of perpendicular lines 548–9
  on travel graphs 252
    velocity–time 256–7
graphs
  of curves 493–516
  distance–time 143–4, 252–3
  exponential 463–4
  of linear inequalities 239–40
  of lines 208–20
  modelling with 247–9
  plotting 496–8
  and proportionality 435–6
  of quadratic functions 448–9
  and rates of change 249–50
  for simultaneous equations 227–8
  transformations of 504–8
  of trigonometric functions 501–3
    sine 493, 501–2, 506–7
  velocity–time 256–7
greatest value 398

HCF see highest common factor
Heron's formula 492
highest common factor (HCF) 12–14, 15–16
  and algebraic expressions 68–9
hyperbola 435
hypotenuse 345, 347, 358

identities 186
imperial units 141–2

improper fractions 156, 168
indices
  in algebra 60, 62–3
  fractions in 45–7
  laws of 49–51, 62, 63
  standard form 52–5, 58, 155, 162
  see also powers; roots
inequalities 234–44
  and bounds 398
inflation 184
inspection, solving equations with 187
  quadratic 443
  simultaneous 222–3
integers
  sequences of 92
  sum of squares of 535–6
  see also whole numbers
intercept (linear functions) 210–11
interest, simple and compound 177–8, 179–80
interior angles 108–9, 380–1, 382
  quadrilaterals 108
  triangles 108–9
inverse functions 368
inverse proportion 432–3, 435
irrational numbers 26
isometric drawings 384, 386–7
isosceles trapezium 114

kite 114

LCM see lowest common multiple
leap years 139
least value 398
length, dimensions of 395, 396
lengths of sides
  and similar shapes 333
  of triangles 333, 357
    and congruence 532–3
    in constructions 289–94
    and Pythagoras' theorem 345–50, 355, 408–9
    and trigonometry 357–71, 470–85
linear functions 83–4, 209–11
  see also lines
linear graphs
  modelling with 247–9
  travel graphs 252–3, 256–7

Index 555

linear inequalities
   and algebra 236–7
   and two variables 239–40
linear sequences 96, 208
   see also arithmetic sequences
lines 105
   equations of 83–4, 213–16, 460–1
   graphs of 208–20
   modelling with 247–9
   intersecting with circles 545–6
   line segments see line segments
   parallel lines see parallel lines
   perpendicular 548–9
line segments 84, 85, 86, 105
   and chords, in circles 131
   constructions with 295–8
   loci of 300
   midpoint coordinates 85, 86
   perpendicular bisectors 296–7
loci, constructing 300–2
long division 8
long multiplication 5–6
lower bounds 30–1, 398–9
lowest common multiple (LCM) 14–16

magic squares 233
mapping shapes, translation for 324–5
maps, four-colour theorem for 129
mass 142, 143
   of solids 277
   units of 140, 141
   volume, and enlargement 334
matchstick puzzles 79–80
maximum value/point
   bounds 405
   cosine 502
   quadratics 448
   sine 501
   tangent 502–3
metric units 140–2
midpoint coordinates 85, 86
minimum value/point
   bounds 405
   quadratics 448, 449
mirror lines 313–14
mirror symmetry 313
mixed fractions 156, 165, 168
modelling with line graphs 247–9

multiples 11
multiplication 4–6
   and brackets 65–7
   decimals in 23–4
   and fractions 166–8
   with indices 49–50, 51, 62–3
   with negative numbers 10
   in standard form 54
   and substituting into formulae 60
   with surds 455, 456
   and vectors 521
multiplying factors 172–4, 175, 176
   and compound interest 177–8

negative numbers 9–10
   and brackets 65
   and inequalities 236, 237
   as powers 47–9, 52
negative vectors 520
nets 379–80, 387, 388
nine-point circle 427
nth terms 92–3, 95, 97–9
number lines 9
   and inequalities 237–8
numbers 1–19
   algebraic proofs 535–6
   astronomical 58
   big numbers 151
   and calculators 151–9
   decimals 23–8
   even 92, 536
   Fibonacci 103
   fractions see fractions
   negative see negative numbers
   odd 92, 536
   percentages 36–41, 172–80, 184
   powers and roots 43–6, 50, 51, 152–3
   negative 47–9
   prime 11, 12, 19
   ratios 169–70
   reciprocals 47–9, 153
   Roman numerals 42
   sequences of 91–9, 208
   standard form see standard form
   sum of squares 535–6
number sequences 91–9, 208
numerator 21

odd numbers
   representing algebraically 536
   sequences of 92

parabolas 448–9, 453
parallel lines 215–16, 220
   and angles 105–6
   gradients of 215–16, 548
   and vectors 520, 522, 523
parallelograms 81, 113, 115
percentage change 172
percentage increase/decrease 172–4
percentages 36–41, 172–80, 184
perimeters 117, 268–9
   and bounds 398
   of circles see circumference
   and enlargement 333
   of sectors of circles 272
   of shapes with semicircles 268–9
periodic functions 501
perpendicular bisectors 296–7, 301–2
perpendicular lines, gradients of 548–9
perpendiculars, constructing 297–8
perspective 311
pi 266, 267, 279–80
plane of symmetry 313
planets 441
plan view 385, 386, 388
Platonic solids 406
plotting graphs 496–8
points
   constructing perpendiculars from 297–8
   distance between 542–4
   loci of 300, 301–2
polygons 135, 380–2
polyhedra 406
position-to-term rule 95
power functions 494
powers 43–55, 151
   in algebra 60, 62–3
   and calculators 43–6, 152
   negative 47–9
   and proportionality 429–30, 433
   sequences of 92
prime factorisation method 13–15, 16
prime factors 11–15, 16
prime numbers 11, 12, 19
prisms 121–2
   and trigonometric problems 484–5
problems
   quadratic equations for 446–7
   simultaneous equations for 228–9

projection drawings 385, 386–7
proofs 531–41
proportion 428–41
pyramids 388, 390, 391
Pythagoras' theorem 344–55, 370
   in 3-D 350, 484–5
   and circles 408–9
   on a coordinate grid 542–4
   and trigonometric problems 370, 371
   in 3-D 484–5
Pythagorean triples 355

quadrants 80–1, 272
quadratic equations 442–53
   and circles 545–6
   factorising 443–4
   formula for 445–6, 457
   problems for 446–7
   and simultaneous equations 460–1
   stretching 506
   translation 504–5
quadratic expressions
   in algebraic fractions 74
   factorising 69–70, 71–2
quadratic functions 494
   plotting graphs 496–7
quadrilaterals 113–17
   angles in 108, 110–11, 193, 380
   cyclic 417–18
   see also rectangles

radius 267
   and chords 408–9
   and tangents 131, 132, 133
   and Pythagoras' theorem 408–9
raising to a power see powers
rates of change 249–50
   and velocity–time graphs 256
rationalising the denominator 456
ratios 169–70
reciprocal functions 494–5
reciprocals 47–9, 153
rectangles 113, 115, 117
   and loci 300, 301
   perimeter 398
recurring decimals 26, 27, 28
reflections 313–14, 324–5, 508
reflection symmetry 313
regular polygons 135, 382

remainders 7
resultant vector 519
reverse percentages 175–6
rhombus 113
RHS (right angle-hypotenuse-side) 532, 533
right angle-hypotenuse-side (RHS) 532, 533
right-angles
   in circles 131–2, 408–9, 414
   and Pythagoras' theorem 345–55, 370
   in 3-D 350, 484–5
   and circles 408–9
   on a coordinate grid 542–4
   and trigonometry 370, 371, 484–5
   in trigonometry 356–77
   in 3-D 484–5
Roman numerals 42
roots 43–6
   and calculators 43–6, 152–3, 154, 344
   see also square roots; surds
rotational symmetry 503
rotations 319–21
rounding 29–31, 44
   multi-stage problems 370
rules for number sequences 94–5

SAS (side-angle-side) 481–2, 532
scalar multiplication 521
scale factors 169
   in enlargements 328–30
   and vectors 522
scientific notation 58
   see also standard form
sectors (circles) 135, 272
segments
   circles 482
   line segments *see* line segments
semicircles 268–9, 272
   angle subtended by 414
   and the loci of line segments 300
semiperimeter 492
sequences 91–9, 208
s.f. (significant figures) 29
shapes 108–22, 267–80, 379–93
   circles *see* circles
   drawings of 311, 384–8
   mapping, translation for 324–5

polyhedra 406
similarity 329, 333–4, 357, 487
on spotty paper 553
transformations 312–29
triangles *see* triangles
and water flow 249–50
see also constructions; graphs; loci
short division 7
short multiplication 4–5
side-angle-side (SAS) 481–2, 532
side elevation 385, 387
side-side-angle (SSA) 293–4
side-side-side (SSS) 291–3, 532
significant figures (s.f.) 29
similar shapes 333–4
   cones 334, 487
   enlargement produces 329
   triangles 333, 357
simple interest 177–8
simplest terms, fractions in 21–2
simultaneous equations 221–32
   and quadratic equations 460–1
sine 357–8, 366–7, 368, 370
   graphs of 493, 501–2, 506–7
   sine rule 470–1, 474–5
sine rule 470–1, 474–5
solids 384–93
   similarity 333, 487
   surface area and volume 120–2, 390–3
   cylinders 276–7, 280
speed 142, 143–4, 246, 265
   and bounds 399
   and distance–time graphs 252–3
   see also velocity
spheres 391, 392
spotty paper 553
square, completing the 448–9
square roots 43, 44
   and calculators 43–4, 152–3, 154, 344
   solving equations with 188
   see also surds
squares 43, 44, 62–3
   and calculators 43–4, 152, 154, 344
   difference of two 71–2

and proportionality 429–3, 433
sequences of 92
sum of, consecutive integers 535–6
squares (shape) 113
SSA (side-side-angle) 293–4
SSS (side-side-side) 291–3, 532
standard form 52–5, 58
   and calculators 152, 155
stellated octahedrons 406
straight lines *see* lines
stretching graphs 506–7
subject of equations, changing 462
subject of formulae, changing 197–9
subtraction 2–3
   decimals in 23
   fractions in 164–5
   and negative numbers 9–10
   and Roman numerals 42
   in standard form 53
   of vectors 519–20
surds 455–7
   see also roots
surface area 120–2
   cones 392–3
   cylinders 276–7, 280
   similar shapes 334
   spheres 392
symbols 245
   for inequalities 235, 237–8
symmetry 313
   cosine functions 502
   and quadrilaterals 113–14
   and reflections 313–14
   sine functions 502
   tangent functions 503

tables of functions 494–5
tangent (tan) 364, 366–7, 368, 371
   graphs of 502–3
tangents (circles) 131–3, 533
   and radius 131, 132, 133
   and Pythagoras' theorem 408–9
terminating decimals 26, 27
term-to-term rule 94
tetrahedrons (triangular pyramids) 390
three dimensions *see* 3-D/3-D objects
time 140, 142

on travel graphs 143–4, 252–3, 256–7
top-heavy fractions 35
see also improper fractions
transformations
   combining 324–5
   enlargements 328–30
   of graphs 504–8
   reflections 313–14, 324–5, 508
   rotations 319–21
   translation 324–5, 504–5
translation 324–5, 504–5
transversals 105
trapezium 114, 116
travel graphs 143–4
treasure island 234
trial and improvement 200–1
triangles
   angles in 108–9, 357–71, 380
   cosine rule for 477–9
   sine rule for 470–1, 474–5
   area of 115, 481–2, 492
   and circles 132, 133, 408–9, 414
   congruent 532–3
   constructing 288–94
   and Pythagoras' theorem 345–55, 370, 371
   in 3-D 350, 484–5
   and circles 408–9
   similar triangles 333, 357
   and trigonometry 356–77
triangular arithmagons 185
triangular numbers 92
triangulation 288
trigonometric functions
   graphs of 501–3
   see also cosine; sine; tangent (tan)
trigonometry 356–78, 469–92
truncated cones 487

units 139–50
   converting between 141
   for area and volume 394
upper bounds 30–1, 398–9

VAT 172
vectors 517–30
   column vectors 324, 518
   using 522–4
velocity 256–7

see also speed
velocity–time graphs 256–7
vertical line graphs
vertically opposite angles 106
volume 120–2

in compound measures 142, 143
of cones 390, 391, 487
of cylinders 276–7, 280
dimensions of 395–6
of pyramids 390, 391

and similar shapes 333, 487
of spheres 391
units of 140, 141, 394

whole numbers 1–19

reciprocals of 48
as solutions to inequalities 235
see also integers

zero powers 51